SHIPWRECKS

SHIPWRECKS

*An Encyclopedia of the
World's Worst
Disasters at Sea*

David Ritchie

Facts On File®

AN INFOBASE HOLDINGS COMPANY

Facts On File, Inc.
11 Penn Plaza
New York, NY 10001

Library of Congress Cataloging-in-Publication Data

Ritchie, David
Shipwrecks : an encyclopedia of the world's worst disasters at sea
/ David Ritchie.
p.   cm.
Includes bibliographical references (p.   ) and index.
ISBN 0-8160-3163-0 (alk. paper)
1. Shipwrecks—Encyclopedias.   I. Title.
VK1250.R57   1996
910.45—dc20   96-15664

Facts On File books are available at special discounts when purchased in bulk quantities for businesses, associations, institutions or sales promotions. Please call our Special Sales Department in New York at 212/967-8800 or 800/322-8755.

Jacket design by Alice Soloway

This book is printed on acid-free paper.

Printed in the United States of America

VB VC 10 9 8 7 6 5 4 3 2 1

To Rebecca Carolyn Woodfin Ritchie, 1916–1975.

Contents

Preface

Any encyclopedia is liable to displease some readers by omitting certain items that the readers think should have been included. This problem is especially great in an encyclopedia of shipwrecks, because limitations of space prevent listing more than a small fraction of all recorded shipwrecks in history. Moreover, particular wrecks have what might be called their fans, who may be disappointed to find their favorite maritime catastrophes left out of such a reference. The author apologizes to such readers and asks them to understand that there simply was not room, even in a large work like this one, to list more than a few hundred of the many thousands of wrecks on record.

Selecting the incidents to include was difficult, because almost any set of criteria used to choose entries was bound to exclude many tragic and noteworthy stories. About the only general rule the author followed in making this selection was that the book should not mention warships sunk in combat, such as the World War II German battleship *Bismarck*. Such sinkings are the special province of military historians. Virtually every other category of sinking, however, was allowed, including warships sunk in storms or other non-combat situations, such as the American Civil War ironclad *Monitor*.

Certain shipwrecks, of course, are so famous that no comprehensive encyclopedia of wrecks could omit them. The sinking of the British liner *Titanic* in 1912 is perhaps the best case in point. The *Lusitania* and *Andrea Doria* are two other celebrated examples.

Beyond such cases, the author has tried to select shipwrecks of particular historical, cultural or technological importance. Among 19th-century shipwrecks, for example, the burning of the *Amazon* demonstrated the danger of fire to wooden-hulled ships, while the loss of the liner *Arctic* showed both the structural weakness of wooden hulls and the need to subdivide hulls into watertight compartments. Some entries in this book were selected for their great loss of life, such as the sinking of the German liner *Wilhelm Gustloff* in World War II—possibly the single worst shipwreck in history in terms of casualties. Other wrecks chosen for this volume illustrate notable natural or technological hazards, including icebergs, storms and boiler explosions.

By the nature of their narratives, shipwrecks lend themselves to lurid treatment. The author has tried to convey the drama of incidents described in this book while avoiding sensationalism, which is best left to television movies and the kind of paperback that goes on sale one month after a catastrophe.

Special thanks should go to my literary agent, Betsy Ryan, for her help and patience on this and other projects; Randy Ladenheim-Gil at Facts On File; the Pratt Library in Baltimore; and the Steamship Historical Society of America, whose collections in Baltimore helped greatly with research. Finally, special thanks should go to Father Andrew Kencis and Father Gregory Abu-Asaly, who helped the author rewrite, in a sense, a vital paragraph in his biography.

A Note on Ship Names

Where a ship listed in this book is named after a person, the wreck, in most cases, is listed with the last name first. A ship such as the *Wyer G. Sargent*, for example, is listed as *Sargent*, with the full name given in the text. Exceptions to this rule include well-known wrecks such as those of the *Andrea Doria* and *Wilhelm Gustloff*.

A

Aden, British liner *Aden* wrecked in a gale on the night of June 8–9, 1897, on the island of Scotora at the southern entrance to the Red Sea. The absence of lighthouses made the coast especially dangerous. Of 86 crew and 34 passengers, 36 crew and nine passengers survived. One boat was filled with women and children and launched but was carried out of sight.

Admella, Australian passenger steamship Eighty-three people are thought to have been killed in the wreck of *Admella* off Cape Northumberland, South Australia, on August 4, 1859. This was one of the most serious wrecks in Australia during the 1800s.

Admiral, American schooner An unconventional vehicle—a steam locomotive—played an important part in rescuing survivors of *Admiral*, which hit the south jetty of the Columbia River bar (Oregon-Washington) in a storm on January 13, 1912. Captain O. S. Wicklund at the Point Adams Lifesaving Station was informed by telephone that a four-masted schooner was in difficulty off the south jetty.

Wicklund proceeded to Fort Stevens and took a steam locomotive (used for repairs to the jetty) out to meet the stricken ship. With him were the locomotive's engineer and fireman. Slowly the men in the locomotive made their way down the track. A fog had reduced visibility almost to nothing.

Then the men saw a man on the track ahead. He was Captain Joseph Bender of *Admiral*, and he was carrying a bundle that turned out to be his baby. "Go get my wife!" he said. The rescuers discovered her a bit farther down the track. A few yards beyond, Wicklund and his party encountered the ship's cook.

The locomotive could carry no more people, so Wicklund and company returned to Fort Stevens.

There they met a lifesaving crew with rescue equipment, which they had placed on a flatcar. The locomotive hooked up with the flatcar and set out again for the wreck.

Wicklund was told that the ship might have demolished part of the trestle, so the rescuers proceeded with caution. They soon found that the report was accurate. The trestle was indeed broken, and a 200-foot gap was visible in the jetty. On the other side of the gap was a group of stranded sailors. After a line was fired across the stretch of water, the men were hauled to safety.

Everyone on board *Admiral* had survived, but the ship itself was nowhere in sight. The wind and seas had driven the ship over the jetty. Despite attempts by a tug to tow the ship, *Admiral* wound up on nearby Peacock Spit, where the wreck soon broke apart.

Admiral Benson, American steamship Sometimes a stranding does not seem serious at first, but later escalates into calamity. Such was the case with *Admiral Benson*, which stranded on the Columbia River bar (Oregon-Washington) near Peacock Spit on the evening of February 15, 1930, with 39 passengers and 39 crewmen on board. The captain sent out a message asking for help. The Coast Guard sent out lifeboats to take off passengers. The crew remained on board.

Soon a strong wind developed, along with heavy surf. The crew went ashore by breeches buoy, and only the captain remained on board. Before long, the winds attained gale force, and huge breakers assaulted the ship. Although *Admiral Benson* started breaking up, the captain remained with his ship for four more days before he finally came ashore.

The wreck disappeared stern-first into the sands. By 1950, only part of the bow was still visible, and that only at low tide. *Admiral Benson* was lost within sight of the spot where the freighter *Laurel* had wrecked the previous year.

See also COLUMBIA RIVER BAR; LAUREL.

Admiral Karpfanger, German training ship This four-masted sailing ship sailed from Port Germein, South Australia, for Falmouth, England, on February 8, 1938, and vanished at sea. Forty sailing cadets were lost with the ship.

Admiral Moorsom, British steamship Five people, including the captain, were killed in the wreck of *Admiral Moorsom*, which collided with the American ship *Santa Clara* in the Irish Sea on January 15, 1885.

Admiral Nakhimov, Soviet passenger liner The 17,000-ton *Admiral Nakhimov* collided with a Soviet bulk carrier, *Pyotr Vasev*, in the Black Sea in 1986. Of 346 crew and 888 passengers on *Admiral Nakhimov*, 398 were killed.

aerial surveys A search from the air can be highly successful in locating shipwrecks. Marine archaeologist Robert Marx recommends conducting an aerial search during a period of flat calm (no waves at all), from 100 to 150 feet altitude, using polarized glasses and a chart of the vicinity. He reports that ballast piles, cannons and anchors and even wrecks covered by sand, may be visible. Iron oxide from buried metal may darken sand above a wreck and make it easier to spot, he adds. Another indicator is a small, lone coral reef or an isolated collection of such reefs, grown up over a wreck.

See also ARCHAEOLOGY.

Affray, British submarine *Affray* disappeared under mysterious circumstances on April 16, 1951, on a training cruise in the English Channel between Falmouth and Portsmouth, England. The submarine departed from Portsmouth around 4 P.M. on April 16, on a training cruise with 75 people on board. Around 9 P.M., *Affray* sent a radio message that she was about to submerge. That was the last communication from the submarine. A search by vessels from several nations, including the United States, France and Belgium, failed to locate the ship. The search lasted for almost three days before it was discontinued temporarily. Later, a ship equipped with a submarine television camera resumed looking for *Affray*. The wreck of the submarine was located on June 14, 1951, near Hurd Deep. The cause of the sinking was not determined, but one possibility is that *Affray* sank as the result of an explosion. The search for *Affray* was a notable early use of underwater video equipment in hunting for shipwrecks.

See also EXPLOSIONS; SUBMARINES; VIDEO.

aft Toward the rear, or stern, of a ship. The opposite of aft is fore, meaning toward the bow.

See also BOW.

Aguila, British steamship In an example of U-boat warfare against British shipping, Germany's U-28 sank *Aguila* off Pembroke, England, on March 27, 1915. The submarine shelled *Aguila*, then fired a torpedo that broke the ship in two. Eight people were killed, including one female passenger and a stewardess, who drowned. *Aguila's* chief engineer and two other men were killed in the shelling.

aircraft lost at sea Aircraft lost during flights over water are sometimes included in shipwreck lore, especially if the aircraft vanished under seemingly mysterious circumstances. A well-known case is the disappearance of a flight of American military aircraft in the so-called Bermuda Triangle (although careful investigation of the incident has shown that the aircraft were not, in fact, lost under unearthly conditions, as some sensationalistic accounts have suggested). Another famous aircraft lost at sea is *L'Oiseau Blanc*, a French biplane that presumably crashed at sea in 1927 while attempting to capture a prize offered for a successful flight across the Atlantic.

See also BERMUDA TRIANGLE; OISEAU BLANC.

Alacrán Reef wreck, Mexico Spanish navigation had a bad reputation in the days of the flota system. Perhaps the survivors of one wreck in 1650 had particular reason to feel that way. A navigational error brought their ship (the name of which is not recorded) to wreck on Alacrán Reef on July 15. Eight people were killed. The survivors managed to survive for almost two months on a small island, then assembled a raft from wreckage and set out toward the mainland. On an island they passed along the way, they discovered survivors from another wreck that had occurred three years earlier.

Alfonso, British steamship Everyone on board except the captain was lost in the wreck of *Alfonso*, which collided with the Spanish collier *Hullera Española* off the coast of Portugal on January 4, 1902. One man was lost on the Spanish vessel.

Alice, French sailing vessel A dog's cries alerted people on shore to the wreck of *Alice*, which came ashore at North Beach Peninsula near the mouth of the Columbia River (Oregon-Washington) during a gale on January 15, 1909.

No sooner had *Alice* come ashore than a dog began howling. His cries brought his master to the scene. (According to historian James Gibbs in his book *Pacific Graveyard*, the dog had survived a shipwreck two years before.) Rescuers assembled on the beach, but their aid was not needed. The crew had already escaped successfully by boat. No lives were lost.

The ship's cargo—approximately 3,000 tons of cement—hardened, and its weight dragged the hull down into the sands.

See also ANIMALS, SHIPWRECKS AND.

Alligator, **American submarine** One of the earliest American submarines, *Alligator* was built in Philadelphia and launched in 1862. Construction delays prevented the submarine from entering service in time to oppose the formidable Confederate ironclad *Virginia* (better known by its former name, *Merrimac*), which caused great destruction of Union ships in Hampton Roads, Virginia, before *Virginia's* famous battle with the Union ironclad *Monitor*. Had *Alligator* been in service a few weeks earlier, it might have succeeded in sinking *Virginia*, or so an engineer employed on the submarine's construction told a Philadelphia newspaper, the *Public Ledger*, in 1862.

Unlike other early submarines, which utilized a screw propeller cranked by hand, *Alligator* reportedly used a peculiar system of 16 oars that operated in the manner of a duck's foot, closing when in forward motion and opening up when moved backward. *Alligator* was sent to Hampton Roads, then assigned to destroy bridges near Richmond and Petersburg, Virginia. The Navy had no faith in the craft's abilities, however, and returned *Alligator* to Hampton Roads almost immediately. The submarine reportedly could barely move at all, and the crew could not obtain air when the vessel submerged. *Alligator* was cut adrift and presumably sank in a storm off the Outer Banks of North Carolina while being towed to Port Royal, South Carolina.

See also MONITOR; SUBMARINES.

almiranta A well-armed galleon that accompanied the Spanish treasure fleets on voyages between Spain and the Americas, the *almiranta* was the smaller of two such galleons that sailed with each fleet. The larger galleon was called the *capitana* and served as the flagship.

See also CAPITANA; FLOTA SYSTEM; GALLEON.

Almiranta de Honduras, **Spanish convoy vessel** On April 2, 1632, *Almiranta de Honduras* was separated from its convoy and wrecked on the Florida shore. The wreck site is thought to have been near what is now Miami.

See also FLORIDA.

Alpena, **American passenger steamer** A severe storm on October 15, 1880, sank the passenger steamer *Alpena* on Lake Michigan, with the loss of 101 passengers and crew. The ship was en route from Grand Haven and Muskegon, Michigan, to Chicago. The storm arose suddenly and caused severe damage to many vessels in harbor. Apparently the ship was virtually shredded by the storm, because small pieces of the ship washed ashore in large quantities, along with vast numbers of apples from the ship's cargo and bodies of victims. The particular storm became known as the "*Alpena* storm."

See also GREAT LAKES; STORMS.

Alvin, **deep-sea submersible** Operated by the Woods Hole (Massachusetts) Oceanographic Institution, *Alvin* is among the most famous submersibles and played an important role in the exploration of the sunken British liner *Titanic*. *Alvin* also took part in the search for, and recovery of, a nuclear weapon lost off the coast of Spain in 1966.

Alvin itself sank in 1968 in more than 5,000 feet of water while preparing for a dive near Cape Cod, Massachusetts. Lifting lines on the craft's tender broke, and *Alvin* sank with its hatch open. *Alvin* was recovered in 1969 with the help of Reynolds Aluminum's submersible *Aluminaut*, which had participated with *Alvin* in the search for the lost nuclear weapon off Spain.

See also PALOMARES INCIDENT; SUBMERSIBLES; TITANIC.

Amazon, **British passenger liner** On her maiden voyage, the 3,000-ton *Amazon* burned and sank in the Bay of Biscay (between France and Spain) on January 4, 1852, killing 140 of 161 people on board. A wooden-hulled paddle steamer, *Amazon* had trouble with bearings overheating. This problem forced the ship to halt during a storm off Portland Bill, England, on January 2. The ship caught fire two days later near the Scilly Isles. The blaze spread despite efforts to put out the fire by pumping water onto it. Part of the problem reportedly was that the captain turned the ship into the wind, a maneuver that merely fanned the flames. It was also reported afterward that the fire kept the crew from shutting the engines down, a move that might have saved the wooden-hulled vessel. The launching of the ship's lifeboats was catastrophic. The falls gave way and upset the lifeboats, spilling their occupants into the water. Only 59 people survived the wreck; 102 were drowned. The destruction of

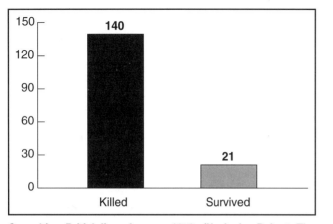

Casualties, British liner *Amazon*, 1952. (Nash, Jay Robert, *The Darkest Hour*. Prentice Hall. 1976)

Amazon added impetus to the move toward iron-hulled ships with screw propellers.

See also CONSTRUCTION; FIRE; LIFEBOATS; PROPULSION.

***Amazon* incident, Tunisia** Salvage sometimes requires unusual techniques and tools. Consider, for example, the stranded Liberty ship *Amazon*, which went onto the beach at Cape Bon, Tunisia, on December 24, 1963. Four days later, the Dutch tug *Zeeland* arrived. Efforts to deliver a line by rocket gun from *Zeeland* to *Amazon* failed. Without such a line, it would be impossible to string a towing cable between the two ships and pull *Amazon* off the beach. In place of rockets, the men on *Zeeland* used a kite; the kite went aloft in a strong wind. As the kite passed over the stranded ship, *Amazon*'s crew fired a rocket gun, which trailed a line over the kite's line and dragged the kite downward. The men on *Amazon* then took hold of the kite's line, and used it to pull a towing cable over from *Zeeland*. *Amazon* was pulled off the beach several days later.

See also SALVAGE.

***America*, American paddle steamship** *America* burned completely in the harbor at Yokohama, Japan, on August 24, 1872. Between 60 and 70 people are thought to have perished. The ship carried hundreds of passengers, most of them Chinese. In a parallel with the "money belt stories" told about Westerners who supposedly sank to their deaths while trying to swim wearing heavy money belts, many of the Chinese on *America* are said to have perished while trying to hang on to boxes of dollars saved in California.

See also MONEY BELT STORIES.

amidship The "midsection" of the ship, between the bow and stern, is vulnerable to damage for various reasons. Because it presents a wide area to any oncoming vessels, this part of the ship is often involved in collisions. (An extremely large vessel such as a supertanker may be so lengthy that another ship, traveling at night, may presume that this long, unlighted section of hull is actually a space between two ships, and steer for the side of the vessel, thinking it represents open water.) Also, this portion of the ship may be subjected to tremendous forces in heavy weather or other extreme conditions, so that leaks may develop amidships, or the hull may even tear in half. Two notable examples of vessels that broke in two are the British liner *Titanic*, which split apart in the vicinity of its fourth funnel while sinking, and the Great Lakes freighter *Edmund Fitzgerald*, which broke apart in a storm.

See also CONSTRUCTION; EDMUND FITZGERALD; TITANIC.

amphorae Ancient wine jars used by the Mediterranean peoples, amphorae are of great value to marine archaeologists as indicators of an ancient shipwreck's age and nationality. Amphorae differ in their size and shape but follow the general pattern of an ovoid body with a tapering bottom and a spout at the top, with handles on either side for lifting. In sunken ships, amphorae often serve as hiding places for octopi. On occasion, an amphora for wine is found with its contents undissipated by sea water. French undersea explorer Jacques Cousteau, for example, reportedly found an amphora still containing wine from Roman times in a wreck near Marseilles. He tasted the wine and found it awful.

See also ARCHAEOLOGY; GRAND CONGLOUE ISLAND WRECK.

***Anangel Liberty*, Greek freighter** There was a time when hardly anyone outside the affected area cared if a ship released pollutants into the waters. In recent years, however, environmental awareness has become much greater and can complicate greatly what otherwise would be a simple salvage operation. An example involves *Anangel Liberty*, which grounded on French Frigate Shoals, a national wildlife refuge in the Hawaiian island chain, in April of 1980. The ship carried more than 19,000 bags of kaolin clay.

When the owner's agent in Hawaii heard the ship was aground, he hired a tug, which sailed for the site. The Coast Guard investigated the situation and decided the owner had not taken adequate precautions against pollution. At that point, the federal government took control of the ship. The Coast Guard called in the Navy.

Soon the federal Environmental Protection Agency and the United States Fish and Wildlife Service were involved too. They favored unloading cargo and fuel from the ship by lighter. That scheme looked impractical, however, because it would take a day for a lighter to reach the freighter and because bringing the lighter alongside the ship was too dangerous.

Eventually, the Coast Guard commander serving as federal coordinator at the scene decided to dump the kaolin clay overboard. *Anangel Liberty* was pulled off the shoal and continued its voyage. There was no discernible damage to the environment. The incident demonstrated how complex the ramifications of a seemingly simple stranding can be.

See also POLLUTION.

anchors   Although anchors, by their size and distinctive shape, can be important indicators of a wreck's presence, they are actually of limited use in identifying specific wrecks. It is hard to assign a date to an anchor, for example, because anchors remained almost constant in shape for centuries. Some changes in construction did occur, however, starting in the early 19th century. Before then, anchors were forged by hand from more than one piece of iron; but after around 1825, anchors began to be cast as single pieces. In the mid-19th century, the stock, or wooden crosspiece of an anchor, was replaced with a metal bar. The now-familiar metal anchor chain also became commonplace in the 19th century. Ships traditionally have carried many anchors, both to replace lost anchors and to provide added safety when stormy weather required the ship to put out extra anchors in order to maintain its position. Spare anchors, dropped during a storm, might be the only way to prevent a ship from being driven onto a reef. Despite its safety value, an anchor has been known to sink a ship on at least one occasion. The spare anchor on a lightship swung against the hull during a storm and knocked out a hole that allowed the ship to fill with water and sink.

See also ARCHAEOLOGY.

Ancona, Italian liner   A submarine flying the Austrian flag reportedly sank *Ancona* on November 8, 1915, off Cap Carbonara, Sardinia, as it was on a voyage to New York. Boats were launched, but they capsized while the liner continued forward under steam. One hundred and ninety-four people were reported killed, including 11 United States citizens. The "Austrian" submarine is believed to have been Germany's U-38.

Andaste, Great Lakes steamship   A curious looking vessel reminiscent of the "pig boats" that plied the Great Lakes in the 1920s, *Andaste* vanished on Lake Michigan on September 9, 1929, with 25 people on board. The ship was an ungainly looking vessel with sides that sloped inward toward the top, and decks full of complicated "self-unloading" machinery designed

to handle cargoes such as coal and iron ore. Dwight Boyer, in his history of shipwrecks on the Great Lakes, writes that *Andaste* was painted an unusual red hue to conceal reddish stains left by chunks of ore that dropped from unloading buckets onto the hull.

Andaste took on a load of gravel at Ferrysburg, Michigan, and departed later that day for South Chicago. The ship passed the Coast Guard station at Grand Haven, Michigan, shortly after 9 P.M. A gale arose on the lake soon after *Andaste* left port.

What exactly happened to *Andaste* thereafter is uncertain. Observers at several points—a Coast Guard station at Holland, Michigan; people at cottages near Grand Haven; and the captain of the steamer *Alabama*, caught in the storm—all reported seeing ship lights during the night. The vessel they saw may have been *Andaste*, but if it was, *Andaste* apparently gave no sign of being in trouble. *Alabama*'s captain, however, had the impression that the ship he saw was not moving.

When *Andaste* was significantly overdue, an air and sea search for the ship began. Wreckage from *Andaste* was found a couple of days later by a tug. Bodies of the crew also washed ashore later. One body, Boyer writes, was that of a man who had been born on a farm on the lakeshore. His body drifted ashore only a few hundred feet from his birthplace.

Boyer also describes an apparent hoax that someone perpetrated with a pencil and a white board. The board reportedly washed up on a beach. Written on it was a message with the initials A.L.A.—the same as Albert L. Anderson, *Andaste*'s captain—stating that the ship could not hold up much longer.

That alleged message was dismissed as a hoax, however, for several reasons. It was not written in proper fashion: a properly written message would have included the ship's approximate position and the cause of sinking. The board was in good condition, unlike wreckage typically discovered on beaches. Perhaps most significant was the fact that ships carried special watertight containers precisely for the purpose of casting such last-minute messages overboard before a vessel sank. Since *Andaste*'s captain presumably would have used such a container for his message, there was additional reason to reject the message on the board as a hoax.

The investigation into *Andaste*'s loss could discover no particular reason for the ship's sinking. The storm was dangerous, of course, but *Andaste* apparently was well-equipped to withstand conditions on the Great Lakes. The federal inspector who had examined *Andaste* earlier that year said he could not think of a more able vessel. The ship had good life preservers. *Andaste* had not been overloaded; on the contrary, the ship was carrying a lighter load than usual. The lifeboat davits appeared to be in good working order.

Inspectors in Chicago had gone over the ship and pronounced it to be in top condition.

In its final report, the jury that investigated *Andaste*'s loss attributed the sinking to reasons unknown. The investigation was not even able to determine where the ship had gone down. The jury emphasized that it found no evidence that carelessness was responsible for the sinking. The exact reason for *Andaste*'s loss remains a mystery.

Andaste had not carried a wireless system, so it was unable to signal that it was in distress.

Boyer reports an incident of animal behavior in connection with *Andaste*'s loss. The ship's mascot was Queenie, a dog of mixed breed (part Airedale) that waited to meet the ship each time it arrived in South Chicago. Queenie did not like lake voyages, so she stayed on shore and greeted *Andaste* with vigorous tail-wagging. When *Andaste* was overdue at South Chicago on its final voyage, however, the dog evidently perceived that something was wrong and became notably agitated, as if aware that the ship was either lost or in trouble.

See also ANIMALS, SHIPWRECKS AND; CLIFTON; GREAT LAKES; WIRELESS.

Anderson, American schooner One of the mysteries of America's Pacific Northwest is the disappearance of *Anna C. Anderson,* which vanished at sea in January of 1869. The ship carried a seven-man crew and a cargo of oysters on its final voyage, and was last seen crossing the bar at Shoalwater in Washington state, headed for San Francisco. Apparently, no trace of the ship was ever found afterward.

What caused the schooner's disappearance is unknown. According to one scenario, however, the ship—carrying a highly perishable cargo—may have put on more sail than necessary, in the hope of cutting travel time to San Francisco. The ship might have paid for all that extra canvas if a wind hit hard and made the vessel capsize before the sails could be taken in.

See also MYSTERIES.

Andrea Doria, Italian passenger liner Named after an admiral of the 16th century, *Andrea Doria* was one of the most beautiful and elegantly appointed liners of the 1950s. On July 25, 1956, *Andrea Doria* collided with the Swedish liner *Stockholm* off Nantucket Island, Massachusetts, and sank the next day. The collision killed 52 people; 1,652 others were rescued. *Stockholm* remained afloat.

The collision occurred in fog at 11:45 P.M. Although *Andrea Doria* and *Stockholm* both were equipped with radar, it displayed only the relative positions of ships it detected. There was still an opportunity for error,

and therefore collision, because ships' officers had to determine the courses of objects displayed on the radar screen. During the final moments before collision, no one on either *Stockholm* or *Andrea Doria* appears to have recognized that the two ships were on courses that would bring them to strike each other.

When radar showed the ships to be only two miles apart, *Andrea Doria*'s lights became visible from *Stockholm. Stockholm*'s third mate, who was on the bridge just then, chose to turn *Stockholm* to the right. At the same time, *Andrea Doria* turned left. Although these turns were meant to avoid collision, they had the opposite result. They placed *Andrea Doria* directly in *Stockholm*'s path.

Stockholm's bow—which was reinforced to cope with icy Swedish waters—struck the right side of *Andrea Doria* and left a hole some thirty feet wide. Captain Piero Calamai did not sound an alarm, so as to avoid creating panic on *Andrea Doria.* He ordered an S.O.S. message sent.

Andrea Doria began listing to the right as water poured in through the huge hole. Soon the list increased to the point where lifeboats could not be lowered on the right side.

Andrea Doria's S.O.S. message brought several rescue ships to the scene, including the great French liner *Île de France.* The captain of *Île de France,* Baron Raoul de Beaudean, had all the lights on his ship turned on, to let *Andrea Doria*'s passengers and crew know that help had arrived. The brilliantly illuminated French liner and other rescue vessels picked up survivors and carried them to shore.

Andrea Doria sank around 10 A.M. on July 26. The wreck lies in 225 feet of water. A yellow buoy marks its site. The wreck became a popular site for diving. Following *Andrea Doria*'s loss, improvements in radar made it possible to determine true courses of ships rather than merely their relative positions. These improvements provided extra protection for ships at sea.

Captain Calamai of *Andrea Doria* reportedly said after the wreck that he had come to hate the sea. Baron de Beaudean, on the other hand, was hailed as a hero for his role in the rescue operations, and the following year was made permanent commander of *Île de France.*

See also COLLISIONS; FOG; NAVIGATION; RADAR.

Andree expedition One of the most famous expeditions into the Arctic, the balloon flight of Swedish aeronaut Salomon August Andree ended in tragedy. Riding a hydrogen-filled balloon launched from Spitsbergen, Norway, on July 11, 1897, Andree and two companions intended to ride the balloon to the north geographic pole. Instead, the balloon came down far

Lifeboats and debris float on surface after Italian liner *Andrea Doria* sinks in Atlantic. (U.S. Coast Guard)

short of its goal, at White Island, a small island east of Spitsbergen. The balloon had spent only three days aloft and had been forced down by the weight of accumulated ice. All three men on the expedition died before they could return to Sweden. The aeronauts' bodies were discovered in 1930.

Angel Gabriel, British sailing vessel   The wreck of the *Angel Gabriel* on August 15, 1635, at Penequid Harbor, Maine, demonstrates how even the safety of a harbor can be illusory. An immigrant ship, *Angel Gabriel* was beset by a storm while in harbor. The vessel is thought to have been driven into shallow water and destroyed by the wind and waves. The 250-ton ship is believed to have been one of the largest, if not the largest, ship destroyed in this particular storm, which also caused numerous other shipwrecks along the Northeast coast.

See also NEW ENGLAND; STORMS.

Anguilla, Lesser Antilles   One of the Leeward Islands, Anguilla has been the site of numerous shipwrecks. In 1772, for example, two large Spanish warships sailing in company with 18 merchant vessels of the New Spain Flota were wrecked off Anguilla. English salvors from nearby islands recovered most of the ships' cargoes.

animals, shipwrecks and   Animal behavior is a minor but colorful element of shipwreck lore. On occasion, an animal's cries have alerted rescuers to a shipwreck, as in the case of the French ship *Alice*, wrecked off the coast of the northwestern United States in 1909. Sometimes a dog has even participated in lifesaving operations, by such feats as swimming to shore with a line tied to him.

A notable shipwreck involving large numbers of animals (including an elephant) was that of the "zoo ship" *Royal Tar*, which burned and sank in New England waters.

The Magna Carta mentions animals carried on board ships and specifies that if any animal escapes from a wrecked vessel alive, local authorities may take control of the vessel.

The Swedish liner *Stockholm* shattered its bow in a collision with the Italian liner *Andrea Doria.*

Stories are told of animals that supposedly perceive somehow, from a great distance, that their masters are in trouble on the seas. Such tales are sometimes cited as examples of "extrasensory perception" and the "psychic" abilities of animals. Reports of this kind are questionable, however, and should be treated with skepticism.

See also ALICE; HARPOONER; ROYAL TAR.

***Anna May*, American trawler** Even a small shipwreck may involve a dramatic rescue. A case in point is the trawler *Anna May*, which sank in a storm on Diamond Shoals, on the Outer Banks of North Carolina, on December 9, 1931.

The trawler's engine stopped, and the boat drifted onto Diamond Shoals, where it filled rapidly with water and sank. All five men on board climbed the mast. They had no life jackets or signals. All they could do was hang on to the mast and hope that someone would see them and come to their aid.

A lookout at the Cape Hatteras lifesaving station sighted the mast sticking up above the turbulent seas, with five men clinging to it. The lifesavers tried to launch a boat from the beach but were unsuccessful. Then mist settled over the waters and concealed the mast and men from view. When a power boat reached

the area where the trawler had sunk, the rescuers could not find the wreck.

The following morning, the mast came once more into view. The trawler's crew was still there. Two boats set out to the rescue. Just as they arrived, the mast fell into the sea and dropped the men into the water. The lifesavers knew their business, however, and rescued all five men. There were no casualties, and the lifesavers of the Outer Banks had another colorful story to tell.

See also OUTER BANKS.

Antigua, Lesser Antilles Storms, reefs and warfare have figured in numerous wrecks in waters around Antigua. The following is a partial list of Antigua's shipwrecks. A hurricane in 1666 reportedly destroyed two unnamed English warships in English Harbor and killed many of those on board. In 1744, an English merchant vessel was wrecked on a bar in the harbor, and an unidentified Spanish privateer was forced ashore by an English warship and wrecked on the southern side of the island. A hurricane on September 13, 1754, destroyed more than 10 vessels near St. John's Harbor. A number of English merchant ships were sunk at St. John's Harbor, and several English warships were lost at English Harbor in a hurricane on August 30, 1772. The 32-gun British warship H.M.S. *De Ruyter* sank at Deep Bay in a hurricane on September 4, 1804, but all the ship's crew was saved. The 10-gun British warship H.M.S. *Guachapin* was wrecked on Rat Island in a hurricane on July 7, 1811. In 1823, the American schooner *Hope* was wrecked on an island on Antigua's northern shore, and the British merchantman *Sisters* was lost on a reef on the southern side of Antigua.

Antikythera wreck, Greece A wreck off the island of Antikythera near Crete yielded to salvage efforts in 1900 numerous items of sculpture, pottery and glassware, including outstanding examples of bronze statuary from Greece's Periclean Age, about 500 to 400 B.C. The wreck is thought to have occurred in the first century B.C. The ship is believed to have been on a voyage from Athens to Rome and manned by coastal raiders. The wreck also yielded a piece of machinery that later was identified as an astrolabe, or mechanical model of the planets and stars. The wreck was discovered in an unlikely manner. A storm in 1900 forced a Greek sailing vessel to anchor near the village of Potama on Antikythera. While waiting for the storm to end, divers went down to search for sponges. One diver landed in the midst of a cluster of statuary and returned with the detached arm of a bronze figure.

See also ARCHAEOLOGY.

apparitions Maritime lore includes many reports of ghostly vessels seen sailing the seas as apparitions long after the actual ships were lost. Such apparitions are reported in many parts of the world.

An example is the phantom schooner said to haunt Gardiner's Bay on Long Island, New York. The apparition was reported seen in the summer of 1881 by a fishing schooner that anchored in Gardiner's Bay at night.

The crew and their guest, a writer for the *New York Sun*, were on deck when they saw what appeared to be a large schooner approaching them at a speed of 10 knots, despite an absence of wind. It appeared that the ship would collide with them; but just before impact, the large schooner allegedly disappeared.

An earlier report of an apparition in waters near Gardiner's Bay dates from 1754. Several men fishing for menhaden between Plum Island and Gardiner's Bay allegedly witnessed a spectral naval engagement above the waters. According to this report, the men saw what appeared to be a battle involving three full-rigged ships. Although the witnesses reportedly were able to see details of the ships' rigging and men on board the vessels, and even saw smoke from the ships' guns, the apparition was silent. The engagement was

said to have been performed with great agility, as by a well-trained crew. The apparition allegedly lasted some 15 minutes before fading gradually from view. According to maritime historian Jeanette Edwards Rattray in her book *Ship Ashore!* about shipwrecks on Long Island, the original report of the phantom naval battle was published in the *New York Gazette* on March 18, 1754, in the form of a letter written from Plum Island.

A similar story involves the New Haven specter ship. This ghostly vessel is said to have been sighted in colonial times above the waters off New Haven, Connecticut.

Perhaps the most famous apparition in the lore of the sea is that of the *Flying Dutchman*. Numerous variations on this story exist. According to one version of this tale, a sea captain named van Straaten foolishly chose to sail his ship in stormy weather around the Cape of Good Hope, at the southern tip of Africa. The ship was sunk, and, with its captain and crew, was supposedly condemned to sail those waters for all time. The *Flying Dutchman* is said to show no navigation lights, but nonetheless to be illuminated somehow. The ship approaches to within perhaps half a mile of another vessel, then disappears.

Natural explanations are possible for many alleged apparitions. The phantom schooner of Gardiner's Bay, for example, has been attributed to St. Elmo's Fire, a visible display of static electricity whose eerie light might be misinterpreted as a ghostly manifestation. The New Haven specter ship is suspected of having been the light from burning methane, or marsh gas, just above the waters. Lightning discharges reflected from clouds conceivably might also take on the appearance, in observers' imaginations, of phantom ships sailing the seas. Another possibility is, of course, that many of these stories are mere hoaxes or hallucinations.

Because they occur in the human mind and have no material existence, apparitions are a different phenomenon from ghost ships, which are actual vessels found adrift or carried ashore with no one on board. A ghost ship may appear to have been abandoned in great haste. A celebrated example of a ghost ship is the *Mary Celeste*, an abandoned sailing vessel that has been the subject of widespread speculation for the past century, in part because of an inaccurate account of the case by British mystery writer Sir Arthur Conan Doyle, creator of Sherlock Holmes.

Likewise, an apparition should not be confused with a ghost wreck, in which inaccurate or misinterpreted records of a shipwreck may lead searchers to seek a wreck, for salvage or some other purpose, where no wreck actually exists.

See also DAVY JONES'S LOCKER; FLYING DUTCHMAN; GHOST SHIPS; GHOST WRECKS; MARY CELESTE; MYSTERIES; MYTHOLOGY; NEW HAVEN SPECTER SHIP; ST. ELMO'S FIRE; SUPERNATURAL EVENTS.

***Arabic*, British passenger liner** Sunk by a German submarine on August 19, 1915, *Arabic* went down only about 50 miles from the spot off the Irish coast where the liner *Lusitania* was sunk by another U-boat only three months before. Although Captain William Finch of *Arabic* took numerous measures to protect his ship against submarine attack, such as steering a zigzag pattern, a torpedo fired by U-24 struck the ship on the starboard side. The wireless was destroyed, so *Arabic* was unable to send a distress call. The ship sank quickly, and a starboard list interfered with lowering boats. Only six lifeboats were launched successfully. The liner sank only nine minutes after the torpedo exploded. Survivors drifted in the boats and on liferafts for more than an hour before being rescued. Forty-four people out of 423 aboard the liner died as a result of the sinking. *Arabic*'s performance in evacuating the ship was much better than that of *Lusitania*, thanks in part to a well-conducted boat drill on *Arabic*. The sinking of *Arabic*, some of whose passengers were Americans, contributed to American anger toward Germany and its policy of sinking unarmed passenger liners without giving warning. Germany defended U-24's commander, one Lieutenant Commander Schneider, by saying that Schneider misinterpreted the liner's zigzag course as an effort to ram his submarine, and sank *Arabic* in self-defense.

See also LUSITANIA; SUBMARINES; TORPEDOES; ZIGZAG.

archaeology Marine archaeology involves the location, surveying, and study of shipwrecks, as well as the recovery and preservation of items from wrecks. A complex discipline, modern marine archaeology was made possible by a variety of inventions, including the self-contained underwater breathing apparatus, or SCUBA, which allows divers to work underwater for extended periods on submerged wrecks.

Archaeologists in recent years have investigated numerous wrecks, some of them thousands of years old, and brought some of their contents to the surface. Recovered items range in size and cultural significance from clay pipes to classical statuary. Other frequently recovered items include coins, firearms, artillery, dinnerware and jewelry. In rare cases, entire ships have been recovered and brought to the surface for display and study. A notable example is the Swedish warship *Vasa*.

Archaeology should not be confused with treasure hunting, the pursuit of economically valuable objects and materials from wrecks, although marine archaeology may involve the finding and retrieval of precious objects such as gold and silver coins. Archaeology is likewise distinct from salvage, which involves the refloating of sunken ships or recovery of materials and objects from them, without systematic study of the wrecks and their contents.

Archaeological surveys of wrecks may reveal much about daily life aboard ship, from the leisure activities of crewmen to the character of their meals. Animal bones found among ballast, for example, may reveal exactly what crewmen ate.

Numerous factors may make projects in marine archaeology difficult, including poor underwater visibility, extremely cold water, strong currents, political obstacles to diving in certain waters, inaccurate positions for wrecks, coral growths or sediment deposits that cover wrecks, and depradations by treasure hunters.

See also SALVAGE.

***Arctic*, American passenger liner** Before the name *Titanic* became a popular synonym for catastrophe at sea, *Arctic* held that distinction. The Collins liner *Arctic*, launched in 1850, was 284 feet long and known for its opulent interior. The ship's 13-knot speed made it unusually fast for its day, and *Arctic* was capable of completing an Atlantic crossing in fewer than 10 days. The liner, however, had two major deficiencies that would destroy it only four years after launching. The wooden hull was one weakness. An iron hull would have provided greater protection. The

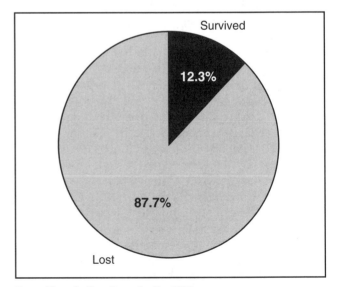

Casualties, Collins liner *Arctic*, 1854.

other deficiency was the lack of watertight compartments. Except for a few pumps, there was no way to contain flooding if something breached the hull.

The final voyage of the *Arctic* began on September 20, 1854, when the liner left Liverpool, England, for New York under the command of Captain James Luce, who made this trip in the company of his young son. On board were 282 passengers and 153 crew members. The passenger list included Mrs. Edward Collins, wife of the founder of the shipping line. With her were her two children, Mary Ann and Henry.

Arctic encountered fog on September 27, as the liner approached North America. Under pressure for a quick passage to New York, Luce maintained a full speed of 13 knots despite the fog and reduced visibility. Luce apparently thought visibility, at one-half to three-fourths of a mile, was adequate to see and avoid any other vessels. Luce did not even take the then-common precaution of posting a crewman to sound a horn that would warn other ships in the immediate area of the liner's presence.

At 12:15 P.M., the liner crossed paths with the iron-hulled French passenger steamer *Vesta*, under the command of Captain Alphonse Duchesne. *Vesta* struck the starboard side of *Arctic*. The collision left three or more holes below the waterline in *Arctic* and tore away 10 feet of *Vesta*'s bow. At first, *Vesta* appeared to be the ship in greater trouble. The French ship lowered two lifeboats, one of which capsized and spilled its occupants into the sea, killing several of them.

At first convinced that *Arctic* was relatively unharmed, Luce prepared to render aid to *Vesta*. Then he recognized that his own ship was in danger too. *Arctic*'s second officer investigated the starboard side and found that water was pouring into the liner. Because *Arctic* had no internal compartments to contain flooding, the ship was in mortal peril. Unless the holes in the hull could be sealed somehow, nothing would prevent the liner from filling and sinking.

Luce immediately took emergency measures. To lighten and elevate the damaged bow, he had the anchors dropped and anchor chains cast overboard. Six pumps were set working to remove water from the ship. The crew also tried to seal the holes by dropping a sail over the side, but found that chunks of iron left there by *Vesta*'s hull made the holes impossible to plug.

With his vessel sinking under him, Luce had to make a difficult decision. He could remain on the site of the collision and obtain help from *Vesta*, or make a run for the shore, and hope to reach land while *Arctic* remained afloat. In what would prove to be a fatal misjudgment, Luce chose a dash for shore. *Arctic*

headed away at top speed and left the damaged *Vesta* behind.

At this point, *Vesta*'s second lifeboat—the one that had been launched successfully—appeared directly ahead of *Arctic*. Unable to avoid the oncoming liner, the lifeboat and its occupants were run down. All but one of the people on the lifeboat were killed. The only survivor was one Jassonet Francois, who grabbed a rope tossed to him by one of *Arctic*'s passengers and was hauled aboard the ship.

Soon it became clear that Captain Luce should have stayed near the French steamer. The full-speed run for shore sent water cascading in through the breaches in the hull, faster than the pumps could keep up with the inflow. In less than two hours, the incoming seawater put out the fires under the boilers. Without steam, *Arctic* stopped about 35 miles from the shore.

The only option left was to put passengers and crew into lifeboats. Luce ordered that women and children should have priority. The stokers disagreed and rushed the boats. A crewman who tried to stop them was killed. The captain was powerless to enforce his own orders. As a result, much of the crew put its own survival first and left passengers, including children and women, to fend for themselves on a sinking ship more than 30 miles from land.

Some crew members, however, remained loyal and obedient to Luce. Among them was apprentice engineer Stuart Holland. Ordered to fire the ship's signal gun at intervals to alert any nearby ships to *Arctic*'s distress, he stayed at the task until his ammunition was exhausted. Meanwhile, passengers and remaining crew were building rafts.

Arctic sank at 4:45 P.M. Captain Luce, in the water, had the horrifying experience of seeing his young son killed when the paddle box—the housing for the ship's huge paddle wheel—bobbed to the surface and then fell upon the boy. Luce and several other men then climbed onto the paddle box.

Survivors (including Jassonet Francois, who had survived the sinkings of *Vesta*'s lifeboat and the *Arctic* in a single day) were scattered across the sea in boats, on rafts, and atop floating debris. During the night, some survivors slipped into the sea and died. The following day, passing ships picked up the survivors they found. Two lifeboats reached land. Three boats that left *Arctic* were never found. Of the 435 people aboard *Arctic*, only about 65 survived. The dead included Mrs. Collins and her children. Edward Collins later would say that Captain Luce, in effect, had murdered the Collins family.

Vesta managed to make port in St. John's, Newfoundland, on September 29. Captain Duchesne and his men received high praise in the press for saving the severely damaged ship. Duchesne's achievement made the loss of life from *Arctic*'s sinking all the more tragic. Had Captain Luce remained near *Vesta* instead of making a dash for land, the French ship probably would have been able to save most, if not all, of *Arctic*'s passengers and crew.

Arctic's loss and *Vesta*'s survival contained two important lessons for shipbuilders. One was the superior strength of iron hulls. The iron-hulled *Vesta* survived; the wooden *Arctic* sank. The other lesson was to build compartments into hulls. *Vesta* had such compartments and used them to survive the loss of much of the ship's bow. Lacking such compartments, *Arctic* filled and sank quickly.

Much of the blame for the *Arctic* catastrophe fell on Captain Luce. Immediately after the collision, he took his mortally damaged ship away, at top speed, from the only ship in the vicinity, namely *Vesta*, and thus isolated his passengers and crew from the sole immediate source of aid. Luce's rush for shore probably hastened *Arctic*'s sinking by accelerating the inflow of water through the holes in the hull. He did not enforce adequate discipline on his crew. Above all else, before the collision, he had maintained maximum speed through fog without even having a crewman sound a horn to warn any nearby vessels of *Arctic*'s presence. *Arctic*'s sinking would remain a pre-eminent symbol of calamity at sea until eclipsed by the magnitude of *Titanic*'s loss in 1912.

See also COLLISIONS; FOG; LIFEBOATS; TITANIC.

Ariosto, American steamship   The wreck of the steamer *Ariosto* on the Outer Banks of North Carolina on December 23, 1899, demonstrated the wisdom of a particular piece of advice from the United States Lifesaving Service: namely, that a ship's crew should never try to reach shore through the surf in their own boats unless and until all hope of help from the shore has disappeared.

Ariosto was en route from Galveston, Texas, to Hamburg, Germany, by way of Norfolk, Virginia, when the ship ran aground about half a mile offshore near Ocracoke Station. The captain, however, had the impression that he had run aground on Diamond Shoals, a few miles north of Ocracoke. (Maritime historian David Stick, in his history of shipwrecks on the Outer Banks, *Graveyard of the Atlantic*, writes that the captain persisted in this mistaken belief even after seeing a red flare to the north in response to the ship's distress signals. Had the ship been stuck on Diamond Shoals, there would have been no land to the north from which a flare might have been launched.)

The captain gave the order to abandon ship, despite the fact that additional flares could be seen on shore—a clear indication that the ship had been sighted and help was on the way. The boats set out from *Ariosto* before everyone had boarded them; thus the captain and several other men were left on the ship.

The boats capsized in rough water. Only two of the 26 people in them were able to swim back to the ship. Moreover, only three of those remaining in the water succeeded in reaching shore alive, and one of them did so under astonishing circumstances. When the surfmen fired a line toward the stricken ship, the line landed on the shoulder of crewman Aleck Anderson, who was trying to stay afloat in the turbulent sea. He wrapped the line around his body and was hauled to shore by the lifesavers. Another man managed to swim to shore, and a third was hauled out of the surf.

Eventually, the captain and five other men remaining on *Ariosto* were rescued. Of 30 men on *Ariosto*, 21 had perished, because the captain gave an abandon-ship order based on a misperception, and because no one had heeded the Lifesaving Service's warning about using a ship's boats to reach shore through the surf.

See also OUTER BANKS.

Armada of the Ocean Sea   A fleet organized by Spain specifically for defense against pirates, the Armada of the Ocean Sea began operating in the early 16th century and was funded by a special levy imposed on all cargoes shipping to and from the Americas. The Armada escorted Spanish convoys from Spain to the Canary Islands, then took up station off the Azores. There the fleet sought out and destroyed pirate ships. The fleet would also meet eastbound convoys and escort them home to Spain. The Armada of the Ocean Sea became highly important to Spanish trade with the Indies. The fleet also was known as the Royal Fleet of Spain.

See also CORSAIRS AND PRIVATEERS; FLOTA SYSTEM.

Arrogante, French Navy ironclad   *Arrogante* sank in a storm off the island of Hyeres near Toulon on March 19, 1879. The lieutenant in command tried to beach the ship, but the vessel would not respond. The sinking killed 47 officers and men.

Arrow, U.S. Army transport ship   The transport *Arrow* was originally the handsome passenger steamer *Belfast*, built in Maine in 1909. During World War II, *Arrow* served as a ferry for supplies and troops in the Hawaiian Islands. On February 13, 1947, *Arrow* was driven by heavy seas onto the shore near Long Beach, Washington. The Army tried at first to protect the ship from looting, but eventually gave up when it became clear that *Arrow* could not be refloated. The wreck became a popular fishing site. In 1949, wreckers cut away all of the wreck that remained atop the beach. The masts were removed and reinstalled as a war memorial at Ocean Park, several miles north of where the ship went ashore.

artifacts Numerous artifacts may be found on a shipwreck. These differ greatly in size, character and state of preservation. Artifacts may range from small items such as coins, buttons and watches to large objects such as artillery. These objects may help to determine the date, nationality and specific identity of a shipwreck. Examples of artifacts found on shipwrecks include bottles, bricks, cannon, coins, firearms, glassware, metal ingots, nails, swords and tableware. Conditions under water may destroy many artifacts, but others are preserved in excellent condition, although they may be covered with crust that requires removal. X-ray photography may help to identify specific artifacts inside heavy encrustation. The recovery and study of artifacts from shipwrecks is among the activities of marine archaeologists, who may be able to reconstruct many aspects of shipboard life from analysis of artifacts. In many cases, artifacts from shipwrecks have revealed much about the cultures that produced the artifacts and the ships that carried them.

A celebrated example of an ancient artifact was recovered from a wreck off the island of Antikythera, near Crete, in 1900. Thought to have occurred in the first century B.C., the wreck yielded a complex piece of machinery that later was identified as an astrolabe, a mechanical model of the planets and stars.

See also ANTIKYTHERA WRECK; ARCHAEOLOGY; DATING OF SHIPWRECKS; EXCAVATION; IDENTIFICATION OF SHIPWRECKS.

artillery Ships in the treasure fleets that operated between Europe and the Americas were generally armed with several pieces of artillery. The number and size of artillery pieces on a ship depended on the size and task of the vessel. A galleon that served as a merchant vessel in a convoy might be equipped with perhaps a dozen cannon. An otherwise identical ship that served as a convoy's flagship and carried a large quantity of treasure, on the other hand, might carry 50 pieces of artillery. Brass artillery generally was preferable to iron, because iron artillery had a tendency to overheat and crack. Good brass artillery had impressive range: a big brass cannon might fire a 12-pound ball to a distance of a mile or more.

See also ARCHAEOLOGY; BOMBARDETA; CANNON; VERSO.

***Ascension,* Spanish convoy ship, Mexico** On voyages between Spain and the Americas during the days of the flota system, a ship might survive great perils along the way, only to be wrecked when entering the apparent safety of a harbor. That was precisely what happened to one convoy ship in 1588. After surviving a storm that lasted for days in the Gulf of Mexico, the 500-ton *Ascension, almiranta* of the New Spain Fleet on a voyage from Sanlucar, Spain, to Veracruz, Mexico, struck a reef and sank at Veracruz. *Ascension* was the last ship of the convoy to enter the

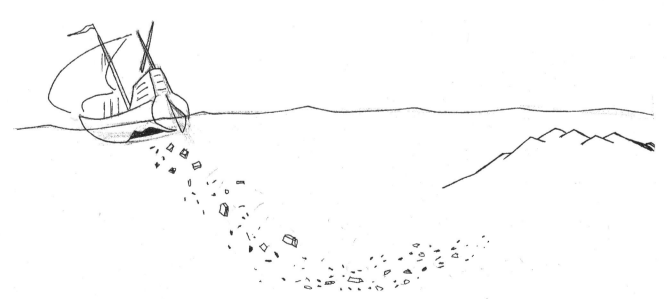

Artifacts are not always found on a wreck itself. In this diagram, a ship has been holed on a reef (right) but is drifting and scattering cargo and ballast across the seabed before sinking.

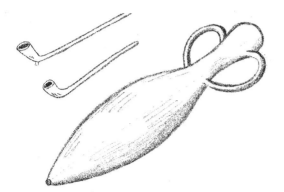

Clay pipes (left) and amphorae (right) are frequently recovered artifacts. (D. Ritchie)

harbor. Most of the ship's cargo of mercury was recovered.

See also ALMIRANTA; FLOTA SYSTEM; MERCURY.

Asia, American passenger steamer   A Great Lakes vessel, *Asia* sank twice in its career, first in 1881 and then again in 1882 after being raised. On its last voyage, *Asia* sailed from Collingwood, Ontario, on September 13, 1882, bound for Sault Ste. Marie, Michigan, under the command of Captain John Savage, with 125 passengers and crew aboard.

Choppy water impeded the ship's progress, and *Asia* consumed large amounts of wood for fuel. Seasickness affected many passengers. At one point, Captain Savage stopped at a small landing and had crew members go ashore to cut trees for firewood. When *Asia* resumed its voyage, the rough weather turned into a gale. Cargo on deck broke loose, and *Asia* had trouble maintaining an even keel.

The situation soon became so dangerous that Captain Savage decided to make for a nearby island. About half a mile from shore, however, *Asia* foundered and cast passengers into the rough water. Although 18 people, including Savage and the first mate, managed to depart the ship in a lifeboat, the boat overturned several times, killing many of those on board, including the mate and captain.

Only two people survived the loss of *Asia:* one Christena Ann Morrison and a teenage boy named Duncan Tinkiss. They clung to the ends of the lifeboat each time it capsized, then climbed back aboard when it was righted. After reaching shore, Morrison and Tinkiss encountered a Native American man who guided them to a settlement at Perry Sound.

The loss of *Asia* demonstrated the dangers of travel on the Great Lakes. Although small by the standards of oceans, the Great Lakes are nonetheless large bodies of water subject to severe weather conditions and,

therefore, potentially dangerous places for ships both large and small.

See also GREAT LAKES; LIFEBOATS.

Astrea, British warship   The sinking of H.M.S. *Astrea* on January 17, 1744, near Portsmouth, New Hampshire, demonstrates the danger of fire on wooden sailing vessels of the 18th century. Anchored in bitter winter weather to take on a cargo of timber, *Astrea* had difficulty heating its interior adequately. Heat originated from a stove, which on the night of January 17 was made especially hot and set the timbers beneath it on fire. A strong wind spread the flames through the vessel. The men on board organized a bucket brigade to fight the fire, but temperatures were so cold that buckets of water were largely frozen by the time they reached the flames. The ship was abandoned and drifted across the harbor to Goat Island, where the vessel burned to the waterline. What remained of the hull sank. In the 19th century, during bridge construction, pilings were driven through the wreck and obliterated much of it. Numerous items were salvaged from what remained of the wreck in the 20th century.

See also ARCHAEOLOGY; FIRE; NEW ENGLAND.

Atlanta, British frigate and training ship   This case is sometimes mentioned in connection with the myth of the so-called Bermuda Triangle, an area of "inexplicably" lost ships and aircraft. *Atlanta* is presumed to have sunk on January 31, 1880, on a voyage from Portsmouth, England, to the West Indies, with some 290 men on board.

The frigate *Atlanta* was built in 1844 and initially named *Juno.* Later the ship was renamed and converted to use as a training vessel. On its last voyage, *Atlanta* stopped in Bermuda to unload two men who had yellow fever. Then the ship continued on its way to the West Indies, and was never seen again. The British Admiralty sent a squadron to search for the lost ship, all the way from Bermuda to Bantry Bay in Ireland. The search failed to locate *Atlanta.* A gunboat reported seeing large amounts of wreckages floating near the Azores, but the debris could not be identified conclusively as coming from *Atlanta.* One possible explanation was that *Atlanta* was sunk in a storm.

See also BERMUDA TRIANGLE.

Atlantic, American steamship   A Great Lakes sidewheel steamer launched in 1848, *Atlantic* was passing Long Point on Lake Erie when it struck the steamer *Ogdensburg* and sank on the night of August 20, 1852.

The ship carried between 500 and 600 crew and passengers. Approximately half the people on *Atlantic* are believed to have drowned, partly as a result of the panic that occurred among the more than 400 immigrant passengers on board. The crew proved unable to maintain order on *Atlantic,* and many passengers tried to abandon ship simply by jumping into the water and swimming away—a fatal mistake. *Ogdensburg* returned to rescue 250 people who took refuge on the floating stern portion of *Atlantic.*

See also GREAT LAKES.

Atlantic, **British passenger liner** The White Star Line's luxury liner *Atlantic* struck a reef and foundered near Halifax, Nova Scotia, on April 1, 1873, as a result of a navigational error. Reportedly, 481 people out of 931 on board were killed. Not one woman on *Atlantic* survived. Only one child lived through the wreck.

Atlantic was one of the best-appointed ships of its time. It was a hybrid of steam and sail, with four masts and four 150-horsepower engines. *Atlantic* had a maximum speed of 12 knots.

The liner's final voyage was the second on the ship for Captain James A. Williams. He was concerned about the ship's coal supply. The coal-burning *Atlantic* had consumed almost 200 tons of fuel to travel the last 670 miles. The chief engineer told Williams that the coal was down to only 127 tons. The captain thought *Atlantic* would need 130 tons or more to reach Sandy Hook, New Jersey. Williams knew he could stop in Halifax, Nova Scotia, for additional coal; but there were good reasons to avoid Halifax. The shipping lane to Halifax was perilous. Also, stopping over in Halifax would be a poor reflection on Williams. No White Star vessel ever had been compelled to make such an unscheduled stop to refuel.

On the other hand, Williams could not ignore the diminishing coal supply, nor the safety of the more than 900 people on board. Moreover, the barometer was falling and indicated that bad weather was on the way. The thought of a fuelless ship, helpless in a storm with hundreds of lives on board, apparently convinced Williams to steer for Halifax.

Atlantic headed for Halifax at top speed. At 10 minutes before midnight on March 31, Williams saw a red light and presumed it was Sambro Light, several miles east of Sambro Island, near Halifax. He did not, however, consult his charts to make sure he had identified the light correctly.

He was wrong. The light on Sambro was white, not red. The captain had mistaken the red light on Peggy's Point for the light on Sambro. The Peggy's

Point light was several miles away from Sambro and marked an area of dangerous reefs. This information evidently was common knowledge to contemporary mariners, but Williams appeared to be unaware of it.

Williams told the officer on watch, Cornelius Brady, to keep a lookout for ice, maintain the same course until 3 A.M., and then call him. Williams then went to his cabin. Fourth Officer John Brown and Chief Officer John Firth relieved Brady on watch at midnight. Brady passed on the captain's instructions to the other officers, and then retired to his cabin.

Although the captain appeared unaware of the danger his error in identifying the lights had created, one account of the wreck says Quartermaster Dunn was concerned for the ship's safety before *Atlantic* struck the reef. He knew something of these waters and told the officers on the bridge to take care that the ship did not run aground. The officers outranked Dunn and told him to mind his place. (According to another account of the ship's last hours, however, Dunn never delivered this warning.)

Captain Williams was asleep at 2:40 A.M. A cabin boy was about to knock on the captain's door, but Brown told the boy not to awaken Williams. The captain remained asleep until 3:15 A.M., when he awakened to cries of "Breakers ahead." *Atlantic* struck the rocks on Mars Head near Halifax.

First a mild vibration ran through the ship. Some on board thought *Atlantic* was dropping anchor. Then a heavier, second shock occurred, and it was clear that the ship was aground. Holed in the side and bottom, *Atlantic* took on water rapidly. Hundreds of people were caught below decks. Some 300 are thought to have drowned in the first several minutes after impact with the reef.

An effort to launch lifeboats was largely unsuccessful. One boat overturned and spilled its occupants (including several men who had rushed the boat, in defiance of Third Officer Brady's order that women should go first) into the water. A wave swept two other boats overboard before they could be launched. Another boat rolled overboard before launching was possible.

A boiler explosion caused the ship to roll over and cast many people into the sea. The seemingly hopeless situation on *Atlantic* forced Third Officer Brady to come up with another, desperate plan to evacuate the remaining people on board. About 90 feet away from *Atlantic,* Brady saw a large rock. Perhaps, he thought, some people could be transferred there. At least the rock offered a firmer platform than the sinking *Atlantic.*

A quartermaster named Owens volunteered to try swimming to the rock with a rope, which would allow passengers to be transferred to the rock. An accomplished swimmer, Owens jumped into the water with one end of the rope tied around his waist. He reached the rock but was unable to climb to the top of it. Finally he gave up and was hauled back aboard the ship.

Brady himself made the next attempt. He managed to reach the top of the rock and affix the line to it. Brady and the two quartermasters then secured four additional lines to the rock, and the men started using a pulley and sling to haul passengers off the ship. Brady swam beside them and pushed them along.

Remaining passengers on *Atlantic* were clinging to the rigging. Some were exhausted and began to fall asleep. Captain Williams and Fourth Officer Brown tried to keep them awake.

Brady became exhausted after ferrying several passengers to the rock and had to be relieved. After resting, Brady reviewed the situation. It was not promising. Approximately 200 people had been transferred to the rock, and it was becoming crowded. It was also a dangerous place, with waves washing over it. Brady decided to swim for nearby Mars Island and arrange to have the survivors transferred there from the rock. Again, Brady went into the water and swam to the island. A fisherman and his daughter helped Brady get word to Halifax about *Atlantic*'s wreck and the dangers facing the survivors.

By 5 A.M., fishing boats began arriving at the wreck and taking survivors off the rock. Soon afterward, the ship finally sank after some or all of the remaining boilers exploded. At 7 A.M., a coded message arrived at White Star's offices in Liverpool. The message informed White Star that *Atlantic* had been wrecked with great loss of life, but that "people including captain [were] saved."

Captain Williams was vilified when news of his navigational error became public. The case against him was strong. He had taken *Atlantic* into perilous waters without referring to his charts. Had he looked at the charts, he would not have mistaken the red light for Sambro Light. He also departed from the bridge, leaving command of the ship in the hands of a subordinate. Moreover, Williams admitted that he had never been to Halifax before, nor even on the coast there; he did not use the lead (an early sounding device) to determine how much water was under the ship; had he been making soundings on a regular basis between midnight and 3 A.M., the ship would not have gone aground. The judge presiding at an

investigation of the wreck said that Williams's conduct in the hours just before the catastrophe deserved "severe censure." Williams's license was revoked for two years.

The pattern observed in the sinking of *Atlantic*—questionable behavior on the part of the ship's master; allegations of a warning ignored; and the subsequent loss of a large, well-appointed liner—are reminiscent of the later tragedy that struck the White Star Line when *Titanic* sank in 1912.

See also NAVIGATION; ROCKS AND SHOALS; TITANIC; WHITE STAR LINE.

***Atlantique,* French passenger liner**   Known as one of the most splendid ships afloat, the 42,512-ton *Atlantique* had a career of less than two years, sailing between Europe and South America. On a voyage from Bordeaux, France, to Le Havre, France, with no passengers on board, the liner caught fire on January 4, 1933. The fire began in a stateroom and spread rapidly. The crew abandoned ship several hours after the fire began. Nineteen crewmen were killed. *Atlantique* was towed to Cherbourg, France, and was sent to the breakers in 1936.

***Atocha,* Spanish galleon**   One of the most famous wrecks in the history of treasure hunting, the 550-ton galleon *Nuestra Señora de Atocha* sailed from Havana for Spain on September 4, 1622, as part of a fleet of 28 ships.

A hurricane hit the convoy in the Straits of Florida. *Atocha* was thought to have been driven ashore at what is now called Matecumbe Key in the Florida Keys. The ship struck a reef and sank. Only five people of some 260 on board survived.

Salvage efforts were organized on several occasions but were generally unsuccessful. At one time, buoys were anchored on the wreck site to mark its location, but the buoys were carried away in a storm.

In 1970, a search of Spanish salvage records in Seville revealed that *Atocha* had gone down in the Marqueas Keys, about 70 miles from Florida, rather than at Matecumbe. A subsequent salvage operation yielded a gold chain, some coins and other artifacts.

The search by 1973 had turned up many more artifacts. Several cannon were discovered on the sea floor in 1975. Some of these cannon appeared to belong to *Atocha*.

The placement of artifacts and treasure on the sea floor indicated that *Atocha* had broken apart in the storm, and the pieces of the vessel had drifted apart, scattering treasure across the seabed. The major portion of the galleon was located in 1981 in slightly more than 60 feet of water.

See also GALLEON; TREASURE.

Augusta, British warship   H.M.S. *Augusta* was sunk in the Delaware River during a British effort to take Philadelphia in 1777. The 64-gun *Augusta* was maneuvering to avoid obstacles placed deliberately in the river by the Americans when the warship ran aground. *Augusta* blew up after some hours of shelling from artillery on shore and sank in the middle of the channel. There the wreck remained until 1869, when *Augusta* was raised and towed to the New Jersey shore. The wreck became a sightseeing attraction for a time, and observers noted that the timbers had been preserved in good condition underwater. Various artifacts from the wreck were sold. The hull started to deteriorate and in time was covered with sand. Part of the wreck was saved, however, and used for oak paneling in a room at Continental Hall, national headquarters of the Daughters of the American Revolution, in Washington, D.C.

averia   A tax placed on all cargoes carried between Spain and the Americas. The tax was intended to support the Armada of the Ocean Sea, which protected against hostile vessels during convoy runs.

See also ARMADA OF THE OCEAN SEA; FLOTA SYSTEM.

Aves Island wrecks, Venezuela   More than 1,200 men reportedly were killed in the wreck of a French fleet on a reef near Aves Island on the night of May 3, 1678. The fleet was supposed to take Curaçao from the Dutch. Of 18 warships and two privateers in the fleet, only one privateer and one warship survived. Not only were the Dutch thus spared attack by the French fleet, but the Dutch also salvaged many of the cannon from the wrecks.

Aviles wreck, Florida   A ship on which one Adelantando Pedro Menéndez de Aviles was traveling in 1572 was wrecked near what is now Cape Canaveral. Everyone on board—30 people in all—survived the wreck and built a small fort on shore, using the debris from the shipwreck. Later, they proceeded on foot to St. Augustine. Two other vessels accompanied Aviles's ship on this voyage. One ship made its way to Havana, Cuba. The other was wrecked elsewhere on the Florida coast, where the crew was murdered and the ship was burned.

See also FLORIDA.

Aygaz, Turkish freighter   A hideous tale of death and survival accompanied the wreck and salvage of *Aygaz*, which capsized after being caught in a storm off the islands near Greece's Peloponnesian peninsula on March 24, 1969. On March 26, the Danish freighter *Lion Cif* sighted the overturned ship still afloat and took the wreck in tow to Pylos, Greece. When the hulk was in the harbor, someone inside the wreck was heard banging on the hull and calling for help. When a hole was cut in the hull near the stern, the ship's second engineer was pulled out of the wreck alive. He and four other men had been trapped in *Aygaz*'s engine room when the ship capsized. Only he survived; his four companions had died of lack of oxygen.

B

"B" powder This extremely dangerous explosive decomposed after lengthy periods in storage and could demolish the ship that carried it. "B" powder was implicated in the explosion of the French battleship *Liberté* at Toulon in 1911.

See also LIBERTÉ.

Bahamas Shipwrecks and salvage have been features of Bahamian life for centuries. Indeed, salvage was the leading occupation of the island until the mid-19th century. Notable shipwrecks in the history of the islands include the following:

The 300-ton Spanish galleon *Santa Clara*, part of the Tierra Firme Armada, was wrecked on October 6, 1564, on the El Mime shoal near Memory Rock in the Little Bahama Bank. No lives were lost, and all the gold and silver on board were recovered.

In 1641, the 680-ton Spanish treasure galleon *Nuestra Señora de la Concepcion*, with some 600 people on board, was wrecked on Silver Shoals after becoming separated from its convoy in a storm. Most of those on board survived by swimming to a sandbar in the vicinity. Few of these survivors lived long after the wreck. Most of some 200 who tried to reach Santo Domingo on boats and rafts died in the attempt. By the time a rescue ship arrived, all those who had stayed behind on the sandbar had died as well. Salvage operations were delayed by weather. When the weather at last became favorable, the sandbar had been washed away, so that it was difficult to locate the site of the wreck. The famous "wracker" Sir William Phips recovered most or all of the treasure from the galleon in 1687.

Tremendous loss of life occurred in 1656 when the 650-ton treasure galleon *Nuestra Señora de la Maravillas*, part of the Tierra Firme Armada, sank in 30 to 36 feet of water on Little Bahama Bank with more than 700 people on board. The ship sank after colliding with another vessel in the convoy at night. Only 56 people survived the wreck.

Some time before 1687, three notable shipwrecks appear to have occurred on Little Bahama Bank. The wrecks, which were shown on a 1687 chart of the bank, included a "Copper Wreck," a "Genovees Wreck" and a "Plate Wreck." The wrecks all were marked within three nautical miles from the bank's edge.

A huge sum in cargo reportedly was lost in August 1800 when the British warship H.M.S. *Lowestoff* and eight merchant vessels, carrying cargo with a value of some 600,000 pounds sterling, were wrecked on Great Inagua Island. The following year, a July hurricane wrecked more than 120 ships in the vicinity of Nassau. Great Inagua Island was also the site of six wrecks in a single day on August 10, 1801, when six English merchant vessels were wrecked simultaneously on reefs there.

See PHIPS, SIR WILLIAM; WRACKING.

Bahía de Uraba wrecks, Colombia A flotilla of four ships under command of Captain Juan de la Cosa was engaged in exploring and mapping the coast of Colombia in 1504 when all four ships were wrecked in a storm at Bahía de Uraba. Of 200 men on the ships, 175 reportedly were drowned.

Bahía Mujeres wreck, Mexico Located at Bahía Mujeres, off the Yucatán Peninsula in Mexico, this wreck involves a ship of undetermined nationality that may have sunk in the early 15th century.

Several possible identifications of the wreck have been attempted, including *San Jerónimo; La Gavarra;* and *La Nicolasa,* a ship of Francisco de Montejo the Elder, Conquistador of the Yucatán. (This last identification, however, appears questionable.) The wreck lies only about 10 feet below the surface and is located inside a reef line that runs in a northeasterly direction from Punta Cancun. Coral has overgrown the wreck site.

The wreck has been the site of intensive archaeological activity following its discovery in 1958, when a small cannon was recovered from the wreck. Several additional cannon were recovered in 1960 and 1961. Two anchors were raised from the wreck in 1961. Armament recovered from the wreck is of the kind used in the early 1600s.

See also ARCHAEOLOGY; CANNON.

Bailey, American schooner   Not all shipwrecks on American shores in the 19th century involved loss of life, nor even difficult rescues. An almost comically easy rescue involved the schooner *A.M. Bailey*, out of Somers Point, New Jersey. The ship went ashore near the Seatack lifesaving station on the Eastern Shore of Virginia during a storm on March 22, 1885. The powerful storm drove the schooner so high on the beach that the four men on board simply jumped down to the sand, with no help needed from the lifesavers. The ship was a complete loss, but the easy rescue made up for it.

ballast   Piles of ballast rock, carried by ships to increase stability by making the vessels "bottom-heavy" and therefore less likely to capsize, are good—but not infallible—indicators of a wreck's location. When a wooden-hulled sailing vessel sank, it commonly left behind a pile of ballast stones where the hull came to rest. Those stones may remain visible on the seabed after hundreds of years and guide archaeologists to the wreck site.

On occasion, however, a ship's crew would throw ballast overboard before the ship took on heavy cargo. The result in such cases would be a pile of ballast stones like that associated with a wreck, even though no wreck actually occurred at the site. (On some voyages, when a ship had especially weighty cargo, the vessel might sail with no ballast at all.)

Ballast rock from Spanish ships can be deceptive, writes marine archaeologist Robert Marx in his book *Shipwrecks in the Americas,* because the Spaniards—known for filthy conditions aboard their ships—would throw garbage such as animal bones and broken glassware into the hold, where the garbage became mixed with the ballast. When the ballast was thrown overboard later, the result was a mixture of rocks and artifacts that might make a modern archaeologist think a wreck had occurred at that site, even though the ship had merely discarded ballast.

Mariners preferred smooth, water-worn ballast rocks as a rule, because the rocks lacked sharp edges that might break through the hulls in heavy seas.

One clever practice to provide ballast on smaller vessels was to take the barrels and casks that had held beer, wine and other liquids and fill them with water as they were emptied. A special advantage of this method was that the sea water could be emptied from the barrels into the ship's hold and then pumped out easily if the ship had to be lightened in a hurry. This was a quicker and easier technique than lifting ballast rocks and heaving them overboard.

See also ARCHAEOLOGY; STABILITY AND INSTABILITY.

Bannockburn, Great Lakes steamship   One of the mysteries of Lake Superior is the disappearance of the steamer *Bannockburn* in 1902, with a crew of 20. A Scottish-built freighter 245 feet long, *Bannockburn* was last seen on the afternoon of November 21, 1902, eastbound near Keweenaw Point, Michigan, with a load of grain taken on at Port Arthur, Ontario, for delivery at Georgian Bay, Ontario.

Among the last to see *Bannockburn* was the captain of the steamship *Algonquin*. He saw *Bannockburn* making its way through haze and chop some 50 miles from Passage Island. Apparently *Algonquin's* captain noticed nothing unusual about *Bannockburn* on this occasion, with one exception: the rapidity with which the ship was lost from sight after the two vessels passed. According to maritime historian Dwight Boyer in his history of Great Lakes shipwrecks, *Bannockburn* vanished from sight unusually fast. The captain of *Algonquin* remarked to his first mate about the other ship's rapid disappearance.

Bannockburn is thought to have left Port Arthur around 9 A.M. on November 21. A few hours later, the ship passed *Algonquin*. The weather turned stormy soon afterward. Gale-force winds swept across Lake Superior and raised large waves. That night, one man on the passenger steamer *Huronic*, on the way to Port Arthur, thought he saw *Bannockburn*. If that was the case, then it must have been the last sighting of *Bannockburn*, because the freighter did not make port at Georgian Bay, and no further news was heard of the ship.

Here the story takes a mysterious turn. A report began circulating several days later that *Bannockburn* was at Slate Island. The story turned out to be groundless. Then another rumor arose: according to a sighting by the ship *Germanic*, *Bannockburn* had been found on the mainland near Michipicoten Island. This report also was false. So was a third story that the ship had turned up at Michipicoten Island itself. A tug went out to Michipicoten Island to search for *Bannockburn*, but found nothing.

The mystery grew deeper. When asked about the ship they allegedly saw near Michipicoten Island, the officers on *Germanic* said they had seen no ship there, and they did not know how the story got started. Moreover, no other ships besides *Bannockburn* were reported missing, so *Germanic* could hardly have mistaken another grounded ship for *Bannockburn*.

One possibility was that the ship had wrecked on Caribou Island, in the eastern part of the lake, just south of Michipicoten Island. Caribou Island's reefs could have made short work of a freighter in a storm. This hypothesis also suffered, however, when an ore carrier reported passing through wreckage many miles southwest of Caribou Island. Since *Bannockburn* was the only ship missing, it was presumed to be the source of the wreckage, which was far from Caribou.

If *Bannockburn* had not wrecked either at Caribou or at Michipicoten, how *had* the ship been lost? Overloading seemed unlikely. The cargo of grain was not excessive. What else, then, might have removed the ship so quickly from the surface of Lake Superior?

The captain of *Algonquin*, among the last to see *Bannockburn*, thought the ship's boilers might have exploded in the several minutes between the moment he saw the vessel and the time he noticed that *Bannockburn* was gone. The fact that no explosion was reported did not necessarily mean that no explosion occurred. Possibly such an explosion would have gone unheard on *Algonquin*, since the ships were a considerable distance apart.

An explosion would account for the ship's sudden disappearance. Moreover, the wreckage was found approximately where winds would have carried it in the days after the presumed explosion of *Bannockburn*. A mystery even surrounded the wreckage, however, for it lay along well-traveled steamer lanes and should have been seen by any of numerous ships if the wreckage had been there for several days. Yet it appears that only one ship, the aforementioned ore carrier, saw the field of debris. Where, then, did the wreckage come from, and how long had it been there before being sighted?

The explosion hypothesis was at odds with the alleged sighting of *Bannockburn* from *Huronic* on the night of the storm. Had *Bannockburn* exploded moments after being seen from *Algonquin*, then *Bannockburn* scarcely could have been sighted from *Huronic* hours later.

Another hypothesis was connected to a piece of evidence found in the lock at the Canadian Soo (Sault Ste. Marie) Canals. When the lock was drained, a steel plate from a ship's bottom was found. There was no proof that the plate had dropped from *Bannockburn*, but the plate's discovery led to speculation. Possibly, if plates were falling from *Bannockburn*'s bottom, then the bottom might have been in such bad condition that the ship's machinery plunged straight through the bottom during the storm, sinking the ship within moments. Yet this theory did not explain why *Bannockburn* seemed to vanish so quickly after being sighted by *Algonquin*. The storm had not yet arisen when those two ships passed. Also, *Bannockburn* had received the highest rating, A-1, from Lloyds.

One contributing factor to the loss of *Bannockburn* may have been the absence of a working lighthouse on Caribou Island. Although the island had a lighthouse, it had been shut less than a week before *Bannockburn*'s last voyage. Perhaps *Bannockburn*'s captain looked for the light and, failing to sight it, misjudged his position and wrecked his ship on the rocks. This explanation, of course, is inconsistent with the finding of wreckage far from the island, and the failure of a search to find a wreck on or around the island.

The mystery of *Bannockburn* remains unresolved. The only pieces of recovered wreckage thought to be from *Bannockburn*, an oar and a life preserver, revealed nothing about the ship's last moments. The wreck must lie somewhere near Caribou Island.

See also EXPLOSIONS; MYSTERIES; OVERLOADING.

bar   A bar is a deposit of sediment beneath the water's surface immediately offshore. Where the bar extends near the surface, it presents a hazard to navigation. Ships may become stranded on the bar and sink, either because of damage to their hulls resulting from striking the bar, or because of pounding from storm-driven waves while stranded on the bar. An example of a bar is the Columbia River bar, at the mouth of the river between Washington state and Oregon. The Columbia River bar has claimed numerous ships over the past 200 years.

Barbados   A member of the Lesser Antilles chain, Barbados has a lengthy history of shipwrecks, selected examples of which follow.

A hurricane on November 1, 1669, reportedly wrecked numerous ships and washed more than 1,500 coffins into the sea from a cemetery on the island. Twelve big English merchant vessels were reported wrecked at Bridgetown in another hurricane on September 1, 1675. The September 27, 1694, hurricane sank 26 English merchant ships at Carlisle Bay, with the loss of more than 1,000 lives. In 1716, a 24-gun pirate vessel under command of one Captain Martel sank a sloop in Carlisle Bay; the pirate ship in turn was sunk the next day by cannon fire from a English warship on the island's eastern shore. A hurricane on August 23, 1758, had catastrophic effects on shipping at Barbados: many vessels were lost in Carlisle Bay, and six unnamed vessels were lost at Bridgetown. Another highly destructive hurricane on October 10, 1780, wrecked more than 20 ships in the vicinity of Barbados and blew many others out to sea, where they apparently were lost without a trace. Waves associated with this storm also washed a building at Bridgetown's Naval Hospital into the sea. A sketchy account of another hurricane on September 2, 1786, reports that all ships in Carlisle Bay were wrecked. Great loss of life allegedly occurred in the wreck of the English slave ship *King George* at Barbados in 1791; of 360 slaves on board, only 80 were reported to have survived.

Barbuda, Lesser Antilles Shipwrecks on and around the island of Barbuda include, but are not limited to, the following. An unnamed Spanish merchant ship carrying the payroll for military garrisons was wrecked off Barbuda in 1695, but all the money was recovered. The *Pearl,* an English slave ship, was wrecked at Barbuda in 1749 with the loss of 70 slaves and 11 crewmen. Another slave ship, the French vessel *Hazard,* was wrecked at Barbuda on a voyage from Africa to Hispaniola, and several dozen slaves were reported drowned. On July 23, 1792, the 24-gun Spanish warship *Lanzerota* was wrecked at Barbuda; the crew was saved although the ship appears to have been almost a total loss. Three English merchant ships were wrecked in 1809: *Farmer,* en route from Britain to Honduras; *Julia,* on a voyage from Cadiz, Spain; and *Kingston,* sailing between England and St. Croix.

bark A sailing ship with at least three masts: a fore-and-aft rig on the mizzen mast; and a square rig on the other masts.

See also BARKENTINE.

barkentine A sailing ship resembling a bark but with a square rig on the foremast only. The other masts had a fore-and-aft rig.

See also BARK.

***Bartlett*, American schooner** The wreck of the *Fannie J. Bartlett* near Montauk, New York, provided the name for a stop on the Long Island Railroad for about 30 years. The ship was wrecked on the beach at Napeague on January 16, 1894, with no loss of life. The ship's nameplate was mounted at a flag-stop along the railway, from which fishermen would ship their fish. The stop became known as "Fannie Bartlett," even though there was no community by that name.

barrier islands These are elongated, sandy islands separating the ocean from a sound, or shallow body of water, that in turn separates the barrier islands from the mainland. New York's Fire Island and the Outer Banks of North Carolina are familiar examples of barrier islands along the Atlantic coast of the United States. The barrier islands' environment may present dangers to shipping, notably offshore shoals.

See also NEAR-SHORE ENVIRONMENT; OUTER BANKS.

Bartley incident In an amazing but evidently true story, reminiscent of the biblical story of the prophet Jonah, English whaler James Bartley reportedly survived being swallowed by a whale on August 25, 1891. The whaling ship *Star of the East* had come upon a pod of sperm whales. One wounded whale took a boat between its jaws and crushed it. As Bartley tried to escape from the boat, the whale seized and swallowed him.

Later that day, a whale was found dead. The whalers spent two days processing the carcass before someone wondered if this might be the same whale that had swallowed Bartley. The whalers cut through to the stomach and saw Bartley's form inside. He was still alive, but unconscious. They carefully freed him. Later, he was able to tell his story.

Bartley said he had seen a pink-and-white "canopy" descend on him, then felt himself being drawn down into the whale's stomach. He reported that the stomach was larger than his body and appeared to be filled with fishes, some of them still alive. He experienced a headache and difficulty in breathing, and perceived tremendous heat, as if being burned in a furnace. Then he fell unconscious.

Maritime historian Edward Rowe Snow writes that editor Henri de Parville of the Paris periodical *Journal des Debats* deliberated for more than four years before deciding to publish an account of Bartley's experience, after checking the details of the story thoroughly for accuracy. Snow adds that Bartley evidently suffered no lingering effects of his ordeal, except for recurring nightmares about it.

See also ESSEX; NYE INCIDENT.

***Barton*, American brig** Almost everything, it seems, worked against the 400-ton brig *Agnes Barton* on its final voyage in 1889, from Navassa in the West Indies to Baltimore with a load of phosphate rock.

The brig leaked badly. Also, the captain reckoned the ship's position incorrectly, so that *Barton*, after about three weeks at sea, found itself off the North Carolina coast, rather than near Cape Henry, Virginia, where the ship was supposed to be. The error was due to northeast winds that had pushed *Barton* toward the south.

The vessel sailed northward toward the mouth of Chesapeake Bay (Maryland-Virginia) but was driven toward the shore. As *Barton* neared land on March 14, the ship came to the notice of the men at Dam

Neck Mills lifesaving station in what is now the city of Virginia Beach. *Barton* was clearly in trouble. The crew flew the American flag inverted as a signal of distress.

The surfmen on shore signaled in response, and *Barton* made straight for the shore. Though driven by strong winds, the brig did not clear the outer bar, and stopped some 750 feet offshore. Immobilized, the ship started breaking up at the stern under the force of the waves. From a relatively safe spot at the bow, the crew watched as the lifesavers set up their Lyle gun and fired a line toward the stricken ship. The first shot failed to reach *Barton,* but the second attempt succeeded, and soon a breeches buoy was rigged and ready to carry men from ship to shore.

Meanwhile, however, *Barton* was moving closer to shore under the force of wind and waves, and the vessel's stern pointed toward the south, so that *Barton* was oriented parallel to the beach, with a list to port. The ship's migration complicated and delayed rescue efforts. To make things worse, *Barton* rolled, so that the line to shore was taut one moment and slack the next.

One by one, the men were brought ashore by breeches buoy. Haste was essential, for nightfall was approaching. On his ride from ship to shore, the ship's captain was washed out of the breeches buoy—the first time this had happened during a rescue in the then-18-year history of the United States Lifesaving Service, as historians Richard and Julie Pouliot point out in their book *Shipwrecks on the Virginia Coast.*

The captain's loss apparently happened as follows. Weakened by his ordeal, the captain had to be helped into the breeches buoy. He was wearing a long overcoat that draped outside the buoy. A crewman, thinking the surf might enter between the captain and his coat, tried to cut away part of the garment but was unable to do so before the buoy was hauled back toward the beach. Without the coat, the captain might have reached shore safely. Instead, he was washed out of the breeches buoy, which came ashore empty.

Rescue operations continued, but the line on the breeches buoy became fouled, and the device stopped working. The rescuers chose to wait until low tide to try to free the line. After dark, the lifesavers built a fire on the beach to let the remaining men on *Barton* know that the rescuers were still present.

The rescue effort ended tragically. The survivors in the rigging were in bad condition by the next morning. When the lifesavers fired a line to them, the men on the ship were unable to haul out a heavier line to operate the rescue system. The lifesavers could not launch a surfboat through the heavy surf. One man on the wreck tried to reach shore by hauling himself, hand over hand, along the line, but was so weak that he dropped away and was lost in the sea. Soon afterward, the ship rolled over and threw the remaining men into the water. They were never seen again. Six men died in the wreck of *Agnes Barton,* and the ship was a $10,000 loss—a huge sum at that time.

See also BREECHES BUOY.

Basseterre, St. Kitts, Lesser Antilles Basseterre has been the site of numerous shipwrecks, largely because of hurricanes but also because of hostilities. In 1629, four vessels were sunk by Spanish cannon at Basseterre during a Spanish attempt to drive away English and French settlers on the island. Thirty-eight years later, in 1667, a Dutch and a French vessel were burned while at anchor in Basseterre by the English, who had sent warships to St. Kitts to take the island from the French.

***Bavarian,* British passenger liner** At 10,376 tons the first passenger ship of more than 10,000 tons to be lost, *Bavarian,* owned by the Allan Line, wrecked on Wye Rock near Montreal on November 5, 1905. No lives were reported lost.

Bay of Ascension wreck, Mexico According to a report by Diego de Landa of Yucatán, a ship with many people on board was wrecked around the year 1542 near the Bay of Ascension in Mexico. The ship reportedly foundered, with only one survivor, who drifted to a nearby small island on a piece of the vessel's mast. He then built a raft and used it to travel to the mainland.

See also MEXICO.

Bay of Santa Maria wrecks, Florida On September 19, 1559, a storm destroyed seven ships in a Spanish fleet that had sailed from Veracruz, Mexico, in June under command of the governor of Florida, Don Tristán de Luna y Arellano. The fleet was anchored in the Bay of Santa Maria at the time. The storm allegedly drove a laden caravel inland to a distance greater than that of a harquebus (firearm) shot from the shoreline.

See also FLORIDA.

"beach pipe" ship This description applies to the ship *Pacific,* which was on its way from Glasgow, Scotland, to New York with a cargo of clay pipes and tiles when the ship went ashore at East Hampton, Long Island, New York, on June 3, 1871. The ship was lightened by throwing cargo overboard and was refloated at high tide. For many years afterward, according to maritime historian Jeanette Edwards Rattray in *Ship Ashore!*, her history of wrecks on Long Island, beachcombers found "beach pipes" in the sands.

beam A length of metal or timber extending from one side of the ship to the other, below decks; the beam, is, so to speak, the "waist" of a ship. The expression "on her beam ends" refers to a situation in which a capsized or heavily rolling ship is virtually on its side in the water. The width of a ship's beam determines its stability to some extent. A broad-beamed ship is likely to be more stable in many sea conditions than a vessel with a narrower beam, simply because the broad-beamed ship is harder to tip over. For this reason, battleships traditionally have been built with very broad beams, to give their big guns a stable platform for firing. Most other military and civilian ships have much narrower beams.

See also CONSTRUCTION.

"beeswax ship," Oregon Except for imprinted pieces of beeswax found near the mouth of the Nehalem River, in the vicinity of Neahkahnie Mountain, on the Oregon coast, there is little evidence for this wreck, which is thought to have occurred around 1769. That evidence is intriguing, however, and appears to be consistent with the hypothesis that a Spanish vessel came to grief there.

The pieces of beeswax bear Arabic numerals (one chunk is marked clearly "67") and the letters "I.H.S.," a monogram for *Jesus*. It is believed that the wreck may be that of the caravel *San José*, which sailed from California on June 16, 1769, and vanished at sea. Historian James Gibbs, in his 1964 book *Pacific Graveyard*, writes that priests in California may have planned to found a new settlement and use the beeswax for candles.

Gibbs also mentions a Native American legend that some white men survived the shipwreck and lived with the natives for a while but were expelled for offensive behavior. One man with blond hair and blue eyes allegedly remained with the natives, however, and fathered children with light complexions.

In connection with that story, Gibbs cites the journals of explorers Meriwether Lewis and William Clark as mentioning a person of mixed ancestry sighted in the vicinity. The Lewis and Clark expedition to the Pacific lasted from 1803 to 1807. A child of mixed blood, produced by a Native American woman and a white survivor of the conjectured shipwreck, might have lived long enough—about 35 years—to have been contemporaneous with the Lewis and Clark visit. Gibbs also cites a similar report of a person of mixed ancestry from the journals of 19th-century adventurer

Ross Cox, who traveled the Columbia River extensively.

See also COLUMBIA RIVER BAR.

***Belle of Clarksville*, American Mississippi River steamboat** Thirty-six people were killed when *Belle of Clarksville* collided with another steamboat on the night of December 14, 1844, somewhere on the lower Mississippi River. *Belle of Clarksville* ran into the other ship's path while trying to avoid shallow water.

***Bennington*, American aircraft carrier** An explosion and fire on the aircraft carrier *Bennington* killed 107 men off Newport, Rhode Island, on May 26, 1954, while the carrier was launching planes. Smoke began emanating from both sides of the ship before an explosion demolished a mess area where many sailors were eating. There is some doubt as to what caused the explosion, but hydraulic oil from a malfunctioning catapult was suspected.

See also FIRE.

***Bennington*, American Navy gunboat** Some 30 people were killed and 80 injured when *Bennington* exploded in San Diego (California) harbor on July 21, 1905.

***Bergh*, American transport ship** The Liberty transport ship *Henry Bergh* was wrecked on the Farallon Islands off the coast of northern California on May 31, 1944. In an amazing rescue, all 1,400 men on board were saved. There were no casualties.

***Berlin*, British passenger liner** The mail packet and passenger liner *Berlin* was traveling from Harwich, England, to Rotterdam, Netherlands, on February 21,

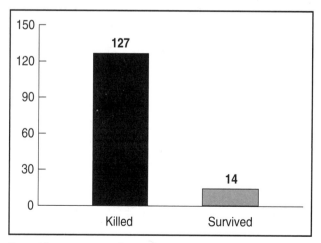

Casualties, passenger liner *Berlin*, 1907. (Nash, Jay Robert, *The Darkest Hour*. Prentice Hall. 1976)

1907, when the ship struck the rocks on the Hook of Holland in stormy weather and rough seas. The ship broke in two, and the impact knocked dozens of people from the foredeck into the sea. Although the wreck occurred close to land, only 16 out of 143 people on *Berlin* were saved. Fourteen of the survivors took refuge on the stern portion of the ship, which rested on the rocks. Casualties included prominent members of the German Opera Company, who were returning home after an engagement in Britain.

See also ROCKS AND SHOALS.

Bermuda   The small island of Bermuda has been the location of many shipwrecks, partly because Bermuda served for centuries as an important port and point of navigation for ships traveling between Europe and the Americas. The many reefs in waters around Bermuda presented a significant hazard to shipping and resulted in the loss of many ships. Dangerous weather conditions in Bermudan waters, such as haze, also have contributed to ship losses there. According to one story, Bermuda itself is named for a Spanish vessel, *La Bermuda*, which allegedly was wrecked there in the early years of the 16th century. (Another account has it that the island was named for a Spanish voyager, Juan Bermúdez.) Notable shipwrecks in Bermuda's history include the following.

In 1533, an unnamed Spanish merchant ship with a cargo of pearls and gold reportedly was wrecked on reefs near Bermuda. There is reason to believe that survivors of this wreck may still have been alive on Bermuda three years later, when a pair of vessels sailing between Santo Domingo and Spain spotted fires burning on the island. Winds and currents prevented the passing ships from putting anyone ashore for an investigation.

In 1543, a Portuguese slave vessel sailing in company with several Spanish merchant ships reportedly wrecked on a reef several miles off the northern shore of Bermuda; 30 survivors of the wreck allegedly used timber from the wreck to build a new craft, on which they sailed to Santo Domingo two months after the wreck.

A hurricane that lasted more than a week in 1551 reportedly destroyed two ships of the Tierra Firme Armada. One warship wound up on a reef, but the ship's cannon and a large quantity of treasure were salvaged. A second ship was likewise wrecked on a reef, but without loss of any treasure on board.

A hurricane on August 1, 1813, destroyed numerous ships at Bermuda. Another destructive hurricane on August 7, 1815, wrecked a large number of vessels, including the 14-gun British warship H.M.S. *Dominica*.

Salvage has been a major occupation on Bermuda because of the large number of wrecks in its waters. Unusually clear waters make wrecks around Bermuda easier to locate than those in many other parts of the world.

See also SEA VENTURE.

***Bermuda*, British passenger liner**   It is hard to imagine an end more catastrophic than that of the 19,000-ton *Bermuda*. The ship caught fire at Hamilton, Bermuda, on June 17, 1930. A few hours after that fire was extinguished, another fire broke out. One person was killed in the second fire. After that fire had been put out, *Bermuda* went back to Britain for repairs. While being repaired, the liner caught fire yet again. This fire totally destroyed the ship's interior. On the way to be scrapped, *Bermuda* ran on rocks and was judged a complete loss.

Bermuda Triangle   This area of the western Atlantic Ocean, bounded approximately by Bermuda, the Bahamas and the southeastern coast of the United States, has a reputation for large numbers of "disappearances" of aircraft and ships, which are said to vanish without trace or explanation.

On close examination, however, many of these "mysterious" incidents cited in popular literature about the Bermuda Triangle turn out to have documented and reasonable explanations. One example, cited by Lawrence David Kusche in his book *The Bermuda Triangle Mystery—Solved!*, involves the Japanese steamship *Raifuku Maru* (often misidentified as *Raiuike Maru*), which allegedly vanished in April 1925, during calm weather, after sending an eerie final message: "It's like a dagger! Come quick! . . . We cannot escape."

Kusche checked Charles Hocking's standard reference work, *Dictionary of Disasters at Sea During the Age of Steam*, and found that the actual story of the Japanese ship's loss differed greatly from that sensational account. *Raifuku Maru* departed from Boston on April 18, 1925, en route to Hamburg with a cargo of grain. The ship ran into stormy weather soon after leaving Boston. By the morning of April 19, *Raifuku Maru* was in trouble. Huge seas had demolished the lifeboats. The ship sent out an SOS as well as a plea in poor English: "Now very danger; come quick." The White Star passenger liner *Homeric*, 70 miles away, responded to the call and steered for the Japanese ship's position, some 400 miles directly east of Boston and just south of Nova Scotia. When *Homeric* arrived, *Raifuku Maru* had a 30-degree list and was helpless in the heavy seas. The liner was unable to pick up any survivors because the Japanese ship's lifeboats were destroyed, and survival was impossible in the water. All 48 on *Raifuku Maru* were drowned.

The facts of the case, then, are much different from the "mystery." The sea was heavy, not calm; the ship did not vanish without a trace, but instead was sighted by another vessel that came to its aid; and the reference to "danger" was transformed somehow into "dagger." Moreover, this case should not even be cited in literature about the Bermuda Triangle, because the Japanese crew perished just off the coast of Nova Scotia, some 700 miles north of Bermuda and well outside the boundaries of the Triangle.

The Bermuda Triangle's reputation as a zone of inexplicable "disappearances" apparently owes much to an article, "The Deadly Bermuda Triangle," in the February 1964 issue of *Argosy* magazine. That article appears to be the origin of the name "Bermuda Triangle" as well. Various authors explored the legend of the so-called Bermuda Triangle over the next several years. Perhaps the most famous of these works is Charles Berlitz's *The Bermuda Triangle*, a sensational work that helped to make the Triangle a subject of public fascination in the early 1970s. Berlitz's book appeared at about the same time as those of Swiss author Erich von Däniken, whose extremely popular works on the subject of UFOs (such as *Chariots of the Gods?*) also contributed to public enthusiasm for "paranormal" events and topics such as the Bermuda Triangle. The UFO craze engendered by von Däniken's books was reflected to some extent in the Bermuda Triangle enthusiasm, which provided an excuse for numerous wild speculations about UFOs, "extraterrestrials" and other bits of modern mythology.

As a social phenomenon, the Bermuda Triangle craze was brief. It was largely discredited by skeptical studies that pointed out numerous natural, explicable phenomena that would account for the "unexplained" losses of ships within the Triangle. For example, the portion of the Atlantic Ocean covered by the so-called Bermuda Triangle is known for frequent, intense storms. In short, there is no need to seek paranormal explanations for ship and aircraft disappearances in the Bermuda Triangle, when more mundane phenomena—such as storms and inaccurate reports of the circumstances surrounding the individual incidents—appear more probable.

See also MYSTERIES; NEUTERCANES; STORMS.

Betsy, American schooner One especially tragic story from the maritime history of Chesapeake Bay (Maryland-Virginia) involves the loss of the schooner *Betsy* on April 22, 1798. The ship was under command of one Captain Duncan, who was accompanied by several members of his family, including his two young

children. In a strong wind and rough seas, the ship began taking on water, and pumps could not keep up with the inflow. *Betsy* began to sink. A terrified crewman climbed the mast. The captain's last act on Earth was evidently to hold his two children in his arms. His body was recovered later, still holding one of the children. The sole survivor of the sinking was the frightened crewman who had scurried up the mast.

Birkenhead, British troopship The expression "*Birkenhead* drill"—meaning men sacrificing their lives so that women and children might be saved—entered the English language following the wreck of the troopship *Birkenhead* on February 26, 1852, off Danger Point near the Cape of Good Hope, South Africa. With Captain Robert Salmond in command, *Birkenhead* was carrying some 680 British troops, sailors and passengers to Algoa Bay in South Africa when the ship struck a rock and began sinking. Captain Salmond gave the order to reverse engines, and *Birkenhead* withdrew from the rock. This move only made the ship take on water more rapidly.

To maintain order, Major Alexander Seton of the 74th Highlanders, in command of the soldiers on board, ordered his troops on deck. They stood there at attention, in uniform, while 20 women and a few children departed in lifeboats. Only after women and children were saved did the troops have an opportunity to leave the ship. According to the story, not one man broke ranks, even though the ship was sinking.

As *Birkenhead* lowered boats to accommodate the troops, the ship broke in half. Seton told his men to swim for safety, although many of them did not know how. Seton, Captain Salmond and more than 400 others were drowned. The 193 survivors included all the women and children aboard.

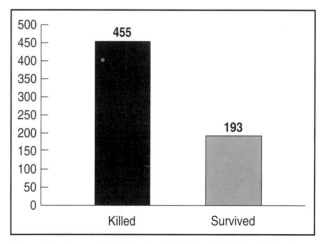

Casualties, troopship *Birkenhead*, 1852. (Nash, Jay Robert, *The Darkest Hour*. Prentice Hall. 1976)

The stern section of *Birkenhead* remained afloat after the ship broke apart. Some 50 troops on that part of the ship were rescued by the schooner *Lioness.*

The behavior of the troops on *Birkenhead* captivated Europe. British author Rudyard Kipling wrote a poem about the *Birkenhead* drill. The King of Prussia admired the British soldiers' behavior so greatly that he had an account of the incident read to his troops.

The *Birkenhead* incident stood in sharp contrast to others, such as the notorious case of the liner *Arctic,* in which men aboard sinking ships rushed the lifeboats and left women and children to drown.

See also ARCTIC; ROCKS AND SHOALS.

Blairgowrie, **British steamship** Twenty-six people were lost when *Blairgowrie* foundered in the North Atlantic on February 26, 1935. A shore station in Ireland picked up a final message from the ship, reporting that two hatches were stove in and the steering gear was gone. A search found no wreckage.

bodies Shipwrecks commonly have resulted in loss of life. In such cases, numerous human bodies have either floated away from the wrecked ship or sunk with it to the sea floor. An ordinary human body, without a life jacket or other flotation aid, is slightly less dense than an equivalent volume of water and floats, but only as long as the lungs are filled with air. If the lungs fill with water, the body sinks. A human body may float at sea for days or weeks before it sinks or is consumed by marine organisms. A body that reaches the seabed tends to be consumed by marine life there, although traces of the body may remain visible. Around the wreck of the British liner *Titanic* on the Atlantic Ocean floor, for example, explorers in the 1980s found numerous pairs of shoes lying side by side on the bottom in orientations that indicated that the shoes marked the former location of a human body.

Bodies or portions of bodies recovered after a ship's loss may provide evidence of the cause of sinking. A badly burned body, for example, would indicate that fire was involved in a ship's destruction. Dismembered bodies would be evidence of an explosion. In a celebrated case of disappearance at sea, that of the steamship *Waratah,* a report of a field of floating body parts has been interpreted as evidence that *Waratah* exploded; the report itself is questionable, however, and so the *Waratah* case appears to remain unsolved.

See also TITANIC; WARATAH.

boilers To generate steam for propulsion, boilers were used on ships beginning in the early 19th century. Water in a boiler was heated by a fire below. Nine-teenth- and early 20th-century boilers used coal or wood as a heat source, but those fuels were replaced by petroleum in the 1900s. Early boilers operated at such low pressures that explosions were a remote possibility. As more advanced boilers with higher pressures came into use, however, the risk of boiler explosions increased. Such an explosion could destroy a ship as effectively as an enemy mine or torpedo. An example of the devastating effects of a boiler explosion is the destruction of the American steam packet *Pulaski* off the North Carolina coast in 1838.

In the mid-20th century, nuclear power replaced petroleum fuel in some vessels, mostly warships such as aircraft carriers and submarines, which had to remain at sea for extended periods and used nuclear power to avoid the need for periodic refueling. The method of propulsion, however, remained essentially the same: using a heat source to vaporize water for steam that operated machinery for propulsion.

See also EXPLOSIONS; MINES; PULASKI; TORPEDOES.

Bokhara, **British liner** *Bokhara* was wrecked on the Pescadores Islands near Formosa (now Taiwan) during a storm on October 10, 1892, on a voyage from Shanghai to Hong Kong. The ship was a total loss; 125 people were killed, and only 23 survived.

bombardeta One of the largest and most elaborate guns carried on European vessels during the age of sail, the wrought-iron *bombardeta* ranged in length from about two feet to more than eight feet and had a bore approximately three to four inches wide. Constructed in much the same manner as a wooden barrel, with "staves" encircled by iron rings and bands analogous to a barrel's hoops, *bombardetas* were designed for destroying enemy ships and for siege work. A *bombardeta* was made of numerous small pieces of iron joined together, and was mounted on a heavy, wheeled oak carriage. Numerous *bombardetas* have been raised from sunken vessels.

See also CANNON.

Bombay, **British line-of-battleship** Ninety-two people were killed when *Bombay* caught fire and blew up off Montevideo, Uruguay, on December 22, 1864.

Boston, **American schooner** In the early days of the United States Lifesaving Service, it was difficult enough to rescue the crew of a stranded ship when the ship stayed in one place after stranding; when the ship began moving, the lifesavers' troubles were compounded.

The three-masted schooner *Boston* went ashore at Virginia Beach, Virginia, during a storm on December

30, 1882, while on a voyage from North Carolina to Philadelphia. That move was deliberate on the captain's part. The ship had started leaking so badly that he headed directly for the beach.

A patrol from the lifesaving station at False Cape, Virginia, burned a flare to warn the ship away, but the schooner continued toward the beach and struck about 600 feet from shore. Lifesavers from False Cape station reached the scene around 10 A.M. and, using their Lyle gun, managed to place a line aboard the ship with only one shot.

To complicate rescue operations, a strong current along the shore began carrying the schooner southward along the beach. The lifesavers had to pick up their equipment and follow the drifting ship. By noon on December 31, however, the lifesavers succeeded in bringing the entire crew ashore by breeches buoy. The crewmen were returned to Philadelphia by way of Norfolk, and the schooner was virtually a complete loss.

See also BREECHES BUOY.

bottles   Among the items most frequently recovered from shipwrecks, bottles may help to establish the date of a shipwreck. A wine bottle of a certain configuration may have originated in a particular decade and thus help to provide an approximate date for a shipwreck. Glass bottles were hand-blown until 1810, when the practice of casting bottles in molds came into use. Therefore, bottles with marks indicating molding must have been manufactured after the first decade of the 19th century. Marine archaeologist Robert Marx writes in his book *Shipwrecks in the Americas* that 95 percent or more of wine bottles found on wrecks from the 17th and 18th centuries were made in England, which had a large bottle-making industry and exported bottles to the rest of Europe.

See also ARCHAEOLOGY.

*Bourgogne***, French liner**   Sheer confusion and panic appear to have killed many of the 571 persons lost in the wreck of *Bourgogne,* which sank on July 4, 1898, in fog south of Nova Scotia's Sable Island, after colliding with the British ship *Cromartyshire.* On a voyage from New York to Le Havre, France, *Bourgogne* collided with *Cromartyshire* at 5 A.M. The crew spoke many different languages, and *Bourgogne*'s captain apparently was unable to make his orders understood. Moreover, many passengers reacted with panic to the collision. Men wielding knives reportedly stabbed and trampled women and children to secure places in lifeboats. The ship sank rapidly. Only about 20 people survived. Some survivors of the wreck were brought to trial for murder but were acquitted. After the wreck, the family

of Anthony Pollock, a passenger killed in the incident, offered a prize of $20,000 for the best lifesaving device. This contest gave rise to a widely used invention: a watertight bulkhead door that could be closed by electrical signal from a ship's bridge.

See also COLLISIONS.

bow   The forwardmost part of the ship, the bow often is involved in collisions between ships. The pointed bow on a large ship may penetrate deeply into another vessel in a collision, creating a hole that allows the second ship to fill quickly and sink. If the bow has been reinforced to contend with icy seas, the destruction may be even greater. The collision between the collier *Storstad* (which had such a reinforced bow) and the liner *Empress of Ireland,* for example, was so destructive that the *Empress of Ireland* sank rapidly, with tremendous loss of life, even though the collision occurred within sight of land on a heavily traveled waterway. Another famous example of a shipwreck caused by collision is the sinking of the Italian liner *Andrea Doria,* which was rammed by the Swedish liner *Stockholm* and sank off Nantucket, Massachusetts.

See also ANDREA DORIA; COLLISIONS; EMPRESS OF IRELAND.

bowsprit   This part of a sailing ship was a lengthy spar or boom that projected forward from the stem, or bow, of a vessel. The bowsprit supported the masts through stays and provided an attachment for sails. Beneath the bowsprit, in many cases, was the figurehead, a decorated wooden sculpture depicting the ship's namesake, such as a celebrity. The bowsprit was often involved in collisions.

Bradish, Joseph, pirate, late 17th century   A minor but interesting figure in the history of piracy is Joseph Bradish, who sank his own ship, the *Adventure,* off Long Island, New York, in 1699.

Carrying a cargo valued at $400,000 for the Far East and Borneo, *Adventure* left London in 1698 with Bradish aboard as boatswain's mate. He was 25 years old. When the ship stopped at an island off the coast of India to take on water, and the captain and other officers went ashore, some crewmen took over the ship, chose Bradish to be their captain, and divided up the cargo among them.

They proceeded to sail for Long Island, where *Adventure* appeared off Sagaponack one day in March of 1699. Lieutenant Colonel Henry Pierson, a leading citizen in the colony of New York, saw the vessel offshore and, with several neighbors, went out by boat to the ship.

Bradish said *Adventure* was on a voyage from London to Philadelphia and requested provisions. Bradish also left jewels and some 2,800 pieces of eight in bags with Pierson.

In the colony, suspicions arose about *Adventure's* actual business. As soon as the ship was unloaded, the pirates sank *Adventure* by firing guns through the bottom. Bradish was captured and was hanged in London. Having accepted the bags of loot from the pirate, Pierson found himself in embarassing circumstances, but powerful friends reportedly interceded for him.

Bradley, **American steamship** The Great Lakes freighter *Carl D. Bradley* sank in Lake Michigan during a storm on November 18, 1958. The ship's loss illustrates the destructive power of waves, even on inland seas such as the Great Lakes. The ship reportedly was hit by two huge waves, fore and aft, at the same time. The ship began breaking up and was split in two by another wave. The ship sank in minutes, killing 34 men. There were only two survivors.

See also EDMUND FITZGERALD; GREAT LAKES; STORMS; WAVES.

Breadalbane, **British sailing vessel** The bark *Breadalbane* was one of many ships that sailed for the Arctic in search of the lost expedition of Sir John Franklin. *Breadalbane* left Britain in 1853 and was sunk by ice in the Canadian Arctic near Baffin Island, in more than 300 feet of water. No one was killed in the sinking. The wreck was located by sonar in 1980. Three years later, an expedition reached the wreck and discovered it to be in good condition after more than a century under water, thanks to the absence of boring organisms in the cold Arctic waters.

See also FRANKLIN EXPEDITION.

breeches buoy One of the most successful and widely used lifesaving devices of the 19th century, the breeches buoy consisted of a life preserver with a canvas seat and was used to haul shipwreck survivors along a line stretched from ship to shore. Simple, lightweight and easily transportable, the breeches buoy also was open, and thus allowed waves and spray to pass through without greatly encumbering the device or its passenger. The breeches buoy replaced the cumbersome and sometimes dangerous "life car," an enclosed lifesaving capsule that had a tendency to fill with water and drown its occupants.

See also LIFE CAR.

Bridgewater, **Australian tanker** When a ship breaks in two, the stern half of the ship is often the more

likely to be salvaged, because it contains the engines and most of the other equipment that makes up the value of the ship. A case in point is the wreck of the tanker *Bridgewater,* which broke in two during a storm about 230 miles northwest of Fremantle, Australia, on January 30, 1962. Another tanker rescued *Bridgewater's* crew. The tug *Yuna* went out the following day and sighted the bow section of *Bridgewater* on the afternoon of February 2. The more important stern section showed up the following morning. *Yuna* took the stern section in tow. On February 4, the weather turned rough. The towline broke on February 6. *Yuna* returned to Fremantle for fresh supplies and additional equipment, then went back to sea on February 9 to look for the stern section of *Bridgewater* again. Yet another storm interfered with the salvage operation, and only on February 20—more than three weeks after the wreck occurred—did *Yuna* succeed in making port with what remained of *Bridgewater* in tow. Several thousand tons of oil were unloaded from the stern section, and the wreck was sold for scrap metal.

See also SALVAGE.

brig Two-masted and square-rigged, the brig was a widespread design for sailing vessels in the 19th century. The brig also carried a large fore-and-aft sail on the mainmast and could be adapted for naval use. Naval brigs could carry up to 20 guns.

brigantine A brig that does not carry a square mainsail.

See BRIG.

Brilliant, **American schooner** A widely cited quotation arose from the wreck of the *Brilliant,* which was destroyed in the first of the Triple Hurricanes of 1839 at Gloucester, Massachusetts. On December 15, 1839, *Brilliant* started to drag its anchors in the storm. The ship grounded some distance from shore, however, with a stretch of dangerous surf between the vessel and the land. The crew climbed into the rigging but were cast into the sea when the ship broke apart and the masts fell. Only one man survived the wreck of *Brilliant.* The bodies of two other men washed ashore. No trace of anyone else on board appears to have been discovered. An onlooker during the schooner's last minutes was quoted as saying, "Were I in their situation, I should want a very clear hope of heaven, and a very strong faith."

See also NEW ENGLAND; STORMS; TRIPLE HURRICANES.

Bristol, **American sailing ship** An immigrant ship, the bark *Bristol* was on its way home from Liverpool,

Breeches buoys can carry shipwreck survivors to shore in safety. (U.S. Coast Guard)

England, when a storm drove the ship onto shoals at Far Rockaway near New York harbor on the night of November 21–22, 1836. A large wave swept away the lifeboats, and *Bristol* started breaking up under the pounding of the sea. The hatches collapsed, and water flooded the hold, drowning most of the immigrant passengers aboard. Eighty-four people on the ship were reported lost.

See also ROCKS AND SHOALS; STORMS.

***Britannic,* British liner** Sister ship to *Titanic* and *Olympic, Britannic* never entered commercial passenger service. Before *Britannic* could be delivered to the White Star Line, the liner was handed over to the British Admiralty in 1914 to be converted into a hospital ship. *Britannic* began duties as a hospital ship the following year. After only a year of such service, *Britannic* was sunk, presumably by a mine, in the Aegean Sea near Port St. Nikolo, on a voyage from Salonika to Mudros. There has been speculation that a torpedo fired by a German submarine sank *Britannic,*

in the manner of the liners *Arabic* and *Lusitania,* but evidence supporting that hypothesis is questionable. Moreover, the Germans are known to have sown mines in the area where *Britannic* sank.

See also ARABIC; LUSITANIA; MINES; OLYMPIC; TITANIC.

Brown's Ferry wreck, South Carolina Thought to have been built (and sunk) in the early 18th century, the Brown's Ferry wreck involved a small, nondescript vessel that might be seen as the colonial maritime equivalent of a modern pickup truck. Nonetheless, the wreck proved important from an archaeological standpoint and was raised from the water and salvaged despite poor working conditions. The wreck was lifted from the Black River at Brown's Ferry on August 28, 1976. Most of the hull had survived the wreck and centuries of immersion. A curious discovery was that of a quadrant, a navigating instrument for use at sea. Why such an instrument should be found on a vessel designed for use on rivers and in near-shore waters has not been determined.

See also ARCHAEOLOGY.

Bruce, **American schooner** Mutineers burned *Robert Bruce* to the waterline at Shoalwater (Willapa) Bay, Washington, on December 16, 1851. According to one story, the crew settled in the vicinity, at a community named Bruceport, after they destroyed the ship. James Gibbs, in his history of shipwrecks in the Pacific Northwest, cites a story in which the ship's cook went mad, set fire to *Robert Bruce* and then made his escape.

Bruiser, **British steamship** Even on a clear, calm evening, with a ship's lights plainly visible, collisions can occur. Under such conditions, *Bruiser* was run down by the collier *Haswell* on a voyage from Hull, England, to London early on the morning of August 19, 1866; 15 people were drowned.

Buena Ventura, **American barge** Though only a lowly barge, *Buena Ventura* went down in the maritime history of New York in December of 1906, when the barge sank in a winter gale off Montauk, Long Island. A brave seaman named Mitchell Bruso, from the tug that had the barge in tow, volunteered to row alone to the sinking barge and rescue the barge's crew. Bruso reached *Buena Ventura* despite the dangerous seas and rescued the barge's captain. Bruso rowed back to the tug and deposited the captain on board, then went out to rescue a seaman who was afloat on a hatch.

Buen Consejo, **Spanish warship** The 70-gun *El Buen Consejo* was wrecked along with the 40-gun galleon *Jesus, Maria y Joseph* off Anguilla in the Lesser Antilles in 1772 while on convoy escort duty.

bulkheads An internal subdivision, or "wall," that divides the ship into two or more compartments, a bulkhead may be made "watertight" by installing special doors that can be closed to contain flooding in case the hull is breached. Bulkheads have provided vital protection for ships in distress.

One dramatic example of bulkheads saving a ship was the survival of the French steamer *Vesta*, which made its way back to port after a collision with the Collins liner *Arctic* in 1854. *Vesta* survived even after losing much of its bow in the collision. *Arctic* lacked such a system of internal compartments and sank with great loss of life.

A bulkhead may be required to withstand tremendous pressure from the sea following a collision. When the liner *Queen Mary* rammed and sank the destroyer *Curaçao* during Atlantic convoy duty in World War II, *Queen Mary*'s collision bulkhead in the bow withstood the full force of the sea until the liner made port.

On the other hand, the protection that bulkheads provide depends on how they are designed and constructed. A system of watertight bulkheads was supposed to make the British liner *Titanic* "unsinkable," but the bulkheads did not extend high enough to contain flooding in the bow after the liner struck an iceberg in the mid-Atlantic in 1912.

See also ARCTIC; CONSTRUCTION; CURAÇAO; TITANIC.

Bunker Hill, **American tanker** *Bunker Hill* exploded on a voyage from Tacoma, Washington, to Anacortes in Puget Sound on March 6, 1964. Five people were killed.

buoyancy A measure of a ship's ability to float on water, buoyancy may be positive, negative or neutral. Positive buoyancy, the kind usually desired, results when a ship weighs less altogether than an equal volume of water. The ship then floats atop the water. Negative buoyancy occurs when a ship takes on water sufficient to sink it.

Submarines submerge and surface through buoyancy control. Admitting water to tanks between the submarine's outer hull and inner, "pressure" hull results in negative buoyancy that allows the submarine to submerge. Pumping compressed air into the tanks expels water and produces positive buoyancy, which lets the submarine rise to the surface. Neutral buoyancy occurs when just enough water is present in the tanks to let the submarine maintain a certain depth. Problems with buoyancy control may sink a submarine, as apparently happened in the wreck of the American nuclear submarine *Thresher*.

See also SUBMARINES; THRESHER.

C

Cabo Catoche wrecks, Mexico The Flota de Nueva España lost two ships near Cabo Catoche on July 18, 1586, on a voyage from Sanlucar, Spain: the 200-ton *Santiago el Mayor* and the 14-ton *Santa María de Begonia*.

Cabot expedition A famous example of a "lost" expedition, John Cabot's 1498 voyage of exploration started at Bristol, England, and evidently ended in catastrophe, for the expedition never returned. Cabot's 1497 voyage to what is now New England gave England a claim to that portion of North America.

See also CORTE REAL EXPEDITIONS.

Cadiz A major Spanish seaport, Cadiz also was dangerous to shipping, partly because of dangerous weather conditions (specifically, a wind known as a "levanter") and partly because of attacks by enemy warships. In the 18th century, Cadiz and Sanlucar replaced Seville as the principal ports of Spain's trade with the New World, because Seville's harbor was too small to contain the large numbers of ships involved in the trade.

See also SANLUCAR.

cairns Piles of stones or other articles built on shore to mark the presence of a shipwreck or the passage of a shipwrecked crew, cairns have served as repositories for documents that provided important information about wrecks and their survivors. The search for the lost Franklin expedition in the Arctic, for example, was assisted by the discovery of a cairn containing a document that provided information on the abandonment of Franklin's ships.

See also FRANKLIN EXPEDITION.

***Cairnsmore*, British bark** *Cairnsmore* buried itself in its own tomb of cement after hitting the sands of the Columbia River bar (Oregon-Washington) on September 26, 1883. The ship went astray in fog and, with a cargo of 7,500 barrels of cement, was too heavily laden to change direction easily when the vessel approached the breakers.

The crew scrambled into the rigging for safety. The men tried launching signal flares, but these were invisible in the fog. The men tried for hours to release their ship from the sands, but finally gave up and took to the boats.

They had two options, neither one promising. They could risk their lives trying to reach shore through the heavy surf, or else they could row seaward in the hope that a passing ship would see them and pick them up.

That latter hope must have seemed slim because of the fog. Yet rescue materialized quickly, in the form of the liner *Queen of the Pacific*, which appeared only about 300 yards from the boats. The liner's crew had heard the men shouting and stopped to pick them up. (*Queen of the Pacific* had gone ashore on nearby Clatsop Spit a few days before.)

A salvage team that visited the wreck of *Cairnsmore* the following day found that water had infiltrated the cement, which was starting to ooze out of the barrels and form a great hardened mass. Entombed in its own cement sepulchre, *Cairnsmore* vanished into the sands.

See also CARGO.

California California's lengthy coast is littered with shipwrecks, some of them dating from the earliest days of European settlement. Fog has been a frequent contributor to wrecks on the California coast. One of the most famous wrecks along the California shore is *Rio de Janeiro*. The Farallon Islands off the coast of northern California also have been the site of notable shipwrecks.

See also FOG; RIO DE JANEIRO.

***Californian* incident** The British liner *Californian* lay surrounded by ice within several miles of R.M.S. *Titanic* on the night *Titanic* sank after striking an

The elegant cruise ship in the background provides a dramatic contrast to the stern section of a ship demolished in an explosion and fire in Los Angeles Harbor in 1976. (U.S. Coast Guard)

iceberg, on April 14–15, 1912. Much of the blame for the tremendous loss of life on *Titanic* was placed on Captain Stanley Lord of the *Californian,* who allegedly was informed that a steamer nearby was firing rockets, but did nothing to help or even to investigate. Because of evident weaknesses in the case against him, however, Captain Lord acquired a coterie of defenders known as "Lordites." The "Lordites" have been persistent and articulate in their defense of the *Californian's* captain, so that controversy over Lord's alleged responsibility in the *Titanic* catastrophe continues to this day.

The facts of the case, in summary, are as follows. *Californian* was on a voyage from London to Boston under Captain Lord's command on the night of April 14–15, 1912. The ship encountered field ice—a broad expanse of ice—and stopped. At 10:20 P.M., Captain Lord told the wireless operator to transmit an ice report.

A few miles away, *Titanic* struck an iceberg at 11:40 P.M. Soon afterward, *Titanic's* fourth officer reported seeing a light ahead. From the bridge, through glasses, he saw a steamer's masthead lights. He reported the sighting to Captain Edward Smith of *Titanic* and asked permission to fire distress rockets. Smith gave permission, and eight rockets went up, one after another.

On *Californian* at 11:00 P.M., the third officer saw a steamship approach from the east, the direction in which *Titanic* was traveling. Captain Lord told him to try contacting the ship by Morse lamp. The unidentified ship did not reply. Lord went next to the wireless operator and asked if he had contacted any ships. The

wireless operator said he had contacted *Titanic* and, on the basis of the strength of her signals, estimated *Titanic* was about 100 miles distant. Lord told the operator to call *Titanic* and inform the liner that *Californian* was stopped in the midst of an ice field. The wireless operator tried to contact *Titanic* but was told curtly to be quiet because *Titanic* was in communication just then with the wireless station at Cape Race, Newfoundland.

At 11:40 P.M., the officer of the watch on *Californian* noticed that the unidentified steamer had stopped. He also thought he saw the ship's lights go out. He thought the ship was a passenger steamer, although Captain Lord disagreed with him on that point. Several minutes later, *Californian's* second officer spoke with Captain Lord about the mysterious ship. Lord gave an order to tell him if the ship came any closer to *Californian.* The captain added that he was going to lie down on the settee in the chart room. Again, *Californian* tried but failed to contact *Titanic* by Morse lamp.

Around 12:45 A.M., what appeared to be a white rocket was seen above the unidentified ship. Three more white rockets were sighted in the following half hour. The second officer, watching from *Californian's* bridge, thought the rockets looked as if they originated from some point beyond the other ship. He contacted Captain Lord and mentioned the rockets. Lord told him to try again to raise the ship by Morse lamp and find out what was happening. Lord also inquired whether the rockets were "private" signals. (Shipping companies had individual recognition signals of various colors, including white, for use when passing other vessels at night; distress signals in par-

The bow of a sunken vessel points forlornly towards the sky. (U.S. Coast Guard)

ticular were white, and usually larger than private company signals.) The second officer said he did not know if the rockets were private signals. Lord told him, "When you get an answer, let me know by [apprentice James] Gibson."

Three more rockets were observed. Gibson and the second officer thought the ship appeared to be moving away toward the southwest. By 2 A.M., the second officer had the impression that the other ship was departing rapidly, with only the stern light and a light at the masthead visible. He told Captain Lord that the ship had sent up eight rockets altogether. "Are you sure there were no colors in them?" Lord asked. He was told all the rockets were white. At 2:45 A.M., the second officer told Lord that no more lights were visible, and the ship was out of sight.

At 4 A.M., the chief officer of *Californian* came to the bridge and learned what had happened over the previous several hours. He awakened Lord and the wireless operator, and told the wireless man to find out what was happening. *Californian* then learned that *Titanic* had struck an iceberg and had radioed that the ship was sinking. Around 5:15 A.M., *Californian* got under way and headed for the position given in *Titanic*'s distress call. At the site of the sinking, *Californian* met *Carpathia*, a liner under command of Captain Arthur Rostron, who had ordered his ship turned immediately on receipt of *Titanic*'s distress call and then raced through a sea full of icebergs to rescue survivors, who were scattered across the sea in lifeboats. *Carpathia* asked *Californian* to remain on the scene and search for any additional survivors. *Californian* stayed in the area until some time between 9 and 10 A.M., then resumed its trip toward Boston.

Californian reached Boston without fanfare. When the *New York Times* contacted Captain Lord, he said that *Californian* was 17 to 19 miles away from *Titanic* when the big liner sank. *Californian*'s role in the tragedy came to widespread notice, however, when one of the ship's crewmen, Ernest Gill, told the *Boston American* that *Californian* had seen *Titanic*'s distress signals that night. Gill said he believed *Titanic* was much closer to *Californian* than the officers on his ship claimed. Gill later testified before both the American and British inquiries into the loss of *Titanic*. His testimony about seeing rockets forced Captain Lord to admit that *Californian* indeed had seen rockets rising from the unidentified ship. Lord also had to admit that the signals might have been distress signals and that he nonetheless had done nothing but try to contact the other vessel by Morse lamp.

This, then, appeared to have been the situation on the night *Titanic* was lost. Captain Lord and his men on *Californian* had seen what looked like white distress signals—eight of them—rising from the unidentified vessel several miles away. *Titanic*, known to have been only several miles from *Californian*, fired approximately eight white distress signals during the period when the signals were seen from *Californian*. Although these observations indicated clearly that a ship might be in trouble nearby, Captain Lord and his crew stood by without attempting to assist the other vessel, except to try unsuccessfully to raise the ship by Morse lamp.

Just as the American inquiry faulted Captain Lord for inaction, the British inquiry into *Titanic*'s sinking had harsh words for the captain. Lord Mersey, who led the British inquiry, wrote as follows:

". . . [The] truth of the matter is plain. The *Titanic* collided with the berg at 11:40. The vessel seen by the *Californian* stopped at this time. The rockets sent up from the *Titanic* were distress signals. The *Californian* saw distress signals. The number sent up by the *Titanic* was about eight. The *Californian* saw eight. The time over which the rockets from the *Titanic* were sent up was from about 12:45 to 1:45 o'clock. It was about this time that the *Californian* saw the rockets. At 2:20 Mr. Stone [the second officer] called to the Master [Captain Lord] that the ship from which he had seen the rockets had disappeared. At 2:20 A.M. the *Titanic* had foundered. It was suggested that the rockets seen by the *Californian* were from some other ship not the *Titanic*. But no other ship to fit this theory has ever been heard of."

Mersey described his conclusions as follows: "These circumstances convince me that the ship seen by the *Californian* was the *Titanic* and if so, according to Captain Lord, the two vessels were about five miles apart at the time of the disaster. The evidence from *Titanic* corroborates this estimate but I am advised that the distance was probably greater though not more than eight to 10 miles. The ice by which *Californian* was surrounded was loose ice extending for a distance of not more than two or three miles in the direction of the *Titanic*. The night was clear and the sea was smooth. When he first saw the rockets the *Californian* could have pushed through the ice to the open water without any serious risk and so have come to the assistance of the *Titanic*. Had she done so she might have saved many if not all of the lives that were lost."

Lord had to resign from the Leyland Line, which operated *Californian*. Despite the chorus of blame directed at him, however, Lord soon found new employment with another steamship line, the Nitrate Producers Steamship Company. His record reportedly was spotless following the *Californian* incident. Lord retired in 1927 and spent the rest of life trying to defend himself against his darkened reputation as "Lord of the *Californian*."

Lord's defenders, the so-called Lordites, have presented detailed and complicated arguments to support the case that *Titanic* must have seen some ship other than *Californian*. The evidence for this argument includes apparent discrepancies between the times when *Titanic* fired rockets and the times when those rockets were sighted by *Californian*. In the last analysis, however, the case against Captain Lord apparently rests on the evidence of the rockets. *Titanic* fired some eight rockets, and the men on *Californian* saw eight rockets. No other vessel near *Californian* that night is known to have fired eight rockets. Therefore, one may presume that *Californian* was close enough to *Titanic* to have reached the sinking ship easily and rescued some, if not all, of the liner's passengers and crew.

Senator William Alden Smith of Michigan, who headed the U.S. Senate inquiry into the sinking of *Titanic*, said of Captain Lord in an address to the Senate, "There is a very strong possibility that every human life that was sacrificed through this disaster could have been spared." Smith added that Lord's inaction laid "a tremendous responsibility upon this officer from which it will be very difficult for him to escape." Almost a century after the *Titanic*'s loss, Smith's verdict on Captain Lord is still widely accepted.

See also LORD, CAPTAIN STANLEY; ROSTRON, CAPTAIN ARTHUR HENRY; SMITH, SENATOR WILLIAM ALDEN; TITANIC.

Callao wrecks, Peru   A powerful earthquake destroyed the port of Callao near Lima on October 28, 1746, along with 23 ships there. Among the ships lost was the 30-gun galleon *San Fermin*. The earthquake killed thousands of people.

See also EARTHQUAKES.

***Cambridge*, American steamship**   A major mid-19th-century shipwreck on the Chesapeake Bay (Maryland-Virginia) was that of the steamer *Cambridge*, which burned on September 16, 1853, while on the way to landings on Virginia's Rappahannock River. There were no fatalities. The ship's engines were salvaged.

***Camorta*, British passenger liner**   One of the first major shipwrecks of the 20th century, the loss of *Camorta* occurred in April of 1902. The ship sank in a storm in the Gulf of Martaban while en route from Madras, India, to Rangoon, Burma. Everyone on board was killed, including 89 crew and 650 passengers.

See also STORMS.

Campeche, Mexico   The current port of Campeche is not identical with the "coast of Campeche," which up to about 1800 meant the entire Yucatán Peninsula.

See also MEXICO.

Canada   With extensive coastlines along both the Atlantic and Pacific oceans, as well as in the Arctic and along the St. Lawrence River and Great Lakes, Canada has been the site of many notable shipwrecks. Canadian waters have been the site of numerous wrecks because many conditions unfavorable to safe navigation have existed there, such as ice, fog, offshore rocks and heavy maritime traffic within confined areas.

An especially great concentration of shipwrecks is located around Sable Island, some 150 miles off the Nova Scotia coast. One of the earliest shipwrecks in the history of European settlements in North America has been excavated at Red Bay, Labrador: a wreck believed to be that of the Basque whaling ship *San Juan*, sunk in 1565. *Erebus* and *Terror*, the ships of 19th-century British explorer Sir John Franklin's calamitous expedition to the Arctic, were crushed in ice and sank in Canadian waters. Perhaps the most famous wreck in Canadian history is that of the liner *Empress of Ireland*, which sank in the St. Lawrence River on May 29, 1914, after colliding with the collier *Storstad*; more than 1,000 persons died in the liner's sinking. One of the greatest explosions in maritime history occurred

The shattered bow of the Canadian passenger vessel S.S. *Princess Kathleen* is clearly visible in this photo. The ship sank near Juneau, Alaska, on September 7, 1952. (U.S. Coast Guard)

in the harbor at Halifax, Nova Scotia, on December 6, 1917, when a French ship carrying explosives blew up after colliding with another vessel; the resulting explosion destroyed much of Halifax, killed some 1,600 people and wiped out the suburb of Richmond.

Another notable shipwreck in Canadian waters involved the French frigate *Le Chameau*, which sank with a load of gold and silver coins off Cape Lornebec, Nova Scotia, in 1725. The warship was on its way from Louisbourg, Nova Scotia, to Quebec with many passengers. A storm off Cape Lornebec capsized the ship, which sank with the loss of almost all lives on board. The wreck was located in 1914, when a helmeted diver exploring a much more recent wreck sighted *Le Chameau* and part of its cargo of silver and gold. The diver intended to start salvage operations on the 18th-century ship but drowned soon after making the discovery and was unable to reveal its precise location. The exact site of the wreck was not rediscovered until some 50 years later. Three amateur divers found the wreck by the simple expedient of dragging a grappling hook and going down to investigate when the hook caught on something. Working under extremely unfavorable conditions including cold water and strong currents, the divers nonetheless managed to recover a large number of artifacts from the wreck, including cannonballs, tableware and a silver pocket watch. This particular salvage operation brought the salvors into conflict with the Canadian government, which required the men to surrender everything recovered from the wreck. The case went to court, and in 1968 the court ruled that the government might claim only 10 percent of what was removed from the wreck and must give the remainder back to the salvors.

A partial list of other notable shipwrecks in Canadian waters follows.

Rough weather on February 26, 1748, sank almost every French warship and merchant vessel in the harbor at Louisbourg on Cape Breton Island, Nova Scotia. Four years later, on October 1, 1752, a hurricane drove ashore or sank more than 50 warships and merchant vessels at Louisbourg. A severe storm on October 7, 1753, destroyed more than 40 large vessels at Cape Breton Island. The 64-gun English warship H.M.S. *Mars,* under command of Captain John Amherst, was wrecked at Halifax, Nova Scotia, in June of 1755. Two other English warships, the 60-gun H.M.S. *Tilbury* and the 10-gun H.M.S. *Ferret,* sank in Louisbourg harbor during a hurricane on September 24, 1757.

On June 28, 1758, the French scuttled several ships, including the 50-gun *Apollon* and the 26-gun *Fidele,* in Louisbourg harbor because too few men were avail-able to man the ships against an anticipated attack by English forces. Three more French warships were burned accidentally at Louisbourg before the English arrived. In another English attack in 1760, 25 French ships were sunk at Chaleur Bay in the Gulf of St. Lawrence, including the 32-gun warship *Marchault,* the 22-gun *Bienfaisant* and the 18-gun *Marquis Marloze.*

In 1761, four notable shipwrecks occurred in the St. Lawrence River. The English merchantman *General Gage* was wrecked on its way from Quebec to London. Another English vessel, the *Isaac and William,* was wrecked on Orleans Shoals en route from Quebec to London, but the ship's cargo was salvaged. The 60-gun French warship *Leopard* arrived with plague among its crew and was burned at Quebec. The English ship *Success* was wrecked near Quebec on a voyage from London.

In 1761, the English merchantman *Margaret & Harriot,* on a voyage from Plymouth, England, to Quebec, was wrecked on rocks near Anticosti Island; one crewman drowned, and the rest of the ship's company had to spend half a year on the island under great hardship. Ten years later, in 1771, the sloop *Grandy* (also called *Granby*) was lost near Lighthouse Rocks in Halifax Harbor with the loss of 16 lives. In 1777, the English ship *Aurora* was wrecked on Sable Island, and the survivors discovered on shore several women who had been stranded there by the wreck of a French ship 16 years before.

Two English warships, the 32-gun transport *Grampus* and the 16-gun *Cupid,* foundered off Newfoundland in 1778. The 12-gun H.M.S. *Spy* also was wrecked in waters near Newfoundland that year. Three English merchantmen were wrecked on the St. Lawrence River in 1783; the ship *Hope* was lost several miles from Tadefase, the *Betsy* was wrecked on Hare Island by strong winds while on a voyage from Quebec to Barbados, and the *Noble* was lost near Quebec while en route from Halifax to Quebec.

Numerous ships were sunk in Halifax harbor during a gale on September 25, 1798, including the English warship H.M.S. *Lynx.* The winter of 1802 appears to have taken a heavy toll on shipping on the St. Lawrence River: 10 ships were reported lost on the river, although only one, *Mary,* was identified. The English warship H.M.S. *Barbadoes* was wrecked on Sable Island on September 28, 1812. The French ship *L'Américaine* was wrecked off Wallace Lake on Sable Island in 1822. That same year, great loss of life was reported when the 10-gun warship H.M.S. *Drake* was wrecked off Newfoundland on June 20.

Canadian waters, as a rule, are not the most hospitable place for exploring wrecks and for salvage work. The water is cold, and ice and stormy weather combine to make conditions unpleasant, if not dangerous.

See also EMPRESS OF IRELAND; FRANKLIN EXPEDITION; SABLE ISLAND; SAN JUAN.

***Canadian Exporter*, Canadian freighter** Sometimes the vagaries of a shipwreck can create eerie effects. One such case involved *Canadian Exporter*, which ran aground at Willapa Harbor in Washington state on August 21, 1921, while on a voyage from Vancouver, British Columbia, to Portland, Oregon. As the ship broke up on a shoal, the sagging bow section of the vessel pulled on the whistle cord and made the ship's whistle blow, as if the ship were mourning its own death, until the cord slackened.

***Cann*, British bark** Despite extremely heavy fog, the men of the U.S. Lifesaving Service at Virginia Beach, Virginia, managed to rescue the crew of the British bark *Joanna H. Cann*, which stranded less than 800 feet from shore on the night of February 10, 1881. The incident involved a captain who thought he was miles away from his actual position.

At first, the only sign of the stranded vessel was a scattering of wreckage along the shore. A surfman from the Cape Henry lifesaving station saw the debris and figured a vessel must be stranded. Through the thick fog, he caught occasional glimpses of a light. The surfman set off a Coston flare to let the men on the ship know they had been sighted.

A boat was launched from shore, and the keeper of the Cape Henry station went aboard *Cann* and offered help. The captain at first thought help was unnecessary. He imagined he was somewhere between the Virginia Capes at the mouth of Chesapeake Bay (Maryland-Virginia) and soon would be freed by a rising tide. When he recognized his mistake, the captain accepted the lifesavers' offer of assistance.

With the help of lifesavers from the nearby Seatack station, the Cape Henry men brought the British crew ashore by breeches buoy. Only about $600, or about 9 percent of the ship's total value, could be salvaged, but the Virginians succeeded in saving the entire crew.

cannon A prominent feature of many shipwrecks from the age of sail, cannon may help to establish the kind of ship involved, its size and approximate date. Bronze cannon are often found marked with their dates of manufacture still readable, because bronze holds up well in the marine environment. Iron cannon, on the other hand, may not show such a clearly legible date because of oxidation. Cannon are not always helpful in determining a wreck's nationality, because cannon from many different countries might be used

on a single ship. Cannon for maritime use were manufactured in many different sizes and configurations.

See also ARCHAEOLOGY; BOMBARDETA; FALCONETE GRANDE; VERSO.

***Caoba*, American schooner** A rumrunner figured in the rescue of *Caoba*'s crew during a storm off the Oregon coast on February 5, 1925. Carrying a load of lumber on deck, the steam-powered *Caoba* started taking on water until the ship was kept afloat largely by the lumber's buoyancy. The engine was helpless against the force of the wind, and before long the rising water doused the fires under the boilers.

The captain ordered all hands into the lifeboats. Two boats left the ship. One was recovered by a tug, but the other had drifted away and was listed as missing with 10 men on board.

The second boat encountered the Canadian rumrunner *Pescawha*, and the men from *Caoba* were rescued. The rumrunner then was seized by the U.S. Coast Guard cutter *Algonquin. Pescawha* was captured with more than 1,000 cases of liquor aboard. This load was thought to be only about one-fourth of the original cargo; the rest presumably went over the side before the Coast Guard seized the rumrunner.

Pescawha's officers were placed under arrest, and the rumrunner was put under guard at Astoria, Washington. The American press responded to the rumrunner's internment with outrage, in view of *Pescawha*'s rescue of *Caoba*'s men from the stormy sea. Internment was seen as a poor reward for such a service.

Caoba eventually drifted ashore, still held afloat by its lumber. Over the years, the wooden hull broke apart and was carried away, leaving only a boiler to mark the spot where the schooner came to rest.

Pescawha came to a tragic end on February 27, 1933, eight years after the wreck of *Caoba* and *Pescawha*'s internment by the Coast Guard. The former rumrunner, now under United States colors, set out on what was described as a whaling voyage.

Powered by a Maxwell automobile engine, the ship headed out during a storm and ran into trouble almost immediately. The engine failed, and the tide carried *Pescawha* into the north jetty at the mouth of the Columbia River (Oregon-Washington). The captain was killed, but the rest of the crew survived despite the rough sea that threatened to dash them on the rocks of the jetty.

The rocks and rough sea together all but pulverized *Pescawha*. Maritime historian James Gibbs, in *Pacific Graveyard*, his history of shipwrecks on the Columbia River bar, says the ship's wheel was the single largest piece of debris recovered by beachcombers after the wreck.

Cape Charles, Virginia Located at the southern tip of Virginia's Eastern Shore, on the northern shore of the mouth of Chesapeake Bay, Cape Charles and the Atlantic shore just north of it have been the site of numerous shipwrecks. An example is *Nuestra Señora de los Godos,* a New Spain Fleet vessel that was wrecked, along with an unidentified brigantine from the same fleet, near Cape Charles during a hurricane in 1750.

See also CAPE CHARLES WRECKS; CHESAPEAKE BAY; NUESTRA SEÑORA DE LOS GODOS.

Cape Charles wrecks, Virginia A fleet consisting of 14 merchant ships was reportedly lost just north of Cape Charles, near the entrance to Chesapeake Bay, during a hurricane in 1706.

See also CHESAPEAKE BAY.

Cape Gelidonya wreck, Turkey One of the oldest shipwrecks ever discovered, this wreck apparently occurred around 1400 B.C. in some 72 feet of water off Cape Gelidonya. The wreck was excavated with support obtained in 1960 from sources including the University of Pennsylvania, and yielded artifacts such as copper ingots, tools, bronze bowls, skewers for shish kebab, and even olive pits left over from crewmen's meals.

See also ARCHAEOLOGY.

Cape Henry, Virginia Located on the southern side of the entrance to Chesapeake Bay, Cape Henry has been the site of notable wrecks, including that of a ship carrying some 300 emigrants from Europe in 1739. The entrance to Chesapeake Bay is bracketed by Cape Henry and Cape Charles, which also has been the site of numerous wrecks.

See also CAPE CHARLES; CHESAPEAKE BAY; SWITZER WRECK.

Cape Horn, South America Like the Cape of Good Hope at the southern tip of Africa, Cape Horn, at the southernmost point of South America, has long been feared for its storms and threat of shipwreck. Avoiding the heavy weather and dangerous seas off Cape Horn was one reason for the building of the Panama Canal. Before the canal was constructed, the only practical passage by sea from the Atlantic Ocean to the Pacific was around Cape Horn.

See also CAPE OF GOOD HOPE.

Cape of Good Hope, South Africa One of the most dangerous areas of the ocean, the waters off the Cape of Good Hope have long been notorious for their stormy weather and heavy seas. Symbolic of the dan-

gers facing ships in these waters is the legend of the Flying Dutchman, the ghostly mariner of myth who allegedly was doomed to sail the waters off the Cape after his vessel was wrecked there. An actual vessel thought to have gone down in those same waters, thus giving rise to one of the great mysteries of the sea, is the steamship *Waratah,* which disappeared without a trace off the South African coast within a few miles of land, on heavily traveled sea lanes.

See also FLYING DUTCHMAN; WARATAH.

capitana A heavily armed galleon, the *capitana* served as the flagship of each treasure fleet operating between Spain and the Americas. The *capitana* was accompanied by a smaller but also well-armed galleon called the *almiranta.*

See also ALMIRANTA; FLOTA SYSTEM; GALLEON.

capsizing A ship capsizes when it loses stability and rolls over beyond recovery. Many influences may cause a ship to capsize, including strong wind, shifting cargo, flooding, heavy seas and collision with other vessels. If a ship rolls over slowly, there may be opportunity for most or all of those on board to escape. In many cases, however, the vessel capsizes so suddenly that many people are trapped within the hull and either drown or are asphyxiated.

There are many famous examples of ships capsizing. One such case involved the French liner *Normandie,* which capsized at its pier in New York City in 1942. The ship rolled over after firefighters poured large amounts of water into *Normandie's* upperworks to put out a fire there; the water made the ship top-heavy and caused *Normandie* to roll over onto its port side. The wreck was not refloated until almost the end of World War II.

Another famous case of capsizing involved the American excursion steamer *Eastland,* which was overloaded and capsized at its pier in Chicago, killing hundreds of passengers.

Novelist Paul Gallico used a capsized ocean liner as the setting for his novel *The Poseidon Adventure,* which described the efforts of a group of passengers to escape from a capsized ocean liner. The book was made into a motion picture starring Gene Hackman and Ernest Borgnine.

See also EASTLAND; NORMANDIE.

***Captain*, British ironclad** *Captain's* low freeboard appears to have been a contributing factor to its loss on the night of September 7, 1870, in the Bay of Biscay. During a gale, the ship rolled to starboard, capsized and sank by the stern. The wreck killed 483 people; 18 survived.

***Captain Bell*, sailing vessel, nationality and date uncertain** Little is known about this wreck, except that it gave the community of Montauk, Long Island, its first teakettle, according to historian Jeannette Edwards Rattray in her 1955 book *Ship Ashore!* Some time in the 1800s, the people of Montauk reportedly recovered a teakettle from the wreck of *Captain Bell*. Unable to identify the strange object, they took it to East Hampton and asked the opinion of one Samuel Hedges, said to be the wisest man in the community. He decided it was the ship's lamp. Rattray reported that the teakettle was preserved at the East Hampton Historical Society museum at Clinton Academy.

caravel One of the most successful and widely used vessels in Europe during the age of sail, the caravel was known for great seaworthiness rather than large cargo capacity. A famous example of a caravel is *Niña*, one of Admiral Christopher Columbus's ships on his 1492 visit to the Americas. The caravel used various forms of rigging, including square sails to utilize trade winds in the Atlantic Ocean. The caravel looks small and round by 20th-century standards but could—and did—sail all the way around the world. The nao was similar to the caravel but was larger and was intended to carry large cargoes between Europe and America.

See also NAO.

Carder narrative, late 16th century One of the most remarkable tales in the literature on shipwrecks and castaways is the story of Peter Carder, a Cornishman who sailed with Sir Francis Drake on Drake's voyage around the globe, beginning in 1577. Carder's story provides not only a glimpse of the practical methods a castaway had to use for survival, but also a grisly glimpse of life among natives whom Carder contacted in his journey back to European civilization.

In September of 1578, Drake passed through the Straits of Magellan. While in these southern waters, Carder and seven other men, including one William Pitcher, became separated from their ship while in an open pinnace at night during bad weather. The men found themselves at sea with neither compass nor provisions.

Two days later, they made their way to land and managed to find food, notably crabs, oysters and roots. Further voyaging in the straits brought the men to an island where they found penguins in large numbers. The penguins provided additional food. The castaways supplemented their diet with fish caught from the sea.

Sailing northward several hundred miles past the River Plata, the men discovered another island with large numbers of seals on it. The men killed and roasted some of the seals before crossing to the north side of the river and going ashore. Six men went to explore woods, while two men remained with the boat.

The exploration party encountered 60 to 70 hostile natives, called "Tapines" by Carder. The natives attacked the Europeans with bows and arrows. The six men who went into the forest were all wounded, and four were captured and evidently never seen again by their shipmates. The survivors of this battle retreated to the pinnace, with the natives in pursuit. The Europeans somehow fought off the natives and managed to escape in the boat to a small island several miles away. There the four survivors tended their wounds. Two of the men died, however, leaving only Carder and William Pitcher alive. To make matters worse, their pinnace was wrecked on the rocky coast.

Carder and Pitcher did not die of their wounds, and food on the island was adequate to sustain life. The castaways ate fruit, crabs and eels. Fresh water, however, was unavailable on the island; and no rain fell to provide drinking water. Before long, the men were reduced to drinking their own urine.

With the pinnace wrecked, and facing death by thirst, Carder and Pitcher devised a desperate plan to reach the mainland and seek fresh water there. They used a 10-foot-long plank to construct a makeshift raft. Taking along what provisions they could carry, the thirsty men set out on the raft for the mainland. Three days and two nights later, they arrived.

One of the first things they discovered on the mainland was fresh water. Carder warned Pitcher not to drink too deeply of the water at first. Pitcher disregarded this warning and drank his fill. Evidently his long drink of water was more than his overstressed system could tolerate, for Pitcher died half an hour later. Carder buried Pitcher's body in the sands and set out along the shore toward Brazil, carrying a sword and shield with him.

The day after Pitcher died, Carder encountered another group of natives. These were less belligerent than the group that had killed Carder's shipmates and received him in friendly fashion. They took Carder to their camp and fed him. Then they went to sleep for the night.

The following day, the natives escorted Carder to their village, a community of about 4,000 people. This was evidently the capital of their country, or at least the residence of their leader, one Caiou, a man about 40 years old. Caiou's village consisted (Carder reported) of only four buildings with 30 or 40 doorways each. Each doorway evidently represented a family's dwelling.

Carder was a careful observer and reported at length on the customs of his hosts. Although Caiou had nine wives, monogamy appeared to be the rule among his people. Exceptions were made for especially valiant men, who were permitted to have two wives each: one wife to care for the children, and another to accompany him to wars.

Caiou's hospitality was superb. He sent out for all manner of foods to see which of them Carder preferred. Instead of stuffing himself, the diplomatic Carder selected only some fowl and fishes, and distributed the rest among the children, thus winning much goodwill for himself.

The castaway found life with Caiou and his people comfortable, and had an opportunity to observe them both closely and at great length. The natives were warlike and merciless to their captured foes. Carder saw firsthand what happened to their captives. When Carder arrived at the village, the men were going off to war. They returned with a captive, who was tied to a post. The victors then got drunk on a beverage made from a root that Carder called "I.P." Intoxicated, the natives danced around their captive and split his skull with a club.

Carder discerned nothing that might be called religion among Caiou's people. They displayed reverence for the moon, particularly the new moon. They evidently greeted the new moon's appearance by dancing, leaping and clapping their hands.

After spending about a year in the village, Carder had learned the natives' language. Caiou evidently saw in Carder the makings of a good warrior and asked him to accompany the army into battle. Carder agreed, and proceeded to improve their weaponry. He showed them how to make shields out of tree bark for protection against arrows. Carder also had them make about 200 clubs. With those clubs and about 100 shields, some 700 men marched off to war, marked (at Carder's suggestion) with red balsam on one leg to distinguish them from their enemies. After three days' march, the army arrived at another village, much smaller than theirs, and were received by volleys of arrows. The shields proved a good defense, however, and the invaders used their new clubs to knock down some 200 defenders. Twenty prisoners were taken, and the rest of the defenders ran away into the woods. Bodies of many of the slain were cooked and eaten. The 20 prisoners also were devoured after being taken to Caiou's village. The looting of the conquered village focused on strong drink, tobacco and cotton beds.

While Carder was living with Caiou's people, a search for the missing men from Drake's expedition was under way. A Portuguese-Brazilian party approached to within a few miles of Caiou's village, but several members of the search party were captured, killed and eaten.

By this time, Carder was evidently homesick and asked Caiou for permission to leave the village. Caiou said yes, and sent Carder on his way with abundant provisions.

Near the town of Bahia de Todos los Santos, Carder encountered a Portuguese man named Michael Jonas. Carder asked him if any Englishmen lived in town. Jonas said that one Antonio de Pava spoke English well and was sympathetic to the English. So, Carder was taken to meet de Pava, who advised him not to let anyone know that Carder understood Portuguese.

There was good reason for such caution. The local authorities were much less hospitable than Caiou's people had been toward Carder. The Portuguese governor, Diego Vas, argued that simply by venturing into Portuguese domains, Carder was in violation of the law, deserved to be sent to prison, then shipped to Portugal and made a galley slave for the rest of his life. Carder contended that he did not enter Portuguese territory of his own will, but was shipwrecked there. Moreover, once he entered Portuguese territory, he had yielded to the authorities willingly.

Nonetheless, Carder was sent to prison, but only briefly. De Pava and some of his friends secured Carder's release from jail. Again, Carder was brought before the governor to argue his case. Diego Vas consulted with his staff and decided the best plan was to release Carder into the custody of de Pava while the authorities wrote home to Portugal for advice on what to do with their visitor. A response to this inquiry was expected to arrive in about a year. (In fact, the response did not arrive for two years.)

While waiting for news from Portugal, Carder served as an overseer in the fields and made some short voyages along the coast on a bark belonging to de Pava. About a year and a half after Carder arrived at the Portuguese community, de Pava advised him to escape before a ship arrived to take him to Portugal. With de Pava's aid, Carder escaped by sea and eventually made his way back to England. Along the way, Carder was captured by English warships and was shipwrecked on the Irish coast. Carder at last returned home in late 1586, just over nine years after leaving England with Sir Francis Drake. He was summoned to Whitehall and spent an hour in conversation with Queen Elizabeth about his adventures. The Queen bestowed a gift of 22 gold coins upon Carder.

cargo Heavy cargo has been a contributing factor in many shipwrecks. A weighty load of phosphate rock, for example, helped to sink the schooner *Lewis A.*

Rommell off the Virginia coast on January 15, 1884. The heavily laden schooner was on a voyage from Charleston, South Carolina, to Baltimore when heavy seas and gale-force winds overcame the vessel off the Little Island lifesaving station at Virginia Beach. The lifesavers, watching from shore, saw the schooner in distress. The surfmen made six trips to the stricken schooner and brought all the crewmen ashore safely. The schooner sank the next day.

Phosphate rock also contributed to the loss of the schooner *Albert C. Paige* on the Virginia shore less than two weeks later, on January 26, 1884. The ship stranded near the Dam Neck Mills lifesaving station at Virginia Beach while on a voyage from Charleston, South Carolina, to New York City. Stiff winds and heavy seas had driven the ship off course. Surfmen from two stations on shore came to the schooner's assistance. A wrecking vessel appeared on the scene soon afterward and tried, without success, to free the stranded ship. Everyone on the schooner was rescued, but the ship eventually was declared a complete loss.

In a similar case from the Great Lakes, an unusually heavy cargo of rails is thought to have sunk the freighter *Benjamin Noble* on Lake Superior in 1914. The overloaded ship, which reportedly left harbor with its anchor pockets almost under water, is thought to have sunk within 25 miles of Duluth, Minnesota, during a storm.

Explosive cargoes have destroyed many ships, especially petroleum carriers in the 20th century. Explosions were also a particular danger for warships in the age of sail. A warship of that time might amount to little more than a great floating keg of powder, vulnerable to any source of ignition that might touch off the explosive. It was not unheard of for a warship to explode while at anchor, when lightning struck the mast and set off powder below decks.

A cargo of gold or silver could be as dangerous as explosives, because such wealth drew the attentions of pirates and privateers. Protecting treasure-laden ships from attack was one reason Spain instituted the flota system to guard its convoys traveling between Spain and Spanish colonies in the Americas.

A strange incident involving a volatile cargo of alcohol may account for one of the most enduring mysteries of the sea, namely the abandoned *Mary Celeste,* found drifting off the Azores in 1872. Many different explanations have been proposed for the abandonment of the ship. According to one of the most plausible of these, tropical heat caused alcohol, carried in barrels below decks, to evaorate and build up gas pressure until the barrel lids blew off. The ship's captain presumably thought the *Mary Celeste* was about to blow sky-high, and ordered all on board into the ship's boat until he was sure the danger had passed. In this scenario, however, he neglected to attach the boat to the ship by a line. A wind then sprang up, carrying the now empty ship away from its crew and passengers, who were left behind in the boat and never heard from again. This scenario, while conjectural, fits the known evidence in the case and in any event is more believable than certain fantasies of a giant squid or extraterrestrial spacecraft making off with the crew and passengers.

Items of cargo, such as coins, snuffboxes and clay pipes, can be useful in dating shipwrecks and identifying the wrecks by nationality. Archaeologists take keen interest in such bits of cargo for the information they may provide about daily life aboard ship.

Shore dwellers in many parts of the world traditionally have shown a keen interest in shipwrecks because of the cargoes on board. Wherever people made only a subsistence living on a less than hospitable shore, a shipwreck could provide a tremendous influx of wealth by local standards. Frightening tales are told of people on shore setting up false navigational signals to lure ships to destruction, then looting the cargo after a ship was wrecked.

See also ARCHAEOLOGY; EXPLOSIONS; FLOTA SYSTEM; GOLD; MARY CELESTE; NOBLE; ROYAL TAR.

Caribbean Sea   For centuries, the Caribbean Sea has been one of the most heavily traveled parts of the ocean. It also abounds in wrecks because of hazards to shipping, from reefs to hurricanes, and during the days of Spain's colonial empire in the Americas presented the extra threat of attack from privateers who preyed on Spanish shipping. Pirates also operated extensively in the Caribbean during the age of sail and took advantage of the numerous islands in the region. For a time, Port Royal, Jamaica, became notorious for the activities of pirates based there. Port Royal also became the site of a sunken city when an earthquake sent much of the community sliding into the ocean in 1692.

See also FLOTA SYSTEM; PORT ROYAL.

***Carnatic*, British mail steamship**   A false sense of security evidently led to the deaths of 27 people in this wreck. On September 12, 1869, *Carnatic* ran onto a coral reef off Shadwan Island at the mouth of the Gulf of Suez. The ship appeared to be in no great danger, so some 230 passengers decided to stay on board. The ship broke in two, however, the following morning. The survivors were rescued from the island.

***Carnegie*, American research vessel**   Constructed by the Carnegie Institution of Washington to serve as a seagoing geophysics research laboratory, *Carnegie* was destroyed in 1929 on a cruise in the Pacific Ocean. On November 29, while the ship was taking on gasoline for fuel, an explosion shook the vessel and blasted a large hole in the deck. There was no hope of saving the ship.

The captain was knocked into the water by the blast. At first he appeared to have suffered only minor injuries, but in fact he was badly hurt and died while being taken to a hospital. The ship's cabin boy was also killed.

Carnegie operated from 1909–1929 and made several cruises to study terrestrial magnetism.

Caronia, British liner Originally part of the Cunard Line, *Caronia* was sailing under the name *Caribia* when the ship was sold to breakers in Taiwan and started, in tow by a tug, on its eventful final voyage in 1974.

Off the Pacific coast of Mexico, the tug and liner encountered a hurricane. The two ships parted company in the storm, although the tug found the liner and resumed towing it several days later.

Near Hawaii, the liner started taking on water and developed a list. The United States Navy's help was requested, and the Navy sent out the salvage vessel *Takelma.* Soon the flooding was overcome, and the liner was brought into Honolulu for repairs before continuing the voyage.

Bad weather struck again as the tug and liner neared Guam. When the tug lost an engine, and the two vessels started moving toward the dangerous coast, the tug cast the liner away. The big ship grounded on a breakwater, then slid off and sank in deep water. The next day, the liner was nowhere to be seen.

Although temporarily lost from view, the ship still presented a potential hazard to navigation. The wreck had to be located. High-resolution side-scan sonar—a system that uses underwater pulses of sound and their returned "echoes" to assemble a graphic image of what lies underwater—was needed to locate and identify the sunken liner. So, a call went out for the sonar equipment, which was then in the Gulf of Mexico and had to be flown to Guam.

The sonar's journey to Guam was just as eventful as the liner's voyage there, writes Captain C. A. Bartholemew in his history of Naval marine salvage. Another piece of equipment took priority over the sonar on the first leg of its flight, so the sonar was stopped temporarily in Houston, Texas. Once the sonar made its way to Los Angeles, it was lost briefly until technicians spotted it and carried it to a plane bound for San Francisco.

At San Francisco, a bomb scare delayed things still further. All cargo had to be removed and examined.

Finally, FBI "sniffer" dogs approved the sonar for shipment. The sonar flew to Guam as the only cargo on the plane. The following day the wreck was located, and ships entering and leaving the harbor could be warned what precautions to take.

The wreck became the responsibility of the Army Corps of Engineers, which decided to award a contract on a competitive basis for the hulk's removal. A Japanese firm won the contract, disassembled the wreck and used a crane to remove it piece by piece. Thus ended the last voyage of *Caribia,* formerly *Caronia.*

Carpathia, British passenger liner The liner *Carpathia* went down in history for its role in saving survivors of *Titanic* in 1912. *Carpathia*'s captain, Arthur Rostron, became a hero for taking his ship at top speed through waters littered with icebergs to save the passengers and crew in *Titanic*'s boats. The rescue operation appears to have been a model of efficiency.

See also CALIFORNIAN INCIDENT; ROSTRON, CAPTAIN ARTHUR HENRY; TITANIC.

carrack A merchant ship with a distinctive combination of triangular bow and rounded stern, used in the Mediterranean Sea in the 1400s and 1500s.

Carroll, American sailing vessel The wreck of the brig *Carroll* off the Outer Banks of North Carolina in 1837 was remarkable for the part that a dog played in rescue operations. *Carroll* left New Orleans on January 25 on a voyage to Baltimore, carrying a cargo including cotton, hides and pork. Also on board were two passengers and the ship's mascot, a dog named Pillow.

In fog, the ship struck Lookout Shoals on the night of February 8, then passed over the bar and back into deep water. The rudder had been carried away. Meanwhile, a strong wind was rising from the southeast, and the captain tried to take *Carroll* ashore before the ship was overwhelmed. About a mile off Cape Lookout, the ship struck the shore and held fast as waves broke over the vessel. At daybreak, an attempt was made to launch a boat, but the boat capsized and was destroyed in the surf. The waves and the distance from shore made it impossible to pass a line from shore to ship, or vice versa. To make matters worse, the weather deteriorated further. Rain began falling, then turned to sleet and hail, and at last snow. Battered by the waves, the survivors on *Carroll* were exposed to freezing temperatures.

Pillow, the dog, saved the survivors by swimming ashore with a rope tied around his neck. The rope allowed the freezing people on *Carroll* to be drawn ashore, and Pillow's brave deed went down in the history of lifesaving on the Outer Banks.

See also OUTER BANKS.

Cartagena, Colombia   One of the most important ports in Spain's American colonies during the days of the flota system, Cartagena was the site of numerous shipwrecks.

See also CARTAGENA WRECKS; CASTILLO SANTA CRUZ WRECKS.

Cartagena wrecks, 1741   In response to an English raid on Cartagena, Colombia, in 1741, the Spaniards sank many ships in the harbor, including six major warships and six galleons. The warships included the 80-gun *San Felipe*, the 70-gun *Galicia*, the 70-gun *Carlos* and the 60-gun *Africa*. Many vessels were sunk deliberately at the mouth of the harbor to block the English fleet's access. The next day, two more Spanish warships, the 60-gun *Dragon* and the 60-gun *Conquistador*, were also sunk.

castaways   This is the general term for survivors of shipwrecks who are stranded in remote locations. The expression also may be applied to people who are put off ships at sea in small boats and forced to drift or sail in them until such time as they are rescued. A large and colorful literature has arisen around the subject of castaways. A familiar example of such literature is Daniel Defoe's novel *Robinson Crusoe*, based on the actual experience of Alexander Selkirk.

See also SELKIRK, ALEXANDER; SERRANO NARRATIVE; TREVESSA.

Castilla, Spanish sailing vessel   The well-armed *Castilla* was lost in a severe storm in Veracruz, Mexico, in 1772. All on board survived, but a large cargo of cochineal was lost.

Castillo Santa Cruz wrecks, Colombia   In 1697, a French fleet attacked Cartagena, and the Spaniards deliberately sank two galleons near Castillo Santa Cruz to block the harbor. The Spaniards proceeded to burn many other ships to deprive the French of their use.

causes of shipwrecks   Shipwrecks may be attributed to numerous causes. Maritime historian John Perry Fish, in his 1989 book *Unfinished Voyages*, cites U.S. Government figures on various causes of shipwrecks on the Atlantic and Gulf coasts for 1906. The 398 wrecks counted in this listing fell into the following categories. (Percentage figures were calculated by this author.)

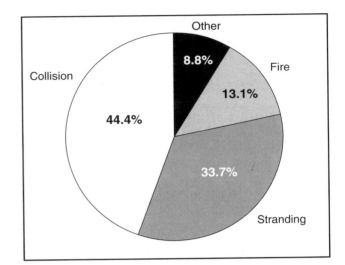

Causes of wrecks, U.S. Atlantic and Gulf coasts. (Fiscal year 1906)

Causes	Number of ships	Percentage
Collision	177	44.4
Stranding	134	33.7
Fire	52	13.1
Foundering	30	7.5
Explosion	3	0.7
Capsizing	1	0.3
Ice	1	0.3
Total	398	100.0

In the largest single category, collisions, Fish cites government statistics on causes (percentages calculated by the author):

Causes	Number of ships	Percentage
Fault of other vessel	60	33.9
Unknown	30	16.9
Fog	26	14.7
Accident	12	6.8
Fault of tug towing	8	4.5
Poor management	7	4.0
Misunderstood signals	7	4.0
Snowstorm	6	3.4
"Unavoidable"	5	2.8
High and "baffling" winds	4	2.2
Tides and currents	3	1.7
Miscellaneous	3	1.7
Carelessness	2	1.1
Pilot error	2	1.1
Lack of proper lights	1	0.6
"Error in judgment"	1	0.6
Total	177	100.0

One may draw several conclusions from the 1906 figures. Collision was by far the leading cause of shipwreck in the areas surveyed, followed closely by stranding, with fire a distant third. When two ships collided, one of the vessels involved was found to be at fault in about one-third of the cases listed. One kind of weather, specifically fog, was responsible for approximately one in every seven collisions. (Snowstorms and high, "baffling" winds were relatively minor factors.) In about one of every six collisions, the cause was unknown.

See also COLLISIONS; FIRE; FOG; STORMS.

Cayman Islands Numerous wrecks have occurred in the waters around the Cayman Islands. Examples include *Morning Star,* a pirate vessel that was wrecked on reefs at Grand Cayman Island during a hurricane in 1722; and *Señor San Miguel,* a Spanish vessel with a cargo of mercury, wrecked on Little Cayman Island in 1730 during a voyage from Spain to Veracruz, Mexico.

Cayo Nuevo wreck, Mexico A 16th-century wreck near Cayo Nuevo, approximately 100 miles north of the Mexican coast near the Yucatán peninsula, has yielded artifacts, notably large cannon, of considerable importance to marine archaeology. Divers from the United States discovered three cannon and an anchor at the site. The divers tried to raise one of the cannon themselves but were unsuccessful. They contacted Mexican authorities and later participated in an expedition, with the Mexican Navy's help, to the site. Analysis of artifacts from the wreck, such as bits of Spanish olive jars, indicate that the ship may have been traveling westward from Spain when the wreck occurred. The ship has not been identified.

See also ARCHAEOLOGY; CANNON.

CEDAM See CLUB OF EXPLORATIONS AND AQUATIC SPORTS OF MEXICO.

Celtic, British passenger liner The 20,000-ton White Star liner *Celtic* was wrecked on December 10, 1928, at Queenstown (now Cobh), Ireland. *Celtic* was trying to enter the harbor in a gale when the ship struck rocks at Roche's Point. No lives were reported lost. Twenty-five of 254 passengers on board were survivors of the wreck of the liner *Vestris* only a month earlier.

See also VESTRIS.

Central America, United States mail steamship *Central America* foundered in a storm on September 11, 1857, while on a voyage from Havana to New York. Of 427 people on board, 160 were rescued.

Challenger, American schooner A victim of fire, *Challenger* burned for days before sinking in the Willapa River in Washington state on November 7, 1904, a few miles north of the Columbia River mouth. The ship carried a cargo of lumber and lime.

While at sea in a gale on November 4 off Tillamook Bay, Oregon, the captain discovered the ship was on fire. Heavy seas prevented *Challenger* from putting in at Tillamook Bay, and the ship continued toward the Columbia River.

Fumes and smoke from the fire made it impossible for anyone to stand at the wheel. The crew signaled for a tug at the Columbia River, but the sea was too rough for a tug to come out. The captain tried hailing a lightship but received no aid there either. The burning ship then proceeded northward to Willapa Harbor, where a tug came out to give *Challenger* a tow. Two hours afterward, the ship had to be scuttled.

Almost everyone involved in this incident was injured in some way. *Challenger's* captain and crew were treated for lung troubles, burns and internal injuries at a local hospital. The tug's captain was knocked down and injured seriously when seas washed over the tug.

Portions of the wreck were brought to the surface in 1934 by a dredge working on the Willapa River.

See also FIRE.

Chameau, French frigate The frigate *Le Chameau* left Louisbourg in Nova Scotia for Quebec in 1725, carrying a cargo of silver and gold, in addition to many passengers. The ship capsized and sank in a storm near Cape Lornebec, Nova Scotia. Nearly all the passengers and crew were killed.

See also CANADA.

Chanduy Reef wrecks, Ecuador During the clichéd "dark and stormy night" in May of 1654, four galleons were on their way to Panama with a cargo of treasure when the *Capitana* of the fleet was wrecked on Chanduy Reef at the mouth of Ecuador's Guayaquil River. The ship broke apart quickly, and nearly everyone on board was killed. Only a little of the treasure was recovered. The rest was soon buried beneath the sands.

See also CAPITANA.

Chapin, American schooner How quickly the sea can destroy a vessel driven ashore was demonstrated by the wreck of *Nahum Chapin,* a three-masted schooner wrecked at Quogue on Long Island, New York, during a gale early on the morning of January 21, 1897. The ship went on the outer bar at 4 A.M. and was demolished in about three hours.

The lifesavers' inability to help the ship was tragic. Lifesavers on shore at dawn could see everyone on *Chapin*, including a child and a woman, clinging to the jib boom and rigging. No boats could be sent out in the heavy seas, and those on the ship were unable to grab and secure lines fired to the ship from shore. One at a time, the ship's occupants were swept away to their deaths in the stormy sea. There were no survivors.

Charlestown, Nevis, Lesser Antilles   The great earthquake of April 6, 1690, destroyed much of Charlestown and sent a large portion of the city, including its principal fort, sliding into the sea. There are few records of this catastrophe. Marine archaeologist Robert Marx reported sighting at least 50 brick structures on a dive at Charlestown in 1961. He also visited the site of the fort and mentioned seeing more than 20 large cannon.

See also NEVIS; PORT ROYAL.

Charon, British warship   The battle of Yorktown in 1781, which provided the climax of the Revolutionary War in America, involved extensive combat between British and French naval vessels. Among the British ships destroyed was the then-new British warship *Charon,* which carried 44 guns and caught fire on the night of October 10, 1781. An American observer named Thatcher reported that a red-hot shot from a French gun set fire to *Charon,* which then drifted across the York River in flames and spread fire to several other vessels before sinking on the Gloucester side of the river. The wreck was identified in 1980. Plans and specifications for the warship made conclusive identification possible. *Charon* was named for the mythical ferryman of the underworld who supposedly carried the souls of the dead across the River Styx to Hades.

See also YORKTOWN WRECKS.

Chesapeake Bay   This great estuary extends northward from Cape Henry and Cape Charles, Virginia, past Baltimore, Maryland, and is separated from the Atlantic Ocean by the Delmarva Peninsula. Chesapeake Bay has been the site of numerous shipwrecks, from earliest colonial times until the present day. Shoals, frequent storms and collisions due to heavy shipping traffic are only three hazards faced by vessels in these waters. The Bay's tributaries, such as the York River, are also sites of numerous wrecks.

See also SWITZER WRECK; TANGIER ISLAND WRECK; YORKTOWN WRECKS.

children found at sea   This curious category of stories involves infants and young children found, dead or alive, at sea under mysterious or especially tragic circumstances. Maritime historian Edward Rowe Snow, for example, has gathered several anecdotes of this kind.

According to one such story, the schooner *Polly* sailed from Provincetown, Massachusetts, for Bay Chaleur in Canada in 1803, with the captain's 10-year-old nephew on board as cabin boy. Off Saint Paul's Island near Cape Breton, the boy thought he heard a young child crying and reported the noise to the captain. At first, the captain was skeptical and thought his nephew had merely heard the cries of gulls. Then the captain heard the wail clearly himself and had to admit it sounded like the cry of a child.

The noise appeared to come from a large rock off Saint Paul's Island. Two men from the schooner—with the cabin boy for company—went by boat to the rock to investigate. There they found a young girl, about to be swept away by the rising tide. The cabin boy rescued the child.

When all were safely aboard the ship, the captain tried without success to find out from the child how she had been stranded on the rock. Despite all further investigations, those circumstances remained a mystery. Apparently the child did not wind up on the rock as the result of a shipwreck, because the weather at the time was calm, and there was no sign of any shipwreck in the vicinity at the time of her discovery and rescue. The crew chose the name Ruth for the little girl, who came to live in the captain's household and eventually married the captain's nephew, her rescuer.

Child's Play, British warship   The whimsically named 24-gun H.M.S. *Child's Play* was sunk at Palmetto Point, St. Kitts, Lesser Antilles, during a hurricane on August 30, 1707. The same storm also sank H.M.S. *Winchester* off nearby Sandy Point. Guns from both wrecks were recovered.

Chippewa, American liner   An interrupted meal figured in the wreck of *Chippewa.* The liner hit the rocks near Montauk, Long Island, New York, in fog early on the morning of June 23, 1908. The impact knocked a hole in the hull, but the ship did not appear to be in immediate danger of sinking, and the men on board sat down to breakfast in the captain's cabin.

One man at the breakfast table that morning was raising a piece of ham to his mouth by fork when a wave broke down the door. The captain told the men to leave. In the boat heading for shore, he discovered he was still holding the fork, which he kept as a souvenir of the wreck.

The ship eventually was hauled off the rocks, on August 4.

Circassian, British steamship See HEATH PARK.

City of Glasgow, trans-Atlantic steamship

What happened to the immigrant vessel *City of Glasgow* is one of the mysteries of the sea. The 1,087-ton, propeller-driven, iron-hulled passenger liner, which sailed between Liverpool, England, and Philadelphia, vanished on a voyage from Liverpool to Philadelphia in 1845, apparently with the loss of all on board.

A vessel presumed to be the missing ship was discovered drifting as a derelict some 600 miles west of Scotland in August of 1854 by the bark *Mary Morris*, out of Glasgow. A boarding party from *Mary Morris* found that all the woodwork on the derelict had been burned. The wreck was identified tentatively as *City of Glasgow* because no other vessel of similar description had been reported lost in those waters over the previous several years.

City of Glasgow had sailed from Liverpool on March 1, 1854, with 399 passengers and 74 officers and crew on board. The voyage was expected to last about a month. By late April, *City of Glasgow* still had not arrived in Philadelphia. According to one hopeful explanation at the time, the ship was thought to have been delayed by ice off the coast of Newfoundland. News from a ship in the Atlantic about that time, however, raised questions about what had happened to *City of Glasgow*.

The ship *Baldaur* reported seeing in mid-Atlantic, on April 21, a large paddle wheel steamer with a black hull, listing markedly to port. There was no sign that anyone was aboard the ship, nor could any smoke be seen from the vessel's funnel.

As *Baldaur* watched, a bark emerged from behind the unidentified steamship and sailed away toward the south. Then fog descended, and *Baldaur* lost sight of the two other vessels. *Baldaur* also sighted numerous biscuit boxes floating on the water.

The situation looked suspicious. Was the listing steamer *City of Glasgow*? Had pirates on the mysterious bark beset *City of Glasgow* and thrown part of its provisions overboard?

The steamer was presumed to be *City of Glasgow*. Yet that identification was dubious. The steamer sighted from *Baldaur* had paddle wheels. *City of Glasgow* was driven by a propeller. (By 20th-century standards, this was roughly comparable to identifying a propeller-driven World War II bomber as a jet airliner of the 1990s.)

Strange stories continued to arrive concerning *City of Glasgow*. A man in Ireland said he had received a letter from one of the missing ship's passengers, to the effect that the ship had foundered and its passengers and crew had made their way to Africa.

Another unusual tale involved a middle-aged Englishman who reportedly kept visiting the offices of the missing ship's owners, the Liverpool and Philadelphia Steamship Company, in Philadelphia, to ask about mail. On these visits, the man had his 12-year-old son with him. The man and boy, according to this story, were seeking news of the rest of their family. The man's wife and other children reportedly had been on *City of Glasgow*. As weeks passed without conclusive news of what had happened to the missing vessel, the man allegedly went mad and had to be confined to an asylum.

The case of *City of Glasgow* apparently continues unresolved. There appears to be no proof, however, that pirates actually attacked the ship and disposed of its passengers and crew in mid-ocean.

See also MARY CELESTE; WARATAH.

City of Honolulu, American passenger liner

This ship had a long and checkered career. Originally the Hamburg America Line's *Kiautschou*, and later renamed *Prinzess Alice* when serving the North German Lloyd Line, the ship became *City of Honolulu* for the Los Angeles Steam Ship Company after World War I and operated between Los Angeles and Honolulu, Hawaii. The ship burned in Honolulu on May 25, 1930, but managed to sail back to California. At 30 years of age, however, the ship was considered too old to make repairs worthwhile, and was scrapped.

City of Portland, American passenger steamer

A famous case of disappearance at sea, the loss of the side-wheel steamer *City of Portland*, operating between Boston and Portland, Maine, occurred during a storm on November 26, 1898. A well-appointed ship with a speed of 10 knots, the *City of Portland* was preparing to leave Boston with an estimated 200 passengers and 100 crew members on board when news arrived from the south that heavy weather was approaching. Captain Henry Blanchard decided to risk the storm and sail for Portland, in the hope of arriving there before the storm did.

This was, however, no ordinary storm. It was one of the most powerful and destructive in the history of the northeastern United States. The weather had deteriorated badly by early evening. Winds reached a velocity of 60 miles per hour a few minutes after 9 P.M., then increased to 90 miles per hour.

Exactly how the *City of Portland* was destroyed is uncertain. Several vessels reported sighting the steamship that evening. Fishing boats allegedly saw the

City of Portland tossing on the waves, but the ship did not respond to a flare signal. Just before midnight, a schooner came close to colliding with a ship that was presumed to be the *City of Portland* and that appeared to have suffered damage. A side-wheel steamer—again, presumably the *City of Portland*—was spotted by yet another ship around 7 o'clock the next morning. Some 45 minutes later, several loud blasts from a steam whistle like that on a large ship were heard at a nearby lifesaving station on shore, but nothing more was heard, and the ship was not visible.

The *City of Portland* never reached its destination. The first evidence of its destruction washed ashore on a beach near Wellfleet, Massachusetts. A man walking along the beach found assorted debris and two bodies, a man's and a woman's. The dead wore life preservers from the *City of Portland*. Additional bodies were recovered later. As far as is known, no one on the steamer survived. The ship is thought to have remained afloat until early evening of November 27, then possibly capsized, collided with another vessel or exploded when water came in contact with the ship's boilers.

The *City of Portland* was only one, although the most famous, of several dozen vessels sunk in this particular storm. Exact figures on the number of dead from the *City of Portland* are not available, because apparently no exact tally of passengers and crew was made. One puzzling element of the *City of Portland*'s loss is why Captain Blanchard did not head for shore when the storm arrived.

See also STORMS.

City of Rio de Janeiro, **American steamship**

Near the end of a voyage from Yokohama, Japan, to San Francisco in February of 1901, the Pacific Mail Steamship Company's 3,548-ton *City of Rio de Janeiro* wrecked on rocks at the Golden Gate after the captain—ignoring the harbor pilot's advice—took the ship through the passage in fog on the morning of February 22. The wreck killed more than 100 people, the captain included.

See also FOG.

Clarke narrative

An English sailor, Richard Clarke of Weymouth, left behind a famous narrative of shipwreck in the North Atlantic. On August 20, 1583, Clarke wrote, he left Saint Johns, Newfoundland, as master of the ship *Admiral,* with General Sir Humfrey Gilbert also on board. The ship headed for the "Isle of Sablon," presumably Sable Island.

A few miles from the island, there was a dispute on *Admiral* about which course the ship should take. The general favored sailing west-northwest, but Clarke thought west-southwest was better. The island was surrounded by dangerous sands, and the ship would run upon them in a few hours by traveling on the course suggested by the general.

Gilbert said Clarke's reckoning was incorrect, and evidently ordered Clarke to sail north-northwest. As Clarke anticipated, the ship ran aground and was wrecked. Clarke and some other men set out from the wreck in a small boat without provisions. One man in the boat, identified in Clarke's story as "Master Hedley," proposed that the men should draw lots to see who would remain in the boat, and who would be put over the side to improve the chance of survival for the rest. Clarke rejected that suggestion.

Lack of food and water took its toll on the company, however, and soon the men were near death. By the seventh day in the boat, they despaired of ever reaching land. Clarke told them that if they did not sight land on the seventh day, they could cast him overboard.

On the seventh day, they did indeed sight land. Wind carried them ashore. Clarke noted that the wind blew south until they reached the shore, then changed toward the north only half an hour after their landfall. Had the wind moved them any direction but south, they would have been lost at sea. For their deliverance, the men praised God.

The men refreshed themselves with berries and with water from a brook. Clarke was impressed with the plant life of the region, including splendid trees. The castaways made themselves a shelter out of tree limbs and fed themselves well on fruit and vegetables. They even found a river full of salmon.

After recovering their strength, the men proceeded north along the shore in their boat. Eventually they were picked up by a ship that delivered them to Biscay, and from there they made their way to England by the end of the year.

Clarksdale Victory, **American Army transport ship**

Clarksdale Victory was wrecked on Hippa Island Reef, British Columbia, on November 24, 1947, while on a voyage from Whittier, Alaska, to Seattle, Washington. The ship reportedly split in two during a storm. Forty-nine on board were killed. There were four survivors.

Clifton, **Great Lakes freighter**

The loss of the freighter *Clifton* on Lake Huron in September of 1924, with 30 on board, involved a peculiar kind of vessel called a "pig boat," presumably named for the resemblance of its rounded back to that of a pig.

Pig boats, also known as "whaleback" boats, were specially designed ore carriers with elongated, rounded hulls almost like those of modern submarines; these hulls let waves wash over the ships in rough weather. Maritime historian Dwight Boyer, in an account of *Clifton*'s loss in his history of Great Lakes shipwrecks, writes that there was a reason for this peculiar approach to ship design.

In theory, a ship could endure heavy seas more easily if its hull offered few obstacles to oncoming waves, such as raised hatchways. At the bow and stern, pig boats had odd, rounded structures in place of the traditional forecastle and superstructure. They were uncomfortable ships to sail in and unpopular with their crews.

Clifton was a pig boat. It had another peculiarity of design: a complex "self-unloading" apparatus on its deck that allowed the ship to take on and unload its cargo of crushed stone even where there were no conventional dockside facilities. This advantage was offset by top-heaviness.

Clifton loaded crushed stone at Sturgeon Bay, Wisconsin, on September 20, 1924, and then set out for Detroit. The ship's route would take it past Presque Isle and Thunder Bay on Lake Huron, to Port Huron, and from there to Detroit, where it would unload its cargo quickly.

Along the way, *Clifton* had to pass the Lansing Shoal Light on a heavily traveled stretch of water off the upper peninsula of Michigan. As the ship passed Old Mackinac Point, a reporting station on shore (a service utilized before the widespread use of wireless and radio) notified *Clifton*'s owners by telegram that the ship had passed there. *Clifton* proceeded from Old Mackinac Point toward Cheboygan, and from there toward the middle of the lake, on the way toward Port Huron.

On the lake, *Clifton* encountered a strong southwest wind and rising seas. Water rolled over the hull. *Clifton* apparently took the change in weather easily. When *Clifton* passed the salvage tug *Favorite*, about 18 hours after leaving Sturgeon Bay, the tug's captain noticed that the pig boat was in no apparent trouble, though large masses of water cascaded over the freighter's decks.

The weather deteriorated further. An intense storm swept across the lake. When *Clifton* failed to appear on schedule at either Port Huron or Detroit, an investigation began. The ship's last reported position was off Forty Mile Point, where *Clifton* encountered the tug *Favorite*. An extensive search by ships and aircraft turned up no sign of *Clifton* over the next few days. Rumors circulated that *Clifton* had found shelter at Oscoda, Michigan, but the rumors were unconvincing, because *Clifton*'s draft was too great for the water there. Also, news would have reached the owners if *Clifton* had arrived at other harbors along the way.

Various ships reported finding wreckage, but none was definitely associated with *Clifton* until the freighter *Glencairn* saw hatch covers floating on the water. Knowing that *Clifton* was missing, *Glencairn* paused to search the immediate area and, after about two hours, found part of *Clifton*'s pilothouse. The wreckage contained the ship's clock, which had stopped and evidently showed *Clifton* had gone down at four o'clock.

What exactly happened to *Clifton* was a matter of debate. The ship's engines were known to be sound, and the ship had passed inspection recently with a good report. It appeared more likely that a large boom on the self-unloading equipment had come loose and swung over the side, causing the ship to become unstable and capsize.

Another possible contributing factor to *Clifton*'s loss was hatch design. Originally, the ship was designed to let waves sweep over the deck unobstructed; hatches therefore were set flush with the hull. The ship had been modified, however, to include traditional hatchways with combings (raised edges) that protruded above the deck. Hatch combings would have offered resistance to the waves, and so the seas might have battered open the hatches.

See also GREAT LAKES.

clipper ships A colorful category of wooden sailing ships, clippers were designed for high speed but had less cargo capacity than other, slower vessels. The term "clipper" is sometimes restricted to approximately a hundred vessels that could make the voyage between New York and San Francisco in 110 or fewer days, or similarly long voyages in comparable time. Clipper ships carried passengers as well as cargo. Their wooden construction, however, left them vulnerable to fire, as in the case of *Great Republic*, the famous and elegant clipper ship that burned at New York in 1853.

See also GREAT REPUBLIC; SNOW SQUALL.

Club of Explorations and Aquatic Sports of Mexico (CEDAM) The first marine archaeological society in the Americas, CEDAM was founded in 1959 and was intended to carry out salvage operations and guard ancient wrecks from looting by foreigners. CEDAM members have taken part in expeditions in Mexico's waters and retrieved many significant artifacts from wreck sites.

See also ARCHAEOLOGY.

Coatzacoalcos wreck, Mexico This wreck and its aftermath provide a glimpse of the widespread practice of smuggling during the days of Spain's flota system. A ship was wrecked on the Mexican shore near Coatzacoalcos, in the vicinity of Veracruz, in 1628 or 1629. When cargo salvaged from the wreck was carried to Veracruz, government officials there found that more than 50 percent of the cargo was contraband.

See also FLOTA SYSTEM.

Coconuts, Long Island, New York This unusual place name, given to a stretch of beach at Montauk, originated with the wreck of the schooner *Elsie Fay* there on February 17, 1893. On its way from Grand Cayman Island in the West Indies to Boston, the ship struck rocks in a snowstorm and broke apart. Part of the cargo was a shipment of coconuts, which washed ashore in great numbers and figured prominently in the local diet for approximately a year afterward. The crew was rescued. The only casualty, apparently, was the ship's parrot.

coins Because they are stamped with their date of minting, coins are extremely valuable in determining the age of a shipwreck. The principle used by marine archaeologists is that a shipwreck is no older than the most recently dated coin found on the wreck. Even when no date is visible on a coin, other features of the coin may be used to establish a date, such as the profile of a monarch in whose reign the coin may have been issued.

See also ARCHAEOLOGY.

Collins Line One of the Cunard Line's early competitors, the American Collins Line was the work of Edward Knight Collins, who started his shipping empire in 1827 with a line between Veracruz, Mexico, and New York. Some years later, he inaugurated a packet line service between New York and Liverpool, England, called the Dramatic Line. In 1850, Collins began steamship service across the Atlantic Ocean. The Collins Line side-wheel paddle steamers *Arctic, Atlantic, Baltic* and *Pacific* were the biggest, fastest and most elegantly appointed passenger ships of their day, at some 283 feet long and approximately 2,800 gross tons each. The United States Government provided Collins with a hefty subsidy to help counter British competition.

The Collins Line was a spectacular success until the liner *Arctic* was lost at sea in 1854 with great loss of life, following a collision with the steamer *Vesta*. More than 300 people, including Collins's wife and children, went down with *Arctic*. Less than two years later, the Collins liner *Pacific* vanished at sea during a passage from Liverpool to New York with approximately 150 passengers aboard.

Although the Collins Line specialized in rapid trans-ocean passages, the company was condemned for running its ships at dangerously high speed. The line's reputation suffered greatly by comparison with that of Cunard, which had had no passenger fatalities at all. Moreover, the Collins Line could not continue regular service with only two liners remaining after the loss of *Arctic* and *Pacific*. The Collins Line folded in 1858. Its great legacy was to establish a model for later trans-Atlantic service, based on a combination of luxury and speed.

See also ARCTIC.

collisions Collisions between ships have been among the leading causes of shipwrecks. Although it may seem unlikely that the only two ships in perhaps a hundred square miles of ocean could come together in the same place at the same time, collisions happen often, for a variety of reasons. Shipping tends to be concentrated in narrow "corridors" or "lanes" of ocean travel, similar in many ways to superhighways for automobiles. As shipping in such lanes becomes highly active, the potential for collisions increases. Collision has been a particular danger in highly crowded harbors. Adverse weather conditions such as fog may make collisions more likely. Inadequate or misunderstood signals between ships also may increase the risk of collision.

Certain construction techniques, such as use of watertight bulkheads and compartments to contain flooding in the event that the hull is breached, have been used to protect ships against sinking after collision, and in many cases have kept stricken ships afloat

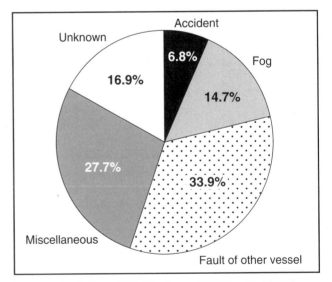

Causes of collisions, U.S. Atlantic and Gulf coasts. (Fiscal year, 1906)

Collisions in harbors are frequent. Here, the Swedish freighter *Nyland* (right) has just sliced into an American grain storage vessel in Hampton Roads, Virginia, on March 17, 1956. (U.S. Coast Guard)

long enough to reach shore. A dramatic demonstration of the wisdom of compartmentalization was the collision between the liner *Arctic* and the steamer *Vesta*. *Vesta* had a compartmentalized hull and survived, whereas *Arctic*, lacking internal divisions to contain flooding, filled and sank. Double sides and bottoms offer additional protection against breaches in the hull, because the inner hull layer may hold even if the outer layer fails.

On the other hand, certain features of ship construction, such as reinforced bows for protection in icy waters, have proven devastating in collisions. The reinforced bow of the collier *Storstad* caused such tremendous damage in a collision with the liner *Empress of Ireland* that the *Empress* sank quickly, with tremendous loss of life, even though the collision occurred close to shore.

In the 20th century, electronic navigation aids such as radar have helped to prevent collision by allowing mariners to perceive the positions of other vessels, even at night or in bad weather. Radar, however, has not prevented all collisions; because radar showed only the relative positions of *Andrea Doria* and *Stockholm*, for example, the two ships collided off Nantucket, Massachusetts, in one of the most famous shipwrecks of the 1950s.

See also ANDREA DORIA; ARCTIC; CONSTRUCTION; EMPRESS OF IRELAND.

Colombia   Cartagena, Colombia, was one of the most important ports in Spain's American colonies during the time of the flota system, and numerous wrecks occurred in and near the port.

See also BAHIA DE URABA WRECKS; CARTAGEÑA; DARIEN WRECK; FLOTA SYSTEM; NUESTRA SEÑORA DE LA CANDELARIA; SAN JUAN BAUTISTA; SANTA MARIA DE BEGONIA.

Columbia River Bar, Oregon-Washington state   A notable hazard to shipping, the Columbia River bar—the area between Willowa Bay and Clatsop Spit—claimed many ships in the 19th century. Some years saw four or five major wrecks. The bar became known as the "Pacific Graveyard."

Columbia River Lightship No. 50, American lightship   Moving a stranded lightship overland to the sea is an unusual engineering job, but it became necessary after this vessel went aground during a storm at McKenzie Head near the mouth of the Columbia River (Oregon-Washington), on November 28, 1899. When the tide went out, the ship was perched so high on the beach that unusual measures were needed to return the lightship to the sea.

The scheme, in principle, was simple: move the stranded lightship a mile across a peninsula to nearby Baker Bay. In the way, however, stood a forest and some less than smooth topography.

The engineers raised the ship from the sand and prepared to haul the lightship seaward, pulled by teams of horses. While those preparations were under way, a path was cut through the forest, and a timber

The bow section of a ship is especially vulnerable to collision damage. (U.S. Coast Guard)

roadbed strong enough to hold the 112-foot vessel was constructed.

After an overland journey of 16 months, Lightship No. 50 was returned to the water. Following repairs at Astoria, Washington, the ship went back on duty, and was retired in 1909.

See also LIGHTSHIPS.

Columbus, American side-wheel steamer *Columbus* burned and sank off Point Lookout, Maryland, on November 27, 1850. This was one of the major wrecks of the mid-19th century on Chesapeake Bay. Nine lives were lost. Parts of the wreck were salvaged.

Columbus expeditions The voyages of Admiral Christopher Columbus to the New World in the late 15th century involved several shipwrecks, most notably the loss of Columbus's flagship *Santa Maria* on his 1492 visit to Hispaniola in what is now the Dominican Republic. In addition to the wreck of *Santa Maria* on his first expedition, Columbus on his second expedition in 1494–1495 reportedly lost several vessels—two caravels named *San Juan* and *Cardera,* and possibly a

third ship named *Gallega*—in a storm at Isabela on Hispaniola in February of 1495.

Columbus appears to have lost no ships on his third voyage, but the fourth voyage, starting in 1502, experienced great trouble from *teredos,* or shipworms, which did such damage to the wooden ships that eventually the pumps could no longer keep up with the water that entered the ships through wormholes in the hulls. One ship, *Viscaína,* was so worm-eaten that it had to be abandoned. Two other vessels, *La Capitana* and *Santiago de Palos,* had to be run ashore at Puerto Santa Gloria, a bay on the northern shore of Jamaica.

Columbus and his party remained there for a year on the grounded ships. The admiral had to cope with mutineers and hostility from the natives, who at first provided food for the stranded Europeans but later became reluctant to support the uninvited visitors. Columbus used deception to intimidate the natives. He knew from an almanac that an eclipse of the moon was expected on the night of February 29, 1504. Columbus told the natives that the Europeans' God would that night display a sign of displeasure with the natives' hostility. The ruse worked. As the moon appeared to vanish before their eyes, the natives pleaded with Columbus to do something. Thereafter, the natives contributed to the expedition's support.

The aforementioned mutineers tried to escape from Jamaica by canoe but were unsuccessful. They returned to Puerto Santa Gloria and tried to capture the camp but lost a battle with Columbus and his loyal men. A rescue ship arrived in June of 1504. Columbus and what remained of his expedition abandoned the two rotten ships and returned to Spain. There, he found that the government was no longer willing to support his expeditions. Columbus died soon afterward.

The point where Columbus ran his leaky ships ashore has been identified as present-day St. Ann's Bay, but no identifiable remains of Columbus's vessels appear to have been discovered.

See also SANTA MARIA; TEREDOS.

Comet, British steamship One of the first passenger steamships, *Comet* was wrecked on Britain's western coast between Glasgow and Fort William, Scotland, on December 13, 1820. *Comet* was carried onto rocks and broke in two. The stern was washed away, but the bow remained on shore.

Comet, British steamship *Comet* collided with the steamship *Ayr* off Kempoch Point on October 21, 1825, while en route from Inverness to Glasgow, Scotland; 70 people were killed.

Commodore Jones, American Union gunboat

A converted ferry, *Commodore Jones* was destroyed on Virginia's James River on May 6, 1864, by a Confederate "galvanic torpedo," an early version of what now would be called a mine.

The Confederates were known to have sown their electrically operated explosive devices in Virginia waters. For their time, the "torpedoes" were sophisticated weapons and could be detonated from a considerable distance. In 1863, the Union gunboat *Commodore Barney* had come close to being destroyed by one of these weapons. It blasted the forward portion of the ship 10 feet into the air and knocked 20 men into the water.

So, the Union forces sent out what, in later decades, would be called a minesweeping party. Three gunboats—*Commodore Jones, Commodore Morris* and *Mackinaw*—were sent up the James River to find and neutralize the Confederate galvanic torpedoes.

An undetected torpedo destroyed *Commodore Jones,* lifting the gunboat out of the water and blasting it to pieces. Forty men were killed. Alerted by the presence of a man running along the shore, the Union forces went ashore and discovered two Confederates and the apparatus they used to set off the torpedoes. The Confederates were captured and interrogated; they eventually told what they knew about the torpedoes, writes Donald Shomette in *Shipwrecks on the Chesapeake.*

See also EXPLOSIVES; MINES; TORPEDOES.

Connecticut, United States

Connecticut waters, with their busy maritime traffic since colonial days, have been the site of numerous shipwrecks. Wrecks include the American merchant vessel *Osprey,* lost near New London in a storm in 1812; the American merchantman *George,* also lost near New London, on October 16, 1817; and the American merchant ship *Mary,* sunk at Darien on March 25, 1817. An interesting part of Connecticut maritime lore is the tale of the New Haven specter ship, an alleged apparition of a vessel lost at sea. The so-called specter ship, however, probably has a natural explanation.

See also NEW HAVEN SPECTER SHIP.

construction

The manner of a ship's construction—including materials, design and workmanship—does much to determine both the vessel's seaworthiness and its likelihood of surviving mishaps at sea. A collision capable of sinking a wooden-hulled vessel,

for example, may have much less effect on a steel-hulled ship. Changes in materials, however, have involved certain trade-offs between one kind of safety and another. For example, the transition from wood to metal in ship construction, beginning in the late 18th century and extending until about 1900, made ships more durable and resistant to storms and other natural hazards, but also increased the danger from collisions. A heavily laden, steel-hulled vessel carries vastly more kinetic energy than a relatively light-weight wooden craft, and therefore the steel ship is likely to do much more damage in a collision than would the wooden ship. When the collier *Storstad* struck the liner *Empress of Ireland* in the St. Lawrence River, near Rimouski, for example, the steel bow of *Storstad* did such tremendous damage that the liner sank almost immediately.

Among the major changes in design affecting ships in the 19th and early 20th centuries were the double hull and watertight bulkheads. Double-hull construction, in which the hull has an inner and an outer "skin" with perhaps a foot of space between them, provides added protection in case the outer hull is breached. Watertight bulkheads serve to contain flooding in the event that something ruptures a vessel's hull.

The effectiveness of such design features depends, of course, on how they are executed. A ship built with only a double bottom, instead of a complete double hull extending across the ship's bottom and up both sides of the hull, is relatively vulnerable to breaches in the flanks of the ship. For maximum protection, watertight bulkheads likewise should extend from the keel to the top of the hull, but considerations other than safety have sometimes led designers to extend watertight bulkheads only partway up from the keel, with calamitous results. The much-advertised watertight bulkheads on the British liner *Titanic,* which supposedly made the ship "unsinkable," actually allowed the liner to sink because they were not high enough to contain flooding in the bow after the ship struck an iceberg. Extending the bulkheads all the way up would have impeded movement from one end of the ship to the other and inconvenienced passengers and crew. So, the bulkheads' height was limited for the sake of convenience, even though that particular design compromise, in effect, sank the ship.

Any internal compartmentalization, however, is better than none at all. A case in point involves the liner *Arctic,* which had no such compartmentalization and sank rapidly after colliding with the steamer *Vesta.* By contrast, *Vesta* had three internal compartments and survived the collision, even after losing much of its bow in the incident. That particular shipwreck also demonstrated the superior strength of iron hulls such as *Vesta*'s over wooden ones like those of *Arctic*.

The quality of workmanship is by no means uniform among shipbuilders. Some ships appear to have sunk simply because their builders did shoddy work.

See also ARCTIC; TITANIC.

coral   A nemesis of mariners and marine archaeologists alike, coral—a complex biological system made up of small, coelenterate animals that build calcareous "houses" for themselves on the sea floor in tropical waters—forms extensive reefs that may extend to within inches of the surface and act, in effect, as barely submerged rocks. Collision with a coral reef can rip out the bottom of a ship. After a ship has sunk on a coral reef, the coral may extend itself over the wreck site and hide much of the wreck from marine archaeologists. The coral then must be broken apart and removed before work on the site can begin.

Corte Real expeditions   The Portuguese explorers and brothers Miguel and Gaspar Corte de Real made three voyages to the northern shores of North America between 1500 and 1502. The explorers are thought to have reached Greenland and what are now the Canadian provinces of Nova Scotia and Newfoundland. The Corte Reals vanished on their final voyage, and no trace of the last expedition was ever found.

See also CABOT EXPEDITION.

Cortez wrecks   In 1519, the Spanish explorer Hernando Cortez, conqueror of Mexico, destroyed all but one of the 10 ships in which he and his expedition had arrived at San Juan de Ulúa. Little is known about the ships, except that they differed in size and were stripped of everything valuable before they were destroyed. These wrecks might be of historical importance if they could be found, but the shoreline has changed since the ships were destroyed, and their remains are believed to lie underground rather than under water. Divers tried to locate the wrecks in 1958 but failed.

corvette   A three-masted sailing ship like a frigate, but smaller, the corvette was used in the 18th century, was fast and could carry as many as 32 guns.

***Cospatrick*, British frigate**   A notable example of the dangers of fire at sea, the sinking of the frigate *Cospatrick* occurred on November 17 or 18, 1874, off Auckland, New Zealand. (Accounts differ on the date.) Only three people on board reportedly survived. More than

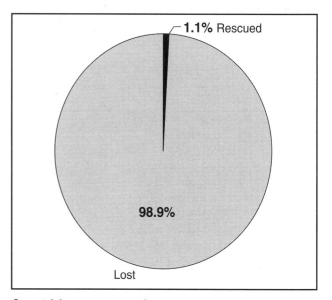

Cospatrick, passengers and crew.

400 others are thought to have drowned in the sinking or died later of thirst in lifeboats.

Cospatrick was built in Burma and launched in 1856, and served as a passenger ship for the Blackwell Shipping Company. The ship also helped to put in place submarine cable in the Persian Gulf in 1863. Later, the Shaw Savill Line bought the vessel and used it to transport emigrants from England to New Zealand.

Cospatrick sailed from England for Auckland, New Zealand, on September 11, 1874, with 429 emigrants on board. The captain's wife and young son accompanied him on the voyage. Soon after midnight, fire was detected in the forecastle, where large amounts of flammable materials were stored, including kerosene and coal. The captain had the ship turned "behind the wind," meaning the wind was blowing from stern to bow. This measure was intended to confine the fire; turning the vessel the opposite way, into the wind, would have helped spread the fire from the bow toward the rest of the ship.

Fire-fighting efforts, however, were complicated by interference from passengers and by problems with equipment. The water pump intended to fight the fire, for example, was in the midst of the blaze and inaccessible. The crew organized a bucket brigade to haul water to the fire, but this process was time-consuming and clumsy. To make matters worse, *Cospatrick* swung into the wind for some reason. Now the wind had an opportunity to fan the fire and spread flames from bow to stern. Before long, the fire was burning uncontrollably.

The fire consumed some lifeboats. Others were too overloaded to launch. An attempt to launch one lifeboat with 40 people aboard ended in tragedy when a rope broke and cast the boat's occupants into the water, reportedly killing all aboard. Two lifeboats were launched successfully, but with only 80 persons in all aboard.

Cospatrick's masts caught fire and fell on the deck, killing many passengers and crew members. Soon afterward, the ship exploded and sank. The lifeboats were not equipped with sails, or with adequate food and water. The occupants suffered greatly from thirst. A storm three days after *Cospatrick* sank, on November 21, separated the lifeboats, and one of them was never seen again. The survivors in the remaining boat reportedly were driven to cannibalism to survive. Only eight of the 41 persons who originally boarded the boat were still alive by the 25th. By that time, the survivors were so thirsty that they began drinking sea water. Three of those eight died in the following three days. Ships passed but either did not see the lifeboat or did not choose to stop. By the time the ship *British Sceptre* picked up the boat's occupants on the 26th, only the second officer, a quartermaster and a seaman were still living. The captain and his family all perished in the sinking. No passengers survived.

It is worth noting that *Cospatrick* was destroyed by fire even though the ship was designed and built with fire safety in mind. Smoking below decks was banned, and security personnel were assigned to patrol the ship and eliminate any violations of fire regulations. The concentration of high flammable materials in the forecastle around the fire pump, however, made these precautions irrelevant.

See also FIRE.

Coston signal An important piece of lifesaving equipment in the late 19th century, the Coston signal was a bright red flare that was ignited on shore to let ships in distress know that someone had sighted them and was aware of their plight. The flare also was used to warn ships away from hazards on shore.

Coubre, **Belgian munitions ship** Laden with weapons and explosives, *La Coubre* blew up at midafternoon in Havana (Cuba) harbor on March 4, 1960, while preparing to unload its cargo. The blast reportedly occurred as grenades were being unloaded. Some 100 people were killed.

See also EXPLOSIONS.

Cousins, **American pilot schooner** Mystery surrounds the case of the pilot schooner *J.C. Cousins*, which came ashore at or near Clatsop Spit, Oregon, at the mouth of the Columbia River, on October 7, 1883, with no one on board.

A handsome, two-masted ship, *Cousins* was operated by the state of Oregon as a pilot boat for two years, from 1881 to 1883. The ship's operations broke what had been a certain captain's monopoly on piloting ships across the Columbia River bar.

On its last voyage, *Cousins* went out to sea on October 6, 1883, to meet approaching vessels. The pilot schooner passed Fort Stevens around noon and was seen anchored off Clatsop Spit that afternoon. Near nightfall, the schooner was seen heading toward the Columbia River bar. At dawn, various ships noticed *Cousins* moving back and forth, sometimes out to sea and sometimes shoreward.

Early on the afternoon of October 7, *Cousins* headed for shore, passed through the breakers and wound up on the beach. When low tide made it possible to visit and examine the wreck, no living people, nor even bodies, were found on board. The schooner's boat was gone, as were the ship's papers and log, although the ship otherwise appeared to be in good order. Several days later, the wreck broke up without yielding any more information about what might have happened to the crew.

The disappearance of the pilot schooner's crew led to much speculation about their last hours on board. According to one fanciful tale related by historian James Gibbs in his book *Pacific Graveyard,* a spectral ship approached *Cousins* and frightened the crew so badly that they raced for shore before the apparition could overtake them. How such an incident would cause the crew to disappear is hard to imagine.

According to another scenario, the schooner's crew was murdered to eliminate competition for the aforementioned pilot-boat monopoly. Gibbs dismisses this explanation as unlikely. He points out that another vessel was chartered at once to continue the work of *Cousins,* until the state of Oregon could build a pilot schooner specifically for that job. It would have made little sense to murder the crew of *Cousins* if another boat and crew were available to take over their duties.

Gibbs apparently favors the suggestion that the pilot schooner hit the Columbia River bar on its way outbound. The frightened crew then supposedly got into the ship's boat, which was then swamped by a heavy swell, tossing the men from the boat and drowning them.

Cozumel Island incident, Mexico In 1519, explorer Hernando Cortez discovered on Cozumel Island a man named Jeronimo de Aguilar. A Spanish native, he reported that he and 17 companions had left Darien en route to the Island of Santo Domingo but were blown off course and shipwrecked in the Gulf of Mexico. Aguilar said the group made its way to Yucatán, but most of the travelers were murdered there by the natives.

See also CORTEZ WRECKS.

Cromwell, American schooner The wreck of *Benjamin C. Cromwell,* a three-masted schooner carrying a cargo of lumber, occurred near the Bellport lifesaving station on Long Island, New York, on February 22, 1904. The story of *Cromwell's* wreck illustrates beautifully the bravery and persistence of the lifesaving crews.

On February 14, *Cromwell* left Charleston, South Carolina, on a voyage to Fall River, Massachusetts. During the northward voyage, *Cromwell* encountered heavy weather and had to cast much of its cargo over the side. Then the ship was surrounded by fog. By the time *Cromwell* reached the New York shore, the ship's crew thought the vessel was 40 miles away from its actual position. The last light they had sighted before running aground was the Diamond Shoals lightship off the North Carolina coast.

Cromwell ran aground on the Long Island coast and began to break apart. The men burned torches to signal their distress. A surfman from the Bellpoint station was watching on shore and replied by burning a flare. He then called on nearby lifesaving stations for help.

The fog and heavy seas together made rescue exceedingly difficult. The sea was too rough to launch a lifeboat, and the fog made it hard to see the ship well enough to put a line aboard by Lyle gun. The lifesavers kept firing the gun, and eventually succeeded in reaching the ship with a line. The line became fouled, however, and unusable.

The only remaining option was to launch a boat despite the dangerous seas. The lifesavers did so. A powerful current swept them away from the ship, however, so that they were forced to return to the beach and try again.

This time, they allowed for the current. They hauled the boat on a wagon to a point farther up the beach before setting out again. As they launched the boat for the second attempt, the ship's masts fell. Soon the ship was demolished completely.

Several men from *Cromwell* remained alive in the water. One man rode toward shore on a floating fragment of the vessel and was hauled from the surf by two lifesavers. The boat was launched again, but the breakers drove it back. The Lyle gun remained workable, and the lifesavers fired it over the wreckage, hoping that the men in the water could seize the line and be hauled to shore. The line became entangled in the wreckage, however, and was useless to the men.

Only two of seven men from *Cromwell* were rescued. The ship and its cargo were a complete loss.

See also LYLE GUN.

crow's nest A platform mounted about halfway up the mast of a ship, the crow's nest traditionally has served as a perch for lookouts scanning the sea for icebergs and other potential hazards. In theory, a lookout in the crow's nest should have the best possible view of the waters ahead of a ship and therefore should be the first to spot dangers. In practice, however, this has not always been the case. On the night when the liner *Carpathia* was rushing to the rescue of survivors from the sinking of the liner *Titanic,* for example, *Carpathia's* lookouts on the bridge proved much better at spotting icebergs ahead. Modern navigational aids such as radar have given mariners a better way to monitor the waters around them, but there still are occasions when ships need a watchful pair of human eyes, preferably at a high elevation on the ship.

See also LOOKOUTS; RADAR; TITANIC.

C-Trader, American freighter The wreck of *C-Trader* on the Columbia River bar (Oregon-Washington) on December 6, 1963, is remembered for scattering its cargo of lumber up and down the coast. The ship scraped bottom on the Willapa shoals, a few miles north of the Columbia River mouth, and began taking on water. Efforts to tow the ship to safety failed when it went aground near the Desdemona Sands light.

This wreck is notable for what happened to *C-Trader's* two sister ships, *Alaska Spruce* and *Alaska Cedar.* The former came near tragedy at almost the site of *C-Trader's* loss, a few days later, when *Alaska Spruce's* steering cable broke and left the ship unable to maneuver. A tug took the damaged ship in tow the next day. *Alaska Cedar* was wrecked at Coos Bay on the Oregon coast almost a year to the day after the wreck of *C-Trader.* As James Gibbs points out in his book *Pacific Graveyard,* all three vessels were built in the same year at the same shipyard, and they all suffered wrecks or serious mishaps within the same period of several months on the same stretch of the Pacific coast.

Cuba Shipwrecks appear to be almost as numerous as fish in the waters surrounding Cuba, which has been one of the most strategically important islands in the world for centuries. According to one estimate by marine archaeologist Robert Marx, more than 700 ships were lost in waters around Cuba between the early 16th century and 1825, for reasons including warfare, storms and navigational errors.

One of the earliest recorded shipwrecks in Cuban waters involved an unnamed vessel that supposedly wrecked on the Cuban coast in the early 16th century. Although the ship's name and the date of the wreck are unrecorded, we do know the names of two people on board: Juan de Rojas and his wife María de Lobera.

The treasure fleets operating between Spain and the Americas accounted for numerous wrecks in Cuban waters. During a storm on May 24, 1556, for example, four ships of the Tierra Firme Armada wrecked on the Cuban shore between Havana and Cape San Anton. On July 18, 1563, six ships of the New Spain Fleet, carrying a large cargo of mercury and various kinds of merchandise, were wrecked on the notorious Jardines Reefs along Cuba's southern coast. Among the people shipwrecked on this occasion was one Archbishop Salcedo.

A hurricane in September of 1616 caused great damage to shipping in ports of Oriente Province, at the eastern end of Cuba. More than 30 ships are thought to have been sunk in this storm.

The New Spain Fleet suffered great losses on September 8, 1628, when a Dutch fleet under command of Admiral Piet Heyn drove the Spanish fleet into Matanzas Bay, where all 24 ships in the Spanish fleet were wrecked.

Another Dutch fleet beset the Tierra Firme Armada in 1638 and waged a two-day battle with the Spaniards. All the Spanish ships but one reached port safely. The lost ship was the 600-ton galleon *Nuestra Señora de Arancacu,* which experienced such damage from Dutch cannon fire that the ship was set afire after its treasure was transferred to other Spanish vessels. The galleon sank at Bahia Honda. Most of the galleon's 20 cannon were recovered later by divers.

The Dutch did not always enjoy notable success in their attacks on Spanish shipping. One Dutch fleet, cruising off Havana in 1640 in hopes of engaging the New Spain Fleet, lost seven warships in a hurricane. Many of the shipwrecked Dutchmen were taken prisoner by the Spaniards.

The New Spain Fleet lost five ships in a storm on December 16, 1711, some 15 miles west of Havana. How much treasure these ships carried was apparently not a matter of public record, but divers reportedly recovered a large sum in treasure by early January.

Sometimes weather destroyed ships in unpredictable ways in Cuban waters. The galleon *Invencible* was riding at anchor in Havana Harbor one day in 1740 when the ship was struck by lightning and exploded. The explosion, similar to the catastrophic Halifax,

Nova Scotia, explosion of 1917, caused extensive damage to the city.

Another spectacular explosion destroyed a Spanish treasure ship in 1748. In a battle near Havana between the New Spain Fleet and an English squadron, one ship in the Spanish fleet ran aground on the shore and was set afire. The ship exploded a few minutes later.

On one occasion, the Spaniards sank three of their biggest warships at the entrance to Havana Harbor, just before surrendering the city to English forces on June 3, 1762. The ships included the 70-gun galleon *Neptuno;* the 64-gun galleon *Asia;* and the 60-gun galleon *Europa.* The English filled three warships with loot and sent them off to England, but the English vessels—*Providence, Lion* and *General Wolfe*—sank at the harbor's entrance.

A devastating hurricane at Havana on October 15, 1768, sank 69 ships and destroyed more than 5,000 buildings in Havana and its vicinity. Another hurricane on October 3, 1780, destroyed 13 British warships on the Jardines Reefs, with the loss of most of the men on board. Yet another hurricane at Havana on August 27–28, 1794, either damaged or demolished 76 ships, including 12 Spanish warships.

See also FLOTA SYSTEM; HALIFAX, NOVA SCOTIA, EXPLOSION; TREASURE.

***Culloden*, British warship** A point on the Long Island (New York) shore was named for this wreck. The 74-gun *Culloden* was pursuing three French vessels off the Long Island shore on January 22, 1781, when a storm blew the ship onto Shagwonggonac (or Shagwong) Reef. The captain tried to take the ship into nearby Fort Pond Bay, but *Culloden* sank off a highland later named Culloden Point. Apparently none of the 600 men aboard was lost. Portions of the wreck were salvaged, and what remained was burned. Part of the hull was still visible in the early 1950s.

Cunard Line The great British shipping firm of Cunard operated liners including the famous *Queen Mary,* which sank the British cruiser *Curaçao* in a collision on a convoy passage in the Atlantic during World War II; and *Queen Elizabeth,* which burned and sank in Hong Kong harbor in 1972.

See also CURAÇAO; QUEEN ELIZABETH; WHITE STAR LINE.

***Curaçao*, British destroyer** While performing zigzag maneuvers during convoy duty on October 2, 1942, the liner *Queen Mary,* then serving as a troopship, struck the destroyer *Curaçao.* The liner sliced the destroyer in two. Out of 439 people aboard the destroyer, 338 were killed. Although badly damaged, *Queen Mary* managed to reach Scotland.

See also ZIGZAG.

current   A continuous mass movement of water within a larger body of water, a current acts in much the same manner as a river and can carry a vessel off course and into many hazards. Currents are especially numerous and unpredictable in the near-shore environment, where many factors, from submarine topography to wave action, may generate currents capable of interfering with shipping and with rescue operations.

See also NEAR-SHORE ENVIRONMENT.

curses   Part of the mythology of the sea, curses are said to afflict certain vessels that have more than their share of mishaps. In the case of the British bark *Melanope*, for example, an elderly female apple vendor who was discovered on board and put off the ship onto a tug was said to have put a curse on the ship. The *Melanope* did indeed have a troubled career that ended with the abandonment of the ship at sea. Other vessels also appear to have encountered numerous troubles, however, even in the absence of alleged curses. So, one ought to eliminate all other possibilities before interpreting any shipwreck as the outcome of a curse.

See also MELANOPE; MYTHOLOGY; SUPERSTITIONS.

***Curtis*, American schooner**   The ingenuity of surfmen from a Virginia lifesaving station saved the *Flora Curtis*, out of Manasquan, New Jersey, from destruction during a storm off Assateague Beach on the Eastern Shore on December 2, 1878. The ship stranded less than a mile offshore and within only three miles of the Assateague Beach lifesaving station at the height of a gale. When surfmen from the station reached the schooner, seas were breaking over the vessel. To haul the ship off the shoal, the surfmen dropped anchors and applied winches. Thus they saved *Flora Curtis* from complete destruction.

See also ANCHORS; LIFESAVING SERVICE.

***Cuyahoga*, Coast Guard cutter**   The Coast Guard cutter *Cuyahoga* was sunk with 11 fatalities on the evening of October 20, 1978, on Chesapeake Bay (Maryland-Virginia) in a collision with the Argentinian freighter *Santa Cruz II*. The cutter sank in only two minutes.

When the cutter's commander saw that a collision was imminent, he ordered full reverse on the en-

gines. This maneuver, however, actually put the cutter squarely in the freighter's path. The freighter's bow struck *Cuyahoga* on the starboard side. The cutter heeled over to a 50-degree angle and flooded swiftly.

The cutter's utility boat rose to the surface, and several injured men were placed aboard it. *Santa Cruz II* stopped to pick up survivors.

Immediately after the cutter sank, it appeared possible that some survivors might be trapped in the wreck and could be rescued, if the wreck could be located and reached in time. A search began for an oil slick that might reveal the sunken cutter's exact location. A fishing boat with a depth-sounder was also enlisted to search for the wreck.

When an oil slick was sighted, the fishing boat made several runs with its depth-sounder. Soon *Cuyahoga* was located. A diver went down to the wreck in the hope of finding someone still alive inside. An examination, however, revealed no survivors inside the wreck.

The wreck was raised, and a patch was placed on the hole made by the freighter's bow. There was no further use for *Cuyahoga*, however, and so the cutter was scuttled off the Virginia coast. With several other wrecks, *Cuyahoga*'s remains now form an artificial reef for fishing.

Donald Shomette, in his book *Shipwrecks on the Chesapeake*, writes that *Cuyahoga* had numerous problems before the collision with *Santa Cruz II*. Those problems reportedly included a faulty electrical system, an inadequate ventilation system and an inaccurate magnetic compass. Shomette also points out that *Cuyahoga* was the sole cutter in the Coast Guard that lacked a radar display in the wheelhouse; moreover, the cutter's radar had failed 12 times or more in the nine months before the collision.

See also COLLISIONS.

***Cyclops*, American naval collier**   The collier (coal carrier) *Cyclops*, built in 1910 at Virginia's Newport News Shipbuilding and Dry Dock Company, vanished at sea in 1918 in one of the great unsolved mysteries of ocean travel. The ship itself was highly unusual and had a bizarre career in its short lifetime. *Cyclops* was designed to carry coal and, to handle that cargo, carried an array of 12 large booms on deck between forecastle and funnels. The ship's sole commander was Captain George Worley, an eccentric man who ran *Cyclops* with tyrannical authority. At times, Worley's behavior went beyond mere eccentricity. He was said to go into drunken rages and chase crewmen around the ship, wielding a wrench. On one occasion, the ship's surgeon and other men on *Cyclops* charged Worley formally with misdeeds including chasing a sailor at gunpoint and talking of handing his ship over to the enemy. Other charges included displaying a "suspicious" light on the masthead—signaling to a U-boat, perhaps? The evidence for these charges was so slight, however, that the Navy apparently took no action against Worley. In any event, severe disciplinarians were not unknown among Navy captains.

It may be significant that Worley was a German national (his real name was Johann Wichman), at a time when the United States was at war with Germany. Worley apparently made no secret of his fondness for Germany. He sang German songs and even boasted that the kaiser once visited *Cyclops* in Kiel (a port in north Germany) and pronounced the vessel "smart." Even this behavior, however, does not appear to have landed him in trouble with the Navy. (The Navy reportedly did send him a mild warning against keeping pets on Naval vessels, after Worley was said to be keeping a pet lion—a gift acquired in Africa—on *Cyclops*. Worley allegedly treated the warning as a joke.)

Nothing on *Cyclops*, then, appeared so far out of order that the Navy felt inclined to intervene. Nonetheless, circumstances on *Cyclops* appeared to be a recipe for trouble; and trouble is what *Cyclops* encountered, in a long string of mishaps even before the ship disappeared.

On January 7, 1918, *Cyclops* sailed from Norfolk, Virginia, to deliver coal to American Navy vessels in South American ports. The ship then would return to Baltimore with a load of manganese ore for the United States Steel Corporation's Fairfield plant in Baltimore. This was not exactly a routine voyage. For one thing, manganese was a strategic metal. It was important for making strengthened steel of the kind needed in warships. That fact made this cargo unusually important to the United States. Moreover, *Cyclops* was not sailing entirely on Navy business. The voyage was also, in a sense, a commercial operation, under the auspices of the South American Shipping Company in New York City. The voyage was arranged with the aid of a German national named Franz Hohenblatt, who worked with the company. On one occasion, Hohenblatt reportedly said he was sorry that America's declaration of war prevented him from returning home to fight for Germany.

The voyage was difficult from the beginning. Worley was suffering from a hernia and was glum. He expressed concern that he might not return from this journey and that he might be buried at sea.

On departure, *Cyclops* came close to colliding with another Navy ship. Worley's capricious behavior manifested itself five days out of Norfolk, when the captain took offense at something the first lieutenant had said and had him placed under arrest without waiting for an explanation. One of the ship's engines failed near Bahia, a port north of Rio de Janeiro. (Later, in Rio, both engines would be inspected and found to be in unsatisfactory condition.)

Cyclops arrived in Rio on January 28. There, *Cyclops* discharged coal and took on manganese ore. Though badly overloaded, the ship proceeded to Bahia. There, *Cyclops* took on a passenger, an American diplomat named Alfred Gottschalk, who was known as strongly sympathetic to Germany. Now the ship had a captain who was a German national and carried a U.S. diplomat with pro-German leanings.

Although *Cyclops* had orders to head straight from Bahia to Baltimore, the ship did not obey those orders. The ship stopped instead in Barbados, West Indies, on March 3. There, Brockholst Livingston, another American diplomat, went on board *Cyclops* to investigate the situation there. Worley thought the stop was necessary to take on more provisions, although the ship evidently had enough supplies on leaving Rio. Nonetheless, Worley had additional food and coal put on board at Barbados. (The added coal was especially puzzling, because *Cyclops*'s coal consumption, on its one working engine, was low.) Tensions on the ship were high, according to Livingston. There was talk of conspiracies and even an execution on *Cyclops* en route to Barbados.

Cyclops left Bridgetown the following day. That apparently was the last anyone on shore ever saw of *Cyclops*. The ship vanished at sea. The Navy did not take much interest in the overdue *Cyclops* until March 23. An extensive search followed the disappearance of *Cyclops*, but no debris from the ship was recovered, nor was any oil slick sighted that might have indicated where the ship went down.

The government approached the South American Shipping Company and asked to speak with Franz Hohenblatt, who had helped arrange the collier's final voyage. Hohenblatt himself had vanished, however, reportedly after burning hundreds of letters he had received from Germany.

Many possible explanations have been suggested for the loss of *Cyclops*. Because the ship was badly overloaded, it is easy to imagine that it merely sank, perhaps in rough weather. (Severe weather appears unlikely, however, in view of the calm conditions reported in the area at that time.) A mechanical mishap is another possibility, since *Cyclops* had serious trouble with its engines on this voyage. An explosion might have occurred, either when coal dust ignited or the ship hit a mine. Possibly a German submarine sank *Cyclops* with a torpedo. If *Cyclops* had exploded or sunk in a storm, however, one would expect at least a little debris to have turned up during the search.

One must also consider the possibility of mutiny. Worley was not a beloved commander. According to another scenario, Worley and Gottschalk—a German national and a German sympathizer, respectively—might have handed the ship and its cargo of strategic metal ore over to the Germans. This explanation would account for the ship's disappearance and the absence of any evidence indicating *Cyclops* sank at sea. The problem here is that little or no solid evidence exists to support this hypothesis. It is virtually unsupported speculation, colorful though the scenario may be.

Even the sea-monster hypothesis once applied to the *Mary Celeste* was revived in an effort to account for the disappearance of *Cyclops*. According to one fanciful account of the collier's last hours, giant squids might have attacked *Cyclops*, devoured its crew and then crushed the ship. This scenario was taken no more seriously than the suggestion that the Germans had built an underwater fortress near Barbados and had used it to blast *Cyclops* to pieces.

Author A. A. Hoehling, in a study of the *Cyclops* incident for his 1984 book *Lost at Sea*, presents a case for sabotage as the cause of the collier's loss. Germany operated a highly effective set of sabotage operations in World War I. Small incendiary devices, produced in a secret factory aboard an interned German liner in Hoboken, New Jersey, were credited with causing approximately 40 fires on Allied merchant vessels. The Black Tom Pier in New York exploded in 1916, destroying ships, trains, barges and ammunition. Moreover, Brazil—*Cyclops*'s destination on the outbound leg of its last voyage—was full of German operatives in World War I. Whatever happened to *Cyclops*, the ship was lost with 309 people aboard, and the collier's disappearance remains as much a mystery today as it was in 1918.

See also DISAPPEARANCES; GHOST SHIPS; MYSTERIES.

D

Dailey, American schooner Nothing better illustrates the dedication of 19th-century American lifesaving crews—and the obstacles they faced in their work—than the wreck of the schooner *Albert Dailey*, which ran aground in fog off Smith Island, Virginia, on January 7, 1883.

The schooner was carrying coal from Baltimore, Maryland, to Bridgeport, Connecticut, when the vessel ran aground about 750 feet from shore, several miles north of the lifesaving station at Smith Island. Several hours passed before a surfman on patrol noticed the ship and burned a flare to let those on board know they had been sighted.

The Smith Island crew responded quickly but had to contend with extremely dense fog, which combined with darkness to make the stricken ship invisible. The men hauled their surfboat to the point where they imagined the ship to be, but could see nothing.

Just before daybreak, they sighted *Albert Dailey*. The lifesavers brought the schooner's men ashore and took them to the Smith Island station. The following day, the ship's captain and crew intended to return to *Albert Dailey*, remove the ship from the beach with the surfmen's help and remove as much of the cargo as they could.

The surfmen could not budge the vessel, however, and so they made arrangements with a local wrecking (that is, marine salvage) company to remove the schooner from the sands. The captain and a representative of the wrecking company stayed on the ship with several other crewmen and wreckers.

Then a heavy snowstorm developed. When the surfmen returned to the ship and asked if the men on *Albert Dailey* wished to be taken ashore, the men said no. They thought their resources were adequate. The wrecking company had a boat on the scene, and the men figured they could signal the lifesaving station, in an emergency, with flags or the ship's foghorn.

As the weather deteriorated, and gale-force winds arose, the surfmen kept an eye on the schooner. A surfman patrolling the beach at 8 P.M. said the ship was no longer visible offshore.

Distinct signs of trouble appeared just before midnight. A patrolman reported finding the ship's hatches and portions of its boat on the beach. Evidently the schooner was starting to break up.

Despite the bitter weather—including high winds and wet snow a foot deep on the beach—the lifesavers set out again for the stranded ship. Tired and chilled, the surfmen finally reached the schooner and saw a horrifying sight.

The hull was under water. Only the masts and rigging remained visible. Apparently the men of *Albert Dailey* had had no time to make a distress signal. All they could do was scramble into the rigging as the sea came aboard.

The lifesavers set off flares to reassure the men on *Dailey* that help was on the way. Reaching the wreck was difficult, however, because of formidable breakers. At last the surfmen did succeed in getting their boat past the breakers, but they had to retreat because of large amounts of debris in the water.

Trying to reach *Albert Dailey* in the darkness, in such dangerous waters, was a prohibitive risk. The wave-borne debris could smash the surfboat. So, the lifesavers returned to shore to await the dawn.

When daylight appeared, the surfmen saw the forlorn, half-frozen men of *Dailey* clinging to the rigging. The men on shore tried repeatedly to shoot a line to the schooner. They succeeded, but the men in the rigging were too cold and exhausted to reach and secure the line.

The rescuers were stymied. They had no way to reach the ship. Securing a line was impossible, and the rough, debris-laden waters around the schooner made an approach by boat too hazardous. So, all the surfmen could do was wait for conditions to improve.

The storm diminished, and on January 10 the rescuers decided to risk setting out by boat, though the sea was still rough and full of wreckage. Although the first few attempts to reach the schooner were unsuccessful, the surfmen boarded *Albert Dailey* at last and rescued four men from the rigging. After carrying the men to shore, the lifesavers returned for the remaining men on *Dailey*. One man died of exposure soon after being rescued. Another had been washed overboard and lost during the night; his body was evidently never recovered. Although the story of *Albert Dailey* is little known, it exemplifies the courage, persistence and energy of the men of the United States Lifesaving Service.

Maritime historians Richard and Julie Pouliot, in their book *Shipwrecks on the Virginia Coast*, add an interesting footnote to this story. The wrecking firm engaged to help refloat *Albert Dailey* was the Cobb Wrecking Company. Its founder, Nathan F. Cobb, left his native Massachusetts with his family in the early 1830s and relocated to Virginia.

As the story goes, Cobb and his family were driven into an inlet on Virginia's Eastern Shore during a storm, and there the Cobbs stayed. Impressed by his experience at sea, Cobb set himself up in the marine salvage business near the present-day community of Oyster, Virginia.

The Cobbs bought an island, which soon became known as "Cobb Island." Their business diversified, and before long the Cobbs were operating a popular hotel that catered to the resort trade. The Cobbs also supplied ducks to New York City restaurants, so that diners there were fed by the same family that battled the elements in shipwrecks off the Virginia coast.

***Dakar*, Israeli submarine**   A former British submarine purchased for the Israeli navy, *Dakar* vanished near Cyprus on January 25, 1968, with 69 men on board. *Dakar*'s disappearance occurred only two days before another submarine, the French *Minerve*, also was lost in the Mediterranean under mysterious circumstances, near the port of Toulon.

See also MINERVE; SUBMARINES.

***Dakota*, American steamship**   One of the most prominent vessels of the American merchant marine, *Dakota* was wrecked, apparently through pure incaution, near Yokohama, Japan, on March 7, 1907. No lives were lost.

Darien wreck, Panama/Colombia border   A large ship carrying supplies and numerous colonists from Santo Domingo to a new Spanish community near Darien was wrecked through navigational error just west of Darien in 1513, with the loss of almost everyone on board.

dating of shipwrecks   Many methods may be used to help establish the date of a particular shipwreck. Historical records may provide useful information. Coins found on a wreck also may indicate its age, because the wreck must be at least as old as the most recent coin found on it (provided the wreck has not been "contaminated" by coins from a later shipwreck at the same site).

Artifacts from the wreck may be subjected to various tests to determine their age. Radiocarbon-14 (better known as carbon-14) dating may be used to establish an approximate date for organic materials such as wood or shells. This method uses measurements of the isotope carbon-14, which is incorporated into all organic material while the organism is alive, to estimate the age of a sample on the basis of how much carbon-14 remains in it. This method has its limitations, however, because the margin of error may be more than a century. Moreover, a date established by the carbon-14 testing of wood may not indicate the actual date of a wreck, because a wooden ship may have been constructed from timbers of an older vessel. A more accurate date may be obtained from material such as charcoal, which is of approximately the same age as the wreck where it was found, having been formed on board shortly before the wreck.

Glassware may be dated by various methods, including counting the number of layers of crust that have built up on the glass over the years under water. The age of ceramics may be established by a process called "thermoluminescence." Electrons released from a ceramic sample are measured as the object is heated in a kiln. Measuring the electron content of the object may help to establish its date with accuracy up to 100 percent.

Various other artifacts found on a wreck may assist in establishing its age, but caution is required, because (1) a certain artifact's age may be difficult to determine, and (2) the date of a given artifact may not coincide even approximately with the date of the wreck. A sword or other artifact recovered from a particular wreck may actually have been manufactured centuries earlier or later. A case in point involves a 19th-century anchor found at a 17th-century wreck site in Florida waters. Using the anchor to set a date for the wreck would have yielded a highly inaccurate result.

Some artifacts, marine archaeologist Robert Marx explains, are virtually useless for determining the date of a wreck because their forms changed so little over long periods. He points out that brass tacks used on a French warship of the 18th century were identical to those found on a Roman shipwreck 15 centuries older.

See also ARCHAEOLOGY; IDENTIFICATION OF SHIPWRECKS.

***Dauntless*, American sloop** Many wrecks are attributed to a captain's error in judgment. One example is the wreck of the sloop *Dauntless* on the Eastern Shore of Virginia on February 21, 1882. A southerly gale was blowing as the sloop returned from New Inlet, Virginia, to its home port of Chincoteague with a cargo of seed oysters. Captain Sewell Collins was advised to put into an inlet before nightfall, rather than attempt a risky entry to Chincoteague Inlet after sundown. The captain pushed on toward Chincoteague, however, with calamitous results.

High seas carried away the cargo from the sloop's deck. Winds shredded the sails. When *Dauntless* approached Chicoteague Inlet, the wind changed direction and began to blow out of the west. The captain saw, belatedly, that he could not enter the inlet safely, and so he dropped the anchors on Fox Shoal near Chincoteague Island. *Dauntless* found itself amid breakers, however, and rapidly filled with water and sank.

Captain Collins was washed overboard and drowned. A young seaman also met his death in the waters. The sole survivor, one John Howard, survived by climbing onto the lower masthead. His position was dangerous at first, because the surf struck the wreck so violently that it threatened to toss him into the water. A falling tide soon reduced that danger, however, and even allowed him to wade ashore before sunrise.

Howard walked to the nearest dwelling. After receiving dry clothes and food, he proceeded to the nearby village and sent out telegrams telling of the deaths of Collins and the seaman—deaths that might have been avoided had the captain put into a safe inlet instead of trying a hazardous approach to Chincoteague in a storm.

***Davis*, sailing vessel** *A.S. Davis*, a big three-masted ship whose home port is unknown, was on a voyage from Peru to Hampton Roads, Virginia, with a cargo of guano when an exceptionally violent storm drove the vessel ashore near the Seatack lifesaving station on the Virginia coast just south of Cape Henry on November 22, 1878.

As soon as the ship ran aground, the crew climbed into the rigging for safety. Seas washed over the ship's whole length and destroyed the vessel quickly. *Davis* went ashore around 6 P.M. on November 22 and was demolished completely by the morning of November 23.

As the sea broke the ship apart, a surfman named John Atwood was walking the beach and saw fragments of the vessel washing ashore. He also saw footprints and followed them into the dunes.

There he found the only survivor of the wreck, one William Minton, who reportedly fell from the rigging and was carried into the surf. Minton survived by holding on to part of the ship's rail. On reaching shore, Minton sought shelter, but the best he could do was dig a hole in the sand and bury himself in it for warmth. There he remained until daybreak, when Atwood discovered him.

The 19 other men on the ship all perished. Seventeen bodies were recovered. The captain and 10 crewmen were buried in a mass grave near the lifesaving station of Cape Henry. The rest of the recovered bodies were buried near the site of the wreck.

This particular storm was remarkable for its intensity and destructive effect. Richard and Julie Pouliot, in their 1986 history *Shipwrecks on the Virginia Coast,* report that the storm destroyed hundreds of buildings in Philadelphia; lifted a schooner from the Chesapeake Bay (Maryland-Virginia) and carried the ship far into the woods onshore; and removed a lifesaving station on Virginia's Eastern Shore from its foundations and carried the building almost half a mile before dropping it, upright, almost half a mile from its original location.

See also LIFESAVING SERVICE.

Davis observation chamber To meet the need for a system that would let salvage workers operate under water while breathing air at atmospheric pressure and moving about freely, inventor Robert H. Davis patented an observation chamber in 1912. The device consisted of a metal cylinder with glass observation ports. A diver could stand or sit inside the chamber and communicate with a tender on the surface by telephone. The observation chamber also came equipped with emergency air supplies in bottles and a "rebreather" that absorbed carbon dioxide from the air. Although the observation chamber had competition for a while from the armored diving suit, or "iron duke," the chamber eventually proved to be more useful in salvage work.

See also DIVING SUITS; "IRON DUKE."

Davy Jones's locker A commonly used expression for the ocean bottom, especially as the resting place of sunken ships. "Gone to Davy Jones's locker" means a vessel was lost at sea. The expression appears to have originated among English-speaking peoples, but how it originated is uncertain and constitutes one of the minor riddles of maritime lore.

See also MYTHOLOGY.

dead water This curious phenomenon has been reported on occasion near coastlines where fresh or brackish water overlies sea water.

According to the Swedish oceanographer Vagn Walfrid Ekman (1874–1954), a sailing ship in dead water may cease to answer its helm, and may become "unmanageable." Although a steamship may remain under control, the ship may lose much of its speed while traveling through dead water. Ekman cites the example of the famed polar exploration vessel *Fram,* which was capable of perhaps four to five knots under ordinary conditions but slowed to only one knot in dead water. Ekman adds that steamships do not appear to be troubled greatly by dead water if they are already moving faster than perhaps five knots.

Dead water has a strange appearance. An unusual pattern of stripes may be seen across the wake of the ship. Stripes extending obliquely aft from the ship's stern may also be reported. The stripes may be described as areas of agitated or smooth water.

Dead water is said to appear abruptly and, in some cases at least, to have sudden and dramatic effects on a ship's progress. The condition may last an entire day or more. A ship entering dead water may slow almost at once to a mere fraction of its usual speed. In similar fashion, a ship may find itself suddenly freed from dead water, so that the vessel resumes normal speed as if a restraining cable is cut.

The effects of dead water are especially dramatic on ships in tow, Ekman reports. Such ships will not respond at all to their helms. If the towed ship encounters dead water in a narrow waterway, the towline must be shortened. Otherwise, the ship may run aground on either shore.

Another remarkable effect of dead water is that a ship that stops its engine in dead water does not coast to a stop, as one might expect, but instead stops short and may even move backward slightly. As the ship stops, the aforementioned stripes in the water may catch up with and pass the vessel. The ship may move backward and forward with the passage of each stripe. Ekman says that the stripes may have a "violent" effect on ships, strong enough to rip a ship away from its moorings.

The influence of dead water appears to be related to the difference in density between surface water and underlying waters, Ekman says. Where such differences are most pronounced, as along the Norwegian coast where fresh water from sources on shore pours out over sea water, the effects of dead water are also notable.

Seamen have suggested various remedies for overcoming the effects of dead water, including pouring oil into the water and having the entire crew run back and forth on deck. The effectiveness of these measures, however, is questionable. Ekman indicates that a more effective method, practiced by tugboats, is to halt and wait until the aforementioned stripes

have passed, then start moving again, full speed ahead.

Dead water has been reported in many parts of the world, including waters around Scandinavia; Canada's Vancouver Island; river mouths of North and South America; and the Mediterranean Sea.

Ekman also cites cases from classical literature in which a vessel propelled by oars or under sail, in the Mediterranean, would be stopped dead in the water by some inexplicable influence. Although such incidents were attributed by the ancients to the remora, a fish that attaches itself to ships and sharks by a suction organ atop its head, Ekman argues that dead water probably was responsible.

***Dearborn,* American schooner** In a mysterious incident, a 1,024-ton schooner was discovered floating bottom up near the Columbia River mouth (Oregon-Washington) on January 4, 1890. There was no sign of what had happened to the crew.

See also MYSTERIES.

deep-sea environment Unlike the shallow-water environment, where many destructive agencies may work to demolish a shipwreck and scatter or bury its cargo, the deep-sea environment is comparatively tranquil and may preserve a wreck for decades or even centuries in good condition.

The deep-sea environment is cold and relatively low in dissolved oxygen. These two factors help to preserve wrecks that sink in deep water. Destructive organisms are also less active in the deep-sea environment. Although wrecks at great depth are more difficult to reach than those in shallow water, the relative inaccessibility of deep-sea wrecks preserves them from looting by souvenir hunters and treasure seekers.

A famous example of a wreck preserved in a deep-sea environment is the British liner *Titanic,* which sank in the North Atlantic Ocean off Newfoundland in 1912 and was located by a joint French-American expedition in 1985. Much of the ship, especially its forward section, still looks almost as it did on the night the liner sank.

See also NEAR-SHORE ENVIRONMENT; SHALLOW-WATER ENVIRONMENT; TITANIC.

***Deering,* American schooner** An outstanding example of a "ghost ship," the five-masted schooner *Carroll A. Deering* appeared mysteriously on Diamond Shoals, off the Outer Banks of North Carolina, on the night of January 30–31, 1921. The ship was discovered there on the morning of January 31, with sails set, but no one on board. The case of the *Deering* has become one of the most famous in the literature of ghost ships, and there has been abundant speculation about how the vessel came to be abandoned.

Launched at Bath, Maine, in 1919, *Deering* was on a voyage from Rio de Janeiro to Norfolk, Virginia, when the ship turned up abandoned on the Outer Banks. The schooner carried no cargo on that voyage and made one stop along the way, at Barbados. The captain was W. T. Wormell. He had replaced one Captain F. Merritt, who had become ill on a previous leg of the ship's voyage, from Boston to Buenos Aires, and was put ashore at Lewes, Delaware, where Captain Wormell took command of *Deering*. The ship reportedly made several stops in South America before setting sail on December 2, 1920, from Rio de Janeiro for Norfolk.

The ship was discovered on Diamond Shoals at 6:30 A.M. on January 31, 1921, by a lookout at the Cape Hatteras Coast Guard station. The wind was from the southwest, and seas were rough. Lifesavers from Hatteras and other stations put out in boats and arrived near the ship several hours later. The men found *Deering* surrounded by breakers. No lifeboats were found on board. A ladder hung over the side. To all appearances, everyone on board had left by boat. The rough sea around *Deering* prevented the livesavers from boarding. The following day, the Coast Guard cutter *Seminole* was sent to investigate. Another cutter, *Manning*, left from Norfolk for the site as well, along with a wrecking tug. Four days later, *Deering* was boarded and was found in poor condition after several days on the shoals. The ship's seams were torn apart, and the hold had filled with water. Refloating the vessel appeared impossible.

The boarders saw evidence on *Deering* that the ship had been abandoned in a hurry. Someone had strewn charts around the master's bathroom. Food was on the stove. Curiously, someone or something also appeared to have disabled the schooner's steering.

Deering was stripped of what could be removed and was destroyed with dynamite several weeks later. Thereafter, analysts tried to determine what had happened to *Deering* before its arrival on Diamond Shoals.

Mutiny was one possibility. Captain Wormell reportedly had told a friend in Barbados that he had no confidence in his crew. There was little evidence, however, to support this hypothesis. Moreover, the mutiny scenario did not account for the whereabouts of the missing crew.

Another suggestion was that pirates attacked *Deering* and captured or murdered its crew. This too was virtually unsupported speculation. Although a man living near Cape Hatteras reported finding a bottle containing a message that pirates had killed *Deering*'s crew, the story was dismissed as a hoax.

A more likely scenario involved a storm at sea. Possibly *Deering*, beset by heavy weather, was carried toward Diamond Shoals and abandoned by the crew, who feared that their vessel would ground on the dangerous shoals along the Outer Banks. One must question this scenario too, however, because a small, open boat is not the safest place to be in a storm at sea. The crew might have been safer aboard *Deering*, even in heavy weather and approaching Diamond Shoals. The strange case of *Deering* is discussed at length in David Stick's 1952 book *Graveyard of the Atlantic: Shipwrecks of the North Carolina Coast*.

See also DIAMOND SHOALS; GHOST SHIPS; OUTER BANKS.

Defence, American privateer   Believed to have been built in Beverly, Massachusetts, in 1779, *Defence* was sunk in the calamitous Penobscot operation that year. The wreck was located in 1972 by a summer class operated by the Massachusetts Institute of Technology and the Maine Maritime Academy. The expedition discovered a brick cookstove and two cannon on the wreck. A study of historical records and of artifacts taken from the wreck allowed the vessel to be identified as *Defence*. Excavations began and continued through 1981. Many supplies and fittings were left aboard the wreck, and the hull was well-preserved compared with many others from the fleet. Study of the wreck revealed much about life aboard the privateer, which must have been extraordinarily cramped with 100 men aboard a vessel less than 100 feet long. Of particular interest during the excavation was the ship's brick stove, which measured some five feet long and wide and was built around a large copper cauldron where the crew's rations of salt pork were cooked. Numerous artifacts such as buttons, tableware and a canister of grapeshot were recovered.

See also PENOBSCOT INCIDENT.

De Grace, American packet ship   Sometimes called *Sylvia de Grasse*, the packet ship *Silvie de Grace* demonstrated, tragically, what could happen in the days before inspections of ships were mandatory. The *de Grace*'s last voyage, in 1849, was extremely short. Burdened by an excessive load of lumber for San Francisco (the ship's owner wanted to make a large profit from the high demand for building materials), the ship had just weighed anchor at Astoria, Washington, when the vessel drifted onto rocks nearby.

With a lighter cargo, the ship might have refloated itself on the high tide; but the weight on board prevented *Silvie de Grace* from moving. The ship remained on the rocks for weeks. At last the owner engaged several schooners to take the cargo of lumber to San Francisco. When those ships arrived, however, they found that the demand for lumber had fallen dramatically. The owner took a great loss, both on his cargo and on his wrecked ship. The wreck of *Silvie de Grace* remained on the rocks for many years. A portion of the ship's anchor chain was preserved by the Oregon Historical Society.

Delaware, United States   One of the most famous shipwrecks in Delaware waters is that of the 16–gun British warship H.M.S. *De Braak*, which capsized and sank near Lewes in 1798 with the loss of 35 crew members. The ship is thought to have carried a large quantity of gold and silver specie and bullion, but Robert Marx reports in his reference book *Shipwrecks in the Americas* that attempts to locate the wreck and bring the treasure to the surface have been unsuccessful. Other notable Delaware wrecks include seven American warships sunk in combat with British forces in Delaware Bay in 1777. Among these ships were the 32-gun warship *Washington* and the 28-gun *Effingham*.

Delphy, American destroyer   In a catastrophic demonstration of the dangers of fog, *Delphy* and six other destroyers in a squadron went aground 75 miles north of Santa Barbara, California, in foggy weather on September 9, 1923. Twenty-two people were killed. The other destroyers were *Chauncey, Fuller, S.P. Lee, Nicholas, Woodbury* and *Young.*

Desdemona, American bark   The Desdemona Sands at the mouth of the Columbia River (Oregon-Washington) were named not for Shakespeare's character, but rather for a ship that was wrecked there on January 1, 1857.

On a voyage from San Francisco, the heavily laden ship arrived off the river's mouth late on December 31, 1856. No pilot was available, and so the captain decided to risk taking the vessel across the bar without a pilot's help.

A more lightly laden ship might have crossed the bar successfully, but *Desdemona* rode so deeply in the water that the ship struck bottom where there was supposed to be deep water. A Coast Guard cutter came to *Desdemona's* aid but was unable to pull the stranded ship off the bar.

As *Desdemona* sank in the sands, the crew started unloading cargo. On January 3, they had to suspend work as a storm passed. After the storm was over, the crew returned to *Desdemona* in a scow to continue unloading. The scow overturned, and a crewman was killed.

The wreck was sold at public auction on January 6, for a mere $215, and was stripped by the buyer. What remained of the ship was visible on the bar for years afterward, but finally sank into the sands and was lost from view.

See also COLUMBIA RIVER BAR.

Detroit, American brig   The wreck of *Detroit*, on the Columbia River bar (Oregon-Washington) on December 25, 1855, had a reasonably happy ending. No one was killed, and the survivors evidently were treated to a good meal afterward.

The ship went aground on the bar and then went free, but the bottom was damaged, and *Detroit* soon filled with water. The terrified crew would not do anything to save the vessel, so the captain gave the order to abandon ship. A pilot boat picked up the men from *Detroit* and carried them to Astoria, Washington, where a holiday dinner awaited them.

The brig did not actually sink. It drifted for about a day and finally went ashore near Tillamook Head, Oregon.

Deutschland, German steamship   A passenger liner traveling from Bremen, Germany, to New York, *Deutschland* struck Britain's Kentish Knock shoals near Harwich during a gale on December 6, 1875, and sank with the loss of an estimated 157 people. One hundred and fifty-five people were reported rescued, most of them by a tug that reached the scene the next day. The great loss of life occurred despite the fact that the wreck took place within sight of land, and the ship was well equipped with life preservers.

When *Deutschland* struck the shoal, the captain ordered full speed astern, but the propeller broke, leaving the ship helpless. Two boats were lowered but capsized in the heavy weather. One boat was righted and drifted away from the wrecked steamship, but with only three people on board. Only one person in this boat was still alive when the boat reached shore.

The storm continued for the following day and a half. Panic apparently contributed to the loss of life on *Deutschland*. Passengers reportedly were terrified at the thought of getting into the boats in such stormy weather. In any event, escape by boat was soon impossible, because the storm demolished the remaining boats.

The captain told passengers to take shelter. To many on board *Deutschland*, this meant climbing the rigging: a fatal error in many cases, as people either froze in the rigging or fell to their deaths.

The tug *Liverpool* arrived the next day to render assistance and found *Deutschland* strewn with frozen corpses. A small fleet of fishing boats also arrived; but rather than help survivors, the boatmen reportedly began to strip the dead bodies of clothing and jewelry, and to loot the ship of valuable furnishings. The men from the tug evidently could do little or nothing to stop these thefts.

See also ROCKS AND SHOALS; STORMS.

Diamond Shoals, North Carolina Among the most dangerous shoals in the world, Diamond Shoals is located along the Outer Banks of North Carolina, near Cape Hatteras, and has claimed numerous ships over the past several centuries, despite such navigational aids as lighthouses. The sands of Diamond Shoals are deposited where two currents intersect. The site of Diamond Shoals can be identified in clear weather by the extreme turbulence of the waters where the two opposing currents meet.

See also OUTER BANKS; ROCKS AND SHOALS.

***Dictator*, Norwegian bark** Seven lives, including those of the captain's wife and young son, were lost in the wreck of the *Dictator* at Virginia Beach, Virginia, on March 27, 1891. On the way from Florida to England with a cargo of pine, the ship encountered heavy weather, began leaking and lost two boats. The captain decided repairs were needed before the bark tried to cross the Atlantic. So, *Dictator* sailed toward Hampton Roads, Virginia.

A gale was blowing as the ship approached Hampton Roads. The ship was off course, because bad weather for days had prevented the captain from taking a sun-sighting to establish his position accurately. For all that time, he had traveled on dead reckoning. As a result, he thought he was near Cape Charles, on the northern side of the mouth of Chesapeake Bay, when in fact he was some 20 miles south of that position. He thought the wide bay mouth was on his ship's port side. Instead, he was off Virginia Beach, and about to run ashore.

The crew of the Dam Neck Mills lifesaving station at Virginia Beach sighted *Dictator* when the ship was about one mile offshore. The sighting was brought to the attention of the Seatack station to the north. The Seatack lifesavers watched as *Dictator* turned to port and headed for the shore. Visibility was poor because of rain and fog.

Dictator grounded on the outer bar about one mile north of Seatack. Surfmen from the Seatack and Cape Henry stations tried to fire a line to the stricken ship with their Lyle gun, but the line fell short. At last, the ship's crew tied a line to a barrel and let the barrel float ashore. Using this line, a breeches buoy was set up and soon was carrying people from the bark to shore. The problem was that *Dictator* turned parallel to the shore and began rolling, so that the breeches buoy was under water one moment and the next moment high in the air.

Seeing what a wild ride the breeches buoy provided, the captain decided to try escape by lifeboat. His wife was terrified of the breeches buoy and would have nothing to do with it. The captain tied a line to the ship's boat and sent it toward the shore with four sailors on board. The plan was to haul people from *Dictator* to shore in the boat, once a line to shore was established for it. The keeper of the Seatack lifesaving station, however, refused to let the boat return. Immediately on launching, he explained later, the boat would have filled with water.

His plan made unworkable, the captain did what he could to save the nine people still on board. He had little time, for the ship was breaking up. He tied a ring life buoy to himself and another to his wife, and tied his son on his back. A wave swept the captain into the sea. His wife was also carried overboard. The captain reached shore alive, but his wife and son were drowned. Ten people survived the wreck of *Dictator*; seven were killed.

After this tragic incident, the keeper of the Seatack station faced an official investigation. One of his superiors criticized him for not using the life car, a special lifesaving device, to rescue people from *Dictator*. The station keeper was asked to resign and did so.

Opinion was divided on the keeper's responsibility and actions in this case. Some thought he was blamed for circumstances beyond his control, including the dead-reckoning errors on the part of *Dictator*'s captain, which had put the ship in danger to begin with.

See also BREECHES BUOY; LIFE CAR.

disappearances On numerous occasions, ships have failed to appear at their destinations as expected, and no trace of the vessels has been discovered, or any communications received, to indicate what happened to the ships en route. Disappearances were commonplace in the years before wireless communications allowed vessels in distress to call for aid. Many different circumstances might account for a ship vanishing at sea, including storms, explosions, collisions, mutiny and fire.

Even in the 20th century, with numerous safety devices and communications systems available, some ships have vanished at sea without leaving any wreckage or other evidence of their passing. Famous cases of 20th-century vessels that vanished at sea include the French liner *Neustria,* which disappeared in 1908 on a voyage from New York City to Marseilles; the British cargo liner *Waratah,* which apparently was lost within sight of land off the South African coast in 1908; and the American freighter *Poet,* which was lost in 1980 en route from the United States to Egypt.

See also MYSTERIES; NEUSTRIA; POET; WARATAH.

diving suits   Early divers were limited to very shallow depths by the relentless increase of water pressure. An unprotected diver can withstand a dive of only a few feet before water pressure becomes too heavy to tolerate. Pressure increases at the rate of one atmosphere (about 14.7 pounds per square inch) for every 33 feet of depth. This means that a dive to 100 feet subjects an unprotected diver to excess pressure of about 45 tons. The deeper one goes, the greater the danger that water pressure will force blood from the circulatory system and into the lungs, thus drowning the diver in his own blood.

One solution to this problem is to supply the diver with compressed air to compensate for the increased pressure on his body. Thus, the water pressure is balanced by increased pressure inside the lungs, and no fatal hemorrhage occurs. This approach required a special, watertight suit with a helmet connected by a hose to an air supply at the surface. A Roman author named Flavius Vegetius, writing in A.D. 375, described a plan for a diving suit using a leather sack for a helmet, with a tube extending up to the surface. There is considerable doubt, however, that a diver actually could have breathed through such apparatus. Leonardo da Vinci considered a design for a diving suit around the start of the 16th century. Almost two centuries later, a French diving suit called a *machine hydrostatergatique,* with a copper helmet, reportedly was tested with less than complete success. In 1783, a Scotsman named Charles Spaulding allegedly drowned in diving apparatus he had invented. In 1784, another design appeared. This one apparently required the diver to wear a large bellows, as in the *machine hydrostatergatique,* and was likewise unsuccessful. Another bellows-based diving outfit by a German named Frederic Drieberg is said to have been tested in 1808. This one required the diver to nod his head continually to operate the bellows. All these designs suffered from ignorance of the most important aspect of diving technology. The apparatus had to do more than merely supply air to the diver. The equipment also had to deliver air under pressure to compensate for increasing water pressure.

An English inventor named William Forder evidently understood the true obstacle to be overcome— that is, supplying air under adequate pressure—and in 1802 came up with a design that used a bellows at the surface to force air under pressure through a hose to a diver wearing a copper helmet. The bellows in this case, however, was too weak to do the job.

Another English inventor, Augustus Siebe, achieved a great advance in 1819 when he designed a diving suit that used an actual pump, not a mere bellows, to force air under pressure to a helmeted diver. His suit worked well in preliminary efforts to salvage the sunken warship *Royal George* at Spithead. The diver's maneuverability was limited in this case, however, because the suit extended only to waist level and was open on the bottom, to allow exhaled air to escape. If the diver bent forward too far, his suit would fill with water. A few years later, Siebe devised an advanced version of his suit. This version enclosed the diver's entire body in a watertight suit, with only the hands uncovered. The diver wore weighted boots to keep him from bobbing to the surface in his inflated costume, and a copper helmet with an escape valve to dispose of the diver's exhaled breath. Invented in 1837, Siebe's full-body suit was essentially the same hard-helmeted diving outfit that has remained in use ever since.

In 1841, an American named Buck Taylor invented a partly successful diving suit with a helmet made of brass and copper. Another American named Abel Blake later devised a suit of his own with the help of two partners. The Blake suit utilized a sheet-metal helmet and a body made of canvas treated with linseed oil. The suit was intended to recover coal from colliers sunk near Stamford, Connecticut. The diver would go down in his suit and use a conveyer belt to transfer coal from the sunken ships' holds to the surface. Blake died in a diving accident.

Early hard-helmet divers sometimes received strange assignments. Historian Joseph N. Gores writes in his 1971 book *Marine Salvage* that an English police officer once turned to divers for help in solving a homicide. Someone had beaten a woman to death with a blunt instrument. The policeman suspected the object was a bottle, and he thought it might have been tossed off a pier. Divers went down to search for the bottle. They found enough fragments to allow the bottle to be reassembled. On the reconstructed bottle, the maker's name was visible, along with a number that indicated the consignment to which the bottle belonged, and even the public house where the bottle was delivered. The police traced the bottle to the buyer, who confessed to the crime.

Hard-helmet divers could accomplish marvelous things, but the technology was clumsy. Supplying air to the diver by a hose was a cumbersome arrangement, and in the early 19th century inventors were already seeking some better design. An experiment in 1825 involved a helmet connected to a tank of oxygen. Another apparatus invented in 1878 disposed of the diver's exhaled carbon dioxide. In 1886, a "demand valve" was patented; it supplied the diver with as much air as needed. By World War I, self-contained underwater breathing units were in use.

Developments continued through the first third of the 20th century. During World War II, French inventors Jacques Cousteau and Emile Gagnan devised what would become the familiar modern SCUBA system, or Aqua-Lung. Gagnan had invented a regulator for automobile fuel supply. This regulator was modified to become the basis for the Aqua-Lung.

In German-occupied France, Cousteau and two companions, Frederic Dumas and Philippe Taillez, began testing their underwater breathing apparatus, which consisted of a cylinder of air and a Gagnan regulator. Their tests had to be conducted in secret to hide their work from the Germans. A shipwreck near Marseilles provided an ideal place for testing. A freighter sunk in a storm rested with its bow on the shore and its stern in 65 feet of water.

The French tests started in 1943. Americans, Britons and Italians were quick to see the tremendous potential of the Cousteau-Gagnan system. The Aqua-Lung was fantastically successful and transformed the business of diving. The diver now was far more maneuverable than ever before.

Cousteau and his associates demonstrated in the 1950s how the new diving equipment could advance salvage operations and marine archeology. Cousteau and his men acted on a report from a diver who told Dumas that he had found large numbers of "pots" in the mud off Grand Congloue Island near Marseilles. The diver thought they might be a grand lobster bed. Dumas thought the pots might be amphorae—earthenware jugs used to transport wine and other liquids by ship in Roman times. Dumas persuaded Cousteau and a professor at the Marseilles Archaeological Museum to seek the shipwreck. Cousteau himself found the wreck while swimming in some 160 feet of water (a depth that would have been unthinkable for divers only a few decades earlier). The wreck yielded more than 8,000 amphorae and thousands of pieces of pottery between 1952 and 1959.

See also ARCHAEOLOGY; GRAND CONGLOUE ISLAND WRECK; SALVAGE.

documents Many documents are available to help locate shipwrecks and provide an idea of the ships' cargoes. For shipwrecks of the late 19th and the 20th centuries, documentation generally is good. In the United States, for example, sources include the Na-

tional Archives; the Coast Guard; the Naval Hydrographic Office; and the U.S. Maritime Commission. All the aforementioned sources are located in the Washington, D.C., area. Lists of ship losses are available from the Public Information Division of the U.S. Coast Guard, including *Principal Marine Disasters 1831–1932*, and *United States Merchant Ship Losses, December 7, 1941–August 14, 1945*. Other American sources include *Records of the Navies of the Civil War*, published by the U.S. Government Printing Office, and *A Guide to Sunken Ships in American Waters*.

British records are available at the British Museum, the National Maritime Museum and Lloyd's of London. All these sources are located in or near London. One rich source of documentation for Spanish shipwrecks in the New World is the Archives of the Indies in Seville. Much documentation of Dutch ship losses in the New World appears to have been either lost or destroyed, so that researchers must seek evidence of Dutch shipwrecks in British or Spanish archives. Likewise, much documentation of French maritime calamities in the New World appears to be unavailable for various reasons.

Even when original documents are available and can be used to locate a wreck precisely, much information in the documents may no longer be accurate. For example, a listing of treasure aboard a sunken vessel may exceed the amount one may expect to find on the wreck, because successful salvage attempts over the years may have gone unrecorded. On the other hand, the widespread practice of smuggling may mean that a ship's manifest lists only a fraction of the treasure actually aboard. A particular ship might have carried perhaps five times as much treasure as the figure recorded in the manifest.

Changes in place names can be another misleading element of documents. The site of a given shipwreck may have had its name changed several times since the ship went down.

See also SALVAGE; TREASURE.

Dogger Bank wrecks, North Sea One day in early March, 1883, a storm sank 45 trawlers and killed 225 men and boys in a particular area known as the "Cemetery." At this particular point near the great fishing ground, gales give rise to a turbulent sea.

See also STORMS.

Dominica, Lesser Antilles What seemed like a safety measure actually brought about the destruction in 1567 of the New Spain Flota under the command of Captain-General Juan Velasco de Barrio in a storm near Dominica. At Veracruz, Mexico, before sailing for Spain, the Captain-General received news that a pair of English fleets, one at the Bahama Channel and the other near Havana, lay in wait to catch the Spanish fleet and its treasure. The Spaniards decided that a safer route was to sail south of Jamaica toward the Virgin Islands and proceed from there toward Spain. Given good weather, this plan might have worked. A storm struck the fleet near Puerto Rico, however, and six large ships in the fleet were lost near Dominica. The storm prevented other ships in the fleet from stopping to rescue survivors. Those survivors who made their way to shore appeared to have been killed, to the last individual, by the fierce Carib tribe.

The Caribs also are said to have slaughtered the survivors of another shipwreck in 1565, when an unnamed Spanish vessel was wrecked on Dominica. A few survivors of the wreck lived to tell the grisly story when another ship put in at the island some months afterward for fresh water and rescued them.

Hurricanes have been a deadly threat to shipping at Dominica. In 1766, an October hurricane destroyed five English merchant vessels. Another hurricane on July 26, 1769, wrecked 13 ships completely. Eighteen unnamed English merchant ships were destroyed in a storm on August 30, 1772. The 40-gun French frigate *Juno* was destroyed in a hurricane on October 9, 1780, with the loss of more than 300 men. Three separate hurricanes in a single year, 1787, sank numerous ships at Dominica; and the August 1, 1792, hurricane wrecked 14 English vessels. A hurricane in August of 1813 destroyed 16 ships.

Doterel, British Navy sloop *Doterel* exploded and sank at Punta Arenas, Chile, with the loss of 143 lives, on April 26, 1880. The explosion was attributed to paint fumes.

draft The amount of water a ship "draws," meaning the distance between the keel and waterline. Some vessels, such as barges, have unusually shallow draft, while others, like battleships or supertankers, have exceptionally great draft.

Dragon, Spanish warship Sixty men were drowned when the 60-gun *Dragon* sank in Mexico's Gulf of Campeche in 1783.

Dresser, American barkentine Lighthouses are meant to aid navigation, but sometimes trouble can result when a ship's master mistakes one lighthouse as another. That was what happened to the barkentine *J.W. Dresser* off the Outer Banks of North Carolina on July 22, 1895.

On the way from Cuba to New York, in a heavy sea and strong wind, the captain saw a lighthouse and thought it was located on Bodie Island, when in fact it was the Cape Hatteras light, a few miles south of Bodie Island. Bodie Island had no dangerous shoals offshore and was safe to approach, so *Dresser* headed for shore to minimize the effects of the sea and wind.

The captain's error had calamitous results. *Dresser* ran aground on Diamond Shoals, one of the most dangerous points on the entire Atlantic coast of the United States.

As maritime historian David Stick points out in his history of shipwrecks on North Carolina's Outer Banks, *Graveyard of the Atlantic,* other factors were working against the stranded ship as well. Most of the men at the lifesaving stations were on vacation; and at the Hatteras station, the only man present—the keeper—was asleep when *Dresser* ran aground. Eventually, the ship was sighted, and two surfboats came out to rescue the men on *Dresser.* All on board the ship survived.

See also BARKENTINE; LIGHTHOUSES; OUTER BANKS.

Drexel Victory, American steamship What exactly happened to *Drexel Victory* is a mystery of the Columbia River (Oregon-Washington). The freighter left Portland, Oregon, for Yokohama, Japan, on the afternoon of January 19, 1947, carrying 5,000 tons of cargo. As the ship crossed the Columbia River bar, *Drexel Victory* suddenly split open between holds number 4 and 5. The ship filled and sank, despite efforts by the Coast Guard to tow it into shallow water and beach it. No one was killed.

The case was mysterious, because there evidently was no shoal or other obstruction that *Drexel Victory* might have hit. It seemed unlikely that the ship, with a draft of only 29 to 30 feet, ran aground in more than 50 feet of water. Another possibility was that *Drexel Victory* had hit a submerged wreck. Yet an investigation revealed no such wreck or other obstruction at the spot where the ship split open. Moreover, *Drexel Victory* was not an aged vessel. It had been built at Richmond, California, only two years earlier, in 1945.

The ship's captain offered structural failure as an explanation for the wreck. An official state panel cleared the captain of any responsibility for the loss of *Drexel Victory.*

Drumcraig, British bark The square-rigged, 1,979-ton *Drumcraig* vanished with all hands on a voyage from Astoria, Washington, to Manila in 1906 with a cargo of lumber. *Drumcraig* was last seen crossing the Columbia River bar (Oregon-Washington).

Duke Campagni, Italian merchant ship With a load of silver specie, *Duke Campagni* left the island of St.

Eustatius in the Lesser Antilles for Amsterdam in 1758, but was wrecked on the north side of the island. No one was killed, and most of the specie were recovered.

Dumlupinar, Turkish submarine   The Turkish submarine *Dumlupinar* (formerly U.S.S. *Bumper*, built in 1944), sank on the night of April 4, 1953, when it was rammed by the Swedish freighter *Naboland* in the Dardanelles near Istanbul. The freighter sustained only minor damage, but *Dumlupinar* sank quickly to a depth of more than 200 feet. Eighty-one men on the submarine died. Five men who were in the conning tower at the time of the collision were saved. Rescue vesseis converged on the scene but were unable to save the men in the sunken submarine. Evidently the men trapped on *Dumlupinar* survived for some time after the sinking, because they reportedly sent a message to the surface, saying they had only enough air for a few hours. Curiously, no one on the sunken submarine appears to have used the escape hatches or the underwater breathing apparatus on the vessel.

See also SUBMARINES.

E

E-11 Although not a shipwreck story, the tale of British Captain Martin E. Nasmith and his submarine *E-11* in World War I illustrates a novel case of salvage. Rather than abandon torpedoes that had failed to hit their targets, Nasmith reportedly brought his ship up to floating torpedoes and recovered them after they had finished their runs. A man would go into the water and remove the detonator from the torpedo, so that it would not explode on handling. Then *E-11* flooded its after-ballast tanks to raise the bow torpedo tubes clear of the water. Sailors would maneuver the spent torpedo back into the tube. Then the outer door of the tube was closed; water was expelled from the tube by compressed air; and the torpedo was brought into the submarine to have its detonator replaced.

See also SUBMARINES.

E-41, **British submarine** This wreck involved a remarkable story of escape from a sunken submarine. The British submarine *E-4* collided with submarine *E-41* during maneuvers in the Irish Sea in July of 1915. Both submarines sank. *E-4* sank so rapidly that its entire crew was drowned. *E-41* went down more gradually, so that the entire crew was able to escape before the sub sank, with the exception of a chief petty officer who was in the engine room when the collision occurred. As *E-41* started sinking, he shut the watertight door in the engine room bulkhead, sealing off the rest of the ship but trapping himself inside. There was only one way out: through a hatch that had about 12,000 pounds of water pressure pressing it shut. The only way to open the hatch was to equalize pressure on the inside and outside. This he did, by opening a valve and letting sea water into the engine room. This in itself was a dangerous operation, because the sea water created a short circuit with the electrical equipment, and the trapped sailor began getting bad electrical shocks when he touched metal. The incoming water compressed the air inside the engine room until he was able to get the hatch open.

His first attempt was unsuccessful. Apparently the pressure was not quite equalized yet, because the hatch opened slightly and then slammed down on his hand, crushing his fingers. On the next try, he managed to open the hatch and was blown out of the submarine and to the surface by an outburst of air. He was rescued and survived.

See also SUBMARINES.

Eagle, **American steamship** An early boiler explosion on Chesapeake Bay involved the steamer *Eagle*, a 110-foot vessel that had the distinction of being the first steamboat to navigate the whole Chesapeake Bay. The ship operated successfully until April 18, 1824, when *Eagle*'s boiler blew up at the mouth of the Patapsco River, Maryland. One passenger was killed, and the captain was burned so badly by steam that he never recovered completely.

This incident occurred less than a year after another such explosion, involving the steamer *Powhatan* in Norfolk, Virginia. *Powhatan*'s boiler exploded on September 20, 1823. No casualty figures for that explosion are available.

See also EXPLOSIONS.

earthquakes Although earthquakes usually do more damage to structures on land than to ships in harbors, a strong earthquake can do significant damage to shipping by generating powerful seismic sea waves, or tsunamis, that can demolish ships in harbors and even carry vessels miles inland. Much of the Alaskan fishing fleet, for example, was destroyed by a tsunami that followed the great Alaskan earthquake of 1964. The crew of U.S.S. *Wateree*, an American naval vessel visiting Peru in 1868, witnessed the destruction of large ships in the harbor there by a tsunami. That tsunami carried *Wateree* far inland and left the ship stranded.

See also JAMAICA; PORT ROYAL; TSUNAMIS; WATEREE.

Eastland, American passenger steamer One of the most notorious shipwrecks in American history occurred next to a pier, when the excursion steamer *Eastland* capsized in the Chicago River on July 24, 1915, killing 852 passengers.

Eastland was one of several steamers assigned to carry passengers from Chicago to a picnic at Michigan City, Indiana. Although *Eastland* was licensed to carry 2,500 passengers and crew, more than 3,500 boarded the ship. *Eastland* developed a list to the left. The ship's chief engineer tried to correct the list by opening a ballast tank on the right side of the ship. The ship continued listing, however, from one side to another. (*Eastland* already had been criticized for instability in a series of tests two years earlier.)

Soon the list increased to more than 30 degrees, and *Eastland* rolled over on its left side and sank beside the pier. Some crew members managed to escape by leaping onto the pier before the ship capsized. The ship was almost entirely submerged. Only some eight feet of the hull remained above the water.

Hundreds of passengers drowned. Some managed to find safety on the exposed right side of the hull. Others wound up in the water, swimming for their lives. Workers at a warehouse beside the river tried to help by throwing lumber and other wooden articles into the water to keep swimmers afloat. One worker used an acetylene torch to cut a hole in the hull so that trapped passengers might escape. For some reason, Captain Harry Pedersen objected and tried to stop the man from cutting the hole. The worker ignored him and continued cutting. Forty people were rescued through that hole. Later, Pedersen was actually arrested for trying to impede the rescue of passengers.

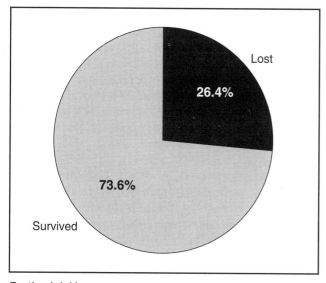

Eastland sinking, passengers.

Although numerous lawsuits were filed against the steamship company, it was held not liable for the catastrophe. An Illinois court ruled instead that the engineer had not filled *Eastland*'s ballast tanks properly.

See also STABILITY AND INSTABILITY.

Edmund Fitzgerald, American freighter In one of the most famous shipwrecks ever to occur on the Great Lakes, the *Edmund Fitzgerald* sank in a storm on Lake Superior on November 10, 1975. Equipment failure appears to have occurred on the ship's last voyage. *Fitzgerald* notified the freighter *Arthur M. Anderson* by radio that *Fitzgerald*'s radars were not working, and asked *Anderson* to maintain a radar watch and help *Fitzgerald* with navigation. *Anderson*, traveling with *Fitzgerald* toward the Lake Huron locks, agreed to do so. Later, *Fitzgerald* disappeared from *Anderson*'s radar screen. *Anderson* tried without success to make visual and radio contact with *Fitzgerald*. An air and sea search failed to locate the missing ship. The Coast Guard eventually found the wreck of *Fitzgerald* in more than 500 feet of water. The ship had broken in two. The vessel is thought to have sunk so quickly that there was no opportunity to transmit a distress signal. The Coast Guard surmised that poorly sealed cargo hatches allowed water to enter, so that the ship lost buoyancy and stability and sank in the heavy seas. According to another scenario, the ship was passing shoals when a wave hit the ship and drove the hull against the bottom. The wreck become the subject of a popular song.

See also BRADLEY; GREAT LAKES; RADAR.

Egypt, British steamship One of the most famous cases in the history of shipwreck and salvage, the sinking of the Peninsular and Oriental Line steamship *Egypt* occurred on May 20, 1922. *Egypt* was rammed by the French freighter *Seine* in fog off Finisterre, France, and sank within 20 minutes in some 60 feet of water. Of 355 passengers and crew aboard, 86 were killed. The ship carried 1,089 gold ingots and 1,229 silver ingots, which were insured for more than a million British pounds. Salvage operations were delayed by the absence of an exact position for the wreck.

In 1928, an Italian salvage firm with a good reputation, the Society for Maritime Recovery (SORIMA), took on the job of locating the wreck and recovering its gold. SORIMA and its vessels *Artiglio* and *Rostro* swept the vicinity of the sinking with a wire strung between the two ships, in the hope of snagging and thus locating *Egypt*. In late August of 1930, SORIMA finally found *Egypt* and identified the ship by sending down a diver in an "iron duke," or armored diving suit, to recover the safe. SORIMA had to leave the site soon afterward.

In December of 1930, SORIMA's ship *Artiglio* was destroyed in another operation that was trying to demolish the wreck of the American munitions ship *Florence* off Quiberon, France. When SORIMA returned to *Egypt* in May of 1931, the firm had a new ship, *Artiglio II*. The new vessel had the world's best collection of deep-water salvage equipment.

Secured in place over *Egypt*, *Artiglio II* started blasting away portions of the wreck until the strong room containing the gold was exposed. This work had to be done carefully, because of the risk that a strong blast might send the heavy gold crashing through the deck and into the hold, where recovery would be more difficult. The onset of winter weather forced *Artiglio II* to leave the site in late November, but the ship returned in May of 1932 and by June was bringing up gold. SORIMA recovered some £80,000 in bullion from the wreck. It took two more years to recover the remainder of the treasure.

SORIMA's experience on this project showed that the iron duke had serious limitations, and that an observation chamber could do the job better. Part of the iron duke's problem was that it could not work in currents exceeding one knot. Moreover, the iron duke's mechanical "hands" were not effective for manipulating objects.

See also DAVIS OBSERVATION CHAMBER; FLORENCE; "IRON DUKE."

Elbe, **German passenger liner**   A collision between the German liner *Elbe* and the British steamer *Crathie* off Lowestoft, England, during a storm on the night of January 30, 1895, left 315 persons dead, according to one report. Only 20 people survived *Elbe*'s sinking. The collision occurred partly because *Crathie*'s lookout and mate were in the galley rather than on the bridge (where they were supposed to be) just before *Crathie* struck *Elbe*. The helmsman on duty saw *Elbe* and tried to contact the mate, but by the time the mate responded and reached the bridge, it was too late to alter course. The German ship sank in only 20 minutes. The storm overwhelmed *Elbe*'s boats. One lifeboat managed to stay afloat for five hours, and its occupants were rescued by a fishing boat. *Crathie* was blamed for the collision, although it was established that *Elbe* had not taken steps to avoid collision even when it was clear that the two ships were going to collide.

See also COLLISIONS.

Elizabeth, **sailing vessel**   Wrecked near Point O'Woods on Fire Island, New York, on July 19, 1850,

Elizabeth sailed on May 17 from Leghorn, Italy. During the voyage, the captain died of smallpox, and an inexperienced mate took command. The mate thought the ship was off the New Jersey coast when it actually was off Long Island, New York, and the vessel wrecked on a sandbar off Fire Island. Among those killed was Margaret Fuller (1810–1850), noted American suffragist and author. According to one account of the voyage, Fuller's young son had contracted smallpox but recovered during the voyage, only to be killed in the shipwreck. A steward reportedly saw the mainmast about to fall on the child, grabbed him, and went overboard; both drowned. Ten people were killed in the wreck, and 11 others survived.

Elizabeth, **German sailing vessel**   One of the worst shipwrecks in Virginia history, the loss of *Elizabeth* involved 27 deaths, including 22 crewmen from the ship and five men from the American lifesaving service.

The wreck occurred near the end of a voyage from Hamburg, Germany, to Baltimore, around midnight on January 8, 1887, near the lifesaving stations at Dam Neck Mills and Little Island in what is now the city of Virginia Beach. The ship stranded in a snowstorm with strong northeasterly winds.

A surfman on patrol sighted the wreck about 1 A.M. and lighted a flare. The snowstorm made response time slower than usual, but by 3 A.M. lifesavers were on the scene, and rescue operations were under way by 5 A.M.

Elizabeth lay about a thousand feet offshore. The lifesavers repeatedly tried firing a line to the ship, but without success. In the daylight, the lifesavers finally had a good look at the stricken ship. The crew was already in a boat on the port side, in the lee of the hull.

Despite heavy seas, the lifesavers managed to launch a surfboat and row out to *Elizabeth*. They found 22 men. The captain and six crewmen got into the surfboat for the trip ashore. A huge wave swamped the two boats, however, and all 29 men were cast into the water. Everyone from *Elizabeth* was killed. There were only two survivors from the surfboat's crew. The ship was a complete loss.

Elmiranda, **American bark**   Some ships carried small menageries of animals on board, as in the case of *Elmiranda*, a three-masted bark from Maine that came ashore at Wainscott, New York, on April 21, 1894. The crew, rescued by breeches buoy, brought with them a parrot and a monkey. The parrot, who rode ashore inside the cook's coat, was soaked but recovered, and was sold for two dollars to someone at the

Georgica lifesaving station. The ship was lightened by throwing coal overboard and was taken off by a tug and lighter.

Emeraude, French submarine   The nuclear submarine *Emeraude* did not sink in this incident, but the commander and nine other sailors were killed on March 30, 1994, when superheated steam escaped from a leak in a pipe in the turbo-generating room. The steam is thought either to have burned the men to death or to have asphyxiated them. *Emeraude* surfaced and used its diesel engines and batteries to return to its base at Toulon, on France's Mediterranean coast.

The French defense ministry said the leak did not affect the submarine's nuclear reactor, nor did the incident present a danger to the environment. *Emeraude* was six years old when the incident occurred. The submarine was on a training cruise with other French naval vessels between Toulon and the island of Corsica.

See also SUBMARINES.

Empress of Ireland, Canadian passenger liner   One of the greatest maritime catastrophes, in terms of lives lost, took place within sight of land on Canada's St. Lawrence River on May 29, 1914, when the Canadian Pacific Line's *Empress of Ireland*, under command of Captain Henry Kendall, sank after colliding with the Norwegian collier *Storstad* in fog. At 2 A.M., Kendall and officers on the *Empress*'s bridge saw the lights of the *Storstad* approaching. The chief officer of *Storstad* saw the masthead lights and red portside light of the *Empress*. Then fog moved in suddenly and hid the two ships from each other's view. To avoid collision,

Kendall ordered full speed astern and sounded the *Empress*'s horn three times. *Storstad*'s chief officer heard the horn blasts and told his captain, Thomas Andersen, what was happening. Andersen likewise ordered full speed astern and sounded his vessel's horn. Moments later, the two ships collided. *Storstad*'s stout bow, reinforced to stand up to ice, smashed into the *Empress* and caused tremendous damage. An attempt to keep the vessels together, so that *Storstad*'s bow would plug the hole in the *Empress*'s side, was unsuccessful. *Storstad* separated from *Empress,* which began sinking immediately. Kendall ordered watertight doors to be shut, but this measure failed because the doors were operated manually, and some were inaccessible because of the inflow of water. Kendall's next plan was to try beaching the ship on the shore, only several miles away, but no steam was available. Helpless, *Empress* sent out an S.O.S. message, and Kendall gave the order to abandon ship.

Reaching the lifeboats on *Empress* was difficult because the ship was listing heavily and affected by a blackout. Three lifeboats were launched successfully. A fourth fell into the river but was righted and used to take off passengers. *Storstad,* though badly damaged, remained afloat. Captain Andersen ordered the ship to return to the site of the collision.

Empress rolled over and sank only 14 minutes after the collision. *Storstad* saved some 50 people from the liner. Other vessels arrived to take aboard some of the 458 survivors from the *Empress.* Loss of life was estimated at 1,024 people, including 840 passengers.

Although an inquiry headed by Lord Mersey (who also had led the British inquiry into the loss of *Titanic* two years before) placed blame for the catastrophe squarely on *Storstad,* a court in Norway reached just the opposite conclusion and found the Norwegian ship not responsible for the collision. Nonetheless, *Storstad*'s chief officer had his license revoked for two years.

What exactly happened on the night of the collision remains uncertain. It has been suggested that *Storstad* made an improper left turn that put the collier on a collision course with the liner. Also, *Empress* was stopped in the water just before the collision, and that halt indicated that Kendall might have been too cautious in his effort to avoid striking *Storstad.* Other evidence indicates that there may have been a problem with *Empress*'s rudder that interfered with steering.

Kendall's career included other dramatic episodes. A later command of his, *Calgarian,* sank in 1918. In 1910, while in command of *Montrose,* Kendall also played an important role in the capture of the British murderer Dr. Crippen, whom Scotland Yard sought for poisoning his wife. Crippen and his mistress, Ethel

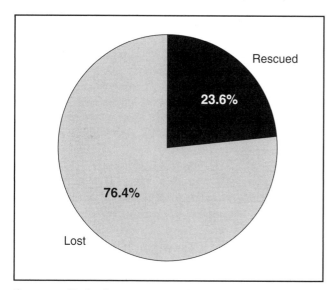

Empress of Ireland, passengers and crew.

LeNeve, were traveling on *Montrose*. Crippen had assumed the name of "Mr. Robinson," and LeNeve, disguised as his son, accompanied him on *Montrose*.

Kendall had read about the Crippen case and became suspicious of "Robinson" and his alleged son. Knowing that Crippen had dentures, the captain told some jokes in an effort to make Crippen laugh. When Crippen did so, his dentures were visible. This and other information led Kendall to contact Scotland Yard by wireless. Scotland Yard sent an inspector across the Atlantic on a fast White Star liner. The inspector arrived two days before *Montrose* and arrested Crippen when Kendall's ship arrived. Crippen was tried, convicted and executed, but his mistress was acquitted.

See also COLLISIONS; FOG; NAVIGATION.

Endurance, British exploration vessel Among the most famous vessels wrecked in the polar regions is *Endurance* (formerly *Polaris*), Sir Ernest Shackleton's ship on his 1912 Antarctic expedition. Caught in ice, the ship was crushed and abandoned and sank in the Weddell Sea between 150 and 200 miles south of the Antarctic Circle on November 21, 1915. Shackleton and his men made their way across the ice to a point just south of Elephant Island, near the South Shetland Islands. On April 9, 1916, Shackleton and his party left the ice behind and set out for Elephant Island in their boats, saved from the wreck of *Endurance*. From Elephant Island, Shackleton and several members of the expedition made one of the most dramatic open-boat journeys in history, to South Georgia Island some 650 nautical miles away. The men left behind on Elephant Island were rescued later.

See also POLAR REGIONS.

Enterprise, American aircraft carrier A series of explosions on *Enterprise* during operations off Hawaii on January 14, 1969, blasted holes in the flight deck and started a fire. The incident killed 27 crewmen. More than 80 others were reported injured. The explosions were attributed to an unsecured bomb that allegedly fell from an aircraft making a landing.

See also EXPLOSIONS.

Enterprize, American sailing vessel A horse played a prominent part in saving survivors from the wreck of the schooner *Enterprize* off the Outer Banks of North Carolina early on the morning of October 27, 1822. Just before dawn, the ship grounded on Chicamacomico Banks, north of Cape Hatteras. Waves started breaking over the craft, and the passengers and crew climbed into the rigging. When it became apparent that the ship was holding together, men climbed down from the rigging and started trying to

pump out the water. The ship's cargo somehow caught on fire, however, and the people on *Enterprize* had to find some way of reaching shore. A horse on board was pushed over the side and reached shore easily, followed by the human occupants of the stricken ship. On shore, the people of *Enterprize* saw the tracks of a cart in the sand and followed them to the nearby community of Chicamacomico, now known as Rodanthe. There they arranged for passage on a schooner on nearby Ocracoke. The schooner departed from Chicamacomico the following day, but the ship encountered rough weather en route, and the schooner's captain was washed overboard and lost.

See also OUTER BANKS.

epidemics Epidemic disease was a particular threat aboard ships during the age of sail. Contagious illnesses such as smallpox could spread rapidly within the confined quarters of a ship, with devastating effects. Disease thus could demolish a ship and its crew as effectively as a submerged rock or an enemy's gunfire. Robert Marx, in his book *Shipwrecks in the Americas*, tells how smallpox destroyed the crews of two Manila galleons that sailed together across the Pacific Ocean in 1657. All 450 people on one galleon died of smallpox during the voyage, while the epidemic killed approximately 200 of the 400 men on the other vessel. Spanish ships were particularly notorious for filthy conditions on board; Marx also quotes an unnamed Englishman of the early 17th century as saying that Spanish ships were "foul" and "beastly," reminiscent of "hog-sties." The Englishman did not seem surprised at these conditions, because he noted that the Spaniards simply did not appear to put anyone in charge of maintaining certain degrees of hygiene aboard their ships.

See also MANILA GALLEONS.

Erasmus, Saint (third century A.D.) Also known as Elmo or Telmo, Saint Erasmus became the patron saint of sailors and had a windlass as his emblem. The luminous display of static electricity sometimes seen in ships' rigging during storms became known as St. Elmo's Fire and was thought to be a sign of the saint's protection.

See also ST. ELMO'S FIRE.

Erfprinz, Dutch warship This was one of the greatest maritime catastrophes in the history of New England. *Erfprinz* sank off Cape Cod, Massachusetts, in 1783 with the loss of more than 300 lives.

Erie, American steamship The Great Lakes steamer *Erie* set out across Lake Erie on August 9, 1841, carrying some 300 Norwegian and German immigrants and some $100,000 that they planned to use to buy land in Wisconsin. Several miles off Silver Creek, New York, the ship burned and sank. In 1854, a salvage operation recovered some $2,000 in coins from the wreck.

***Erria,* Danish motorship** A cargo-passenger liner of the East Asiatic Company of Copenhagen, *Erria* caught fire while anchored at the mouth of the Columbia River (Oregon-Washington) early on the morning of December 20, 1951. Three crew members and eight passengers were killed, out of 114 persons in all on board.

The fire, which was thought to have originated from a shorted wire, proved extremely difficult to extinguish and burned for several days. The heat was so intense that rivets popped out of plates in the hull.

When the fire at last was out, the wreck was towed to Portland, Oregon. There, what remained of the cargo was unloaded. The ship then was towed to Holland to be rebuilt as a freighter, with no passenger capability.

***Ertogrul,* Turkish frigate** Political intrigue figures in the case of *Ertogrul,* a poorly constructed frigate that foundered in the Sea of Japan on September 19, 1890, with the loss of 587 lives. The stories of intrigue involve Osman Pasha, a mysterious military leader who had tremendous influence (and numerous enemies) in the Turkish government. He served in the Crimean War and distinguished himself in combat, then embarked on a political career that took him to the highest levels of the Turkish government. Much of his career was surrounded by mystery, however, and even his original nationality was uncertain.

The Sultan of Turkey reportedly sent Osman Pasha on a voyage to Japan aboard *Ertogrul,* which was unsuitable for ocean travel because of structural weakness and malfunctioning engines. The frigate sank in a storm, and rumor has it that the purpose of the voyage was to make sure that Osman Pasha died at sea.

***Essex,* American whaler** The whaling vessel *Essex,* out of Nantucket, Massachusetts, is apparently the only reasonably large ship ever to be sunk by a whale. On November 20, 1820, *Essex* encountered an exceptionally large and aggressive sperm whale that rammed the ship twice. The damage was severe. Two days later, the whaler sank, and the 20-man crew, in three boats loaded with provisions, began a long and arduous voyage.

The Galapagos Islands were the nearest land to the point where *Essex* sank. The winds were unfavorable for trying to reach the Galapagos, however, and so

Captain George Pollard, Jr. decided to head south in the hope of catching a west wind that would drive the boats toward South America. At first, the boats caught a wind that carried them southward, according to the captain's plan. The weather then became rough for a time. Next, the wind reversed direction and blew the boats northward, in the direction from which they had come. By the end of November, the boats were located less than 500 miles from the spot where *Essex* sank. Then the wind started driving the boats southward again.

Although the boats were heading once more in the right direction, they also were running short on drinking water. The men suffered from thirst under the tropical sun. A scheme to catch rainwater in the sails proved unworkable, because the rainwater picked up salt from the sails and became undrinkable. Food supplies ran low, and the boats began leaking and had to be bailed out often.

On December 20, the boats reached land, a small and uninhabited island. Edible plants, birds and eggs provided food, and a spring on the island supplied fresh water for drinking. The island's food resources did not appear adequate for 20 men, however, and so the company—minus three men who chose to remain on the island—set out in the boats again. The winds continued driving the boats in a southerly direction. (The three men on the island were rescued about two months afterward.)

The first death among the crew occurred on January 8, 1821, when the second mate expired. He was buried at sea. Then a storm scattered the boats. One boat under the command of First Mate Owen Chase became separated from the other two boats. Chase and his men proceeded eastward, while Captain Pollard and the two boats under his command traveled along a parallel but more southerly course toward South America.

The next month was one of hideous suffering for the boat crews. The sun was intensely hot, and their rations were reduced to a few ounces of bread daily. One man in Chase's boat died on January 20. Another of Chase's party died on February 8, after going mad. Other deaths occurred in Captain Pollard's group. The remaining sailors reportedly ate the bodies of their dead mates in order to survive. Pollard's group soon was diminished by one boat. One night, the second boat under Pollard's command, with three men aboard, drifted away and was never seen again.

Chase's group, now reduced to three, was rescued on February 15 by the British ship *Indian.* Pollard and his men had to wait longer. At one point, Pollard's group decided that one of their number should be killed for food so that the rest of the party might live.

The men drew straws, and one Owen Coffin drew the short straw and was shot to death. Only two men, including Pollard, were left alive when rescued by the American whaler *Dauphin* on February 23.

All the survivors of the *Essex* returned to Nantucket. Perhaps the islanders decided that the men had suffered enough, for none of the surviving crew members of the *Essex* appears to have been censured for their conduct (including cannibalism and homicide) in the drifting boats.

Captain Pollard took command of another whaling vessel. After a second shipwreck in the Pacific, he returned to dry land and stayed there for the rest of his life. Owen Chase became a whaling captain himself but eventually quit whaling because of poor health. In later life, he allegedly suffered from serious mental illness that included a fear of starving to death.

***Estonia,* Estonian car/passenger ferry** More than 900 people were killed when the ferry *Estonia* sank in the Baltic Sea on September 28, 1994, in strong winds and high seas.

***Eurydice,* British frigate** *Eurydice* was serving as a training ship when it capsized in a storm and sank off the Isle of Wight on March 24, 1878, killing some 400 people. Only two survivors were reported. The storm arose suddenly and appears to have sunk the ship within several minutes. Observers on shore saw the storm sweep over *Eurydice*. When the storm had passed, the ship had vanished. Later, it was learned that ports on the main deck had been opened to let air into the mess. When the storm hit *Eurydice,* water entered through the open ports, and the ship capsized.

***Eurydice,* French submarine** *Eurydice* appears to have exploded while submerged on a voyage between St. Tropez, France, and Toulon, France, on March 4, 1970. The submarine's whole complement of 57 men died in the wreck. The cause of the explosion is unknown.

See also EXPLOSIONS; SUBMARINES.

***Evening Star,* American passenger ship** A hybrid of steam and sail, *Evening Star* was a famous liner of its day and operated between New York and New Orleans. On either March 3 or October 3, 1866 (accounts differ on the date), *Evening Star* encountered heavy weather and foundered. Only nine people out of 270 on board survived.

excavation Shipwrecks in shallow water may be excavated to recover artifacts. Various methods and technologies are used for excavating wrecks. Artifacts

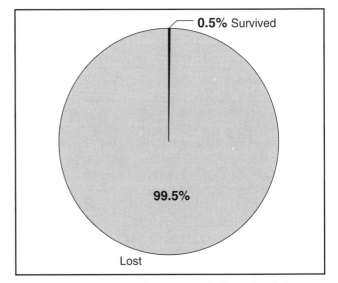

Survivors, British frigate *Eurydice*, 1878. (Nash, Jay Robert, *The Darkest Hour*, Prentice Hall, 1976)

may be sent to the surface in wire-mesh baskets or fuel drums. Divers may carry small bags with them for recovering and storing small articles.

One widely used excavation tool is the airlift, which uses compressed air forced into a metal tube to create suction and carry articles to the surface. The airlift is recommended for use on silty or muddy wreck sites. The airlift can direct sediments raised from the bottom away from the wreck site, thus improving visibility underwater. An airlift with a diameter of six inches or less is preferred, according to marine archeologist Robert Marx, because airlifts with larger diameters are hard to control and may result in damaged or lost articles. The airlift is akin to the hydrolift, a similar device that utilizes water pressure instead of air pressure to raise materials from the bottom.

Another tool for excavation is the prop-wash. Invented early in the 20th century to remove silt from oyster beds, the prop-wash consists of a metal tube, bent at a 90-degree angle, that fits over a ship's propeller and directs the propeller's wash downward. The propeller generates a "whirlpool" action that is highly effective at removing unconsolidated sediment, and even coral in some cases. A prop-wash may remove up an inch of sand per minute from a wreck. Controlling the device's speed is important, however, because an overly vigorous prop-wash may displace articles from the wreck as well as sediment. Marx writes that he once saw a powerful prop-wash blow a six-pound cannonball more than 50 feet from its initial location. The prop-wash's usefulness as an excavation tool was discovered in the early 1960s, when salvors working on a wreck in Florida waters tried using a prop-wash to carry clear surface water down to the bottom in order to improve visibility. The salvors found that the prop-wash was highly effective in excavating the site. The effective depth of a prop-wash is a function of its diameter and the maximum velocity of the propeller. A large prop-wash may be able to excavate a large hole at a depth of 50 feet.

Water jets (water hoses for underwater use) and air jets (which operate on the same principle, but use air instead of water) may be used to remove sediment from a wreck.

The difficulty of excavating a wreck varies greatly from one site to another. Some wrecks are easily accessible, whereas others may lie buried under coral, which is extremely difficult to remove.

Marx emphasizes the importance of systematic operation and of keeping records properly while working on an excavation. Such careful work can avoid confusion later.

See also ARCHAEOLOGY.

excursion ships   These passenger vessels were popular in the 19th and early 20th centuries for pleasure trips before modern highways and the automobile made land transportation much easier. Excursion ships were commonly used to carry large numbers of passengers short distances—perhaps 10 or 20 miles—on pleasure trips.

In some cases, excursion ships were given to top-heaviness because of tall superstructures needed to give passengers space to walk on deck. Instability could be a problem, as in the case of the American steamer *Eastland,* which capsized at its dock with great loss of life.

Because so many passengers could crowd onto a single excursion ship, a fire or collision could result in tremendous loss of life, as occurred when the American excursion ship *General Slocum* burned and the British excursion vessel *Princess Alice* was rammed and sunk by a collier.

See also EASTLAND; GENERAL SLOCUM; PRINCESS ALICE.

explosions   Explosive cargoes and fuels have caused many shipwrecks. Cargoes such as gunpowder, coal, oil and petroleum products, alcohol and even grain may explode and cause enough destruction to sink a vessel. Explosions from various fuels may bring about the complete loss of a ship. Tankers in particular have been subject to such explosions, which in some cases have both demolished the ship and spread pollution and destruction throughout the immediate vicinity. Other explosive events have occurred when cold water came into contact with the hot boilers of a steam-propelled vessel. The ship's chance of sur-

Fire often accompanies explosions. Shown here is the S.S. *Sansenina*, which exploded, burned and sank in Los Angeles Harbor in 1976. (U.S. Coast Guard)

viving an explosion without loss of life depends on various factors including the force and location of the explosion; the character of the explosive material; the construction (materials and design) of the vessel; the preparedness of its master and crew; and the ship's nearness to shore and/or to qualified assistance.

explosives   Deteriorated explosives on warships could pose as great a threat as enemy guns. After long periods in storage, explosives could become unstable and extremely dangerous. Among ship losses

Explosions can rip a vessel apart. The burning object in the background is part of a deck structure that was blasted off the ship in the foreground and landed on an oil company terminal dock.

attributed to deteriorated explosives are the Japanese warship *Mikasa,* destroyed in a dockyard in 1905; the British battleship *Bulwark,* which exploded off Sheerness in 1914, with only 12 survivors; the German light cruiser *Karlsruhe* in 1914; and the Japanese cruiser *Tsukuba* in 1918. The destruction of the Japanese battleship *Kawachi* in 1918 and the Italian battleship *Leonardo da Vinci* in 1915 has also been attributed to unstable powder.

See also "B" POWDER; EXPLOSIONS; KAWACHI; LIBERTÉ.

Express, American steamship The Potomac Transportation Line's steamship *Express* was wrecked in a storm on Chesapeake Bay (Maryland-Virginia) on October 23, 1878, on a trip from Baltimore to Washington, D.C.

The ship left Baltimore on the afternoon of October 22 and encountered no problems with the weather until around midnight. Then the wind picked up, and in a couple of hours had reached gale velocity. Large waves began to batter the ship and wash over the deck. Then the wind intensified still further.

The captain found himself facing unattractive options. West of him was an uninviting shoreline of cliffs, while to his east lay dangerous shoals.

The best plan, he decided, was to make for shelter at Hooper's Straits on the bay's Eastern Shore. That was many miles away, however, and the ship did not complete the trip.

An enormous wave struck *Express* and put out the fires under the boilers. The ship was powerless now, and soon lost much of its upper deck to another wave. Then *Express* rolled over.

The survivors clung to whatever they could find that would float. The ship's quartermaster had an especially dreadful experience while awaiting rescue, writes Donald Shomette in his history *Shipwrecks on the Chesapeake.*

Drifting with assorted wreckage including barrels of oil, the quartermaster saw a schooner approach and stop nearby. Evidently the men on the schooner saw him but did not care enough to pick him up. They hauled aboard the barrels of oil and other cargo from the wreck, then departed, leaving the quartermaster adrift. Eventually, another passing schooner saved him.

Sixteen people on *Express* were killed, and 15 survived. The storm also damaged numerous other ships on Chesapeake Bay.

Exxon Valdez, oil tanker One of the largest oil spills in United States history occurred on March 24, 1989, when the tanker *Exxon Valdez* struck a rock in Prince William Sound, Alaska, and lost 11 million gallons of crude oil.

F

F-4, American submarine The tragic loss of *F-4* (also known as *SS 23* or *Skate*) on March 15, 1915, was the first submarine loss in the United States Navy. The submarine sank in about 300 feet of water off Oahu, Hawaii, while running submerged. The sub was designed for a maximum depth of 200 feet.

At first, the Navy hoped that some of the crew might have survived, and made preparations for rescue. Two divers went down to 190 feet and later to 215 feet, but saw no sign of the sunken vessel. Air bubbles and an oil slick on the surface were attributed to *F-4*.

An initial attempt to raise the sub by passing a sling around it was unsuccessful. The next attempt involved sweeping a wire under the submarine and trying to bring it up to the surface. This effort also failed. It now was clear that the submarine was full of water, and no one on board was left alive.

Although rescue was no longer an option, the Navy was determined to recover the submarine to see what caused the sinking. Using a pair of scows and a lifting apparatus, the salvors moved *F-4* into shallow water by a series of short lifts. Although poor weather complicated the job, *F-4* rested in less than 50 feet of water by May 25. Pontoons then were attached for buoyancy, and *F-4* made a final journey to a dry dock in Honolulu. (Pontoons would become an important element of later submarine salvage jobs.)

An examination of the wreck showed that battery acid had eaten through rivets, and water had leaked in through the rivet holes. This finding resulted in design modifications for American submarines.

This operation demonstrated how difficult it was for divers to work at the depth of the sunken submarine. One diver reportedly felt no weariness while on the bottom but collapsed after returning to the surface and was unable to work again for days.

See also PONTOONS; SUBMARINES.

falconete grande A curious cannon, contemporaneous with the verso, the wrought-iron falconete grande resembled the verso but had a very long barrel of unusual construction, with alternating bands and sleeves. The *falconete grande* is thought to have been more than 10 feet long. An example of the *falconete grande,* though poorly preserved, was raised from the Bahia Mujeres wreck off the Yucatán Peninsula in Mexico.

See also BAHIA MUJERES WRECK; CANNON; VERSO.

Falkland Islands A remote group of islands in the South Atlantic Ocean near South America, the Falklands provided a much-needed shelter and source of provisions for ships making their way around stormy Cape Horn, at the extreme southern tip of South America. A ship that experienced severe storm damage while going around the Cape, but managed to remain afloat, might make its way back to the Falklands for repairs. A celebrated clipper ship, *Snow Squall,* did exactly that after being caught in a gale and driven ashore in the Straits of Le Maire near Cape Horn in 1864.

See also SNOW SQUALL; STORMS.

fathom A unit of depth measurement, one fathom is commonly interpreted as equivalent to six feet. In practice, however, the fathom's exact value varied considerably during the age of sail. Mariners defined it, for working purposes, as the span of a man's outstretched arms. A large man's armspan was considerably greater than a small man's, and thus one man's "fathom" might be as much as a foot longer or shorter than another's. In this work, the standard six-foot value is used.

Felicidad, Spanish schooner Captain José de Castillo lost *Felicidad* in Veracruz, Mexico, in 1808 when the ship exploded after being struck by lightning.

Fern Glen, British vessel Not all wrecks occur in fog or storms. Sometimes a wreck takes place in splendid weather, on a starry night. Such was the case with *Fern Glen,* an 818-tonner that ran ashore on Clatsop Spit at the Columbia River bar (Oregon-Washington) early on the morning of October 16, 1881, on the way to Portland, Oregon, to take on a load of grain. The ship's master mistook the light at Tillamook Rock on the Oregon coast for another at nearby Point Adams, and shipwreck was the result. The weather changed for the worse soon after *Fern Glen* went ashore, but the crewmen managed to escape in a lifeboat and were picked up by a tug.

ferries   Designed to carry passengers and cargo on regular service over short distances, ferries have experienced numerous wrecks, many as a result of heavy weather. Collisions may be a particular danger if the ferry operates in heavily traveled waters such as a harbor. Also, a ferry typically has numerous openings, such as access doors for automobiles, that can admit large amounts of water in rough weather unless secured carefully. Many injuries and fatalities are possible in ferry wrecks, because ferries can carry large numbers of passengers.

See also HERALD OF FREE ENTERPRISE; KIANGYA; STELLA.

1591 fleet   According to English records, a 75-ship Spanish fleet that left Havana for Spain in 1591 was beset by numerous storms, and at least 29 ships in the fleet were lost. Many of them sank off the Florida coast. The ships had no treasure on board.

See also FLORIDA.

***Figogna,* Italian bark**   The United States Lifesaving Service during the late 19th century had to contend not only with foul weather and heavy seas, but sometimes also with language barriers and catastrophic misunderstandings.

An outstanding example of those last two problems was the wreck of the Italian bark *Figogna* at Virginia Beach, Virginia, on the morning of February 27, 1883. *Figogna* was on the way from Parma, Italy, to Baltimore, Maryland, carrying iron ore.

The lifesavers at the Little Island station saw the bark anchored offshore in about 36 feet of water, and the surfmen rowed out to *Figogna.* None of the ship's crew spoke English. After labored and unsuccessful attempts to communicate with the Italians, the surfmen learned at last that the ship was leaking seriously.

The keeper of the Little Island station thought his men should go to work at the pumps to remove water from the bark's hold, but the Italian captain—thinking the Americans might be salvage men, and afraid of

losing authority over his ship—would not let them start pumping.

The lifesavers contacted the Italian consul in Norfolk, and soon the consul's office sent a telegram saying that a salvage ship was on the way. The lifesavers went back to the bark.

The captain must have had a change of heart, for the Americans were allowed to help with pumping until after sundown. Then the surfmen returned to shore in their boat, only to return again the next morning and find the bark sinking. The water had almost reached the level of the deck.

Something had to be done and quickly. The Italian captain was so protective of his authority, however, that he declined all offers of assistance and ordered everyone except his crew to leave the ship.

At this point, winds began blowing the vessel out to sea. The American lifesavers remained close by in their boat, in case they had to rescue the Italians.

Later that day, the Italians abandoned *Figogna* in their own boats, still refusing the American lifesavers' offers of aid. The captain and mate stayed on the bark until the ship showed unmistakable signs of going down. Hastily, the captain and mate were taken off *Figogna,* which then sank about 10 miles off the Little Island station.

The bark's loss was probably preventable. With the lifesavers' help, *Figogna* most likely could have been saved. The captain's distrust and fear of sacrificing his authority, however, destroyed the ship as effectively as a fire or explosion.

The suspicions of *Figogna*'s captain may have been mild compared to those of some foreign visitors to the United States. Foreigners in American waters sometimes had peculiar notions about the United States and its customs. As late as 1889, for example, some Britons appeared to think the American mainland was inhabited by cannibals who would devour shipwrecked sailors.

See also WINGATE.

fire   Risk of fire has proven almost impossible to eliminate entirely. In the days before iron and steel hulls, ships were made almost entirely of wood, cloth and other flammable materials, and the complete destruction of ships by fire was commonplace. One notable tragedy in this category was the loss of the British passenger steamer *Amazon* in 1852. Even the adoption of metal hulls did not reduce the risk of fire as much as one might have expected, because ships continued to use large amounts of flammable material in their construction, and because such ships carried large amounts of fuel for the engines that propelled them. The burning of the liner *Morro Castle* off the

Wrecks of passenger liners are widely publicized. (U.S. Coast Guard)

New Jersey coast in 1934, for example, demonstrated how destructive fire could be, even in modern ships of predominantly metal construction. In at least one case, the design and building of the American passenger liner *United States*, fire prevention measures were taken to such lengths that the only wooden objects on board were said to be a piano and a chef's chopping block, and even pictures on stateroom walls were executed with non-flammable paints.

See also AMAZON; MORRO CASTLE.

fishing fleet, Columbia River, Oregon-Washington Some 200 fishermen drowned when a fleet of small fishing boats suddenly encountered gale-force winds from the southwest while sailing off the Columbia River mouth on May 4, 1880. The boats were overturned and sunk.

***Florence*, American munitions ship** Sunk off Quiberon, France, in 1917 by a German time bomb, *Florence* sank in shallow water and presented a hazard to navigation. So, the French government arranged with an Italian salvage firm, the Society for Maritime Recovery (SORIMA), to destroy the wreck with explosives. The job was difficult and dangerous, because the wreck still contained hundreds of tons of unexploded munitions. SORIMA's ship *Artiglio* was destroyed, with the loss of 12 of 19 crewmen, when the munitions on the wreck exploded on December 7, 1930. The munitions went off following the explosion of the last charge meant to demolish the wreck. This huge explosion created a column of water 600 feet high that

landed on *Artiglio* and sank the salvage vessel at once. The company replaced the lost ship almost immediately with a new craft, *Artiglio II*. Both *Artiglio* and *Artiglio II* were involved in salvage operations on the British liner *Egypt*.

See also EGYPT.

Florida For a variety of reasons, Florida has had numerous shipwrecks. Florida waters are strewn with hazardous shoals and reefs; hurricanes occur often; and during the three centuries of the flota system, Spanish treasure fleets passed Florida on a regular basis. Selected wrecks in Florida waters include the following.

In 1525, a caravel belonging to a Spanish expedition was lost in the vicinity of Cape St. Helen. Native Americans are believed to have killed all the 200 survivors of the wreck.

Twenty years later, in 1545, another, unidentified vessel reportedly was wrecked somewhere on the Florida coast, and natives are thought to have killed some of the 200 crew members and made slaves of the rest.

In 1567, Spaniards exploring Tampa Bay and vicinity found a Portuguese trader who, after emerging as the lone survivor of a shipwreck, had been taken prisoner by natives, who had killed everyone else from the ship.

A massacre reportedly followed the wreck of two vessels lost in a storm off Cape Canaveral in 1571 or 1572. As survivors of the wrecks were making their way overland to St. Augustine, natives allegedly slaughtered them.

A rum-laden vessel was destroyed by an unusual cause in 1768 while passing through the Florida Straits. Lightning set the ship on fire, and the ship burned completely, with the loss of all lives on board.

See also ALMIRANTA DE HONDURAS; AVILES WRECK; BAY OF SANTA MARIA WRECKS; FLORIDA KEYS; GULF OF FLORIDA WRECKS; PUERTO ESCONDIDO WRECK; SANTA CATALINA.

Florida Keys Shipwrecks have been numerous in the waters surrounding the Florida Keys, a chain of small islands extending southwest from the southern tip of Florida. The Keys are surrounded by dangerous reefs and shoals, and severe weather occurs there frequently. For anyone interested in working on shipwrecks, however, the Keys offer a splendid environment, including warm waters and good underwater visibility.

See also FLORIDA.

flota system This convoy system was established by Spain in the mid-1500s to transport cargoes to and from the New World. Two separate convoys, or flotas (fleets) of vessels would leave Spain each year. Each flota included four well-armed galleons of 300 tons each or more, plus two pataches (smaller vessels) of 80 tons, and perhaps several dozen merchant ships, or naos. One flota sailed in the spring and the other in early autumn.

The flotas, as a rule, would put in first at Martinique or Guadeloupe in the Caribbean, then divide into separate groups with different destinations. Some ships would proceed to Cuba, Hispaniola, Honduras, Jamaica, Mexico and Puerto Rico. The galleons and pataches would accompany ships bound for Nuevo Reino de Granada (now Colombia), Venezuela and the Isthmus of Panama. The galleons would stop at two ports—Cartageña and Nombre de Dios—before sailing for Havana. At Havana, the warships would wait for ships from the various Spanish colonies to gather before accompanying the fleet back to Spain. One great weakness of this arrangement was that many vessels were left without the warships' protection after the fleet split up on reaching the Caribbean. Those ships were left defenseless against pirates.

A new system was introduced in 1564. Two armed galleons and two pataches accompanied each of the two fleets that left Spain each year. The New Spain Fleet left Spain in the spring, and the Tierra Firme Flota in the autumn. The bigger galleon in each flota was called the *capitana* and served as flagship. The smaller galleon was known as the *almiranta*. Ships bound for Honduras and the Greater Antilles would accompany the New Spain Flota. Hazardous weather in the Gulf of Mexico between October and February forced the flotas to spend the winters at Veracruz, Mexico, before sailing home in late winter or early spring.

The Tierra Firme Fleet would leave Spain in August or thereabouts and spend the winter in Cartagena after taking on treasure at Nombre de Dios. In January, the fleet would return to Spain and might join the New Spain Fleet along the way for the voyage home.

Later, the Spaniards added a third fleet, known as the Tierra Firme Armada or the Silver Fleet. This fleet was assigned exclusively to transporting treasure and consisted of several galleons and pataches. These ships were about 600 tons on the average, although some galleons in the Silver Fleet might attain 1,000 tons. The Silver Fleet was heavily armed and carried hundreds of marines. Under the three-fleet system, the Tierra Firme Fleet sailed in March (about the same time as the Silver Fleet), and the New Spain Fleet departed from Spain in May or June.

Although the flota system was organized to provide protection against pirates and other dangers, many ships in the Spanish treasure fleets were lost to hazards including storms, grounding, poor navigation and fire. Shipwreck was the greatest threat to the fleet. Very few ships were lost in mid-ocean because the weather there was generally favorable, and there was no danger of running aground in deep water. In the Indies, however, hurricanes, reefs and shoals multiplied the dangers to the vessels.

The eastward voyage from the West Indies to Spain was generally more hazardous than the westward trip from Spain. On the previous leg of the voyage and during the prolonged stay in the Caribbean, ships had their hulls weakened by teredos, or shipworms, boring molluscs that destroyed timbers. Also, the route homeward took the ships past many hazardous reefs.

See also GALLEON; NAO; REEFS; TEREDOS; TREASURE.

Flying Dutchman A famous example of maritime lore of the supernatural, the story of the Flying Dutchman has been popular for almost 200 years and exists in many different versions. They all involve, however, the story of a ship and sailor condemned to sail the seas forever, or at least until some intervention sets him free.

According to one version of the legend, the Dutchman was a captain named van Straaten who made the error of trying to sail around the dangerous Cape of Good Hope, at Africa's southern tip, in stormy weather. In this version, the ship was wrecked and its crew was killed, but the vessel and men were forced to sail their ship through the afterlife, always on the same spot of ocean where they were wrecked. In another variation on the legend, the captain's name was von Falkenberg.

German poet Heinrich Heine wrote his own version of the Flying Dutchman legend, *Memoirs of Herr von Schnabelwopski*, in which the captain is permitted to go ashore once every seven years to try to attain his freedom by winning the hand of a maiden. This version of the story provided the basis for German composer Richard Wagner's early opera *Der fliegende Hollander*. In Wagner's version, the captain was named van Derdeeken.

The apparition of the Dutchman's ship has been reported seen repeatedly at night in the waters off the Cape of Good Hope. The ship is described as carrying no navigational lights, but nonetheless luminous. The apparition allegedly approaches within perhaps half a mile of another vessel, then disappears.

Although the legend of the Flying Dutchman may be pure imagination or the result of hallucination, the story may have its origins in some natural phenomenon such as lightning or static electricity, which could produce a glow reminiscent of a spectral sailing vessel.

See also APPARITIONS; MYTHOLOGY; ST. ELMO'S FIRE; SUPERNATURAL EVENTS.

***Flying Enterprise*, American freighter** *Flying Enterprise* encountered heavy weather on a voyage from Hamburg, Germany, to the United States in December 1951. On December 28, off Land's End, England, the ship developed a 30-degree list to port. All passengers and crew except the captain were taken off the ship. By January 2, the list had increased to 80 degrees; thus the ship was, in effect, lying on its side. After a tug's mate went on board, the ship was taken in tow toward Falmouth, but the line parted, and the ship sank on January 10. Just before the ship sank, the captain and tug's mate walked down the funnel and onto the tug.

fog A cloud lying directly atop the water, fog has played a significant role in many shipwrecks. Fog reduces visibility and thus increases the risk of collisions between ships as well as navigational errors that cause ships to run onto rocks or shoals, or into icebergs. The danger from fog has been especially great in waters off the northeastern United States and Canada's maritime provinces, where high humidity and temperature differences between air and water can produce thick fog. Even relatively light haze can reduce visibility significantly. Modern technologies such as radar and satellite fixes have reduced the danger

from fog by making more accurate navigation possible, but this particular threat has not yet been eliminated entirely.

foghorn A sound generator, the foghorn has been widely used on ships for decades to produce an audible warning signal during conditions of reduced visibility. The familiar foghorn signal is a bass tone similar to that produced by air horns on locomotives.

food The saying that an army travels on its stomach might be applied to navies and individual ships as well. In the age of sail, when a vessel might be out of sight of land for months or even years at a time, what the crew ate might make the difference between health and debility; shipwreck and success. Considering what Spanish sailors had to eat during the centuries of the flota system, it is surprising the sailors and ships fared as well as they did. Robert Marx, in his book *Shipwrecks in the Americas,* lists daily rations for crews of galleons and merchant naos as follows: two pounds of biscuit, one quart of water and one quart of wine. Four days per week, each man was given eight ounces of dried fish and two ounces of beans or peas. The remaining three days of the week, the men each received 1.5 ounces of rice and eight ounces of salt pork. There was also a small weekly ration of cheese, olive oil and vinegar. The crews caught fresh fish at sea to supplement this Spartan diet. Note the absence of fresh fruit, which can provide vitamin C, which is an "antiscorbutic," or scurvy-preventing

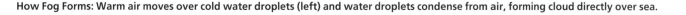

How Fog Forms: Warm air moves over cold water droplets (left) and water droplets condense from air, forming cloud directly over sea.

agent. The absence of foods rich in vitamin C accounted for numerous cases of scurvy on ships during long voyages.

See also FLOTA SYSTEM; NAO; SCURVY.

fore Toward the bow, or nose, of a ship. The opposite of fore is aft, meaning toward the rear or stern of a vessel.

See also AFT; BOW.

fore-and-aft Parallel to a ship's length. A ship "rigged fore-and-aft" had sails carried on a stay or gaff, as distinct from a "square-rigged" vessel. Schooners and sloops are familiar examples of vessels rigged fore-and-aft.

See also SCHOONER; SLOOP; SQUARE-RIGGED.

forecastle Sometimes called the "fo'c'sle" for short, the forecastle consists of the upper deck in the front of a ship. The forecastle commonly provides a place for the crew to sleep and eat. Quarters in the forecastle can be decidedly uncomfortable in heavy weather, as waves may make the ship pitch and cause the forecastle to rise and fall many feet at a time. The forecastle also can be a vulnerable point in collisions between ships.

See also COLLISIONS.

Forfarshire, British coastal steamer Of 63 people on board, 45 were killed when *Forfarshire* was wrecked in a storm on rocks at Harkers on a voyage from Hull, England, to Dundee, Scotland, on September 7, 1838.

Forrestal, American aircraft carrier *Forrestal* was launching aircraft for strikes against North Vietnam on July 29, 1967, when fire broke out on the carrier. The fire killed 134 men and destroyed 25 fighter aircraft. The fire reportedly began when a fuel tank dropped from an aircraft preparing for takeoff. Bomb explosions left holes in the flight deck. Many of the men killed in this incident reportedly died when they leaped off the flight deck to avoid being burned by advancing flames.

See also FIRE.

foundering The condition in which a vessel sinks after taking on large amounts of water, as in a storm at sea.

See also CAUSES OF SHIPWRECKS.

France, French battleship *France* struck Basse-Nouvelle reef off Quiberon, France, and sank on the night of August 25–26, 1922. Of 900 people on board, only one was lost.

Franklin, American steamship A notable case of successful lifesaving efforts, the wreck of the paddlewheel steamer *Franklin* occurred on July 17, 1854, at Westhampton Beach on Long Island, New York. A gale was blowing, and there was heavy fog. Under the command of Captain James Wooten, *Franklin* struck the outer bar some 400 yards from the beach. Although Wooten had anchors put out in an attempt to keep the ship from drifting onto the beach, the chains broke, and *Franklin* was driven ashore. Wooten appears to have responded coolly and responsibly to the crisis. He had his men reassure the passengers and told all on board to put on life jackets. The first mate began firing *Franklin*'s signal gun to let people on shore know that the ship was in distress. A number of small boats with volunteer crews put out to the ship. Townspeople also responded and waited on the beach to rescue survivors. Because of Wooten's calm, professional response to the crisis, and because local residents came to the rescue, everyone on *Franklin* was rescued.

Franklin expedition, British Explorer Sir John Franklin's expedition to the Arctic in 1845 ended in the destruction of his two ships and the total loss of his 129-man crew. The loss of Franklin's ships and men exercised on the English-speaking world a fascination that is probably unequaled by any other maritime catastrophe, with the possible exception of the sinking of the British liner *Titanic* in 1912. Perhaps no other maritime tragedy has done more than the Franklin expedition to encourage exploration of the polar regions.

Franklin and his men aimed to find the Northwest Passage, a rumored sea route through the Arctic regions of North America between the Atlantic and Pacific oceans. Such a passage seemed possible, because what we know as the Canadian Arctic, though then largely unexplored, was thought (correctly) to be an archipelago. It was conceivable, then, that a passage of clear water might be found amid the archipelago's ice. Earlier expeditions, notably those of 16th-century British voyager Martin Frobisher and 17th-century Danish explorer Jens Munk, had tried but failed to find the Northwest Passage. Munk's 1619–1620 voyage ended in tragedy. Sixty-one of 64 men with him died of cold and scurvy; only Munk and two of his companions managed to return home in one of the expedition's ships.

Franklin thought prospects for finding the Northwest Passage looked better in the mid-19th century, given adequate vessels and provisions. The vessels on his expedition were *Erebus* and *Terror*, three-masted sailing ships that already had served in the Antarctic under Sir James Clark Ross between 1839 and 1843. *Erebus* and *Terror* had been strengthened for protection in icy waters and appeared well-suited for another polar voyage. Ross himself was offered command of the expedition to find the Northwest Passage but declined. So, command of the expedition went to Franklin.

Franklin had had a distinguished military career. He joined the Royal Navy at age 14, participated in combat during the Napoleonic wars and was present at Trafalgar. After Napoleon's defeat, the British Navy had to look for new exploits and chose to specialize in Arctic exploration. Franklin was involved here too, and served in 1818 as second-in-command during a voyage to Spitzbergen, Norway, with Captain David Buchan.

Franklin also participated in an 1819 expedition to North America, to sail from Hudson's Bay north into the polar ocean and map the Arctic coast of Canada. On this voyage, prefiguring what would happen to his final Arctic expedition, Franklin lost 10 men to hunger and cold, partly because of his limited knowledge of conditions in the Arctic. Franklin himself came close to starving on this journey, which reportedly included incidents of murder and cannibalism.

Despite the alleged horrors of this expedition, Franklin was promoted to captain and returned to the Arctic in 1825–1827. On this voyage, he mapped hundreds of miles of coastline. Afterward, he was knighted for this achievement. He went on to serve in Australia for six years as governor of Van Diemen's Land (now Tasmania) before taking command of his final expedition to the Arctic.

Erebus and *Terror* underwent extensive renovations for the 1845 voyage. Their bows were plated with iron for increased strength. A new heating system was installed, and whole steam locomotives were installed in the holds for emergency use. The locomotives were fitted with screw propellers. In addition to everything else, the ships were loaded with food, fuel and other provisions sufficient to last three years.

Just before Franklin sailed for the Arctic, he was ill with influenza. His wife, Lady Jane Franklin, placed a Union Jack over his legs to keep him warm. Franklin was horrified. "Don't you know that they lay the Union Jack over a corpse?" he said.

The expedition sailed down the Thames River and toward the Arctic on May 19, 1845. By the end of July, Franklin and his men were in the Arctic, at Baffin Bay. Two whaling vessels, *Prince of Wales* and *Enterprise*, encountered *Erebus* and *Terror* there while Franklin waited for suitable conditions to cross the bay. Franklin's ships were secured to an iceberg on which his men had set up an observatory. The captain of *Prince of Wales* reported finding the expedition well. The whalers' visit was the last contact Franklin and his men would have with the outside world.

Franklin did not return. By late 1847, the Admiralty became worried and dispatched three expeditions— one to Lancaster Sound, another to Bering Strait and a third (traveling overland) to the Mackenzie River— to search for Franklin and his men. None of these three expeditions discovered a trace of the Franklin expedition.

The British government next offered a hefty reward of £20,000 to anyone who could and would "render efficient assistance" to Franklin and his men. An additional £10,000 was promised to anyone who proved capable of relieving the Franklin crews or even providing information contributing to relieving them.

Many ships were searching the Arctic for Franklin by the latter half of 1850. Americans as well as Britons joined the search. One expedition discovered on Victoria Island pieces of wood that might have come from *Erebus* and *Terror*, but no positive identification was possible.

The first breakthrough came on August 23, 1850, when H.M.S. *Assistance*, under command of Captain Erasmus Ommanney, discovered traces of the Franklin party on Devon Island. Here at last was solid evidence, in the form of clothing, empty tins that once contained preserved meat, and other debris.

Later, on nearby Beechey Island, a cairn, or pile of rocks, was discovered. The cairn appeared to indicate that Franklin and his men, or at least some party of Europeans, had assembled it. The cairn contained no documents or other information, however, that might indicate the whereabouts of the Franklin expedition.

The search now focused on the area around Beechey Island. More evidence of Franklin's crew turned up at Cape Spencer on Devon Island. A stone hut was discovered there, along with other evidence including more food tins, items of clothing and pieces of newspapers printed in September of 1845.

On August 27, the graves of three of Franklin's men—William Braine and John Hartnell of *Erebus*, and John Torrington of *Terror*—were discovered on Beechey Island. Dates on the headboards showed that all three men died early in 1846. The graves and other evidence found on Beechey Island showed that Franklin's men apparently had passed the winter of 1845–1846 there. The cause of death for the three men was not immediately apparent, but scurvy and spoiled tinned meat were suspected.

By the time the graves were discovered, hope was diminishing that Franklin and any of his men might be found alive in the Arctic. Nonetheless, more expeditions departed in search of him. Lady Jane Franklin waged a tireless campaign to find her husband. A popular song called "Lord Franklin" referred to her efforts:

> In Baffin's Bay where the whale-fish blow,
> The fate of Franklin no man may know. . . .
> Ten thousand pounds I would freely give,
> To say on earth that my Franklin lives.

Rumors emanating from the Arctic were not encouraging. The *Toronto Globe* of October 23, 1854, carried a report that Franklin had died of starvation. The paper's source was John Rae, an experienced Arctic explorer who claimed to have heard from the native Inuit people that Franklin's ships had been crushed in the ice, and that the men had died in large numbers on an overland journey during which survivors ate the bodies of the dead.

Rae informed the Admiralty that his discoveries resolved "beyond a doubt" that Franklin's expedition had perished. Rae acquired from the Inuit various items from the Franklin expedition, including one of Franklin's decorations. Despite Rae's testimony, which was second-hand, questions remained about what had happened to Franklin and his men.

The British government at this time was involved in the Crimean War and decided against using its resources on any additional expeditions to find Franklin. Other, privately organized expeditions continued to travel to the Arctic in search of Franklin, however, and eventually turned up more conclusive evidence of his party's loss, including skeletons of expedition members and a written statement, dictated by Captain F. R. M. Crozier, that Franklin had died on June 11, 1847. The note was found in a cairn and dated April 25, 1848.

When Crozier composed his note, the ships were trapped in ice near King William Island, and the expedition already had lost nine officers and 15 enlisted men. The rest of the expedition evidently perished in an overland march.

Franklin was hailed in England as a tragic hero. The British public reacted later with revulsion and outrage when reports reached Europe that members of Franklin's hungry party evidently had practiced cannibalism on their deceased comrades during the overland march. (Evidence of knife marks on bones indicated that these reports were accurate.)

Forensic expeditions that visited Beechey Island in the 1980s disinterred the bodies of the three sailors buried there and took tissue samples for analysis. The bodies were found to be in good condition because of the cold environment, which retarded decay. The tissue samples contained extremely high levels of lead, which may have contributed to the deaths of the three men and to the failure of the expedition. Sources of lead were numerous on Franklin's ships, notably the meat tins, which were soldered carelessly and exposed the contents to lead contamination from the solder. Lead poisoning would have made the men ill and possibly affected their judgment.

See also POLAR REGIONS.

freeboard The distance between the waterline and gunwale of a ship, freeboard may be an important factor in shipwrecks. Generally speaking, the smaller the freeboard, the more likely the ship is to founder. Some early ironclads capsized and were lost in part because of very low freeboard.

See also CAPTAIN; MONITOR.

frieze of Phidias One of the stranger tales of shipwreck and salvage involves the frieze of Phidias taken from the Parthenon in Athens, Greece. In 1802, when Greece was at war with the Turks, the British diplomat Thomas Bruce, earl of Elgin, decided to take the frieze and ship it to Britain (supposedly for safekeeping). Bruce had sections of the frieze loaded aboard the brig *Mentor*. The ship struck a reef near Kythera in a storm, however, and sank in 60 feet of water with the frieze aboard. Elgin tried repeatedly to have the artistic treasure recovered and finally succeeded with a team of divers from Samos. The frieze was concealed on shore and guarded there for two years until the sections could be shipped to England. Eventually, Elgin is believed to have made a handsome profit. According to one report, the frieze cost him £5,000, a figure that included the loss of the ship; he sold it to the British government for £35,000. The frieze is displayed in the British Museum.

frigate A three-masted naval vessel ranging between 750 and 1,400 tons, the frigate in the 18th century could carry as many as 64 guns. Nineteenth-century frigates increased dramatically in tonnage because of iron plating.

G

galleon Developed from the design of the shorter nao, the galleon emerged in the 16th century as a vehicle for maritime trade. The galleon had serious flaws including top-heaviness, however, and could be notably unseaworthy when loaded. Armed galleons with several decks of heavy guns were especially unstable. To overcome these shortcomings, Spanish Admiral Pedro Menendez de Aviles pushed for construction of ships called galeoncetes, which had longer keels and better sailing characteristics than galleons. Galleons and galeoncetes represented steps toward the development of frigates, the fast warships that played an important part in naval history in the 17th century.

General Slocum Though little noted today, the burning of the excursion steamer *General Slocum* in New York's East River on June 15, 1904, was a catastrophe, with 1,021 killed. Interpreters of the incident have placed much of the blame on Captain William Van Schaick, although responsibility for those deaths does not appear to be his alone.

Van Schaick was in command on that day, when *General Slocum* took on board an estimated 1,400 to 1,500 passengers near Throg's Neck in the Bronx, for a day-long school picnic. The ship left the pier around 9 A.M. On the way up the East River, in the vicinity of 130th Street, fire reportedly was discovered in a paint locker, although another account says the fire was found in a cabin filled with gasoline and other highly flammable materials. A third report says that a stove blew up. The steamer's wooden construction allowed the fire to spread rapidly.

Manhattan Island was only about 1,000 feet away, and the ship could have reached it easily. Yet Captain Van Schaick had the ship turned toward North Brother Island, much farther away. This decision gave the fire longer to spread, under the influence of a strong wind. Meanwhile, crew members who tried to put out the fire found the fire-fighting equipment inoperable.

Passengers gathered at the stern and were trapped there by the fire. Many of their life preservers reportedly had rotted and were torn apart as passengers fought over them. In any case, the efficacy of the life preservers must have been doubtful: according to one account, their manufacturer had placed metal bars inside them to bring them up to mandatory lawful weight!

Captain Van Schaick beached his ship on the rocks of North Brother Island, leaving the stern in some 30 feet of water—more than enough to drown many passengers who fell or jumped into the river from the stern. Tugs finally came near enough to the burning ship to rescue passengers. Although Van Schaick and other crew members were criticized later for their alleged failure to help save passengers, three crewmen were cited for responsible behavior and bravery in the face of great danger. Engineers Everett Brandow and George Conklin stayed at their posts as the ship burned around then; Brandow survived the wreck, but Conklin died. Crewman William Trembly rescued women and children from the water. According to one account, bodies lay so thick upon the water near

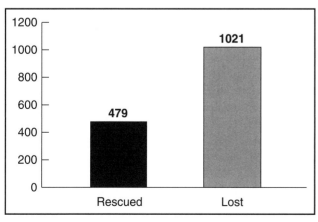

General Slocum, **passengers and crew.**

the steamer's bow that they formed a bridge of sorts, across which survivors could walk to shore.

General Slocum burned to the waterline. Only 407 were saved. Most of the dead were women and children. The destruction of the ship was dramatized later in a motion picture called *Manhattan Melodrama.*

Captain Van Schaick was charged with manslaughter and with failing to give his crew adequate training in lifesaving methods and fire prevention. Tried and convicted, he was sentenced to 10 years in prison but was pardoned in 1908. Although much of the responsibility for the loss of life on *General Slocum* does appear to have been the captain's, two New York City safety inspectors were fired after the wreck.

See also FIRE.

General Warren, American steamship Forty-two people were killed in the wreck of *General Warren* on Clatsop Spit, Oregon, on January 28, 1852. A well-appointed passenger ship, *General Warren* encountered heavy weather and large swells.

When a pilot came aboard at the Columbia River bar, he decided to wait until the weather improved before trying to make the crossing. The captain and passengers told the pilot that the ship might not stay afloat much longer. At last the pilot acceded to their requests and took the ship in, although he said he would not take responsibility for what might happen along the way.

The ship was taking on so much water that the captain ordered *General Warren* run aground. Soon the vessel started breaking up. Most of the lifeboats were smashed by the seas.

Several volunteers went ashore in the one remaining lifeboat to seek help. They reached nearby Astoria in three hours and reported *General Warren*'s plight to the master of the bark *George and Martha.*

A whaleboat with provisions and crew went out toward *General Warren*, but nothing was left of the passenger ship by the time the boat arrived. The seas had destroyed the ship totally. According to one report, the bodies of a young married couple were found on the beach later, still holding each other by the hand.

Genovesa, Spanish galleon The 54-gun galleon *Genovesa* was on a voyage from Cartagena, Colombia, to Havana when the ship was wrecked on a reef at Pedro Shoals, Jamaica. The ship is believed to have been carrying gold and silver worth more than three million pesos. The English frigate H.M.S. *Experiment* rescued survivors of the wreck and took aboard much of the galleon's treasure. Some of the treasure remained on the wreck and was buried by sand. Marine archaeologist Robert Marx, in his book *Shipwrecks in*

the Americas, writes that he has examined artifacts said to have been recovered from this wreck by treasure hunters and has determined that they came from another, later Spanish wreck in the vicinity of the *Genovesa* wreck.

See also JAMAICA.

George & Susan, American whaler Although *George & Susan* itself was not wrecked, Captain Ebenezer Nye had a harrowing adventure during a voyage on the ship in 1849. He and several other men from the vessel had fastened onto a dead whale near sundown and started towing the whale toward the ship. They lost sight of the whaler's lights in the darkness, however, and were lost in the vast Pacific Ocean.

Nye conferred with the other men in the boat, and they decided to try reaching the Marquesas Islands, some 2,000 miles away. Food and water soon ran out, but supplies were replenished unexpectedly one day when a porpoise leaped out of the sea and landed in the boat, where it was eaten by the hungry men.

After 15 days, one of the men went mad and jumped into the ocean. Another man killed himself in the same manner four days afterward. A third man jumped into the sea and died on the 20th day. Captain Nye and his two remaining companions came within sight of an island in the Marquesas group the following day. The boat drifted ashore. Almost too tired to move, Nye managed to crawl to a pool of fresh water on the island, drink some of the water to regain his strength and carry water back to the other men in the boat, using the only available container: his shoe. Friendly natives rescued Nye and his companions and took them to a nearby island, where the whalers regained their health. From there, Nye and his men went to Tahiti, where the captain took command of a schooner bound for San Francisco. The schooner capsized during the voyage, however, killing three men. Nye and five other survivors had to wait 22 days before an English merchant vessel picked them up and carried them to Hawaii. The men were able to survive because the schooner's hull remained afloat and contained adequate provisions. On his way back to the United States from this voyage, Nye spent a total of 44 days in open boats at sea.

ghost ships This category includes alleged apparitions of ships, as well as cases of actual vessels found abandoned at sea, for no apparent reason, in good condition. Among the most famous cases of apparitions is the story of the New Haven specter ship, which is said to have appeared off Connecticut after the presumed loss of a merchant vessel. Abandoned

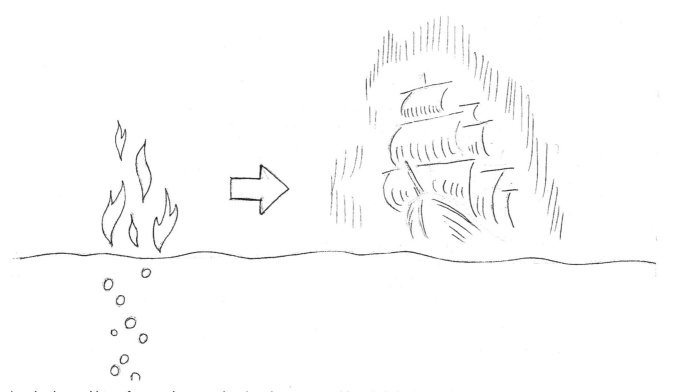

Imagination could transform methane gas, burning above water with eerie light, into a phantom ship (right). (D. Ritchie)

vessels that are considered "ghost ships" include the brig *Mary Celeste* and the schooner *Patriot.* Although bizarre speculation is often associated with reports of ghost ships, most such cases, if not all, can be explained by haste, changes in weather and negligence. It has been suggested, for example, that the *Mary Celeste* was left abandoned, sailing the seas unmanned, following the captain's failure to attach the lifeboat to the ship by a line when circumstances forced a hasty evacuation of the vessel.

See also DEERING; FLYING DUTCHMAN; MARY CELESTE; NEW HAVEN SPECTER SHIP; PATRIOT.

ghost wrecks As distinct from authentic wrecks, ghost wrecks are those that either exist only in the imagination or have had the facts of their cases distorted almost beyond recognition. Robert Marx, in the 1987 edition of his book *Shipwrecks of the Americas,* mentions that several groups of allegedly professional wreck hunters spent more than $100,000 seeking the wreck of a Spanish vessel that supposedly sank in 1656 in the Florida Keys. Marx writes that his research revealed the ship actually sank in the Bahamas.

See also DOCUMENTS; MYTHOLOGY; SALVAGE; TREASURE.

***Giambatista Primo,* Italian bark** Foreign crews in American waters during the late 19th century owed

much to the efforts of the U.S. Lifesaving Service. A case in point is the wreck of *Giambatista Primo,* a Genoese bark that ran onto shoals near the Hog Island lifesaving station on Virginia's Eastern Shore on October 22, 1880.

High winds and heavy surf prevented the lifesavers from launching their surfboat directly from the beach, so they hauled the boat to a nearby inlet and launched it there instead. The storm was so strong, however, that the men could row no farther than the inlet's mouth. The boat drifted onto the beach.

Meanwhile, the Italian vessel needed help urgently. The station keeper took three men with him and walked several miles south to the Cobb Island station and enlisted men there to help row.

Eventually, the lifesavers reached *Giambatista Primo* and rescued the crewmen, who were preparing to swim to a schooner anchored nearby. The Italians stayed at the Cobb Island station for two days and then were sent to Norfolk. The Virginia lifesavers even retrieved from the beach such of the Italians' clothing and personal effects as they could find, and sent the articles to the Italian consul in Norfolk. The ship itself was a complete loss.

***Glenmorag,* British sailing vessel** *Glenmorag*'s last voyage was eventful, to say the least. After leaving New York for Melbourne, Australia, on August 16,

1895, the three-masted vessel was imprisoned briefly in an ice field that came close to sinking the ship.

Glenmorag eventually made its way toward Astoria, Washington, and arrived off the Columbia River mouth on March 18, 1896. There, fog and lack of wind accomplished what the ice field could not. The becalmed ship drifted onto the beach at Ilwaco, Washington.

Glenmorag's stranding went unseen from shore because of the fog. Thus, the sailors had to attempt to rescue themselves. They lowered two boats. One reached shore safely, but the other boat was caught by the sea and smashed against the ship, killing two men. They were the only fatalities. Twenty-five others from the ship survived.

An attempt to refloat the ship was unsuccessful. Everything that could be removed from the wreck was stripped away, and the hull disappeared into the sands.

Gneisenau, German training corvette Thirty-eight men were drowned and 100 injured when *Gneisenau* sank in a storm at Malaga, Spain, on December 16, 1900.

gold The word "gold" is almost synonymous with shipwreck in some respects, because of rumors concerning treasure ships that supposedly sank with vast quantities of gold and silver on board. Such rumors especially surround Caribbean shipwrecks, because of the great amounts of gold and silver shipped eastward from Spain's colonies in the Americas during the days of the flota system.

Certain shipwrecks have indeed given up large quantities of gold in salvage operations. A well-known example of such operations involved H.M.S. *Edinburgh,* a gold-laden British cruiser sunk by a German submarine off the Russian port of Murmansk during World War II. Divers descended more than 800 feet to recover 431 gold bars from the cruiser's wreck. Would-be treasure hunters are cautioned, however, that the percentage of gold-bearing wrecks is actually small; the presence of gold may be mere rumor; someone else may have recovered the gold years or even centuries before; locating the wreck may be difficult, if not impossible; and, depending on the wreck's location, official permission may be required to conduct salvage operations.

"Pirate treasure," specifically chests full of gold and other loot buried on obscure islands for safekeeping, is a prominent element of maritime lore. The "treasure map" that supposedly marks the site of such buried wealth has become a symbol of get-rich-quick schemes. This legend, too, is largely imaginary. Bury-

ing treasure, in a primitive equivalent of a savings account, does not appear to have been part of the buccaneers' culture; any such loot was more likely to be spent than hoarded.

Goodwin Sands, England The shoals at Goodwin Sands, off the coast of Kent near Deal, have been the site of numerous wrecks, reportedly including a number of Spanish treasure galleons.

See also ROCKS AND SHOALS.

Gordon, Bruce, castaway, 18th century A colorful story of shipwreck involves one Bruce Gordon, also known as "the polar Crusoe" for his alleged adventures in the Arctic following the wreck of a whaling vessel in 1757.

According to a story published by maritime historian Edward Rowe Snow, Gordon sailed from Aberdeen, Scotland, in 1757 on the whaling ship *Anne Forbes,* bound for Greenland waters. The captain drank heavily, and his irresponsible behavior brought the ship into an ice field, where the vessel was crushed and sank rapidly. Gordon was the only survivor. The wreck returned to the surface the following day, upside down. Gordon gained entrance to the vessel and found a supply of biscuits. He then got drunk on the alcohol stores and slept.

On awakening, he heard what he thought were human voices outside the wreck. He investigated and found several polar bears devouring the remains of several men from the ship, including the captain. Gordon shouted at the bears in an effort to drive them away. Instead, they advanced on him. Gordon retreated and fortified the wreck against them. Then he dipped into the alcohol again and went to sleep.

The bears did not trouble Gordon again for a while. He collected supplies from within the ship and at last succeeded in building a fire. Before long, however, a bear forced its way into the cabin where Gordon was sleeping. Gordon was awakened by the noise of the bear eating his food supplies. He fell upon the animal with a knife and killed the bear with two stabs in the heart. He then skinned the animal and removed meat from its body. The skin he used for a rug.

The bear was a nursing female, and her cub, another female, was not far away. The hungry young bear showed up outside the wreck. Something in the cub's manner apparently touched Gordon's sympathies, for he let her enter. The cub allegedly reacted with joy at the sight of her mother's skin, but then became saddened on seeing that she was dead. Gordon felt sorry for the cub and offered her biscuits. The cub accepted them and became, in effect, Gordon's pet. He named her Nancy and fed her on frozen blubber. She allegedly became as tame as a domestic dog and kept him company through the Arctic winter.

When spring arrived, Gordon began making plans to return to civilization. He did not know his exact location, however, and therefore was unsure where the nearest land might lie. He prepared an observation post atop a nearby iceberg and even dug a cavern inside the iceberg, thinking he might retreat there for safety if and when the ice broke up and the wreck sank.

Soon the ice did begin breaking apart. Gordon found himself and the bear on a drifting mass of ice, which still encased the wreck. Nancy went fishing. Nancy's efforts, however, were not always helpful. When the iceberg drifted near land, and Gordon tried to draw the attention of a woman on the beach by shouting at her, Nancy let out such a terrifying roar that the woman fled.

After months of drifting, Gordon decided to make for land. With the bear in tow, he set out toward the south-southwest. Soon he found traces of men and dogs, and followed them to shore. He improvised a muzzle for the bear to keep her from attacking the dogs and men, should Gordon ever catch up with them.

Eventually, Gordon reached a small settlement and was told that he was in Greenland. The settlers were said to be the descendants of a Norwegian colony. Gordon and Nancy became part of the community. After several months, the bear disappeared, and Gordon never saw her again.

When Gordon heard news of whaling and sealing ships a few miles to the south, he said good-bye to his friends and set out by canoe. He was picked up by a Dutch vessel. Gordon was told that slightly more than seven years had passed since he had left Scotland. Several weeks later, Gordon was back in Scotland. His story was not widely believed at first, but in time his accurate reports of Arctic topography earned his tale a certain degree of acceptance.

See also CASTAWAYS.

Gowanburn, **British steamship**   Wrecking crews stood in considerable danger when trying to reach a stranded vessel, as the case of *Gowanburn* demonstrates. The 4,000-ton steamship went ashore in fog at the Blue Point lifesaving station on Fire Island, New York, on March 14, 1907. Lifesavers from several stations on shore came to the stranded ship's aid. By breeches buoy and lifeboat, they started hauling the steamer's Chinese crew to shore.

The following day, the tug *Rescue* arrived on the scene. The tug was part of a wrecking fleet sent to try to refloat the steamer. With the tug on the scene, the

lifesavers handed operations over to the wrecking team and went to have dinner.

The tug, however, was not suited for this particular situation. The men simply did not have the expertise to handle their boat (which was not the boat ordinarily used for such work, but another that had been acquired in New York) in the surf.

Despite rising seas, the crew of the boat made two trips successfully between the steamer and the tug. On the third trip, however, during an attempt to put a hawser aboard *Gowanburn*, a wave threw steersman Edward Johnsen into the water. As the remaining men in the boat tried to rescue Johnsen, they turned the boat broadside to the waves, and it began taking on large amounts of water. Frightened, the men abandoned Johnsen to the sea and rowed quickly for the beach.

Johnsen tried to swim for an oar that the boat had dropped. Then he turned instead toward a ring buoy that someone had tossed from the steamship. Before he could reach the buoy, he went down.

Surfmen from the lifesaving stations set out to rescue Johnsen. They recovered only his cap, the ring buoy and the floating oar. Johnsen was gone. His body washed ashore several days later. The ship was refloated and towed to New York.

Jeanette Edwards Rattray, in her history of shipwrecks on Long Island, relates an anecdote about the Chinese crew rescued from *Gowanburn*. The men were taken to a lifesaving station for a meal. One of the lifesavers, who served as cook, prepared a large quantity of rice for the Chinese, thinking it was their preferred food. The Chinese rejected the rice, however, and demanded to be fed, Western style, on pancakes and beef!

Grand Congloue Island wreck, Mediterranean Sea   This wreck of a Roman merchant vessel, discovered in the early 1950s by a diver off Grand Congloue Island near Marseilles, was one of the greatest discoveries in the history of marine archaeology and demonstrated the superiority of the newly developed self-contained underwater breathing apparatus (SCUBA) for such work.

The wreck was spotted first by a diver who noticed large numbers of what he described as "pots" on the sea floor. His report came to the attention of a colleague of SCUBA inventor Jacques Cousteau. Soon an archeological expedition was at work in chilly water that restricted working time on the bottom to only 17 minutes per dive. Despite the uncomfortable conditions, the expedition recovered thousands of amphorae (wine jars) and examples of Roman pottery from the wreck.

Archaeologists eventually were able to determine much about the ship's history. It belonged to a prominent Roman, Marcus Sestius, who is mentioned in Livy's *Annals of the Roman People.* The vessel sailed from the Greek island of Delos in 230 B.C. carrying 10,000 amphorae of wine to Massalia, now known as Marseilles. Along the way, the ship stopped at the Gulf of Gaeta in Italy to pick up additional cargo, including more amphorae and a shipment of pottery. Apparently the ship was overloaded. It is thought to have sunk in a storm.

The wreck revealed much about Mediterranean shipping in Roman times. The vessel was large: roughly the size of a frigate of the 1800s. Evidently it was a sailing ship, because such a large vessel could not have been propelled solely by slaves working oars. The wreck also indicated that the shipbuilders used lead sheathing on the decks, as well as copper nails coated with lead. Analysis of the cargo showed that the Romans must have used mass production techniques to manufacture pottery, because the dinnerware found on the wreck was standardized. This expedition was the first occasion on which underwater television was used in archaeological salvage, historian Joseph Gores writes in his 1971 book *Marine Salvage.*

See also AMPHORAE; DIVING SUITS; SALVAGE; VIDEO.

Grant, **American steamship** One of the first propeller steamboats in service in America's Pacific Northwest, *U.S. Grant* carried passengers and freight between Astoria, Washington, and Baker Bay. The captain and his brother were performing maintenance on the engine on December 19, 1871, at Fort Canby when the ship went adrift in a storm and was driven ashore at Sand Island on the Columbia River bar. The two men escaped in a boat and spent the night drifting in it, in freezing weather. They were recovered alive the next day. *Grant* was lost completely. James Gibbs, in his history of shipwrecks on the Columbia River bar, reports the curious fact that *Grant* was built by a farmer, Clinton Kelly.

Great Britain, **British steamship** The trans-Atlantic steamer *Great Britain* was built by the illustrious engineer Isambard Kingdom Brunel and was launched in 1843. The ship had a troubled history. *Great Britain* ran aground at Dundrum Bay in Ireland in 1845 and was not refloated until almost a year later. The steamer remained in service until 1886, when the ship sustained heavy damage from a storm off Cape Horn, at the southern tip of South America. To prevent mutiny by his crew, the captain beached the ship on the Falkland Islands. There *Great Britain* was bought

for use as a floating storage vessel but was eventually abandoned. After public interest in the historic vessel intensified, *Great Britain* was towed home to England for exhibit.

See also FALKLAND ISLANDS; GREAT EASTERN.

Great Eastern, **British steamship** The largest ship in the world at that time (693 feet long), *Great Eastern* did not actually sink after striking rocks off Montauk, New York, on August 27, 1862, but the ship sustained heavy damage. The rocks tore a hole 86 feet long in the hull. *Great Eastern* had a double hull, however, and the inner hull remained intact, thus saving the ship. *Great Eastern* was designed by the great engineer Isambard Kingdom Brunel, who also was responsible for the famous *Great Britain.* Four years after the mishap off Montauk, *Great Eastern* was used to put in place the first trans-Atlantic cable.

See also GREAT BRITAIN.

Great Lakes A set of inland seas located between the United States and Canada, and connected to the Atlantic Ocean by the St. Lawrence River, the Great Lakes have been the sites of many notable shipwrecks. Storms have contributed to the toll of shipwrecks on the Great Lakes, because cold fronts moving south from Canada toward the United States often generate intense storm activity. Winter storms on the Great Lakes can be especially dangerous to shipping because of their intensity and because ice may form on a ship's upperworks and thus make the ship more likely to capsize. Waves in Great Lakes storms may reach impressive size; the lakes themselves are hundreds of miles in length and may offer winds a lengthy "fetch," or continuous passage over water, in which to generate large waves. Many shipwrecks on the Great Lakes have involved freighters, because of the heavy freight traffic across the lakes. There also has been extensive passenger traffic across the Great Lakes in the past two centuries, with a corresponding number of passenger vessels wrecked and large numbers of fatalities.

See also BANNOCKBURN; EDMUND FITZGERALD.

Great Liverpool, **British paddle steamer** *Great Liverpool* struck a reef and sank between Cape Finisterre and Corcubion on February 24, 1846. Two women and a child were killed when their boat capsized.

Great Republic, **American passenger steamer** Not to be confused with the famous clipper ship by the same name, the sidewheel passenger steamer *Great Republic* was built at Greenport, New York, in 1866 and spent some time in trade with China before the ship's owners, concerned about high operating costs, laid up the vessel at San Francisco. There *Great Republic* was bought by one P. B. Cornwall, who put the ship into freight and passenger service along the Pacific coast. The ship did good business in this trade and was known for making fast passages. *Great Republic's* coastal service lasted less than a year, however, and ended in shipwreck at the mouth of the Columbia River (Oregon-Washington) in 1879.

Great Republic reached the mouth of the Columbia River on the night of April 18 and took aboard a pilot. Shortly after midnight, the ship started across the bar.

According to Captain James Carroll's testimony at a hearing, he saw Sand Island through glasses and mentioned it to the pilot, who had not yet seen it. The captain said he thought the ship was too close to the island. "I do not think we are in far enough," the pilot replied. The captain repeated his warning and told the pilot, "Port your helm and put it hard over." The pilot reportedly waited several minutes before carrying out the captain's instructions. (Later, the pilot testified that he had miscalculated the strength of the tide.) The ship went aground.

Since the grounding occurred at high tide, the ship was stuck with little chance of being refloated. Moreover, the barometer was falling, thus indicating that a storm was on the way. The captain sent the purser to nearby Fort Canby for help. Tugs and steamers arrived soon afterward. Passengers were sent ashore. The crew stayed aboard in the hope of refloating *Great Republic*.

Great Republic started breaking apart almost as soon as it ran aground. As the next high tide approached, waves accompanying a developing gale put heavy strains on the hull and prevented tugs from coming to the ship's aid. As the ship worked on the spit, steam pipes disconnected. Malfunctioning bilge pumps failed to remove water. A bad situation became steadily worse, until the crew and the few remaining passengers went ashore. One boat capsized and killed 11 of 14 men on board. The captain and pilot were the last to leave the ship.

After an inquiry, the pilot's license was suspended for a year. Captain Carroll's license was suspended for six months, but he appealed the decision successfully. Some of the cargo was salvaged, and parts of the wreck remained visible in the river until around 1900. The site of the wreck was named Republic Spit.

Great Republic, American clipper ship   The masterwork of the famous 19th-century American shipbuilder Donald McKay, *Great Republic* has been described as the most splendid wooden sailing ship ever constructed. Equipped with luxuries and decorations including stained-glass windows, the four-masted vessel was intended to beat all competition in the clipper-ship trade. Fire destroyed the ship in New York on December 26, 1853, however, before it could set out on its maiden voyage to Liverpool. What remained of the ship was sold and rebuilt, and sailed for a number of owners over the next two decades. The ship was abandoned following a storm off Bermuda in 1872.

Great Western, British steamship   Designed by Isambard Kingdom Brunel, who also designed *Great Eastern* and *Great Britain*, *Great Western* was the first exclusively steam-powered ship to be used for regular travel across the ocean. Much smaller than the enormous *Great Eastern*, *Great Western* carried passengers for a time but eventually carried only freight. *Great Western* had a lengthy career. Almost half a century after its first trip across the Atlantic, the ship was wrecked on the beach at Fire Island, New York, on January 26, 1876, and was a total loss, although no one was killed. Only a few miles away, off Montauk, *Great Eastern* gashed open its outer hull on a rock in 1862 but was saved by its inner hull, which remained intact.

Great Western apparently missed by only six hours the distinction of being the first ship to cross the Atlantic Ocean exclusively on steam power. That honor evidently went to the packet *Sirius*, which arrived in New York from Dublin six hours ahead of *Great Western* in 1838.

See also GREAT BRITAIN; GREAT EASTERN.

Grenada   Swept frequently by hurricanes, Grenada is located in the Lesser Antilles and has been the site of numerous shipwrecks. One highly destructive hurricane on October 10, 1780, reportedly wrecked numerous vessels, including 19 Dutch merchant ships in Grenville Bay; *Prince Frederick Adolph*, a Swedish merchant vessel, in St. George's Harbor; and various French and English merchant ships in various ports on the island.

Griffin, French sailing vessel   One of the earliest cases of a sailing vessel disappearing on the Great Lakes, the loss of the 40-ton *Griffin* on September 19, 1679, is thought to have taken some 30 lives. Built by the French explorer Rene-Robert La Salle, *Griffin* was a supply ship and is thought to have been en route from Green Bay, Wisconsin, to Fort Niagara, New York, when the vessel was lost. What exactly happened to *Griffin* is, of course, subject to conjecture, but stormy weather on the Great Lakes is a possible explanation for the ship's disappearance.

See also GREAT LAKES.

Griffith, **steamer** One of many steamships to be lost on the Great Lakes, *G.P. Griffith* caught fire and sank on Lake Erie on June 17, 1850, on a voyage from Buffalo, New York, to Chicago. The ship carried 321 people altogether, including English, German and Irish immigrants as passengers. Only 26 reportedly survived the fire and sinking, and 295 were killed. The fire is said to have started in the cargo hold. The captain appears to have responded coolly to the crisis and headed for shore, where he hoped to beach the ship and put off his passengers safely. The crew assembled the passengers on deck. Then the fire escaped from the hold, advanced along the deck and drove passengers into the water. No children from *Griffith* survived, and only one woman lived through the catastrophe. The loss of *Griffith* led to passage of federal laws governing inspection of boilers, hulls and lifeboats on ships.

See also FIRE; GREAT LAKES.

Guadeloupe, Lesser Antilles Perhaps the most famous shipwrecks in Guadeloupe's history occurred in 1603, when the New Spain Flota, under command of Captain-General Fulgencio de Meneses, put in there to load fresh water. A wind brought about the loss of three ships, including the 45-gun, 700-ton *San Juan Bautista.* The captain-general left a large party of men behind for a salvage operation, but they came under attack from Native Americans (specifically the Carib people) soon after the fleet left Guadeloupe, and the salvage team recovered nothing from the wrecks. Apparently someone succeeded in salvaging items from the wrecks, however, because some months after, a French pirate ship captured by the Spaniards was found to be carrying several bronze cannon from *San Juan Bautista.*

Another Spanish vessel named *San Juan Bautista*—this one a merchant ship—sank in 1609 at Guadeloupe, in the same vicinity where the above mentioned three ships had been wrecked. Again, the Caribs kept the Spaniards from carrying out salvage operations.

On August 12, 1666, French and English fleets engaged in battle near Guadeloupe. More than 12 large French warships were sunk, and the English lost two vessels. The British fleet was destroyed only two days

afterward, however, by a hurricane that struck the island. The entire British fleet—15 ships in all—was wrecked in the storm.

Another hurricane on October 6, 1766, destroyed more than 50 large English vessels at Guadeloupe, in addition to 12 slave ships wrecked in the vicinity. More than 40 ships reportedly were lost at and around Guadeloupe in a hurricane on September 6, 1776. In 1809, four warships were wrecked, including the French warships *Loire* and *Seine,* destroyed by the British; the 18-gun English H.M.S. *Carieux,* wrecked on Maria Galante Island; and the 12-gun English H.M.S. *Unique,* which burned at Basse-Terre.

Guadalupe, **Spanish frigate** Under command of Captain Juan Gil del Barrios, *Nuestra Señora de Guadalupe,* also known as *La Tetis,* was wrecked on Chinchorro Reef off the Mexican coast during a voyage from Honduras to Spain, on December 5, 1772. The ship carried 29 chests of silver, of which 26 were recovered.

Guernsey, **British steamship** Lost off Cap de la Hague (Cape La Hague), France, on the night of April 8, 1915, *Guernsey* ran on the rocks with such force that the captain was thrown overboard from the bridge and was never seen again. Of 19 on board, 12 survived.

Gulf of Florida wrecks To understand what devastation hurricanes could inflict on shipping in the waters around Florida during the days of sail, consider the following list of vessels wrecked in the Gulf of Florida during a single hurricane on the single day of October 22, 1752: the British merchant ships *Alexander, Dolphin, Lancaster, May* and *Queen Anne;* American merchant vessels *Rhode Island* and *Statea;* a Spanish schooner and Spanish man-of-war, both unidentified; and three other ships, likewise unidentified.

See also FLORIDA; STORMS.

"gunpowder ship," American brig Known officially as the *Live Oak,* this vessel is remembered on Long Island, New York, for the extensive damage it caused in Southampton one night in July 1814. After catching fire at sea, the ship, loaded with 900 kegs of gunpowder, ran ashore at Shinnecock Point and exploded. The ship was blown to bits. One bit of iron from the vessel was recovered half a mile away.

See also EXPLOSIONS.

H

Hai Chu, Chinese steamship *Hai Chu* hit a mine and sank near the mouth of the Canton River on November 8, 1945. Of some 2,000 soldiers, 100 civilians and crew on board, only 300 people reportedly survived.

Haisborough Sand, England Located off the eastern coast of England at Norfolk County, the shoals at Haisborough Sand and Hammond's Knoll have been the site of so many shipwrecks that the area has come to be known as the Devil's Throat.

See also ROCKS AND SHOALS.

Halifax, Nova Scotia, explosion Sometimes, a shipwreck spreads destruction all around it. A case in point is the explosion of the French freighter *Mont Blanc,* loaded with explosives, in the harbor at Halifax, Nova Scotia, on December 6, 1917. The explosion destroyed much of Halifax, killed an estimated 1,600 people, injured perhaps 8,000 others and left perhaps 2,000 more people missing. Damage was estimated at more than $30 million in all.

The explosion occurred after *Mont Blanc*—loaded with TNT, benzene and picric acid—collided with the Belgian relief vessel *Imo.* The collision reportedly occurred in broad daylight and clear weather and was attributed later to confused signals from *Imo.*

Imo's captain tried to avoid collision by reversing the ship's engines. This apparently had just the opposite effect from that which he intended, and pointed *Imo's* bow at *Mont Blanc. Imo* struck *Mont Blanc,* setting the French ship on fire. Then *Imo* headed for shore. The men of *Mont Blanc* tried for a while to fight the fire but soon gave up and abandoned ship. They reached shore and ran into the woods for shelter.

Mont Blanc exploded 17 minutes after the collision, when the fire set off TNT in the ship's holds. It was one of the greatest artificial explosions in history before the age of nuclear warfare, and was heard 60 miles away. The blast lifted *Imo* out of the water and deposited the ship on shore. The community of Richmond was virtually erased; the blast left only one telegraph line in Halifax working; the telegraph operator stayed at his post but finally left when told that his wife was dying.

Although *Mont Blanc* was blasted to pieces, *Imo* was rebuilt and given the new name of *Guvernoren.* The renamed vessel operated for four more years before finally being lost in a shipwreck off the Falkland Islands.

See also EXPLOSIONS.

Hampshire, British naval cruiser The sinking of H.M.S. *Hampshire* by a German mine on June 5, 1916, was one of the most famous sea catastrophes in British history and is the center of a mystery involving Lord Kitchener, Britain's secretary for war, who was lost with *Hampshire* on a wartime voyage to Russia.

Kitchener was one of the most prominent military men in Britain. His face, with a penetrating gaze and a distinctive heavy mustache, appeared on a famous recruiting poster. For his performance in the Boer War, he was named a viscount and awarded the Order of Merit. In World War I, he set in motion a great expansion of the British army.

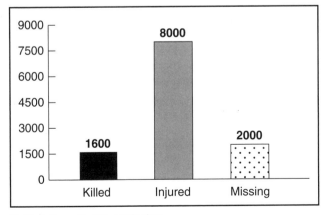

Halifax, Nova Scotia, explosion.

Kitchener had numerous foes in the British government. Apparently some powerful men would have been pleased to see him dead. With that thought in mind, some conspiracy theorists have suggested that Kitchener's final voyage was in fact a trap to destroy him by sinking *Hampshire.*

No proof of any such plan or action has been offered, but the circumstances of *Hampshire's* sinking are indeed mysterious. For one thing, security was evidently poor, so that word of Kitchener's upcoming voyage was public knowledge weeks before *Hampshire* departed for Russia.

Also, it was reported in the 1980s, after a study of British Naval Intelligence documents, that the Germans had intercepted a signal from a British destroyer to the effect that mines had been swept clear from a channel west of Orkney—the channel that *Hampshire* used on its last voyage.

This signal was transmitted several times from the destroyer to the Admiralty and must have alerted the Germans that the British had some pressing reason to clear mines from that channel. The Germans sent the submarine *U-75* to sow more mines in the channel. One of those mines destroyed *Hampshire.*

Sending the signal to the Admiralty, rather than to an ordinary shore station, indicated that something or someone very important might be on a British ship traveling through the aforementioned channel. In that case, the signal was practically as good as a direct message to the Germans.

At the same time, according to one report, British Naval Intelligence learned that a German submarine was still prowling in the area where Kitchener and *Hampshire* were to travel—yet Kitchener was not informed of the submarine's presence. Kitchener then sailed into catastrophe.

This much is known: Around 7:45 P.M. on June 5, during an intense storm, two explosions shook *Hampshire.* The first explosion presumably came from a mine; the second may have been from a boiler. Lights went out, and the ship lost electrical power. Because the boats were launched by an electric-powered system, abandoning *Hampshire* was difficult. One boat was launched manually but was smashed against the cruiser's side. Only 12 men out of 665 on board escaped from the sinking ship. One survivor said he had seen Kitchener on deck before *Hampshire* sank, but Kitchener's body reportedly was never recovered. *Hampshire* sank rapidly. By 8 P.M., the cruiser was gone.

Kitchener's death stunned the British public. The effect of his death on Britain has been compared to that of John F. Kennedy's assassination on the American public in 1963. Rumors of sabotage and intrigue circulated after Kitchener died. The exact circumstances of his death and the loss of *Hampshire* remain mysteries of the sea.

See also MYSTERIES.

Hans Hedtoft, Danish cargo/passenger ship

In a wreck reminiscent of the loss of *Titanic* 47 years earlier, the Danish ship *Hans Hedtoft* struck an iceberg and sank on its maiden voyage, between Greenland and Denmark, on January 30, 1959. All 95 people on board were lost. The ship transmitted only three short radio messages before sinking. The first message said the ship had struck an iceberg; the second, that the ship was filling quickly; and the third, that the engine room was flooding. *Hans Hedtoft* was built for year-round service between Denmark and Greenland.

See also TITANIC.

harbors

Although harbors are commonly viewed as shelters from storms and other commonplace threats to shipping, the harbor environment itself contains many dangers. Intense traffic within a confined area such as a harbor, for example, creates a great potential for collisions. The harbor area may contain hazards such as rocks and shoals, and a pilot's guidance may be necessary to avoid them. Submerged wrecks also may be present, especially during or immediately after wartime. Collisions with bridges, buoys and other such objects are additional hazards of the harbor environment. Hazardous cargoes—including many explosive, flammable and toxic materials—may be present in harbor areas and add their own particular dangers. Many calamitous wrecks and associated events have occurred in harbors. Two famous examples are the Halifax, Nova Scotia, and Texas City, Texas, explosions, where ships with explosive cargoes blew up and caused widespread damage on shore.

See also EXPLOSIVES; HALIFAX, NOVA SCOTIA, EXPLOSION; TEXAS CITY EXPLOSION.

Harpooner, British transport

A dog named King helped save numerous lives, and a baby was born, when *Harpooner* ran onto a reef off Newfoundland on the morning of November 9, 1816. *Harpooner* was on its way from Quebec to London with 385 men, women and children on board.

The dog's tale of heroism began the moment *Harpooner* hit the reef. The dog grabbed the captain's sleeve and pulled him toward the cabin. There the captain found that lighted candles had fallen and set the cabin on fire. He and several sailors extinguished the fire.

Breaking apart under the assault of waves, the ship lay about 300 feet from a large rock offshore. Five men in a boat managed to reach the rock, but the boat was smashed, so they could not return to the ship. One of the men called out to the captain to release a log line, so that the men could secure it when it floated ashore. Currents, however, prevented the log line from reaching the men on the rock.

By this time, *Harpooner*'s situation was desperate. The ship was about to fall to pieces. The captain turned to King for help. After tying a line to the dog's collar, the captain pointed to the men on the rock and told the dog to go to them. Being a Newfoundland, King was a great swimmer. He managed to carry the line to the rock, and soon rescue operations began. One by one, people from *Harpooner* were hauled ashore by sling.

One of the first women ashore was pregnant. Less than two hours after she reached shore, she gave birth to a son.

Another remarkable rescue was that of an elderly subaltern, the last person to leave the ship. When all others on board had been either rescued or lost in the sea, the old man jumped into the water and floated to shore.

Two hundred and eight people, including the captain, were killed in the wreck of *Harpooner*. One hundred and seventy-seven, plus a brave dog, survived.

Harusame, Japanese destroyer *Harusame* sank in a gale off Cape Shima, Japan, on November 23, 1911. Of 60 on board, 45 drowned.

Harvest Home, American bark Fog and a faulty chronometer contributed to the loss of *Harvest Home* on January 18, 1882, on the coast of Washington state near the mouth of the Columbia River.

The ship was heading through fog in a northwesterly direction, for Port Townsend. Then the helmsman heard a sound highly unusual at sea: the crowing of a rooster.

Immediately after the rooster crowed, the ship ran onto the beach. The captain was astonished. By his reckoning, the vessel should have been six miles out to sea. His estimates were based, however, on readings from a malfunctioning chronometer.

The rooster belonged to a farm only a few yards from the beach where *Harvest Home* went ashore. The wreck became a tourist attraction.

hatches Openings in a ship's hull that are designed to admit people and materiel, hatches are, in a sense, structural weak points and present certain dangers in heavy weather. A rough sea can tear away hatch covers and leave a ship's hold open to flooding, thus sinking the vessel. Stresses placed on a deck by heavy seas may overcome, or "spring," fasteners used to secure the hatch covers, and thus open the ship to the sea. On the other hand, hatchways also may be valuable avenues of escape for people on a sinking (or even sunken) ship.

Sprung hatches are thought to have sunk the Great Lakes car ferry *Milwaukee*, which was lost on Lake Michigan on October 22, 1929, during a storm. According to one speculation, excessive stresses resulting from the storm may have twisted the deck and sprung hatches leading to spaces below deck. Filled with water, those spaces would have dragged the ship down, so to speak.

See also MILWAUKEE.

Hawke incident, United Kingdom One of the most famous collisions between two vessels occurred on September 20, 1911, when the 7,350-ton British cruiser *Hawke* encountered the giant White Star liner *Olympic*, sister ship to *Titanic*, in the Solent (channel between Isle of Wight and England). The captain on *Olympic* at the time was E.J. Smith, who commanded *Titanic* on its catastrophic maiden voyage in 1912.

Olympic and *Hawke* traveled on parallel courses for a while. When the two ships were between 100 and 300 yards apart, something appeared to draw them together, and they collided. *Hawke*'s bow was badly damaged, and the collision ripped two holes in *Olympic*'s side some 80 feet from the liner's stern. No one was killed on either vessel. *Olympic* put passengers ashore by tender and then returned to home port at Southampton. Despite extensive damage, *Hawke* proceeded under its own power to Portsmouth.

Although the cruiser was widely presumed to be at fault in the collision, the Admiralty proved to the satisfaction of a court of inquiry that the speed and great displacement of *Olympic*, in effect, had generated hydrodynamic forces that "pulled" the cruiser into *Olympic*'s side. The court agreed with that assessment, and its ruling was upheld on appeal. Captain Smith was not blamed for the collision, however, because *Olympic* had been under the harbor pilot's command when the collision occurred.

The incident now is seen as evidence that the new generation of giant liners represented by *Olympic* and *Titanic* produced, when in motion, hydrodynamic forces of which the ships' commanders and crews were still largely ignorant. These forces apparently caused the collision between *Hawke* and *Olympic*. In similar fashion, hydrodynamic effects generated by *Titanic* came close to causing a collision in 1912. As *Titanic* left port at Southampton, its passage drew the liner *New York* away from its berth. Only quick action by Captain Smith on *Titanic,* and by tugboats in the harbor, prevented the two liners from colliding.

See also TITANIC.

Heath Park, Scottish bark   The sailing vessel *Heath Park* left Perth Amboy, New Jersey, on November 25, 1876, on a voyage to London. *Heath Park* was loaded with a heavy cargo of slate. Soon after the ship left port, bad weather set in. Within two days of leaving Perth Amboy, *Heath Park* was taking on large amounts of water through seams in the hull. The captain ordered men to work hand pumps, but before long the pumps could not stay ahead of the inflow of water.

Two options were available. *Heath Park* could head for Nantucket, Massachusetts, the nearest land; but to get there, the ship would have to cross the dangerous Nantucket Shoals. The captain decided a wiser choice was to head for Long Island, New York, instead. He also gave orders to cast some of the slate cargo overboard to lighten the ship.

The rough weather continued. After six days, the men on *Heath Park* sighted another ship and sent up a distress flag. The other vessel, the steel-hulled *Circassian* out of Liverpool, pulled alongside *Heath Park* and took the leaking ship's crew aboard. Every man on *Heath Park* was rescued. Moments later, *Heath Park* sank.

Bound for New York, *Circassian* made its way through heavy seas. Then the ship went aground on the Long Island shore near Bridgehampton, about a quarter-mile from a lifesaving station.

The situation was grave. *Circassian* could not survive for long under the repeated blows of the heavy seas. Yet the sea was too rough to launch a boat to rescue the men on board the stricken ship. Moreover, it seemed impossible to shoot a line to the vessel successfully, because *Circassian* was too far from land; gale-force winds were blowing and darkness was falling, thus the livesavers could not aim the line accurately and the men on *Circassian* would be unable to see the line even if it reached the ship.

The keeper at the livesaving station decided to wait out the night. The stout-hulled *Circassian* seemed likely to last that long.

The next day, the livesavers began firing rockets to carry a line to *Circassian.* At last they succeeded. The men on the ship secured the line, and the lifesavers put out from shore in a boat, guided by the line. All 47 men on *Circassian,* including the 12 men rescued from *Heath Park,* were taken safely to shore.

The story of *Circassian*'s wreck, however, was just beginning. As the storm abated, a wrecking company began salvage work on the vessel, which lay upon the bar offshore. After several days' work, however, the weather became stormy again. The wrecking company discontinued work on *Circassian* for the duration of the storm, sent some of the workers ashore and left 31 others on board to watch the ship. Those left on board included 10 Native Americans of the Shinnecock tribe on Long Island. They were virtually the only able-bodied men in a community of some 200 Native Americans.

As the storm intensified, *Circassian* wound up balanced, so to speak, on the bar. The ship rested on the bar amidships, with its bow and stern hanging out over empty water. This situation put excessive stress on the hull amidships, and *Circassian* broke in two. As men on the beach watched, the mainmast broke at its base and fell into the water. The men on *Circassian* climbed onto the remaining masts and rigging to save themselves. There, however, they were in a highly exposed position. The hull had filled with water to the upper decks, and waves sent spray flying some 80 feet into the air.

Lifesavers on shore tried repeatedly to shoot a line by mortar to *Circassian* but were unsuccessful, because the line was wet and frozen. Either the shots fell short of the ship, or else the wind blew them off target. Meanwhile, the men on *Circassian* tried to save themselves. Three of them lashed themselves to a cork float in the hope that it would keep them alive if they fell or were washed into the sea.

Circassian was breaking up. A series of powerful waves shattered what remained of the ship. Several of the remaining men on board were washed into the sea. Others climbed the mizzenmast. Their cries were audible on shore. Slowly, the mizzenmast dipped toward the water. At last it reached the surface, and the men clinging to the mast were washed away.

Four men survived the ordeal on *Circassian:* the three who had lashed themselves to the cork float, plus another who clung to it. The loss of life on *Circassian* struck the Shinnecock community especially hard. The 10 Shinnecock men who died in the wreck had supported, in one way or another, some 30 people in their community.

Helen, French sailing vessel   Wrecked at Southampton on Long Island, New York, on January 17, 1820, *Helen* had a poignant link to the United States Military Academy at West Point.

A Frenchman named Louis Berard—brother of Claudius Berard, the Academy's librarian—was bringing a collection of books for the Academy's library with him from France on *Helen* when he was lost in the shipwreck. Although Berard was killed, his box of books survived the wreck and was retrieved from the beach.

A woman in Sag Harbor knew Claudius Berard's wife, recognized the name on the box and contacted the Berards by mail. The books eventually were delivered to West Point, where Claudius Berard had to keep them because the government did not have the funds to buy them.

Heraklion, Greek ferry The ferry *Heraklion*, carrying passengers and cargo between Crete and the port of Piraeus near Athens, was caught in a storm in the Aegean Sea in the early hours of December 12, 1966, and sank with the loss of 230 lives of the 281 passengers and crew on board. Automobiles on the ferry's lower decks broke loose and started battering the ship's sides. One vehicle knocked a hole in the ship, and the ferry began to fill and sink. The ferry reportedly sank in only 15 minutes.

Herald of Free Enterprise, British ferry Operating between Zeebrugge, Netherlands, and Dover, England, *Herald of Free Enterprise* capsized and sank on March 6, 1987, in the English Channel. The ferry was designed with a low bow in order to let automobiles roll on and off freely. The low bow meant that the bow doors were close to the waterline. At a rate estimated at 200 tons per minute, water started entering through the bow doors as the ferry sailed from Zeebrugge to Dover. Several minutes later, the quartermaster noticed that the ferry did not respond to the wheel. The ship developed a strong list and then rolled over onto its right side. A large rescue operation involving ships and aircraft converged on *Herald of Free Enterprise*. Some 190 people are thought to have died in the sinking. There was one happy surprise in this catastrophe: when a doctor checked a number of supposedly dead bodies, he discovered that two of them were still alive.

heroism and cowardice Crises tend to bring out either the best or worst in human behavior, and shipwrecks are no exception. In some cases of shipwreck, captain, crew and passengers have behaved with dignity and courage. In other instances, cowardice and panic have been the rule. Of stories of heroism at sea, perhaps the most famous in Anglo-American maritime lore is that of the crew of the British liner R.M.S. *Titanic*, enforcing the ancient rule of "women and children first" as passengers entered the lifeboats. A particular instance of heroism in the *Titanic* story is that of Fifth Officer Harold Lowe, who took the lifeboat under his command back to search for survivors in the water while other lifeboats stood off.

Another celebrated case of heroism at sea is that of the British troopship *Birkenhead*, which was wrecked in 1852 near the Cape of Good Hope. The troops on *Birkenhead* assembled on deck, stood at attention, and remained that way until the ship went down. The troops reportedly obeyed the order to stay in place, even while their wives and children pleaded with them to save themselves.

At the opposite extreme from such stories is that of the Collins liner *Arctic*, which sank in 1854 after colliding with a French vessel off Cape Race, Newfoundland. According to one account of the wreck, the stokers rushed the boats and left passengers to save themselves as best they could.

See also ARCTIC; BIRKENHEAD; TITANIC.

Hesperus, fictional schooner "The Wreck of the *Hesperus*," a poem by Henry Wadsworth Longfellow, is one of the most famous fictional depictions of a shipwreck. The poem tells of a schooner's master who takes his young daughter with him on a voyage. Both are killed when the ship is driven onto rocks during a snowstorm. Several excerpts from the poem follow:

> It was the schooner *Hesperus*,
>   That sailed the wintry sea;
> And the skipper had taken his little daughter,
>   To bear him company. . . .
> Down came the storm, and smote amain
>   The vessel in its strength;
> She shuddered and paused, like a frighted steed,
>   Then leaped her cable's length.
> "Come hither! come hither! my little daughter,
>   And do not tremble so;
> For I can weather the roughest gale
>   That ever wind did blow."
> He wrapped her warm in his seaman's coat
>   Against the stinging blast;
> He cut a rope from a broken spar,
>   And bound her to the mast. . . .
> She struck where the white and fleecy waves
>   Looked soft as carded wool,
> But the cruel rocks, they gored her side
>   Like the horns of an angry bull. . . .
> At daybreak on the bleak sea-beach,
>   A fisherman stood aghast
> To see the form of a maiden fair,
>   Lashed close to a drifting mast. . . .

Maritime historian Edward Rowe Snow investigated the circumstances of the poem's composition. He reported that although Longfellow based the poem on an actual set of incidents, he rearranged and modified them considerably.

Longfellow wrote the poem following a series of hurricanes that struck New England within two weeks in December of 1839. A heavy snowfall began at midnight on December 14. The storm demolished some 20 schooners in the harbor (including three sunk at their moorings) and drove 21 other ships ashore.

One of the ships affected was the schooner *Hesperus,* which was driven up a dock. The ship's jib boom was rammed into the third story of a building across the street. Another vessel caught in this storm was demolished, and 17 bodies washed ashore at Cape Ann, Massachusetts. Among the bodies was that of a woman lashed to the windlass bits of a schooner.

Longfellow noticed news reports of these incidents and decided to write a ballad based on them. He apparently erred in thinking the schooner *Hesperus* was wrecked near Gloucester, Massachusetts, on a reef called Norman's Woe, when *Hesperus* actually had been in Boston harbor when the storm struck.

There was another discrepancy between the poem and the results of the storm. The young, fair maiden described by Longfellow was not actually discovered dead on the beach following the storm, lashed to a portion of a wrecked schooner. The woman described in the news report was 55 years old.

***Hibernia*, British steamship**   On November 24, 1868, during a voyage from New York to Glasgow, Scotland, *Hibernia* broke a propeller shaft and started taking on water. The ship sank in the North Atlantic; 78 lives were lost, but 55 people were rescued.

Highborn Cay wreck, Bahamas   Discovered by divers in 1965 off Highborn Cay, this wreck has been an important site of modern marine archeology. The wreck is located in about 20 feet of water and has been overgrown by coral. One salvage operation started in 1966, continued through May of 1967 and recovered some armament and portions of the rigging. A few smaller items also were recovered, including what appeared to be a harpoon with a shaft more than six feet long. Further investigation of the site in the 1980s revealed that some of the ship's timbers were preserved beneath the ballast stones that marked the site of the wreck. The wreck exhibited evidence of construction techniques used in 16th-century vessels.

Apparently the ship was at anchor when it sank, because two anchors were found near the wreck. The ship's remote location and the large amount of armaments on board has led to speculation that the wreck is that of a pirate vessel, although there are other possibilities.

See also ANCHORS; BAHIA MUJERES WRECK; CANNON; MOLASSES REEF WRECK.

Hispaniola   This island, now comprising Haiti and the Dominican Republic, is the site of numerous shipwrecks, only a few of which are mentioned here.

Perhaps the most famous shipwreck in Hispaniola's history is *Santa Maria*, the flagship of Christopher Columbus on his voyage to the New World in 1492. *Santa Maria* sank on a reef near Cape Haitian. Two more of Columbus's ships, from his second voyage, are thought to have been wrecked in a hurricane at Hispaniola in 1494.

Columbus might have prevented the loss of 26 ships of a 30-ship fleet that departed Santo Domingo in 1502, had the governor not ignored Columbus's advice. A fleet of 30 caravels with treasure on board was about to sail for Spain when Columbus saw evidence of an approaching hurricane and tried to keep the fleet from sailing. The governor disregarded Columbus's advice, however, and the fleet left for Spain. Columbus turned out to have been correct: soon after leaving port, a hurricane struck the fleet and destroyed 26 of the 30 ships in it, with a loss of more than 500 lives.

In 1545, two devastating hurricanes struck Santo Domingo on August 20 and September 18. The first hurricane destroyed numerous ships at the port. The second storm destroyed some 18 to 20 vessels that had not been wrecked in the earlier hurricane.

Another storm in 1551, in the Bahama Channel, destroyed a treasure galleon, the 200-ton *San Miguel,* which was loaded with gold and silver. The galleon lost its rudder and mainmast, then drifted until it was wrecked on a reef approximately 90 miles from Puerto de Plata. No one was killed in the wreck, and divers salvaged all the treasure on board.

An incident in 1673 demonstrated that privateering ships—a significant cause of shipwrecks—were themselves vulnerable to wrecking. Poor navigation caused the English privateer *Jamaica Merchant* to wreck on Isle de Vache (literally, Cow Island; also known as Vacour or Vaca) on February 25. Another privateer came to the rescue several days later and picked up the wrecked ship's complement. The celebrated buccaneer Henry Morgan was on board *Jamaica Merchant* when it was wrecked.

The New Spain Fleet encountered a hurricane in September of 1724 near the Bahama Channel on the way to Bermuda. Several ships sank with an undetermined amount of treasure near Samana Bay. More than 120 people were killed, although salvage operations reportedly were completely successful on all but one of the wrecked vessels. Another storm on October 5, 1737, demolished the town of Santo Domingo and numerous ships in the harbor.

The 18-gun British sloop of war H.M.S. *Cormorant* exploded—allegedly by accident—at Port-au-Prince in 1796. Of the 121 men in the ship's crew, 95 were reported lost.

See also COLUMBUS EXPEDITIONS; CORSAIRS AND PRIVATEERS; FLOTA SYSTEM.

Hoboken fire, New Jersey One of the most hideous maritime catastrophes in American history occurred on June 30, 1900, when a fire on the North German Lloyd Line pier in Hoboken, New Jersey, spread to four passenger ships at the pier, killing 326 people and injuring more than 200 others. The fire allegedly started in bales of cotton, then spread to barrels of whisky and caused them to explode. The wooden pier caught fire. Forty longshoremen on the pier were allegedly caught in the flames.

Soon the fire spread to four liners, the *Main, Bremen, Saale* and *Kaiser Wilhelm der Grosse.* All but *Kaiser Wilhelm* were destroyed. Tugs pulled *Kaiser Wilhelm* away from the pier, and the crew put out the fires on board. No lives were lost on *Kaiser Wilhelm.*

The other three liners were not saved, despite all efforts to extinguish the fires and rescue passengers on board. Portholes on the ships were only 11 inches wide, too small for an adult to pass through. Would-be rescuers watched from boats only feet from the ships as passengers tried unsuccessfully to escape through the portholes, then were burned to death in plain view of the onlookers.

From *Main* came an astonishing tale of survival. Men on a tugboat saw someone reaching through a porthole and signaling with a torch. The tugboat's crew started cutting through the hull and rescued 15 men who had survived in a coal bunker deep inside the ship.

See also FIRE.

Hobson, American destroyer On April 26, 1952, the U.S. Navy destroyer *Hobson* was struck by the American aircraft carrier *Wasp* during an Atlantic crossing and sank with the loss of 175 men. Sixty-one

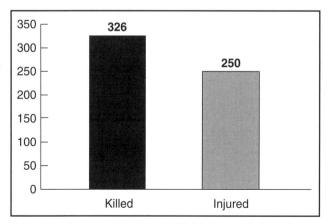

Casualties, Hoboken, N.J., fire, 1900. (Nash, Jay Robert, *The Darkest Hour.* Prentice Hall. 1976)

men were rescued. The collision reportedly occurred as *Wasp* was turning into the wind to recover a flight of aircraft. Cut in two by the collision, *Hobson* sank in four minutes. *Hobson*'s captain, who was lost with his ship, was blamed by a board of inquiry for failing to compensate correctly for the carrier's turn.

See also COLLISIONS.

Home, American steamship A casualty of an especially fierce hurricane in 1837, the paddle-wheel packet *Home* operated between New York and Charleston, South Carolina, and was off Cape Hatteras on October 9 when the storm overcame the vessel. *Home* was taking on water faster than pumps could expel it. Captain Carleton White told passengers to help bail out the ship, but this measure also proved ineffective.

As *Home* passed Cape Hatteras, the captain turned the ship toward land in the hope of beaching the vessel. *Home* made little progress, however, in the heavy seas. Soon the water put out the fires under the boilers, and the ship had to try to make land on short sail.

Home struck the beach late that night, some six miles from Ocracoke Village on the Outer Banks of North Carolina. Order on the ship appears to have vanished at that moment. Two men grabbed the only two life preservers on board and departed the ship, leaving behind some 130 other people. A number of women and children were gathered on the forecastle, and most of them were killed when the forecastle broke away from the rest of the ship. One elderly, overweight woman was rescued by islanders after drifting ashore tied to a settee.

Only 40 people on *Home* were saved, including the captain, 20 crewmen and 20 passengers. The two men who stole the life preservers reached shore safely. The bodies of many of the wreck's victims washed ashore. Of *Home* itself, everything but the boilers was demolished.

The wreck of the *Home* resembled that of the British liner *Titanic* 75 years later, in that both ships carried more people than their lifesaving equipment could accommodate. After the *Home* catastrophe, Congress passed legislation requiring all seagoing ships to have a life preserver for every individual on board.

Hong Koh, Chinese steamer A combination of shipwreck and riot, the loss of *Hong Koh* on March 18, 1921, reportedly killed more than 1,000 people, either in the riot or in the sinking. The aged vessel was carrying more than 1,100 Swatow and Amoy Chinese passengers into the harbor at Swatow, China. The Swatow passengers insisted on going ashore at their home port, whereas the Amoy passengers demanded to be put ashore at Amoy. Apparently, there was vicious animosity between the two communities, and armed violence was about to break out between the Amoy and Swatow contingents as the ship approached the harbor. A riot began when the ship's pilot declared that a sandbar would prevent entry to the harbor. The captain and crew restored order briefly with the help of firearms and a hose. Then the ship struck a reef, and the passengers began using knives and axes to fight their way into lifeboats. The captain was drowned, and only a few on board escaped with their lives.

hull Many shipwrecks occur when a ship's hull, or "skin," is breached, allowing water to enter and flood the ship's interior. The ship then sinks as a result of lost buoyancy.

It is not widely appreciated how thin and fragile a typical ship's hull is. It has been said that if a large modern ship were reduced somehow to desktop size, with everything in its original proportions, the hull would be about as thin as aluminum foil.

Even a hull made of inch-thick steel, the thickness used to build the British liner *Titanic,* will not withstand a collision with an iceberg or another vessel at any considerable speed. A glancing blow against an iceberg in the North Atlantic ripped open *Titanic's* hull and sank the liner on its maiden voyage in 1912, and *Titanic's* sister ship *Olympic* sustained serious damage to its hull in a collision with the British cruiser *Hawke* several months before *Titanic's* loss.

One protection against shipwreck resulting from hull damage is to build a double hull, with both inner and outer layers. In that case, if the outer hull is

Metal-hulled ships can actually be fragile. (U.S. Coast Guard)

breached, the inner hull prevents the ship from filling and sinking. This design has been used in many vessels, notably the famous 19th-century liner *Great Eastern.* (One grisly story associated with *Great Eastern's* hull involves a worker who allegedly was sealed inside the hull during its construction. According to the story, his skeleton was discovered between the inner and outer hull when the ship was scrapped.)

Extremely stout hulls are a characteristic of icebreakers, special vessels designed to break open passageways through thick ice. The extremely thick, uniquely designed hulls of icebreakers allow the ships to ride up over thick ice and crush it under the vessel's weight.

Wooden-hulled ships, during the age of sail and the transition to the age of steam-powered vessels, were vulnerable to attack by shipworms, or teredos. These organisms—actually not worms at all, but molluscs with the capability to bore through wood or even rock—could leave a wooden hull riddled, rotten and liable to break apart.

See also CONSTRUCTION; GREAT EASTERN; TEREDOS.

***Hunt,* American schooner** The wreck of *Augustus Hunt* on January 22, 1904, on Long Island, New York, exemplifies the dangers and difficulties of lifesaving in the early 20th century. A four-masted collier, *Hunt* went aground in a gale off Quogue. Just before the ship struck the bar, a lookout reported seeing a light ahead. Although the mate thought the light belonged to a steamer, the light was actually that of the Shinnecock lighthouse.

An extremely heavy sea was running. The ship was driven so deeply onto the bar that *Hunt* held firm while the sea swept over the schooner with devasta-

Wooden-hulled sailing ships looked impressive but were vulnerable to fire. (U.S. Coast Guard)

ting effect. The men of Quogue lifesaving station tried to assist *Hunt,* but had trouble seeing the vessel. Fog reduced visibility, and the ship's lights had been knocked out when *Hunt* struck the bar. The men on shore were able to hear the cries of *Hunt*'s men, however, and made an unsuccessful attempt around 3 A.M. to put a line aboard the ship with their Lyle gun. Three to four hours later, the lifesavers heard three of the ship's masts fall with a tremendous noise. The fourth mast fell several minutes later.

Two men survived the wreck. They perched at first on the jib boom, then made their way to the forecastle and jumped from there onto a piece of wreckage floating in the water. That piece of the ship was carried close to shore, and the men on it were rescued. The bravery of one lifesaver was outstanding. At the risk of his life, he went into the breakers with a line tied around his body, climbed onto the piece of wreckage and brought one of the wreck's survivors back to shore. Another lifesaver leaped into the water to rescue the other man on the floating wreckage.

Jeanette Edwards Rattray, in her history of shipwrecks on Long Island, reports that both the aforementioned lifesavers were awarded gold medals by the government for their bravery. What was left of the wreck was sold for $15.

hurricanes Tropical storms of exceptional size and violence, hurricanes have been responsible for numerous shipwrecks. A seemingly safe harbor may in fact offer little or no protection against the waves and winds of hurricanes, as the record of numerous shipwrecks in the Caribbean region indicates. A hurricane may be several hundred miles in diameter, and its destructive effects, such as dangerous waves, may extend far beyond the actual boundaries of the storm.

Winds within a hurricane may exceed velocities of 100 miles per hour and generate waves capable of sinking even large modern vessels. A peculiarity of hurricane structure is the "eye," a zone of calm air at the center of the hurricane. The eye is surrounded by winds of extreme velocity, which become less intense as one moves toward the periphery of the storm.

Hurricanes are an export mechanism, so to speak, for tropical heat. They transfer that heat from the tropics to higher latitudes during a period of several months, usually in the autumn. In the Atlantic, hurricanes typically do most damage in the Caribbean region and along the Gulf and South Atlantic states of the United States. Some hurricanes have reached far to the north, however, and have caused widespread destruction in areas as far north as New England.

The expression "hurricane" now is used to describe such storms in both the Atlantic and Pacific Oceans. For many years, it was customary to call Pacific hurricanes "typhoons." Another old custom, applying exclusively female names to hurricanes, has been discontinued in recent years. Both male and female names now are applied to the storms.

See also STORMS; WAVES.

***Hussar*, British frigate**   On November 3, 1780, *Hussar* ran aground in New York's East River while trying to evade capture by revolutionary forces. The ship struck a shoal off Pot Rock, near what is now 134th Street. *Hussar* sank quickly, killing 12 crewmen and a number of American prisoners imprisoned in the hold. The exact location of the wreck is uncertain.

See also TREASURE.

I

icebergs Huge blocks of ice that break off from glaciers and drift toward shipping lanes in lower latitudes, icebergs have been responsible for numerous incidents of damage to ships. Collision with an iceberg caused the most celebrated shipwreck of the 20th century, namely the loss of the British liner *Titanic* in 1912. As a result of *Titanic*'s sinking, the International Ice Patrol was formed to track movements of icebergs in the North Atlantic.

Icebergs occur in various sizes, shapes and colors. Some have the familiar "alpine" configuration, with one or more mountain-like peaks. Others are "tabular" in configuration, with flat tops. "Growlers" are relatively small icebergs. The color of an iceberg depends partly on how much rock is included in it. Some icebergs are reportedly very dark and difficult to detect visually.

Even a small iceberg can pose a serious threat to shipping, because of its great mass and resistance. An iceberg may be so hard that striking it is equivalent

Icebergs are a hazard to shipping, as in this drawing of the *Titanic*.

to a collision with a submerged rock and can sink a ship easily.

Experiments in destroying icebergs with explosives have been fruitless. An energy release equivalent to that of a small nuclear weapon would be required to destroy a typical iceberg. The only practical defense against icebergs is to detect, track and avoid them.

Ships that collide with icebergs are more likely to survive if they hit the iceberg directly rather than at an angle. A "head-on" collision may damage a ship's bow but probably will leave the vessel afloat. A glancing blow to an iceberg, on the other hand, may extend damage along much of the ship's flank and cause the craft to sink quickly. A collision of this latter kind sank *Titanic*.

See also HANS HEDTOFT; INTERNATIONAL ICE PATROL; TITANIC.

identification of shipwrecks Modern shipwrecks are generally identified as they occur, but identifying wrecks of earlier centuries may be difficult. In the case of wooden ships, the entire structure of the ship itself may be gone, leaving behind only ballast and various artifacts to identify the ship's nationality and identity. As a rule, marine archeologist Robert Marx points out, the chance of a positive identification increases with the number of articles a salvor recovers from a wreck.

There are problems in using artifacts to identify a wreck, however, because the site may have been "contaminated" by other artifacts that were deposited after the wreck occurred. For example, another wreck may have occurred at the same location and scattered artifacts over the site. Another possibility is that articles were thrown from, or otherwise lost by, a passing ship at some date after the wreck and landed on the site. Marx cites the case of a salvage operation in Florida waters that found a 19th-century anchor on the site of a 17th-century wreck. The anchor had caught on the wreck and been abandoned. The salvors would have erred greatly in dating the shipwreck on the basis of that anchor.

Another possibility is that a given wreck will include items older than the wreck itself. Marx writes of a Spanish sea captain in the early 18th century who wrote of using a sword dating from the 16th century. In another case, a 17th-century ship carried cannon recovered from a ship sunk in the mid-16th century. Sometimes the age discrepancy between wrecks and their cargo is extreme; Marx mentions a 19th-century shipwreck that yielded a statue from Roman times.

Determining the nationality of a wrecked ship is likewise difficult if the vessel carried articles from different countries. A Spanish ship might carry numerous items of English manufacture, as well as articles from other European countries and their colonies in the western hemisphere.

Sometimes, specialists are called in to help identify wrecks by nationality on the basis of seemingly unlikely clues. Marx tells of one wreck near Jamaica that was identified as a Dutch merchantman. A zoologist studied fish bones found on the wreck site and found that they belonged to North Sea herring, a fish not native to Caribbean waters. The herring bones, together with Dutch artifacts discovered on the wreck, helped establish the ship's Dutch nationality. Marx adds that geologists may be able to identify ballast rock by its country of origin, and that information too may help in identifying a wreck by nationality.

See also ARCHAEOLOGY.

immigration Many shipwrecks in the 18th and 19th centuries involved immigrant vessels on their way westward from Europe to America. Economic hardships and other problems in Europe caused millions of families to risk the dangerous Atlantic crossing in the hope of attaining a better social and economic environment. As one might expect under such circumstances, traveling conditions were generally unpleasant. Large numbers of immigrants were loaded onto ships almost in the same manner as livestock. If and when an immigrant ship encountered heavy weather or other difficulty and began to sink, the immigrants on board were, in many cases, likely to drown. A notorious example of an immigrant vessel coming to grief was the wreck of a British ship with some 300 German Protestant immigrants bound for Virginia on board, in the early 18th century.

See also SWITZER WRECK.

Industry, American bark One of many vessels that came to grief on the Columbia River (Oregon-Wash-ington) bar, *Industry* already had had a rough voyage when the bark arrived off the Oregon coast in March of 1865. On a voyage from San Francisco, the ship had encountered stormy weather, and some tanks of fresh water on board had been broken.

When the pilot boat came out to meet *Industry*, no pilot came on board. Instead, *Industry* was expected to follow the boat into the river mouth. *Industry* ran aground and ripped off the rudder. The ship came free but grounded again only a few feet away.

For his passengers' safety, the captain had a boat lowered. A large swell demolished the boat, however, and killed the first officer, who was in charge of it.

A storm was approaching, and around nightfall the ship's occupants climbed into the rigging. The heavy seas began breaking apart the vessel. The next morning, the passengers and crew started building rafts.

One raft was launched successfully and carried five survivors across the bar. Soldiers from nearby Fort Stevens met them in a lifeboat and rescued them. Several passengers on another raft were swept overboard, and another passenger on that raft reportedly perished from exposure.

Of eight passengers, only two survived the wreck. Crew members who had stayed on *Industry*, so as to give passengers places on the rafts, were killed when the ship broke apart. Only seven of 24 people on *Industry* survived.

International Ice Patrol A multinational organization devoted to monitoring icebergs and their movements in the North Atlantic Ocean, the International Ice Patrol was established in response to the sinking of the British liner *Titanic* following a collision with an iceberg in 1912.

See also ICEBERGS; TITANIC.

***Iowa*, American freighter** In an incident both tragic and mysterious, 34 men were killed in the wreck of the freighter *Iowa* at Peacock Spit on the Columbia River (Oregon-Washington) bar on January 12, 1936. Caught in a gale while crossing the bar outbound, the freighter lost a fight with powerful winds and was driven onto the notorious Peacock Spit. An S.O.S. message from *Iowa* brought the Coast Guard cutter *Onondaga* to the scene. By the time *Onondaga* arrived, however, almost nothing of *Iowa* remained visible above the waters. No one on the freighter survived to tell what exactly had happened to *Iowa*. Two possibilities are that the ship experienced damage either to the rudder or to the steering engine and was swept onto Peacock Spit as a result.

***Iredale*, British sailing vessel**   A large and attractive ship, of rugged iron and steel construction, *Peter Iredale* was built in England in 1890. The ship's hulk became a landmark of sorts on the Oregon coast after *Iredale* wrecked at Clatsop Beach on October 25, 1906.

The captain testified that he had intended to wait offshore for a pilot, but a strong wind and current "prevailed," and *Iredale* went ashore. Portions of the masts broke and fell, and the captain was astonished that no one was killed. A surf boat from Point Adams took the men ashore.

Iredale had a colorful history even after its wreck. A Japanese naval vessel shelled the Oregon coast one night early in World War II. The shells struck near, but apparently did not damage, the wreck of *Iredale*. The wreck and Clatsop Beach were strewn with barbed wire during the war in case of invasion. Over the years, the wreck became a favorite subject of artists and photographers.

"iron duke"   An armored diving suit, the "iron duke" was supposed to let a diver breathe at normal atmospheric pressure while protecting him from intense water pressure by encasing him in a rigid shell, yet allowing him to move freely. The iron duke appears to have originated in the early 18th century with a design by English inventor John Lethbridge, whose suit had a rigid shell but left the diver's arms exposed. This design would not have worked in practice, because the openings for the diver's arms would have defeated the entire purpose of the rigid shell. Various other designs were put forward in the 1800s, none of them feasible.

A German company, Neufelt and Kuhnke, produced a workable iron duke in 1923. It consisted of a metal shell with articulated metal "hands" for exterior work. The suit carried its own air supply in cylinders and had a ballast tank to provide negative or positive buoyancy (that is, to let the suit sink or rise, respectively). This iron duke played an important part in salvage on the wreck of the British liner *Egypt*.

See also DIVING SUITS; EGYPT.

***Isidore*, American bark**   The maritime literature on precognition and premonition includes the tale of the bark *Isidore*, which sailed from Kennebunkport, Maine, on November 30, 1842.

A snowstorm began as the ship departed. Wreckage from *Isidore* drifted ashore at Cape Neddick Nubble soon afterward. Historian Edward Rowe Snow reports that a strange presentiment of calamity characterized the bark's departure: some women were sobbing out loud as *Isidore* left port.

Snow also mentions the alleged experience of Thomas King, a seaman who reportedly dreamed, two nights before the bark sailed, that *Isidore* and its crew would be lost. King was so upset that he went to the bark's captain and asked to be released from his contract, but the captain scoffed at King's dream.

Still reluctant to sail, King concealed himself in the woods and watched until he saw *Isidore* sail out of the harbor. King came under criticism at first for refusing to sail on *Isidore*, but was respected for his decision after news of the ship's loss arrived.

It should be noted, however, that tales of alleged premonitions and precognition can be manufactured after a ship's loss at sea, and therefore should be viewed with at least a normal degree of skepticism.

See also PRECOGNITION AND PREMONITIONS.

***Italia*, Italian airship**   Though not a shipwreck in the nautical sense, the loss of the Italian airship *Italia* on May 25, 1928, is nonetheless a sad part of the history of Arctic exploration.

Under command of explorer Umberto Nobile, the gas-filled airship departed Italy on April 15 on the first leg of a journey to the North Pole. *Italia* stopped at King's Bay, Spitzbergen, Norway, at the northern tip of Scandinavia, to meet a supply ship.

On May 23, the ship reached the North Pole. *Italia* encountered heavy weather on the return to Spitzbergen, however, and was forced down on the icecap on May 25.

Nobile and several of his companions were stranded on the ice with supplies including a tent, a radio and enough provisions for a month and a half. The airship itself was carried away by the storm with seven people still on board, and was never seen again.

Injured and unable to travel 60 miles to the nearest land, Nobile sent out radio messages giving his position. A huge international rescue effort followed. Nobile was rescued by a Swedish aircraft on June 24. A Russian icebreaker rescued the rest of the expedition's survivors on July 10.

A tragic element of the rescue operation was the disappearance of famed Norwegian polar explorer Roald Amundsen, first man to reach the South Pole. Amundsen and several companions set out in an aircraft to search for Nobile on June 18. No one from Amundsen's party ever returned.

J

Jamaica Although numerous shipwrecks have occurred in Jamaican waters, large wrecks are few, because the island was not considered an important colony of Spain, and few large vessels visited Jamaica. On the other hand, the sunken city of Port Royal, submerged in an earthquake, has been a major site of marine archaeological activity. Among the wrecks in Jamaican waters are those of Columbus's two ships *Capitana* and *Santiago,* lost on his fourth and final voyage to the Americas.

See also COLUMBUS EXPEDITIONS; PORT ROYAL.

Jameson, American schooner The wreck of the schooner *Frank Jameson* in 1877 played an important part in mobilizing public support for the then-newborn U.S. Lifesaving Service. The schooner was bound from Maine to Richmond, Virginia, with a cargo of ice when a storm drove the ship ashore at the Smith Island station on Virginia's Eastern Shore, just north of Cape Charles, on November 25, 1877. The storm demolished the ship. At that time, the station was closed, and the lifesavers were off duty. A lighthouse keeper on the island knew of the schooner's presence but presumed, erroneously, that the ship was merely anchored and riding out the storm. Only one crewman survived the wreck of *Jameson.* He was discovered and rescued by the lifesavers, who finally had been summoned hours after the wreck occurred. Had the station been manned on a full-time basis, the surfmen probably would have seen the wreck and responded in time to save most or all of the men on the stricken schooner. This was one of two almost simultaneous wrecks that helped increase public support for the government lifesaving service.

See also LIFESAVING SERVICE; OSSIPEE.

Jardines Reefs, Cuba An extremely dangerous set of reefs on Cuba's southern coast near the Isle of Pines, the Jardines Reefs reportedly destroyed six ships of the New Spain Fleet on a single day in 1563.

On July 18, the 150-ton *capitana* of the fleet, *San Juan Bautista,* along with five other large ships including the 350-ton *San Salvador,* the 300-ton *Santa Margarita* and the 250-ton *San Juan,* sank in water perhaps 24 feet deep or less. Despite the shallowness of the water, salvage attempts are said to have been largely unsuccessful. The cargo included mercury.

See also CUBA; FLOTA SYSTEM; MERCURY.

John & Lucy, American sailing vessel An early wreck in American waters, *John & Lucy* provides a glimpse of maritime commerce and cargo in the colonies. During a voyage from Rhode Island to New York, the ship was wrecked at Montauk on Long Island, New York, on March 22, 1668. The vessel carried 15 men along with two sheep, two goats, three mares, the ship's dog (named Lyon) and several cats. The ship apparently struck a rock and was stuck upon it all night. At daybreak, the crew abandoned the stricken ship so quickly that three men were left behind. The men in boats proceeded to New London, Connecticut, where a sloop and a bark were engaged to sail out to *John & Lucy.* Bad weather delayed the ships for several days. The men left on *John & Lucy* were rescued.

Jonah, biblical prophet One of the most famous stories of survival at sea, the tale of the prophet Jonah is told in the Book of Jonah in the Old Testament. The narrator is not identified but is presumed to be Jonah himself.

Jonah is told by God to go to the city of Nineveh, on the Tigris River, and preach repentance to its people, for the sins of Nineveh have come to God's attention. (The city's sins are not listed specifically in the Book of Jonah but are thought to have included witchcraft, sexual immorality and unsavory business practices.)

Instead of obeying God's command, Jonah flees to the port city of Joppa and embarks on a ship bound for Tarshish, which may have been located near what is now Gibraltar. God sends such a great storm upon the ship that the vessel soon is close to breaking up. The pagan seamen entreat their particular gods to quell the storm, but their prayers have no effect. They throw their cargo overboard in a desperate attempt to save the ship.

At last, the captain, going below and finding Jonah asleep, demands that Jonah arise and call on God to save the ship. Meanwhile, the sailors cast lots to determine who is responsible for bringing the storm upon them, and the lot indicates that Jonah is the one.

In response to the sailors' questions, Jonah explains that he is a Hebrew, and he worships the God who made the land and sea. Aware that Jonah is trying to flee from God, and that the sea is becoming rougher all the time, the mariners ask what they can do to escape the storm's violence. Jonah tells them to cast him into the sea, because his disobedience has brought the storm upon them. Then, he tells them, the storm will abate. The sailors throw Jonah into the sea as directed, and the sea grows calm.

God sends a huge fish to swallow Jonah. (The biblical text says specifically that the animal is a fish, not a whale, as many modern retellings of the story have it.) Jonah remains inside the fish for three days and three nights. Jonah, from inside the fish, cries out for deliverance. At God's command, the fish casts Jonah out onto dry land.

Next, God repeats his command to Jonah to go and preach repentance to the Ninevites. This time, Jonah obeys. The city will be overthrown in 40 days, he warns, unless Nineveh collectively repents of sin. The Ninevites listen to Jonah and turn from their evil ways. Even the king puts off his royal robes and wears sackcloth instead. He also issues a proclamation, telling the people to give up evildoing. In consequence, God has compassion on the city and does not allow the city's destruction.

Jonah, however, is disappointed. He actually wished to see Nineveh destroyed, and was outraged when the city was spared.

K

K-13, British submarine A small but calamitous mechanical malfunction appears to have sunk *K-13* during a test dive on January 29, 1917. A light on the control panel glowed green, indicating that ventilating doors in the boiler room were closed. The doors were in fact still open, and on diving, the submarine flooded in its aft compartments and sank. Thirty-four seamen reportedly drowned. Forty-eight others remained alive in the dry forward compartments. Because the submarine sank in reasonably shallow water (only about 60 feet deep), escape and rescue operations were possible. Two men tried to escape through the conning tower, reach the surface and bring help. One of the men died in the ascent, but the other succeeded. A rescue operation brought food and air through hoses to the sunken submarine, sustaining the men aboard until the sub could be raised. When the submarine was hauled to the surface, the remaining 46 survivors were freed through a hole cut in the hull. The submarine later was refitted and recommissioned as *K-22*.

See also SUBMARINES.

Kaiser Wilhelm der Grosse, German passenger liner The big and handsome *Kaiser Wilhelm* was rammed by the British steamer *Orinoco* off Cherbourg, France, on November 21, 1906. Five passengers were killed, and the German liner experienced heavy damage. *Kaiser Wilhelm* also was involved in the great Hoboken, New Jersey, fire of 1900 but escaped with only minor damage in that incident.

See also HOBOKEN FIRE.

Kaiyo Maru, Japanese observation vessel Sent to observe an undersea volcanic eruption in 1952 in the Bonin Islands, a volcanic island chain extending southward from the vicinity of Tokyo, *Kaiyo Maru* and another vessel arrived at the scene just as a spectacular eruption was occurring. Although the ships tried to maintain a safe distance from the erup-tion, *Kaiyo Maru* strayed over the top of a volcanic vent and was blown up when the submarine volcano erupted just after noon on September 24. No one on the vessel survived.

Kaptajn Nielsen, Danish dredge The large dredge *Kaptajn Nielsen* capsized and sank in the harbor at Brisbane, Australia, on September 18, 1964. Two men were killed.

Around 11:15 P.M., as the captain left the bridge to go to his day room, he heard the noise of winches raising the suction pipe on the dredge's starboard side. The ship heeled slightly to one side, as normally happened during that operation. Ordinarily, the vessel would have resumed its usual attitude, but this time the dredge rolled over, trapping the crew inside the hull.

A seaman named Eric Poulsen escaped from the overturned ship and swam four miles to shore, then ran two miles to a residence on Moreton Island and reported the incident. Rescue operations began immediately.

Divers from a local SCUBA diving club reached the scene and began investigating the wreck. They found the crew still alive, in cabins half-filled with water. One by one, the survivors were rescued. The divers explored the vessel thoroughly to make sure that no one was left aboard.

Two men in the engine room escaped through one of the large tubes through which sand was pumped during dredging. Once free, they sat on the keel until rescued.

The reasons for the capsizing were a mystery. Apparently there was no evidence that the ship had grounded; and the chains to the main hopper doors were unbroken, thus ruling out the possibility that the doors had opened and released part of the dredge's load.

Apparently, the capsizing took only a few seconds. A diver who reached the wreck noticed that dishes found in the sunken vessel were unbroken. The diver surmised that the dredge overturned so quickly that the dishes fell into the water rather than directly onto the deck as the vessel capsized.

***Kawachi*, Japanese battleship** One of the most impressive warships of its time, equipped with 12 12-inch guns, *Kawachi* was destroyed in a mysterious explosion as the ship entered Tokuyama Bay, Japan, on July 12, 1918. The blast ripped the battleship in half and killed some 500 of 900 men on board. What caused the explosion is not certain, but one theory is that an explosion in a magazine in the lower hold set off a much more powerful explosion that destroyed the vessel.

See also EXPLOSIONS; MYSTERIES.

***Kawanoura Maru*, Japanese steamship** *Kawanoura Maru* was slammed into another steamship, the *Hozui Maru*, in Kobe, Japan, by a tsunami, or seismic sea wave, on June 15, 1896. According to one report, both ships sank, and 178 men aboard them were killed. This particular tsunami devastated the northeastern coast of Japan and is thought to have killed more than 28,000 people within several minutes. Fishing boats returning home from a day's work found a vast area with bodies and debris floating on the water. Investigators concluded later that the tsunami was generated when part of the seabed collapsed.

See also TSUNAMIS.

keel The "spine" of a ship, so to speak, the keel is the lowermost longitudinal structural member of a vessel. The keel is the first element of the ship to be laid down during construction. It also tends to be the heaviest portion of the ship, so that a ship is likely to sink with the keel downward and thus land upright on the bottom. This is true even if the ship capsizes (that is, rolls over) at the surface, provided the vessel has enough time to right itself on the way to the bottom. Although the keel is formed in many cases from two or more pieces that are joined to form a single structural member, the keel may be manufactured as a single unit, with no joints or welds. An interesting case of a keel built as a single unit may be seen in *San Juan*, a Basque whaler excavated at Red Bay, Labrador.

See also SAN JUAN.

***Kenmure Castle*, British steamship** Heavy seas in the Bay of Biscay on February 1, 1883, washed away the entire superstructure of *Kenmure Castle*. Only one boat was launched, with 16 on board. Thirty-two people were killed, including the captain.

***Kent*, British troopship** The 1,350-ton troopship *Kent* sank in the Atlantic Ocean during a gale on February 19, 1825, while on a voyage to Bengal. *Kent* caught fire and burned, killing 81 people. More than 500 people were rescued by other ships.

The fire is thought to have started when a lantern ignited a spill of whisky. Captain Henry Cobb tried to save the ship by having a portion of the lower decks flooded to prevent the fire from reaching the magazines. This measure protected the magazines for a while, but the flooding caused *Kent*'s bow to dip into the sea.

As Cobb was about to issue an order to abandon ship, the brig *Cambria* appeared on the scene. In the rescue operation, Cobb and the crew gave strict priority to the wives and children of the soldiers on board. The captain gave orders to "cut down" any man who tried to enter a boat before all women and children were saved. The men on *Kent* were well-disciplined, however, and did not try to rush the boats.

Another vessel, the *Caroline*, arrived to assist in rescue operations just as the final lifeboat left *Kent*. Two hours later, the fire finally reached the ship's magazines, and *Kent* exploded with some men still left on board, clinging to the rigging. Somehow, 17 men survived the explosion and were rescued from the ocean later.

The rescue operation is especially remarkable in that it was conducted at sea, during a gale, using fragile boats removing survivors from a badly listing ship, and still managed to save 87 percent of those on board. The bravery and discipline of the troops on *Kent* have been compared to that of the soldiers on the troopship *Birkenhead*, whose name became a synonym for bravery and obedience to orders in the face of death.

The sinking of *Kent* produced an interesting anecdote that has parallels in other tales of catastrophes at sea. One sailor reportedly tied 400 sovereigns (heavy coins) in a handkerchief around his neck and would not leave them behind, even though their weight seemed sure to drown him in the sea. "You'll sink with it," Cobb reportedly warned him. Similar stories are told of other wrecks.

See also BIRKENHEAD; FIRE; MONEY BELT STORIES.

***Kiang Hsin*, Chinese steamship** *Kiang Hsin* was bombed and sunk by Japanese aircraft on June 28, 1938, near Yochow on the Yangtsze River, with the loss of more than 1,000 lives. The ship was raised, then sunk again during the Chinese Civil War, at Shanghai, on September 5, 1949.

***Kiangya*, Chinese steamer** The 2,100-ton coastal steamer *Kiangya* was carrying more than 3,000 people when it hit a Japanese mine and sank near Shanghai on December 3, 1948. Only about 700 people survived the explosion and sinking. Between 2,700 and 2,800 people are thought to have died. The overcrowded conditions on the steamer were due to refugees fleeing Communist forces.

***Kien Yuan,* Chinese steamship**   *Kien Yuan* sank in a collision with another vessel, the *Tai Ping,* in Bonham Strait near Chusan Island, China, on January 27, 1949. Both ships sank. More than 1,500 people are believed to have been killed.

***Kincora,* British steamship**   In fog, not even reducing speed and sounding the ship's siren can guarantee safety. *Kincora* took those precautions but was run down nonetheless by the White Star liner *Oceanic* in fog off Tuskar Rock in St. George's Channel (between England and Ireland) early on the morning of August 8, 1901. *Kincora* sank in seven minutes, with the loss of seven crewmen.

Kingston/Port Royal wrecks, Jamaica   In October of 1744, a hurricane sank 105 ships in Kingston harbor and Port Royal. The total is thought to include 95 merchant vessels and nine warships, including the 50-gun H.M.S. *Albans,* the 50-gun H.M.S. *Greenwich* and the 14-gun *Bonetta.* The storm also is said to have destroyed warehouses and wharves. On July 13, 1815, a hurricane and earthquake struck Kingston simultaneously and brought about the loss of some 40 to 50 small vessels at Port Royal and a dozen large craft at Kingston.

See also JAMAICA.

***Kjobenhavn,* Danish passenger steamship**   Years after war, mines may continue to be a deadly hazard. *Kjobenhavn* was passing through what was considered a safe route when the ship struck a mine off the coast of Jutland and sank within 10 minutes. Out of 350 passengers and 52 crewmen, 216 passengers and 45 crew were rescued. The explosion occurred in the early morning hours and knocked out the ship's electrical system and lighting, so that it was difficult to get people on deck in the darkness.

***Klose,* American schooner**   This wreck was the focus of a short-lived mystery. The derelict schooner *C.A. Klose* drifted ashore near Fort Canby, Oregon, on March 26, 1905. The ship was upside down, with its keel pointed skyward, so the crew was presumed to be lost. The crew turned up safe and sound several weeks later. They had abandoned ship on March 21 when it looked as if *Klose* were about to founder.

Another ship picked them up and put them ashore upon making port.

Knight expedition, British   An early 18th-century Arctic explorer, James Knight, an employee of the Hudson's Bay Company, sailed into the bay in search of the Northwest Passage, the rumored sea route through the far North between the Atlantic and Pacific Oceans. More than 40 men accompanied him. The Knight expedition never returned. More than 40 years later, the Hudson's Bay Company finally learned that the expedition was shipwrecked on Marble Island. Some members of the expedition survived for some years after the wreck but eventually died of cold and malnutrition. The native Inuit people reportedly observed a tragic scene as the last two survivors of the expedition stood on the island watching for a relief party. According to the story, the men sat down and wept. After a while, one of the men died. His companion tried to dig a grave for him but was so weakened that he, too, fell down and perished in the effort. Shipwrecks were numerous in the early days of Arctic exploration.

See also FRANKLIN EXPEDITION; POLAR REGIONS.

knot   A measurement of speed equivalent to one nautical mile (6076.1 feet) per hour. One knot equals about 1.15 miles per hour. Although ships on the ocean measure their speed in knots, vessels on American inland waterways measure theirs in miles per hour.

***Kobenhaven,* Danish sailing vessel**   A five-master, *Kobenhaven* was on a voyage from the River Plate (Uruguay-Argentina) to Australia with 75 people on board when the ship was lost under mysterious circumstances off Tristan de Cunha. The final message from the ship, on December 22, 1928, gave its position as 900 miles off the island. The vessel and crew then disappeared at sea and were neither seen nor heard from again. *Kobenhaven* was presumed to have foundered in a storm.

See also MYSTERIES.

***Kyzikes,* Greek steamer**   Wrecked on the Outer Banks of North Carolina in a storm on December 3, 1927, *Kyzikes* went ashore near Kitty Hawk.

The ship broke in two. The frightened men on the bow saw what looked like the lights of a rescue ship beside them. Then, the men understood that the apparent rescue ship was merely the stern fragment of their own vessel, from which their fellow crewmen were returning their signals. The men on the stern boarded the bow section by an improvised gangplank. Four lives were lost.

L

L-24, British submarine Built in 1919, *L-24* went down with 48 men when rammed by the British dreadnought *Resolution* off Portland Bill, England, in fog on January 10, 1924. Although *Resolution* carried special listening equipment to detect submarines nearby, it apparently failed to detect *L-24*, which was running submerged just before the collision. For reasons unknown, the submarine rose to the surface directly in the dreadnought's path and was rammed. The submarine sank in about 180 feet of water with the loss of all hands. The collision occurred during maneuvers in which two other submarines, *K-2* and *K-12*, had struck and damaged each other earlier.

See also SUBMARINES.

Lady Elgin, American side-wheel steamer In a case somewhat similar the loss of the British liner *Titanic* in the North Atlantic more than 50 years later, the excursion ship *Lady Elgin* was sunk in a collision on Lake Michigan in the early morning hours of September 8, 1860. The cruise, a fund-raising occasion, brought together a crowd of merrymakers on board, and the ship was brightly illuminated for the event.

Out of the darkness came the schooner *Augusta of Oswego*. The schooner's captain presumed he had the right of way and would not yield to the steamer, although *Lady Elgin* was plainly visible, and the vessels were on a collision course. *Lady Elgin*'s men could not see *Augusta of Oswego*, because the schooner ran dark—without lights—that night. Moreover, high winds and rain suddenly beset the two ships just before the collision, reducing visibility.

Augusta of Oswego rammed *Lady Elgin*, then reportedly sailed away without rendering assistance, leaving the side-wheel steamer sinking in a storm. Fewer than 100 people survived the sinking; 287 are thought to have been killed. The schooner's captain was arrested and placed on trial, but was found not guilty because he technically had not violated the law. Ship masters at that time had broad powers of discretion in navigat-

ing their vessels, even though the results might be catastrophic.

Augusta of Oswego had a blighted career thereafter. Widely despised, the ship became a symbol of catastrophe, and its notoriety lasted for decades, until the vessel was wrecked in a storm near Cleveland, Ohio, in 1894.

The parallels between *Lady Elgin* and *Titanic* are close and numerous. Both ships were filled with well-off passengers when they sank; both were lost at night, as the result of a collision, *Lady Elgin* with a schooner and *Titanic* with an iceberg; and in both cases, only a small fraction of those on board survived the wreck.

In another parallel, opprobrium descended on a particular ship and its master after each incident. In the *Lady Elgin* sinking, *Augusta of Oswego* and its master, one Captain Matson, were accused but acquitted. In *Titanic*'s case, Captain Stanley Lord of the liner *Californian* is thought to have been within several miles of *Titanic* on the night of the sinking, but failed to come to *Titanic*'s aid.

Lake Maracaibo wrecks, Venezuela Pirates scored a victory over Spanish forces at Lake Maracaibo in 1669. To combat the pirates, who under the leadership of Captain Henry Morgan were raiding communities on the lake, the Spaniards assigned three frigates, which anchored near a fort at the lake's entrance. Undaunted, the pirates captured one frigate and destroyed another by use of a fire ship. The Spaniards burned the third frigate to keep the pirates from capturing it.

Lakonia, Greek liner Originally a Dutch passenger ship, *Lakonia* was sailing under Greek ownership when the vessel caught fire and burned off Madeira on December 22, 1963. One hundred and twenty-eight people—33 crew members and 95 passengers—died either of the fire or of drowning.

Larchmont, American steamship The passenger steamer *Larchmont* sank near Montauk Point, Long Island, New York, on the night of February 11–12, 1907, after colliding with the coal schooner *Harry P. Knowlton.* Of 170 people on *Larchmont*, 131 were lost, and 93 bodies were recovered. The *Knowlton* also was lost.

Las Hormigas wreck, Peru A pilot's profession could be hazardous in more ways than one, as this wreck demonstrated. A big merchant ship on a voyage from Panama to Callao, Peru, was wrecked on rocks at Las Hormigas, several miles from Callao, on February 27, 1632. All on board were killed except the pilot and one other man. For losing the vessel (writes Robert Marx in his book *Shipwrecks in the Americas*), the pilot was hanged.

Laurel, American freighter Sometimes when a ship comes to grief, the captain and his would-be rescuers find themselves at odds. A case in point is the experience of Captain Louis Johnson of *Laurel.*

The lumber-laden freighter was carried onto Peacock Spit at the Columbia River (Oregon-Washington) bar during a storm on June 16, 1929. Despite the dangerous sea conditions, the Coast Guard managed to rescue everyone from *Laurel* except a young seaman, who was killed when the ship broke in two, and Captain Johnson.

The captain refused to leave his ship. He chose instead to stay on board and protect the cargo, as he said later, from salvagers. He hoped that the afterportion of the wreck would be carried onto the beach. When the bulkheads collapsed, however, he gave up and flew a white flag, the signal that he was ready to be taken ashore.

During his two-day watch on the disintegrating *Laurel*, the captain could be seen walking the deck. Although he said he did not want to become a hero, that was the reputation he acquired.

Laurentic, British liner Converted from a White Star passenger liner to a naval cruiser, *Laurentic* in January of 1917 struck a mine off the mouth of Lough Swilly along the Irish coast, and sank in about 130 feet of water, killing 354 of 745 people on board. On board were more than 3,000 gold ingots bound for Halifax, Nova Scotia, to pay for war materials. Britain could not afford to lose the gold, and salvage efforts began at once. The man in charge of salvage was Commander Guybon Damant. He had a distinguished record as a diver.

Damant set out for the wreck site and soon found the task was going to be extraordinarily difficult.

Laurentic lay on its left side at an angle of 60 degrees. The decks were only a few feet below the surface. That meant divers on the sunken ship's deck would have to contend with waves during any storms that occurred. To make matters worse, blocks on lifeboat falls were swinging like great pendulums from their davits, posing a grave threat to divers. The blocks had to be cut loose before salvage could start.

Then there was the threat from U-boats to consider. A submarine could put a torpedo into the salvage vessel as it floated above the wreck. On at least one occasion, Damant had to flee the scene when someone reported seeing a submarine's periscope. A diver working on the wreck at the time was dragged away and had to be hauled in as the vessel ran.

The divers blasted their way into the ship and, in a few days, reached the room where the gold was stored. From there, the salvage appeared to be merely a matter of hauling the gold to the surface. Several boxes of gold bars were recovered in two days.

A gale swept down on the ships, however, and Damant and his crew had to leave site for a week. On returning, divers found that the storm had damaged the wreck greatly. The passageway to the gold now was all but closed. The battering that *Laurentic* took from the storm had compressed the passageway to a mere foot and a half. There was nothing to do but resume blasting in order to open the passageway anew.

Once that work was finished, a new and awful surprise met Damant's team. The gold was no longer where it had been. It had spilled out of the room and into the wreckage deep inside the ship. The only course of action was to start cutting down into the wreck with explosives—a difficult, time-consuming and dangerous procedure. How dangerous it was, the men learned when a diver was trapped by a steel plate that fell on him. He was rescued by another diver, who located him by following the air bubbles from the trapped man's suit.

By September of 1917, Damant and his men had recovered some £800,000 of the approximately £5 million on board. Because the United States had entered the war, the gold was no longer needed so urgently, and the Admiralty called a halt to the salvage effort on *Laurentic* for the rest of the war. Salvage operations resumed after the war, in 1919.

When Damant and his crew returned to the wreck, they found new dangers awaiting them. The superstructure, weakened by blasting, was collapsing. Nonetheless, Damant and his men went back to work and brought more gold worth £470,000 out of the wreck.

All of a sudden, there appeared to be no more gold, although almost £4 million was supposedly still down there. Damant reached the disheartening conclusion that most of the gold was buried even more deeply in the vessel's holds.

The next year brought nothing but frustration. Two portions of the superstructure collapsed into the work area amidships, and sediment deposited in the work area by storms had hardened into a rock-like material made still stronger by the metal debris within it.

Damant and his team tried explosives, dredges and other means to clear the work area. Nothing worked. At last he decided to use water under high pressure, delivered by underwater hoses, to clear away the hardened mass. Work went slowly, but in 1922 the workers recovered some £1.5 million. The following year, the divers brought up an additional £2 million. That left only about £240,000 unrecovered. To find the last of the gold, Damant blasted away the bottom layer of *Laurentic*'s wreck and laid bare the sand below. There was the remaining gold.

Of more than 3,000 ingots, only 25 were left on the sea floor. Damant and his men had recovered more than 99 percent of a vast sunken treasure by the remarkable method of cutting apart a sunken ocean liner with explosives. Most remarkable of all, no one on the salvage team was killed in more than 5,000 dives.

See also DIVING SUITS; SALVAGE; TREASURE.

lead In the days before echo sounding devices that used sound pulses reflected off the seabed to estimate the depth of water under a ship's keel, vessels relied on "the lead" to determine how deep the water was beneath them. The technique was simple. Someone on board would cast over the side a lead weight attached to a line, then retrieve the lead after it touched bottom. Measuring the length of line allowed the user to estimate how much water was below. This technique was cumbersome but reasonably accurate, and helped prevent shipwrecks by alerting crews to dangerously shallow waters.

One colorful (though possibly fictional) story of the lead and its use concerns a ship's master who supposedly could tell his whereabouts off the New England coast by tasting the mud clinging to the lead when it was brought up. One day, the story goes, his crew decided to play a trick on him, and coated the lead with soil taken from a woman's property on Nantucket. The captain supposedly tasted it and exclaimed, "Nantucket's sunk, and here we sit, right over old Marm Hackett's garden!"

***Lena*, Norwegian bark** Sometimes shipwrecks occur because of misunderstood signals. Such was the case with *Lena*, a bark that went ashore near Hog Island on Virginia's Eastern Shore on December 26, 1884, while en route from Natal, Brazil, to Philadelphia.

Blown off course by strong winds, *Lena* was heading for the shore near the lifesaving station at Hog Island just before 4 A.M. when a surfman noticed the ship's running lights and burned a red flare to warn the vessel away. *Lena* mistook the warning flare for a pilot signal, however, and proceeded to run onto a shoal about one mile offshore.

The lifesavers at Hog Island prepared to launch their boat, but the surf was too high. About all the surfmen could do was wait and see if perhaps the seas would bring the stranded ship closer to shore, so that a line could be fired to it with the Lyle gun.

Gradually, *Lena* worked its way shoreward, but not close enough to receive a line. The lifesavers tried three times to shoot a line to *Lena*, each time unsuccessfully. Meanwhile, the turbulent sea made it difficult to reach the stranded ship by boat.

When it became clear that the Lyle gun was useless under the circumstances, the keeper of the lifesaving station decided to try launching the surfboat. The attempt failed. No matter how hard they pulled on the oars, the breakers kept pushing the surfboat back to the beach. A second effort, at a different point on the beach, also failed.

The rescuers then tried another plan. They tied a line to a barrel and released it into the surf, in the hope that currents somehow would carry the barrel to the ship. This scheme too was unsuccessful.

These attempts occupied much of the day. Near nightfall, the lifesavers built a bonfire on the beach. The fire signaled the people on *Lena* that the lifesavers were still on the job, and helped warm several dozen people who had assembled on the beach to assist in the rescue. The warmth must have been welcome, because freezing rain began to fall that evening.

On the night of December 27, fog settled over the area. *Lena* was no longer visible. Around 4 A.M., the station keeper glimpsed a dark mass through the fog, figured it was *Lena*, and sent out the surfboat.

Rowing through water covered with wreckage, the rescuers reached the ship—or rather, what remained of the vessel. *Lena* had broken up in the pounding sea. Only the cabin and stern portions of *Lena* had survived.

The lifesavers found two men still alive, plus the body of the captain. The surfmen pulled the survivors off the wreck. Eight on *Lena* were killed, partly because of a misunderstood signal.

***Leocadia*, Spanish warship** The 34-gun *Leocadia* was wrecked near Punta Santa Elena, Ecuador, in 1800, with more than two million pesos in treasure on board. The ship also carried passengers and a number of English prisoners. The wreck killed 140 people. Most of the treasure was recovered within days after the wreck.

Leona, American schooner This wreck involved one of the most dramatic and dangerous rescues in the history of the United States Lifesaving Service in the late 1800s. *Leona,* on a voyage from New York City to West Point, Virginia, stranded near the Hog Island lifesaving station on Virginia's Eastern Shore during a storm on March 2, 1886.

The lifesavers responded quickly, using a new piece of equipment—a self-righting, self-bailing surfboat equipped with a mast and sails. Their new boat was slow to reach the stranded schooner, however, because sub-zero temperatures had frozen the waters, and the surfmen had to spend several hours breaking a path through the ice to *Leona.*

When the rescuers reached the schooner, they found the vessel in bad shape. A cargo of phosphate rock was knocking holes in the hull, while seas broke over the ship. The upperworks were coated with ice. About the only sheltered place on deck was a small area in the lee of the cabin. There the surfmen found Leona's crew, still alive but in desperate need of help.

The rescuers themselves were not much better off. The station keeper saw that there was no way to return to shore until the wind diminished. So, the lifesavers remained aboard *Leona* for several hours, hoping for a change in the weather. All the while, the schooner appeared to be in danger of breaking up, and the wind combined with the below-zero temperatures to produce an unearthly chill.

Leona broke in two around nightfall. The crew and surfmen had to escape in the surfboat. The men tried to row ashore but made no progress against the storm. They dropped an anchor in an effort to hold their position, but the anchor was almost useless. At last they tried to set sail for shore and relative safety, but the fierce wind destroyed the sails and pushed the boat out to sea.

So, the rescued and rescuers found themselves all in need of rescue, on (as the expression has it) a dark and stormy night. Their boat was stable, but it provided little shelter from the icy winds. Thus they passed a horrible night, freezing and never far from being washed overboard.

A schooner picked them up on the morning of March 3, about five miles south of the lifesaving station at Smith Island, some 30 miles from their point of departure. Although half-frozen and exhausted, the men in the surfboat were made of stern stuff. Only

six hours after their rescue, they were ready to return in the surfboat to shore.

They spent the night at the Smith Island lifesaving station, then set out at daybreak for Hog Island, despite the still-blowing gale, which made their northward progress slow. Along the way, they encountered a steamer that towed them on the last leg of their journey home.

The medical record shows how rugged the 13 men involved in this rescue really were. Richard and Julie Pouliot, in their history of shipwrecks on the Virginia coast, report that only two of the men had to be hospitalized for the effects of their ordeal.

Leona was a complete loss. Part of the sails was all that could be salvaged. The cargo of phosphate rock, as noted earlier, contributed to the wreck by grinding against, and knocking holes in, the bottom of the vessel. Phosphate rock cargo was a factor in other wrecks of the time.

See also CARGO.

Leonardo da Vinci, Italian battleship In an early use of compressed air to refloat a sunken vessel, the Italian navy brought up the battleship *Leonardo da Vinci,* which was sunk by a German bomb on August 2, 1916. The warship sank near Taranto (Italy) harbor, killing 249 men. The wreck settled on the bottom upside down, with keel upward and upperworks buried in the mud.

Holes in the hull were repaired, the ship's ammunition was removed, the compartments inside the hull were made watertight, and the wreck was pumped full of air, one compartment at a time. Complicating the salvage operation was the need to remove the upperworks that had become buried in the mud. Their removal was accomplished from within the wreck, since there was no way to approach them from outside.

The ship came up easily, on September 17, 1919. The following day, the hull—still upside down—was placed in drydock. Righting the hull posed a problem that was soon solved. The hull was removed from drydock and taken to a specially dredged basin. There, water was pumped into compartments on one side of the hull. The added weight caused the hull to right itself. The battleship's huge gun turrets were recovered separately from their resting places in the mud where the ship had sunk.

See also SALVAGE.

Leonardo da Vinci, Italian passenger liner The 33,000-ton liner *Leonardo da Vinci* burned at La Spezia, Italy, on March 3, 1980. No one was killed, but the liner was destroyed.

***Lexington,* American steam packet** Although no exact figure is available, the burning of *Lexington* on Long Island Sound on January 13, 1840, killed more than 100 people. Under command of Captain George Child, the 220-foot ship was carrying passengers and a cargo of cotton from New York to Stonington, Connecticut. It was a bitterly cold night, and ice littered the waters of the sound.

Shortly after dinner, the passengers were gathered in the main cabin when someone noticed smoke emanating from the smokestack casing and from bales of cotton on deck. According to one explanation, the fire started when the smokestack overheated and ignited woodwork and cotton.

A wind fanned the fire. Efforts to put out the blaze failed. The fire disabled the steering gear, and the packet began sailing in circles. The wind thus had an opportunity to spread the fire to all parts of *Lexington.*

The captain told the passengers, "Take to the boats," and panic broke out. A rush for the boats occurred, and the overloaded boats capsized. Among those killed was the captain.

Only five people survived the burning of *Lexington,* by clinging to bales of cotton thrown overboard. Second Mate David Crowley rode a bale of cotton for two days and nights before making his way ashore near Riverhead, New York.

As in modern times, entrepreneurs were quick to cash in on the catastrophe. They had bales of cotton recovered from the wreck woven into *"Lexington* shirts" and sold them.

Jeanette Edwards Rattray, in her history of shipwrecks on Long Island, points out several notable aspects of the *Lexington* tragedy. Poet Henry Wadsworth Longfellow, author of "The Wreck of the *Hesperus,"* one of the most famous poems ever written about a shipwreck, was on the passenger list of *Lexington* for its final voyage but was not actually on board; he had been delayed and was unable to make the voyage. His poem was published the day after *Lexington* was lost. *Lexington's* pilot, Captain Stephen Manchester, was later involved in another shipwreck several miles from where *Lexington* came to grief.

See also FIRE; HESPERUS.

***Liban,* French steamer** One hundred and fifty people of the 240 on board are thought to have died in the wreck of *Liban,* which collided with the steamship *Insulaire* near Marseilles, France, on June 7, 1903. The collision occurred in daylight. The cause was not ascertained. *Liban* sank in less than 20 minutes.

***Liberté,* French battleship** *Liberté* exploded in Toulon harbor on September 25, 1911. Lookouts on nearby ships sighted fire emanating from the battleship's foredeck at 5:30 A.M. Although the captain had the forward magazines flooded, they blew up several minutes later. The explosion not only destroyed *Liberté* but also caused great damage on shore. The explosion was attributed to old, unstable "B" powder, which was implicated in numerous other explosions on warships in the early 20th century. Of more than 700 men in *Liberté's* crew, 235 were killed and hundreds were injured. More than 100 crewmen were ashore on leave; otherwise, the toll from the explosion might have been much higher.

See also "B" POWDER; EXPLOSIONS.

lifebelts These now-familiar lifesaving devices, consisting of lightweight material such as cork sewn in fabric packages, are designed to be worn or carried by people leaving a sinking vessel. The lightweight contents of the lifebelt make the user more buoyant and, in theory at least, more likely to survive in the water until rescued. Experience allegedly has fallen short of theory on occasion, however, notably in the burning of the excursion ship *General Slocum* in New York's East River on June 15, 1904. Reportedly, some lifebelts on that vessel dragged their users down to their deaths because the manufacturer had put iron bars in the lifebelts to increase their weight to the mandatory minimum figure.

See also GENERAL SLOCUM.

lifeboats The history of lifeboats has been largely one of lessons learned through tragic experience in shipwrecks. Perhaps the most important of such les-

A list can make it difficult to lower lifeboats. (U.S. Coast Guard)

sons involved the sinking of the British liner *Titanic,* which put to sea with enough lifeboats for only a fraction of its total number of passengers and crew. (Technically, *Titanic*'s owner, the White Star Line, appeared to be within the law by providing an inadequate number of lifeboats, because British Board of Trade rules did not actually require the company to make sure a seat in a lifeboat was available for every single person on board.) Although designed primarily to keep survivors of shipwrecks afloat and in reasonable safety for only brief periods after a ship goes down, lifeboats have proven adequate, under capable handling, for extended sea journeys on some occasions.

Lifeboats have been involved in dramatic stories of seamanship and survival, notably the rugged boat journey that British polar explorer Ernest Shackleton and members of his party undertook after the wreck of their ship, the *Endurance,* in the Antarctic in 1915. The boat journey covered a distance of more than 600 nautical miles, under severe conditions, between Elephant Island (just northeast of the South Shetland Islands near Graham Land in Antarctica) and South Georgia.

See ENDURANCE; POLAR REGIONS; TITANIC.

life car   A mid-19th-century lifesaving apparatus, the life car consisted of an enclosed canvas receptacle used to transport shipwreck survivors from the wreck to the shore. The life car was hauled along a line stretched between ship and shore. Though sometimes successful, the life car tended to fill with water during rescue operations, so that some people actually drowned in the device that was supposed to save them. Use of the life car eventually was discontinued in favor of the simpler and safer "breeches buoy."

See also BREECHES BUOY.

life jacket   A floatation device designed to be worn by passengers on a ship, the life jacket (also known as a life vest) consists of an inflatable plastic balloon, or some buoyant material encased in fabric, configured roughly in the manner of a vest or jacket and worn on the body in similar fashion. The life jacket is designed to keep the wearer afloat and in an upright position until rescue occurs. Life jackets are manufactured in brilliant colors for maximum visibility. Such devices have been in widespread use for more than a century and have saved countless lives, but their protective capability is limited in many situations.

Lifesaving Service   Established in 1878, the United States Lifesaving Service became known for its heroic efforts to assist ships in distress along American

shores. It had the advantage of a dedicated and brilliant superintendent, Sumner Kimball (1834–1923). The service utilized numerous lifesaving stations and beach patrols to detect and help vessels in distress. Rescue operations commonly involved the launching of surfboats to remove people from wrecked ships. Other widely used pieces of lifesaving apparatus included the Lyle gun, used to fire lines to stricken ships, and the breeches buoy, a vehicle for transporting people, one at a time, from ship to shore.

See also BREECHES BUOY; LYLE GUN.

life vest   See LIFE JACKET.

lighthouses   For more than 1,500 years, from the days of the giant *pharos,* or lighthouse, at Alexandria, Egypt, to modern times, lighthouses have served as aids to navigation and have warned mariners away from especially dangerous points on coastlines. Foghorns also were installed at some lighthouses for an extra measure of warning and safety.

For many years, lighthouses had to be manned, because automatic equipment was either unavailable or inadequate for the task of operating a lighthouse. The "lonely lighthouse keeper" became a symbol of solitude in this period. That symbolism has endured, although automation has largely taken over the lighthouse keeper's job.

There was a limit to the protection that even the best-designed and most efficiently maintained lighthouse could provide, because a ship's master might mistake a given lighthouse for another at a nearby location, and steer a wrong course straight into danger on the basis of that error.

Some lighthouses have become famous for their architecture and color schemes, such as the striking "barber pole" decoration of the Cape Hatteras lighthouse on the Outer Banks of North Carolina. The seaborne equivalent of the lighthouse was the lightship.

See also LIGHTSHIPS; OUTER BANKS.

"Lighthouse Tragedy, The"   A wreck that killed five people near Boston provided the subject for an early literary effort by Benjamin Franklin, a poem entitled "The Lighthouse Tragedy." On November 3, 1718, George Worthylake, keeper of *Boston Light,* reportedly was en route by boat with his wife Anne, his daughter Ruth and a companion to nearby Lovell's Island when their boat capsized, killing all on board. Franklin's poem became highly popular. It was reprinted in maritime historian Edward Rowe Snow's 1954 book *Amazing Sea Stories Never Told Before.* A few stanzas of the poem follow:

Oh, George, this wild November
We must not pass with you,
For Ruth, our fragile daughter,
Its chilly gales will rue.

So, home to Lovell's Island
Takes us when falls the sea
To the old house where comfort
And better shelter be.

* * *

With wild nor'wester came this morning,
Cold and clear the heartless day
Come, wife, take Ruth, the pull will be long,
So—in the boat I'll row you away.

* * *

Now they reach the open channel
Where the flood tide breasts the gale
Rears a toppling wall of water,
Making Anne's cheeks grow pale.

Quick the prow is upward borne
George in Anne's arms is tossed
Husband, wife and child together
In the chilly waves are lost.

Frenzied clasp of wife and daughter
Bears the sturdy swimmer down
Save the boat upon the water
Nothing of their fate is known.

Snow points out that the facts of the tragedy differ considerably from Franklin's account of it, in that there actually was no storm that day. According to Snow, Franklin considered the poem "wretched" but was flattered when it sold well.

lightships   The floating equivalent of lighthouses on land, lightships were anchored at various points at sea to warn of dangers such as rocks or shoals, or to mark important points for navigation. The Nantucket lightship, for example, was stationed near Nantucket Shoals off southern New England. Assignment to a lightship was hazardous duty, because another vessel might ram and sink the lightship by accident. Such an event occurred on May 16, 1934, when the British passenger liner *Olympic* struck the Nantucket lightship and killed seven of the lightship's crew.

See also LIGHTHOUSES.

Linchoten report   An outstanding case of incorrect information about losses among Spanish shipping, this report originated with a Dutch historian named Linchoten, who claimed that 99 of 100 large vessels in the Tierra Firme Flota were wrecked in the Florida Channel in 1589. He added that only 14 or 15 of 220 ships that sailed in 1589 from Spanish possessions in the Americas made their way successfully to Spain and Portugal. These claims are not supported by Spanish records, says marine archaeologist Robert Marx, who cites Linchoten's report as an example of misinformation.

***London*, British combination sailing vessel and steamship**   In one of the greatest maritime catastrophes to that date, *London* sank on January 11, 1866, in a severe storm off Land's End, England. Waves put out the fires under the boilers, and pumping was not adequate to save the ship. Of 236 crewmen and passengers, more than 220 were lost.

Long Island, New York   Located between the Atlantic Ocean and Long Island Sound, Long Island has been the site of numerous shipwrecks on both its southern and northern coasts. One especially dangerous point for ships has been off Plum Island, at the extreme eastern tip of Long Island. Famous shipwrecks on Long Island include the burning of the steam packet *Lexington* in 1840.

See also LEXINGTON; POCAHONTAS.

lookouts   Although modern technology such as radar has done much to make ocean travel safer by alerting crews to dangers at sea, the eyes of human lookouts have traditionally done the most to detect and identify such dangers. The familiar "crow's nest," a platform mounted partway up a ship's mast, was designed as a vantage point for lookouts, who also might be stationed at the bow as well as on the bridge or at other locations around a ship. The lookouts would watch for such phenomena as icebergs, the lights of other ships and the telltale breakers that indicated the presence of shoals or shorelines. The lookout's technique commonly was to scan large sections of the sea with the unaided eye, looking for anything out of the ordinary. Then, if something unusual showed up, the lookout would use binoculars (or whatever other visual devices he might have) to take a close look at the anomaly before alerting the bridge. Lookouts were by no means infallible; many different factors, from haze to the darkness of a moonless night, might interfere with their work and allow a ship to sail into danger. The role of lookouts was an important element of the investigation into the sinking of the British liner *Titanic* in 1912.

See also RADAR; TITANIC.

Lord, Captain Stanley (1877–1962)   Known as "Lord of the *Californian*," Lord was in command of the Leyland liner *Californian* as it lay stopped in an ice field several miles from the sinking liner *Titanic* on the night of April 14–15, 1912. Lord was aware that a ship nearby was firing what appeared to be distress signals, yet he took no measures to investigate the signals and assist the other vessel (which he learned afterward had been *Titanic*) beyond an unsuccessful attempt to raise the unidentified ship by Morse lamp. Had Lord sailed only a few miles to *Titanic*'s side, most or all of the stricken liner's passengers and crew might have been saved. That was, at least, the conclusion of the official American inquiry into the loss of *Titanic*. The official British inquiry also faulted Captain Lord for his inaction on the night of *Titanic*'s sinking. Lord acquired defenders, known collectively as "Lordites," who thought the judgments of him unfair and tried to clear Lord's reputation. Their efforts had only limited success, however, because of the correspondence between the number, times and color of *Titanic*'s distress rockets and those seen by *Californian*. Controversy between critics and defenders of Captain Lord has continued to the present.

See also CALIFORNIAN INCIDENT; TITANIC.

Los Triangulos wreck, Mexico In 1524, the governor of Santiago de Cuba, Alonso Zuazo, sailed to Mexico to visit explorer Hernando Cortez but was shipwrecked on Los Triangulos. The 43 survivors of the shipwreck obtained water from a small cay nearby and managed to build a small boat from the wreckage of their ship. In that small vessel, they sailed to Veracruz. There is some uncertainty about the site of the shipwreck; but according to marine archeologist Robert Marx, Los Triangulos appears to be the most likely spot.

See also CORTEZ WRECKS.

Louisbourg wrecks, Nova Scotia, Canada On June 28, 1758, the French at Louisbourg scuttled several warships because too few men were available to use them against an anticipated attack by the British. Before the English arrived, three more warships were burned by accident at Louisbourg: the 74-gun *Entreprenant*, the 64-gun *Capricieux* and the 64-gun *Celebre*.

See also CANADA.

***Louisiana*, American sidewheel steamer** The rescue operations that followed *Louisiana*'s collision with another ship showed how smooth and effective such operations can be when passengers stay calm and a ship's officers and crew know their business.

Part of the Baltimore Steam Packet Company's fleet, *Louisiana* collided with the steamer *Falcon* off Smith Point in Chesapeake Bay near the mouth of the Potomac River early on the morning of November 14, 1874.

Louisiana was nearing Smith Point when the lookout saw the light of *Falcon* nearby and informed the pilot.

Although *Louisiana* was well-lighted and should have been easy to see and avoid, *Falcon* headed for *Louisiana* and did not alter course. *Louisiana* blew its whistle, but the other ship did not respond.

The captain, who had been sleeping, was awakened by the whistle and came to see what was happening. He ordered the wheel turned first hard aport, then hard astarboard, in a last-minute effort to avoid collision.

Immediately after he gave the order, however, the ships collided. *Falcon* hit *Louisiana* amidships. Then the two ships separated, and *Louisiana* began to fill with water.

The crew's behavior was a textbook example of how to respond to such a crisis. All went to their emergency stations in a cool and well-disciplined manner. Passengers also remained calm.

Meanwhile, *Falcon* remained in the area. The steamer had experienced only slight damage to its bow. *Falcon* came alongside *Louisiana*. A hawser was passed to *Falcon* from *Louisiana*. Gangplanks were run between the two ships, and passengers were transferred to *Falcon* along with their personal baggage. *Louisiana*'s crew even managed to save the ship's safe.

The captain was the last to leave the sinking *Louisiana*. The only casualties on *Louisiana*, writes Donald Shomette in his history *Shipwrecks on the Chesapeake*, were a canary and a horse.

Falcon proceeded to Baltimore. An investigation found the Baltimore and Charleston Line, which operated *Falcon*, at fault for the collision. Salvage operations succeeded in recovering *Louisiana*'s engines, which were installed in another ship.

See also COLLISIONS.

***Louis-Philippe*, French packet ship** Communities on Long Island, New York, were more beautiful after the wreck of *Louis-Philippe*, which was lost on the beach near Bridgehampton and Southampton on April 14, 1842. The ship's cargo included shrubs and trees, which washed ashore and were planted in local gardens. (No one was killed in the wreck.) Maritime historian Jeanette Edwards Rattray noted in *Ship Ashore!*, her history of shipwrecks on Long Island, that a pink "Louis-Phillipe" rose, double and fragrant, from that particular wreck, bloomed in her garden each summer.

***Lupatia*, British bark** A dog was the only survivor of this wreck, which occurred during a storm at Tillamook Rock on the Oregon coast on January 2, 1881. That evening, the crew of the Tillamook lighthouse heard someone cry, "Hard aport!"

The men figured a ship was in difficulty just off-shore, and so they lighted lanterns and built a fire to warn the ship that it was too near the shore. Despite the darkness, the men could see a sailing vessel several hundred feet offshore. A running light could be seen, and it looked as if the ship had avoided wrecking.

At daybreak, however, one of the ship's masts could be seen above the water between the Tillamook Rock and Tillamook Head. The vessel had wrecked on the rocks during the night. The ship, *Lupatia,* had been on a voyage from Japan to the Columbia River.

A search revealed the bodies of 10 men washed up along the shore. A burial party discovered a dog, an Australian shepherd, who apparently had survived the wreck. The dog was sent to, and became the pet of, a friend of *Lupatia's* first officer, who lived in nearby Astoria, Oregon.

The exact cause of *Lupatia's* wreck was not determined, but one possibility is that the weather was too bad for *Lupatia* to take bearings, and that the nearness of shore might have given the ship erroneous compass readings.

Lusitania, British passenger liner

On the morning of May 1, 1915, the German embassy in Washington, D.C., had printed in New York newspapers the following warning:

NOTICE

Travellers intending to embark on the Atlantic voyage are reminded that a state of war exists . . . that the zone of war includes the waters adjacent to the British Isles; that, in accordance with formal notice given by the Imperial German government, vessels flying the flag of Great Britain or of any of her allies are liable to destruction in those waters and that travellers sailing in the war zone on ships of Great Britain or her allies do so at their own risk.

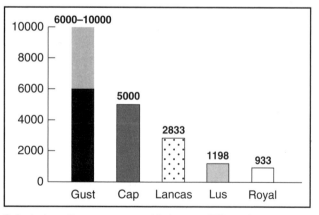

Selected wartime passenger ship losses, 20th century.

In one of the great coincidences of maritime history, this notice appeared in the New York *World* beside an advertisement for the Cunard Line and its huge liner *Lusitania.* Less than one week later, *Lusitania* would sink after being hit by a U-boat's torpedo off the southern coast of Ireland, during a voyage from New York to Britain under the command of Captain William Turner.

Lusitania sailed from New York on May 1, 1917, the same day the aforementioned warning from Germany appeared in the New York press. Also at sea that week was 32-year-old Kapitanleutnant Walther Schwieger, commanding the German submarine *U-20.* He and his crew were busy sinking British shipping. On May 5, *U-20* sank the schooner *Earl of Latham* off the Old Head of Kinsale, along the southern coast of Ireland. *U-20* sank two more ships on May 6. The liner *Candidate* took a torpedo from *U-20* near the Coningberg lightship at St. George's Channel. Another civilian vessel, *Centurion,* was hit by a torpedo from *U-20* soon afterward. No one was killed in these attacks. It was well established, then, that a German submarine was active off the southern coast of Ireland and constituted a deadly threat to shipping. The Admiralty sent out a warning by wireless to that effect on May 7. The Admiralty also broadcast a message repeatedly to all British ships, warning them to avoid headlands (points where submarines were known to operate) and travel at full speed. For some reason, however, *Lusitania* stayed close to shore, steered a straight course through the waters where *U-20* was active, and traveled slowly. Although Captain Turner reportedly took some measures to ensure the safety of his passengers and crew, such as closing watertight bulkheads, the liner's slow speed and steady course combined with its nearness to shore to make the ship an ideal target for Schwieger.

U-boats were able to operate successfully off British shores because Britain's coastal defenses were minimal. The Royal Navy was spread over much of the globe in wartime and could not spare large numbers of ships to protect the southern Irish waters. The best the Navy could do was to assign the aged cruiser *Juno* to that area. *Juno's* armament was virtually useless against any but cumbersome, slow-moving targets. So, Schwieger was able to operate essentially unopposed in the seas off southern Ireland.

Just before *Lusitania* was sunk, Captain Turner reportedly did not know his position and steered toward land to look for familiar landmarks. He saw the Old Head of Kinsale and knew he was near Cork Harbor. This approach to the shore, however, put *Lusitania* off a headland—prime hunting ground for submarines—at just the moment when *U-20* was in the vicinity. To make the situation worse, Turner took this occasion to take a four-point bearing, a position-finding operation that required the liner to steer a straight course for some 40 minutes. Such a course made it easy to put a torpedo into the ship.

Schwieger and *U-20* noticed *Lusitania* around 1 P.M. on May 7. The submarine dived to slightly more than 30 feet and headed at high speed for the liner. At 2:09, *U-20* was in position for a shot and fired a torpedo. A lookout on the liner cried, "Torpedoes coming on the starboard [right] side!" Schwieger noted that the torpedo hit the ship behind the bridge. An unusually large explosion followed and sent a cloud rising high above the first funnel. Schwieger figured a second explosion, of coal or gunpowder or perhaps a boiler, must have occurred immediately after the torpedo struck. Schwieger recorded in his log that the ship's bridge and superstructure over the point of explosion were torn apart and that fire broke out and spread to the bridge. *Lusitania* heeled over and started sinking quickly by the bow. The liner sank in about 18 minutes. Rescue vessels, including *Juno,* soon arrived to pick up survivors.

Schwieger reported observing "confusion" on board *Lusitania.* He decided to leave the area without putting another shot into the stricken liner. Evidently Schwieger had some humanitarian concerns, for he mentioned in his log that he could not fire another torpedo when so many people were in the water, trying to save themselves.

The British, however, saw nothing humanitarian in Schwieger's actions. The official court of inquiry into *Lusitania*'s sinking found that "the loss of the said ship and lives was due to damage caused to the said ship by torpedoes fired by a submarine of German nationality whereby the ship sank. In the opinion of the Court the act was done not merely with the intention of sinking the ship, but also with the intention of destroying the lives of the people on board." Of 1,959 who were on *Lusitania,* 1,198 were lost. Ninety-four of 129 children on board were killed. There were 35 infants on *Lusitania.* Only four survived.

The loss of *Lusitania* was a propaganda victory for Britain, which used the sinking to depict the Germans as monsters and murderers. The Germans countered this propaganda assault by pointing out that the British had been warned, and adding that Germany considered *Lusitania* to be an auxiliary cruiser of the Royal Navy. The Germans also said Britain was using the liner to transport contraband of war.

It has been suggested that *Lusitania* was armed and was transporting Canadian troops as well as munitions on its final voyage. There appears to be no evidence that *Lusitania* was equipped with guns, nor that the ship carried Canadian troops. As for munitions, *Lusitania* is thought to have carried more than 40,000 cases of rifle ammunition and some empty shrapnel casings. Another suggestion is that the large explosion observed by Schwieger—a blast apparently much larger than a torpedo would produce—originated when munitions on *Lusitania* blew up, although it also is possible that this explosion was caused by a boiler.

Rumors of conspiracy have surrounded the *Lusitania* incident for decades. According to these stories, Britain supposedly set up *Lusitania* to be sunk in the hope that the calamity would draw the United States into the war in Europe. Although the sinking did provoke outrage in the United States because American passengers were on the liner, and the United States did enter the war in 1917, there is no conclusive evidence to show that the liner's loss was the result of any such plot by the British government.

Nonetheless, many mysteries surround the sinking of *Lusitania.* Among these is the behavior of Captain Turner. In submarine-infested waters, he nonetheless made his ship a splendid target for torpedoes by steering a straight course, at leisurely speed, close to land, for some 40 minutes before *U-20*'s attack. Under such circumstances, Schwieger could hardly have missed a huge target like *Lusitania.* Turner should have been farther from shore, steering a zigzag course at high speed to minimize the chance of successful U-boat attack. Yet he did just the opposite.

There appears to be no adequate and universally accepted explanation for Turner's actions. Turner himself, at the inquiry into *Lusitania*'s sinking, could not provide an adequate account of his behavior. For example, he admitted he was much closer to land than he should have been. He also said he was near land because he thought submarines were more likely to lurk farther out at sea. The wreck commissioner, Lord Mersey (who also presided over the British inquiry into the sinking of *Titanic*) found Turner's explanation hard to believe, and said he did not understand the captain's reasoning. Submarines were known to operate close to headlands such as the Old Head of Kinsale. Moreover, the Admiralty had provided clear instructions to avoid such areas and to make the U-boats' job more difficult by traveling at high speed and using the zigzag.

It has been suggested that Turner was merely a poor captain, unable to understand simple instructions from the Admiralty. Yet as A. A. Hoehling points out in his treatment of the *Lusitania* incident in his 1984 book *Lost At Sea,* it is hard to see Turner as incompetent. His record was good, up to the day *Lusitania* was sunk. Moreover, as *Lusitania*'s captain, he held a position of extreme prestige and responsibility. Cunard hardly would have awarded such a command to an inept master.

The results of the inquiry also are puzzling. Lord Mersey, after listening to Turner's own admission that he had done almost everything wrong, nonetheless praised Turner as a "skilled and experienced" master and said that the captain should not be blamed for the sinking of his vessel. Mersey said that the advice given Turner was not meant to deprive him of the right to exercise his own judgment. Mersey added that Turner's actions should not be interpreted as incompetence or negligence.

Then there is the matter of steam. *Lusitania* needed steam but was curiously unprepared to generate large amounts of it. Although *Lusitania* was traveling through a war zone and needed speed to evade enemy submarines, the liner was operating with six of its 25 boilers—almost one-fourth of its capacity—shut down. This meant the ship could not attain top speed. Two reasons given for shutting down so many boilers were that stokers were hard to find just then, and that the ship was short on coal. Possibly stokers were scarce at that time, but *Lusitania* still reportedly had 6,000 tons of coal on board.

Another mystery is why *Lusitania* sank so rapidly. It is tempting to suspect that contraband munitions on *Lusitania* exploded and did such tremendous damage that the ship sank quickly, but as noted earlier, this explanation is not fully supported by evidence.

Captain Turner survived the sinking of a later command, the *Ivernia,* which was torpedoed off the Greek coast in 1917. More than 150 soldiers and crewmen on board reportedly died in the loss of *Ivernia.* Turner spent the rest of the war on shore. He became commodore of the Cunard Line in 1921, was awarded the Order of the British Empire, and died, reportedly of cancer, in 1933. Schwieger was killed in action in 1917 while commanding *U-38.*

See also CUNARD LINE; EXPLOSIONS; SUBMARINES; SHIPWRECKS, SOCIAL IMPACT OF; TORPEDOES.

Lyle gun, lifesaving apparatus The Lyle gun was essentially a mortar that fired a projectile trailing a small line to a ship in distress near shore. The vessel's crew then used the small line to pull a stouter line on board and start livesaving operations.

The gun was the invention of a U.S. Army lieutenant named David Lyle, at the Springfield Armory in Springfield, Massachusetts. Lyle improved on a British design by Captain G. W. Manby that used a mortar to cast a line to ships.

Lyle made his gun out of bronze, which was lightweight and resisted corrosion. The line attached to the projectile was stored in a special box with pegs in it. Coiled around the pegs, the line unrolled from the box free of tangles.

The Lyle gun had a range of about 400 yards, or roughly a quarter of a mile. In its final version, the gun was about two feet long and had a 5.5-inch breech and 2.5-inch bore.

Lyle began experimenting with designs for the lifesaving gun in 1877 and finished a report on it in 1878. In the report, Lyle gave Manby credit for the design on which the Lyle gun was based.

There were problems with the Lyle gun, including high breech pressure, a result of the tight fit required to obtain maximum range for the projectile. Eventually, however, the Lyle gun was given credit for saving thousands of lives in shipwrecks.

M

MacGregor, American paddle steamer A boiler on Mississipppi steamer *Helen MacGregor* at Memphis, Tennessee, on February 24, 1830, killed almost 60 people. More might have been killed had iron stanchions not stopped a part of the boiler that was blown into a dining room where several dozen people were having breakfast.

magazine A storage area on a warship where gunpowder, shells or other ammunition or explosive materiel is kept, a magazine has been involved in numerous wrecks, when something has touched off the explosives inside and demolished a ship. Magazine explosions have wrecked numerous warships, notably the French battleship *Liberte*. An especially dangerous kind of explosive in the 20th century has been "B" powder, which became unstable after a few years in storage and could go off without warning.

See also "b" POWDER; EXPLOSIVES; LIBERTE.

Magna Carta The Magna Carta, one of the earliest and most famous documents in British constitutional history, includes what is thought to be the first known law governing shipwrecks in Britain. It specifies that if a human, dog or cat escapes alive from a wrecked ship, the vessel and everything in it may not be considered a wreck (that is, available to anyone who cares to recover its cargo), but shall be taken over by local authorities.

Magpie, schooner Presumably an American vessel, *Magpie* was involved in a dramatic story of shipwreck and shark attack off the coast of New England in 1826. On August 27, *Magpie* was caught in a storm and sank quickly. Two of the crewmen went down with the ship. The rest of the crew, in the water, made their way to the ship's longboat. The boat capsized when they tried to board it. A few men climbed onto the overturned boat, while the rest held on to the gunwales. Eventually, they managed to right the boat and start bailing it out.

Then the shipwrecked men saw a shark's fin cutting the water nearby. The boat capsized again, and the men found themselves in the water with the shark. Terrified, the men tried to scramble back atop the boat. In doing so, they created a disturbance in the water. Such a disturbance is known to attract sharks, which apparently interpret the commotion as the struggle of weak and vulnerable prey.

The noise in the water soon attracted more than a dozen additional sharks. One shark attacked, then another. Before long, the sharks had killed all but two men, Tom Meldrum and Jack Maclean. They succeeded in righting the boat again and climbed into it. Safe in the boat for the moment, they slept for a while and then began scanning the sea for ships.

The men knew they would die if not rescued very soon. They had no provisions and no way to sail the boat toward land. When they saw the sail of a passing brig, they tried to attract the attention of the ship's crew but were unsuccessful. In desperation, Meldrum decided to swim toward the brig and try to draw its attention.

The plan appeared virtually suicidal. The sea was filled with sharks, and Meldrum would have to swim a long distance through their midst. Maclean tried to talk Meldrum out of his decision to swim for it, but Meldrum was determined. As Meldrum went into the water, Maclean splashed his jacket in the water to draw the sharks' attention away from the swimmer. At least one shark noticed Meldrum in the water, however, and swam up to him. Before the shark could attack Meldrum, someone on the brig noticed him. A boat was lowered, and Meldrum and Maclean were rescued.

See also SHARKS.

Maine, United States The state of Maine has an extensive coastline and has been the site of numerous shipwrecks, notably the loss of several American warships in the Penobscot incident in 1779. Other significant shipwrecks in Maine waters include the warship H.M.S. *Astrea*, which was burned by accident in the Piscatauqua River in 1743 with the loss of several crewmen; the English merchant vessel *Phoenix*, wrecked in Casco Bay in 1758; and the American schooner *Charles*, which was wrecked on a reef near Portland Lighthouse in 1807 with the loss of 16 of 22 crew members.

See also PENOBSCOT INCIDENT.

Maine, **American battleship**   The destruction of the battleship *Maine* in Havana harbor on February 15, 1898, was at that time the greatest single catastrophe in the history of the United States Navy. The incident did much to impel the United States toward war with Spain. The circumstances of the ship's destruction remain mysterious.

Tension was rising at the time between Spain, which wanted to retain its colonies such as Cuba, and the United States, which had expansionist ambitions and was encouraging a Cuban insurgent movement. When *Maine* was sent to Havana, a circular was distributed in the city urging "death to the Americans."

Captain Charles Sigsbee of *Maine* thought extraordinary security precautions were advisable during the battleship's visit to Havana. For example, he put armed sentries on duty, and *Maine* maintained steam in two boilers rather than the usual one, in case quick response to danger should be required.

Sigsbee was in his cabin at about 9:40 P.M. when an explosion, possibly followed by a second one (eyewitness accounts differ on this detail), shook the ship and destroyed *Maine*'s powerplant. The battleship immediately began listing to port and caught fire amidships.

When Sigsbee ordered lifeboats lowered to rescue men in the water, he found that all but three of the ship's 15 lifeboats were destroyed. Nonetheless, the crew managed to start rescue operations. Nearby ships assisted.

Seeing that *Maine* could not be saved, Sigsbee gave the order to abandon ship. As *Maine* settled into the water, explosions continued. In all, three officers and 258 enlisted men were lost.

Sigsbee reported to Washington that he had not determined the cause of the explosion. At first, it was attributed to an accident. That explanation struck some Americans as unlikely, however, and then-President William McKinley found himself under strong pressure to go to war with Spain over the incident. Theodore Roosevelt, then assistant secretary of the navy, criticized McKinley for resisting calls for war.

Yet McKinley decided to wait for a report from a naval board of inquiry before deciding what action he might take.

The board attributed the explosion to a mine that made ammunition in the ship's magazines blow up. This verdict was based on observations by divers who examined the wreck and saw that hull plates and the keel were forced inward, as if by an explosion outside the hull. The board cleared Sigsbee and his men of responsibility for the explosion but did not lay blame on anyone in particular.

This sober, conservative judgment did not prevent war. Supported by the Hearst press, Congress declared war on Cuba on April 25. The resulting Spanish-American War lasted less than a year and stripped Spain of possessions including Cuba, the Philippines and Puerto Rico, which then went to the United States.

Apparently, the government of Spain was not responsible for the destruction of *Maine*. The evidence points instead to two groups: Spaniards acting without their government's knowledge, and Cuban rebels trying to draw the United States into involvement with Spain.

Critics of the board of inquiry's conclusion—specifically, that a mine destroyed the ship—have argued instead that an internal explosion might have been responsible. An internal explosion might have had any of several origins, including a bursting boiler or fire in the ship's coal bunker. Evidence for the internal-explosion hypothesis can be summarized roughly as follows: A mine would have caused a single explosion, but some witnesses to the ship's destruction reported hearing two initial blasts. Also, the explosion reportedly cast up a smaller amount of water than would be expected from a mine going off, and there was little or no evidence of dead fish in the water following the explosion. Exploding mines commonly leave behind large quantities of dead fish and other marine animals.

None of this evidence, however, amounts to proof that an internal explosion wrecked *Maine*. Reports of a second initial explosion may have been in error; a mine directly under the ship, or at a considerable depth, would not throw up large amounts of water; and an exploding mine might merely have stunned fish in the vicinity, thus allowing them to swim away once they recovered. Moreover, the boilers that night were operating at considerably less than their intended pressure of 120 pounds per square inch, and there was no sign of fire in the coal bunker before the explosion. The most significant evidence against the internal-explosion hypothesis, however, is the condition of the hull plates and keel. An explosion within the hull would have forced the plates and keel outward, rather than inward, as divers found them.

The sinking of *Maine* had a strong influence on American political rhetoric. One of the most famous slogans in American history, "Remember the *Maine*," was used immediately after the incident to support the cause of war with Spain. The slogan allegedly originated with a patron of a bar in New York City.

See also EXPLOSIONS.

Maine, **American whaler** This whaling crew was a resourceful lot. After their ship was wrecked on Clatsop Spit at the Columbia River (Oregon-Washington) bar on August 25, 1848, they were determined to make their way home to Massachusetts. Since no ship was available, they made their own. The whalers bought a ship's boat, modified it for ocean travel, and sailed away in their little craft for San Francisco, where they embarked on another ship for the long trip back to New England.

Manantico, **American schooner** *Manantico's* wreck on the Virginia coast on October 31, 1887, shows how a captain's error in reckoning could be deadly.

On a voyage to Richmond with a cargo of lumber, *Manantico's* captain was unsure of his position in a storm. He thought he was off Cape Charles, at the northern end of the mouth of Chesapeake Bay, when he actually was off Cape Henry, at the southern end of the bay's mouth—an error of some 15 miles.

So, the captain turned toward what he thought would be the entrance to the bay, and safety. He wound up instead heading for shore near the lifesaving station at Cape Henry, as heavy seas began to demolish his ship before it even grounded.

The captain tried dropping anchors, but they would not hold. Driven by wind and waves, the schooner struck hard on a sandbar. The impact tossed the captain into the sea. He died before he could reach shore. A few minutes earlier, shifting cargo had crushed the ship's cook to death. The rest of the crew climbed into the rigging and were rescued by lifesavers using a breeches buoy.

Three other ships were also wrecked in the vicinity by this same storm. One of these wrecks, the schooner *Carrie Holmes*, provided dramatic evidence of the storm's power. The storm drove *Carrie Holmes* so far up onto the beach that her crew simply leaped off the ship and waded ashore to safety.

Mandoil II, **Liberian tanker** *Mandoil II* collided with the Japanese freighter *Suwaharu Maru* in the Pacific Ocean, 340 miles off the northwest coast of the United States, on February 28, 1968. Both ships caught fire

and were abandoned. Survivors included *Mandoil II's* mascot, a parrot.

Manila galleons For some 250 years, the Manila galleons sailed at a rate of perhaps two to four per year, on an almost annual basis, between Acapulco, Mexico, and Manila in the Philippine Islands. The voyage from Manila to Acapulco was extremely hazardous, and many ships were lost. Sailing from Manila to Acapulco took as long as eight months, and perhaps a third of the men on each ship would die en route from causes such as scurvy, starvation and smallpox. The record of one particular voyage in 1657, when two galleons sailed together, indicates that three-fourths of the men involved died during the voyage, apparently from smallpox. Despite the dangers of the voyage across the Pacific, the Manila galleons continued to sail from 1565 to 1815. These galleons were exceptionally large and, in the 1700s, might attain 2,000 tons.

See also FLOTA SYSTEM; GALLEON.

Maria Louisa, **sailing vessel** A population of cats on Gardiners Island, at the eastern tip of Long Island, New York, was reportedly descended from a Maltese cat that survived the wreck of *Maria Louisa* on December 25, 1812. A salvage worker saw the cat holding on to a floating fragment of wood. He had the cat rescued and took it home wrapped in a handkerchief. The cat had many descendants, one of which was named Maria Louisa after the wrecked ship.

Marine Sulphur Queen, **American tanker** In a widely publicized case of disappearance at sea, the 554-foot tanker left Beaumont, Texas, for Norfolk, Virginia, on February 2, 1963, with a cargo of molten sulfur on board. The last reported communication from the ship was a routine radio message on February 3. The message indicated the vessel was west of Key West, Florida. Nothing more was heard from *Marine Sulphur Queen*, nor was anything ever seen of the ship again except some debris and a life jacket believed to have come from the vessel.

Martinique, Lesser Antilles This island has a long history of shipwrecks from various causes, including storms, warfare and even volcanic eruption. In 1636, for example, the Spanish warship *San Salvador*, en route to Venezuela, was wrecked in shallow water on the southern shore of Martinique. The Spaniards set fire to the wreck before abandoning it. Then the ship exploded before the island's French residents had a chance to recover any of its cargo, which included military supplies intended for a Spanish assault on the Dutch at Curaçao.

Thirty years later, in 1666, the English governor of Barbados sent five ships to capture six French vessels in Bay of All Saints on Martinique. Although the French set all six of their vessels afire, the English evidently managed to put out the fires and save five of the ships. (One sank.) The English had little time to enjoy their achievement, however, because a storm the next day sank all the English ships while the English were removing loot from the French vessels.

There are conflicting accounts of the circumstances behind a set of wrecks at Martinique in 1667. According to one story, an English fleet burned 20 French warships and merchant vessels in the harbor at Fort-de-France. Another version of this tale says that the attack occurred at Governor's Bay and involved the destruction of 19 French warships and assorted other vessels.

More than 20 large French vessels are said to have been lost, along with numerous lives, at Cul-de-Sac Bay during a hurricane on August 3, 1680. Military action by the British brought about the destruction of two French warships and 30 French merchantmen at Martinique in 1745.

Twenty-eight French ships and eight English vessels were destroyed at Fort-de-France in a hurricane in October of 1766; 27 other ships also were reported lost at other locations. Two hurricanes struck Martinique in quick succession in 1779; the second storm destroyed more than 70 ships on the southern side of Martinique.

The hurricane of October 12, 1780, was one of the most destructive ever to strike Martinique and is said to have wrecked 40 French troop transports there, in addition to several large French warships that were lost with all hands. The British also suffered greatly from this storm: three English warships, two of 28 guns each and one of 24 guns, were lost on the western side of Martinique.

Another hurricane in September of 1788 is said to have wrecked more than 50 large French vessels and washed the community of Caravel, along with most of its residents, into the ocean.

The eruption of Pelée, Martinique's great volcano, on May 8, 1902, devastated the city of St. Pierre and wrecked vessels in the harbor.

See also RODDAM; RORAIMA.

Mary Celeste A celebrated example of a "ghost ship," the two-masted brig *Mary Celeste* was found deserted in the North Atlantic Ocean between Portugal and the Azores on December 5, 1872. The ship carried a cargo of crude alcohol. The lifeboat was missing, there was some damage to the sails, and the cargo hatches had been torn off. The last entry in the

logbook was dated November 25. That meant the ship had sailed, abandoned, for nine days before being discovered. Evidently the ship had been abandoned in a hurry, because the seamen's belongings were still in their quarters. Arthur Conan Doyle, creator of the fictional detective Sherlock Holmes, wrote a celebrated story based on the facts of the case, but introduced many errors through his account, notably by misidentifying the ship as the *Marie Celeste* and by reporting that the aforementioned lifeboat was still in place when the ship was found. That latter error—the matter of the lifeboat—led future students of the case astray and brought about all manner of bizarre speculation as to how the captain, crew and passengers could abandon the ship without taking to the lifeboat. At one point, abduction by an extraterrestrial spacecraft was suggested as a possible explanation for the ship's abandonment. A less exotic scenario is that something on board alarmed the captain, who ordered everyone into the lifeboat for safety. In the rush to leave, the captain neglected to tie the lifeboat to the ship with a cable. Before the crew and passengers could return to the *Mary Celeste*, the wind blew up and the ship sailed away, leaving the lifeboat behind.

See also GHOST SHIPS.

Maryland, United States Shipwrecks seem as numerous as waterfowl in Maryland waters, which include both the Atlantic coast of the state as well as portions of Chesapeake Bay. Numerous British ships were lost in Maryland waters in the late 18th century, including the 74-gun warship H.M.S. *Culloden*, sunk in a storm in 1781, and several other warships—the 44-gun *Charon*, the 28-gun H.M.S. *Guadeloupe* and the eight-gun H.M.S. *Vulcan*—that were scuttled in Chesapeake Bay that same year.

Mary Rose, English galleon In one of the earliest and most spectacular shipwrecks in New England history, the galleon *Mary Rose* exploded in Boston Harbor on July 27, 1640, when something set off gunpowder on board. (Reportedly, someone had used a candle carelessly to provide light in the hold.) According to the journal of Governor Winthrop of Massachusetts, the ship exploded around dinnertime. The blast evidently killed all but one man, who was rescued by a ferryboat and later could remember nothing of the explosion, nor of his rescue. The ship was salvaged.

Massachusetts, United States Dominating the coast of Massachusetts is Cape Cod, the lengthy, curved hook of land that has been the site of numerous shipwrecks from early colonial times to the pres-

A severe storm broke apart the tanker *Pendleton* off Chatham Bar, Massachusetts, on February 18, 1952. (U.S. Coast Guard)

ent. Numerous shoals off the Massachusetts coast also have claimed a large number of ships. Adding to the perils of shipping in Massachusetts waters are frequent, violent storms. Examples of notable shipwrecks along the Massachusetts coast include the 32-gun British warship H.M.S. *Solebay,* wrecked at Boston Neck on December 25, 1709, with the loss of its entire crew, and the sloop-of-war H.M.S. *Hazard,* lost near Boston in 1714, likewise with the loss of all hands.

See also CITY OF PORTLAND; NANTUCKET; PORT FORTUNE INCIDENT; SPARROW HAWK; STORMS.

masts and spars Large vertical timbers or metal columns extending upward from the deck of a ship, masts provided a temporary refuge for many sailors when waves washed over the decks during a shipwreck. Horizontal members, or "spars," attached to masts also could supply temporary havens for sailors during a wreck, as could the rigging, or system of ropes attached to the spars and masts.

The safety that masts and spars provided could be illusory, however, because the ship might roll over and pitch men clinging to them into the sea. Also, during cold and stormy weather, survivors who went aloft might find themselves in danger of death from exposure. In some cases, survivors had to spend extended periods on masts or in rigging before rescuers arrived.

Masts, spars and rigging were prime targets for lifesavers trying to shoot a line aboard a vessel, using a Lyle gun, a modified mortar that shot a special projectile trailing a line to a vessel in distress. If all went as hoped, the projectile would land on a mast, spar or piece of rigging, and the attached line could be used to rig a breeches buoy or other piece of lifesaving equipment to carry survivors to shore.

A ship that lost its masts in a storm was said to be "dismasted."

See also RIGGING.

Matanzas Bay wrecks, Cuba On September 8, 1628, a Dutch fleet forced the New Spain Fleet into Matanzas Bay near Havana, where all 24 vessels in the Spanish fleet wrecked on shoals. The Spaniards reportedly did not put up a fight.

See also CUBA; FLOTA SYSTEM.

***Mauna Ala*, American freighter** A wartime blackout that extinguished navigation aids and radio beacons along the Pacific coast of the United States brought about the wreck of *Mauna Ala.* The freighter was on its way to Honolulu in December of 1941 when, immediately after the Japanese attack on Pearl Harbor, the ship received an order to proceed to the nearest port at once. The ship complied, but its officers had not been told that a blackout was imposed on the coast.

Near the Oregon coast, *Mauna Ala* encountered another ship that warned the freighter to halt. *Mauna Ala* slowed down for a while, but the captain later ordered full speed ahead because he expected to sight a lightship. Instead of the lightship, the men of *Mauna Ala* soon saw breakers ahead. The ship grounded on the Columbia River bar and broke in two a few days later. Most of the ship's cargo—including 60,000 Christmas trees—was lost.

May Queen, American bark Sometimes a wreck has slightly ludicrous results when cargo washes ashore. Consider, for example, the *May Queen* and its load of coconuts.

On the morning of April 3, 1886, the ship was on its way home to Baltimore from Colombia with more than $7,000 worth of coconuts on board (a substantial cargo, in the days when the ship itself was valued at only $4,000), when it stranded just north of the Little Island lifesaving station at Virginia Beach, Virginia. About a third of the coconuts were salvaged, but many more wound up scattered along the beach or caught in fishing nets.

So numerous were the coconuts that even after the locals had gathered as many as they cared to have, coconuts remained all over the sands to refresh passersby. People walking on the beach would break open the coconuts, drink the milk inside and discard the hulls on the sand. For years afterward, coconuts could be seen all along the beach at high tide.

See also CARGO.

Medora, American steamship Among the worst calamities to occur in American waters in the early 19th century was the destruction of the sidewheel steamer *Medora* in Baltimore harbor on April 14, 1842. The ship, which belonged to the Baltimore and Norfolk Steam Packet Company, was leaving the wharf for its sea trials when the boiler exploded. The boiler flew into the air, then fell back to the deck. The ship was demolished, and great clouds of steam escaped. *Medora* sank next to the wharf. Twenty-six people were reported killed, and 38 injured. *Medora* was raised and rebuilt, and finally went back into operation under the name *Herald*. The steamer continued in service until 1885.

See also EXPLOSIONS.

Medusa, French frigate In one of the most horrible tales in maritime history, *Medusa* ran aground on a reef off the African coast while on a voyage to Senegal,

on July 1, 1816, with 250 people on board. Of these, 155 did not survive the voyage.

The wreck was attributed to the negligence of the captain, who ignored the responsibilities of command in order to attend a party. When *Medusa* ran onto the reef, drunken crewmen rushed for the boats and left the ship with some 170 people, including many women and children, still on board. The boats eventually reached the African shore.

Those left behind assembled a large raft, on which 150 people set out, without taking food or navigational tools. (A few men who were hopelessly drunk stayed behind on *Medusa.* Only three of them were discovered alive when rescuers reached the ship almost three months afterward.)

The raft drifted for 12 days. Its occupants went without food and water for all that time. At one point, mutineers tried to kill the officers on board and cut the ropes that held the raft together. The mutiny was suppressed, and one of the mutineers was killed. Later, the mutineers tried again to take over the raft. This time, numerous deaths resulted.

Only 16 people remained alive when a sloop from Senegal found the raft and took the survivors on board. Seven of them died on the way to hospitals.

Melanope, British bark A mysterious wreck on the Columbia River (Oregon-Washington) bar, the case of *Melanope* ended happily, or at least safely, for all involved. The dismasted ship was found drifting near the river's mouth one day in December of 1908, with no one on board except a small dog. The sails were torn, and one of the boats was missing.

The bark was discovered by the steamship *Northland,* which took *Melanope* in tow and brought the derelict vessel to Astoria, Washington, where the wreck was sold to a new owner who converted the ship into a barge.

The mystery of the crew's whereabouts was resolved weeks afterward. The crew had abandoned *Melanope* after the ship was dismasted in a storm. In their hasty departure, the crew left behind their canine mascot.

Melanope served some time as a barge and then was scrapped. Thus ended a troubled career that reportedly included one captain's suicide (he is said to have gone mad and jumped overboard into shark-filled waters) and the death of a passenger (described by maritime historian James Gibbs as an "Indian princess") who died of alcohol abuse while at sea.

merchantman A trading ship of the age of sail, the merchantman carried cargo and passengers. Although it could be armed for self-defense, the merchantman was not designed specifically for armed engagement of an enemy, as warships were. Merchantmen often were vulnerable to attack by corsairs, pirates and privateers.

See also CORSAIRS AND PRIVATEERS.

mercury The liquid metal mercury was an important commodity in the days of Spain's flota system, because mercury was used to refine the precious metals that were the economic mainstay of the convoys traveling between Spain and the Americas. The "mercury amalgamation process" used in refining the precious metals required large quantities of mercury, which were extracted from a Crown mine at Huancavelica in Peru. Some supplies of mercury also came from Europe. Pools of mercury may still be seen on the seabed in some locations, marking the spot where a flota vessel with its shiny liquid cargo went down.

See also FLOTA SYSTEM; QUICKSILVER GALLEONS.

***Mermaid*, American fishing boat** A sad story from the annals of the U.S. Coast Guard involves the fishing boat *Mermaid*, which lost its rudder during a storm on the Columbia River (Oregon-Washington) bar on January 14, 1961. *Mermaid* sent a radio message for help. Three Coast Guard boats, two from Cape Disappointment station and another from Point Adams station, left to help *Mermaid*.

One Coast Guard boat, *Triumph*, and another boat managed to put towlines aboard *Mermaid*, but *Triumph*'s line broke. *Triumph* overturned. Only one crewman managed to escape and was rescued by *Mermaid*. The second Coast Guard boat that had put a line aboard *Mermaid* then overturned as well.

The third Coast Guard boat rescued three men from the second overturned boat and carried them to a nearby lightship. The waves battered the boat against the lightship's side, however, so that the boat soon sank.

Before another rescue attempt on *Mermaid* could be attempted, the fishing boat broke apart, killing the three men on board. Either seven or eight men (accounts differ on the total number) were killed in this incident.

***Merry*, American schooner** An interesting coincidence marked the wreck of the four-masted schooner *Miles M. Merry*. The ship was wrecked near the Moriches lifesaving station on Long Island, New York, at exactly the same spot where the vessel had run aground some two years earlier, in 1907. After the first grounding, *Merry* was refloated essentially un-

damaged. On the second occasion, however, heavy seas accompanying a gale broke the ship in two. The Moriches lifesavers rescued the men of *Merry*, as well as a wrecking crew that was on the scene. What remained of the wreck burned in March of 1909.

messages Before the age of wireless communications, ships in distress had few means of informing potential rescuers of their problems. The famous "message in a bottle" method, in which a written report was placed in a watertight container and cast into the sea in the hope that it would be found eventually, was used in some maritime catastrophes. This approach clearly was of no use in summoning immediate assistance, but nonetheless generated many colorful stories. (American fantasy author Edgar Allan Poe once wrote a fanciful tale of maritime calamity under the title "Ms. Found in a Bottle." The abbrevation "Ms." stood for "manuscript.") Some shipwrecked sailors who managed to reach shore deposited written accounts of their ships' destruction in canisters and placed the containers in cairns— monuments made by piling up loose rocks. The messages commonly included a request that finders make a copy of the original before passing it along to the proper authorities; this probably was a wise precaution, because there was no guarantee that the finders themselves would reach home safely.

Various kinds of visual signals, such as flags, could communicate messages to ships within certain ranges under the right conditions. In the early days of 20th-century steamship travel, company signals included rockets of various colors. Similar to Roman candles, these fireworks were used at night, when daytime visual signals would have been useless.

A particular kind of rocket, which exploded with a loud noise and released a shower of "stars," was used to indicate a ship was in distress. In the famous *Californian* incident, involving a liner known to be close to *Titanic* on the night of the great ship's sinking, observers on the *Californian* saw eight rockets of this kind rise from a ship nearby. Since *Titanic* fired eight rockets like those seen from *Californian*, this evidence has been used to argue that the master of *Californian*, Captain Stanley Lord, could and should have responded to the signals by getting under way and traveling to *Titanic*'s side.

In the age of wireless messages, two famous codes were widely used for signaling that a ship was in distress. One was C.Q.D.; the other, and later, code was the famous S.O.S., which was easier to send and to recognize. According to the one story, the wireless operator on *Titanic* switched from C.Q.D. to S.O.S., at a fellow crewman's suggestion, as the ship was sinking.

See also CAIRNS; CALIFORNIAN INCIDENT; LORD, CAPTAIN STANLEY; TITANIC; WIRELESS.

***Metropolis,* American steamship** The wreck of *Metropolis* on January 31, 1878, was one of the most significant in the history of North Carolina's Outer Banks. The final voyage of *Metropolis* began in Philadelphia, where the ship took on railway workers and 500 tons of iron rails for a railroad-building project in Brazil.

The ship—in poor condition for a sea voyage—left Philadelphia on January 28 with 248 people on board. Soon a rough sea developed, and the vessel started taking on water. Several feet of water accumulated in the hold, from a leak near the rudder. Coal was thrown overboard to lighten the ship. Although *Metropolis* was within easy reach of the great harbor at Hampton Roads, Virginia, with its repair facilities, the ship continued on its southward course instead of putting in there. Meanwhile, passengers were suffering badly from seasickness, and the iron rails below decks started shifting with the rolling of the ship.

After the coal was jettisoned, the pumps were able to counteract the leak for a while. Before long, however, other leaks developed, and the pumps finally gave out. The rising water posed a threat to the fires under the boilers.

Suddenly, a giant wave rolled over the ship, carrying away much of the superstructure, as well as several lifeboats. The wave also doused the fires, leaving *Metropolis* powerless in a violent sea.

Metropolis still had most of its sails, and the captain had the ship turned toward shore. In the distance he could see a lighthouse at Currituck Beach, North Carolina.

On the beach, two men were out for a morning walk, to see what might have washed ashore in the storm during the previous night. One of them sighted *Metropolis* offshore. A crowd could be seen on deck. The faint sound of their voices could be heard over the stormy waters. One of the men on shore went for help to the lifesaving station at Currituck Beach.

Some of the people on *Metropolis* decided to take their chances in the water, and leaped overboard. Six others set out for shore in the last remaining lifeboat; they tried to tow a line to shore but were unsuccessful. Most chose to remain with the ship, however, rather than risk their lives in the turbulent sea.

The lifesavers were alerted to the ship's plight and set up their mortar on shore to fire a line to *Metropolis.* The first shot missed. The second shot reached the ship, but the second mate, who took hold of the line, did not know how to attach it, and the line broke.

Then the lifesavers discovered they were out of powder for the mortar. More powder was available at the station, but that was miles away, and the only means of rapid transportation—two ponies—had been sent off on other business. So, there was no way to bring more powder rapidly to shoot another line to *Metropolis.* A neighbor had powder at his home, however, and soon the mortar was ready for firing again. When the lifesavers fired their two remaining shots, however, each time the line snapped, and the projectile passed far over *Metropolis* and landed in the sea. Now the frustrated lifesavers had powder, but no more projectiles to shoot.

All this time, *Metropolis* was breaking up under the assault of the storm. The people remaining on board had no lifeboats left, and many of them had no life preservers either.

In a desperate effort to carry a line to shore, the ship's quartermaster jumped into the sea with a line between his teeth. He soon had to let go of the line, however, and concentrate on saving himself.

The mainmast fell. The sea washed many of those on board into the water. Many were killed by debris in the water. Others died of exhaustion and the cold. There were 85 fatalities.

See also OUTER BANKS.

Mexico The seas around Mexico hold numerous wrecks, and the clarity of Mexican waters does much to encourage marine archaeology there. Many wrecks date from the time of the flota system, when large convoys carried treasure and other cargoes on a regular basis between Spain and the Spanish colonies in America. Wreck sites from this era tend to be concentrated on Mexico's eastern coast, because most trade was with Spain. Some shipping did occur across the Pacific to and from Mexico, as in the case of the famous Manila Galleons; but trade between Mexico, Peru and Panama was discouraged because of the potential for smuggling in such trade. Mexico is home to the Club of Explorations and Aquatic Sports of Mexico (CEDAM), the famous marine archaeological society.

See also ALACRAN REEF WRECK; ASCENSION; BAY OF ASCENSION WRECKS; CLUB OF EXPLORATIONS AND AQUATIC SPORTS OF MEXICO; COATZACOALCOS WRECK; COZUMEL ISLAND INCIDENT; FLOTA SYSTEM; MANILA GALLEONS; NEW SPAIN FLEET, 1590; NUESTRA SEÑORA DEL JUNCAL; PANDORA; RIO ALVARADO WRECKS; SAN ANTONIO DE PADUA; SAN JUAN DE ULUA WRECKS; SAN MIGUEL; SANTA MARIA LA BLANCA; SANTIAGO; VERACRUZ; VERACRUZ WRECK; YUCATÁN WRECKS.

Middle Ground shoal, Virginia   Among the most notorious shoals in the waters of colonial America was Middle Ground, which lay midway between Cape Henry and Cape Charles at the entrance to Chesapeake Bay. The shoal was forever changing position, so that even mariners who knew of its existence were in danger from it. Numerous ships were wrecked on Middle Ground in the early 18th century. Among them was the merchant ship *Richmond*, which sailed directly into the shoal on April 4, 1738, ran aground, and was abandoned after water flooded the hold through opened seams. The crew left the ship so rapidly that they did not lower the sails. When a salvage team arrived later at the spot where *Richmond* ran aground the ship was nowhere to be seen. It is not known whether the ship sank on the shoal or whether it was driven away, sails still set, by a wind.

A remarkable survival story involving Middle Ground occurred when the Scottish ship *Success* arrived at the mouth of Virginia's York River on December 31, 1745. The ship dropped anchor there, but hours afterward a storm ripped the vessel from its moorings and drove *Success* out into the bay, where the ship struck Middle Ground. *Success* sank so rapidly that four men were lost immediately. The other crewmen left the wreck in the ship's longboat, but the storm carried them past the Virginia capes and out to sea. Although the boat carried no provisions, the men managed to survive at sea until they reached Cape Henry at last.

See also ROCKS AND SHOALS.

Mikhail Lermontov, Soviet passenger liner   The 20,000-ton *Mikhail Lermontov* was lost in a storm near New Zealand on February 16, 1986. Only one person, a crewman, appears to have lost his life. Everyone else on board—229 crew members and 409 passengers—survived. The loss of *Mikhail Lermontov* was one of two major calamities to strike Soviet passenger ships in 1986. The other such incident was the loss of *Admiral Nakhimov*, following a collision with another ship in the Black Sea.

See also ADMIRAL NAKHIMOV.

Milwaukee, Great Lakes car ferry   The "car ferry" was a large, highly specialized ship built to carry railroad freight cars across Lake Michigan. Several railroads operated such car ferries. *Milwaukee* set out in a storm on October 22, 1929, from Milwaukee, Wisconsin, to Grand Haven, Michigan, with a load of railroad freight cars carrying merchandise as varied as peas and automobiles. To leave port in such weather was dangerous, because the storm was one of the most intense ever experienced on Lake Michigan.

Moreover, the ferry did not have a radio to send out a distress call in case of emergency.

The ship passed U.S. Lightship 95 near the harbor entrance at Milwaukee, and was never seen again. The lightship's captain saw that the ferry was rolling and pitching heavily in the stormy lake waters.

When the ferry was a day and a half overdue at Grand Haven, *Milwaukee*'s absence became cause for serious concern. On October 24, the steamer *Colonel* passed a field of floating wreckage off Racine, Wisconsin, and stopped to recover some of the debris. None of the wreckage, however, could be identified positively as belonging to the car ferry.

An air and sea search failed to turn up any sign of the missing vessel. Then the bodies of two *Milwaukee* crewmen were recovered off Kenosha, Wisconsin. Several more bodies of men from the car ferry were found later. One of the ship's lifeboats was discovered in a field of wreckage with four bodies on board; the men evidently had died of exhaustion and exposure.

The ferry's message case—a special, watertight container designed to be thrown overboard with a last message inside—was discovered in the surf near South Haven, Michigan. The message inside was from the ship's purser, A. R. Sadon. Dated October 22 at 8:30 P.M., the message said the ship was taking on water fast, the sea gate (a barrier at the stern) was bent, and the "flicker" was flooded. "Flicker" was the name for the crew quarters, beneath the car deck, immediately aft of the engine and boiler rooms. He also said the ship had turned around and headed back toward Milwaukee.

What specifically sank the big car ferry? The ship was inspected in August of 1929 and had passed. Even a ship in good condition might fail in the face of a terrible Great Lakes storm, however, and so the investigators had to consider many possibilities.

Perhaps the cargo had worked loose somehow and smashed through the ferry's side as *Milwaukee* rolled in the heavy seas. Another scenario was a boiler malfunction or engine failure that left the ship powerless and helpless amid huge waves.

Of particular significance was the purser's message about the flooded flicker. Since the flicker was located next to the engine and boiler rooms, perhaps all of them flooded, causing the ship to sink.

The captain of the car ferry *Grand Haven* suggested that when *Milwaukee* turned around in the heavy sea to return to Milwaukee, the sea gate at the stern was torn away, allowing the seas to enter and flood the car deck. What happened next is conjecture, but Dwight Boyer, writing an account of the ship's loss in his history of Great Lakes shipwrecks, indicates that the stresses placed on the ship by the storm may have twisted the car deck and sprung the "scuttle hatches," or entrances that allowed access to spaces below the car deck. If the scuttle hatches had been sprung and carried away, then the compartments below the car deck, including the flicker, would have been open to the sea and filled.

A watch found on one of the bodies recovered from the wreck had stopped at 9:45. If the time recorded by the purser in his message was accurate, then the car ferry must have remained afloat for more than an hour after the message was cast into the sea. Had *Milwaukee* carried a radio, a distress call might have brought help in time to save at least some of the men on board.

The ferry's captain came under strong official criticism for taking *Milwaukee* out in such weather. A government report to the U.S. Secretary of Commerce pointed out that other car-ferry captains had had the wisdom to keep their ships in port during the storm, and that *Milwaukee*'s captain had exercised notably poor judgment.

See also GREAT LAKES.

***Mindora*, American bark** Sometimes, a shipwreck involves interesting coincidences, as in the case of the American barks *Mindora* and *I. Merrithew*, which both were lost on the same day—January 12, 1853—on the Columbia River (Oregon-Washington) bar.

Mindora came to grief on a voyage from San Francisco to Portland, Oregon. Currents dragged the ship away from its anchorage off Sand Island near the Columbia River mouth and carried *Mindora* onto a shoal, where waves started breaking the vessel apart. When the captain gave the order to abandon ship, the crew lowered a boat into the rough waters. The boat started to fill with water, but the men bailed vigorously and managed to stay afloat long enough to reach nearby Astoria, Washington.

The following day, the captain set out for the wreck in a schooner, only to find that *Mindora* had disappeared. The vessel had drifted off the shoal and finally come to rest in Shoalwater Bay, several miles north of the river mouth.

That same day, *Merrithew* also grounded at the river mouth, on Clatsop Spit. The coincidences did not stop there. *Merrithew* had loaded next to *Mindora* at San Francisco, crossed the Columbia River bar on the same day as *Mindora*, and—as did *Mindora*—drifted away again after the crew abandoned ship. Currents carried *Merrithew* ashore at North Head, just north of the river mouth.

See also COLUMBIA RIVER BAR.

***Minerve*, French submarine** *Minerve* was running submerged on its way to the port of Toulon on Janu-

ary 27, 1968, when the submarine sent a radio message saying that the vessel was running smoothly. That was its last communication. The submarine did not arrive in port, and a week-long search by sea and air failed to find *Minerve*. The submarine was presumed sunk with all 52 men on board.

See also SUBMARINES.

mines Explosive devices scattered in the sea during wartime to sink or damage enemy vessels, mines have presented a serious threat to non-combattant vessels. Mines may take any of several forms. Some are contact mines designed to explode when a ship's hull touches them. Others may explode in the presence of a magnetic field that accompanies the metal hull of a passing vessel. Mines may be moored at a certain place or scattered to float freely in the sea. A mine may remain dangerous for long after it has been moored or released.

Although the popular image of a mine is that of World War II, namely a black, spherical object with "horns" protruding from it, present-day mine technology has advanced far beyond that of the 1940s. Modern mines are far more sophisticated in their function and discriminating in their targets. The current American CAPTOR system (short for "en*cap*sulated *tor*pedo"), for example, is said to consist of a torpedo housed in a cylindrical canister and activated by a computerized audio monitoring system. CAPTOR listens (so to speak) for the particular kind of noise, or "acoustical signature," that indicates an appropriate target such as an enemy submarine or surface vessel. When such a target approaches within range, CAPTOR releases its torpedo, which homes in on the target to destroy it. This system is intended to reduce the threat to non-hostile civilian shipping as well as friendly naval vessels.

See also TORPEDOES.

***Minotaur*, British frigate** *Minotaur* was lost in a storm off the coast of Holland on December 22, 1810. Only two boats could be launched, with 110 people in them. The remaining 570 people on *Minotaur* were left to save themselves as best they could, but none survived.

Molasses Reef wreck, Turks and Caicos Islands, West Indies Located north of Hispaniola, at the southeastern end of the Bahamas chain, the Molasses Reef wreck lies in about 20 feet of water on the western edge of Caicos Bank near West Caicos island. The wreck is thought to be the oldest yet discovered in the New World and has been an important site of modern marine archaeology. The ship's business at the time of its sinking, however, remains mysterious.

A great variety of weapons was found at the wreck site, ranging from crossbows to swivel guns. (Indeed, the ship appears to have been carrying little except armaments.) This evidence of weaponry appears to indicate that the wreck dates from the latter part of the 15th century. Hollow iron shot (equivalent to modern grenades) found at the site contained granular material, thought to be gunpowder, that evidently had remained dry for hundreds of years underwater. Although the ship's nationality has not been determined for certain, analysis of its weaponry and other items found at the site appears to indicate a Spanish origin for the vessel. Possibly the ship was engaged in exploration and/or capturing natives for use as slaves.

Apparently, nothing is known for certain of what happened to the crew of the sunken ship. Survivors may have made their way ashore and been murdered by natives. Maritime historian Donald Keith has suggested, however, that any survivors of the wreck may have spent the rest of their lives marooned on a nearby island. Slaving activities appear to have depopulated the Caicos Islands by the early 16th century, so that explorer Ponce de Leon did not see a single village in the whole length of the Bahamas while sailing there in 1513.

Two particularly grim bits of evidence emerged from the wreck: sets of leg irons, metal cuffs that would have been used to restrict the mobility of prisoners or slaves. According to a photo caption in George Bass's 1988 anthology *Ships and Shipwrecks of the Americas*, the irons were discovered in the locked position, so it seems reasonable to think they were locked around someone's legs when the vessel sank. This evidence does not constitute proof, however, that the ship was engaged in the gathering of slaves.

See also ARCHAEOLOGY; BAHIA MUJERES WRECK; HIGHBORN CAY WRECK.

Monck narrative

This story concerns the adventures of one Captain Monck, who survived shipwreck in the Arctic but later perished after a rebuke from a king.

Monck was ordered by King Christian IV of Denmark to sail into what is now the Canadian Arctic in search of a passage between America and Greenland. Monck set out with two ships and a total of 64 men on May 16, 1619, for Hudson's Straits.

Ice-filled waters made going difficult, but there was enough room to maneuver, so the ice did Monck and his ships no great harm. The weather on this voyage was peculiar. The ships allegedly encountered icy conditions one day, and the next day enjoyed almost balmy temperatures.

Monck and company arrived at Hudson's Straits on July 17. He renamed the waters Christian's Straits in honor of the Danish king. When he stopped at an island near Greenland, Monck sent men ashore to see if the island was inhabited. The next day, natives were seen on shore. They were armed, but the Danes had no great difficulty in disarming them. The Danes eventually gave them back their weapons, however, and received some food in return.

Monck's little fleet tried to leave the island on July 19 but was forced back by ice. He made another attempt on July 22 but encountered poor weather and so much ice that Monck had to take shelter near other islands. On August 9 he proceeded west-southwest, and the next day anchored near a large island that he named Snow Island for its snowy cover.

Monck and his men made their way to 63 degrees, 20 minutes north latitude. Then the ships were enclosed in ice, and Monck had to pass the winter there. The men built huts for shelter against the approaching winter. The explorers also investigated the island to see if it was inhabited. No inhabitants could be seen, although they did find a stone painted with a curious horned image that reminded them of the devil, as well as arrangements of stones that they took to be altars. Evidence of animal sacrifices, in the form of bones, lay everywhere around these sites.

The Danes laid up a supply of firewood and fresh meat for the winter. Monck reported killing a polar bear himself, and the men found its meat delicious. They were not prepared adequately for the Arctic winter, however, and suffered greatly when it arrived. They fell ill and died one after another.

Evidently the problem was scurvy, for the men's symptoms matched those of the disease, including loose teeth and swollen gums. So many perished that by March Captain Monck himself was performing sentry duty. Monck lay at the point of death by early June, but survived. By that time, only three of the 64 men who left on the expedition were still alive. These few survivors were saved by some unidentified root that relieved their symptoms. On June 18 the men caught some fish, and soon regained enough strength to plan their return to Denmark.

Sailing in the smaller ship, and leaving the larger one behind, the men were confronted by ice and trapped in it at one point, but soon were freed by a change in weather. A storm dismasted their ship, but eventually the survivors made their way back to Denmark. The king was pleased to see Monck again, having giving the explorer up for lost.

The king also, however, was the agent of Monck's death, in a most peculiar way. As Monck prepared for another expedition, the king pointed out that Monck's errors had cost him two ships already. Monck was angered and gave the king a less than tactful reply. Irritated, the monarch pushed his cane angrily against Monck's chest. Monck's reaction was extreme: he went home, took to his bed, and would not eat. Ten days later, he died.

money belt stories   Among the most colorful bits of shipwreck lore are the "money belt stories," according to which a passenger or crew member, unwilling to part with worldly wealth even in the face of imminent death, stuffs his money belt or other clothing with gold or heavy coins and is dragged down by his weight in the sea. How many of these stories are true, and how many are mere invention, it is difficult to say.

An example of a money belt story involves a sailor on the British troopship *Kent,* which was destroyed in a fire at sea during a gale in 1825. The sailor reportedly tied 400 sovereigns (coins) around his neck in a hand-kerchief. "You'll sink with it," the captain warned him. According to the story, the sailor fell into the sea and was lost while trying to lower himself and his treasure into a lifeboat.

The opposite of a money belt story is what one might called an "orange story." In this kind of tale, a wealthy passenger, preparing to leave a sinking ship, leaves material riches behind and takes something of comparatively little value instead. A passenger on the British liner *Titanic* in 1912, for example, reportedly left a box full of securities in his cabin as the ship was sinking, but took along an orange.

See also KENT; TITANIC.

Monitor, American Union ironclad   Among the many ships lost off the Outer Banks of North Carolina is the Union ironclad *Monitor,* which in 1862 stopped the Confederate ironclad *Virginia* (formerly *Merrimac*) from destroying the Federal fleet in Hampton Roads, Virginia.

The battle of the ironclads took place on March 9, 1862. Although the two ships battered each other at close range for hours, neither one attained a conclusive victory, and the fight is widely considered a draw.

The historical importance of the *Monitor-Virginia* duel was tremendous, however, in that it marked the end of the age of wooden warships. The Confederate ironclad had demonstrated its superiority over wooden vessels by demolishing much of the Union fleet in Hampton Roads before *Monitor* arrived.

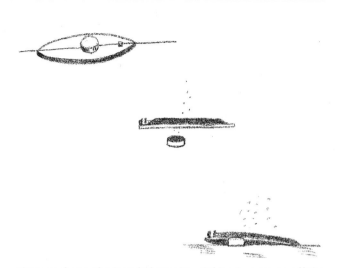

Diagram shows the ironclad *Monitor* sinking in a storm off the North Carolina coast. The hull came to rest upside down, atop a turret. (D. Ritchie)

Virginia was destroyed afterward to prevent the ironclad from falling into Union hands, and in 1862 *Monitor* sank off the Outer Banks while under tow to Wilmington, North Carolina.

The loss of *Monitor* was due partly to heavy weather and partly to the ironclad's design, which was compared to "a cheesebox on a raft." The deck extended only a few inches above the water, so as to minimize the ship's profile and provide the smallest possible target for enemy gunners. About the only superstructure was a rotating cylindrical turret housing two cannon.

There was no watertight seal around the turret's rim, and thus water poured through the seam between turret and hull in rough weather. On the ship's final voyage, *Monitor* took on so much water that the ironclad sank.

Monitor's wreck rests on the bottom near Cape Hatteras. The wreck is still largely intact and has been photographed extensively. *Monitor* capsized while sinking and lies upside down. The turret separated from the hull, which came to rest at an angle atop the turret.

Monmouth, American sidewheel steamer   The steamboat *Monmouth* was sunk off Wolf Trap Light in Chesapeake Bay on October 14, 1856, after a collision with the brig *Windward.* Seven lives were lost.

Monongahela, American whaler   Presumed lost in the Arctic Ocean in 1853 or 1854, *Monongahela* occupies an interesting niche in the lore of shipwrecks, because the ship's loss is said to have destroyed material evidence of the whaler's alleged encounter with a sea serpent.

According to maritime historian Edward Rowe Snow in his 1954 book *Amazing Sea Stories Never Told*

Before, Monongahela left New Bedford, Massachusetts, on October 1, 1850, on a voyage to the North Pacific Ocean. The whaler was under command of Captain Jason Seabury. Slightly more than a year later, on January 13, 1852, *Monongahela* was sailing the Pacific in company with another vessel, *Rebecca Sims,* when a lookout sighted "white water," the sign of a whale on the surface. The captain studied the disturbance with his spyglass but decided it was merely a school of porpoises, not a whale. The captain then went below to have breakfast but was interrupted by a terrified crewman who said he had seen something in the water that was not a whale.

The captain went to investigate and reportedly saw something with shiny black skin vanish beneath the waves. The creature allegedly reappeared a few minutes later and was visible on the surface about three-fourths of a mile from the ship. The monster was said to resemble a huge rope several feet wide, weaving in a sinuous motion. As the ship approached the strange animal, crewmen reportedly could hear the monster making a curious sobbing noise.

According to the story, Captain Seabury understood what a prize the sea monster would make, and asked for volunteers to try killing the monster and reducing its blubber to oil. A moment later, Seabury had his volunteers. Before boats could be lowered, however, the sea serpent vanished again. The beast was sighted again a few minutes later. A gale was developing, and Seabury was reluctant to lower boats in such weather. Eventually, the sea serpent lay so near *Monongahela* that the captain decided to risk sending out the boats to attack the monster.

Seabury went out in one of the boats and soon was beside the creature. The monster was wounded by two harpoons. As the serpent raised its head, a third harpoon reportedly went into one of the animal's eyes. The beast then knocked the captain into the sea before diving to an estimated depth of more than a mile and remaining submerged for some 16 hours. When the sea serpent reappeared on the surface, it evidently was dead and was surrounded by what appeared to be pieces of lung tissue. The serpent turned out to have life in it yet, however, for the animal allegedly went into convulsions and emitted an eerie, terrifying noise before expiring.

The whalers reportedly examined the monster's body and found it to be a male with a length of 103 feet, seven inches, and 49 feet, 11 inches in circumference at its widest point. The head was said to be elongated and flattened, the back black, and the belly yellow with a white stripe that extended most of the length of the body. The skin was said to be dotted with dark spots. The examination reportedly indicated that the animal breathed in the manner of a whale, through two spiracles or "spout holes." Other alleged features of the animal included four "paws" that the creature apparently used for swimming. The head was described as having 94 sharp teeth as large as a man's thumb. In the animal's stomach, the men reportedly found a blackfish and pieces of squid. The skeleton reportedly was preserved after being stripped of flesh. Removing the blubber allegedly was difficult because it was extremely elastic. The oil derived from the blubber was said to be as clear as water and to burn quickly.

Alonzo Sampson, a boat steerer on *Rebecca Sims,* the ship that accompanied *Monongahela,* mentioned the sea serpent in a book titled *Three Times Around the World.* According to Snow, Sampson said the sea serpent had a head like that of an alligator, but 10 feet long. The tail resembled a snake's, he added, and on either side of the body the sea serpent had two small fins near the head. Sampson claimed that the bones were cleaned and kept aboard *Monongahela* but were lost with the ship when *Monongahela* vanished at sea.

After the ship's alleged encounter with the sea monster, *Monongahela* reportedly sailed for the northern Pacific Ocean and was never seen again, although a cask with the ship's markings on it was said to have been recovered in the Arctic Ocean. A brig also reportedly found the quarterboard from the *Monongahela* and sent the wreckage to New Bedford, Massachusetts, writes Snow. The U.S. Navy sent a ship to search for any survivors from the presumed wreck of *Monongahela,* and learned on this voyage that a ship, possibly *Monongahela,* was lost in the autumn of 1853 near the island of Atka in the Aleutian chain between Alaska and Siberia. According to another account, published in 1855, the ship supposedly was lost in a gale in the fall of 1853.

The loss of *Monongahela* is remembered today primarily for the fanciful tale of its encounter with the sea serpent. Numerous other accounts of meeting sea serpents may be found in 19th-century maritime literature, although evidence of such alleged encounters (as in UFO reports in our own time) seems to have had a strange way of disappearing before critical investigators could examime it. The sea serpent reports are reminiscent of legends of giant octopi attacking ships. There appears to be only one actual case of a "sea monster" attacking and sinking a ship, namely the whaler *Essex,* which was struck and sunk by a whale in the Pacific Ocean.

See also ESSEX; OCTOPI.

Montejo wrecks, Mexico   Conquistador Francisco de Montejo, after arriving in Mexico's Yucatán in 1527, had two of his vessels—a caravel and a brigantine—burned at Punta Soliman. American marine archaeologist Robert Marx visited the site of the wrecks in 1957 and recovered items including an anchor and an iron cauldron.

Montserrat, Lesser Antilles   This island has been the site of many shipwrecks, a selected list of which follows. A hurricane in September of 1666 wrecked numerous French warships at Montserrat. A hurricane on September 21, 1747, destroyed several vessels, including two English merchantmen; another hurricane on October 24 wrecked an English ship. Eight unnamed British merchant ships were destroyed at Plymouth Harbor on Montserrat in a hurricane on September 13, 1754. In another hurricane in October of 1766, numerous English merchant ships on a voyage to Europe were destroyed near the island.

Morning Star, French bark   The hazards of the Columbia River (Oregon-Washington) bar—and of trying to make a difficult passage without a qualified pilot—are illustrated by the tale of *Morning Star,* which arrived at the Columbia River's mouth early in July of 1849 and found no pilot available. The captain waited for several days, then grew impatient and decided to try crossing the bar without a pilot's help.

The captain knew something of the bar, but his information was out of date, and the ship ran aground near Sand Island, on the northern shore of the river mouth. *Morning Star* began taking on water. The sea was rough and attempts to lower the boats were unsuccessful. The rudder broke away. Then *Morning Star* rose from the bar and drifted free, though it was damaged seriously.

Rescuers on shore saw the ship's plight and made their way to *Morning Star* in a canoe. They removed the crew to the safety of the shore and spent a day pumping out water from the holds. With a new rudder installed, the ship sailed later to Portland, Oregon, and the cargo was sold.

See also COLUMBIA RIVER BAR.

Moro Maru, Japanese hospital ship   A wartime mystery, the sinking of *Moro Maru* near Manila Bay in the Philippines in 1944 was attributed to American action. Japan lodged a complaint in Geneva against the United States for the sinking of the hospital ship. To find what had sunk *Moro Maru,* American divers went down to investigate the wreck. Bullet holes in the decks indicated that the ship had indeed been strafed. Yet the divers reportedly found no damage sufficient to have sunk the vessel; nor did they find charts and books, which appeared to have been removed. The absence of bodies aboard the ship was also strange. If *Moro Maru* had been sunk by enemy action, there almost surely would have been bodies left aboard. Yet everyone appeared to have gotten off the hospital ship. It was suggested that the crew had sunk the ship intentionally by opening the sea cocks.

Morro Castle, American passenger liner   *Morro Castle* caught fire and burned off the New Jersey coast while on a voyage between Havana and New York on September 8, 1934. The liner drifted ashore at Asbury Park, New Jersey, and was later hauled away to be scrapped. Of 435 passengers and crew, 133 were killed. The ship's loss occurred under mysterious circumstances, including the death of the captain just before the fire broke out. The acting captain was brought to trial, convicted and sentenced to two years in jail for negligence, but that ruling was overturned. What actually caused the fire is uncertain, but some evidence indicates a crewman with a long criminal record may have set the blaze deliberately.

See also FIRE.

Moskenstraumen, Norway   Located near Norway's Lofoten Islands, the Moskenstraumen is a dangerous coastal passage between four and five miles long, characterized by powerful currents. Ships miles from the Moskenstraumen are said to make substantial course adjustments to allow for the currents' influence.

mud and silt   These fine-grained sediments may help to preserve the wreck of a wooden vessel by protecting the wood against attack by teredos, or shipworms. Diver and marine archaeologist Robert Marx, for example, has reported diving on two large Spanish wrecks, dating from 1740, in the harbor at Cartagena, Colombia, and finding them remarkably well-preserved after many years buried under such conditions. Marx points out that the wreck's weight tends to push it down quickly into the mud and silt and thus hide the wood almost immediately from shipworm attack. Such conditions are both bane and blessing for marine archaeologists, however, because the fine sediment that preserves the wood may make visibility practically zero during excavations.

See also TEREDOS.

mysteries   Many ships have disappeared at sea under mysterious circumstances, and some of those cases have been publicized widely. Outstanding examples include the steamship *Waratah,* which evidently disappeared only a few miles off the South African coast, in busy sea lanes; the sailing vessel *Mary Celeste*, discovered drifting at sea with all its crew missing after apparently having been abandoned in haste; the U.S. Navy collier *Cyclops*, which disappeared at sea during World War I under circumstances that strongly suggest German involvement in the ship's loss; and the immigrant steamship *City of Glasgow*, which never arrived at its destination in Philadelphia after a voyage from Liverpool.

In the days before wireless communication, it was not unusual for vessels to be lost at sea without a trace. Numerous causes (such as waves, storms, explosions, mechanical malfunction, fire, or collision with other ships or with icebergs) could account for such losses. Moreover, the sea is so huge that wreckage from a ship might go unnoticed in its vastness. Wireless communications made such losses less frequent by allowing a stricken ship to notify others immediately of its plight and position.

Freak storms may be responsible for some cases of ships lost at sea without a trace. Intense but highly localized storms have been reported on occasion, and some of these storms may have sufficed to sink ships of considerable size.

Colorful tales of the supernatural tend to attach themselves to tales of vanished ships. One example is the story of the New Haven specter ship, an apparition that supposedly was witnessed above the waters off New Haven, Connecticut, following the unexplained loss of a sailing vessel in colonial times.

In the 1970s, a body of mythology about the so-called Bermuda Triangle became popular. The Bermuda Triangle, also known as the "Devil's Triangle," is a section of the western Atlantic Ocean between Bermuda and the southeastern United States in which large numbers of ships and aircraft are said to have disappeared under mysterious conditions that supposedly included unusual weather and magnetic phenomena. Unidentified flying objects (UFOs) also figure in Bermuda Triangle lore. The Bermuda Triangle does not appear to deserve its sinister reputation, since careful study of reports of "disappearances" in that region have revealed that the various ship and aircraft losses actually occurred under conditions much different from the lurid tales that generated the myth of the "Devil's Triangle." In short, the Bermuda Triangle evidently is no more dangerous than any other, similarly well-traveled area of the ocean, and the wild stories associated with the Bermuda Triangle have generally been dismissed as sensationalism.

One of the strangest tales associated with a vanished vessel is that of the sea monster allegedly killed by the crew of the whaling ship *Monongahela*. The putative monster is said to have resembled a giant serpent and to have yielded considerable quantities of oil when its blubber was processed. Any material evidence of this alleged encounter was lost with the ship, which reportedly disappeared in the Pacific Ocean. (Marine monsters of various kinds, notably giant octopi, have been suggested as possible explanations for the disappearances of ships at sea. The most charitable way to describe such tales is to say that they are groundless. Tales of "ghosts" and other supernatural phenomena associated with various individual shipwrecks likewise deserve to be met with skepticism.)

Even when it is known where a ship sank, and what circumstances were responsible for its sinking, mysteries still may surround the vessel's loss. A famous case in point is the British liner *Lusitania*, which was sunk by a German submarine off the Old Head of Kinsale, Ireland, during World War I. Although the admiralty and the captain of *Lusitania* were aware that an enemy submarine was operating in the vicinity at that time, *Lusitania* steered a straight course off a headland, at modest speed—circumstances ideal for U-boat attack. Why *Lusitania*'s captain put his ship in such a vulnerable (and easily avoidable) position has not been explained satisfactorily on the public record.

Among the minor mysteries of maritime lore is the origin of the expression "Davy Jones's Locker," meaning the deep sea as a graveyard for lost ships and sailors. Who Davy Jones may have been, and how the ocean floor came to be known as his "locker," are mysteries that have never received a conclusive explanation.

See also BERMUDA TRIANGLE; CITY OF GLASGOW; CYCLOPS; DAVY JONES'S LOCKER; DISAPPEARANCES; LUSITANIA; MARY CELESTE; MONONGAHELA; MYTHOLOGY; NEW HAVEN SPECTER SHIP; OCTOPI; POET; STORMS; WARATAH.

"Mysterious Bank" This feature of charts of waters near Grand Cayman Island indicates how waters—and charts—can change over time. Located west of the island, the bank is an area of shallow water, only several fathoms deep. Sixteenth-century navigators reported a small island in this vicinity, but around the beginning of the 17th century the island appears to have vanished. Apparently the bank represents a tiny island that has been visible above the water at some times and submerged at others.

mythology Myths surround accounts of many shipwrecks. Some of these are minor embellishments to the actual stories. A familiar example is the report that the orchestra on the *Titanic* played the hymn

"Nearer, My God, To Thee" as the ship was sinking, when the evidence appears to indicate that the orchestra did not do so.

A more familiar set of myths surrounds stories of the Bermuda Triangle, an area of the Atlantic Ocean in which numerous unexplained disappearances of ships and aircraft are said to have occurred, and paranormal phenomena are widely believed to occur frequently. According to some elements of Bermuda Triangle mythology, extraterrestrial beings have manipulated the atmosphere and magnetism in that portion of the sea so as to capture humans and their craft for study. Bermuda Triangle lore became highly popular in the United States in the mid-1970s, following publication of a bestselling book on the subject by author Charles Berlitz.

Shipwreck reports themselves may be myths. Treasure hunters in particular have found that numerous records of sunken ships are pure fiction. Extensive library research and other investigation may be required to determine the truth or falsehood of such stories before salvage operations begin.

Colorful myths involving sea creatures may arise following shipwrecks. An attack by a hypothetical giant octopus, for example, was suggested as an explanation for the disappearance of the crew from the *Mary Celeste.*

Certain natural phenomena also may give rise to myths concerning shipwrecks. The tale of the New Haven specter ship, for one, may be a mythologized account of flammable methane gas rising to the surface of waters off New England, igniting and burning with an eerie light, and then being interpreted as a spectral image of a wrecked vessel.

A centuries-old myth of the sea is that of Davy Jones, an evil being who is said to preside over the ocean depths (hence their popular name, "Davy Jones's Locker") and to be associated with shipwrecks. In his novel *Peregrine Pickle,* 18th-century British novelist Tobias Smollett describes "Jones"—actually a hoaxer in disguise—perching in a ship's rigging to terrify mariners.

The source of the Davy Jones myth is mysterious. It appears to have arisen among the English-speaking peoples, but otherwise little is known of its origin. Although his prosaic name would appear to indicate the monster was modeled after an actual person, perhaps a mad captain who led his ship and crew to destruction, there evidently is no record of any such officer or ship's master by that name to whom the myth could be traced. Davy Jones might be a personification of St. Elmo's Fire, the electrostatic glow that sometimes appears in a ship's rigging before or during an electrical storm; but this explanation does not account for the particular name "Jones" received.

Myths surrounding shipwrecks may be viewed as an attempt to dispel mystery by inventing some explanation, even a fantastic one, for the loss of the vessels.

See also BERMUDA TRIANGLE; MARY CELESTE; NEW HAVEN SPECTER SHIP; OCTOPI; TITANIC.

N

Nachi, Japanese cruiser An intelligence bonanza came out of this wreck. On November 5, 1944, the cruiser *Nachi* was sunk by bombs, torpedoes and rockets while trying to escape from Manila Bay in the Philippines. Divers sent down to examine the wreck came up with huge amounts of paper money and—more valuable still—with extensive plans and orders for Japan's defense against the imminent Allied invasion.

names More than one shipwreck may involve a vessel with the same name. Commonplace names listed in maritime historian Robert Marx's book *Shipwrecks in the Americas* include *Active, Adventure, Africa, Albert, Albion, Alexander, Amelia, Ann* (or *Anne*), *Astrea, Barbados* (or *Barbadoes*), *Betsey* (or *Betsy*), *Britannia, Brutus, Caesar, Caroline, Catherine, Cato, Commerce, Cornelia, Diana, Dispatch, Dolphin, Eagle, Echo, Edward, Eliza, Elizabeth, Enterprize, Europa, Experiment, Fame, Fanny, Favorite, Friends, Friendship, George, Hannah, Harriet, Hazard, Hope, Industry, Jamaica, Jane, John, Joseph, Kingston, Lark, Liberty, Lion, Lively, London, Lucy, Martha, Martin, Mary, Molly, Nancy, Nelly, Pacific, Patty, Peace, Pearl, Peggy, Perseverance, Polly, Providence, Rebecca, Robert, Rodney, Sally, San Juan, Santiago, Sarah, Savannah, Seaflower, Sisters, Speedwell, Suffolk, Swan, Thomas, Three Friends, Union, Victoria, Virginia, Warren, Warwick* and *William*. When trying to locate a wreck by a certain name, therefore, one should make sure that one has not selected, by mistake, another wreck with an identical name.

Pirate ships apparently had a tradition of misleading names, for many vessels had names out of keeping with their villainous business. Hugh Rankin, in his book *The Pirates of Colonial North Carolina*, lists pirate ships with names such as *Happy Delivery* and *Blessings*. The name *Revenge* appears to have been popular among pirate ships; Rankin actually cites one pirate vessel called *New York Revenge's Revenge*. Other pirate ships had colorful names such as *Bravo, Flying Horse* and *Night Rambler*.

nao A Spanish merchant vessel in the age of sail, the nao carried much of the trade between Spain and its colonies in the Americas. Many ships wrecked in the Caribbean were naos. A famous example of a nao is *Santa Maria*, the flagship of Christopher Columbus's expedition to America in 1492.

See also COLUMBUS EXPEDITIONS; SANTA MARIA.

Native Americans Although horror stories are told of Native Americans slaughtering or enslaving European survivors of shipwrecks along the Atlantic coast of North America during the colonial period, it should be noted that the natives sometimes received their unexpected guests in a friendly manner. A case in point is the wreck of a ship at Pleasant Bay on Cape Cod in 1626. The natives informed Massachusetts Governor William Bradford of the wreck and told him the survivors needed help. Europeans visiting the Americas in colonial days, on the other hand, were known to abuse the hospitality of their native hosts.

See also COLUMBUS EXPEDITIONS; PORT FORTUNE INCIDENT; SPARROW HAWK.

Nautilus, British sailing vessel Twenty-seven people were killed in the wreck of *Nautilus* during a storm near Macao on November 19, 1803. There were 19 survivors.

navigation Errors in navigation have been responsible for numerous shipwrecks. In the 18th and early 19th centuries, navigation was often highly inexact. Latitudes of ports were not always known with certainty, and navigation tables contained significant computational errors. Also, such navigational aids as existed then, including lighthouses, were not absolutely reliable, because they could be misinterpreted by a captain who was not extremely familiar with the stretch of coast they occupied. As a result, the captain might set an incorrect course and sail his ship into dangerous shoals. Observations of the sun, made with sextants, could provide a reasonably good estimate of a ship's position; but favorable conditions for such sightings were not always available. Eventually, the invention of reliable machines for carrying out calculations made more accurate navigational tables available and thus made navigation safer and more reliable. Modern navigational aids include radio and radar beacons and position fixes obtained by satellite.

See also LIGHTHOUSES; LIGHTSHIPS; RADAR; RADIO.

near-shore environment Many wrecks occur in this environment, which may be defined as extending perhaps two miles offshore and several hundred yards inland. The near-shore environment poses numerous hazards to ships, including rocks and shoals, which may rip out the bottom of a ship or entrap the vessel in sands; strong currents, which can carry a ship off its intended course and toward other hazards; wrecks, which may extend to within a few inches of the surface and cause severe damage to ships that strike them; heavy traffic, which increases the risk of collision between ships; and surf, which may help to destroy a stranded ship and impede rescue efforts. During severe storms, the near-shore environment may extend a considerable distance inland, as when a storm surge raises sea level and floods inland areas. It is not unusual for a storm to send large ships inland on a surge and leave them stranded far from the beach.

Over the centuries, the near-shore environment has had its man-made hazards, such as "wreckers," who reportedly would set false navigational lights on shore to confuse mariners and bring their ships to destruction so that shore folk could prey on the wrecked ships and their cargoes. The near-shore environment also has offered a measure of safety for sailors in trouble, however, especially after the establishment of well-equipped and adequately staffed lifesaving stations.

See also CURRENT; ROCKS AND SHOALS; WRECKERS.

Needham, American merchant ship A major shipwreck in colonial America, the loss of *Needham* occurred on February 21, 1738. The ship burned, on its maiden voyage from New England to Virginia, near West Point, Virginia. Virtually no cargo was on board at the time, and no lives were lost.

Neustria, French passenger liner *Neustria* vanished at sea en route to Marseilles, France, after sailing from New York on October 27, 1908. No figures are available on how many people were lost with the ship. *Neustria* was equipped to carry more than 1,000 passengers, many of them in steerage; but the number of passengers on an eastward voyage probably was much fewer.

See also DISAPPEARANCES.

neutercane A meteorological phenomenon described as an isolated, violent storm that covers a small area, appearing and disappearing rapidly, the neutercane is said to be only a few miles in diameter, to cause great swells in the ocean and to generate numerous tornadoes and waterspouts. Although meteorologists apparently disagree on whether or not neutercanes actually occur, pilots report unpleasant encounters with them. Such storms might be responsible for certain incidents in which aircraft and vessels at sea simply "disappear" without a trace.

See also STORMS.

Nevis, Lesser Antilles Beset by warfare, storms and earthquakes, this island has a long history of shipwrecks and even a sunken city. The sunken city came to be when an earthquake on April 6, 1690, shook the island and sent much of the community of Charlestown sliding into the sea. Apparently no records are available to indicate how many buildings and lives were lost, but exploration by marine archaeologist Robert Marx in 1961 indicated that at least 50 buildings were visible above the sea floor and possibly many others were buried under sand. Marx reported seeing more than 20 large cannon underwater at a fort that was destroyed in the earthquake. The fort lies only eight to 10 feet below the surface.

Here is a selected list of shipwrecks at Nevis. In 1667, an English warship in Nevis Roads was blown up by accident on April 10 during a battle between French and English forces, killing most of the ship's crew. A hurricane on September 21, 1747, destroyed eight ships at Nevis. Another hurricane on September 4, 1779, destroyed several big French warships in a fleet then anchored near Charlestown. On January 25, 1790, H.M.S. *Solebay*, a 28-gun British warship, was wrecked at Nevis Point while being pursued by French vessels; *Solebay*'s crew burned the ship and then made their escape to land. Twenty unnamed merchant vessels were destroyed near Charlestown and Nevis Point in a hurricane in August of 1790. The 14-gun British warship H.M.S. *Drake* was lost on a reef in 1804, but all the crew survived. A reef also claimed the English merchant ship *Grace* on January 30, 1808; the ship was a complete loss, but the crew and a portion of the cargo were saved.

New England, United States The beaches and waters of New England are littered with thousands of wrecks dating back to the earliest days of European exploration and settlement. Several factors combined to make wrecks especially numerous in New England. Maritime traffic was very active; storms were numerous and violent; rocks and shoals were plentiful. In the days when wooden ships predominated, shipping was especially vulnerable to such hazards. Even in the age of iron and steel hulls, wrecks have occurred frequently in New England.

See also ANGEL GABRIEL; CITY OF PORTLAND; HESPERUS; ROCKS AND SHOALS; PORT FORTUNE INCIDENT.

New Hampshire, United States Although it has only a short coastline, New Hampshire has been the site of some notable shipwrecks. These include the English merchantman *Friends Adventure,* which sank while leaving Portsmouth on a voyage to Jamaica in 1760; three unnamed merchant vessels that were wrecked on Appledore Island in 1780, with the loss of many lives; and the American merchant ship *Commerce,* which was wrecked on Portsmouth Beach on May 14, 1817.

New Haven specter ship, Connecticut A story from 17th-century New England, the case of the New Haven specter ship may be seen as part of the literature on "ghost ships." Puritan religious leader Cotton Mather recorded the case of a new but unseaworthy ship that had departed from Rhode Island for England in 1646 but apparently foundered at sea. The ship did not reach its destination, nor did any news of the vessel reach New England via ships returning from England.

A pastor in New Haven wrote to Mather that some months after the ship set sail (and presumably was lost at sea), an "apparition of a ship in the air" appeared above New Haven harbor, following a thunderstorm. The aerial phantom ship appeared about an hour before sunset and was said to resemble the lost ship. The spectral ship at first appeared to have its sails filled with a strong wind, on a northward course, and was observed for half an hour by many witnesses. The ship approached within a stone's throw of the shore. Then witnesses apparently saw the ship maintop blown away, then the mizzen-top and finally all the masts. The phantom ship then appeared to careen and overturn, and finally disappeared into a "smoky" cloud, which dissipated and left only clear air behind. Witnesses allegedly could distinguish the colors of the ship's components.

The incident was interpreted as a sign from God, showing the people of New Haven what had happened to the ship. Various interpretations of this sighting are possible. One interpretation is that methane, or "marsh gas," arising from underwater collected near the surface, was ignited (possibly by electricity associated with the passing thunderstorm) and burned with a flame that was transformed by active imaginations into the image of a ship. New England is seismically active, and some geologists believe that methane commonly escapes from the Earth's interior to the surface in such areas.

See also GHOST SHIPS.

New Jersey, United States Perhaps the single most famous maritime catastrophe in New Jersey history is the Hoboken fire in 1900. Four passenger ships caught fire at the North German Lloyd Line pier. More than 300 people died in the fire, and more than 200 others were injured. The earlier history of shipwrecks in New Jersey waters includes the loss of the 18-gun privateer ship *Castle del Rey* near Sandy Hook in a storm in 1704, with only 13 survivors from a crew of 145; the 34-gun Spanish warship *Juno,* sunk on October 29, 1802, near Cape May with the loss of all 425 people on board; and a great number of ships, their names unrecorded, that sank near Cape May in a hurricane on September 3, 1821.

See also HOBOKEN FIRE.

New Jersey and Virginia, American battleships These two American warships occupy a special place in the literature on shipwrecks, because they were sunk on purpose, by aerial bombardment, to show the capabilities of air power. The battleships were sunk near Diamond Shoals on the Outer Banks of North Carolina on September 5, 1923, by Army aircraft under the command of Brigadier General Billy Mitchell. The aircraft operated from a temporary airfield set up on the Outer Banks. Mitchell's planes dropped 1,100-pound bombs on the *Virginia* and sank the battleship in half an hour. The *New Jersey* was more difficult to sink but also was sent to the bottom several hours later. The exercise demonstrated that aircraft could pose a lethal threat to large warships. The ships were destroyed as part of reductions in American warships mandated by a naval limitations treaty after World War I.

New Spain Fleet, 1589 The New Spain Fleet joined forces with the Tierra Firme Armada and the Tierra Firme Fleet in Havana to form a huge convoy of approximately 100 ships for protection against the

English. The convoy left Havana on September 9 and encountered a hurricane. Several vessels sank, including the *Almiranta* of the New Spain Fleet.

New Spain Fleet, 1590 More than 1,000 people died, and cargo worth more than 2 million pesos was lost, in wrecks caused by an intense storm in the Gulf of Mexico in November of 1590. The New Spain Fleet set sail from Sanlucar, Spain, on August 1 with 63 ships. In the storm, 16 vessels were lost on the coast of Mexico. The rest of the fleet managed to make port at Veracruz on November 8. The 280-ton *La Trinidad* was lost while attempting to enter Veracruz harbor in the storm. The 220-ton *Nuestra Señora del Socorro* was lost at Veracruz. A 180-ton Portuguese ship, *La Piedad*, was lost at Veracruz, with only 18 survivors. Another Portuguese ship of 130 tons was lost in the vicinity of Veracruz. Twelve other ships in the fleet also were wrecked.

See also FLOTA SYSTEM; STORMS.

New Spain Fleet, 1600 A calamitous storm on September 12 killed perhaps 1,000 men and destroyed six ships of the 60 in the New Spain Fleet on this voyage. The fleet encountered the storm about 60 miles off the coast of Villa Rica, Mexico. Three of the lost ships sank soon after the storm struck. Two other ships vanished and were presumed lost. Another ship was wrecked on the Tabasco shore. Eight additional ships were lost later in the storm, at locations including the Medellin River and Isla Verde. Lost vessels included the 300-ton *San Pedro*, the 300-ton *La Caridad* and the 100-ton *La Catalina*. The destroyed ships and their cargo had an estimated total value of 10 million pesos.

New Spain Fleet, 1610 A hurricane struck on September 10, shortly after the New Spain Fleet reached Veracruz, and wrecked numerous frigates in the vicinity.

New Spain Fleet, 1615 The New Spain Fleet, consisting of 41 ships on this voyage, encountered a storm off Islas Tranquilo and Arena, Mexico, on August 30, 1615. The 500-ton *San Miguel*, carrying wine, mercury and other cargo, broke in two and sank so rapidly that neither the cargo nor anyone on board was saved.

New Spain Fleet, 1631 A hurricane evidently wiped out the 19-ship New Spain Fleet completely on this voyage, about one week after the fleet left Veracruz, Mexico. The *capitana* of the fleet sank 24 miles north of Bajo de las Arcas, with the loss of 300 people. There were 35 survivors. What happened to the rest of the fleet is not known.

New Spain Fleet, 1641 The New Spain Fleet and a protective squadron were traveling together when they encountered a hurricane on September 27, 1641, and lost five ships of the New Spain Fleet on the Florida coast. Additional ships sank at sea. The *almiranta* of the fleet went adrift and was wrecked on a reef north of Hispaniola. The reef came to be known as Silver Shoals because of the silver that was on the ship. Most of the treasure was recovered.

See also SILVER SHOALS WRECK.

New Spain Fleet, 1715 The fleet lost four ships when a storm struck Veracruz, Mexico, on March 28. Damage to shipping and the city from this storm was extensive.

New Spain Fleet, 1725 The fleet's *capitana* burned at Campeche Sound in the Gulf of Mexico. More than 400 men were killed.

New York, United States From earliest colonial times, New York waters have claimed numerous ships. The Dutch ship *Tiger* burned and sank near Manhattan in 1614. Another Dutch vessel, *Prins Maurits*, was wrecked on Fire Island in 1657 while carrying immigrants to New Amsterdam (now New York City), but Native Americans rescued everyone on board. A 12-gun Spanish privateer with 133 men on board exploded in a fight with a local privateer off Long Island's eastern tip in 1719, killing 42 Spaniards. In 1777, there were several notable ship losses in New York waters, including the Irish merchant ship *Diamond*, which hit rocks and sank at the mouth of the East River near Manhattan; the British warship H.M.S. *Liverpool*, lost on the southern shore of Long Island; and the 24-gun American warship *Montgomery*, which was captured and destroyed by the British on the Hudson River. Eight unnamed ships sank in a single storm at New York City on January 11, 1796. Another destructive storm on September 4, 1821, sank numerous vessels in New York City, including 10 large vessels sunk at the Quarantine and a dozen other large ships sunk at Public Store Dock Number 12. Among the most notorious shipwrecks in New York history is the burning of *General Slocum*, an excursion steamer, in the East River on June 15, 1904, with more than 1,000 lives lost.

See also GENERAL SLOCUM; TIGER.

Niagara, passenger liner One of the great stories of modern salvage involves the wreck of the trans-ocean liner *Niagara*, which departed from Auckland, New Zealand, for Vancouver, British Columbia, on the night of June 18, 1940, with $12 million in gold bullion from the Bank of England on board.

The liner hit a mine less than four hours after leaving port, and drifted for two hours before sinking in almost 450 feet of water at 5:30 A.M. on June 19. A ship rescued the passengers and crew later that morning, and attention turned to recovering the tons of gold inside the wreck. The salvage operation was led by Captain J. P. Williams, using the steamer *Claymore* as salvage vessel.

The first challenge was locating the wreck. Its exact position at the time of sinking was not known, because of the two hours *Niagara* had spent drifting after hitting the mine. While trawling the sea floor in search of *Niagara, Claymore* had a frightening experience. A green object in the water near *Claymore* turned out to be a floating mine covered with sea growth. The salvage vessel evidently came within several feet of being blown to pieces.

The search for the wreck took weeks. At last, on January 31, 1941, a cable caught on some submerged object. When a sounding lead was dropped over the side, it came up again bearing traces of paint like that on the sunken vessel. By February 2 (after another close call involving a mine), the wreck had been located. Divers descended to the wreck in a specially constructed diving bell, because the depth was too great for divers in traditional apparatus.

Niagara lay on its side. Evidently the ship had struck a pair of mines, because it had two large holes in the hull. Now that the wreck was found, the salvage team had to find a way to reach the room where the bullion was stored. Using a model of the sunken ship, the salvors on *Claymore* could follow the work of the chief diver, John Johnstone, as he investigated the wreck and communicated with the surface by telephone.

Explosives, it turned out, were the only solution. So, the salvors started blasting their way into *Niagara.* The work lasted another five months, during which time the frequent explosions began to demolish *Claymore* as well as *Niagara;* at one point work had to stop while the salvage ship was repaired.

Eventually, divers reached the bullion room, and the grab started hauling boxes of gold to the surface. In less than two months, more than 500 gold ingots with a value of about $9 million were salvaged.

See also GOLD.

Niantic, American whaler

The strange career of *Niantic* began in 1835, when the ship was built in Connecticut as a packet. In 1844, the ship was converted for service as a whaler, and in 1848 *Niantic* left New England on a whaling voyage to the Pacific Northwest. While *Niantic* was at sea, gold was discovered in California, and the great gold rush was on. *Niantic's* captain learned of the gold rush when the whaler

stopped in Peru. The captain decided that potential profits were greater in ferrying prospectors to California than in whaling, so he proceeded to the Isthmus of Panama and took on board 246 California-bound seekers after gold. Fares were $150 to $250, depending on accommodations. When *Niantic* reached San Francisco, most of the crew departed with the passengers to join the gold rush, and the ship—like many others in the harbor—was left virtually deserted.

Local realtors bought *Niantic,* removed the masts and rigging and turned the vessel into San Francisco's first "storeship," a new category of craft intended to provide housing, offices and commercial space to relieve a real-estate crunch brought on by the sudden growth in the city's population. In 1851, a fire destroyed more than 20 blocks of the waterfront and burned *Niantic* as well. The burned wreck was covered with landfill after the fire and thus preserved from further destruction. The wreck was uncovered in 1978 during excavations for a new building. (By this time, the wreck site was many blocks from the shore.) Thousands of artifacts ranging from firearms to bottles for alcoholic beverages were recovered from the vessel. *Niantic* thus provided a rare and detailed look at the merchandise sold in San Francisco in gold rush days. Like the so-called Water Street wreck in New York City, *Niantic* is a good example of how maritime archaeology sometimes occurs under city streets.

See also WATER STREET WRECK.

Nicolasa, Spanish supply ship

La Nicolasa was wrecked at Isla Cancun, Mexico, in 1526 while on a voyage from Cuba to Veracruz. The wreck became a notable archaeological site in the 20th century. CEDAM, the famous Mexican marine archaeology society, recovered several cannons from the wreck in 1959.

Niobe, German naval training vessel

The four-masted *Niobe* sank in a storm off Kiel, Germany, on July 26, 1932. The ship apparently sank so quickly that there was no opportunity to lower lifeboats. Sixty-nine men were killed, but 40 others were rescued.

Noble, American steamship

Benjamin Noble, which sank in a storm on Lake Superior in April of 1914, has been described as a victim of America's economic troubles, which then included extremely high rates of unemployment.

In such a time, men were desperate for jobs and were willing to tolerate unsafe working conditions in return for a paycheck. Perhaps that is the reason no one appears to have spoken up about the extremely heavy load of rails loaded on the *Noble* at Conneaut, Ohio, for delivery to Duluth, Minnesota.

According to historian Dwight Boyer in his book *Ghost Ships of the Great Lakes,* the ship's normal loaded draft was 17 feet, but on this voyage *Noble* exceeded 18 feet. Boyer also cites an unnamed dock employee as saying that *Noble* left harbor with its anchor pockets all but submerged.

Mild weather allowed the ship to complete the first portion of its voyage, through the Soo Locks, apparently without serious incident. *Noble* cleared the locks successfully on April 25, 1912.

Immediately after *Noble* left the Soo, a gale approached from the north. A fog settled over the water, followed by strong winds, then rain, sleet and snow. Had the storm arrived earlier, *Noble* would have had an opportunity to turn and find shelter along the shore. As it happened, however, the steamer was out on the lake, unprotected, with a dangerously heavy cargo, when the weather turned bad. To make matters worse, the cargo limited the ship's speed to perhaps only nine knots, so that *Noble* could not hasten to safety. The ship simply had to plod along, overloaded and vulnerable, and battered by the seas.

The storm was one of the most severe in years. Somehow, *Noble* appears to have survived this leg of its passage. Approaching Duluth harbor, however, the ship faced an unanticipated problem.

Access to Duluth harbor was through a narrow canal with concrete walls on both sides. The two piers at the canal's lake end were marked by kerosene lights. The seas during this gale were so huge, however, that one of them reached some 10 feet above the canal wall and washed out the south light. There was no way to relight the beacon until the storm subsided. That left only one light burning at the canal entrance—not enough to allow a safe passage, because there was no way to tell from a distance which light was burning. A wrong guess could bring a ship to destruction.

Noble did not make harbor at Duluth. Presumably, the captain saw only one light burning at the canal entrance, and chose to head for the nearby port of Two Harbors, Minnesota, about 30 miles to the northeast, rather than risk destruction at Duluth.

On the way to Two Harbors, heavy seas overcame *Noble,* which sank with the loss of some 18 men. Bits of debris from the ship were found later on shore. The steamer is thought to have sunk near Knife Island—so quickly that the crew had no opportunity to escape.

Boyer uses *Noble*'s tragic fate to illustrate many changes that have occurred in American shipping since 1914. Today, owners would be much less likely to send out a ship in such an overloaded state; unions would make it impossible to assemble a crew for such

a voyage; and the Coast Guard has the power to halt any ship leaving port so heavily overloaded. Conditions were different then, however, and so *Noble* went out with an excessive load of rails and was lost with all hands.

See also CARGO.

Nordby incident   One of the most peculiar reports from the literature on conditions at sea comes from the Danish steamship *Nordby.* Although *Nordby* was neither sunk nor even badly damaged, a set of highly anomalous phenomena allegedly beset the ship. The phenomena reportedly appeared on May 8, 1902, the day of the great eruptions of the volcano *soufrière* on the island of St. Vincent and the volcano Mount Pelée that destroyed the steamships *Roddam* and *Roraima* in the harbor at St. Pierre on the island of Martinique.

Nordby, under command of Captain Eric Lillienskjold, was several hundred miles from the island. The captain went to the bridge to make an observation and noticed that the weather seemed much warmer than normal, and the heat kept increasing. By early afternoon, the heat was so remarkable that everyone on board was discussing it, and "[you] could almost see the pitch softening in the seams" of the vessel, the captain reported later.

Lillienskjold described what happened next: "Then, as quick as you could toss a biscuit over its rail, the *Nordby* dropped—regularly dropped—three or four feet down into the sea. No sooner did it do this than four big waves, that looked like they were coming from all directions at once, began to smash against our sides. This was queerer yet, because the water a minute before was as smooth as I ever saw it."

The captain had all hands piped on deck. The crew battened down everything in preparation for a storm. What followed was a storm of sorts, but unlike anything else the captain had ever witnessed. Here is his account of the phenomenon:

> There was something wrong with the sun that afternoon. It grew red and then dark red and then, about a quarter after 2, it went out of sight altogether. The day got so dark that you couldn't see half a ship's length ahead of you. We got our lamps going, and put on our oilskins, ready for a hurricane. All of a sudden there came a sheet of lightning that showed up the whole tumbling sea for miles and miles. We sort of ducked, expecting an awful crash of thunder, but it didn't come. There was no sound except the big waves pounding against our sides. There wasn't a breath of wind.

The captain called this occasion "the most exciting time I've ever been through." The waves impressed him greatly. "Every second there'd be waves 15 or 20 feet high, belting us head-on, stern-on and broadside, all at once," he related. "We could see them coming, for without any stop at all, flash after flash of lightning was blazing all about us."

The water temperature also was unusual, Lillienskjold said: " . . . [The] queerest part of it was the water itself. It was hot—not so hot that our feet could not stand it when it washed over the deck, but hot enough to make us think that it had been heated by some kind of a fire."

Even animals were behaving in bizarre fashion, according to the captain: "Something else we could see, too. Sharks! there were hundreds of them on all sides, jumping up and down in the water. And sea birds! A flock of them, squawking and crying, made for our rigging and perched there. They seemed like they were scared to death."

This strange set of phenomena continued for hours and terrified the crew: "The waves, the lightning, the hot water and the sharks, and all the rest of the odd things happening, frightened the crew out of their wits. . . . Mighty strange things happen on the sea, but this topped them all."

The captain remained on the bridge all night. Around 2 A.M., he reported, the unusual conditions ceased as suddenly as they had arisen. *Nordby*'s crew waited until daylight, then established their position (some 700 miles off Cape Henlopen) and resumed their voyage. "None of us was hurt, and the old *Nordby* pulled through all right, but I'd sooner stay ashore than see waves without wind and lightning without thunder," Lillienskjold said. His account of the incident was printed in Charles Morris's 1902 book *The Volcano's Deadly Work*, which also included extensive coverage of the eruption at Mount Pelée on the island of Martinique, as well as the simultaneous eruption of the volcano Soufrière on the island of St. Vincent.

The conditions *Nordby* experienced may or may not have been linked with the eruptions of the two volcanoes, but at least were coincident with them. Also, the captain's report of the unusually warm water would appear to indicate that volcanic activity might have been associated somehow with the strange events that he reported.

See also RODDAM; RORAIMA.

Norfolk, Virginia Norfolk and its adjacent waters have been the site of many notable shipwrecks, including the greatest maritime calamity that the Americans suffered in the war for independence. That incident occurred in 1779, when British Admiral George Collier and his men burned and wrecked almost 150 American merchant and naval vessels in Norfolk and

vicinity. Only six years later, in 1785, a number of heavy storms caused great damage to shipping in the Norfolk area; one storm drove a number of ships deep into the woods in Portsmouth. In another gale on July 23, 1788, numerous ships were demolished and sunk at Norfolk. A hurricane in 1821 had similar results.

See also SWITZER WRECK.

Norge, Danish steamship The *Norge* was bound from Copenhagen to New York with 703 passengers and 71 crew on June 28, 1904, when the ship struck the Rockall shoals near the Hebrides at about 7:30 A.M. The bow was ruptured, and the ship began to fill and sink. Although there was an attempt to rush the boats, the third mate reportedly reimposed discipline by threatening to kill anyone who entered the boats without permission. One boat was demolished during launching when a tackle failed, dropping one end of the boat and spilling some of its passengers into the sea; a wave then smashed the boat to pieces against the hull. A second boat reached the water with its occupants aboard but then also was smashed against the ship by a wave and destroyed; several additional passengers were killed in this incident. Some lifeboats were launched successfully and pulled away from the sinking *Norge*. Some passengers leaped directly into the water and drowned. The *Norge* sank some 20 minutes after striking Rockall. The captain reportedly intended to go down with his ship but was rescued nonetheless.

The lifeboats drifted for several days. Eventually, passing vessels picked up the survivors. Of 774 individuals aboard the ship, 701 allegedly died in the shipwreck. Deaths associated with the wreck were not limited to those who actually died in the sinking. At least one relative of a shipwreck victim was discovered dead beside a railroad track later, evidently having committed suicide. On December 24, 1904, the Maritime and Commercial Court in Copenhagen found the captain not guilty of negligence. Although there was suspicion that the *Norge* had sailed in an overcrowded condition, no blame was attached officially to the directors of the shipping line.

See also ROCKS AND SHOALS.

Normandie, French passenger liner The burning and sinking of the French liner *Normandie* at its pier in New York City on February 9, 1942, brought an end to the career of what was arguably the most magnificent liner ever built.

From the start, the French planned the ship to be huge, fast and elegant. The designer was Russian émigré Vladimir Yourkevitch. His design was a dramatic departure from the traditional scheme of ocean liners. The hull he designed for the new French liner would let the ship travel as fast as her great British competitor, *Queen Mary*, but use 20 percent less horsepower and much less fuel. (For *Queen Mary*, Britain's Cunard Line had considered but turned down Yourkevitch's ideas.)

At 1,029 feet in length the first liner longer than 1,000 feet, *Normandie*—known initially as "T6" at the Penhoet shipyard in St. Nazaire where the liner was built—was also, at that time, the heaviest ship ever launched, at 27,657 tons. The completed vessel looked like nothing else afloat. Instead of the straight, near-vertical stem of traditional ship designs, *Normandie* had a flared clippership bow. Three massive funnels like gigantic opera hats rose from the superstructure. Even minor elements of the liner were distinctive works of design, such as the elegantly curved wave deflector at the bow. On its maiden voyage to New York in 1935, *Normandie* set a world record by traveling 744 nautical miles in a single day, at an average speed of just under 30 knots. *Normandie* on this voyage took the famed Blue Ribbon, the award for fastest trans-Atlantic crossing, from the Italian liner *Rex*. On arriving in New York, *Normandie* dwarfed all other vessels around, even the giant excursion steamers. The great liner's passage had stripped the lower portion of the bow completely clean of paint.

Normandie was in New York when war broke out in Europe in 1939. The liner would never put to sea again. The brief remainder of its life would be spent at its pier in Manhattan. The Allies hoped to use *Normandie* as a troop transport, in the manner of *Queen Mary* and *Queen Elizabeth*. A skeleton crew of 115 men remained on board after 900 other crew members returned to France. The French crew maintained the ship's elaborate fire control system, at that time considered among the best in the world. When the United States government seized the ship, however, this system was discontinued.

The United States seized *Normandie* on December 13, 1941, and immediately began preparing to convert the liner into a mammoth troopship. Many of the ship's magnificent artworks were removed. What happened next was one of the great tragedies in the history of ocean travel.

On February 9, 1942, sparks from a civilian worker's blowtorch set fire to a pile of life preservers on *Normandie*. The fire spread quickly through the great ship's interior. The liner's fire control system had been discontinued by this time, and fire-fighting equipment on the scene was inadequate to contain the blaze. Smoke from the burning ship spread over New York City and into adjacent Nassau County. Ninety-three men were injured and two were killed in the fire.

Fireboats converged on the burning ship and pumped vast quantities of water into *Normandie*. The weight of the water made *Normandie* top-heavy. The liner started to list away from the pier. New York City's mayor, Fiorello LaGuardia, showed up at the scene and told the press, "Everything is all right now." The mayor was mistaken. *Normandie* was about to capsize. Vladimir Yourkevitch, the ship's designer, urged Navy authorities to open the seacocks, valves in the ship's bottom that would let seawater rush in. With the seacocks open, Yourkevitch explained, *Normandie* would settle a few feet to the bottom in an upright position. Refloating the liner thereafter would be easy. The Navy refused to listen to Yourkevitch, however, and the ship's list increased. Soon *Normandie* rolled over on its left side. The rims of the huge funnels came to rest just inches above the ice-filled waters.

There was talk of sabotage after *Normandie* sank, but later investigation established that carelessness and ineptitude had been responsible for the liner's loss. One amusing aspect of the sinking was that cameramen were barred from the scene just before *Normandie* rolled over, although all of New York could see what was happening.

The man in charge of salvage was Navy Commander William A. Sullivan. He and his men set to work within days of the sinking, preparing the giant ship for refloating. The superstructure was cut away, and divers sealed all openings below the water. The Navy worked at this preliminary phase of the job for more than a year.

On August 4, 1943, pumps went to work removing water from the liner's interior, and *Normandie* began to rise slowly. By August 10, the ship had reached a 45-degree angle. *Normandie* finally attained an even keel again on October 27. On November 3, the liner was towed away to a Brooklyn pier. Some hope remained for rebuilding *Normandie* for troopship duty, but the government decided to have what remained of the vessel scrapped. A New Jersey scrapping firm handled that task, and the last remnant of the once great liner was removed from the water on October 6, 1947.

About all that remains of *Normandie* is a selection of artworks removed from the liner before its destruction. A statue of a Norman knight now occupies part of the lobby of an apartment building in New York City, and panels from the entrance to the dining salon now adorn the doors of a church in Brooklyn. The ship's wheel, seared by the fire, wound up on display at New York's South Street Seaport.

See also FIRE; QUEEN ELIZABETH.

Noronic, Canadian passenger steamship Built mostly of flammable materials, *Noronic* burned at a pier in Toronto on September 17, 1949. Of almost 700 people on the ship, more than 100 were killed (accounts differ on the number of fatalities). Fourteen people thought to be on the ship were never found. The catastrophe brought about revision of regulations and safety measures affecting Great Lakes shipping.

North Bend, American schooner A remarkable shipwreck involved the *North Bend*, which was cast ashore by the winds and waves, then freed by the sea later in good condition. *North Bend* went onto Peacock Spit near Cape Disappointment at the Columbia River (Oregon-Washington) bar on January 25, 1928, while trying to cross the bar without a pilot. A tug failed to budge the schooner. Subsequently, winds and waves pushed *North Bend* high onto the beach and thus preserved the ship from destruction by the sea. The ship remained in that relatively safe position for almost a year. In the winter of 1928–29, waves removed the sand from around the ship, which floated free and, with some human assistance, was refloated in Baker Bay on February 11, 1929. Still in good condition, the hull was converted into a barge.

North Carolina, American passenger steamship Part of the Baltimore Steam Packet Company, the luxurious steamer *North Carolina* burned near the mouth of Chesapeake Bay early on the foggy morning of January 29, 1859, with two lives reported lost.

North Carolina was en route from Baltimore to Norfolk, Virginia, when fire broke out in a linen storage room. The captain had the engines stopped and went to investigate the fire. He found it had spread into the staterooms. A water hose was rigged to fight the fire, but soon the flames were out of control.

The captain and crew remained calm. Passengers were roused from their staterooms and assembled on the lower deck. According to Donald Shomette in his 1982 history *Shipwrecks on the Chesapeake*, one family, Mr. and Mrs. Crayton and their baby, had a perilous escape. Unable to leave their stateroom through the door, the family escaped through the window, then found they had to slide down a stanchion. Mr. Crayton then wrapped the baby in a blanket, dropped the child into the cold water and leaped overboard himself. He kept his wife and child afloat until the family was rescued by a lifeboat.

Launching lifeboats was difficult because of the intense heat. As one boat reached the water, its tackle was burning. When all boats were lowered, they were lashed together on the captain's orders. Several crewmen on an improvised raft joined the lifeboats. The captain and a few other men remained on board. After the ship was searched to see if anyone had been left behind, the lifeboats pushed away from the burning ship. The men on the raft climbed aboard the lifeboats.

With the captain's boat in the lead, the lifeboats proceeded toward the nearby Smith Point Lightship, where they remained for a few hours until a passing steamer took the survivors on board for the remainder of their voyage to Norfolk. The captain and crew received high praise for their coolness and courage during the crisis.

Two people are thought to have died in the burning of *North Carolina*. They included one Thomas Curtis, who apparently drowned after jumping overboard, and Isaac Waterson, a steward who was a very sound sleeper and is believed to have perished in his bunk during the fire.

Shomette writes that two unsuccessful attempts were made to salvage *North Carolina,* and the wreck still rests at the bottom of Chesapeake Bay near the mouth of the Potomac River.

See also FIRE.

northeaster Also known as nor'easters or northeast storms, northeasters are characterized by storms or strong winds originating from the northeast.

Northeasters are commonplace along the Atlantic coast of the United States and are generated by the passage of frontal weather systems from northwest to east across North America. Such winds and storms have contributed to numerous wrecks along the Atlantic coast of the United States. A strong northeastern wind can drive ships easily onto the Eastern seaboard.

A northeaster should not be confused with a hurricane, which is a cyclonic storm that originates in the tropics and typically follows a slow, curving path northward. Hurricanes affecting the United States typically reach hurricane force in the Caribbean Sea before moving northward, whereas northeasters originate in the north and send their winds southward. Also, northeasters occur more frequently than hurricanes.

The southern Atlantic and Gulf Coast states of the United States are especially vulnerable to hurricanes, whereas northeasters are more closely associated with the Middle Atlantic and New England states.

Northeast Passage   Many shipwrecks in the age of sail resulted from attempts to find a northeast passage, or navigable sea route, between Europe and the Pacific Ocean, along the northern coast of Russia. Mariners knew that if such a route could be found, it might cut thousands of miles off journeys between Europe and eastern Asia (specifically China) and spare ships the hazardous, stormy passage around the Cape of Good Hope at the southern tip of Africa.

Many attempts were made to locate the Northeast Passage, and many expeditions ended in catastrophe in the Arctic. An example is the Barents expedition of 1596, which resulted in the shipwreck of the Dutch explorer William Barents and his crew on the northern coast of Novaya Zemyla in the Russian Arctic. Barents died on this expedition, his third in search of the Northeast Passage. (Some 300 years after Barents' final visit to the Arctic, a Norwegian sealing vessel visited the spot where Barents and his men had spent the winter following the wreck of their ship. The Norwegian ship's captain found some of the Dutchmen's belongings, preserved by the icy environment.)

Another shipwreck that occurred in the search for the Northeast Passage was that of Sir Hugh Willoughby's expedition in 1553. The English explorer commanded a fleet of three ships but lost two of them— and their crews—on the Kola Peninsula. The men evidently were asphyxiated by carbon monoxide from a stove. One ship on this expedition succeeded in reaching what is now Russia's Arctic port of Archangelsk, and sent a representative to Moscow to meet Ivan the Terrible. The British negotiated a trade agreement with the Russians on this visit but did not complete the Northeast Passage.

The Russians themselves established a northeast passage, using sturdy sailing craft called kochis. Small but rugged and versatile, a kochi had a sail and could even be dragged over the ice in the manner of a sledge.

The search for the Northeast Passage had an equivalent in the Canadian Arctic. Europeans spent centuries seeking a northwest passage for vessels sailing westward toward the Pacific. Just as the quest for the Northeast Passage cost many ships and lives, the search for the Northwest Passage was also expensive in terms of life and vessels. In neither case did Europeans locate a northern sea route like the one they had imagined. Europeans therefore had to be content with lengthy, hazardous passages around the southern tips of South America and Africa until canals were built at Suez and Panama to shorten sea routes to the East.

See also NORTHWEST PASSAGE.

***Northern Pacific*, American transport ship**   With more than 2,500 passengers on board, most of them wounded soldiers, the transport ship *Northern Pacific* ran aground on Fire Island, New York, on January 1, 1919, on a voyage from France to New York. Fog and a rough sea impeded rescue efforts, but the ship at least grounded firmly in the sand and was in no danger of breaking up. The Navy and Coast Guard removed the men from *Northern Pacific* by boats and breeches buoy.

***Northfleet*, British passenger frigate**   *Northfleet* collided with a Spanish steamship off Dungeness, England, on January 22, 1873, while on the way to Tasmania with many immigrants on board. *Northfleet* broke up quickly. Some 30 people were killed.

North German Lloyd Line   One of the major trans-Atlantic passenger carriers in the late 19th and early 20th centuries, North German Lloyd (also known by its German initials, NDL) operated liners including *Kaiser Wilhelm der Grosse, Bremen, Main* and *Saale.* Those four liners were all present at the company's piers in Hoboken, New Jersey, when the great fire broke out there on June 30, 1900, and destroyed the *Saale,* killing 99 people.

See also HOBOKEN FIRE.

Northwest Passage   The search for the fabled Northwest Passage, a navigable sea route between Europe and China, through what is now the Canadian Arctic, preoccupied European explorers for centuries. Numerous expeditions set out for the northern part of North America to seek a passage through the icebound islands there. On these expeditions, many ships and lives were lost.

Perhaps the most famous of these expeditions is that of British explorer Sir John Franklin, who was lost with his entire party of 129 men and both his ships, *Erebus* and *Terror,* on an 1845 voyage. The ships were caught in the ice and sunk. Franklin died and was buried in the Arctic. The last surviving members of the expedition appear to have perished on an overland journey. Many expeditions were sent out to search for Franklin, and in doing so opened up many areas of the Canadian Arctic to exploration.

The Northwest Passage, like its northeastern counterpart, was never realized in the form that Europeans imagined. Not until 1905 did Norwegian explorer Roald Amundsen succeed in completing the Northwest Passage, on the ship *Gjoa;* and even then, it never became the successful trade route that optimists had once hoped it would be.

See also FRANKLIN EXPEDITION; NORTHEAST PASSAGE.

***Nuestra Señora de Atocha y San Josef*, Spanish convoy ship**   Catastrophe could strike Spain's convoy ships anywhere, at any time, during their voyages between Spain and the Americas. Sometimes a ship would survive ordeals at sea, then be wrecked scant feet from shore. The 400-ton *Nuestra Señora de Atocha y San Josef*, for example, was part of the New Spain Fleet on a voyage from Havana to Spain in 1641. Among the few ships (and possibly the only ship) of the fleet to survive a hurricane in the Bahama Channel, the vessel managed to make port at Santiago de Cuba and make repairs. Then the ship set out from Santiago de Cuba for Havana. Another storm struck near Havana, however, and wrecked the ship only a few yards from the Fort of La Puntal.

See also CUBA; FLOTA SYSTEM.

Nuestra Señora de la Balvanera, Spanish galleon The 470-ton galleon was wrecked in 1788 on reefs near San Carlos, Chile, with the loss of the entire crew.

Nuestra Señora de la Candelaria, Spanish galleon This 600-ton galleon was wrecked on a reef when departing from Cartagena, Colombia, with the Tierra Firme Armada in 1626.

See also FLOTA SYSTEM.

Nuestra Señora de la Concepcion, Spanish galleon More than 500 men were killed in the sinking of this galleon at Veracruz, Mexico, in January of 1732.

Nuestra Señora del Juncal, Spanish convoy ship Part of the New Spain Fleet during a voyage in 1631, this ship—the *capitana*, or flagship, of the fleet—sank in a hurricane near Mexico's Bayo de las Arcas, with the loss of 300 lives. Only 35 people survived the wreck.

See also FLOTA SYSTEM.

Nuestra Señora de los Godos, Spanish sailing vessel *Nuestra Señora de los Godos*, part of the New Spain Fleet, was lost in a hurricane near Cape Charles, Virginia, on August 18, 1750. Several other ships from the fleet also were lost at various points along the coasts of Virginia and North Carolina. *La Galga* and an unidentified brigantine were lost on the Virginia shore north of Cape Charles, while four vessels were lost off Cape Hatteras. Two ships, the galleon *Zumaca* and the *Capitaña Nuestra Señora de Guadalupe*, made their way to safety in Norfolk but were lost soon afterward in another hurricane.

See also CHESAPEAKE BAY.

Nye incident An American whaler named Peleg Nye reportedly survived near-swallowing by a sperm whale in March of 1863. Although Nye presumed that a certain whale had been killed, the whale struck Nye's boat with its lower jaw, and Nye fell into the whale's mouth. As the whale closed its jaw, Nye was trapped by the legs.

The whale sounded, diving into the ocean. Nye fell unconscious. The whale then died and floated back to the surface. Nye also returned to the surface; eventually recovering from his ordeal. He reportedly lived to age 79.

See also BARTLEY INCIDENT; ESSEX.

O

O-5, American submarine   A hair-raising rescue operation occurred after *O-5* sank near the Panama Canal in October of 1923. Most of the crew managed to escape before the submarine sank, but three men were trapped inside as *O-5* sank in 40 feet of water. One crewman was trapped in the engine room for several minutes after the sinking but succeeded in opening the escape hatch and was blasted to the surface by escaping air. The other two men, in the torpedo room, had a harrowing wait for their rescue. First they had to wait 12 hours while cables were put in place around *O-5* and the submarine was brought to the surface. The cables snapped, however, and *O-5* fell back to the bottom before the men could get out. They were then forced to wait an additional 16 hours before being rescued at last.

See also SUBMARINES.

O-9, American submarine   The aged *O-9*, built in 1918, submerged during maneuvers with other submarines off Portsmouth, New Hampshire, on June 16, 1941, but never returned to the surface. Divers located the wreck three days later. The submarine evidently descended too deeply for safety and was crushed by water pressure. Exactly what caused the sinking was not determined. All 33 men on board were lost.

See also SUBMARINES.

Ocean Monarch, American immigrant ship   The 1,300-ton packet *Ocean Monarch,* owned by the Train Line in Boston and under command of Captain James Murdoch, was carrying some 380 people on the morning of August 24, 1848, when the ship caught fire and burned off Great Ormes Head near Liverpool, England. Of the crew and passengers on board, 176 reportedly died in the loss of the *Ocean Monarch.* The exact number of passengers on the ship on this voyage is uncertain, however, because so many immigrant families with young children were aboard that a precise count was difficult to make.

Ocean Monarch entered the Irish Sea from Liverpool harbor around 8 A.M. Later that morning, the ship was sighted by the yacht *Queen of the Ocean,* owned by Thomas Littledale, a Liverpool merchant. Also in the vicinity was *Affonso,* a Brazilian frigate under command of the Marquis d'Lisboa; the Marquis had on board many distinguished guests, including the Prince de Joinville.

Exactly how the fire began on *Ocean Monarch* was unclear. According to one report, the fire started when a passenger in steerage set a fire to cook his lunch. Another account of the incident said a candle had been dropped into inflammable material.

Whatever the fire's cause, it spread rapidly. A passenger came on deck and reported that a cabin below was filled with smoke. Captain Murdoch investigated and discovered his ship was on fire at the stern. He then gave orders to douse the fire with water, and to turn the ship before the wind so that the wind would have less opportunity to spread the fire to the rest of the vessel. These measures were inadequate, however, and the fire (Murdoch recalled later) spread as quickly as "lightning." Soon the whole stern was aflame.

The fire spread rapidly through the rest of the ship. *Ocean Monarch* appears to have been a floating tinderbox, in effect, because highly inflammable wooden bulkheads had been installed to convert the ship into an immigrant vessel.

Captain Murdoch watched as fire spread with tremendous intensity from the stern and the midsection of the ship. Passengers fled toward the bow, screaming in terror. Murdoch saw women leap overboard with children in their arms, then sink and perish in the sea. Watching men, women and children die in this manner, Murdoch wrote later, brought to mind the saying: "In the midst of life we are in death."

The captain tried to maintain order but was unable to calm the passengers. Although he told them that several vessels were nearby, and urged them to stay calm so as to make rescue easier, he heard no reply except howls of fear and cries for aid.

Unable to suppress panic among his passengers, the captain then gave an order to let go the anchors. This measure, he hoped, would bring the ship's head into the wind and possibly confine the fire. This too proved ineffective. Murdoch watched as the mizzenmast and then the mainmast caught fire, burned and fell overboard. At last the foremast went overboard as well, taking with it large numbers of people who were clinging to the jib boom in hope of escaping the flames. Some of them were able to remain afloat by clinging to spars in the water, but many drowned.

Chaos on *Ocean Monarch* made the situation still worse. Murdoch's orders could scarcely be heard above the noise, and his orders could barely be executed amid the confusion. Nonetheless, Murdoch gave orders to put the ship's boats in the water. Two boats were lowered successfully. Fire spread to the remaining boats, however, and burned them before they could be lowered.

Seeing that hope of escape destroyed, the passengers became more terrified and desperate than before. It was, Murdoch said with vast understatement, a "painful moment." Large numbers of passengers jumped overboard. The captain ordered any movable objects that would float to be thrown over the side so that people in the water might cling to them.

Even the two boats that were lowered evidently did little to help the struggling men, women and children in the water. A passenger on the Brazilian frigate *Affonso*, one Sir Thomas Hesbeth, reported that the two boats from *Ocean Monarch* headed for Liverpool instead of remaining on the scene to help with rescue. If the boats had remained near *Ocean Monarch* and transferred survivors to rescue vessels, more lives probably would have been saved.

A passenger on *Ocean Monarch*, one Mr. Gregg, a businessman from Salem, Massachusetts, thought the fire had started somewhere under the first-class accommodations on *Ocean Monarch*. He reported later that the fire spread so quickly that, only 20 minutes after the fire was discovered, it was no longer possible to remain below decks. Apparently Gregg returned to his stateroom to retrieve a valuable piece of luggage but was almost overcome by the fire and had to be hauled onto deck through a skylight.

Gregg noted with disapproval the behavior of *Ocean Monarch*'s crew. He reported later that the crewmen seemed intent on saving themselves rather than helping the frightened, suffering people on board. The only "seamanlike" behavior the crew exhibited, Gregg said, was to bring the ship to anchor. Even then, apparently, things went catastrophically wrong:

Gregg said that some women and children were seated near the cable and were drawn into the sea when the the crew let go the anchors.

The passengers, on the other hand, provided heroic assistance to one another, Gregg reported. He described how one stewardess was killed while trying to haul some 25 pounds of gunpowder out of a cabin. She went below to get the powder and supposedly was suffocated. The powder blew up but apparently did not do much damage.

Littledale, on *Queen of the Ocean*, was among the first to see that *Ocean Monarch* was in trouble. He saw the ship hoist a distress flag and headed for the stricken ship at top speed. On arriving near *Ocean Monarch*, Littledale had the yacht's boat lowered and sent to the burning vessel to render what assistance was possible. A heavy swell prevented the boat from approaching too near *Ocean Monarch*, but thirty-two people were saved from the waters.

Sir Thomas Hesbeth reported a spectacular story of heroism in the rescue operations. A seaman from *New World*, a packet boat on its way to New York, made his way to *Ocean Monarch* and personally lowered 100 people, including many women and children, to waiting boats below. The seaman stayed with the burning ship until everyone had left.

Affonso lowered four boats to assist *Ocean Monarch*. The Marquis d'Lisboa was in one boat and Prince de Joinville in another. The prince in particular was cited for his tireless efforts to rescue survivors, who were trying to remain afloat in the sea or clinging desperately to the poop (extreme stern) and bowsprit of the burning *Ocean Monarch*. The boats from *Affonso* had trouble approaching *Ocean Monarch* closely, however, because so many survivors were in the water around the stricken ship.

Before he left his ruined vessel, Captain Murdoch threw the topgallant yard overboard with the help of two seamen and the ship's carpenter. He ordered anyone who could hear his order to jump over the side and hang on to the spar, which was made fast to the ship with a rope. At that point, Murdoch had to leave the ship himself, because flames were all around him. He hung on to the spar for about half an hour until a rescue party from *Queen of the Ocean* picked him up. By 3 P.M., *Ocean Monarch* had burned to the waterline.

The individual stories of survivors were reported in the following days and weeks. One Irish lady was rescued by her brother, who grabbed her by the hair as she was sinking into the sea. *Affonso* reached port with two unclaimed children, a girl and a boy, on board. One Anna Roper, though injured, grabbed her child, took hold of a rope, leaped overboard from

Ocean Monarch and clung to the rope until rescued. An entire family named Sullivan, with five children, was lost except for one child and the mother.

See also FIRE.

Ocracoke Bar wrecks, North Carolina   A hurricane on September 1–3, 1772, caused tremendous damage to ships at Ocracoke Bar on the Outer Banks of North Carolina. More than a dozen ships, including frigates of considerable size, were lifted upon the waters and carried far inland. Fifty or more people are thought to have died.

Ocracoke Inlet, North Carolina   Ocracoke Inlet, on the Outer Banks, has been the site of many notable shipwrecks. These include nine ships sunk at or near the inlet in a hurricane on October 7–8, 1749; six vessels sunk in a gale on August 2, 1795; and 20 ships sunk at the inlet or on Ocracoke Island in a hurricane in September 1815.

See also OUTER BANKS.

octopi   The lore of shipwrecks includes at least one reference to a giant octopus attacking a sailing vessel. Although there appears to be no documented case of such an incident, a hypothetical, huge octopus was implicated in the mystery of the *Mary Celeste*, which was found deserted and drifting in the North Atlantic Ocean between the Azores and Portugal on December 5, 1872. An author named J. L. Hornibrook, writing in the British publication *Chambers' Journal* in 1904, cited anonymous American "scientists" to the effect that a giant octopus might have beset the *Mary Celeste* and devoured its crew, leaving the ship unmanned. Maritime historians have not taken this explanation seriously.

Such tales probably owe something to the Norse myth of the *kraken*, a giant octopod said to live in the ocean depths. The fearsome reputation of octopi in general appears to be largely imaginary. That reputation may stem in part from the writings of 19th-century French novelist Victor Hugo, who in his novel *Toilers of the Sea* depicts a huge octopus eating a man alive. Octopi actually are known for a shy and retiring disposition.

There is, however, at least one documented case of a sea animal sinking a ship. This incident involved the whaler *Essex*, which was rammed and sunk by a whale in 1820, some 1,500 miles west of the Galapagos Islands in the South Pacific Ocean.

See also ESSEX; MARY CELESTE.

Ogeron, Tortugan pirate ship   It is hard to imagine a more colorful crew than that of *Ogeron*, a warship built under orders from the French governor of Tortuga, an island near Haiti. The ship had a crew of 500 pirates and was sent to help capture Curaçao. *Ogeron* was wrecked in a storm off the western coast of Puerto Rico in 1673. Many of the pirates made their way to shore, only to be slaughtered by Spaniards the following day.

Oiseau Blanc, French aircraft   Although not a shipwreck, the disappearance of *L'Oiseau Blanc*, or "The White Bird," during a trans-Atlantic flight in 1927 is sometimes included in shipwreck lore.

A white-painted biplane, the aircraft was flown by French aviators Charles Nungesser and Francois Coli from Le Bourget field near Paris, in the hope of winning a $25,000 prize put up by a French-born American businessman for a successful airplane flight between France and New York. Nungesser and Coli took off on the morning of May 8, 1927. Between Paris and the English Channel, four other French fliers provided the white aircraft with an escort. Then *L'Oiseau Blanc* proceeded alone from the French coast across the Atlantic.

There was a false report that the two French aviators had reached New York. In fact, they and their aircraft were never seen again; or at least, there was no definite, confirmed sighting, although reports came in from Newfoundland; St. Pierre (a small island south of Newfoundland); Rockland, Maine; Seguin, Maine; and Casco Bay, Maine. Presumably, the airplane went down at sea.

Maritime historian Edward Rowe Snow speculated in his 1976 book, *Maritime Mysteries and Dramatic Disasters of New England*, that Nungesser and Coli crashed in Casco Bay, in the vicinity of Jewel Island and Halfway Rock Light on the Maine coast.

Oler, American schooner   This shipwreck provided dramatic evidence of the dangers of towing a ship in heavy weather. The four-masted schooner *Wesley M. Oler* encountered a hurricane on a voyage between Orchilla Island, off the coast of Venezuela, and New York in November of 1902. The ship managed to make port at Nassau on November 7. A salvage vessel was found to tow the badly damaged schooner to New York, and left with *Oler* in tow on November 30. On December 2, the two ships encountered severe weather again, and early on the morning of December 5 the towline snapped. *Oler* was lost on the open sea, at night, in a tempest. The salvage vessel headed for port at Hampton Roads, Virginia. *Oler* was driven ashore at Hatteras Inlet on the Outer Banks of North Carolina. The hull was submerged, but the masts remained upright. A search for survivors located only bodies. Most of the dead men were found in sleeping garments: evidence that the broken towline had caught them unprepared.

olive jars Comparable to the amphora of Greek and Roman days, the olive jar was used widely to store liquids on board ship and is commonly found on shipwrecks. Manufactured in Seville, Spain, the olive jar was a humble piece of pottery, usually with no date of manufacture on it. The olive jar held several gallons of liquid on the average. Configurations of olive jars changed over the years, so the shape of an olive jar may be used to establish an approximate date for some shipwrecks.

See also ARCHAEOLOGY.

Olympic, **British passenger liner** Although *Olympic* was not sunk, the liner had an eventful career. *Olympic* was sister ship to *Titanic* and resembled *Titanic* so closely that photographs of the two are often confused with each other. On one voyage during World War I, off the coast of Ireland near Lough Swilly, *Olympic* came upon the British battleship *Audacious*, which had just struck a mine and was sinking. *Olympic* stopped, took aboard most of the warship's crew, and then tried to take *Audacious* in tow. The battleship sank, however, before it could be towed to shore. In May of 1918, while serving as a troop carrier, *Olympic* came under attack by the German submarine *U-103*.

Olympic avoided the U-boat's torpedo, then rammed and sank the submarine. Part of *U-103*'s crew was rescued by an American destroyer. In 1934, *Olympic* collided with and sank the Nantucket lightship. Seven crewmen on the lightship were killed.

See also LIGHTSHIPS; TITANIC.

Ondine, **French submarine** On a voyage from Cherbourg to Toulon, *Ondine* disappeared on October 4, 1928, with 43 men on board. What happened to *Ondine* is not known for certain, but a Greek freighter is thought to have collided with and sunk the submarine as *Ondine* was running at night on the surface.

See also SUBMARINES.

Oneida, **American frigate** *Oneida* was on its way from Yokohama, Japan, to the United States when it was rammed and sunk by the British steamship *Bombay* 20 miles from Yokohama on the night of January 23, 1870. One hundred and twenty of 176 men on *Oneida* were killed. Although the British ship's captain had to appear before a board of inquiry and was given a reprimand, he was allowed to keep his master's papers.

Ontario, **American steamship** A notable case of fire at sea involved the steamer *Ontario*, which was on a voyage from Baltimore to Boston when the ship caught fire in April of 1912. The crew fought the fire

The liner *Olympic* collided with and sank the lightship *Nantucket*.

The British liner *Olympic,* seen here, struck and sank the lightship *Nantucket* on May 15, 1934.

for three days before the ship was beached at Montauk Point, Long Island, New York, on April 10. All 72 passengers and crew were removed safely. Soon after the ship was evacuated, *Ontario* exploded. The blast blew off the deck, leaving only the hull behind. The wreck was hauled away the following month.

Historian Jeanette Rattray Edwards notes that *Ontario* was beached within 1,000 feet of the point where another ship owned by the same line—*George Appold*—was wrecked in 1889.

The wreck of *Ontario* occurred within a week of a much greater calamity: the loss of the British liner *Titanic,* which sank after colliding with an iceberg in the North Atlantic. Like *Titanic, Ontario* was able to send a distress message by wireless.

See also EXPLOSIONS; FIRE.

Orange Town, St. Eustatius, Lesser Antilles   Orange Town and the shipping in its vicinity suffered greatly from storms during the 18th century. Twenty English merchant vessels from a large fleet were sunk off Orange Town during a hurricane in October of 1737. Every house in the community was destroyed in a hurricane in August of 1772. Orange Town was completely demolished again in the hurricane of October 9, 1780, which killed between 4,000 and 5,000 people and wrecked several Dutch ships, killing all on board.

On April 6, 1690, an earthquake sent most of the island's principal settlement sliding into the sea and killed several hundred people.

See also PORT ROYAL.

***Orcutt,* American schooner**   The wreck of the *Calvin B. Orcutt* on December 23, 1896, at Chatham, Massachusetts, illustrates the difficulties of livesaving operations in the late 19th century. The schooner, with nine crew members aboard, came too near shore during a blizzard and struck the outer bar at Chatham.

There was a lifesaving station at Chatham, but its men were unable to help *Orcutt* because of the severity of the storm. Another lifesaving station existed at nearby Orleans, and that station was in a better position to reach the stranded ship; but telephone lines between Chatham and Orleans were out of service, and the weather was so bad that Orleans did not yet know of the shipwreck.

The Chatham men managed to contact a nearby lighthouse. From there, the call for help went by telegraph to the Orleans railroad station, where a man took the message and carried it several miles by hand—traveling on foot through heavy snow and suffering permanent damage to his vision from the bitter weather—to a home with a telephone. A phone call from there finally brought the news of *Orcutt's* plight to the Orleans livesaving station.

The men at Orleans went into action as fast as they could, but the weather slowed them down. The snow was deep, and the horse that hauled their boat across the beach soon became tired, so that the men had to help move the boat. The men succeeded in launching the boat and eventually reached the wreck, but visibility was so poor that they had trouble seeing *Orcutt*. The sea was so rough that there was no chance of bringing the boat alongside *Orcutt* and rescuing the ship's crew; moreover, *Orcutt* was too far from shore to fire a line to the vessel. Battered by the heavy seas, *Orcutt* broke apart in the storm, and all on board were killed. The wreck of *Orcutt*, and the obstacles that livesavers had to overcome even to reach the ship, led to the establishment of a new lifesaving station.

See also LYLE GUN; STORMS.

Ordovic, British bark   The need for a pilot was made unmistakably clear in the case of *Ordovic*, which was unable to find a pilot to guide the ship into Hampton Roads, Virginia, on November 16, 1889. Unwilling to wait, the captain tried to bring the ship in by himself, even though it was night and he did not know where the channel was. *Ordovic* promptly ran aground near the lifesaving station at Cape Henry, Virginia. The ship was evidently unharmed, and a tug pulled *Ordovic* free the following day. Although no harm was done, the lesson was plain: wait for the pilot.

Oregon, United States   Numerous wrecks have occurred along the Oregon coast since navigation began there. The most wreck-strewn waters are probably those around the Columbia River bar, at the mouth of the Columbia River between Oregon and Washington state.

See also COLUMBIA RIVER BAR; DESDEMONA.

Oregon, British steamer   The Cunard steamer *Oregon* was lost off Center Moriches on the southern shore of Long Island, New York, on March 14, 1886. Just before 4 A.M., the ship collided with an unidentified schooner, which sank immediately afterward. The collision knocked three holes in *Oregon*, which also began to fill and sink. Several vessels came to *Oregon*'s rescue and took off all passengers and crew safely. *Oregon* sank early that afternoon.

Oriskany, American aircraft carrier   Forty-three men were killed when *Oriskany* caught fire in the Gulf of Tonkin off Vietnam on October 26, 1966. The fire reportedly started with magnesium flares in a locker. Many of the fatalities were pilots trapped in the fore-castle area of the ship and overcome by smoke. Most of the dead were officers.

See also FIRE.

Orpheus, British warship   The steam corvette *Orpheus* struck reefs off Manukau Harbor, New Zealand, and sank on February 7, 1863. Heavy seas capsized the ship's launch. A steamer came to help *Orpheus* but was unable to approach closely. Of 260 men on *Orpheus*, 190 were killed.

Orriflamme, Spanish treasure ship   Originally French (hence its non-Spanish name), *L'Orriflamme* was carrying some 700 people and a cargo worth more than four million pesos when the ship was wrecked in a storm near Valparaiso, Chile, in 1770. Survivors were few, and salvage operations yielded little.

Ossipee, American brig   The wreck of *Ossipee* is one of two that occurred virtually at the same time on the Virginia shore and helped mobilize public support for the then-infant lifesaving service. During a gale on November 25, 1877, *Ossipee* went ashore several miles south of the Assateague Island lifesaving station on Virginia's Eastern Shore, just south of the Maryland line. The station was inactive at the time, because its winter season extended only from December 1 through the end of April.

The brig was on a voyage from Spain to New York with a cargo of fruit and nuts, and had been driven far off course by the storm. *Ossipee* began breaking up as soon as the vessel went ashore. Two men were killed in the rescue operation. The keeper of the lifesaving station said later that the entire crew of *Ossipee* could have been saved if his station had been open.

The loss of *Ossipee* occurred within 12 hours of another wreck, that of the schooner *Frank Jameson*, near the Smith Island lifesaving station on the Eastern Shore near Cape Charles, Virginia. These two wrecks together demonstrated the need for year-round operation of lifesaving stations and helped mobilize public support for the government lifesaving service.

See also JAMESON; LIFESAVING SERVICE.

Outer Banks, North Carolina   A chain of barrier islands along the coast of North Carolina, the Outer Banks are known as the "graveyard of the Atlantic" because of the large number of ships sunk here over the past several centuries. Perhaps the most dangerous point along the Outer Banks for shipping is Diamond Shoals, near Cape Hatteras. At Diamond Shoals, two currents converge and drop large amounts of sand just below the ocean surface. Many ships have become trapped on Diamond Shoals. The sand may obtain an unbreakable grip on a vessel, which then may have to be destroyed because refloating the ship is impossible.

Shipwrecks provided a livelihood for residents of the Outer Banks for many years. Homes were built of wood taken from shipwrecks there, and local folk took advantage of cargoes that washed ashore. When government lifesaving operations were organized in the 19th century, many residents of the Outer Banks began to make their living by rescuing mariners in distress. The work was dangerous, but the "bankers" did it brilliantly, and their valor and energy are almost legendary in the annals of lifesaving.

See also ROCKS AND SHOALS.

overloading   This practice has contributed to many shipwrecks by making ships ride too low in the water, thus making them susceptible to foundering. Although the dangers of overloading are obvious, financial considerations have overriden safety on many occasions, and ships have been sent to their destruction with excessive loads on board.

In the early 20th century, ship traffic was not monitored and inspected as closely as today, and there was nothing to stop a ship's owner from sending out dangerously overloaded vessels in the hope of making a bigger profit, short-sighted and dangerous though that policy was. Overloading could be done easily in difficult economic times, because ships' masters and crews were reluctant to protest and thus risk losing their jobs when employment was scarce.

A well-known case of a ship that evidently sank through overloading involved *Benjamin Noble,* a Great Lakes freighter that sank in 1914 on Lake Superior after sailing with an extremely heavy load of rails. The ship was lost between Duluth, Minnesota, and the nearby port of Two Harbors while trying to make port in a storm. Dwight Boyer, in his history of Great Lakes shipwrecks, writes that an economic depression apparently contributed to the loss of *Benjamin Noble,* because the crewmen feared for their jobs if they objected to the overloading of the ship.

See also GREAT LAKES; NOBLE.

P

packet In the 18th century, packets were mail-carrying ships so-called for their packets of mail. The expression in the 19th century came to mean merchant ships that operated on a regular basis over specific routes.

paddle wheels Before the screw propeller became a commonplace means of propulsion, steamships utilized paddle wheels, or arrays of paddles on rotating wheels that pushed the ship through the water. Paddle wheels could be located at the stern of a vessel or on either side. The latter arrangement was preferred for ocean-going vessels, whereas the stern-mounted paddle wheel was used widely on rivers and other inland waterways, such as the Mississippi River. Side-mounted paddle wheels were contained in housings called "boxes." These might be decorated with filigree and the name of the ship. The paddle wheel was a much less efficient means of propulsion than the screw propeller and had virtually disappeared by the end of the 19th century.

Padre Island wrecks, Texas The Padre Island wrecks occurred about 10 miles offshore from the modern community of Port Mansfield, Texas, in 1554, and involved ships of the New Spain Fleet that operated between Spain and Spain's colonies in the Americas. Four ships left Veracruz, Mexico, for Spain in 1554. The ships encountered a severe storm, and three of them—*San Esteban, Espiritu Santo* and *Santa Maria de Yciar*—were driven ashore off the barrier islands along the Texas coast just north of the Mexican border. The fourth ship managed to reach Cuba but had to be abandoned.

Of some 300 people on the three wrecked vessels, possibly half drowned, and many of the rest are thought to have died of starvation and attack by natives during an overland journey to Mexico. A few survivors reached Mexico by boat. Two of the wrecks, thought to be those of *Santa Maria de Yciar* and *Espiritu*

Santo, were destroyed in the 20th century by dredging and treasure hunting, respectively. The third wreck, believed to be *San Esteban*, was excavated by archaeologists between 1972 and 1976. Artifacts recovered from the wrecks included coins, weapons and navigational instruments. Weapons retrieved from the wrecks included swivel guns, small breech-loading cannon approximately 6.5 to 10 feet long.

See also ARCHAEOLOGY; CANNON.

Palomares incident, Spain In an unusual case, the United States Navy in 1966 had to help the Air Force find a missing hydrogen bomb that was thought to have fallen into the sea off Palomares, Spain, following a midair collision between a B-52 bomber and a KC-135 tanker. The search involved two deep-diving submersibles, Reynolds Aluminum's *Aluminaut,* and *Alvin,* operated by Woods Hole Oceanographic Institution. The submersibles were needed to conduct a visual search, because acoustical surveys were difficult in the irregular bottom topography. *Alvin* sighted the bomb on March 15, 1966, after following a furrow on the bottom. Recovery was difficult, because the bomb rested on a steep slope. A first attempt to recover the bomb failed when the line broke. The bomb fell back to the seabed, and the search had to start over. *Alvin* found the bomb again on April 2. On April 7, the bomb was hauled to the surface.

See also ALVIN; SUBMERSIBLES.

***Pamir*, German sailing vessel** One of the most magnificent and beautiful of all sailing vessels, *Pamir* was built in 1905 by Hamburg's Bloehm and Voss shipyard for owner Reederei F. Laeisz, whose ships specialized in making speedy voyages. The ship had a long series of owners after Laeisz, and eventually became a training ship.

Pamir was on a voyage from Buenos Aires to Europe in September of 1957 when the ship encountered a hurricane in the Atlantic. On September 21, *Pamir* sent out a distress message that gave the ship's position and said *Pamir* had a list of 45 degrees. The ship had lost its sails and was in danger of sinking. Although nearby ships began steering immediately to *Pamir*'s position, *Pamir* went under before they could arrive.

According to a survivor's account, *Pamir*'s mast snapped in the storm. The winds blew the ship over onto its side. The crew put on life jackets and prepared to abandon ship, but the extreme list made it impossible to lower boats. The ship capsized. Some survivors held on to wreckage. A group of 15 survivors managed to reach a lifeboat floating nearby.

Another group of 24 men saw a vessel nearby and tried swimming to it, but the other ship evidently did not see them, and steamed away. All 24 men in the group were lost. Eighty-one men altogether perished in the wreck of *Pamir*.

Pamir is thought to have sunk because of instability. The ship did not have a deep keel, and thus it capsized more easily than a deep-keeled vessel would have. Also, survivors indicated that they did not have enough time to shorten sail before the ship capsized.

See also STABILITY AND INSTABILITY.

***Pandora,* Spanish sailing vessel** A freakish incident sank the 600-ton *La Pandora* and another vessel, the 700-ton *San Buenaventura,* at the entrance of the port of San Juan de Ulua, Mexico, during a voyage with the New Spain Fleet in 1597. An anchor on *La Pandora*'s bow became caught in *San Buenaventura*'s rigging while the ships were sailing in close proximity; thus entangled, the ships collided and sank.

Park squadron, Cuba In a massive loss of ships and lives, 13 English warships under command of Sir Hyde Park were wrecked on the Jardines Reefs on Cuba's southern coast on October 3, 1780, during a hurricane. The squadron was on a voyage from Jamaica to Florida. Most of the crewmen are believed to have been killed in the wrecks. The ships included the 74-gun *Thunderer,* the 64-gun *Stirling Castle,* the 44-gun *Phoenix,* the 42-gun *La Blanche,* the 28-gun *Laurel,* the 28-gun *Andromeda* and the 24-gun *Deal Castle.*

passenger ships The most famous shipwrecks generally involve passenger ships, for several reasons. Their large size tends to make their wrecks spectacular; they carry many passengers, whose plight makes the news; the loss of a large passenger ship is a great commercial loss, so that it becomes business news; rescue operations may be intensive and exciting; passenger ships may come to grief in many dramatic ways, from collision to fire; and the crisis of shipwreck tends to bring out the best and worst in behavior among passengers and crew alike.

Perhaps the most widely known example of a passenger ship's wreck is that of the British liner R.M.S. *Titanic,* which sank after striking an iceberg off Newfoundland in 1912. *Titanic*'s loss resulted in more than 1,000 deaths.

Mysteries surround many passenger shipwrecks. A well-known example is the liner *Lusitania,* which was torpedoed and sunk by a U-boat off the Irish coast in 1915. At least one U-boat was known to be operating in those waters, yet *Lusitania* sailed in such a manner as to present a perfect target for submarine attack. Moreover, the liner sank with unusual rapidity. The mysteries involved in *Lusitania*'s loss were not dispelled at the official inquiry into the liner's loss, and remain as puzzling now as they were in 1915. Another famous mystery involving a passenger liner is the disappearance of the Blue Anchor liner *Waratah,* which vanished off the South African coast with all on board in 1909. Although the ship was notably unstable and may have capsized in a storm, there appears to be no conclusive explanation for the liner's disappearance.

See also ALPENA; AMAZON; ANDREA DORIA; ARCTIC; ASIA; ATLANTIC (both); BERLIN; BOURGOGNE; DEUTSCHLAND; EASTLAND; ELBE; EMPRESS OF IRELAND; EVENING STAR; GENERAL SLOCUM; GRIFFITH; HOBOKEN FIRE; KIANGYA; LADY ELGIN; LAKONIA; LARCHMONT; LONDON; LUSITANIA; MORRO CASTLE; NORGE; NORONIC; PRINCESS ALICE; PRINCESS SOPHIA; PRINCIPE DE ASTURIAS; PRINCIPESSA MALFADA; QUETTA; RIO DE JANEIRO; SAN FRANCISCO; TAYLEUR; TITANIC; VESTRIS; WARATAH; WILHELM GUSTLOFF; YARMOUTH CASTLE.

***Patria,* French passenger liner** In what appears to have been a terrorist attack, *Patria* sank at Haifa (in what is now Israel) on November 25, 1940, after three explosions ripped through the vessel. The ship was expected to carry 1,900 immigrants to Palestine; 279 people were killed.

***Patriot,* American schooner** A mysterious example of a ghost ship, the story of the schooner *Patriot* began when the *Patriot* set sail from Georgetown, South Carolina, on December 30, 1812. The ship's destination was New York. Passengers included Theodosia Burr Alston, 29-year-old daughter of former United States vice-president Aaron Burr and the wife of South Carolina governor John Alston. When the *Patriot* did not arrive in New York as expected, an investigation began. A storm was known to have occurred near Cape Hatteras as *Patriot* supposedly passed there. One day in January, *Patriot* reportedly drifted ashore at

Nags Head, on the Outer Banks of North Carolina. No one was found on board, although some reports indicate an oil portrait of a woman strongly resembling Theodosia Burr Alston was recovered from a deserted ship—presumably *Patriot*—that came ashore near Nags Head about this time.

Apparently, the *Patriot* mystery has never been resolved, although possible solutions to the puzzle have been suggested. One hypothesis is that pirates killed the passengers and crew of the *Patriot*. This hypothesis receives some support from the reported deathbed confessions of two alleged pirates who are said to have claimed responsibility for the taking of *Patriot* and the deaths of her crew and passengers.

See also GHOST SHIPS.

Paul, Saint, shipwreck of

On his journey to Rome in A.D. 59–60, the apostle Paul was shipwrecked at Malta, just south of Sicily. This shipwreck is one of the most famous in history, if only because it involved the apostle. The story is told in chapters 27 and 28 of the Acts of the Apostles, in the New Testament.

Paul was a prisoner at the time, but had claimed his right as a Roman citizen to be tried before Caesar himself. Just before sailing for Rome, Paul and several other prisoners were put in the care of a centurion named Julius. The ship made several stops, including one at Myra in Lycia, part of what is now Turkey. There, Paul, the centurion and the other passengers were transferred to an Alexandrian vessel bound for Italy with a cargo of grain. From there, the ship sailed toward Cnidus, a coastal city some 170 miles east of Myra, and then toward the island of Crete, about 200 miles off the southern coast of Turkey. The going was difficult, but eventually the ship reached Fair Havens, near the community of Lasea, on Crete's southern coast.

It was autumn, when the Romans considered sailing on the Mediterranean extremely dangerous. The harbor on Crete was not a good place to spend the winter, so the ship moved on toward Phoenix, another harbor on Crete's southern shore, and presumably a more suitable place for wintering. The voyage from Fair Havens to Phoenix was short—only about 50 miles—and started well, with a gentle south wind.

Before long, however, that soft south wind was replaced by "Euroclydon," a fierce northerly wind similar to the "northeasters" on the Atlantic coast of the United States. Caught in the tempest, the ship was swept along to the southwest. As the ship passed a small island called Cauda, some 25 miles from Crete, the island supplied enough shelter for the men on board to secure the lifeboat, which evidently was towed behind the ship and had to be hauled aboard.

Another menace—distant, but still worth worrying about—was Syrtis, a point on the African shore near Tripoli feared for its sands. The men on board were concerned that the ship might be driven all the way across the Mediterranean and lost on Syrtis's shoals. To reduce this risk, either the sea anchor was dropped or the mainsail was lowered (there is some uncertainty about what exactly the sailors did, because the Greek expression evidently has more than one possible translation). They also passed ropes under the ship itself to hold the hull together, and threw the ship's cargo and tackle (spars and other equipment, perhaps including the mainsail) overboard. Paul's prediction was coming true.

Though the ship remained afloat, the storm continued for so many days that those on board lost hope of survival.

After some two weeks in the storm, the ship approached land, The mariners took soundings and found that the vessel was in shallow water: first 120 feet, then 90 feet. The sailors evidently decided to abandon ship, for they went to lower the lifeboat, pretending that they were going to drop anchors from the bow.

Paul knew what was happening, however, and told the centurion that the sailors were needed on board: "Unless these men abide in the ship, ye cannot be saved." (Acts 27: 31) Alerted, the soldiers cut the rope to the lifeboat, and the boat fell away.

Paul knew that shipwreck was imminent. So, he urged his companions to eat something to keep up their strength. He also reassured them that everyone on board would survive the wreck.

At dawn, they saw the ship was off a beach on the island of Malta, where the ship could be run aground. The sailors cut loose the anchors and made for the beach. Before it could reach the beach, however, the ship grounded on a sandbar. The bow was stuck fast, and waves started to demolish the stern.

To keep the prisoners from escaping, some of the soldiers wanted to kill them; but the centurion, wishing to spare Paul's life, prevented the soldiers from carrying out their murderous plan. The centurion told those who could swim to make for the shore, and non-swimmers to grab whatever would float, and hold on. All 276 people on board reached land safely, as Paul had said they would.

Peacock, American sloop of war

The wreck of the 18-gun *Peacock* on July 18, 1841, is typical of ships destroyed on the dangerous Columbia River bar between Oregon and Washington state. Engaged in charting the Pacific Ocean, *Peacock* ran aground on the bar after trying to cross it using inaccurate charts.

The men tried to lighten ship by tossing cannon and shot overboard, but the anchor chain broke, and *Peacock* lay helpless in the surf. The pumps soon gave out. That night, the ship broke on the shoal, and the men abandoned ship. The crew boarded a schooner and resumed their survey.

See also COLUMBIA RIVER BAR.

Peacock Spit, Columbia River bar, Oregon-Washington state   One of the most dangerous spots along the Pacific coast of the United States, Peacock Spit has been the site of notable wrecks, including those of the steamer *Rosecrans* in 1912 and the freighter *Iowa* in 1936. The spit extends seaward from Cape Disappointment at the north shore of the Columbia River mouth.

See also COLUMBIA RIVER BAR; IOWA; ROSECRANS.

Pearl Harbor wrecks, Hawaii   The Japanese attack on Pearl Harbor on December 7, 1941, left the harbor strewn with damaged and sunken vessels. Much of the United States Navy had been destroyed or incapacitated at a single blow.

Nonetheless, as Captain C. A. Bartholemew points out in his history of United States Navy marine salvage operation, conditions were favorable for salvage. The Navy yard was practically untouched by the attack; the needed staff was still available for salvage; engineering officers were at hand; and good industrial support and an engineering contractor were available.

Also, the day before the Japanese attack, a naval reserve officer with expertise in salvage, Lieutenant Commander Lebbeus Curtis, had arrived in Hawaii, where he stayed for months to help with salvage operations.

Salvage at Pearl Harbor was a huge, complex and difficult undertaking. Many of the sunken or damaged ships were large, had numerous compartments, and contained explosives and other hazardous materials. Human remains also were distributed widely on the sunken vessels, and had profound emotional effects on salvage workers. Other hazards included volatile liquids such as gasoline, which could produce vapor explosions; unexploded Japanese bombs; and the ships' own ammunition. Bartholemew points out that no mishaps took place in handling ammunition during the cleanup at Pearl Harbor.

Among the first steps was to repair lightly damaged ships. These included the battleships *Maryland, Pennsylvania* and *Tennessee;* the cruisers *Helena, Honolulu* and *Raleigh;* and the destroyer *Helm.* All these vessels were either back in service or en route to the West Coast for further repair by mid-February.

Some ships were easy to salvage. The destroyer *Shaw,* for example, was in a floating drydock at the time of the attack. The drydock sank, but the *Shaw* remained afloat. Although the destroyer's bow was blown away when a magazine exploded, it was reasonably simple to keep the ship afloat long enough to reach another drydock.

The battleship *Nevada* was beached and thoroughly flooded, but managed to sail for Puget Sound under its own power in May of 1942. After patching with concrete, the battleship *West Virginia* was floated by pumping and compressed air, and was in drydock by September of 1942. The battleship *California* also was refloated, and headed for Puget Sound in April of 1942.

One of the most outstanding salvage jobs at Pearl Harbor involved the battleship *Oklahoma,* which took several hits from torpedoes and capsized. Although there were no plans to return the battleship to service, the wreck had to be removed. Returning *Oklahoma* to an upright position called for fantastically complicated salvage work. It was accomplished by building a long row of "headframes"—40-foot-tall towers built directly on the capsized ship's side—and passing wire ropes over them to a row of 21 electric winches on shore. After the hull was sealed and pumped full of compressed air, the ship was gradually pulled upright. The righting lasted until June of 1943.

The most famous wreck at Pearl Harbor, the battleship *Arizona,* was not salvaged. The wreck was stripped of useful material and left in place. It now stands as a memorial to those killed in the attack.

See also EXPLOSIVES.

***Peerless*, American schooner**   Even when a vessel strands in calm weather, there is no guarantee of a happy outcome. Weather can change suddenly, with devastating results. A case in point is the loss of the schooner *Peerless,* out of Baltimore, near Cape Charles, Virginia, on December 1, 1878.

Peerless was on its way out of Chesapeake Bay when the ship stranded in the early morning, some five miles from the lifesaving station at Smith Island, Virginia. The sea was smooth. Several hours later, lifesavers boarded the vessel, but the captain declined to leave, and the lifesavers returned to shore.

The calm, however, did not last long. The wind rose quickly in the morning and became a gale by midday. The lifesavers returned to *Peerless* but were unable to bring their boat along because of rough seas, despite three attempts to do so. The masts then fell, and the hull broke apart. The men on *Peerless* held on to the rigging and were rescued from the waters and brought to shore. Such rescues were commonplace in the history of the U.S. Lifesaving Service.

See also LIFESAVING SERVICE.

Pelagia, **American freighter**   On a voyage from Norway to Baltimore, Maryland, *Pelagia* encountered a gale and heavy seas, and sank on September 15, 1956. Thirty-three of 38 men on board were lost.

Pelican, **American excursion boat**   Forty-five people were killed in the wreck of *Pelican*, which capsized off Montauk Point on Long Island, New York, on September 1, 1951. Nine people survived. A strong wind blew from the northeast that morning. There was a heavy sea. Nonetheless, the boat went out at 10 A.M. for recreational fishing. An hour later, the captain decided to halt the excursion and return to shore. Reportedly, one of the craft's two engines failed when *Pelican* was 10 miles off Montauk Light. The boat capsized after a large wave struck it, at 2:15 P.M. *Pelican* carried many life jackets, but only one passenger had thought to wear one. Nearby vessels picked up survivors. *Pelican* remained afloat and was towed later to Montauk. Ten bodies were discovered in the cabin. Other bodies were recovered from the water, although some bodies were never found. It was pointed out at a subsequent inquiry that the boat should have carried only 20 passengers.

See also EXCURSION SHIPS.

Penobscot incident, Maine   This catastrophe occurred as part of a Revolutionary War expedition to dislodge British forces at Fort George at Majabagaduce, Maine, in July of 1779. A convoy of 41 Revolutionary vessels under command of Commodore Dudley Saltonstall sailed from Boston to the Penobscot River in Maine. The expedition also included Lieutenant Colonel Paul Revere and Brigadier General Peleg Wadsworth, as well as large numbers of foot soldiers.

Although the Revolutionary forces outnumbered the British (who had far fewer men and only three sloops with 56 cannon in all), the British defended the fort successfully for weeks. The siege was so lengthy that the British forces in New York had time to learn what was happening and sent six ships—including a man-of-war with 64 guns—to save Fort George from capture.

The British ships arrived on August 13 and took the Americans by surprise. Saltonstall ordered a retreat up the Penobscot River. The American warships, however, moved faster than their transports, which fell behind. The transports were grounded in shallow water and abandoned by their crews, who made their way ashore and then had to set out on foot for distant Boston. The British captured only three American ships. The Revolutionary forces destroyed the rest of their fleet by fire, explosion and scuttling. Ships with 140 cannon in all were lost in this military catastrophe. The Americans lost more than 450 men; the British, only about 70. Saltonstall was drummed out of the Navy. Wadsworth received a strong reprimand. Revere was subjected to court-martial but acquitted.

John Perry Fish, in his history, *Unfinished Voyages*, writes that during the rout of the Revolutionary forces, Wadsworth told Revere to assist a supply vessel, but Revere disobeyed the order and kept on retreating instead. There was an irony in this situation, Fish adds, because Wadsworth's grandson, poet Henry Wadsworth Longfellow, depicted Revere as a hero in Longfellow's famous poem, "The Midnight Ride of Paul Revere."

See also NEW ENGLAND.

Pettingill, **American schooner**   The saving of *E.L. Pettingill* demonstrated beautifully the skill and resourcefulness of the men of the United States Lifesaving Service in the late 19th century.

The schooner was traveling from Chile to Hampton Roads, Virginia, with a valuable cargo of nitrate of soda when the ship became lost in fog and ran aground at low tide on a sandbar off the Dam Neck Mills lifesaving station at Virginia Beach.

A tug was not needed to pull *Pettingill* off the bar, thanks to the clever work of surfmen who went out to the grounded vessel and deployed anchors that kept the ship from working its way toward the beach as the tide came in. Held in place by the anchors, the schooner was lifted off the sandbar as the tide rose, and was freed unharmed.

Phénix, **French submarine**   *Phénix* vanished at sea on June 15, 1939, off Cam Ranh Bay in French Indochina (now Vietnam) with 71 men on board. *Phénix* submerged during an exercise with a French cruiser but did not return to the surface. After two days, the submarine was presumed lost. Oil slicks seen in the area of the sinking were attributed to the sunken submarine.

See also SUBMARINES.

Philadelphia, **American warship**   A small gunboat, only 53 feet long, *Philadelphia* nonetheless is of historical importance for its role in General Benedict Arnold's battle with British forces at Valcour Island in Lake Champlain near Plattsburgh, New York, on October 11, 1776.

Arnold led an assault on Quebec in late 1775 but had to withdraw early the following year, and went south along Lake Champlain with his troops. As Arnold fled, the British perceived an opportunity for military operations that, if successful, would separate New England from the rest of the colonies.

The British confronted the Americans at Valcour Island and sank two American warships, *Philadelphia* and the schooner *Royal Savage*. *Philadelphia* sank in about 60 feet of water. Although the Americans stole away in the night, the British later caught up with them and destroyed most of the American fleet. The fight with the American fleet delayed the planned British campaign so long that the British had to abandon their plan with the onset of winter.

The wreck of *Royal Savage* was discovered in 1932 and raised in 1934. The vessel's bottom was about all that remained. The discovery of *Royal Savage* led to a search for *Philadelphia,* which was discovered in 1935. *Philadelphia* was found to be in good condition when raised from the bottom, and eventually was given to the Smithsonian Institution in Washington, D.C.

Phips, William (1651–?), salvage expert A shrewd New Englander born in Maine, Phips went down in history as an outstandingly successful salvage specialist. After serving an apprenticeship with a shipwright, he moved to Boston and set himself up as a shipowner and trader. On trips to the Caribbean, he heard reports of a Spanish treasure fleet that had been lost in a hurricane on a bank south of the Bahamas on November 15, 1643.

On investigation, he learned that the wrecks actually had occurred. According to one report he gathered, a galleon from the fleet sank on a reef near Turks Island in the Bahamas. He also bought a treasure map and used it to interest England's Duke of Albemarle in the treasure hunt. The duke in turn approached King Charles II, who apparently saw salvage as a good way to enrich the treasury.

In 1684, Phips was put in charge of the British frigate *Rose of Algier* and sent back to the Caribbean to recover the sunken treasure. The expedition was unsuccessful, and Phips returned to England empty-handed in 1695.

With Albemarle's help, however, Phips managed to return on a second expedition in 1696. This voyage was a spectacular success. Phips brought back to England in 1687 more than 30 tons of precious metals and pearls worth some £ 300,000 in all. Phips received one-sixteenth of the recovered treasure. He also was made a knight and named governor of Massachusetts. Phips's success reportedly set off a great enthusiasm in England for treasure hunting: swindlers parted numerous investors from their money in salvage schemes.

See also SALVAGE.

Phoenix, American steamship The wreck of the *Phoenix* in 1819 is of historical importance because the vessel was the second steamship to sail on Lake Champlain. The first was *Vermont,* sunk in 1815. A side-wheel steamer, *Phoenix* caught fire and sank off Colchester Point in 60 to 110 feet of water. Some of the ship's machinery was saved and used in another ship, *Phoenix II.* According to one story, a candle in the galley set the ship on fire.

See also VERMONT.

Phoenix, British frigate *Phoenix* encountered a hurricane and was wrecked on the coast of Cuba at Cabo de la Cruz on October 4, 1780. Approximately 200 men were killed on *Phoenix* and on its companion vessel, *Badger.* There were only a few survivors. This particular storm destroyed a dozen British ships altogether, with a loss of more than 3,000 lives.

Pieter Corneliszoon, Dutch passenger liner This liner was launched in 1926 and burned twice in its career: once while being fitted out and again on November 14, 1932, in Amsterdam. The second fire destroyed the ship.

pig boats This curious category of freighter sailed on the Great Lakes in the late 19th and early 20th centuries. Also known as "whaleback" ships, the pig boats resembled modern submarines in some respects, though they were designed for surface travel.

The pig boats had peculiar rounded backs that were designed to offer minimum resistance to oncoming seas. Pig boats also had two rounded turrets at bow and stern, instead of more conventional superstructures. The ships lacked portholes and were known as highly unpleasant places to be, especially during storms. Pig boats were unpopular with crewmen.

The theory behind the pig boat's design was that a ship stood the best chance of surviving heavy seas by letting them roll aboard without resistance. Therefore, the pig boats had (for example) hatch covers set flush with the decks, with no combings, or raised edges, to obstruct waves sweeping over the decks. In principle, the pig boat's design was sound. In practice, however, it left something to be desired. *Clifton,* a notable shipwreck on Lake Huron, was a pig boat.

See also CLIFTON; GREAT LAKES.

pilot A mariner well-acquainted with a particular port or other highly localized body of water, the pilot traditionally has gone out in a boat to meet ships and guide them safely into port. The pilot's expertise enables him to steer ships clear of shoals and other hazards of which a ship's captain may not be aware.

pilot boats These small vessels carried pilots between ships and shore. Although pilot boats ordinarily were not glamorous or mysterious craft, a mystery surrounds at least one pilot boat, the *Columbia,* which vanished one night in the late 1870s or 1880s off Fire Island, New York.

A telegraph operator at Fire Island reported later that he saw a signal from *Columbia* on the night the vessel vanished. Then the light went out, and soon afterward the operator saw a steamer cruising around the area as if searching for something. The ship remained in the vicinity until daylight and afterward reported colliding with another vessel. Strangely, no evidence of the pilot boat or its crew was ever reported found, although the wreck, if it occurred, must have taken place close to shore. The case was not a major shipwreck but was sufficiently puzzling to be mentioned in historian Charles Burr Todd's 1907 book *In Olde New York* and in Jeanette Edwards Rattray's 1955 book *Ship Ashore!,* a history of shipwrecks on Long Island.

See also PILOT.

***Pinmore*, British bark** Sometimes a crew can lose their ship even if the ship survives an ordeal at sea, and the crewmen escape unharmed. A case in point involves the bark *Pinmore,* abandoned at the mouth of the Columbia River in 1901. On a voyage from Mexico to Portland, Oregon, the ship encountered a storm. The ship heeled steeply to one side and could not recover. The ballast shifted, and the crew feared the ship was about to capsize. The captain gave the order to abandon ship, and the men took to the boats. The next day, a passing steamer picked up the men and carried them to nearby Astoria, Washington. Once on shore, they saw their ship in the harbor. Another vessel had taken *Pinmore* in tow as salvage.

Pinmore continued sailing for years afterward but was sunk by a German raider in World War I. Maritime historian James Gibbs, in his book *Pacific Graveyard,* writes that *Pinmore* was sent to the bottom on February 19, 1917, by Count Felix von Luckner, of the raider *Seeadler.* The count had served on *Pinmore* before he joined the German merchant marine. Before destroying the ship, the count went aboard, saw the bunk where he had slept, and even visited the stern rail in which he had carved his name years before. He then returned to *Seeadler* and had *Pinmore* sunk.

***Pioneer*, American submarine** A Confederate submarine, *Pioneer* was designed to attack Union ship-

ping. Construction began late in 1861, and within a few months *Pioneer* was undergoing trials in Lake Ponchartrain near New Orleans, Louisiana. In these trials, *Pioneer* reportedly succeeded in sinking a barge with a bomb towed behind the submarine. *Pioneer* never went into action against Union shipping, however, because the submarine was scuttled in Lake Ponchartrain when New Orleans was evacuated. *Pioneer* was about 20 feet long, six feet wide and four feet deep. A stern propeller, cranked by hand, provided propulsion.

Pioneer was the work of a remarkable team that included James R. McClintock, Baxter Watson and Horace L. Hunley; this team also collaborated on two other submarines for the Confederacy. After the loss of *Pioneer,* the three men began work on a submarine equipped with a battery-powered electrical engine—the same kind of propulsion system that Germany's U-boats used for submerged running more than 50 years later, during World War I. The technology of the 1860s was inadequate for building such a system, however, and so the design had to be changed in favor of a muscle-powered drive. This vessel reportedly did not perform very well. It was swamped by rising seas and sank while under tow.

The team's third submarine had a lengthy record of sinking and being recovered. During a night cruise on the surface of the harbor in Charleston, South Carolina, the submarine was swamped by a passing steamship. Its hatches open, the submarine filled with water and sank. Only the captain managed to escape. The submarine was raised and put back in service under Hunley's supervision. Hunley died on board when the submarine sank in 54 feet of water near Charleston. The submarine reportedly made a steep dive and buried its nose in the mud. Efforts to refloat the craft immediately and free its crewmen failed, and all the men aboard, including Hunley, died of asphyxiation. The submarine was raised and named *Hunley* in its late inventor's honor. The craft succeeded in sinking the Union Corvette *Housatonic* off Beach Inlet near Charleston on February 17, 1864. The submarine used a "spar" torpedo that consisted of an explosive charge mounted on the end of a spar extending forward from the craft's bow. This arrangement was easier to control than earlier, towed torpedoes such as the one used in the tests at Lake Ponchartrain. The modern "torpedo," a fast-moving, self-propelled device with an explosive charge on its nose, had not yet been invented during the War Between the States.

See also SUBMARINES; TORPEDOES.

pipes Clay pipes for smoking can be useful in establishing the date of a shipwreck, because such pipes, as a rule, can be dated to within a decade of their manufacture. The size and shape of the bowl changed in distinctive ways over the centuries, and many pipes were imprinted with the name or initials of the maker. Marine archaeologist Robert Marx, however, argues that the diameter of a pipestem's bore (the hole running lengthwise through the middle of the stem) should not be used to date clay pipes, because the bore diameter bears no relationship to date of manufacture. Clay pipes are especially common on wrecks of Dutch and English ships, although a few such pipes have been found on Spanish shipwrecks too.

See also ARCHAEOLOGY.

pitch   (1) Vertical motion of a ship's bow and stern as the vessel pivots around a point amidships. Pitch can become extreme in a vessel making its way through heavy seas. (2) A dark, tarry material used to "caulk," or fill, seams between planks in a wooden ship's hull to keep out water.

See also CONSTRUCTION; ROLL; YAW.

Pocahontas, **American brig**   Among the most tragic situations is when observers on shore want to render aid to a ship in distress but simply are unable to do so. All they can do is watch while a ship goes to pieces offshore and the crew perishes. Such a case involved the brig *Pocahontas,* which was wrecked on December 29, 1839, off Plum Island at the extreme eastern tip of Long Island, New York. A captain at Plum Island noticed a ship in trouble about half a mile offshore during a storm that morning. He hurried to the beach and saw the ship being battered to pieces some 450 feet offshore. He saw three apparently dead men on the vessel, plus two others hanging on to the bowsprit. The heavy sea made rescue impossible. As

the captain and several companions watched from the beach, the men of *Pocahontas* were swept away and drowned. The last man on *Pocahontas,* as he was washed off the ship, grasped a rope and tried to save himself, but failed. An examination of papers, luggage and debris washed ashore established that the ship had left Cadiz, Spain, in October for Newburyport, Massachusetts.

Maritime historian Jeanette Edwards Rattray, in her history of shipwrecks on Long Island, writes that *Pocahontas* may have anchored offshore the previous night but dragged anchor and struck a reef stern-first. Rattray adds that if the ship had come ashore only one-fourth of a mile to either side of the reef, *Pocahontas* would have struck a smooth beach in safety.

Poet, **American freighter**   Originally the Liberty ship *General Omar Bundy, Poet* was launched in 1944 and, after World War II, spent years idle in the "mothball fleet" on Virginia's James River. *Poet* was carrying a cargo of grain to Egypt as part of the U.S. State Department's Food for Peace program when the ship vanished at sea on October 25, 1980, during a storm.

An extensive air search involving U.S. and Canadian planes, and covering an area of almost 300,000 square miles, discovered not a trace of *Poet.* The final known communication from *Poet* was a personal radiotelephone call from a crewman to his wife. Although an alarm signal was reportedly detected at a marine radio station in Baltimore on October 26, the Coast Guard reported, on inquiry, that it had received no such signal.

Because no confirmed distress signal was ever received, and because no physical evidence of the ship's sinking was ever discovered, what happened to *Poet* remains conjecture. According to one hypothesis, the

The disappearance of the *Poet* is a modern mystery of the sea. (U.S. Coast Guard)

ship capsized in heavy seas and sank quickly. The Coast Guard speculated that one of the ship's holds might have flooded in the storm. However *Poet* sank, thirty-four men were lost with the ship. This incident resembles others in which reasonably large vessels have disappeared at sea without a trace, despite subsequent searches for evidence of sinking.

See also STORMS; WARATAH.

polar regions Shipwrecks in the polar regions have been numerous, especially in the early days of Arctic exploration. Notable examples of ship losses in the Arctic include the Knight expedition in the early 18th century and the abandonment of *Erebus* and *Terror*, the ships of Sir John Franklin's expedition, in 1845. Ships of the days before steel-hulled construction could not withstand pressures imposed by ice, and were crushed and sunk. Poor understanding of conditions in the Arctic was another reason for the numerous catastrophes on these expeditions. Many explorers did not understand fully how to prepare for survival in the Arctic, and stocked their ships with clothing and other supplies that proved ineffective against the bitterly cold environment. The British, although known as leaders in polar exploration, seemed especially slow to learn about the dangers of the polar realms. Their ignorance resulted in the loss of many men. By contrast, explorers from other countries, such as Norway and the United States, succeeded often in their polar explorations by making a careful study of the polar environment and ways in which the native peoples survived there. Many early expeditions to the Arctic were aimed at finding the Northwest Passage, a rumored clear-water route between the Atlantic and Pacific Oceans. The Northwest Passage turned out to be a mere myth, but the search for it brought about many shipwrecks and great loss of life.

See also ENDURANCE; FRANKLIN EXPEDITION; KNIGHT EXPEDITION.

pollution In the 20th century, pollution has been an increasingly serious consequence of shipwrecks, esecially where oil tankers are involved. A single tanker wreck may release enough oil to befoul many miles of beach.

In such cases, there is considerable controversy over how to handle cleanup activities. According to one school of thinking, detergents should be used to remove as much of the the spilled oil as possible. A contrary argument is that the affected area will recover better if such treatment is not used, and the ecosystem is left to cleanse itself of oil.

The profound emotional impact of oil spills (especially when oil kills sea mammals such as seals), however, provides a powerful incentive to attempt cleanup by any means possible, rather than give the politically dangerous appearance of doing nothing in the face of environmental calamity.

pontoons Large, cylindrical, air-filled floats, pontoons have been used widely to provide buoyancy for sunken vessels in salvage operations. A notable use of pontoons involved the Submarine Pontoon Salvage Method, developed by Lieutenant Commander Julius Furer for the United States Navy. Chains were placed under the wreck and attached to flooded pontoons. The pontoons then were filled with compressed air and provided lift to raise the wreck from the bottom. Furer's system used pontoons 32 feet long and sheathed in wood. Six of these pontoons could lift more than 400 tons. The wooden sheathing allowed the pontoons to be used in conditions where an unprotected steel pontoon would have been punctured and made useless. Furer's system was used to raise the wreck of submarine *F-4* off Hawaii in 1915.

"Poor Englishman Cast Away, A" This castaway story with a happy ending describes the experience of an unnamed Englishman who reportedly was cast away with a companion on a small island off Scotland in 1615. Their boat was thrown upon a rock and broke apart, but the two men successfully made their way to shore.

A bleak environment awaited them. They could find no grass, nor trees, nor anything else that might support human life. The only shelter they could find was a pair of stones with another stone resting atop them. The stones evidently were arranged that way for fishermen to dry fish.

They did find eggs and other edibles along the shore. A greater problem was thirst, because they could find no fresh water except rainwater that gathered in small hollows.

The men built a shelter of sorts from the wreckage of their boat, and lived in it for some six weeks, trying to encourage each other. One day, however, the Englishman's companion disappeared. What happened to him was not clear, but presumably the man fell to his death from a rock while searching for birds' eggs. The Englishman was so despondent over his friend's death that he considered suicide, but changed his mind when he considered that the sin of suicide would result in damnation.

In addition to loneliness, the Englishman soon suffered the loss of his only tool, a knife, which he figured was stolen by a bird of prey. With great difficulty, he fashioned a new knife from a large nail that he extracted from the boards of his hut.

Winter came, and with it new miseries. His clothing was inadequate against the cold. On some snowy

Pollution accompanies many wrecks. (U.S. Coast Guard)

days, he could not leave his hut at all. Somehow he survived for almost a year under such conditions.

His rescue came at last in 1616, when a Fleming by the name of Pickman—known for his skill at marine salvage—visited the island. Some of Pickman's men went ashore and climbed a rock to seek birds' eggs. From the rock, they saw the Englishman and were so startled that they fled without offering him any help.

At first, the newcomers were not sure what to make of the castaway, but before long his pleas for help overcame their fears, and they went to rescue him. He was taken aboard their boat at the same point where he was cast ashore the previous year.

The men on Pickman's ship gave the Englishman proper care, and a few days later his condition was much improved. He was put ashore at Londonderry,

Ireland, and with financial help from friends was able to return home to England.

port (1) The left side of a ship, from the viewpoint of someone facing toward the bow, or front of the vessel. The opposite of port is starboard, meaning the right side of the ship. Although turns once were described as "to port" and "to starboard," they now are described as "left" and "right," respectively.

(2) A porthole, or window, in the ship's side.

(3) A navigable harbor and associated community with facilities for receiving and accommodating ships.

See also AFT; BOW; FORE.

Porter, American packet-sloop The wreck of *David Porter* at Eaton's Neck on Long Island, New York, in January of 1827 provides a glimpse of traveling

Even a little wreck like this sunken yacht means work for the Coast Guard. (U.S. Coast Guard)

Tankers, with their flammable cargoes of petroleum, can spread destruction and pollution over wide areas if wrecked. (U.S. Coast Guard)

conditions and social conventions in those days, thanks to an account written by a survivor, Maria Sayre, years after the wreck. She was 13 years old at the time of the voyage.

Porter operated between Sag Harbor, New York, and New York City on a weekly basis. A one-way voyage took three days. It was the custom for travelers to take along their own provisions, and so they would board the vessel carrying biscuits, pies, roast fowl and other victuals prepared at home beforehand.

Porter left Sag Harbor on the afternoon of September 19 with a cargo of whale oil. As a fiddler entertained the passengers, the vessel encountered foul weather. The storm continued through the night. Two women took turns holding a lantern over the binnacle so that the captain could see which way he was steering.

At daybreak, the ship was off Eaton's Neck. Nearby was a hazardous, U-shaped reef with the opening of the U toward Long Island Sound. The ship headed for shore and passed through the mouth of the U, but was headed for the rocks.

Maria Sayre's uncle carried her topside with some difficulty, because the ship was listing. The weather was still stormy, and waves battered the ship. Maria wrote later that the waves resembled mountains topped with snow.

To keep her from being washed away, Maria's uncle fastened her to a pump near the companionway—but not too securely, so that she might escape if the ship went down.

At this point, the ship's cargo of whale oil came in handy. Someone spread the oil on the waters, and the waves became a manageable swell. (The oil also covered the passengers.)

Porter broke in two when it hit the shore. The female passengers made their way ashore and took shelter at first under bushes. Then they saw a small house nearby and headed for it. (Maria recalled how the bushes and briars along the way shredded her dress.) The occupants of the house, a woman and her two sons, took in the shipwrecked women and fed them with gingerbread and chicken.

The men tried to recover trunks and other luggage from the wreck. When they finished, the wreck had been completely demolished.

The shipwrecked men and women made their way to New York in a barouche and wagon supplied by a neighboring household. The women took time to secure new hats or other head coverings. (Maria actually took time to note what the other women were wearing, including a pink satin hat trimmed with flowers and a calash made of black lace and reeds. The men's hats, she added, looked "hideous," because the soaking made the wide brims droop. Maria said the men's hats looked like mushrooms.) Eventually, Maria and company reached New York safely. Apparently Maria arrived at Brooklyn's Fulton Ferry to the sound of music, for she reported that one of her uncles had a little music box in his pocket and had wound it up just before greeting her.

Port Fortune incident, Massachusetts This incident was minor in terms of property lost (only one small sailboat) but violent, and cost two French explorers their lives. The case involved French explorer Samuel de Champlain (for whom Lake Champlain along the Vermont-New York border is named).

In the early 17th century, the French had settled at Port-Royal, near the mouth of the St. Croix River, in the vicinity of what is now the border between Maine and the province of New Brunswick. From this base, the French sent an exploration party southward on September 5, 1606, under command on Jean de Poutrincourt. His party included Champlain.

The expedition sailed on a bark with a little sailboat in tow. After spending several days along Cape Cod, Massachusetts, the expedition proceeded toward Nantucket Island. The ship ran aground on shoals near Nantucket and lost its rudder. The crew managed to steer the craft to the mainland and found an anchorage on the shore of Nantucket Sound. They named this location Port Fortune.

An encounter with the local native population turned violent after the Frenchmen found a hatchet missing and presumed the natives had stolen it. The explorers fired their guns at the natives, who fled. Frightened and angry, the natives retaliated. They showered the French camp on shore with arrows. Two Frenchmen were killed, and two others were wounded.

The explorers buried their dead. According to one report, the Native Americans desecrated the graves of the two Frenchmen, disinterred their bodies and subjected the corpses to indignities. The surviving Frenchmen returned to the beach, drove away the natives and reburied the bodies.

The French departed, then encountered bad weather and had to return to Port Fortune. The expedition killed several natives in a series of small battles. On departing, the Frenchmen lost their sailboat, which was driven ashore and destroyed by waves. This was one of the first shipwrecks recorded in what later would be known as New England.

***Port Philip*, British steamer** A novel salvage operation followed the wreck of *Port Philip*, which sank after colliding with the American supply ship *Proteus* in the vicinity of New York harbor in fog in late 1918.

Port Philip went down with hundreds of Ford Model T automobiles and trucks on board, disassembled and in crates. The vehicles were intended to transport troops.

Before salvage began on the trucks and automobiles, however, World War I ended, and the British government had no more interest in the vehicles. The wreck could not be allowed simply to sit there, because it was dangerous to navigation. So, the U.S. Army arranged with a salvage firm to dispose of the sunken ship and its contents.

The company thought of a clever—and remunerative—approach to salvaging the autos and trucks. Each crate that was brought up was opened, and water was allowed to drain away. Then the sections of autos and trucks were immersed in tanks of oil for a while. Next, the parts were removed from the oil bath, cleaned and assembled into finished vehicles, which then were sold to waiting buyers.

See also SALVAGE.

Port Royal, Jamaica In addition to sunken vessels, the literature on marine archaeology contains accounts of sunken cities—communities that were destroyed by earthquake and cast beneath the sea. Perhaps the most famous of sunken cities is Port Royal, Jamaica, which was destroyed in an earthquake on the morning of June 7, 1692. A watch recovered from the sunken city in 1959 indicated that the watch had stopped at 11:43.

Founded in the mid-17th century after the British took Jamaica from Spain, Port Royal provided a base for privateers, such as Henry Morgan, who preyed upon Spanish shipping. Privateers enjoyed a welcome in Port Royal only briefly, however, until Britain and Spain signed a peace treaty in 1670. In the following 22 years before the earthquake, Port Royal became a thriving commercial center with a population of approximately 8,000 and an extensive waterfront. Three major forts (Fort Carlisle, Fort Charles and Fort James) protected the community.

Port Royal was built on unconsolidated material that behaved essentially as a liquid during the earthquake. The waterfront disappeared into the sea. Thames Street and the buildings along it were engulfed by the waters. The King's Warehouse, a long wooden building running parallel to the waterfront, was demolished within moments. Fort Carlisle and Fort James sank into the sea.

St. Paul's Church was also destroyed in the earthquake, but its rector, Emmanuel Heath, survived. He had been at the church early that morning, reading prayers in the hope that his example would influence the folk of Port Royal toward piety. After prayers

were finished, Heath left the church to have a meal with John White, acting governor of Jamaica. White had just proposed having wine before the meal when the earthquake struck. "What is this?" asked Heath, alarmed. "It is an earthquake," the governor replied. "Be not afraid. It will soon be over." The earthquake was indeed over quickly, but it left some 2,000 people dead and more than half of Port Royal destroyed and submerged.

Heath went out to do what he could for the survivors of the earthquake and soon was reading prayers before a kneeling group of frightened townspeople. Meanwhile, the ground continued to shake. Heath compared the ground motions to the rolling of the seas. For safety, Heath spent the night on a ship in the harbor, while privateers looted what was left of Port Royal.

Some 3,000 persons died of epidemic disease after the earthquake. Survivors founded a new community called Kingston on the other side of the harbor.

Although salvage operations began immediately after the earthquake, they were less than completely successful, partly because the city's ruins lay in water too deep for divers. Excavations conducted between 1966 and 1968 recovered more than 50,000 items from the wreck of Port Royal. Working conditions underwater were extremely dangerous, and marine archaeologist Robert Marx reports that divers were trapped on occasion when brick walls fell on them.

See also ARCHAEOLOGY; JAMAICA.

Poseidon, British submarine *Poseidon* sank on June 9, 1931, and demonstrated the lifesaving capabilities of the Davis Submarine Escape Lung, a device that allowed individual crew members to breathe underwater while making their way to the surface. After colliding with the Chinese steamer *Yuta* in the South China Sea, *Poseidon* sank in two minutes, in 120 feet of water. Thirty-one men escaped, 13 were drowned and eight were trapped alive within the sunken submarine. Of those eight, two men drowned inside the submarine before they could escape; a third was killed by hitting his head on the rim of the hatchway; and a fourth died of ruptured lungs when he made the mistake of holding his breath during the ascent. Diminishing water pressure during the rise to the surface caused his lungs to burst.

See also SUBMARINES.

Potalloch, British sailing vessel Not only did *Potalloch* go ashore at Shoalwater Bay, Washington, on November 26, 1900, but the vessel also came close—inadvertently—to bringing another ship to destruction some months later.

Potalloch was sailing toward Puget Sound to load grain when the ship went ashore in fog. Apparently no one was killed or injured, and the crew was able simply to drop a ladder over the side and step ashore.

Months passed before *Potalloch* was refloated. Meanwhile, the big, impressive ship gave a passing German bark, *Professor Koch*, the wrong impression. En route to the Columbia River, the German ship sighted *Potalloch* and presumed it was heading for the Columbia River too.

The Germans steered for *Potalloch*, thinking they would follow the big vessel in. They had no idea they were heading straight for shore until a steamer met them and warned them that *Potalloch* was aground.

precognition and premonitions A colorful but questionable element of shipwreck lore involves precognition and premonitions. Precognition may be defined as the alleged ability to see a shipwreck before the event actually occurs. Premonitions may be defined as intense but apparently groundless fears that a vessel will come to harm.

According to these definitions, precognition involves a reasonably detailed and accurate perception of a wreck that has yet to take place, whereas a premonition involves merely a fear that tragedy will overtake a particular vessel.

Perhaps the most famous example—or alleged example—of precognition in a case of shipwreck is found in American novelist Morgan Robertson's 1898 book *Futility*. The novel describes the wreck of a fictional ocean liner that bears an extremely close resemblance to the real British liner *Titanic*, under circumstances much like the actual wreck in 1912, 14 years after the novel was published.

There is reason to question whether the similarities in this represent a genuine case of precognition, however, because other circumstances and processes could account equally well for the resemblance between Robertson's tale and the actual loss of *Titanic*.

Likewise, reports of premonitions should be viewed with skepticism. Imagination may transform fears experienced before an event into a mysterious "warning" or other perception that catastrophe was about to happen before what was feared occurred. Also, it is possible in many cases that reports of alleged premonitions were invented to attract publicity after a shipwreck or other such event.

See also ROBERTSON, MORGAN; TITANIC.

President Hoover, American passenger liner Owned by the Dollar Line, the 21,936-ton *President Hoover* hit a reef near Taiwan on December 10, 1937, during a voyage to Manila from Kobe, Japan. Passengers and crew were removed successfully from the

liner, but efforts to refloat the ship were unsuccessful. The wreck was sold in 1938 to Japanese breakers and was scrapped.

President Madison, American liner *President Madison* capsized and sank on March 23, 1933, at Seattle. One man drowned. The liner was refloated several weeks later. Sold to a Philippine buyer, the ship was renamed *President Quezon*. It was wrecked again off Tanegashima, Japan, with the loss of one life. This time, the ship was a complete loss.

Princess Alice, British excursion ship *Princess Alice*, one of the finest excursion ships in Britain, sank in the Thames River on September 3, 1878, with more than 700 people on board after a collision with the collier *Bywell Castle*. Almost 650 people are believed to have drowned.

Princess Augusta, German immigrant ship *Princess Augusta* was wrecked at Sandy Point on Block Island, Rhode Island, in 1738 on a voyage from Amsterdam to New York. Three hundred and fifty immigrants had left Amsterdam, but by the time of the wreck, 250 passengers and some crew members had already died from drinking contaminated water.

Princess Sophia, Canadian steamship On its way from Skagway, Alaska, to Vancouver, British Columbia, the passenger ship *Princess Sophia* encountered an intense snowstorm and went off course. The ship struck a reef and sank on October 27, 1912, with the loss of all 346 passengers and crew.

Princeton, American warship The United States Navy's first screw steam warship, *Princeton* was involved in a tragic explosion during a public demonstration of its armament on February 28, 1844, on the Potomac River.

Princeton was, for its time, a revolutionary piece of design and engineering. It incorporated numerous features of what later would be called stealth technology. The ship could move quickly and quietly, without releasing great amounts of smoke, and thus could slip up on an opponent undetected.

Built at the Philadelphia Navy Yard, *Princeton* was largely the work of Captain Robert F. Stockton. He designed for the ship two huge 12-inch guns that shot shells weighing more than 200 pounds apiece. The guns were named "Oregon" and "Peacemaker." Of the two, Peacemaker was said to be the better constructed.

Building Peacemaker presented unusual problems. It was a wrought-iron gun, meaning it was manufactured in separate pieces that then were welded together. The welding process was difficult. Ordinarily it was used on much smaller weapons. Welding the great components of Peacemaker together was a highly challenging job, especially around the breech. Stockton was convinced that Peacemaker had great potential, however, and he even paid for its testing.

Peacemaker's trials succeeded brilliantly. Stockton described the finished gun as "perfect" and said he believed that no charge of powder could damage it. Peacemaker was mounted in *Princeton*'s bow on a rotating carriage.

After the guns were installed on the ship, Stockton conducted a promotional campaign for the warship and its magnificent weapons. To show off his wondrous vessel, he invited the public and government officials to take trips on the Potomac on board *Princeton*, and witness the firing of Peacemaker. Loaded with perhaps 30 pounds of powder, the gun would fire a gigantic cannonball a distance of several miles. Stockton claimed the gun was so accurate that it could hit a target the size of a barrel, 90 percent of the time, from half a mile away.

At a demonstration on February 20, Peacemaker shot its great cannonball almost four miles—a tremendous achievement for the time. President John Tyler and numerous dignitaries from the capital attended another demonstration on February 28. Also present were former First Lady Dolley Madison, and a young socialite named Julia Gardiner, daughter of Senator David Gardiner of New York.

Princeton steamed down the Potomac toward Mount Vernon, Virginia. Peacemaker was fired twice. Then the guests went below to dine. Afterward, Stockton was asked to fire the great gun once more, although Peacemaker was still hot from the earlier demonstrations. Stockton agreed, and Peacemaker was prepared for another shot, with 25 pounds of powder.

This time, the gun exploded. It blew apart near the breech and sent chunks of metal ripping through the crowd that had gathered on deck. Among the dead were Senator Gardiner; the secretary of state, Abel Upshur; and the secretary of the navy, Thomas Walker Gilmer. President Tyler was below decks and escaped injury. Julia Gardiner fainted on hearing that her father was dead.

Stockton himself called for an investigation into the catastrophe. The investigation did not put blame on Stockton or on his officers, although it was revealed that poor-quality iron was used in the gun's construction, and that Stockton had not obtained final approval of the gun from the Ordnance Department.

Results of the Peacemaker explosion included the invention of a new gun that could perform as well as Peacemaker; in a few years, this line of development led to the famous Dahlgren cannon that were used with great success during the War Between the States.

Donald Shomette, in his 1982 book *Shipwrecks on the Chesapeake*, writes that Stockton went on to become a war hero and a United States senator. President Tyler married Julia Gardiner several months after the Peacemaker explosion.

See also EXPLOSIONS.

***Principe de Asturias*, Spanish passenger ship**   With almost 600 passengers and crew on board, *Principe de Asturias* was on a voyage from Barcelona to Buenos Aires, and proceeding at high speed through fog, when the ship struck a reef at Ponta Boi on the coast of Brazil in the early hours of March 5, 1914. The boilers exploded, and the ship sank rapidly in approximately 120 feet of water. Although a French ship rescued many survivors, 445 people drowned.

***Principessa Iolanda*, Italian passenger liner**   Believed to be the only passenger liner ever to sink immediately upon launching, *Principessa Iolanda* was launched at Riva Trogoso on September 21 or 22, 1907 (there is disagreement on the date), but capsized and sank only a few yards from shore. The liner was scrapped where it sank. *Principessa Iolanda* was sister ship to *Principessa Malfada*, which sank in 1927 following a boiler explosion at sea.

See also PRINCIPESSA MALFADA.

***Principessa Malfada*, Italian passenger liner**   Sister ship to *Principessa Iolanda* (believed to be the only passenger liner ever to sink immediately upon launching), *Principessa Malfada* sank during a voyage to South America, on October 25, 1927. When a propeller shaft broke, sea water poured into the hull and caused a boiler explosion. Passengers panicked as the ship started to capsize, and more than 300 of 971 passengers on board reportedly were killed.

See also PRINCIPESSA IOLANDA.

***Prins Maurits*, Dutch transport and immigrant ship**   A significant early shipwreck in colonial America, *Prins Maurits* was wrecked at Fire Island, on what is now Long Island, during a storm on the night of May 8, 1657. The ship was a complete loss, but all passengers, 160 immigrants and soldiers, were rescued. Native Americans gave them a friendly reception and guided them to New York (then called New Amsterdam). The wreck occurred near present-day Carman's River.

***Priscilla*, American barkentine**   The wreck of *Priscilla* on the Outer Banks of North Carolina on August 18, 1899, is remembered for the heroism and skill of a particular lifesaver: Rasmus S. Midgett, of the Gull Shoal station.

Priscilla sailed from Baltimore on August 12 for Rio de Janeiro, with a crew of 12 and two passengers, the captain's wife and 12-year-old son. (Another of the captain's sons was serving as part of the crew.)

Along the way, the ship ran into the great San Ciriaco hurricane, one of the most powerful and destructive storms in United States history. The ship survived the hurricane itself but was damaged so severely that *Priscilla* went ashore near the Gull Shoal station.

The ship soon came to the attention of Rasmus Midgett, who was on patrol south of the station between 3 A.M. and sunrise. The ship was already in perilous condition. The captain had had part of the rigging cut away, and the masts had fallen. Waves were breaking across the ship with terrific impact. Maritime historian David Stick, in his history of shipwrecks on the Outer Banks, writes that a single wave washed away the captain's wife and sons.

Midgett could see there was no time to return to the station for assistance. He would have to do the best he could, then and there; and his best was superb.

Huge waves were breaking on the beach. Between waves, however, the water receded and gave Midgett an opportunity to run toward the ship just long enough to shout instructions at the men huddled on the ship. Then he ran back to shore before the next wave came in.

Midgett made this trip seven more times, rushing out to the ship in the lull between waves, and back before the next wave arrived. On each trip he hauled a man from the ship to shore, then turned and went back.

Soon, only three men remained aboard *Priscilla*, but they were too battered and exhausted even to climb down the ropes over *Priscilla*'s side and meet Midgett. The brave lifesaver made his way to the ship again and hauled himself up the ropes to the deck.

Midgett proceeded to carry the three men, one at a time, on his shoulders, from the wreck to the beach. He saved them all, with no help from anyone else. At last, he marched to the station along with the 10 men he had rescued. For this rescue, Midgett received the Gold Lifesaving Medal of Honor.

Midgett had participated, two days earlier, in efforts to help the schooner *Aaron Reppard*, another ship wrecked in the San Ciriaco hurricane.

See also OUTER BANKS; REPPARD.

Puerto Escondido wreck, Florida   A nao from the Tierra Firme Armada was separated from the fleet during a storm in 1576 during a voyage from Havana to Spain. The ship, damaged and about to sink, managed to make its way to Puerto Escondido before sinking.

See also FLORIDA; NAO.

***Pulaski*, American steam packet**   The wreck of the steam packet *Pulaski* off the North Carolina coast in 1838 is a notable story of survival at sea. A sidewheeler of 680 tons, slightly more than 200 feet long, *Pulaski* left Charleston, South Carolina, on June 14, 1838, and headed northward. Some 200 people were on board. Passengers included one Major Heath, whose presence on *Pulaski* would turn out to be a matter of survival for many on board.

The sea turned rough, and a wind arose from the east. The ship began pitching markedly in the seas, causing seasickness among passengers. Late that night, Major Heath was on the way to his cabin when he paused at one of the boilers and saw that the steam pressure was 30 inches, apparently an unusually high reading. Heath mentioned this reading to an engineer and was told there was no danger, because the boilers (the engineer said) could stand considerably higher pressures than that. About 30 minutes later, the first mate heard a whistling noise from that boiler and judged that the water level in the boiler must be too low. He was about to advise the aforementioned engineer to lower the temperature in the boiler before adding fresh water.

Then the boiler exploded. Steam rushed through the ship's interior, killing many sleeping passengers. Major Heath looked into one cabin and found its occupants—all dead—scattered around the deck.

The explosion blasted a hole in the right side of the vessel. Water poured in. The first mate ordered the ship's four lifeboats lowered. He planned to stay near the ship and pick up as many survivors as possible. (Why the first mate did not inform passengers of the ship's imminent sinking, then fill the boats before lowering them, is an interesting question. Possibly he feared setting off a panic, with consequent loss of boats and lives, if he tried to fill and launch the boats after telling passengers the ship was sinking.)

Major Heath was on his way forward when the sea washed him overboard. He saved himself by taking hold of a line and climbing back aboard. Then the mast fell, and *Pulaski* split in two. The forward section, virtually under water by this time, floated away from the rest of the ship. Major Heath was on the forward portion.

Part of the promenade deck broke away but remained afloat, and many survivors floated away with it. Other passengers clung to floating furniture, pieces of wood and an improvised raft. Nine survivors, including the first mate, were in a boat. Another boat carried 11 additional people, most of them women and children.

The first mate was urged to make for shore but chose to remain in the area of the wreck until dawn. When daybreak arrived, the two boats under his command started toward the North Carolina coast, approximately 30 miles away.

The boats steered northwest, so that the wind and current were with them, and took several hours to reach the coast. In the distance, the boats' occupants saw the low profile of the Outer Banks. The first mate faced a difficult decision. Should he try to land his charges directly on the beach—a potentially dangerous operation, as large breakers were present—or sail along the shore in search of an inlet that would let the boats pass through to the comparatively safe waters of the sound on the other side of the barrier islands? The latter course seemed safer in theory, but night was approaching, and the mate decided it was too risky to remain at sea in open boats for a full night. The mate took his boat in first. It capsized in the breakers. Six men reached shore safely, but the boat's other occupants, including two women, were drowned. The second boat also capsized in the breakers, but all on board survived and made their way to the beach. The women and children were suffering considerably from exposure, so they lay down in a sheltered location and were covered with sand, which served as a blanket of sorts. Some of the men went looking for help and soon found a house where the survivors were received with hospitality.

Out at sea, 23 survivors on the floating fragment of promenade deck had the advantage of an undamaged boat that had remained attached to their piece of the vessel. After two days, they decided that someone should take the boat and try to reach land. Six men set out in the boat, while the remainder of the survivors stayed behind. Several people perished each day, including a clergyman with his wife and child, who were swept away together by a large wave. When only five were left alive on the piece of promenade deck, Major Heath and his party appeared in the distance. Thinking it was a rescue vessel, a passenger named Smith swam for it. Evidently he came near Heath's group, but then stopped swimming for some reason and sank. The six men in the boat took four days to reach land, but finally came ashore near the spot where the first mate and his group of survivors had landed several days before.

Major Heath and some 20 other survivors on the forward section of *Pulaski* faced a grim situation. The forward section was in danger of breaking up. The men managed to pass a line under the floating remnant of the ship and thus hold it together. Heath and an officer from *Pulaski* had trouble dissuading some of the thirsty survivors from drinking salt water. This group of survivors spent a whole day and night drifting on the forward section of the packet. On the morning of the second day, they saw what appeared to be land in the distance. They also encountered another floating piece of the wreck with four survivors on it. Now there were 26 survivors hanging on to fragments of *Pulaski*.

As the survivors drifted within a mile of shore, some wanted to try landing on the beach. Heath could see the powerful breakers, however, and decided any attempt at landing would be calamitous. He advised the group to wait until they could find a safer place to land. Under other circumstances, a few might have ignored Heath's counsel and swum for shore, but the wind changed and started pushing the survivors back out to sea.

At this point, as in many other cases of this kind, the thought of cannibalism appears to have occurred to some in Heath's party. Someone suggested drawing lots to determine who would die so that others in the party might have food to live. Heath's advice here saved the group from what could have become a grisly situation. He told the men that they must not sink to the "brute" level while they still had life in their bodies. Heath's moral authority must have been tremendous, for apparently there was no further thought of cannibalism.

A gale arose on the third day after *Pulaski*'s destruction. The rain relieved the men's thirst slightly, but starvation was starting to drive some of the men mad. On the fifth day, the schooner *Henry Camerdon*, sailing from Philadelphia to Wilmington, North Carolina, rescued the men. The schooner also searched for, and found, the floating bit of promenade deck with its few survivors.

One particular survival story from the wreck of *Pulaski* had an especially happy ending, according to historian David Stick in his 1952 book *Graveyard of the Atlantic: Shipwrecks of the North Carolina Coast.* One young man and young woman survived on a raft. Before they were rescued, they pledged to marry each other. After their rescue, the young man confessed that he had lost all he had in the wreck and was completely penniless. That did not matter, the young lady replied; no poverty could be worse than the ordeal they had just survived. She still wanted to marry him; and marry they did. Afterward, the young man learned that his bride was the heiress to a substantial estate.

See also EXPLOSIONS; OUTER BANKS.

Punta de Araya wrecks, Venezuela   The Dutch had a great need for salt, as a preservative for fish. So, the Dutch established a salt industry in Venezuela, at Punta de Araya, around the year 1600. The Dutch presence there was not to the liking of the Spaniards, who sent a fleet of ships to Punta de Araya, destroyed 22 Dutch vessels and killed all the Dutchmen at the facility.

Q

Queen (Queen of the Pacific), American passenger liner   This ship came close to catastrophe on an early voyage but survived, only to succumb to fire years later. Under its original name, *Queen of the Pacific*, the vessel went into service in 1882. On September 5, 1883, the ship ran onto Clatsop Spit on the Columbia River bar (Oregon-Washington) in dense fog. The ship was unable to escape under its own power, and a small fleet of powerful tugs soon arrived to attempt a rescue. The tugs pulled on the liner for hours before succeeding at last, during high tide.

Under the new name of *Queen*, the ship caught fire off the coast of Oregon on February 27, 1904. Fourteen people on board were killed before the ship arrived at Puget Sound. The ship was sold to Japanese interests and sailed to Japan to be scrapped.

Queen Charlotte, British frigate   Fire destroyed *Queen Charlotte* off Leghorn, Italy, on March 17, 1800. The ship sank quickly, drowning all but a few of the 700-man crew. An American ship rescued the survivors.

Queen Elizabeth   One of Cunard's two greatest liners (*Queen Mary* was the other), *Queen Elizabeth* came close to capsizing while on convoy duty as a troopship during World War II. During a storm off Ireland in February of 1944, *Queen Elizabeth* rolled 37 degrees to port but recovered. Sold to Chinese shipping tycoon C. Y. Tung after being taken out of service in 1968, *Queen Elizabeth* was sent to Hong Kong and converted into a floating school called *Seawise University*. The ship caught fire on January 9, 1972, and rolled over and sank in Hong Kong harbor. The liner was scrapped where it sank.

Quesnel, American whaling vessel   *Edward Quesnel* was wrecked between Montauk and Amagansett on Long Island, New York, in May of 1839. Although the ship was a complete loss, some of its cargo of whale oil was saved. As many as 12 men were killed.

Quetta, British steamship   *Quetta* struck a reef off Cape York, Australia, and sank on March 1, 1890. More than half, or 146, of 282 people on board were killed. Mortality was heavily concentrated among steerage passengers, Lascars and Javanese.

quicksilver galleons, Spanish   Known as the "quicksilver galleons" because they carried a cargo of mercury for use in amalgamating silver, *Nuestra Señora de Guadalupe* (1,000 tons) and *Conde de Tolosa* (1,500 tons) were on the way westward to Havana when caught in a hurricane near Samana Bay, off the northern shore of Hispaniola, on the night of August 24, 1724. *Guadalupe* was driven onto a shoal in the bay and settled in an upright position. The ship did not break apart, and most of the more than 600 passengers on board managed to reach shore. *Tolosa* anchored at the mouth of the bay for a while but soon was driven onto a reef. Most of the more than 600 people on board were killed.

Spanish attempts to recover the sunken cargo of mercury were unsuccessful. The Dominican government assumed authority over the *Guadalupe* wreck site in 1976, and Dominican naval divers retrieved many items, including coins and cannon from the wreck. The wreck also yielded numerous luxury items made in Europe and intended for sale in the New World. *Tolosa* also was located on a nearby reef and was an even richer source of artifacts than *Guadalupe*. The two wrecks together provided a valuable look at trade in luxury items between Spain and its colonies in the 18th century.

See also GALLEON; TREASURE.

R

R-6, American submarine   *R-6*, also known as *SS 83*, sank at its moorings at San Pedro, California, on September 26, 1921, when a crewman opened an inner torpedo tube door while the outer door was open. The raising of *R-6* is a classic example of submarine salvage.

R-6 had sunk under good conditions for salvage. The sub sank on an even keel in a harbor, in fairly shallow water (32 feet), with almost all hatches open. The crew had escaped and was ready to help with salvage. A submarine tender was right next to *R-6* when the submarine sank.

As Captain C. A. Bartholemew, United States Navy, writes in his history of naval marine salvage, there were three possible approaches to raising *R-6*. One was to raise the sub with pontoons. This was not the first choice. The salvors decided to keep it in reserve because it required so much effort.

Another method was to seal all openings on the submarine and pump air into the vessel through salvage lines. This technique was complicated and involved much work by divers.

So, the salvors chose a third approach. They would install plugs on open hatches and pump *R-6* out. This was the simplest method.

The salvage operation began the day after *R-6* sank. Pumping started several days later. At first, pumping was unsuccessful. Apparently water was entering somewhere as fast as pumps could remove it.

The leaks could not be located, however, and so the salvors decided to change tactics. They tried sealing the vents and blowing air into the submarine while the pumps were running. This approach also failed.

The next step was to increase pumping power and try again. The more powerful pumps worked for a while, but then the pump motors flooded. Once they were repaired, work resumed, and soon the submarine was almost pumped out.

Divers went down to the submarine, entered the hull and blew the auxiliary ballast tanks, followed by the main ballast. *R-6* started rising. The sub was down by the stern, however, and this bow-up attitude interfered with pumping. All the water flowed to the stern and left the pumps sucking air.

Moreover, the submarine was still too heavy to be hauled into shallower water. Salvors again entered the submarine to blow the fuel tanks and close all air outlets to allow the engine room to be blown free of water. Gradually, the submarine rose.

The operation took more than two weeks, but by October 13, *R-6* bobbed to the surface. Bartholemew observes that *R-6*'s salvage was in many ways a typical salvage effort, in that diving conditions were poor; plans had to be altered as conditions changed during the operation; many techniques were used; and numerous mishaps occurred. Methods used on the salvage of *R-6* were also used on later salvage operations.

Conditions are not always so favorable for salvage when submarines sink. In many cases, submarines have sunk in water so deep that salvage was vastly more difficult, if not impossible.

See also SUBMARINES.

radar   A system that uses reflections of pulses of electromagnetic energy to detect and locate objects, and to display their images in visual form on a monitor, radar has proven a great aid to navigation. Radar also has increased the safety of ocean travel tremendously by allowing ships to establish the positions and monitor the movements of other vessels in the vicinity even in darkness, fog or storm. Nonetheless, radar has not been completely effective in preventing collisions and other calamities at sea. For example, the wreck of the Italian liner *Andrea Doria,* which sank after colliding with the Swedish liner *Stockholm,* occurred despite the use of radar.

radio   Radio communications have provided great improvements in maritime safety. Ships may use radio to monitor broadcasts that provide weather forecasts and other information about possible hazards to navigation. Ships in distress also use radio to summon assistance. Radio beacons also serve as navigational aids. There are limits to the security that radio technology provides, however, because a ship in distress may find itself unable to transmit a call for help, either because the radio equipment has been disabled or because catastrophe strikes so suddenly that there is no time for a transmission. Also, radio distress calls may be ineffective if no assistance is in a position to reach a stricken vessel before the ship founders. (This was the case with the Danish liner *Hans Hedtoft,* which sank after striking an iceberg, even though the ship was able to transmit repeated distress messages.) Radio, which can carry voice transmissions as well as other kinds of communication, is distinct from wireless, an early form of electronic communication that was limited to "dot-dash" code.

See also WIRELESS.

Ramapo incident   This incident involved one of the largest storm-generated waves ever to have its height estimated with reasonable accuracy.

Waves up to 50 or 60 feet high are reported often in storms. It is difficult to estimate a wave's height with precision, however, unless the wave is sighted in a setting whose geometry is known.

Such an opportunity occurred to U.S.S. *Ramapo,* which was steaming through a storm in the Pacific Ocean on February 7, 1933, when an observer on the bridge saw seas astern reaching above the crow's-nest on the mainmast.

Calculations based on the known length of *Ramapo* (477 feet, 10 inches) and a presumed wave length of 1,180 feet (about a quarter-mile) yielded a height of 112 feet for the wave, or about the same as an 11-story building.

See also WAVES.

Ranger, American merchant ship   The many dangers to shipping in the mid-18th century are demonstrated by the sad career of *Ranger,* lost in 1766 at Cape Henry, Virginia. On a visit to Barbados just before the ship's destruction, *Ranger*'s sails were lost in a fire that destroyed the port of Bridgetown. *Ranger* managed to assemble enough sailcloth to make a voyage to Norfolk, Virginia, but there another fire destroyed that set of sails too. The ship at last was refitted but then was wrecked in a storm at Cape Henry.

Rawson, American schooner   Even serious illness could not stop the lifesavers at the Cape Lookout station on North Carolina's Outer Banks from coming to the aid of the schooner *Sarah D.J. Rawson,* which was wrecked there on February 9, 1905.

The men were weak and sick with influenza that day. Fog limited visibility to perhaps a mile. Nonetheless, station keeper William Gaskill went up to the tower to keep watch for stricken ships. When the fog parted for an instant, Gaskill thought he saw a ship's mast on Lookout Shoals. He proceeded on the assumption that a ship was in distress, and so the ailing lifesavers went out into the cold and fog.

Meanwhile, waves were pounding *Rawson* to pieces. By the time the lifesavers reached the ship, two of the ship's three masts were gone, and the rigging and deckhouses had been carried away.

Gaskill and his men tried repeatedly to approach the ship through the floating wreckage surrounding the vessel, but were unsuccessful. As night fell, the boat had to return to shore.

The lifesavers did not return to the station. Instead, they anchored their boat downwind from *Rawson,* so that they might intercept anyone who was washed overboard from the schooner.

At daybreak, the lifesavers tried again to reach the ship. At first they were unsuccessful; but at last they came near enough to *Rawson* to throw a line aboard. A sailor on the schooner tied it around his waist, leaped into the sea, and was hauled aboard the boat. This operation was repeated six times, once for each of the men still aboard the schooner. The shipwrecked men were rowed back to shore, and fed and housed at the station by the sick lifesavers.

For this rescue, nine gold lifesaving medals were bestowed on the men at the Cape Lookout lifesaving station.

reefs   A reef is a formation of rock, sand or coral at or very near the surface of the water. Because it does not extend above the water, a reef is a potential hazard to navigation. Numerous ships have been lost when they ran on reefs and tore out their bottoms, or became stuck on reefs during storms and were pounded to pieces by the waves.

Regulus, American naval supply ship   No one was killed on *Regulus* when typhoon Rose hit Hong Kong on August 17, 1971, but the storm demonstrated what damage a cyclone can cause to shipping. *Regulus* and 25 other ships were driven ashore, and a ferryboat capsized with no apparent survivors.

Reina Regenta, Spanish cruiser   On a voyage from Cadiz, Spain, to Tangier, Morocco, *Reina Regenta* encountered an intense storm, capsized and sank on March 11, 1895, 12 miles off Bajos d'Aceitunois. All

402 on board were lost. The wreck was located a month later in more than 600 feet of water.

Reppard, American schooner The schooner *Aaron Reppard* was wrecked on August 16, 1899, on the Outer Banks of North Carolina. *Reppard* left Philadelphia on August 12 with a cargo of coal, bound for Savannah. When a strong wind arose, the captain anchored the ship offshore, near the border between Virginia and North Carolina, and hoped to ride out the storm.

As maritime historian David Stick points out in his account of *Reppard*'s wreck in his book *Graveyard of the Atlantic*, however, this was no ordinary storm. It was the great San Ciriaco hurricane of 1899, one of the most violent and destructive storms in American history.

Foot by foot, the storm dragged *Reppard* toward the shore, until the schooner finally was carried into the surf on the Outer Banks. The eight-man crew climbed into the rigging as soon as the ship went ashore. With each wave, the ship thumped hard against the bottom, making it difficult for the men on *Reppard* to hang on.

On the beach, the sailors saw a group of perhaps 20 men trying to get their attention. These men were lifesavers from the stations at Gull Shoal, Little Kinnakeet and Chicamacomico.

The lifesavers tried to fire a line to the stricken schooner. The first shot parted from its line. The second shot fell short. The third shot reached the ship, but the men were unable to reach the line because of the vibrations from the hull pounding on the bottom.

The first man to die was a passenger. Dislodged from the rigging, he fell toward the deck. On the way down, he caught his leg in a rope, and the wind battered him to death against the mizzenmast.

At that point, the ship began breaking up. The mainmast and foremast fell, casting the people on them into the sea. The men who survived the fall of the masts made their way to shore, where the lifesavers met them. Of the eight men on *Reppard*, only three survived.

The San Ciriaco hurricane lasted nearly a month, killed thousands of people along its course, and sank seven ships on the Outer Banks of North Carolina alone. The Diamond Shoals lightship was driven ashore, and six ships along the Outer Banks were lost at sea; they vanished as if they had never existed.

Among the heroes of the San Ciriaco storm was one Rasmus S. Midgett, a surfman at the Gull Shoal station on the Outer Banks. Midgett singlehandedly rescued 10 men from the stern of a wrecked vessel without even returning to the station to report.

See also PRISCILLA.

Republic, British steamship The White Star Line's *Republic*, under the command of Captain William Sealby, collided with the Lloyd Italiano Line's *Florida*, Captain Angelo Ruspini commanding, in fog 26 miles south of Nantucket, Massachusetts, on January 23, 1909. More than 400 passengers were aboard *Republic*, and *Florida* carried some 900 Italian immigrants bound for North America. At 5:47 A.M., officers on *Republic* heard *Florida*'s whistle off the port bow. The *Republic* turned hard to port and sounded its fog horn twice to indicate a left turn. For reasons that are not clear, *Florida* responded by turning hard to starboard, so that the two ships were certain to collide. Despite *Republic*'s efforts to avoid collision, *Florida* struck the British liner amidship. *Florida*'s bow crumpled, but the ship remained afloat. *Republic* began to fill with water and sink.

The response of the British and Italian masters and their crews drew praise later. A cool-headed engineer on *Republic* activated injector valves that allowed cold water to enter the boilers gradually and lower their pressure. This action may have prevented a catastrophic explosion. On *Florida*, Captain Ruspini told his officers to reassure passengers that the ship was not in danger of sinking. Next, Ruspini had a sail dropped over *Florida*'s bow to diminish leaks. Then he headed for *Republic* to render assistance. On arriving beside the British ship, Ruspini offered to take *Republic*'s passengers aboard, and Captain Sealby and his men began making preparations for the transfer.

Sealby kept order on *Republic*. He emphasized that there was no danger but told passengers to prepare for transfer to another vessel. The calm, professional attitude of the officers reassured the passengers. Although only 10 lifeboats were available on *Republic*, and a choppy sea made the transfer operations difficult, everyone was taken off *Republic* by 12:30 P.M. except a few crew members.

One who stayed behind on *Republic*, wireless operator Jack Binns, became a hero for spending 14 hours at his set, contacting nearby ships to aid in the rescue. "Ship's sinking, but will stick to the end," Binns told one vessel.

The White Star liner *Baltic* made a dramatic dash to help *Republic* but was stopped temporarily by the dense fog. *Baltic* and *Republic* drifted a few miles apart for some 12 hours, setting off bombs and sounding horns to indicate each other's location. Finally Binns signalled that *Baltic* was on course, and *Baltic* arrived at the scene in time to take some of the passengers. This transfer was easier than the first, because the fog was lifting.

Republic was still afloat. Thinking the ship might be salvaged, Sealby asked for volunteers to return to *Republic*. Thirty-six men stepped forward. The revenue cutter *Gresham* and the U.S. Navy destroyer *Seneca* took *Republic* in tow, with the Anchor Line's ship *Furnessia* behind to help with steering. As the ships approached shallow water, *Republic* began filling more rapidly, and it became clear that the ship would sink. Everyone left *Republic* except Sealby and his second officer. The two men tried to ignite blue flares (the signal to cut the cables attached to *Republic*), but the flares were wet and would not burn. Sealby fired his revolver instead as a signal. The men climbed into the rigging as the ship settled. The captain and second officer wound up in the water and were picked up by a lifeboat.

Jack Binns's heroism at the wireless was recalled three years later, when another wireless operator, this time on the White Star liner *Titanic*, informed the world that the ship was going down.

See also COLLISIONS; FOG; TITANIC; WIRELESS.

rescues   When a ship is stranded or sinking, rescue efforts can be complicated, dangerous and time-consuming. Although modern technology, such as helicopters, has improved the effectiveness of rescue operations, there are still limits to what rescuers can do to save lives on a stricken ship. Now as always, much depends on the seaworthiness of the ship, the state of its emergency equipment and the competence of its master and crew; the response of passengers (if any) to a crisis situation; the nature and severity of the emergency; nearness to shore; availability of rescue ships in the vicinity; and weather and sea conditions.

Famous rescue operations in maritime history involve vessels such as the British liner *Republic*, whose wireless played an important role in alerting rescuers

Rescue operations are assisted by more advanced technology than was available in the early and mid-19th century. (U.S. Coast Guard)

to the ship's plight in 1909, and the Cunard liner *Carpathia*, which raced at night through a sea strewn with icebergs to rescue the few survivors of the liner *Titanic*, which sank in 1912 after striking an iceberg in the North Atlantic.

Some of the most outstanding rescue stories come from the annals of the United States Lifesaving Service. The American lifesavers, operating out of small stations along the shores, risked their lives on a regular basis to save the passengers and crews of vessels stranded offshore. Dunbar Davis, keeper of the Oak Island lifesaving station on the Outer Banks of North Carolina, exemplified the stamina and resourcefulness of the men of the Lifesaving Service. In a single hurricane in August of 1893, he had to render assistance to five vessels near Cape Fear.

American lifesavers of the late 19th and early 20th centuries relied largely on muscle power to reach stricken ships and bring their crews ashore. Technology in the form of the breeches buoy and Lyle gun, however, also helped haul shipwrecked crewmen and passengers to safety.

Some notable rescues have involved brave animals as well as brave people. For example, a dog named King helped save many lives when the ship *Harpooner* ran onto a reef off Newfoundland on the morning of November 9, 1816. When rough seas and currents interfered with efforts to put a line ashore, the captain tied a line to King's collar and sent the dog swimming shoreward. King succeeded, and soon rescue operations began.

In some cases, rescue has been difficult or impossible even when a ship lies within a few feet of the

Helicopters are important to rescue operations. (U.S. Coast Guard)

shore. Cases in point include the steamer *Eastland*, which capsized at its Chicago pier in 1915, trapping many passengers within the hull; and the German liner *Saale*, which burned near shore at Hoboken, New Jersey in 1900. Portholes on *Saale* were too small for people trapped inside to use to escape, and would-be rescuers had to watch helplessly from boats alongside the liner as the people on board burned to death.

See also BREECHES BUOY; CARPATHIA; HARPOONER; HOBOKEN FIRE; LIFE CAR; LYLE GUN; REPUBLIC.

Rhein, German steamship Only two months after the wreck of the German sailing vessel *Elizabeth* at Virginia Beach, Virginia, with the loss of 27 lives, *Rhein* was also stranded on the Virginia shore, though with a less tragic outcome.

Rhein ran aground near the lifesaving station at Hog Island on Virginia's Eastern Shore on March 8, 1887, in fog. The ship's whistle alerted surfmen, but the fog made it hard for them to find the ship. At last the surfmen reached *Rhein*, which by this time was being battered by large waves.

The keeper of the Hog Island station reassured the Germans that they were in no danger. He sent a surfman back to shore to send a telegram to the German consul in Baltimore, requesting help.

The next day, the 1,023 passengers on *Rhein* were transferred to a nearby steamer. The cargo was cast overboard. *Rhein* was freed from the sands and continued its voyage safely to Baltimore. Not one life was lost.

See also ELIZABETH.

Rhode Island, United States Rhode Island's maritime history includes numerous shipwrecks, several examples of which follow. A German vessel, *Princess Augusta*, was wrecked at Sandy Point on Block Island in 1738, after a calamitous voyage in which some two-thirds of the passengers and crew on board are said to have died after drinking tainted water. Some 350 German immigrants were on *Princess Augusta* for this voyage. In 1777, two British warships, H.M.S. *Triton* and H.M.S. *Syren*, were wrecked near Point Judith. The following year, seven British warships were reported burned and sunk in Narragansett Bay, including H.M.S. *Juno*, H.M.S. *Lark* and H.M.S. *Orpheus*, each 32 guns. A hurricane on September 23, 1815, wrecked some 35 ships, including seven schooners and nine brigs, at Providence.

Rhode Island, American packet ship The captain of *Rhode Island* on an abbreviated voyage in 1846 was Stephen Manchester, who had survived the burning of *Lexington* in 1840. On the night of November 1,

1846, *Rhode Island* lost its rudder during a storm off Crab Meadow Beach, Long Island, New York, while on a voyage from Stonington, Connecticut, to New York. The captain managed to put in at Cow Neck, near Tuckahoe, New York, and dropped anchors to keep the ship from being destroyed on the rocks. Whaleboats brought all aboard *Rhode Island* ashore, and the rescuers were awarded gold medals.

See also LEXINGTON.

rigging The complex of ropes and other components that serves to suspend and operate sails, rigging provided a temporary refuge to many sailors during shipwrecks, when waves began washing over the deck, or a ship settled deeply into the water. The rigging itself could become a dangerous place, however, during storms or when the ship rolled and cast men in the rigging into the water. Sailors who spent extended periods in the rigging during and after a shipwreck might risk death by exposure. Nonetheless, many seamen did survive prolonged stays in the rigging and owed their lives to its elevated position.

The rigging was a prime target for lifesavers trying to reach a stricken ship with the Lyle gun, a small mortar that shot a projectile trailing a line. If all went as hoped, the projectile would land in the rigging, where crewmen could reach the line and use it to establish a link to shore by breeches buoy.

In cold weather, ice buildup on rigging could make a ship top-heavy and more likely to capsize. For this reason, it was necessary to clear ice from ships frequently during winter passages.

Ships' masts, spars and rigging were frequently the location of "St. Elmo's fire," a luminous accumulation of static electricity. Although essentially harmless, this phenomenon has been associated, through superstition, with various supernatural influences.

See also MASTS AND SPARS; ST. ELMO'S FIRE.

Rio Alvarado wrecks, Mexico In 1558, a fleet of Spanish merchant ships bound from the Caribbean to Mexico encountered a storm near Veracruz. Two ships were lost in the vicinity of Rio Alvarado. Sixty people were killed.

See also MEXICO.

Rio de Janeiro, American steamship Near the end of a voyage from Yokohama, Japan, to San Francisco in February of 1901, the Pacific Mail Steamship Company's 3,548-ton *City of Rio de Janeiro* wrecked on rocks at the Golden Gate after the captain—ignoring the harbor pilot's advice—took the ship through the passage in fog on the morning of February 22. The wreck killed more than 100 people, the captain included.

See also FOG.

Ripple Rock, Seymour Narrows, British Columbia

This menace to navigation, which is thought to have claimed approximately 120 ships, was destroyed on April 7, 1958, in what was said to be the most powerful non-nuclear explosion to that date. Some 2.75 million pounds of high explosive were used to blow up the rock.

Rising Sun, Scottish frigate

Of 112 people on *Rising Sun*, 97 were drowned when a hurricane struck Charleston, South Carolina, on September 3, 1700. Twelve of the 15 survivors were on shore when the storm arrived. Only three survivors were actually on the frigate when the hurricane hit.

Robertson, Morgan (1861–1915), American author

Robertson is best known for his 1898 novel *Futility*, which has been interpreted as a case of "precognition" because the wreck of an imaginary ocean liner in the story resembled in so many ways the wreck of the British liner *Titanic* in 1912.

In Robertson's story, a fictional ocean liner named *Titan* strikes an iceberg and sinks. The liner in the story is virtually identical in many respects with the actual *Titanic. Titan*'s displacement was 70,000 tons; *Titanic*'s, 66,000. *Titan* was 800 feet long; *Titanic*, 882.5 feet. *Titan* had 2,000 passengers aboard; *Titanic* had 2,230. Both ships had three propellers, a top speed of 24 to 25 knots and a capacity of about 3,000 people. Both ships sailed in April and were damaged on the starboard side by striking an iceberg.

Perhaps it is unwise to make much of the similarities between the fictional *Titan* and the actual *Titanic*, for two reasons. First, collisions between ships and icebergs were commonplace occurrences in the late 19th and early 20th centuries, and so it must have seemed reasonable to presume that such collisions would continue to happen. Second, it probably took no particular act of precognition to extrapolate trends in ship design (bigger ocean liners, carrying more passengers) and envision an imaginary "superliner" much like *Titanic*.

Robertson wrote more than a dozen novels on maritime themes. His novel *Futility* appears to have brought him no great profit, even after the wreck of *Titanic*.

See also PRECOGNITION AND PREMONITIONS; TITANIC.

rocks and shoals

Among the greatest threats to shipping are rocks and shoals along coastlines. Colli-

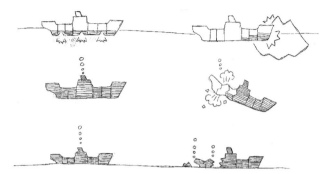

Hazards of the near shore environment include

sion with a submerged rock can rip open a ship's hull and cause the vessel to founder quickly, while contact with a shoal may trap a ship in sands and make refloating the vessel impossible. One of the most notorious shoal areas is Diamond Shoals, off the Outer Banks of North Carolina, a place so dangerous to shipping that it is known as the "graveyard of the Atlantic."

Although it should be easy, in theory, to avoid a well-known and well-charted area of shoals, in practice the task has proven to be more difficult. For example, a ship's master might have to decide between steering a course well out to sea, thus avoiding the shoals but adding time and expense to the voyage; and staying close to shore, thus saving time and money but exposing the ship to the risk of striking a shoal. Such a choice would appear to be easy, if safety were the only consideration. Tight budgets and competitive pressures may take priority over safety, however, and put ships on courses straight onto deadly shoals. Errors in navigation also have been responsible for shipwreck on shoals. Although manned lightships used to be placed on some shoals to warn other ships away, lightships now have been largely replaced by unmanned, automatic beacons.

See also DIAMOND SHOALS; LIGHTSHIPS; OUTER BANKS.

Roddam, British steamship

Caught along with the British steamer *Roraima* in the harbor at St. Pierre, Martinique, during the eruption of the volcano Mount Pelée in 1902, *Roddam* was damaged severely by a nuée ardente (fiery cloud) from the mountain and barely managed to make its way to the open sea after the catastrophe. Captain Freeman of *Roddam* said he watched as St. Pierre was destroyed: "I witnessed the entire destruction of St. Pierre. The flames enveloped the town in every quarter with such rapidity that it

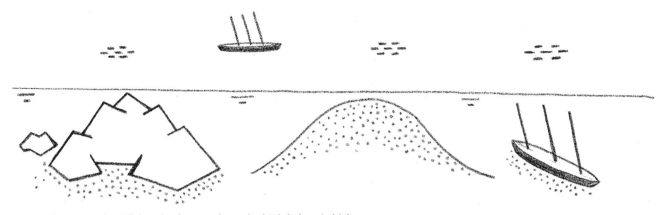

rocks (left), shoals (middle) and submerged wrecks (right). (D. Ritchie)

was impossible that any person could be saved. . . . [The] day was suddenly turned to night, but I could distinguish by the light of the burning town people distractedly running about on the beach. The burning buildings stood out from the surrounding darkness like black shadows. All this time the mountain was roaring and shaking, and in the intervals between those terrifying sounds I could hear the cries of despair and agony from the thousands who were perishing. These cries added to the terror of the scene, but it is impossible to describe its horror and the dreadful sensations it produced. It was like witnessing the end of the world."

Here is how Captain Freeman described his ship's ordeal:

I went to anchorage between 7 and 8 [A.M.] and had hardly moored when the side of the volcano opened out with a terrible explosion. [A] wall of fire swept over the town and the bay. The *Roddam* was struck broadside by the burning mass. The shock to the ship was terrible, nearly capsizing her.

Hearing the awful report of the explosion and seeing the great wall of flames approaching the steamer, those on deck sought shelter wherever it was possible, jumping into the cabin, the forecastle and even into the hold. I was in the chart room, but the burning embers were borne by so swift a movement of the air that they were swept in through the door and portholes, suffocating and scorching me badly. I was terribly burned by these embers about the face and hands, but managed to reach the deck. Then, as soon as it was possible, I mustered the few survivors who seemed able to move, ordered them to slip the anchor, leaped for the bridge and [rang] the engine for full speed astern.

The ship's surroundings were nightmarish, the captain reported: "One of the most terrifying conditions was that, the atmosphere being charged with ashes, it was totally dark. The sun was completely obscured,

and the sun was only illuminated by the flames from the volcano and those of the burning town and shipping. It seems small to say that the scene was terrifying in the extreme."

Roddam still had power, but it was some time before the ship regained steering capability, as the captain explained: "The second and the third engineer and a fireman were on watch below and so escaped injury . . . but the men on deck could not work the steering gear because it was jammed by the debris from the volcano. We accordingly went ahead and astern until the gear was free, but in this running backward and forward it was two hours after the first shock before we were clear of the bay."

On the way out of the harbor, *Roddam* passed the burning *Roraima*, described thus by Freeman: "As we backed out we passed close to the *Roraima*, which was one mass of blaze. The steam was rushing from the engine room, and the screams of those on board were terrible to hear. The cries for help were all in vain, for I could do nothing but save my own ship." When Freeman last saw *Roraima*, the ship was settling by the stern.

Once *Roddam* cleared the harbor at St. Pierre, Freeman took his ship to nearby St. Lucia. Not only had the ship "presented an appalling appearance" on arriving at St. Lucia, but the vessel also kept breaking out in flames, according to Freeman: "Dead and calcined bodies lay about the deck, which was also crowded with injured, helpless and suffering people . . . The woodwork and the cabins and everything inflammable on deck were constantly igniting, and it was with great difficulty that we few survivors managed to keep the flames down. My ropes, awnings, tarpaulins were completely burned up."

The captain of the British ship *Etona* visited *Roddam* at St. Lucia on May 11, three days after the nuée ardente descended on St. Pierre, and described the damage to the vessel: "The *Roddam* was covered with a mass of fine bluish gray dust or ashes of cementlike appearance. In some places it lay two feet deep on the decks. This matter had fallen in a red-hot state all over the steamer, setting fire to everything it struck that was burnable, and, when it fell on the men on board, burning off limbs and large pieces of flesh. This was shown by finding portions of human flesh when the decks were cleared of the debris. The rigging, ropes, tarpaulins, sails, awnings, etc., were charred or burned, and most of the upper stanchions and spars were swept overboard or destroyed by fire. Skylights were smashed and cabins were filled with volcanic dust. The scene of ruin was deplorable."

At St. Lucia, Freeman assembled the survivors and conducted a search for the dead and injured. "Some," he recalled, "I found in the saloon where they had . . . sought for safety, but the cabins were full of burning embers that had blown in through the portholes. Through these the fire swept as through funnels and burned the victims where they lay or stood, leaving a circular imprint of scorched and burned flesh. I brought 10 on deck who were thus burned; two of them were dead, the other survived, although in a dreadful state of torture from their burns. Their screams of agony were heartrending . . ." Later Freeman discovered a sailor's body in the forecastle of the ship. "The body was horribly burned," Freeman related, "and the sailor had evidently crept in there in his agony to die."

According to one estimate, 18 people were killed on *Roddam*. The eruption of Mount Pelée is thought to have killed some 30,000 people in St. Pierre; only six individuals from the city survived. The May eruption of Pelée destroyed an area of some eight square miles.

See also RORAIMA.

roll A ship's tendency to turn around its longitudinal axis, roll can be dangerous if it routinely exceeds several degrees, because it makes the vessel liable to capsize. A top-heavy ship may exhibit an excessive tendency to roll. Increasing ballast may compensate for a tendency to roll.

See also BALLAST; STABILITY AND INSTABILITY.

***Roosevelt*, American polar exploration vessel** Although the famous *Roosevelt* was not actually wrecked on this occasion, it came close. Explorer Robert Peary reported that on the night of November 12, 1908, some 450 miles from the North Pole, an ice pack moved shoreward.

Lying in his bunk around midnight, Peary heard the noise of grinding ice outside. He went on deck to investigate. For a while it appeared that *Roosevelt* would be pushed aground. A huge iceberg pressed against the ship's side.

Peary was not afraid that the ice would crush the ship, but he did fear that the encroaching ice might push the ship over on its side, spilling coals and setting the vessel on fire. So, every fire on *Roosevelt* was put out.

When the tide turned around 1:30 A.M., the danger was over, but Peary reported that the ship did not return to an even keel for months.

See also POLAR REGIONS.

***Roraima*, British steamship** *Roraima* was present—and was demolished—at the calamitous eruption of the volcano Mount Pelée at St. Pierre on Martinique in the Caribbean, on the morning of May 8, 1902. This eruption also destroyed the city of St. Pierre. The volcano had been in eruption for more than a month already and had cast vast amounts of ash over the island. Maritime traffic continued into and out of the harbor, however, and on May 8 the passenger steamer *Roraima*, under command of Captain G. T. Muggah, arrived at St. Pierre. Several other ships were also in the harbor at this time, including the British steamer *Roddam* and the cable ship *Grappler*.

Just before 8 A.M., about an hour after *Roraima*'s arrival, Mount Pelée let loose a nuée ardente, or "fiery cloud," one of the most destructive of all volcanic phenomena. The nuée ardente is a cloud of ash, rock and superheated gas that flows downslope along the flanks of a volcano and incinerates or melts virtually everything in its path, devastating the land as effectively as a nuclear explosion. Whatever animal life survives the heat and shock of the nuée ardente is likely to asphyxiate in the toxic gases it carries.

The nuée ardente from Pelée was described as a black cloud dotted with flames. It rolled over St. Pierre, carbonizing trees, ripping roofs off buildings and either roasting or gassing the population. Then the nuée ardente went on to destroy the ships in the harbor. Here is how one eyewitness to the destruction, the French traveler Comte de Fitz-James, described the scene:

> From a boat in the roadstead . . . I witnessed the cataclysm that came upon the city. We saw the shipping destroyed by a breath of fire. We saw the cable ship *Grappler* keel over under the whirlwind, and sink as though drawn down into the waters of the harbor by some force from below. The *Roraima* was overcome and burned at anchor. The *Roddam* . . . was able to escape like a stricken moth which crawls from a flame that has burned its wings . . . (Morris 1902)

Passengers on *Roraima* were preparing for breakfast when the nuée ardente arrived. A steward shouted, "The volcano is coming!" Then the fiery cloud struck *Roraima*, lifting the ship out of the water and then dropping it back into the sea. Knocked off their feet, passengers were scalded by steaming hot mud from the cloud that poured in through broken skylights and portholes. The noise was terrific and was described by the ship's purser as resembling "a thousand cannon." Assistant Purser Thompson on *Roraima* recalled later:

> The wave of fire was on us and over us like a lightning flash. It was like a hurricane of fire. I saw it strike the . . . *Grappler* broadside on and capsize her. From end to end she burst into flames and then sank. . . . Wherever the mass of fire struck the sea the water boiled and sent up vast clouds of steam. The sea was torn into huge whirlpools that careened toward the open sea. One of these horrible hot whirlpools swung under the *Roraima* and pulled her down on her beam ends with the suction. She careened way over to port, and then the fire hurricane from the volcano smashed her, and over she went on the opposite side. The fire wave swept off the masts and smokestack as if they were cut off with a knife. (Morris 1902)

Captain Muggah was on the bridge as the *nuée ardente* arrived. A crewman saw the captain standing upright, bracing himself for the cloud's impact. He shouted to "heave up," or raise the anchor. Then the volcanic cloud struck. Ellery Scott, mate of *Roraima*, remembered the scene on the bridge:

> As I was looking at [the captain], he was all ablaze. He reeled and fell on the bridge with his face toward me. His mustache and eyebrows were gone in a jiffy. His hat had gone, and his hair was aflame, and so were his clothes from head to foot. I knew he was conscious when he fell, by the look in his eyes, but he didn't make a sound. (Morris 1902)

Roraima heeled over, and Muggah was cast into the water. Later a crewman found him in the water, so badly burned that the crewman did not recognize him. Though in great pain, Muggah wanted to rejoin his ship, and pleaded to be put back aboard. The crewman and several other survivors built a crude raft and put the captain on it. Muggah's body was recovered later.

Scott was one of only a few men on board who were still capable of doing anything. Here is how he described the scene on what remained of *Roraima*:

> It was still raining fire and hot rocks, and you could hardly see a ship's length for dust and ashes, but we could stand that. There were burning men and some women and two or three children lying about the deck. Not just burned, but burning, then, when we

got to them. More than half the ship's company had been killed in that first rush of flame. . . . The cook was burned to death in his galley. He had been paring potatoes for dinner, and what was left of his right hand held the shank of his potato knife. The wooden handle was in ashes. All that happened to [the] man in less than a minute. . . .

> My own son's gone, too. It has been his [turn] at lookout ahead . . . that morning, when we were making for St. Pierre, so I supposed at first when the fire struck us that he was asleep in his bunk and safe. But he wasn't. Nobody could tell me where he was. I don't know whether he was burned to death or rolled overboard and drowned. . . . (Morris 1902)

Out of 47 crew members on *Roraima*, only 28 survived. There were only two survivors among the passengers, a young girl and her nurse.

See also RODDAM.

Rosecrans, American tanker

One of the most tragic wrecks in the history of the Columbia River bar (Oregon-Washington) is that of *Rosecrans*, which sank in 1913 with the loss of 33 men. Only three men survived the sinking.

The tanker's wreck came at the end of a checkered—and often calamitous—career. Originally named *Methven Castle*, the vessel was launched at Glasgow in 1884. The ship's next owner named the vessel *Columbia*. Eventually the ship wound up serving the United States Army as a transport during the Spanish-American War and was renamed *Rosecrans*. The Army found the ship too expensive to operate, however, and the vessel passed over to an oil company that converted it into a tanker.

On March 12, 1912, the tanker was caught in a gale and driven onto rocks on the California coast several miles north of Santa Barbara. Two crew members were killed. A salvage company managed to haul the ship off the rocks and deliver it to San Francisco to have a large hole in the hull repaired. Half a year later, the ship caught fire and burned while taking on oil, but was salvaged again, rebuilt and restored to service.

The final voyage of *Rosecrans* was a trip from San Francisco to Portland, Oregon, with a cargo of crude oil. The ship encountered a gale and wound up on the Columbia River bar at Peacock Spit, on the north side of the river mouth. The last message from *Rosecrans* read, in part, SHIP BREAKING UP FAST; CAN STAY AT MY STATION NO LONGER. *Rosecrans* broke into two pieces. The crew climbed into the rigging but were swept from it into the sea and were drowned.

Despite the perilous weather, a surf boat made its way to *Rosecrans*. By this time, only four men were left on the tanker, clinging to the mast. In his eagerness to be rescued, one man jumped into the water but drowned in his effort to reach the surf boat. The remaining three men were rescued.

Because the weather was so violent, the crew of the surf boat decided not to attempt a return to shore. They dropped the rescued crewmen instead at a nearby lightship. The loss of *Rosecrans* was attributed to a navigational error. Apparently the captain lost his bearings in the storm and mistook the North Head light for the lightship, so that the tanker ran onto the spit.

Rostron, Captain Arthur Henry   Captain Rostron of the Cunard liner *Carpathia* supervised the rescue of survivors from *Titanic* on the night of April 14–15, 1912, after *Titanic* sank following a collision with an iceberg in the North Atlantic Ocean. Rostron steered a course through an ice-strewn sea at top speed to reach *Titanic*'s last reported position. After picking up the survivors and boats, *Carpathia* headed for New York and deposited them safely on shore.

This rescue was perhaps the most dramatic incident in Rostron's career at sea. He eventually became commodore of the Cunard fleet.

See also CALIFORNIAN INCIDENT; TITANIC.

Roumania, British steamship   Off the coast of Portugal, *Roumania* encountered an intense storm on October 27, 1892, and was torn apart. The wreck killed 113 people.

Royal George, British warship   More than 900 men died in the wreck of *Royal George*, a battleship that sank at Spithead on August 29, 1792. (One report says the sinking occurred several years earlier.) Carelessness appears to have been the cause of the sinking. The ship was being careened, or tilted to one side, to conduct a repair just below the waterline on the right side of the vessel. In this case, the ship was tilted toward the left side. The gunports on that side were left open, however, and admitted large amounts of water. The warship sank in shallow water with its masts protruding above the surface.

The wreck of *Royal George* was involved in an historic episode in salvage operations in the early 19th century. In 1819, an inventor named Augustus Siebe designed a diving suit that combined a helmet with a waterproof jacket that extended to waist level. A pump at the surface delivered compressed air to the helmet. The jacket was open at the waist so that exhaled air could escape. Siebe's suit reportedly worked well in efforts to salvage *Royal George*, although the diver had to remain approximately vertical so that water would not fill his suit.

Eventually, however, *Royal George*—a threat to navigation in such shallow water—was destroyed with explosives. One Colonel Pasley was put in charge of the demolition project. He used iron containers filled with gunpowder, set off by wires attached to electrical batteries on the surface. The wreck was destroyed after several tons of copper and some timber were salvaged.

See also DIVING SUITS; SALVAGE.

Royal Tar, American steamship   Also known as the "zoo ship," the paddlewheel steamer *Royal Tar* was destroyed in one of the strangest and most colorful shipwrecks in New England history. On October 21, 1836, for a voyage from St. John, New Brunswick, to Maine, *Royal Tar* took on board a cargo of circus animals including several lions and Arabian horses, a leopard, a tiger, an elephant named Mogul, two camels, some monkeys and assorted reptiles. Also on board were 85 passengers who included members of a brass band. Altogether, the little ship was carrying 106 people in addition to its exotic cargo. The ship was overloaded. Moreover, three of the ship's five lifeboats were left behind to make additional room on board.

The voyage started in lively fashion, with a concert on deck by the band. On the second day out, however, Captain Thomas Reed saw an ominous overcast ahead, and the wind started rising, tossing the little ship about. Captain Reed decided to put into Eastport, Maine, for safety. The weather remained unfavorable for the next two days, but by that time the captain had decided he had no more time to wait. So, *Royal Tar* set out again.

The ship was supposed to deliver the circus to Thomaston, Maine. Before *Royal Tar* could reach Thomaston, however, the wind increased to gale force. Once again, Reed headed for safety along the shore, this time in the shelter of coastal islands. Meanwhile, however, trouble was developing with the boilers. A leak had left the water level in the boilers too low, and they overheated, setting fire to wooden supports used to strengthen the deck where the elephant stood.

The crew tried but failed to contain the fire. Captain Reed at first did not tell the passengers that the ship was on fire, because he did not want to cause panic. Several members of the crew made matters worse by taking one of the two remaining lifeboats and heading for shore, leaving only one lifeboat for approximately 100 people left on board.

As the passengers were about to have a meal, the captain told them at last that the ship was on fire. Fanned by strong winds, the fire spread through the ship. Reed tried to sail toward land, but *Royal Tar* began drifting seaward instead. The last remaining lifeboat seemed the only hope of saving anyone on board, so Reed took to the boat and stationed it near the burning ship to pick up passengers who jumped from the deck. Meanwhile, the terrified animals, notably the elephant, raised a tremendous din. Some of the animals were shoved overboard in an effort to save at least a few of them. Mogul the elephant stayed on board for a while, bellowing from fear, but eventually leaped into the water and tried to reach shore. The lions and other big cats were left in their cages, because it was thought that their release would endanger humans.

According to one report, a passenger on *Royal Tar* was unwilling to part with his worldly wealth and paid for that attachment with his life. His pockets filled with heavy silver dollars, he sank as soon as he reached the water and never came up.

A revenue cutter appeared on the scene and took aboard the people Captain Reed had rescued in his boat. The cutter was carrying explosives, and its captain hesitated to approach the burning *Royal Tar*. So, it was up to Captain Reed to rescue as many people as he could. He made numerous trips to *Royal Tar* and ferried as many survivors as possible to the cutter. After rescue operations were finished, the still-burning steamer drifted out to sea until it sank and the waters finally put out the fire. In all, 74 people survived the burning of *Royal Tar*. Thirty-two died. Captain Reed was hailed as a hero for his rescue efforts. Mogul the elephant died in the sea, and his huge carcass washed ashore several days afterward.

See also STORMS.

Royston Grange, British cargo vessel   A huge explosion wrecked both ships when *Royston Grange* col-lided with the Liberian tanker *Tien Chee* in the River Plate near Montevideo, Uruguay, on May 11, 1972. The blast killed 84 people, presumably including 10 who were never found. The cause of the collision is uncertain. Oil spilled from the tanker's broken hull and coated local beaches. Fire then broke out, and soon both ships were demolished in an explosion.

rusticles   A curious phenomenon observed on certain sunken vessels, "rusticles" are elongated, icicle-like formations formed by bacteria acting on iron and steel hulls. The bacteria use iron from the hulls in their metabolism and generate long, reddish rusticles that extend downward from the ships. The rusticles consist of dead bacteria and oxidized iron, which gives rusticles a characteristic red hue. As bacteria on the hull's surface die and are replaced by new generations of bacteria, the dead bacteria are displaced outward, away from the hull, to form rusticles. Rusticles are extremely fragile and may break off under their own weight after some years, piling up around a wreck. Rusticles were found in large amounts on the wreck of the British liner *Titanic* when the wreck was explored by French and American expeditions in the 1980s.

Ruth, American paddle wheel steamer   While doing Union Army duty during the War Between the States, *Ruth* caught fire and burned off the Missouri shore on August 3, 1863, after leaving St. Louis for Vicksburg, Mississippi, with the payroll for General Grant's army on board. Thirty men were killed. Although the ship was destroyed, the payroll was saved.

S

S-4, American submarine The Coast Guard cutter *Pauling* struck *S-4* on the afternoon of December 17, 1927, as the submarine returned to the surface following a test run, less than a mile off Cape Cod, Massachusetts. As *S-4* sank, *Pauling* stopped, lowered its boats and sent a radio message for help. Rescue vessels arrived converged on the site.

Some crew members on *S-4* remained alive in the control room and torpedo room, but the men in the control room soon were flooded out and had to retreat to the engine room. Temperatures inside the sunken submarine were only slightly higher than freezing, and the men had no cold-weather clothing.

By the time a diver reached the wreck, 22 hours after the sinking, only the men in the torpedo room responded to his rapping on hatch covers. The salvage team at the surface decided the best plan was to try bringing *S-4* to the surface by pumping out the ballast tanks. This approach failed. Meanwhile, the men in the torpedo room were running out of air.

One diver had a nightmarish experience. He set foot on the submarine in the midst of the damage caused by the collision. A storm at the surface was creating rough water. As his rescue vessel above slid into troughs between waves, his air line and then his life line (or tether) looped and were caught on pieces of wreckage, so that he was trapped on the deck of the sunken submarine. Another diver had to go down and rescue him. That diver—despite a dangerous tear in his diving suit—took some two hours to free his trapped comrade by cutting away wreckage with a hacksaw, and later received the Medal of Honor for this courageous rescue.

The men on *S-4* remained alive and communicated with the rescuers by messages tapped out in Morse code. As their air was about to run out, they asked, "Is there any hope?" The rescue team responded that they were doing all they could. The last message from the trapped men came through at 6:15 A.M. on December 19. "We understand," they said. "All is well."

Heavy weather had prevented divers from connecting an air line to the torpedo room. When divers finally managed to do so, it was too late to save the men in the torpedo room. The air in the room was found to contain seven percent carbon dioxide, or 2,333 times the concentration ordinarily found in the air.

The salvage of *S-4* required 564 dives in all. The submarine was raised on March 17, 1928, and later used in a test of safety devices that were installed after the vessel was raised. *S-4* then was sunk again, this time deliberately, in 60 feet of water with ballast tanks flooded. The aim of this test was to raise the sunken submarine and free an imaginary crew trapped inside. The test was unsuccessful, because the engine room developed a leak while on the bottom, and only the prow reached the surface during the attempt to refloat the submarine. After the *S-4* tragedy, the Navy adopted an "escape lung" that was supposed to give individual crewmen on a sunken submarine a chance of reaching the surface.

See also SUBMARINES.

S-5, American submarine A telephone call from the deep saved the crew of *S-5* after a mechanical malfunction left the submarine in trouble off the eastern coast of the United States during World War I. *S-5* was on patrol, submerged, and tried to surface. The stern ballast tanks were pumped out successfully, but the forward tanks remained filled. Thus *S-5* rose to the surface with only the tip of the stern above water. A radio distress call was impossible under the circumstances, and so the crew ejected the telephone buoy, a communications device that allowed phone contact with the surface. The buoy rang for more than 30 hours, unanswered. The troopship *General Goethals* finally passed near the buoy, heard the rings, and sent six men in a boat to see what was happening. They made contact with the men trapped inside the submarine, and rescue operations began. Men from the troopship cut a hole in the exposed bit of *S-5*'s stern so that air could enter, then removed a hull plate to let the submarine's crew escape. Twenty-eight men were rescued after 40 hours in the half-sunken submarine.

See also SUBMARINES.

S-19, American submarine Even when a salvage operation becomes difficult, it pays to persevere. That lesson is clear in the case of the United States Navy submarine *S-19*, which ran ashore at Nauset Beach near Orleans, Massachusetts, on January 13, 1925. A tug passed a line to the stranded submarine and pulled, but the only effect was to make *S-19* heel over several degrees. After the crew was removed from the submarine, two tugs pulling in tandem tried again to move *S-19*, but again without success. Now the submarine was heeled over some 40 degrees. Operations continued, but by late January the sub was still stranded and was actually working its way inshore.

It was clear that some new approach was needed. So, the salvors set up a shore tackle. This apparatus consisted of a big buoy moored in place with several anchors. A line was passed from the submarine through a block on the buoy, and from there to a purchase on shore. A winch on shore assisted in pulling the submarine off the beach. Two tugs also pulled on *S-19*. The submarine inched off the beach and at last was refloated on March 18, more than two months after running aground. At times during the salvage operation, *S-19* heeled over 90 degrees (that is, lay on its side). This incident demonstrated the durability of submarines.

See also SUBMARINES.

S-48, American submarine *S-48* was stranded not once, but twice, on January 29, 1925, near Portsmouth, New Hampshire. First the submarine was grounded on rocks near Jaffey Point. Then, later that night, *S-48* floated off the rocks and drifted into Little Harbor. There the sub grounded on sand, with a 34-degree list.

The double grounding had damaged the hull, and the ship had several leaks. Salvors working out of the nearby Portsmouth Navy Yard used an anchor to keep the submarine in place, and tried to pump out the hull.

It soon became clear that pumping would not work, because too many leaks were involved. So, the salvors used a different tactic. They pumped compressed air into the hull and ballast tanks. With a tug alongside for assistance, *S-48* was refloated and towed to the yard. Captain C. A. Bartholemew, U.S.N., writes in

his history of Naval marine salvage that this operation was extraordinarily economical. The entire job cost only $3,400.

The stranding of *S-48* occurred only about two weeks after the submarine *S-19* grounded on Cape Cod, Massachusetts, and required a lengthy, difficult salvage operation.

See also SUBMARINES.

S-51, American submarine *S-51* sank on September 25, 1925, 15 miles east of Block Island, Rhode Island, in Long Island Sound, with 37 crewmen aboard. The submarine was cruising on the surface when it was rammed by the liner *City of Rome*. *S-51* sank in 132 feet of water. Nine men who were in the vicinity of the conning tower at the moment of collision escaped, but only three of those men remained alive in the water by the time *City of Rome* stopped and sent boats to pick them up. Navy divers later located the wreck but found it flooded, with no one aboard left alive. The Navy set out to raise the submarine. Salvage was lengthy and complicated, and the submarine was not raised until July 5, 1926. The *S-51* tragedy was one of many that occurred before the navies of the world began equipping submarines with adequate escape systems.

See also SUBMARINES.

Sable Island, Canada Noted for its heavy concentration of shipwrecks, Sable Island is located some 150 miles off Nova Scotia and is known to have more than 500 wrecks dating from early colonial times to the modern era.

See also CANADA; TREASURE.

sabotage In wartime, sabotage is a significant concern to shippers and captains, because a bomb or incendiary device slipped aboard a vessel in port can destroy the vessel as effectively as a mine or torpedo. German saboteurs during World War I are thought to have been especially skilled at inserting incendiary devices on ships leaving New York. Sabotage can be difficult to prove, however, because so much evidence is likely to be destroyed in a shipwreck.

See also EXPLOSIONS; FIRE.

Sacramento, Portuguese warship The armed galleon *Sacramento* was part of a convoy of 60 vessels that sailed from Portugal to Brazil in 1668. Some 1,000 people are believed to have been on board *Sacramento* for this voyage. The ship ran aground in stormy weather on a shoal at Banco de Santo Antonio near Bahia (now Sao Salvador, Brazil) on May 5, when the pilot decided to try taking the ship into the harbor despite the fact that darkness was falling. *Sacramento* subsequently was driven off the shoal, foundered and sank. Only 70 people survived the wreck.

One interesting aspect of the wreck is that it was found to contain bronze guns from the 16th century. This information indicates that good bronze cannon from the 1500s remained effective almost 100 years after their manufacture, salvage expert Roger Smith notes in an essay in George Bass's 1988 anthology *Ships and Shipwrecks of the Americas.*

See also CANNON; ROCKS AND SHOALS.

Sagamore, **American schooner** This wreck stands out in the maritime history of the United States because of a bizarre incident immediately after the collision. On the night of May 11, 1907, the four-masted schooner *Sagamore* was carrying a load of coal from Virginia to Boston when the ship collided with the Norwegian steamship *Edda* near Martha's Vineyard, off the coast of Massachusetts. *Edda* struck *Sagamore* on the bow. As the two ships then moved apart, *Sagamore*'s bow swung around so that the bowsprit— the long timber projecting forward from the bow— swung across *Edda*'s bridge and swept up the Norwegian ship's captain, who then found himself on the vessel that his own ship had struck. As *Sagamore* was sinking, the Norwegian captain presented himself to the master of *Sagamore* and joined the schooner's men in the longboat.

See also COLLISIONS.

sails Although sails were essential to maritime technology for many centuries, they presented dangers to shipping. A ship trying to make a fast passage, for example, might put on too much sail, and then capsize when a strong wind struck the ship unexpectedly, before the sails could be taken in.

A case in point involves the American schooner *Anna C. Anderson,* which disappeared at sea with seven on board in January of 1869. The ship was on a voyage from Oysterville, Washington, to San Francisco with a highly perishable cargo of oysters. According to one hypothesis, the ship put on an extravagant amount of sail in the hope of making a fast passage to San Francisco, but a heavy wind struck the ship and made it capsize.

Sailing vessels were classified according to the kind and number of sails they carried. Some sails were square-rigged, or set at a right angle to the ship's long axis. Other sails were arranged fore-and-aft, or parallel to the ship's long axis. Vessels such as brigantines and barkentines might have combinations of both kinds of sails. Schooners were characterized by fore-and-aft sails.

Square-rigged, or square, sails, were designated (from bottom to top of mast) as courses, topsails, topgallants, royals and skysails.

See also SCHOONER.

St. Barthélemy, Lesser Antilles Located in the Leeward Islands, St. Barthélemy has been the site of numerous shipwrecks. Many of those wrecks have occurred in storms. An intense storm in September of 1791 wrecked three unnamed ships here; ten other ships, likewise unidentified, were reportedly wrecked in the main harbor by a hurricane on August 1, 1792; another hurricane on October 7, 1811, destroyed 40 vessels, the majority of them American ships that had sought shelter from the storm in the harbor; an additional 60 vessels were destroyed in the harbor by a hurricane on September 18, 1815; and a hurricane in September of 1819 demolished much of the community on shore while wrecking all the ships at St. Barthelemy.

St. Catharis, **British ship** The case of St. Catharis illustrates how easily inaccuracies can enter records of maritime catastrophes, and how misleading those errors can be. *St. Catharis* was wrecked off the Caroline Islands in the Pacific Ocean on April 16, 1891. The wreck is sometimes listed, however, as having occurred on the Outer Banks of North Carolina, in the North Atlantic Ocean. According to historian David Stick in his book *Graveyard of the Atlantic: Shipwrecks of the North Carolina Coast*, this strange translocation apparently began when someone misread "Caroline Islands" as "Carolina Island." Error led to further error thereafter, until a writer for America's Federal Writers' Project, in the 1930s, mentioned in a guidebook to North Carolina that Chicamacomico on the Outer Banks was the site of a burial mound of British seamen who supposedly had drowned in the wreck of *St. Catharis* there in 1891. There was in fact no such mound at Chicamacomico, because *St. Catharis* sank in a different ocean, thousands of miles away. Evidently *St. Catharis* was confused with *Strathairly*, another British vessel that did sink off the Outer Banks at about the same time *St. Catharis* was wrecked in the Caroline Islands. Nonetheless, Stick reports that residents of the Outer Banks would relate how their parents had told them about the horrible wreck of *St. Catharis* there; that bloodstains on the floor of a lifesaving station on the Outer Banks were attributed to bodies from the wreck of *St. Catharis*; and that a widely used reference work, the *World Almanac and Book of Facts*, listed *St. Catharis* as having been wrecked off a nonexistent "Carolina Island." The case of *St. Catharis* is a good example of how simple error, imagination and false memory can alter the true story of a wreck dramatically.

See also OUTER BANKS; STRATHAIRLY.

St. Elmo's fire A luminous accumulation of static electricity often seen in the rigging of ships during stormy weather, St. Elmo's fire commonly takes the form of a pinkish glow concentrated at points such as the tips of masts or spars. St. Elmo's fire may have given rise to many tales of apparitions and supernatural influences at work on ships at sea. In modern times, the same phenomenon has been witnessed on aircraft. "St. Elmo" in this case appears to be derived from the name of St. Erasmus, patron saint of mariners.

See also APPARITIONS; ERASMUS, SAINT; SUPERNATURAL EVENTS.

***St. James*, Portuguese sailing vessel** Wrecked off Madagascar in the spring of 1586, *St. James* carried more than 500 people, of whom only about 60 are said to have survived.

According to one account of the wreck, the captain was among the first to leave the ship by lifeboat. Most of the people on board were simply left behind to save themselves as best they could.

About 70 people crowded into a repaired lifeboat and set out for the African shore. There was a horrible scene as those in the overloaded boat used sabers and other weapons to drive away swimmers who tried to climb aboard.

A cruel form of triage followed, as the Portuguese nobleman in command of the boat selected those who looked too weak to continue on the voyage. They were dropped into the sea.

The captain, who had left his ship immediately after wrecking it, was given command of another ship, which he also sailed to its destruction.

St. Kitts, Lesser Antilles One of the Leeward Islands, the small island of St. Kitts has been the site of numerous shipwrecks. Indeed, the history of St. Kitts appears to be, in large part, a story of ship losses resulting from warfare and destructive storms. A selection of St. Kitts shipwrecks follows.

In 1629, in a Spanish assault against the French and English presence on the island, the Spanish sank four ships at Basseterre. The newly appointed governor of Santiago, Cuba, was among those killed when a merchant ship of the New Spain Flota was wrecked on St. Kitts in 1630. A hurricane in 1642 destroyed 23 English vessels at Basseterre, but apparently few lives were lost because many crewmen were on shore. A pair of hurricanes in 1650 wrecked 28 merchant ships from various countries at St. Kitts; the wrecks killed many people

and involved the loss of cargoes worth more than half a million pounds sterling. In a hurricane in June of 1733, 12 ships were lost at Basseterre, and another vessel newly arrived from Philadelphia was destroyed with a complete loss of cargo and lives. Two hurricanes on September 21 and October 24, 1747, wrecked 24 English merchant vessels at Basseterre. Some 200 people are thought to have died in the wreck of an English privateer at Sandy Point in a hurricane in 1758. An especially destructive storm on October 11–12, 1780, reportedly destroyed more than 100 ships of various nationalities at St. Kitts and killed thousands of people. The 18-gun American privateer *Earl of Cornwallis* sank at Basseterre in 1781 with the loss of many crewmen. A hurricane on August 12, 1793, resulted in the loss of 30 American and English merchant ships at St. Kitts. The hurricane of July 23, 1813, destroyed 17 ships at St. Kitts, including 10 American vessels that had been captured as prizes of war.

St. Lucia, Lesser Antilles Selected shipwrecks from St. Lucia's history include, but are not limited to, the following. A hurricane on October 10, 1780, sank several ships at St. Lucia, including the 74-gun British warship H.M.S. *Cornwall*; the 32-gun H.M.S. *Vengeance*; and English and American merchant ships. The 32-gun British warship H.M.S. *Thetis* was wrecked on the western side of St. Lucia in 1781.

St. Martin, Leeward Islands Located in the Lesser Antilles, St. Martin has been the site of several notable shipwrecks. In 1631, for example, an unnamed Dutch merchant vessel reportedly was wrecked off St. Martin while being pursued by ships under the command of the Spanish Admiral Azevelo. As the admiral's ship was picking up survivors from the wreck of the Dutch vessel, a storm arose suddenly and sank the admiral's ship too. Altogether, only eight people are thought to have survived the two wrecks. One hundred and seventy years later, in 1801, the 32-gun British warship H.M.S. *Proselyte* was wrecked on a reef that now is called Proselyte Reef after the incident. No lives were lost. Marine archaeologist Robert Marx explored the site in 1960 and found that coral had overgrown much of the wreck, but some portions of the wreck lay on a sandy bottom beyond the reef.

***Saint Peter*, Russian sailing vessel** Famed Danish explorer Vitus Bering was on a voyage to Russia's Far East when his ship, *Saint Peter*, was wrecked on a barren arctic island in 1741. Bering died on the island on December 8 of that year. On this expedition, Bering became the first European explorer to see the coast of Alaska.

St. Vincent, Lesser Antilles   Famous as the site of the 1797 naval battle in which Britain's Admiral Horatio Nelson defeated the Spanish fleet commanded by Admiral Jose de Cordoba, St. Vincent also is known for a long list of shipwrecks. The 50-gun British warship H.M.S. *Experiment* and the 40-gun French warship *Juno*, for example, both were destroyed by the same hurricane at St. Vincent on October 10, 1780, with the loss of virtually all hands. A mysterious wreck involved an unnamed, large ship that reportedly drifted ashore one day in 1793, on the eastern side of St. Vincent, with no one on board.

See also GHOST SHIPS.

salvage   The process and business of recovering wrecked ships and their cargo, salvage ranges in scale from the raising of sunken small craft to the refloating of sunken ocean liners and warships. A ship may be refloated in a salvage operation, or it may be left on the bottom and its cargo removed. In some cases, the wreck may have to be disassembled on the sea floor in order to reach the cargo. Salvage can be extremely dangerous, especially to divers working on a sunken wreck. A famous salvage operation of modern times involved the French passenger liner *Normandie*, which burned and sank at its pier in New York City during World War II. *Normandie* was refloated and towed away for scrapping.

See also NORMANDIE.

San Antonio de Padua, Spanish convoy ship   Life on some convoys traveling between Spain and the Americas during the days of the flota system must have seemed like one storm after another. Sailing with the New Spain Fleet on a voyage from Cadiz in 1600, the 300-ton *San Antonio de Padua* sank in a hurricane on September 12 off the Mexican coast, along with several other vessels. After the storm passed, the remaining ships of the convoy proceeded to Veracruz, Mexico, and arrived there on September 26. Reaching Veracruz, however, did not protect them from further storms. Eight additional ships were lost in more stormy weather there. The crews cast overboard much of their cargoes—as well as anchors and cannon—to keep their vessels afloat. On this voyage, the convoy lost two vessels that carried large quantities of mercury, which was important to the extraction of precious metals.

See also FLOTA SYSTEM; MERCURY; STORMS.

San Ciriaco hurricane, 1899   Storms have caused great numbers of shipwrecks, but few storms have been more destructive of shipping than the San Ciriaco hurricane of 1899. The storm lasted almost a month and devastated the eastern seaboard of the United States. Along the Outer Banks of North Carolina alone, seven ships were lost on the beach, and the storm drove ashore the Diamond Shoals lightship.

See also OUTER BANKS; STORMS.

sand   Shipwrecks that settle on a sandy bottom may disappear beneath the sand in short order. Currents that remove the finer sediment from the seabed and leave behind only the coarser sand may carry the sand rapidly over a wreck, so that 10 or 12 feet of sand may cover a wreck within a few weeks after the ship went down. Diver and marine archaeologist Robert Marx points out that this happened with the *Atocha*, which went down in 1622 in the Florida Keys. *Atocha* sank on the boundary of the Gulf Stream, where currents of one to three knots carried sand quickly over the wreck and buried it under an average of about 12 feet of sand within two months of the sinking.

San Diego, United States Navy cruiser   Thought to have been sunk by German mines sown by submarine, *San Diego* went down on July 10, 1918, 10 to 20 miles off Point O'Woods on Long Island, New York. Although the Navy destroyed many of the mines, some drifted ashore on Long Island. A Coast Guard officer helped neutralize one mine on the beach at Moriches. After it was rendered harmless, he reportedly hauled it in his own boat to East Moriches and handed it over to the Navy.

See also MINES.

San Felipe, Spanish warship   The *capitana* of the Tierra Firme Armada on a voyage between Spain and Cartagena in 1610, the 850-ton, 42-gun *San Felipe* was wrecked near Bon Aire Island, Venezuela, along with another ship in the fleet. Divers recovered all the cannon from the two wrecks and much of the cargo from *San Felipe*.

See also CAPITANA; CARTAGENA; FLOTA SYSTEM.

San Francisco, American steam packet   Built in 1853, *San Francisco* was a gigantic ship for its time. It could carry 1,600 people and was 280 feet long. On its maiden voyage from New York to California, the ship encountered an intense storm off the North Carolina coast. The storm intensified and sank the ship on January 14, 1854, despite heroic efforts to save the vessel. A single wave washed away more than 150 men who were trying to clear debris off the decks. Rescue vessels saved 450 survivors, but 300 people are thought to have been lost.

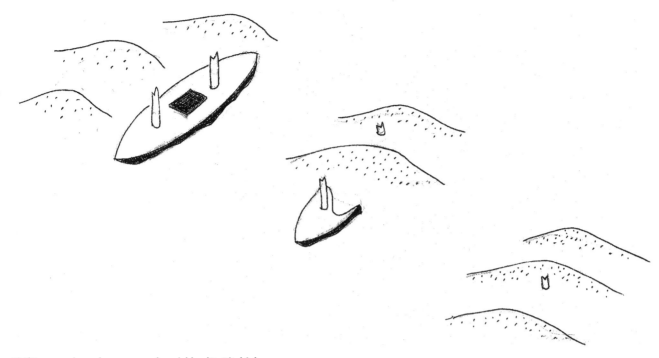

Shifting sand can bury a wreck quickly. (D. Ritchie)

***San Geronimo,* Spanish cargo ship**   Also known as *El Retiro,* this vessel was wrecked on a reef several miles south of Cabo Catoche, Mexico, on August 6, 1751. The wreck occurred near Isla Mujeres. *San Geronimo* carried a cargo of mercury.

***San Jose,* Spanish sailing vessel**   The positions of ballast, cannon and other items from a wrecked vessel may reveal much about the last moments of the ship. A case in point is *San Jose,* one of 21 Spanish ships that were wrecked off the Florida Keys during a hurricane in 1733. Diver and marine archaeologist Robert Marx investigated the wreck of *San Jose* and explained, in his book *Shipwrecks in the Americas,* what an excavation indicated about the sequence of events when the ship sank. The ship evidently struck a reef offshore, where the water was about 10 feet deep. Another possibility is that the ship was carried completely over the reef. In either event, the ship hit the sandy bottom approximately a quarter-mile nearer shore, in water about 20 feet deep. Here the ship lost its rudder, as well as several cannon and a large amount of cargo. The major portion of the hull continued on its way for about another 250 feet, then sank in 30 feet of water. Most of the ship's cannon were found here, either directly atop ballast rock or very near the main portion of the lower hull. A trail of ballast rock extended between this location and the location of the other group of several cannon. Marx

concluded from this evidence that the ship must have lost a portion of its stern at the point where the several cannon nearest the reef were found. The ship appears to have remained largely intact thereafter, until it sank. This conclusion is supported by the group of cannon found in or very near the main portion of the wreck.

***San Jose,* Spanish warship**   With soldiers and silver aboard, *San Jose* set out from Concepcion, Chile, early in 1650. The ship was wrecked on March 26 near Valdivia, Chile. Most of the men on board made their way successfully to shore but are thought to have been murdered there by natives.

***San Juan,* possible Basque whaler, Labrador**   Although no positive identification has been made, a wreck on the bottom of Red Bay, Labrador, is believed to be that of the Basque whaling ship *San Juan,* sunk in 1565. The wreck lies about 100 feet off the northern shore of Saddle Island, on a slope that places the wreck in approximately 20 to 40 feet of water. *San Juan* is thought to have sunk with a cargo of up to 1,000 barrels of whale oil on board.

The ship was a three-masted vessel slightly more than 70 feet long, with a cargo capacity of approximately 250 tons. The keel is remarkable in that it appears to have been cut in a single piece from a tree, rather than assembled from more than one piece.

This approach eliminated structural weaknesses that would have resulted from joining several pieces to make the keel.

Between 1980 and 1984, Parks Canada conducted an excavation and survey program in which the wreck was mapped, taken apart, brought to the surface in pieces for study and recording, and finally reburied on the bottom. This project produced large latex molds of sections of the wreck under water. The molds provided an accurate representation of the wreck, down to small details such as the grain of timbers.

The wreck believed to be *San Juan* is important evidence of a Basque whaling community in Labrador in the 16th century. It is not known exactly when the Basques arrived in Labrador, but by the mid-1500s they had more than a dozen ports there. Most of the ports were located along the Strait of Belle Isle. The whalers are thought to have hunted both the right whale (*Balaena glacialis*) and the bowhead whale (*Balaena mysticetus*). Bones of both species have been found in large numbers in the vicinity of the former Basque whaling community and traced to the whalers' activities. According to one estimate, the Red Bay whalers are thought to have killed some 200 whales per season. The whaling operations appear to have been highly lucrative, because in those days before petroleum supplanted whale oil as a fuel, whale oil was extremely valuable. An individual ship might carry its own value in whale oil home to Basque country in a single voyage. The whaling industry in Labrador is thought to have produced perhaps 30,000 barrels of oil per year.

Although evidently profitable, the whaling industry in 16th-century Labrador also appears to have been dangerous. The whalers had to contend with ice and severe weather. Some whalers remained in Labrador until almost the end of the year, when freezing harbors forced the ships to return home to Europe.

Wrecks of two other large 16th-century Basque vessels also were discovered in Red Bay, in addition to various small craft.

See also ARCHAEOLOGY; ESSEX.

San Juan Bautista, **Spanish treasure galleon** This 600-ton galleon was one of four ships lost in 1634 when the Tierra Firme Armada struck a reef on arriving at Cartagena, Colombia, after a voyage from Portobello, Panama. The galleon's cannon and load of treasure were recovered. Also lost were the 450-ton *Nuestra Señora del Rosario,* which was salvaged later; the 600-ton *Los Tres Reyes;* and the 80-ton *Nuestra Señora del Carmen.* The last two ships sank because they simply were too leaky to remain afloat. The following week, a fifth ship—an unnamed merchant vessel—struck one of the wrecks and was lost too.

See also FLOTA SYSTEM.

San Juan de Ulúa wrecks, Mexico The New Spain Fleet, under command of Captain-General Francisco de Luxan and Admiral Juan de Ubillo, found an unpleasant situation waiting for them when the fleet reached San Juan de Ulúa in Mexico after a voyage from Sanlucar, Spain, in 1568. Eight English ships under command of John Hawkins were in port. The two groups arranged a truce, but it was short-lived. Battle soon erupted between the English and Spanish forces, and the Spanish *almiranta,* the 500-ton *Santa Clara,* blew up and sank with its cargo of mercury. Several English vessels also were sunk during the battle. Among the English ships that escaped destruction was *Judith,* under command of Francis Drake, the famous privateer.

See also ALMIRANTA; MERCURY.

Sanlucar, Spanish port Located at the mouth of the Guadalquivir River, Sanlucar was the site of more than 200 shipwrecks on a dangerous sandbar over three centuries when Spain's treasure vessels were sailing between Europe and the New World. Sanlucar and Cadiz supplanted Seville as the principal ports for the Indies trade as Spain's fleet grew too numerous to continue using the small harbor at Seville.

See also CADIZ.

San Miguel, **Spanish convoy ship** Catastrophe could strike quickly during convoy runs between Spain and Spanish colonies in the Americas. The 500-ton *San Miguel,* for example, was caught in a storm while sailing with the New Spain Fleet off the Mexican coast in 1615. The ship broke in two and sank so rapidly that neither the crew nor any of the cargo could be saved.

San Narciso wrecks, Virgin Islands and vicinity The San Narciso hurricane, as it came to be known, caused extensive damage to shipping, especially vessels of the Royal Mail Fleet, in and around the Virgin Islands on October 29, 1867. Small in extent but packing tremendous winds, the storm lifted a 2,738-ton liner from the ocean and deposited the ship on rocks, breaking it in two. On that ship, 123 people were killed, and only 22 survived. More than 600 people on various ships are thought to have died in this storm.

Santa Ana, **Spanish sailing vessel** A shoal in Acapulco's harbor was named after this big ship, which was wrecked on the shoal in 1781 during a voyage from Peru.

Santa Catalina, Spanish merchant ship The 350-ton *Santa Catalina* was part of a Spanish fleet that encountered a hurricane in the Bahama Channel off Florida in 1589. The ship sank in deep water. Two other merchant ships in this fleet sank also, as did the *almiranta* of the fleet. The *almiranta* is thought to have carried treasure.

See also FLORIDA.

Santa Maria The flagship of Admiral Christopher Columbus on his 1492 visit to the Americas, *Santa Maria* made the trans-Atlantic voyage in company with two other vessels, *Niña* and *Pinta*. *Santa Maria*, believed to have been either a nao or a carrack, ran aground on a shoal on the reefs of Cap-Haïtien near Cibao on Hispaniola (now part of the Dominican Republic) and could not be pulled free. Columbus and his men had to unload hardware and stores from the ship, and used timber from the vessel to build a community named La Navidad. The lower portion of *Santa Maria*'s hull remained on the reef, along with the ship's ballast stones, about four and a half miles from shore. The wreck of *Santa Maria* is thought to be the first recorded shipwreck of a European vessel in the New World. Columbus left 39 men behind at La Navidad and then returned to Spain with the rest of the expedition.

Some three centuries after the wreck of *Santa Maria*, one of the ship's anchors was discovered in Grande Riviere near what is now the village of Limonade Bord-de-Mer, Haiti. In 1939, American naval historian Samuel Eliot Morison surmised that *Santa Maria* had run aground on one of several shoals near Limonade Bord-de-Mer. About 10 years later, a pilot glimpsed what appeared to be the wreck of a ship inside the barrier reef at Cap-Haïtien. Although the exact whereabouts of the wreck apparently remain unknown, expeditions in the mid-1950s and afterward uncovered artifacts including an anchor, grapeshot and iron bars like those used as ballast on warships.

Although several so-called reconstructions of Columbus's ships have been made, opinions differ about the size and design details of *Santa Maria*, *Niña* and *Pinta*. *Santa Maria* is thought to have had a capacity of less than 100 tons. (Capacity was measured by how many wine barrels, or "tuns," a ship could carry.) A reconstruction of *Santa Maria* built in 1892 for the 400th anniversary of Columbus's voyage is said to have handled wretchedly. The ship had a tendency to "yaw," or veer significantly from the intended course. Heavy pitching and rolling also were problems with the reconstructed vessel. This poor performance may have been due in part to inaccuracies in the reconstruction and to ignorance of how the original ships were constructed and ballasted.

See also ANCHORS; COLUMBUS EXPEDITIONS; NAO; PITCH; ROLL; YAW.

Santa Maria, Spanish frigate Also known as *Santa Marta*, this 38-gun frigate was carrying military materials as part of a squadron when wrecked in 1780 some two miles off Mexico's Yucatán coast.

Santa María de Begonia, Spanish merchant ship The 700-ton nao *Santa María de Begonia* was wrecked at Veracruz, Mexico, in September of 1604 with a cargo of mercury on board.

Santa Maria de los Valles, Spanish galleon This 1,500-ton galleon burned and sank off Acapulco, Mexico, on December 23, 1668. Of 778 people on board, 330 were killed.

Santa María la Blanca, Spanish merchant ship On January 21, 1555, the 220-ton *Santa María la Blanca* was wrecked in, or in the vicinity of, the port of San Juan de Ulúa in Mexico. According to one account, the ship was lost in the harbor. Another report says the ship was wrecked on reefs while leaving San Juan de Ulúa. All the ship's cargo was salvaged, but 85 people died in the wreck.

See also MEXICO.

Santiago, Spanish convoy ship The *Santiago* and three other ships of the New Spain Fleet were lost on the Yucatán coast of Mexico on a voyage in 1659. Some 300 survivors were rescued two months later. *Santiago* was wrecked on Cozumel during heavy weather. Where exactly the other three ships were wrecked is not known.

Santo Cristo de Maracaibo, Spanish galleon One of a trio of big galleons bringing mercury to Veracruz, Mexico, this vessel was wrecked, with two companions, on the coast of Campeche, Mexico, in 1719.

Sargent, American merchant ship Though not exactly a ghost ship, *Wyer G. Sargent* was a remarkable case nonetheless. Abandoned near Cape Hatteras in March of 1891, the ship drifted across the Atlantic Ocean and was sighted again in December of 1892, having drifted some 6,000 miles in 20 months and two weeks.

See also GHOST SHIPS.

Savannah, American steamship The historic *Savannah*, first vessel to use steam power to cross an ocean, was wrecked on Fire Island, New York, on November 5, 1821. All 11 men on board were killed.

Savannah was launched in 1818 at Corlear's Hook on New York's East River. A paddle-wheel vessel, *Savannah* completed a voyage from Savannah, Georgia, to Liverpool, England, in 1819. The voyage lasted 26 days. On this voyage, the ship also visited Copenhagen, Denmark; Stockholm, Sweden; St. Petersburg, Russia; and the Russian port of Kronstadt.

Jeannette Edward Rattray, in her 1955 book *Ship Ashore!*, a chronicle of shipwrecks along the Long Island shore, relates a remarkable story about the wreck of *Savannah*. A money-filled trunk belonging to Captain John Coles was cast upon the beach and broken open by wave action, scattering silver and gold along the sands. The sole witness to the wreck, one Smith Muncy, was reportedly such an honest man that he handed over to the local authorities every dollar he found from Coles's chest.

schooner A sailing ship with two or more masts and all its lower sails rigged fore-and-aft, the schooner played an important part in 19th- and early 20th-century maritime commerce. Schooner wrecks are numerous off the eastern coast of the United States, especially in northeastern waters. Some schooners attained tremendous size by the standards of sailing vessels. Schooners with six and even seven masts were constructed. Only one seven-masted schooner was ever built: *Thomas W. Lawson,* believed to be the biggest purely sailing ship in history. The giant ship handled poorly, however, and was wrecked off the Scilly Isles on December 14, 1907.

***Scorpion*, United States nuclear submarine** The attack submarine *Scorpion* sank with all 99 men on board off the Azores on May 21, 1968. The submarine is thought to have been sunk by one of its own torpedoes.

On a voyage from the Mediterranean to Norfolk, Virginia, *Scorpion* sent its last message on May 21, giving the submarine's position as 35 degrees, 7 minutes north latitude and 41 degrees, 42 minutes west longitude; speed 18 knots; and course 290 degrees, meaning the ship was traveling west-northwest. The submarine was traveling submerged at the time.

After that message, there was only silence. *Scorpion* did not arrive in Norfolk as anticipated, on May 27. A large-scale search was initiated but was not immediately successful. At one point, a mysterious radio message from "Brandywine," the code name for *Scorpion,* was received; but the message apparently was sent by one of several other ships bearing that name.

Later, a study of recordings from the Navy's secret undersea listening network turned up evidence of what had happened to *Scorpion.* The system had recorded what appeared to be an underwater implosion (that is, the noise of a ship being crushed by water pressure) at a depth of approximately 2,000 feet, some 400 miles southwest of the island of San Miguel in the Azores. This was *Scorpion*'s location immediately after the submarine's last transmission. There was speculation that the submarine had struck a "seamount," or submerged volcanic mountain, in the manner of an aircraft flying into a mountain in foggy weather.

In November of 1968, a ship equipped with underwater video cameras located and photographed, at a depth of about 10,000 feet, wreckage that was identified as belonging to *Scorpion.* At one point, the submarine's loss was attributed to mechanical problems involving pipe joints and the ship's deballasting system. Later, however, it was suggested that the explosion of one of the submarine's own torpedoes had sunk *Scorpion.*

In 1993, the Navy released a report indicating that one of *Scorpion*'s torpedoes had become armed somehow. When expelled from its tube in hopes of saving the ship, the torpedo apparently turned and homed in on the *Scorpion,* striking and sinking the submarine. The wreck of *Scorpion* was one of two known losses of American nuclear submarines during the 1960s. The other was the sinking of the submarine *Thresher* off the New England coast in 1963.

See also SUBMARINES; THRESHER.

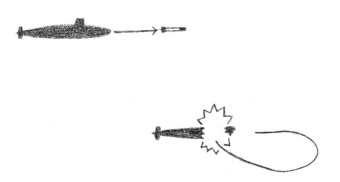

The U.S. submarine *Scorpion* is thought to have been sunk by one of its own torpedoes. (D. Ritchie)

scurvy This disease, caused by a vitamin C deficiency, was a major cause of death among sailors at sea for centuries. Scurvy is characterized by symptoms including weakness; loosened teeth; bleeding gums; and a tendency for old wounds to reopen. The British navy recognized in the 18th century that certain foods acted as "antiscorbutics," or preventives against scurvy, although the specific role of vitamin C in their effectiveness was not established until the 20th century. British ships carried limes to provide vitamin

C for crews: hence the nickname "limeys" for British sailors and even for the British people in general. Other good sources of vitamin C available to sailors included fresh, undercooked meat from seals and penguins. These animals helped prevent scurvy among explorers in the polar regions on many expeditions. Scurvy was one reason why large numbers of Spanish sailors perished on the dreadful voyages of the Manila Galleons across the Pacific Ocean between the Philippine Islands and Acapulco, Mexico.

See also MANILA GALLEONS; POLAR REGIONS.

scuttling This term describes the practice of opening a ship's hull deliberately to the sea in order to sink the vessel. In modern times, scuttling is commonly accomplished by opening "seacocks," or valves that admit sea water to the hull. Explosives also may be used. A ship may be scuttled for a variety of reasons. One military application of scuttling is to sink a ship in a channel, so as to block movements of enemy vessels. A ship also may be scuttled to deprive an enemy of its use.

Scyllias, diver, probably fifth century B.C. Mentioned in the writings of the Greek historian Herodotus, who wrote in approximately the middle of the fifth century B.C., Scyllias was said to be the greatest diver of his day and to have recovered much valuable property from wrecks of Persian ships. Evidently Scyllias was disgruntled with his Persian masters, for Herodotus reports that the diver defected to the Greeks, who were Persia's foes at the time. Herodotus expresses skepticism, however, about a tale that Scyllias swam 10 miles under water to reach the Greek forces. Herodotus thought it more likely that Scyllias made the journey by boat.

***Seabird*, Great Lakes passenger steamer** The side-wheeler *Seabird* was destroyed by fire on April 9, 1868, during a voyage from Chicago to Milwaukee, with the loss of as many as 103 lives. The exact number is uncertain, because no passenger manifest was available. The fire reportedly started when a steward discarded hot ashes on the windward side of the vessel. The hot ashes blew into open holds, set fire to straw, and thus ignited the blaze that consumed the ship.

See also FIRE.

seaquakes Earthquakes occurring beneath the ocean can have dramatic effects on ships. These events are called "seaquakes" and may be misinterpreted as a collision with an uncharted shoal.

Seaquakes produce effects on ships that are comparable in many ways to buildings' responses to earthquakes on land. A seaquake may begin with a rumbling sound, followed almost immediately by shocks that cause the ship to vibrate or even lurch to a stop, as if the vessel had struck an underwater object. The ship may experience a series of such shocks.

The shocks are attributed to a kind of seismic wave known as a p-wave (short for primary or pressure wave). The p-wave works in much the same way as two billiard balls striking each other; one particle of water receives the wave's energy from the particle next to it, in a highly efficient transfer. A p-wave travels through sea water at almost a mile per second. Ordinarily, it does not produce any visible change in the sea surface.

Initial p-waves reaching a ship from a seaquake may not be perceived as vibrations. Instead, they may produce a loud booming noise as their energy is transferred to the atmosphere. More palpable vibrations are likely to follow, although in some cases the sound may be unaccompanied by trembling of the ship.

Vibrations, when they occur, may last up to several minutes. A duration of 15 seconds to one minute appears to be typical. During this time, the ship may vibrate vigorously, causing heavy objects on deck to bounce perhaps six inches into the air.

Damage from such vibrations may be extensive. A report published in 1967, for example, describes damage to a vessel off the Solomon Islands during a seaquake on June 15, 1966. Damage included a broken cathode-ray tube, a smashed tube in a barometer, vacuum tubes dislodged from their sockets in a wireless transmitter and a broken fuel line. The ship also took on water, although none could be seen leaking in after the seaquake. Presumably, seams had opened during the quake and admitted water, then closed again after the vibrations ceased. The ship's masts whipped markedly, and a frightening rattling noise came from the funnel.

The effects of a seaquake on ships at sea have been studied in detail, notably in the case of a quake that occurred in 1932. An earthquake in Mexico on June 3 was felt as a violent vibration on a ship 60 miles away, in more than 4,500 feet of water. Another vessel to the southwest, about 70 miles from the epicenter of the earthquake, had a similar experience, although in this case the vibrations were less energetic but longer in duration. In neither case was any change observed in the condition of the sea.

Conditions elsewhere were more severe. A vessel 115 miles from the epicenter was shaken so strongly, for a period of three minutes, that the engines were shut down. A change was observed in the pattern of swells, and the sea surface became confused. Another ship some 130 miles from the epicenter vibrated for more than a minute.

Aftershocks, or lesser earthquakes following the principal shock, over the next few days also were correlated with effects on ships at sea. The effects included noises like gunfire, heavy vibrations, pitching and rolling motions, and what appeared to be small white objects (possibly dead fish) strewn over the sea surface.

Although seaquakes do not appear to constitute a major threat to shipping, they may account for many reports of a ship grounding briefly on an uncharted shoal that cannot be found on a later search.

Other marine phenomena associated with earthquakes include tsunamis, or seismic waves. Tsunamis are large very long waves that may be imperceptible in mid-ocean but can rise and produce huge, highly destructive breakers on reaching shore.

See also TSUNAMIS.

Sea Venture, English sailing vessel An outstanding case in marine archaeology, the wreck of *Sea Venture* (also called *Sea Adventure* in some accounts) occurred on June 7, 1609, off St. George's Island at the northeastern tip of Bermuda. Under command of Christopher Newport, *Sea Venture* was the flagship of a group of nine vessels carrying 600 colonists from Plymouth, England, to Jamestown, Virginia. The ships encountered a hurricane that separated *Sea Venture* from the other vessels.

Sea Venture experienced heavy weather for four days and eventually was driven onto a reef. All 150 people on board made their way safely to shore. The ship's longboat was made ready for sea and sent out with eight men on board to bring a rescue expedition from Jamestown. The longboat did not return, however, nor did rescuers show up from Virginia. The stranded colonists on Bermuda built two pinnaces and eventually arrived at Jamestown.

The wreck of *Sea Venture* was discovered in 1958 but remained unexplored for 20 years. An excavation began in 1978. Study of the wreck indicated that *Sea Venture* may have been as much as 75 feet long. A cannon and large quantities of shot were recovered from the wreck, along with pottery and cooking implements. Ming porcelain from China also was retrieved. The wreck is important in the annals of marine archaeology because its artifacts provide a detailed picture of what colonists carried with them on such voyages, and because the artifacts could be dated reliably. Accurate dating of the artifacts helps to establish correct dates for other shipwrecks on which similar items are found.

The wreck of *Sea Venture* also reportedly had a major effect on English literature. The wreck is said to have given playwright William Shakespeare the idea for his play *The Tempest*.

See also ARCHAEOLOGY.

Selkirk, Alexander, castaway (1674?–1721) A Scottish castaway whose adventures supplied the basis for Daniel Defoe's novel *Robinson Crusoe*, Selkirk was the sailing master of the *Cinque Ports*, an English privateer that was heavily damaged in encounters with Spanish vessels in the South Pacific during the War of the Spanish Succession.

Apparently because of the ship's condition and because of a disagreement with the captain, Selkirk left the vessel in September of 1704 when *Cinque Ports* stopped at Juan Fernandez, a small island about 400 miles west of Valparaiso, Chile. The captain evidently was glad to see Selkirk leave and had him deposited on the island with all his possessions.

According to one account of Selkirk's departure, the captain considered Selkirk's conduct to be mutiny and thought exile on Juan Fernandez was a suitable sentence. Just before the ship left, Selkirk had a change of heart and tried to reboard *Cinque Ports*, but was not allowed to return. The ship sailed away, leaving Selkirk on the island.

Selkirk's belongings consisted of some bedding and clothing, a gun with bullets and powder, tobacco, several books (including a Bible), a hatchet, a knife and some nautical equipment. At first he took shelter in a cave but was driven from it by the noise of sea lions roaring nearby. Later, he constructed two huts, one for cooking and the other for sleeping. Goats on the island provided him with milk and meat. Their skins served as clothing after his initial garments wore out. He also fed on lobsters found along the shore, and on various vegetables.

In his first four years on the island, Selkirk had only one set of visitors, and they were less than friendly. When two Spanish frigates stopped at Juan Fernandez, the Spaniards for some reason chased Selkirk up a tree. The Spaniards soon departed, and Selkirk had the island to himself again.

Selkirk burned signal fires to alert passing ships to his presence. On February 1, 1709, the British privateers *Duke* and *Duchess* dropped anchor at Juan Fernandez. The captain saw the fire and proceeded cautiously, in case it was some kind of trap.

The following day, he sent a party ashore to investigate. The sailors met Selkirk and took him aboard, although they had trouble understanding him. Years of isolation, with no one for conversation, had left Selkirk so unused to talking that he had trouble making himself understood. Selkirk also had trouble readjusting his diet to the fare of civilization.

After leaving the island, the ships sailed northward to attack Spanish shipping. Selkirk was put in charge of one of the Spanish vessels captured. The privateers spent several months preying on Spanish vessels and eventually returned to England.

Selkirk's share of the loot made him reasonably wealthy. He bought himself some elegant clothing and returned to Scotland in 1711, but reportedly was unhappy there and regretted leaving his peaceful island. He married a local woman but left her to go back to sea, where he died on a ship off the African coast in 1721, at age 47. In 1868, a tablet commemorating his stay on the island was installed on Juan Fernandez.

Senator, Great Lakes automobile carrier Lost in a collision with the ore carrier *Marquette* on October 31, 1929, with seven known killed or missing, *Senator* was one of many ships to be wrecked on the Great Lakes during an especially calamitous period in late 1929. The collision occurred in fog off Manitowoc, Wisconsin, about midway between Milwaukee and Green Bay.

Marquette and *Senator* were traveling along the western shore of the lake, the former sailing southward from Escanaba on Green Bay, and the latter northward from Kenosha. *Senator* was taking this route in order to avoid the dangerous Grays Reef and Manitou passages.

The ships encountered each other in the fog at about 10:20 A.M. When it became apparent that they were on a collision course, both ships ordered full astern, and tried to turn. It happened that both ships turned in the same direction, however, and collided. *Marquette*'s bow penetrated the side of *Senator*, which started to list, and sank rapidly. The ship's list prevent launching lifeboats, but some crew members managed to put life rafts into the water. A fishing boat that happened to be in the vicinity at the time of the collision helped with rescue operations. Twenty-one people were saved from the wreck. The dead included the captain of *Senator*.

Marquette experienced serious damage to its bow. Dwight Boyer, in his history of shipwrecks on the Great Lakes, tells how that damage to *Marquette* helped save the life of *Senator*'s radio operator, who had leaped over the side as *Senator* went down. The wireless operator made his way through the rough, cold water to *Marquette*, climbed up an anchor chain, and hauled himself to safety through the gaping hole in the ship's bow.

The Manitou Passage (which *Senator* was trying to avoid by traveling the western route) is located be-

tween the mainland and North and South Manitou Islands. The waters here are filled with shipwrecks. Boyer cites one study that revealed 96 wrecks listed in lighthouse keepers' logbooks. Some 200 sailors killed in shipwrecks are reportedly buried in a field near a cemetery on South Manitou Island.

See also COLLISIONS; GREAT LAKES; MILWAUKEE; WISCONSIN.

Serrano narrative The lore of castaways includes the story of Pedro Serrano, who allegedly spent two years on Southwest Key, an island off the coast of Central America. According to one story, Serrano found himself marooned on an island that lacked water, grass and wood. A close look at the island's resources, however, revealed that it was not as barren as it appeared at first glance. Serrano found edible shellfish on the shore and also a population of turtles. These animals provided him with food to eat and liquid to drink. A turtle shell allowed him to collect rainwater for drinking.

Next he turned his attention to making fire, so that he might signal passing ships. Although no trees grew on the island, there was flammable material at hand. Serrano collected dry seaweed and planks from shipwrecks to use as fuel. By diving into the waters around the island, he also found stones with which to strike fire. There was a danger that rainfall would put out his fire, but he solved that problem by using a large turtle shell to form a rainshield.

Clothing was a greater problem. Unprotected from the sun, he had to run into the water when the day's heat became too much for him to bear. He let his hair grow long, so that eventually his hair and beard extended to his waist.

Serrano allegedly lived for three years under these conditions. Then, one day, he suddenly found he had a companion on the island. Another castaway appeared, having survived the wreck of his vessel.

The newcomer saw the smoke from Serrano's fire and made his way toward it. When he met Serrano, however, the new castaway ran away in terror, thinking the hairy, wild-looking Serrano was actually the devil in human form, come to incite despair in him.

Serrano relieved his fears by reciting the *Credo*, or Apostles' Creed. The new arrival reasoned that the devil would not have that testimony on his lips. The two men then got acquainted with each other, and Serrano offered his new friend such comforts as the island could provide.

It was not a completely harmonious relationship. Serrano and his companion quarreled on occasion but made peace afterward.

The two men established a regular schedule of activities. Certain times were allotted for fishing, gathering fuel and so forth. They took great care to keep the fire burning, so that passing ships might see it and come to rescue them.

Several ships did pass in the three years after Serrano came to live on the island, but none stopped. Possibly the crews were afraid of running onto shoals near the island and becoming castaways themselves. After his companion arrived, Serrano reportedly had to wait four additional years before a passing vessel in 1534 saw the smoke from the fire, stopped, and sent a boat ashore to investigate.

The boat's arrival was a replay of Serrano's first encounter with his fellow castaway. The men in the boat were so frightened at the appearance of the men on shore that they started rowing back to the ship. Serrano and his friend managed to talk them into coming ashore, however, and thus were rescued. Serrano survived the voyage to Spain, but his friend from the island died during the voyage.

After returning to civilization, Serrano allegedly kept his long hair and beard as mementos of his long stay on the island. He evidently became something of a social lion, and crowds would pay to have a look at him. The German Emperor is said to have granted him an income for life. Serrano reportedly died in Panama.

Seyne, **French passenger liner** The aged *La Seyne,* 36 years old, collided with the British liner *Onda* on a voyage to Singapore on November 14, 1909, and sank, reportedly killing 101 of 162 passengers on board.

shallow-water environment Although identical in many cases with the near-shore environment, the shallow-water environment may extend for considerable distances offshore. The shallow-water environment is characterized by warm waters (compared to the cold waters of the deep-sea environment), high concentrations of dissolved oxygen and an abundance of organisms, including destructive organisms that may demolish or conceal wrecks. Waves and currents also may help to destroy wrecks, conceal them under sediment and scatter their cargoes. Wrecks in shallow-water environments are also vulnerable to damage and looting by careless divers, souvenir hunters and treasure seekers, although location in shallow water also makes wrecks more easily accessible to legitimate archaeologists and responsible salvors and divers.

See also DEEP-SEA ENVIRONMENT; NEAR-SHORE ENVIRONMENT.

Shark, **American naval schooner** The wreck of *Shark* on September 10, 1846, gave rise to a place name in Oregon. The 300-ton vessel arrived at the Columbia River in August after a voyage from Honolulu, and took on a self-proclaimed pilot who had survived the wreck of the sloop of war *Peacock* five years before. *Shark* ran aground almost immediately after the so-called pilot came aboard, but floated free as the tide came in. On its departure, *Shark* ran aground again, on Clatsop Spit, and this time was unable to free itself. The ship broke apart, and a piece of the vessel, with a cannon on board, drifted ashore at Tillamook Head, a few miles to the south. That point was named Cannon Beach to commemorate the cannon's recovery.

See also COLUMBIA RIVER BAR; PEACOCK.

sharks In many cases, sharks have attacked survivors of shipwrecks in the water and thus added to the death toll from the wrecks. Sharks are attracted to the kind of irregular, struggling motion made by a swimmer. Presumably, the shark interprets vibrations generated by the swimmer as those of distressed and vulnerable prey, and homes in on their source. Although persons in shark-infested waters have been advised to avoid struggling, so as to minimize the risk of shark attack, such advice is difficult to heed in the circumstance of shipwreck.

Where one shark appears, others may follow, until the waters where a ship has sunk are filled with curious and excitable sharks. When sharks detect blood in the water, the result may be a "feeding frenzy," in which the sharks devour anything and everything that looks as if it might be food. (There is even an account of a shark biting down on the whirling propeller of a boat.) In such a situation, few swimmers are likely to survive. Sharks reportedly have attacked and evidently tried to overturn boats on occasion, but there is some question whether these incidents represent deliberate attempts to capsize the boats and cast their occupants into the water.

It should be noted that not all species of sharks are known to attack humans. Indeed, some sharks are not flesh-eaters at all. Moreover, in view of the importance of shark fisheries to supply fresh fish for humans, it appears that a human is far more likely to eat a shark than vice versa.

A notable case of mass shark attack occurred after the sinking of the schooner *Magpie* off the New England coast in 1826. Only two men from the ship survived its sinking and a subsequent mass attack by sharks. They reached temporary safety on the ship's longboat but knew they could not survive long there without provisions. One of the survivors was rescued from the sea after a lengthy swim through water full of sharks to draw the attention of a passing brig.

His brave effort was successful, and both men were saved.

See also MAGPIE; NANCY.

Shaw, American schooner Among the most controversial wrecks in Virginia history, *Fannie K. Shaw* went ashore during a storm at Virginia Beach on December 9, 1876, on a voyage from Georgia to Baltimore. The captain, John Belano, wrote a letter to a newspaper, accusing the lifesavers at Cape Henry Station of cowardice and calling for an official investigation. Belano said that of the lifesavers at Cape Henry, only two had come to his ship's assistance after Shaw displayed a distress signal. According to Belano, everyone on board would have died, had Belano and the first mate not brought some of the men ashore in the schooner's boat. Belano said that he went to the lifesaving station after reaching shore and brought the station's keeper and a surfman to complete rescue operations. Apparently Belano's accusations were groundless. This early accusation against the men of the lifesaving service, however, is more than offset by numerous accounts of the surfmen's daring and self-sacrifice.

See also LIFESAVING SERVICE.

sheathing Hoping to find a way of defeating the highly destructive teredo, or shipworm, Europe's navies conducted experiments in sheathing their wooden-hulled vessels with metal. Spanish experiments with lead sheathing reportedly began around 1508 and ceased in 1567, when the king decided the added lead made ships too slow. (The practice appears to have been reinstituted briefly in the early 1600s, however, on Spanish ships bound for the New World, to protect the ships from teredo attack during the winter months in the harbor at Veracruz, Mexico.) Copper sheathing was used on many British ships in the 18th century and was adopted elsewhere in the early 19th century. The arrival of metal-hulled ships in the 19th century made anti-teredo sheathing unnecessary thereafter.

See also TEREDOS.

Sherrod, Mississippi River steamboat *Ben Sherrod* burned on or about May 9, 1837, with the loss of 150 lives, en route to Louisville. The ship was engaged in a race with another steamboat when wood fuel and a barrel of whisky ignited, and the ship caught fire.

Shinnecock (Ponquogue) Light, Long Island, New York Located near the eastern tip of Long Island, on the Atlantic Ocean, the Shinnecock light operated between 1858 and 1931, when an automatically operated skeleton tower took over its duties. The lighthouse had a fixed light from 1858 to 1914 and a flashing light thereafter.

Although lighthouses are supposed to help prevent shipwrecks, the building of the fixed-beam Shinnecock light was blamed in part for the wreck of the sailing vessel *John Milton* on February 20, 1858. That same year, the lighthouse at Montauk Point, at the extreme eastern end of the island, switched from a steady to a flashing signal.

This change caused confusion for Captain Ephraim Harding on *John Milton*, passing off Long Island's southern shore in a snowstorm on February 20. Unaware that the lights looked different now, the captain misidentified the Shinnecock light as Montauk and turned north, thinking he had open water ahead when in fact he was heading straight for the shore. The ship ran onto the rocks five miles west of Montauk. Everyone on board perished. The next morning, historian Jeannette Edwards Rattray writes in her book *Ship Ashore!*, the ship's bell was found resting on a pair of beams, seemingly tolling for the dead.

Rattray reports that another ship's master, Captain Henry Babcock of the whaling ship *Washington*, encountered much the same situation that destroyed *John Milton*, but was saved by his own caution. Homeward bound to Sag Harbor, New York, from a cruise in the Pacific, *Washington* was passing Long Island when the captain became puzzled at the sight of a steady light on shore. It looked like the Montauk light, but the captain had taken his position by the sun the previous day and was sure the ship could not be off Montauk yet.

His crew told him the light must be Montauk, but Babcock was not persuaded. He gave orders to stand offshore. His judgment was proven correct. What looked like the Montauk light was actually the Shinnecock light. But for the captain's caution, *Washington* might have been wrecked in the same manner as *John Milton*.

See also LIGHTHOUSES.

shipwreck, process of Most shipwrecks in the Western Hemisphere have happened according to the following pattern, writes marine archaeologist Robert Marx in his book *Shipwrecks in the Americas*. The shipwreck occurs in shallow water. Either at once or soon afterward, the ship begins breaking apart. In the case of a wooden vessel, the first portion of the ship to be lost is the superstructure, which tends to float and may wash ashore near the wreck site. The rest of the hull is lost. The wood is carried away on the waves or destroyed by teredos (shipworms), leaving behind resistant, heavy items such as ballast stones and cannon. These items, however, may be buried quickly in

The stern disappears as the Italian liner *Andrea Doria* sinks in the North Atlantic. (U.S. Coast Guard)

mud or sand. If that happens, before long there may be no trace of the wreck's whereabouts.

The wreck of a modern, metal-hulled ship proceeds in a different manner. The highly resistant hull may endure for years after the wreck occurs. In time, however, even a stout metal hull may be broken apart and carried away by wave action, if the hull is not scrapped on the spot. Shifting sands may bury an entire hull.

When a ship sinks in deep water, it may capsize at the surface and begin its descent to the seabed upside down. During the descent, however, the hull tends to right itself and start falling with the keel downward, since the keel is the heaviest portion of the vessel. Given enough time to right itself, the ship therefore will land on the bottom in an upright position.

If the ship floods completely, or almost completely, at the surface before starting its descent, then the wreck may reach the bottom largely intact, because of equal pressure both inside and outside the hull. A wreck that sinks with many internal compartments still dry, however, may be crushed and demolished further by increasing water pressure on the way to the bottom.

Perhaps the most famous illustration of this effect may be seen in the wreck of the British liner *Titanic* at the bottom of the Atlantic Ocean. *Titanic* broke in two at the surface during its sinking. The hull split apart between the third and fourth funnels. The bow section, which had largely filled with water already, proceeded to the bottom and landed there essentially intact, be-

cause the water-filled interior equalized pressure with the sea outside. The stern section, on the other hand, appears to have gone down with numerous compartments still filled with air. These compartments apparently collapsed during the descent, with the result that the stern section was crushed and fragmented on its way to the sea floor. The stern section reached the seabed in many pieces, unlike the bow, which was still essentially in one piece when it landed.

A wreck may be surrounded with a debris field consisting of cargo and other items that spilled from the hull or were cast overboard deliberately during the sinking. Debris may continue settling to the bottom for hours after a ship actually sinks. In *Titanic*'s case, lightweight bits of debris continued falling to the ocean floor long after the two major portions of the hull had finished their descent. After such a slow descent, even fragile items such as china cups may be preserved in good condition on the sea floor.

See also CONSTRUCTION; TITANIC.

shipwrecks, social impact of   As in any other calamity, a shipwreck may have substantial impact on society. Effects may range from legislation or new regulations intended to discourage or prevent similar catastrophes in the future, to declarations of war. The sinking of the liner *Lusitania* by a German submarine, for example, helped to draw the United States into World War I by generating anti-German sentiment.

Perhaps the most significant shipwreck in terms of its impact on society was the sinking of the British

Fire at sea is a notable cause of shipwrecks. (U.S. Coast Guard)

liner *Titanic* in 1912. The loss of *Titanic* led to formation of the International Ice Patrol to protect shipping against the danger from icebergs; brought about reforms in safety regulations, specifically those governing provisions for adequate numbers of lifeboats; provided a popular image for catastrophe; gave wireless technology a significant boost; and generated a huge literature on the topic of that particular wreck.

On a different level, some localized societies have actually derived their material wealth from shipwrecks in one way or another. Salvage, for example, was one of the principal industries of Bermuda for many years, on the strength of the numerous wrecks in the island's waters; and on the Outer Banks of North Carolina, wood from shipwrecks drifted ashore in such great quantities that for many years it was used as building material on the islands.

See also LUSITANIA; TITANIC.

***Shubert*, American schooner** The difficulties and complexities of rescue work on American shores in the late 19th century are exemplified by the case of the schooner *Sarah Shubert*, which stranded off Little

Machipongo Inlet on Virginia's Eastern Shore on October 4, 1884, near the lifesaving station at Parramore Beach.

Surf was heavy, and a gale was blowing from the northeast. The surfmen from the station launched their boat but needed some two hours to cover the short distance (only some 200 yards) to the stranded vessel. On arriving at the ship, the rescuers found that the five-man crew had climbed into the rigging to escape the seas that were sweeping over the deck.

There was no way to bring the surfboat directly alongside the schooner, because the boat might get swamped. The best plan—risky as it seemed—was to attempt a rescue from the bowsprit. So, the surfmen told the crew to descend from the rigging and make their way toward the bow. While the crewmen did so, the lifesavers returned to the beach and bailed out their little craft. When the men on the schooner signaled that they were ready, the lifesavers set out again.

Back at the ship, the lifesavers tossed a line to the crew on *Shubert*, but the crewmen failed to catch it, and the surfboat drifted past the schooner. The rescu-

Harbors are sites of numerous wrecks and fires. (U.S. Coast Guard)

ers went back to the beach and tried again. This attempt succeeded.

Secured by a line to *Shubert*, the lifesavers then started the delicate, time-consuming business of taking the men off the schooner. The process was complicated and dangerous, because the boat was in constant danger of being swamped, and because the men had to wait for the right moment to leap into the boat. Eventually, however, all five men were rescued and taken to shore. The ship and cargo were a complete loss.

See also BOWSPRIT.

side-wheel steamers This category of ship was widely used in the 19th century and was propelled by two large paddle wheels, one on either side of the hull, approximately amidships. The wheels—which were several stories in height—were housed in casings, or "boxes," with the blades exposed only at the bottom. The rotary motion of the wheels propelled the ship as the blades "bit" into the water.

Many early steamships were built on this design. It was used on large ocean-going vessels such as the famed Collins liner *Arctic*, which sank in the North Atlantic in 1854 after colliding with an iron-hulled French vessel. Another famous sidewheeler was the excursion ship *General Slocum*, which burned in 1904 in New York's East River, with more than 1,000 killed.

The boxes on side-wheel steamers were sometimes works of art, decorated with intricate filigree patterns. Some vessels, notably certain steamships on the Mississippi River, had a single paddle wheel mounted at the stern, with no box around the wheel.

The scale of shipwrecks—even relatively modest ones—is enormous. Human figures are at bottom, center. (U.S. Coast Guard)

Side-wheel propulsion was used on large ships well into the early 20th century. The wheels worked reasonably well but were replaced eventually with the more efficient screw propellers.

Silver Shoals wreck, Bahamas   A hurricane in 1641 struck a Spanish convoy off the coast of Florida. Five ships were wrecked. Another vessel was damaged so badly that it drifted onto a reef in the Bahamas and was wrecked there, on a reef called Silver Shoals. One of the wrecked vessels was located a few days after the storm, several miles from shore, with a few survivors on board. Other survivors had tried to swim to land, the rescuers were told, but had been devoured by sharks.

Simoda Bay wrecks, Japan   Numerous ships in Simoda Bay were damaged or destroyed by a tsunami on December 22, 1854. The tsunami was estimated to be 50 to 75 feet high and apparently was associated with a powerful earthquake that struck the main island of Honshu on that date and caused extensive damage to Osaka and other cities. An officer on a frigate anchored in Simoda Bay reported later that the waves tossed ships at anchor against one another and damaged them severely. He also said that water in the bay rose and fell dramatically for hours after the initial wave struck.

See also TSUNAMIS.

***Sirio*, Italian immigrant ship**   The wreck of *Sirio* demonstrated how panic can kill as effectively as fire or explosion in a shipwreck. More than 400 persons are believed to have died when the 4,141-ton *Sirio* was wrecked on rocks on August 4, 1906, during a voyage to Cadiz. Of 1,214 people on board, 442 died in the wreck. The ship was sailing outside regular shipping lanes and was said to be carrying immigrants illegally.

Skuldelev knarr, **Viking sailing vessel, Denmark**

Though better known for their fearsome war craft, the longboats, the Vikings also made extensive use of the knarr, a sturdily built cargo vessel used to ply the stormy North Atlantic Ocean. The wreck of a knarr was excavated from 1957 to 1962 in Roskilde Fjord near Skuldelev, Denmark. The wreck dated from around 1000 A.D. The knarr in this case was some 54 feet long and about 15 feet wide, and was built largely of oak and pine. The ship was equipped with a single square sail. It appears that the knarr was essentially a big open boat and provided no shelter for people on board during rough weather. This kind of vessel is thought to have been used on Norse voyages to North America in pre-Columbian times.

sloop A single-masted sailing vessel, rigged fore-and-aft, with one headsail jib, and the mast set well forward.

See also FORE-AND-AFT.

Smith, Senator William Alden (1859–1932)

Senator Smith of Michigan, a member of the Senate Commerce Committee, headed the U.S. Senate's inquiry into the sinking of the British liner *Titanic* in 1912. Smith and his inquiry came under strong criticism in Britain, where it was thought that Americans had no business investigating the loss of a British liner. The British government ultimately adopted a policy of not commenting on the American investigation, so as to avoid the appearance of trying to interfere with the inquiry.

Smith saw the inquiry as an opportunity to shed light on the operations of shipping trusts. He used government authority to ensure that White Star Line chairman J. Bruce Ismay, a survivor of the wreck, would be present to answer the panel's questions. Twenty-nine crew members also received subpoenas and were instructed to appear before the Senate panel.

The American inquiry was less formal in its approach than the official British inquiry headed by Lord Mersey. The Senate panel allowed witnesses great freedom to tell their stories in their own words and thus succeeded in uncovering much information about the wreck.

The British press portrayed Smith as an incompetent clown and rustic politician. Although critics faulted him for ignorance of maritime matters (he asked one witness what an iceberg was made of, and was told, "ice"), he tended to ignore such criticisms. He once said that energy is often preferable to learning.

In a speech to the Senate after the inquiry was done, Smith praised the character of *Titanic's* Captain E. J. Smith but pointed out that the captain's overconfidence had contributed to *Titanic's* loss. The senator added that some lifeboats were not fully loaded, and the boats were manned poorly. He also castigated Captain Stanley Lord of the liner *Californian,* which had been within several miles of *Titanic* as the great liner sank, and said Lord bore a great responsibility for his inaction on that night. Senator Smith stopped short of blaming Ismay for *Titanic's* rush through an area where a hazard from ice was known to exist; but Smith did point out that Ismay's presence on *Titanic* had provided an incentive to high speed.

Smith's inquiry contributed to new legislation aimed at making ships safer and imposing some regulation on the free-for-all environment of wireless communications.

See also CALIFORNIAN INCIDENT; LORD, CAPTAIN STANLEY; TITANIC; WIRELESS.

Snow Squall, **American clipper ship**

A famous clipper ship, *Snow Squall* was caught in a severe storm in the Straits of Le Maire near Cape Horn in 1864 and damaged badly when driven aground. The ship managed to make its way to the Falkland Islands in the hope of making repairs, but the damage proved irreparable, and the ship's master sold the vessel to the Falkland Islands Company, which grounded the ship and used it to store wool. The ship eventually was abandoned, and a dock was built over the top of its hull. Marine archaeologists later took an interest in *Snow Squall* and removed much of the hull.

See also CLIPPER SHIPS; FALKLAND ISLANDS.

sonar The word "sonar" is short for "sound navigation and ranging." The term refers collectively to a variety of systems that use acoustical energy transmitted through sea water. Sonar may be used to detect the presence of an object underwater, estimate its size and range, and even produce a visual image of it. One variety of sonar used to find and explore shipwrecks is side-scan sonar, which uses high-frequency acoustic pulses of short duration. Reflections of these pulses are processed to yield an image of the sea bottom and objects on it. In some cases, the resulting image has almost the resolution of a good photograph. This system has been used successfully to locate wrecks including H.M.S. *Breadalbane* in the Arctic and *Titanic* on the floor of the North Atlantic.

See also BREADALBANE; TITANIC.

songs Popular songs and ballads about shipwrecks are so numerous that even a selected listing would fill several pages. Literary ballads about shipwrecks include the famous British ballad "Sir Padric Spens," about a mariner who is forced by political pressure to put to sea in a stormy season with a load of dignitaries on his ship; the vessel is wrecked, and the last one sees of the official passengers is their hats floating on the waters.

Ballads may be written from the viewpoint of women on shore, mourning the loss of their men at sea; a case in point is a ballad about Lady Jane Franklin, who helped organize several expeditions to search for her husband Sir John Franklin, a famed British explorer who was lost with all on his two ships during an expedition to the Canadian Arctic in the mid-19th century.

Twentieth-century songs about shipwrecks include some 300 works about, or somehow associated with, the wreck of the British liner R.M.S. *Titanic* in 1912. These songs have titles such as "The *Titanic's* Disaster," "My Sweetheart Went Down with the Ship" and "Just As the Ship Went Down." Among the most famous of late 20th-century songs about shipwrecks is folksinger Gordon Lightfoot's ballad "The Wreck of the *Edmund Fitzgerald,*" about the Great Lakes freighter that sank in a storm with the loss of all hands.

See also EDMUND FITZGERALD; FRANKLIN EXPEDITION; TITANIC.

Sophia, American merchant ship   *Sophia* was destroyed by a pitch pot heated in the wrong location. On May 5, 1789, the ship was anchored in Maryland's Chester River near Chestertown when the ship's carpenter tried to heat a pitch pot on board the vessel. This was a mistake. The pot should have been heated on shore. How great a mistake it was, the carpenter soon saw. The pot spilled by accident and set the ship on fire. The flames spread rapidly through the ship's recently tarred rigging, and soon *Sophia* was destroyed completely. No one on board was killed.

See also FIRE.

S.O.S.   This widely used international distress signal was conceived as a replacement for the Morse code distress signal C.Q.D., which predominated early in the 20th century. The S.O.S. signal (sometimes said to stand for "save our ship") was easier to remember and to recognize than the previous distress signal. The first use of the S.O.S. signal in a shipwreck is thought to have occurred in the sinking of the British liner R.M.S. *Titanic* in 1912.

See also TITANIC; WIRELESS.

soundings   Depth measurements, or soundings, have been vital to navigation along coastlines and on inland waterways. A sounding may be measured either in feet or in fathoms, a fathom traditionally being roughly six feet. The time-honored method of conducting a sounding was to toss a weight, or "lead," over the side on a line and retrieve it, measuring the depth by the line. Modern echo-sounding devices, which calculate depth on the basis of how long a reflected pulse of sound takes to return from the bottom, have supplanted the old method.

According to some legends of the sea, highly experienced sailors could tell where they were by tasting the mud on the lead after it was hauled up from the bottom. One such tale concerns a New England captain whose crew reportedly once tried to trick him by coating the lead with soil from a garden on Nantucket. The captain, so the story goes, took a taste and exclaimed that Nantucket had sunk!

See also FATHOM.

Spanish Armada, invasion fleet   A fleet of 127 ships sailed from Lisbon, Portugal, on May 28, 1588, in an effort by King Philip II of Spain to invade England. The ships carried some 30,000 men altogether. The armada had to fight several battles at sea, but was largely destroyed by severe weather rather than naval action, during an attempt to sail around Scotland and Ireland. As many as 10,000 men are thought to have been killed. Only about half (64) of the original 127 ships returned to Spain.

Spanish treasure fleet   Twelve ships in this fleet were wrecked in a hurricane on September 2, 1552, while preparing for a voyage from Veracruz, Mexico, to Havana and from there to Spain. Much of the ships' cargo was recovered.

Sparrowhawk, Dutch sailing vessel   The tiny *Sparrowhawk* was on a voyage from Formosa (now Taiwan) to Japan when a hurricane off the coast of Korea began to demolish the vessel. The crew managed to bring *Sparrowhawk* to an island about 15 miles from the Korean mainland, but found no place to anchor. Waves knocked a large hole in the hull and washed many men on deck into the sea. Thirty-six men are said to have survived the wreck. Twenty-eight men were killed, including the captain. The wreck occurred on August 15, 1654.

Sparrow Hawk, sailing vessel   In 1863, a storm uncovered the wreck of a small ship at Pleasant Bay on Cape Cod, Massachusetts. The remains of the vessel were collected and removed, and later reassembled for exhibit in Boston. Although not identified precisely, the wreck is thought to be that of *Sparrow*

Hawk, which was transporting 40 people to Plymouth, Massachusetts, in 1626 when the wreck occurred.

The recovered wreck also has been linked with a shipwreck cited by Massachusetts Governor William Bradford in his history of Plymouth Plantation for the years 1620–1647. Bradford mentions that a ship with many passengers aboard ran aground in Pleasant Bay in the winter of 1626. This ship was said to be on a voyage to Virginia when the wreck occurred. The captain was ill, and the ship reportedly was running out of provisions after more than a month and a half at sea. Friendly natives saved the survivors of the wreck and notified Bradford of the wreck and the survivors' need for assistance. According to one account, the ship was repaired but was destroyed by another storm and abandoned. This incident has historical significance as an early shipwreck in colonial America.

See also NATIVE AMERICANS.

***Squalus,* American submarine** *Squalus* is famed for the successful rescue operation that followed its sinking on May 23, 1939, during a dive off Portsmouth, New Hampshire.

The submarine sank because an electrical control panel did not show correctly the condition of all openings where water might enter. An air inlet remained open when the dive began, so that the submarine filled partially and sank to the bottom in about 240 feet of water.

The captain knew that rescue was possible at such a depth. He told the men to remain quiet and conserve their air supply. The following day, rescue operations began, using a bell that was lowered and positioned over the submarine's escape hatch. Thirty-three men were brought to the surface. Twenty-six others were killed in the sinking.

Squalus was refloated almost four months later. The sinking of *Squalus* resembled in some ways that of the British submarine *K-13,* which also sank because of a malfunctioning electrical control panel.

See also K-13; SUBMARINES.

square-rigged A square-rigged ship had sails arranged on spars mounted perpendicular, or square, to the ship's length. A brigantine is an example of a square-rigged ship.

See also FORE-AND-AFT.

stability and instability Instability has been a major cause of shipwrecks. An unstable ship is liable to capsize. Top-heaviness has been a problem with many vessels. A top-heavy ship may have trouble recovering from a roll or list, and continue rolling until it capsizes. Even a well-designed ship may encounter

problems with top-heaviness under certain conditions, as when a winter storm causes large amounts of ice to form on the ship's upperworks.

One famous case of instability causing a ship to sink is the loss of the American passenger steamer *Eastland,* which capsized at its pier in Chicago, Illinois, in 1915, killing 852 passengers.

A ship with a low center of gravity (the "balance point," one might say, of the vessel) tends to be more stable than a vessel with a high center of gravity. The lower the center of gravity, the more easily the ship can recover from a roll. Various steps may be taken to lower the center of gravity of a top-heavy ship, such as adding ballast.

See also EASTLAND.

***Stage,* Danish training ship** *Georg Stage* collided with the British steamship *Ancona* on the night of June 25, 1905. Twenty-two people, most of them boys, were drowned.

***Star of Bengal,* American bark** *Star of Bengal* was wrecked in a storm near Coronation Island, Alaska, on September 20, 1908. More than 100 people were killed, most of them Asian cannery workers.

***State of California,* American steamship** Forty people were killed in this wreck, which occurred on August 17, 1913, when *State of California* hit a shoal and sank rapidly in Gambier Bay, 90 miles from Juneau, Alaska. A passing vessel rescued approximately 80 survivors.

***State of Washington,* American river steamer** A boiler explosion destroyed this sternwheel steamer on the Columbia River during a voyage from Astoria, Washington, to Portland, Oregon, with an oil barge in tow on June 23, 1920. Damage was so extensive that a hawser connected to the barge was the only thing that kept the steamer afloat. One crewman was killed, and six others were injured.

***Stella,* British Channel ferry** *Stella* sank on March 30, 1899, after hitting Black Rock at the Casquets off the coast of France, while on a voyage from Southampton, England, in dense fog. Of some 200 people on board, about 100 went down with the ferry. The wreck was noted for the self-sacrifice of men who obeyed the rule of "women and children first" as the ship was being evacuated.

See also FERRIES.

stern The rear, or aft, portion of a ship. The ship's name and the name of its home port are commonly displayed on the stern. Although the stern does not appear to be as vulnerable to collision damage as the forward-pointing bow, the stern usually contains the fragile rudder and propellers, damage to which can disable a ship.

See also BOW.

Stevens, American schooner Sometimes a salvor has a nice piece of work drift simply into his path. That was what happened after the schooner *Emily Stevens* stranded on Clatsop Spit at the Columbia River (Oregon-Washington) bar on February 8, 1881. The crew gave up on their vessel and abandoned it, considering it a complete loss. That judgment was premature, however, for the schooner drifted off the shoal and out to sea, where a tug encountered the not-too-badly-damaged vessel and towed it to Astoria, Washington. The tug's master was awarded $950 for salvaging the ship.

storms Violent weather is one of the leading causes of shipwrecks. Storms may drive vessels ashore, onto rocks or shoals. High winds have dismasted sailing ships, ripping open their decks and leaving them to be flooded. Storm-driven waves may overwhelm ships. Cold-weather storms may cause ice to accumulate on the upperworks of ships, so that the vessels become top-heavy and capsize.

Even large vessels may be in danger from storms. Particular dangers may include rolling, which in extreme cases may cause a ship to capsize, and wave impact, which may smash portions of the hull or even extend far above the waterline to damage the upperworks. Cases of a large wave demolishing a ship's bridge are not unknown. Stresses imposed by storms may cause a ship to disintegrate, although modern steel-hull construction has made such incidents less likely than in the days of all-wooden vessels.

Weather forecasting has become much more reliable in the 1900s than in earlier centuries, but severe weather remains a major threat to shipping nonetheless, partly because local weather conditions can be highly unpredictable. A forecast of acceptable weather conditions for a given region may not rule out the possibility of highly localized storms arising suddenly and posing serious danger to shipping.

Strathairly, British steamship Bound from England to Cuba with a load of iron ore, *Strathairly* became stranded in fog on the Outer Banks of North Carolina near Chicamacomico lifesaving station around 4:30 A.M. on March 24, 1891. The ship's whistle of distress drew the attention of a patrolman on the beach, who burned a light to let the ship's crew know that some-

one had heard the signal. The patrolman went to get help, and a lifesaving team from Chicamacomico arrived at the scene only an hour after the steamer's stranding. The sea was very rough, and haste was required; but the fog made it impossible actually to see the ship. When the fog lifted around 10 A.M., *Strathairly* could be seen at last, lying in pieces in the surf. The ship had broken in two. Three men on board, including the captain, had been killed by the fall of the mainmast. The remaining 23 men on board had gathered on the bow section.

With the ship now visible, the men on shore tried firing a Lyle gun to carry a line to *Strathairly*. The shot fell short, as did a second attempt. A third shot reached the stricken ship, but the line broke. Further attempts were also unsuccessful, because the lines kept breaking. Meanwhile, the men on *Strathairly* were suffering severely from injuries and exposure. By midafternoon, one man on *Strathairly* became so desperate that he donned a life belt and leaped into the sea. He reached the shore alive, but just barely. The remaining survivors on *Strathairly* (three men had died on board by that time) jumped into the sea later that afternoon. Seven men survived. Ten bodies were recovered, but the bodies of the remaining nine men on *Strathairly* were never found.

The story of *Strathairly*'s wreck did not end here. A series of errors in recording and reporting the wreck led to confusion between *Strathairly* and another British ship, *St. Catharis*, that was wrecked on the Caroline Islands in the Pacific Ocean about the same time. One error led to another, and eventually even some residents of the Outer Banks came to believe that *St. Catharis*, rather than *Strathairly*, had been wrecked on the North Carolina coast.

See also LYLE GUN; OUTER BANKS; ST. CATHARIS.

Strathblane, British sailing vessel A faulty chronometer appears to have contributed to the loss of *Strathblane* on November 3, 1891, on a voyage from Honolulu to the Columbia River. The ship wrecked on the Oregon coast near Ocean Park. Seven people were killed, including Captain George Cuthell. Evidently the inaccurate chronometer led Cuthell to think he was 60 miles off the coast when his ship went ashore. Heavy surf made rescue operations difficult, and all but one of the vessel's boats were damaged or destroyed by the seas. In a heroic effort to reach safety, one damaged boat was repaired and launched, but capsized only a few feet from the ship and drowned all on board. The waves demolished *Strathblane* completely within hours after it struck the shore. The bodies of those killed in the wreck were buried in a cemetery at Ilwaco, Washington.

***Strathmore*, British clipper ship** *Strathmore* was wrecked on the Crozet Islands in the Indian Ocean on June 30, 1875. Of 88 people on board, 44 were killed in the wreck, and five more died while stranded on a small island for six months. Three of the fatalities occurred as a result of frostbitten feet. The castaways sustained themselves largely by eating birds and herbs that they found on the island. The 39 eventual survivors were rescued on January 21, 1876, by an American whaling vessel.

See also CASTAWAYS.

submarines Several features of submarines' design make them especially vulnerable to sinking. One is their submersible character. Mechanical malfunction or some other cause may prevent a submarine running beneath the surface from rising again. Also, the low profile of submarines makes them difficult for other ships to see under certain conditions. As a consequence, a submarine may be rammed and sunk by accident when another ship fails to see the submarine in time to change course and avoid it. At least one American submarine in peacetime, the nuclear submarine *Scorpion* in 1968, appears to have been sunk by an accident involving one of its own torpedoes. Although designed to withstand extreme pressure when submerged, a submarine's inner pressure hull may be vulnerable to collision damage, and crack under even a seemingly light impact with another vessel on the surface. A submarine crew may be rescued from the vessel after sinking, if the craft remains intact on its way to the bottom; if the water is not too deep for rescue operations; and if rescuers can reach the submarine before the oxygen on board is exhausted. Submarines have played a prominent role in causing shipwrecks, notably in such cases as the sinking of the British liner *Lusitania* in World War I and the German liner *Wilhelm Gustloff* in World War II.

See also LUSITANIA; SCORPION; THRESHER; WILHELM GUSTLOFF.

submersibles Manned undersea craft capable of diving to great depths and withstanding tremendous pressures, submersibles have been used to investigate shipwrecks and supply observational details that remote video equipment could not provide. Among the most famous submersibles is *Alvin*, of the Woods Hole Oceanographic Institution in Massachusetts. *Alvin* was used to explore the wreck of the British liner *Titanic* after the wreck was located by a joint French-American expedition in 1985. On its visits to *Titanic*, *Alvin* utilized a tethered, mobile camera system called "Jason Junior" to enter the wreck and photograph portions of its interior. Despite the tremendous amount of information and striking photo images they may yield, submersibles are not used extensively to explore shipwrecks, partly because of extensive demand for their services and because operating such craft is very expensive.

See also ALVIN; TITANIC; VIDEO.

suelto A small, single vessel (as distinct from a ship sailing in convoy) between Spain and the Americas during the era of the flota system, a *suelto* was able to visit out-of-the-way places not frequented by convoys. This freedom carried a disadvantage with it, however, because the individual *suelto*—unlike a convoy ship—could not take advantage of armed escorts for protection from corsairs and other hostile ships. Despite this hazard, many *suelto*s sailed between Europe and the Americas. Also, the lack of protection was not complete, since Spain kept a squadron of several galleons, known collectively as the Windward Armada, in the Caribbean Sea to provide some defense for *suelto*s and settlements in the region.

See also FLOTA SYSTEM.

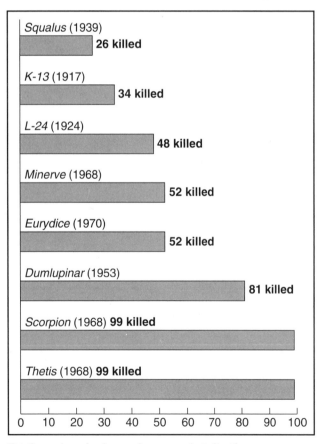

Deaths, submarine losses in noncombat situations, 1917–1970. (Nash, Jay Robert, *The Darkest Hour*, Prentice Hall. 1976)

***Suevic*, British cargo/passenger vessel** The White Star Line's small (12,000-ton) *Suevic* became stranded on Stag Rock at the Lizard, a dangerous stretch of shoreline on Britain's Cornish coast, on March 17, 1907. The bow was stuck on the rocks, but the stern remained afloat. The ship was salvaged by an interesting procedure. Because most of the machinery and other material that composed the ship's value was located in the after portion of the vessel, *Suevic* was blasted in two by explosives immediately astern of the bridge. The bow remained on the rocks, and the stern was towed away to have a new bow added. *Suevic* continued in service until 1942, when the ship was scuttled to prevent the Germans from taking possession of it.

See also SALVAGE.

***Sultana*, American steamer** A Mississippi River side-wheeler, *Sultana* exploded and burned on the night of April 26-27, 1865, after stopping at Vicksburg, Mississippi, during a trip from New Orleans, Louisiana, to Cincinnati, Ohio. Some 2,400 Union soldiers were on board, including many prisoners recently freed from Confederate prisoner of war camps.

A boiler exploded as the ship passed the Hens and Chickens Islands. The ship burned to the water line in the fire that followed the explosion. Approximately 1,500 people are thought to have died in the wreck of *Sultana,* although estimates of fatalities differ.

See also EXPLOSIONS; FIRE.

***Sunshine*, American schooner** A three-masted schooner of 326 tons, built in 1875 at what is now Coos Bay, Oregon, *Sunshine* is the center of a mystery of the sea. On a voyage from San Francisco to Oregon, *Sunshine* departed on November 3, 1875, and was not reported seen again for the next 15 days. Then the wreck of *Sunshine* was seen floating bottom-up off Cape Disappointment, on the northern side of the Columbia River mouth. The wreck washed ashore on November 22. No sign was found of the 25 persons on board *Sunshine* for its final voyage. There appears to be no explanation of what happened to the ship and those on it.

supernatural events The lore of the sea is full of stories of seemingly supernatural happenings, including apparitions of wrecked ships and ghostly mariners.

One widely told story of a supernatural occurrence at sea involves a ship's master who reportedly receives a mysterious message, either written on a slate or whispered to him, to steer a certain course. In some versions of the story, he is told that a human life depends on his following that instruction. The captain obeys and arrives just in time to save survivors of a shipwreck from death at sea. The bearer of the mysterious message is commonly supposed to be an angel.

"Haunted" vessels are also widely reported. "Ghosts" of crewmen or a deceased captain may be alleged to walk the decks of a ship. Such tales are almost always highly dubious, because many phenomena, from the creaking of a ship's members to a stray beam of moonlight, might be misinterpreted as a ghostly presence by an imaginative or superstitious witness; nor should the effects of rum on a sailor's perceptions be discounted.

A curious story in this category involves the mythological figure of "Davy Jones," a monstrous being that once was thought to appear in the rigging of ships just before they came to grief. A watery grave came to be known as "Davy Jones's locker."

Alleged apparitions of ships include the *Flying Dutchman,* a spectral sailing vessel said to haunt the waters off the Cape of Good Hope at the southern tip of Africa, and the New Haven specter ship, an apparition reported seen above the waters off New Haven, Connecticut.

Although such tales are entertaining, one ought to allow for hallucination, hoaxes and lively imagination when assigning a cause to reports of supernatural events at sea. Apparitions and so-called hauntings also may have natural explanations, such as St. Elmo's Fire (visible accumulations of static electricity) or flammable gases burning just above the waters.

Faith in supernatural powers that supposedly inhabited certain areas of water was part of Native American belief in colonial and pre-colonial times. Natives traveling certain stretches of water in canoes were said to toss food overboard to propitiate the spirits of the waters.

See also APPARITIONS; DAVY JONES'S LOCKER; MYSTERIES; MYTHOLOGY; NEW HAVEN SPECTER SHIP; ST. ELMO'S FIRE.

superstitions Numerous superstitions have attached themselves to shipwrecks. One such belief, for example, is that a renamed vessel supposedly will come to an untimely and unpleasant end. Superstitions, which typically involve prohibitions on certain practices, are distinct from myths, which usually involve fantastic beings such as giant octopi or supernatural figures such as the goblin-like Davy Jones.

See also DAVY JONES'S LOCKER; MYTHOLOGY; OCTOPI.

superstructure The portion of a ship above the main deck, the superstructure includes the bridge, rigging, funnels and many other structures. A too-high superstructure may make a ship top-heavy and therefore unstable.

surfboat An essential item of lifesaving work in the early days of the United States Lifesaving Service, the surfboat was a wooden boat with oars, designed to force its way through surf to reach vessels in distress offshore. The surfboat was commonly dragged to the beach on a four-wheeled wooden vehicle called a surfboat carriage. Operating the surfboat required great skill and tremendous muscle power on the part of the surfmen.

The operation of a surfboat—and the many dangers facing the boat and its crew—may be seen in the story of the schooner *Pearl Nelson,* which stranded about 450 feet offshore on the Virginia coast while en route from Wilmington, North Carolina, to Plymouth, Massachusetts, on February 24, 1882. The ship stranded in powerful winds and heavy seas near the False Cape lifesaving station, just north of the Virginia-North Carolina border.

The lifesavers from False Cape dragged the boat to the beach on its carriage and launched it into the surf. When the men reached the ship, their boat was dashed against the schooner with such force that the surfboat had to be taken aboard *Pearl Nelson* for repairs.

After repairs were completed, the lifesavers faced an additional problem. The schooner's crew—having seen the surfboat almost smashed to piece—declined to attempt the passage to shore in such a fragile craft.

So, the lifesavers returned to the beach in the surfboat and prepared to rescue the schooner's crew by breeches buoy. Eventually, all the men on *Pearl Nelson* were brought safely ashore. *Pearl Nelson* was pulled free by a tug the next day and towed to nearby Norfolk.

See also BREECHES BUOY.

surf zone The area along the shore where breakers arise and collapse, generating a dangerous expanse of turbulent water, the surf zone has been a special hazard to shipwrecked crews and their rescuers, because the turbulence makes it difficult to launch and maneuver rescue craft from shore. The waves also may contribute to the rapid destruction of a stranded vessel.

See also NEAR-SHORE ENVIRONMENT.

***Susanna,* Scottish merchant ship** Not even a ship moored in a seemingly secure anchorage is completely safe from wrecking. A case in point is the Scottish merchant vessel *Susanna. Susanna* was anchored at Port Tobacco Creek near Nansemond, Maryland, in January of 1749 when severe weather caused the creek (and much of Chesapeake Bay as well) to freeze over. *Susanna* was caught in the ice, which sliced through the hull. When the ice melted, *Susanna* sank.

***Swan* incident, Chesapeake Bay** The perils of shipboard life in the 18th century were many, and even a seemingly unlikely chain of events could destroy a ship. The experience of the brigantine *Swan* is a case in point. *Swan* was at a wharf in Maryland on July 21, 1753, when a candle flame ignited rum vapors as a cabin boy was filling a bottle from a hogshead of the liquid. The burning vapors caused the hogshead of rum to explode, and before long the ship had burned. The cabin boy was killed.

See also EXPLOSIONS; FIRE.

Switzer wreck, Virginia Many shipwrecks have involved immigrant vessels on their way from Europe to the Americas. An early example of such a wreck is that of a ship that carried some 300 German Protestants, known as "Switzers," from England to Virginia in 1738. The expedition was organized by one Colonel Brown.

The ship left England in August and experienced a highly unpleasant crossing of the Atlantic. The passengers suffered from tainted water and wretched food. Contagious disease killed some 60 of the passengers and crew. On top of these hardships, the vessel encountered rough weather.

The voyage was supposed to take two months. It lasted five months instead. By the time the immigrant ship approached the Virginia shore, provisions were exhausted.

At last, the vessel reached the Virginia capes and entered the mouth of Chesapeake Bay. The captain's plan was to anchor in Hampton Roads. The passengers were so near starvation, however, that they prevailed upon him to anchor immediately in Lynnhaven Bay and go ashore to find provisions. Although a storm was approaching, the captain agreed.

The search for provisions was unsuccessful. The captain and several passengers left the ship and explored a sandspit or island for a while but apparently found nothing that would help the suffering Switzers. Meanwhile, a winter storm arose from the northwest, destroyed the shore party's boat and left the captain and his companions stranded on the island, with no way to return to the ship.

The wind also wrecked the immigrant ship. One anchor chain parted, and the other anchor began dragging. Helpless, the ship was driven onto the shore. The seams parted, and water poured into the hull, drowning many of the passengers below decks.

Two small craft tried to reach the stricken ship. Colonel Brown, who had arrived some days earlier on another vessel and had been waiting in nearby Hampton for the immigrant ship's arrival, was in one of the two vessels that made their way to the Switzers. Among those in peril on the wrecked vessel were the colonel's four daughters.

The rescue craft were too small to carry all the survivors to safety, however, and many of the shipwrecked Switzers had to be put ashore at the nearest convenient point, despite the severe and chilly weather. Some of them apparently died of exposure on the beach, while others walked into and were lost in a marsh.

Of the 300 Switzers who left England on this voyage, fewer than 60 survived the wreck. All of Colonel Brown's daughters survived. The people of Virginia, led by Governor Gooch, received the survivors hospitably. The ship, however, appears to have been virtually a total loss. The wreck also created what the 20th century knows as a public relations problem. The loss of the immigrants and ship served to discourage further immigration.

See also IMMIGRATION.

Sylph, British warship A British sloop of war, *Sylph* was part of a blockade against American shipping in Long Island Sound, New York, in 1815. On January 16, 1815, a heavy snowstorm beset *Sylph* off Long Island's southern coast. The storm reduced visibility and was accompanied by large swells and strong winds. Captain Henry Dickens knew his approximate position, but was unable to judge it precisely and thus steered inadvertently onto a bar. Although Britain and America had been at war from 1812 to 1814 (a peace was arranged in December of 1814, about a month before the wreck of *Sylph*), the Long Islanders made a brave effort to rescue the men on the sloop. Winds and waves made it impossible to launch a boat at first, but eventually the Americans managed to reach *Sylph* and rescue the only six men left alive on the vessel. The rescue boat then returned to shore, where the Long Islanders cared for the shipwrecked Britons. The wreck is believed to have killed 127 people. The bodies of some of them washed ashore and were buried on Great South Beach.

See also STORMS.

T

Tabasco wrecks, Mexico Late in 1571, four merchant vessels from the Flota de Nueva España were wrecked on the Tabasco coast while on a voyage from Sanlucar, Spain, to Veracruz, Mexico. The ships included the 886-ton *La Magdelena,* the 550-ton *La María,* the 400-ton *Santa Catalina* and the 300-ton *San Juan.* The ships carried mercury and other cargo, most of which was recovered.

tacking In nautical terminology, "tacking" refers to the practice of changing course by altering the set of the sails. An individual change of course is called a tack, and a ship may be said to be on a starboard tack or port tack, depending on the direction of the change in course. "Tacking" may refer to a zigzag course produced by a series of individual tacks.

***Tamarac,* British (?) vessel** What we know of this wreck comes from the account of an anonymous clergyman who traveled on the *Tamarac* from Liverpool, England, on a voyage to New York and was wrecked at Islip, Long Island, New York, on January 3, 1837. According to his account, the voyage was a string of tragedies. One man on board was killed when a load of iron dropped on him. The cook jumped overboard and drowned after being punished for serving breakfast late. The mate suffered severe head injuries when a block fell from the yardarm and struck him. Then the ship was wrecked at Islip. No one was killed, but the ship was a complete loss.

***Tang,* American submarine** One of the most remarkable tales of shipwreck involves the sinking of the submarine *Tang* in World War II. On its last voyage in 1944, *Tang* went to the Taiwan Strait between the Chinese mainland and the island of Formosa (now Taiwan) and waited for Japanese ships to appear.

Tang sank numerous ships in the Taiwan Strait but was sunk at last by one of the submarine's own torpedoes, which traveled in a circle after firing, and blasted open three compartments on *Tang.* Nine men escaped from the stricken submarine immediately after the torpedo struck. Forty-nine men were killed, and 30 others remained alive in dry compartments as *Tang* settled to the sea floor some 180 feet down. The survivors on the seabed then had to listen to Japanese depth charges going off around them, because the Japanese did not know *Tang* had been sunk by one of its own torpedoes.

The trapped sailors made their predicament worse by burning secret papers, thus consuming precious oxygen. The atmosphere on board turned even worse after an electrical fire began in the forward battery compartment and released smoke into the air. Seventeen men trapped in the sunken submarine died there. Thirteen men managed to escape from the submarine by using the Davis Submarine Escape Apparatus, a self-contained underwater breathing device. Five of 13 failed to reach the surface alive; three others died after reaching the surface; and five were captured by the Japanese. Fifteen men in all were captured from *Tang.* Only nine of the 88 men on board *Tang* for this patrol survived both the sinking and the rigors of life in prisoner-of-war camp.

See also SUBMARINES.

Tangier Island wreck, Virginia One of the mysteries of marine archaeology is the story of the Tangier Island wreck. Tangier is a small island in Chesapeake Bay. Stories used to circulate on the island that a pirate vessel was wrecked on the island in 1610.

In 1926, a discovery on Tangier allegedly provided evidence that a shipwreck of some kind indeed had occurred there centuries earlier. A gale in February of 1926 reportedly uncovered the upperworks of a ship. Watermen from the island explored the wreck, dipping into the hold with oyster tongs to see what they might recover.

According to the story, the men retrieved several objects, including dishes and a battle-ax with a small stiletto concealed in the handle. The dishes were sold to an antique dealer, and someone from nearby Crisfield, Maryland, bought the ax for $10.

By April, word of the curious find had reached Baltimore, and before long the ax was brought to Baltimore's Peabody Institute for study by experts. They found that the still-sharp ax was made of Damascus steel, of such high quality that it was still unaffected by oxidation weeks after being removed from the water.

The ax was reportedly described as a medieval "pole ax" used widely in Latin countries. A brass shield on the ax could not be interpreted. The stiletto had a blade eight inches long. Before the ax could be taken to New York for further study, however, the artifact reportedly disappeared and was never relocated.

It is uncertain whether the tale of the Tangier Island wreck and the mysterious ax recovered from it were accurate, or whether the story was merely invented. Although there appears to be no material evidence to support the story, many artifacts are known to have survived centuries of immersion in good condition.

Moreover, there appears to have been a Spanish presence in Chesapeake Bay long before the first English settlement there in the early 17th century. Historian Donald Shomette, in his book *Shipwrecks on the Chesapeake,* describes numerous examples of Spanish expeditions and influence in the region, and suggests that the vessel allegedly lost on Tangier Island might have been a Spanish caravel that was sent to the bay to observe English fortifications believed to be under construction at Point Comfort, Virginia.

See also ARCHAEOLOGY; MYSTERIES.

***Tayleur*, British immigrant ship** Intended to carry immigrants to Australia, *Tayleur* sank on the second day of its initial voyage, near Dublin, Ireland, on January 20, 1854. Of more than 500 people on board, 349 were killed, including some 250 women and children. Although the ship was reportedly unstable and difficult to maneuver, the wreck appears to have occurred when anchor chains broke in heavy weather and allowed the ship to be driven onto shoals at Lambay Island.

***Telephone*, American side-wheel steamer** Advertised as the fastest sternwheeler in the world, the exquisitely appointed passenger steamer *Telephone* was destroyed by fire near Astoria, Washington, on November 20, 1887. During a fast passage on the Columbia River, the ship caught fire. Captain U. B. Scott turned the ship and ran it onto the river bank at a speed of 19 knots. Panic broke out among the passengers, who swarmed over the crewmen who were trying to preserve order. The passengers jumped onto the beach and made their way from the burning ship to safety. The captain had to leap through the pilot house window to escape, because the ladder had been consumed by flames. Firemen on shore put out the blaze, but only the hull survived the fire. All but one person on board, a drunken man, lived through the calamity. After the fire, the ship was rebuilt, and was even more elegant than the original *Telephone* but not quite as fast.

teredos, marine organisms Better known as shipworms, teredos are burrowing molluscs that can destroy the hull of a wooden ship in a matter of weeks or months. In the centuries before metal sheathing and all-metal hulls solved the shipworm problem, teredos were capable of sinking ships and indeed contributed to the failure of Christopher Columbus's fourth and final expedition to the New World. Teredos caused such extensive damage to Columbus's ships that they could not remain afloat. Columbus had to run his vessels ashore on the northern coast of Jamaica and wait there until a rescue vessel arrived.

See also COLUMBUS EXPEDITIONS; CONSTRUCTION; SHEATHING.

***Texanita*, Liberian tanker** *Texanita* collided with another Liberian tanker, the *Oswego Guardian,* and exploded on August 21, 1972, in fog off Cape Agulhas, South Africa. Only three men from *Texanita* survived. Forty-seven others were killed. The tanker sank in only four minutes. *Texanita* had unloaded its cargo, and its tanks were filled with highly explosive fumes at the time of the collision.

See also EXPLOSIONS.

Texas, United States With its lengthy coastline, Texas has had many notable shipwrecks and other maritime catastrophes. In 1533, for example, three Spanish treasure ships of the New Spain Fleet were wrecked on Padre Island; what happened to the crews of two of these ships is apparently unknown, but survivors of the third vessel reportedly were slaughtered by natives. Only two survivors of these wrecks are known for certain.

The hurricane of September 4, 1766, wrecked five Spanish ships on Galveston Island, including *El Nuevo Constante* and *La Caraquena,* also known as *Guipuzcuana.* Most people on these ships were saved.

Modern maritime calamities along the Texas shore include the Texas City explosions and fire of 1947, in which more than 550 people are thought to have been killed.

The Texas City, Texas, catastrophe of 1947 destroyed the waterfront. (U.S. Coast Guard)

Texas City, Texas, explosion   Located on Galveston Bay 10 miles north of the city of Galveston, Texas City was the site of a tremendous explosion on April 16, 1947.

More than 2,000 tons of extremely flammable fertilizer made with ammonium nitrate caught fire in the hold of the French cargo ship *Grandcamp*. Efforts to put out the fire with water failed, and steam jets were directed onto the fire instead. The steam raised the fertilizer to a temperature of 350 degrees, at which point the fertilizer exploded.

The explosion simply obliterated *Grandcamp*. Pieces of the vessel flew through the air and were recovered later at distances of up to five miles. The blast ignited oil dumps at Texas City. A second huge explosion followed when another vessel, *Highflyer*, had its cargo of ammonium nitrate ignited. *Highflyer* was destroyed, along with another ship, the *Keene*, beside it.

The explosions and fire at Texas City destroyed much of the community, killed 552 people and injured some 3,000. Two hundred people were missing after the catastrophe. More than $100 million in damage was reported.

See also EXPLOSIONS; HALIFAX, NOVA SCOTIA, EXPLOSION.

Thaxter, Celia, American poet (1836–1894)   Thaxter is remembered mainly for one of her poems, "A Tryst," which was published in 1874 and is sometimes cited in connection with the wreck of the British liner *Titanic* 38 years later. The poem describes a collision between a ship and an iceberg, with the loss of all on board. One stanza conveys the flavor of the work:

> O helmsman, turn thy wheel! Will no surmise
> Cleave through the midnight drear?
> No warning of the horrible surprise
> Reach thine unconscious ear?

Students of *Titanic*'s loss have suggested, or at least hinted, that Thaxter's poem might represent a precognition of *Titanic*'s collision with an iceberg in 1912. It takes a great leap of imagination, however, to see in "A Tryst" any identifiable references to the wreck of *Titanic*.

Thaxter spent most of her life on an island off the New Hampshire coast where her father served as a lighthouse keeper. She therefore must have been familiar with maritime lore and probably would have had no trouble incorporating tales of shipwrecks and icebergs into stories of her own.

See also PRECOGNITION AND PREMONITIONS; ROBERTSON, MORGAN; TITANIC.

***Thetis*, British frigate**   One of the most famous stories in the history of marine salvage is that of H.M.S. *Thetis*, a 46-ton frigate that sank near Brazil's Cape

Ship wreckage from the Texas City catastrophe. (U.S. Coast Guard)

Frio in 1830 with hundreds of thousands of dollars' worth of gold aboard. *Thetis* sailed from Rio de Janeiro on December 4, 1830, and sailed directly into cliffs two nights later. A current carried the ship away from the cliff, and *Thetis* sank some 1,800 feet away.

Conditions appeared unfavorable for salvage. The water was deep, currents were rapid, and storms occurred often in the vicinity. Yet Captain Thomas Dickinson thought salvage was possible. He had a diving bell built from a warship's iron water tank and utilized a pump to maintain adequate air pressure inside the makeshift bell. By late January of 1831, he was at Cape Frio, ready to start salvage operations.

The wreck of *Thetis* lay in water 35 to 70 feet deep, in a narrow cove. The situation required a derrick from which to suspend the bell. To make room for the derrick, he used explosives to remove part of the

northeastern cliff at the cove. To build the derrick, he used the spars and masts of *Thetis*, which had washed ashore nearby. When completed, the derrick weighed 40 tons and was more than 150 feet long.

Dickinson's bell was a success. He recovered some 16 percent of the sunken treasure by late May. Then operations using the bell had to be suspended when a storm wrecked the derrick. Delayed but not defeated, Dickinson continued work, using a smaller bell suspended from ropes stretched across the cove from one cliff to the other. This arrangement worked, and Dickinson recovered some three-fourths of the treasure.

For political reasons, Dickinson was replaced as leader of the salvage operation, but it continued nonetheless and soon had recovered almost all the sunken gold. When Dickinson returned to England, he reportedly found that one of his superiors had tried to take credit for Dickinson's work at the salvage site. Eventually, Dickinson received credit for his work, as well as a substantial salvage award.

See also SALVAGE; TREASURE.

Thetis, British submarine   *Thetis* sank on June 1, 1939, off Great Ormes Head in the Irish Sea because of an equipment malfunction. The captain and a lieutenant made their way out of the sunken submarine through an escape hatch and reached the surface. They told rescuers that the remaining men on *Thetis* were suffering from lack of oxygen. Two more men escaped several hours later.

Salvage teams attempted to pass cables around the submarine; the stern was above the surface, allowing salvors to try cutting a hole in the hull. Before any more men from *Thetis* could be rescued, however, the submarine slipped away and sank completely with 99 men still on board. They died of asphyxiation. Their bodies were recovered when *Thetis* finally was brought to the surface weeks later. The submarine was refitted and sent back into service as the *Thunderbolt*, and was sunk by an Italian warship in 1943.

See also SQUALUS; SUBMARINES.

Three Rivers, American steamship   The burning of the steamship *Three Rivers* in Chesapeake Bay on the night of July 4, 1924, was especially tragic in that it involved the deaths of five newsboys—children who delivered newspapers—who worked for the *Baltimore Sun*. The boys played in a band that promoted the newspaper. The band had performed that day at Crisfield, Maryland, and the boys were returning to Baltimore on *Three Rivers*. (The ship was named for the Patuxent, Potomac and Rappahannock Rivers, on which it traveled.) The fire, said to have been caused by a cigarette, reportedly started in the ship's saloon. Ten persons, five adults and five children, died in the fire. The ship's upperworks burned, but the metal hull survived and later was converted into a barge.

The newsboys' band was a colorful institution in the Baltimore of the 1920s. Famed bandleader John Philip Sousa conducted the band in one concert. On another occasion, baseball player Babe Ruth led the band in an original composition called "Battering Babe."

See also FIRE.

Three Saints, Russian sailing vessel   This voyage was a memorable experience for passenger Alexander Baranof, a merchant. After the ship was wrecked in 1790 off Unalaska Island, Alaska, Baranof spent the winter on the island, then used a native boat to complete his journey to Three Saints Bay, some 600 miles away.

Thresher, American nuclear submarine   One of two U.S. nuclear submarines lost at sea in the 1960s (*Scorpion*, sunk in 1968, was the other), *Thresher* sank on April 10, 1963, about 220 miles east of Cape Cod, Massachusetts, during what was supposed to be a routine cruise to check repairs made recently to the submarine. *Thresher*'s designation was SSN-593. The submarine rescue vessel *Skylark* accompanied *Thresher* on this voyage.

After *Thresher* submerged for a test dive on the morning of April 10, *Skylark* received a message from the submarine. It began, "Have position up angle," and added that the sub was attempting to blow its ballast tanks. This apparently meant that the submarine was inclined considerably off the horizontal, and the crew was trying to correct the angle by pumping water out of ballast tanks. Another message allegedly came through soon afterward but was garbled and included what sounded like the noise of the submarine breaking up. *Thresher* did not return to the surface. All 129 persons on board, including several civilians, were killed.

Some evidence of the sinking was discovered on the surface over the next few days, including an oil slick and bits of cork and plastic that might have come from *Thresher*. This evidence was not enough to determine reliably what had happened to *Thresher*, however, and the Navy used advanced undersea search technology including the famous bathyscaphe *Trieste* to find and investigate the submarine's wreckage. The bathyscaphe was a submersible that consisted of a spherical chamber suspended under a large "float" filled with gasoline. Because gasoline is less dense than water, the float acted as a balloon does in air, providing buoyancy to lift the craft back to the surface after its mission on the seabed was done.

Trieste found a shoe cover similar to those worn by reactor specialists on board *Thresher*. Other pieces of debris also were visible. On a later dive, *Trieste* found an extensive debris field that was identified as belonging to the wreck of *Thresher*. *Trieste* recovered some of the debris and brought it to the surface for study. One piece of debris was inscribed "593 boat," indicating it had been part of *Thresher*.

The loss of *Thresher* was attributed to mechanical failure. According to one theory, a small leak developed while the vessel was submerged, and the inflow of water caused an electrical failure that resulted in the submarine's destruction. Presumably, the power

The U.S. submarine *Thresher*, shown here in a diagram, apparently developed mechanical trouble (left), sank below crush depth (dotted line, center), imploded and was scattered in numerous pieces across the seabed. (D. Ritchie)

failure left *Thresher* unable to rise to the surface and the sub collapsed under tremendous water pressure when it sank below its "crush depth."

See also SCORPION; SUBMARINES; SUBMERSIBLES.

Tierra Firme Armada, 1659   Three hundred men survived the wreck of the nao *Santiago*, which wrecked on Cozumel, Mexico, during a storm. The survivors were rescued after two months. Three other ships from this fleet were also lost.

***Tiger*, Dutch sailing vessel**   An example of the dangers of fire on wooden vessels, the wreck of *Tiger* occurred early in 1614 on a voyage to map the coast of what would become the northeastern United States. Under the command of Captain Adrian Block, *Tiger* was anchored during bitter winter weather near Manhattan Island when the ship's stove set fire to the galley. The highly flammable materials of the ship (including pitch and tar used to make seams in the hull waterproof) allowed the fire to consume the

vessel, and the ship sank. Block and his men built another ship, named *Onrust*, to replace *Tiger*. The expedition later returned successfully to the Netherlands. A wreck believed to be that of *Tiger* was discovered during a subway excavation in New York City some three centuries later.

See also FIRE.

***Titanic*, British passenger liner**   The wreck of the Royal Mail Steamer *Titanic* on the night of April 14–15, 1912, in the North Atlantic, is probably the most famous single shipwreck, although not the most costly in terms of loss of life. The liner struck an iceberg and sank with the loss of 1,517 lives. The ship did not carry enough lifeboats for all on board.

Titanic belonged to the White Star Line, rival to Cunard. Built between 1910 and 1912 at the Harland and Wolff yard in Belfast, Northern Ireland, *Titanic* was 882.5 feet long and 92.5 feet across the beam, with 45,000 tons displacement. The ship had a crew of 700.

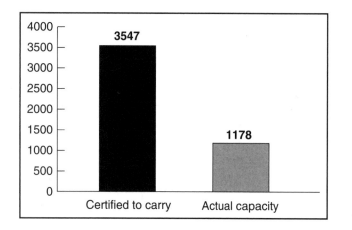

The ship was considered practically "unsinkable" because of its compartmentalized hull. Watertight doors in bulkheads could be activated to seal off one compartment from another and, in theory, to contain flooding if anything should breach the hull in a given compartment.

At the time, damage from a collision affecting two adjacent compartments appears to have been the worst damage imaginable. The ship proved unable to cope, however, with a glancing blow from an iceberg, which laid open six watertight compartments at the bow. As the bow went down, water from flooded compartments spilled over the inadequate bulkheads into adjacent compartments, so that the ship flooded progressively and sank.

Titanic's departure from Southampton, England, on April 10 was marked by an ominous incident involving the liner *New York*, which was moored at Berth 38. *Titanic*'s passage caused *New York* to tear loose from its moorings and move toward *Titanic*. The quick work of Captain Smith on *Titanic* helped prevent a collision. Smith gave the order "Full astern" as soon as he saw what was happening. The order stopped

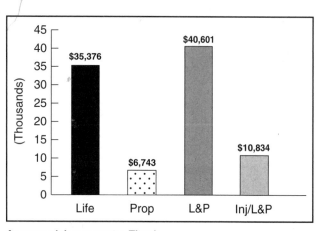

Average claim amounts, *Titanic*.

Titanic's forward motion, and *New York* missed *Titanic*, although by only a few feet. The incident later was interpreted as an indication that liners had become so large that their performance was not yet understood clearly.

Titanic received numerous wireless messages warning of ice before the collision occurred. *Mesaba*, for example, sailing ahead of *Titanic*, warned at 9:40 P.M. on April 14 that she had encountered heavy pack ice and numerous icebergs.

The circumstances of *Titanic*'s collision with the iceberg are not entirely clear. According to one account, there was haze over the water, although other descriptions of the weather that night indicate that visibility was excellent, with stars on the horizon casting reflections on the water. The aforementioned message from *Mesaba* described weather as "good" and "clear."

Also, in one attempt to account for the collision, the iceberg was described as black. Yet, eyewitnesses on *Titanic* saw the iceberg pass the ship and mistook the iceberg for a sailing vessel—hardly the interpretation one would expect of a black iceberg. Also, the International Ice Patrol, formed after *Titanic*'s loss to monitor icebergs in the North Atlantic, reportedly has no record of ever seeing an iceberg of that color.

The first to spot the iceberg was lookout Frederick Fleet, in *Titanic*'s crow's nest. "Iceberg, right ahead," he reported on the telephone to the bridge. The first officer tried to turn to port (that is, left) and pass around the iceberg, but the liner sideswiped the iceberg with a noise that was compared to the tearing of a long strip of cloth. Pieces of ice fell through open portholes.

An inspection showed that the first six compartments were holed, and that the ship would fill completely and sink in a matter of hours. The crew tried to maintain calm among passengers while advising them to assemble on deck with their lifebelts. *Titanic* sent out one of the most famous distress messages in history: "CQD MGY I REQUIRE ASSISTANCE IMMEDIATELY STRUCK BY ICEBERG IN POSITION 41 46 N 50 14 W." (MGY was *Titanic*'s wireless identification.) Later, in another historic signal, *Titanic* would become the first ship ever to use the new distress code, S.O.S., in an emergency.

Among the ships that picked up *Titanic*'s message was the Cunard liner *Carpathia*, under command of Captain Arthur Rostron. He had his vessel turn immediately and raced to *Titanic*'s position through waters filled with icebergs.

As *Carpathia* came to the rescue, *Titanic* sank by the bow. The forward funnel collapsed and fell into the water, killing many people in the water. As the stern

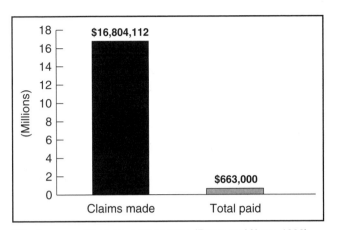

Titanic case, claims vs. settlements. (Eaton and Haas, 1986)

rose into the air, the ship broke in two between the third and fourth funnels. The bow section fell to the ocean floor, while the stern remained afloat for a few minutes before sinking.

One especially controversial element of *Titanic's* wreck was the role of the liner *Californian*, which allegedly lay several miles from *Titanic* on the night of the catastrophe but did not come to *Titanic's* aid, even though *Californian's* crew saw a ship consistent in appearance with *Titanic*, as well as rockets that matched the description of *Titanic's* distress signals. Captain Stanley Lord of *Californian* became notorious for inaction in this case, and was known afterward as "Lord of the *Californian*," even though he had an otherwise exemplary record as a ship's master. Lord acquired a highly vocal group of defenders, known as "Lordites."

Carpathia arrived at *Titanic's* position several hours later and picked up survivors. By this time *Californian* also was aware of *Titanic's* loss and proceeded to the scene. *Carpathia* left *Californian* to search the area, then proceeded to New York.

Numerous myths and dubious stories have arisen around accounts of *Titanic's* loss. One such story, evidently, is that the ship's orchestra played the hymn, "Nearer, My God, to Thee," as *Titanic* sank. According to another questionable report, the orchestra played the hymn "Autumn." It has been suggested that the latter story arose when someone confused the hymn with a piece of popular music, "Songe d'Automne" ("Autumn Song"), which was part of the orchestra's repertory.

An industry of sorts has developed around the *Titanic* wreck, producing books, motion pictures and various memorabilia about the liner's loss. Numerous films have dramatized the wreck, notably the 1953 motion picture *Titanic*, starring Clifton Webb and Barbara Stanwyck, and the 1958 movie *A Night to Remem-*

ber, with Kenneth More and Alec McCowen. One of the passengers, Denver socialite Molly Brown, became the subject of a famous American musical, *The Unsinkable Molly Brown*. Authors of fiction and nonfiction have devoted numerous works to the wreck. The best-known nonfiction work about *Titanic* is probably Walter Lord's *A Night to Remember*. Lord also wrote a sequel entitled *The Night Lives On*. Michael Davie's *Titanic: The Death and Life of a Legend* is a thorough examination of the liner's loss.

Titanic's influence on popular culture has been tremendous. The ship's name has become a synonym for calamity at sea, and "rearranging the deck chairs on the *Titanic*" is now a commonly used expression for an inadequate response to a crisis. The wreck brought about improved safety standards for passenger vessels and led to the formation of the International Ice Patrol.

Among the casualties of *Titanic's* sinking were Captain Edward Smith, who reportedly stood on the bridge as it went under; President William Howard Taft's aide, Major Archibald Butt, who allegedly vowed to shoot the first man who tried to reach the lifeboats before women and children were put aboard; New York retail store magnate Isidor Straus and his wife Ida, who remained together and both perished, even though Mrs. Straus had an opportunity to get into a lifeboat; and Colonel John Jacob Astor, for whose family the Waldorf-Astoria hotel in New York City was named.

Widely perceived as a villain in the aftermath of the sinking was White Star Line's president, Joseph Bruce Ismay, who survived the wreck. According to popular sentiment, Ismay should have gone down with his

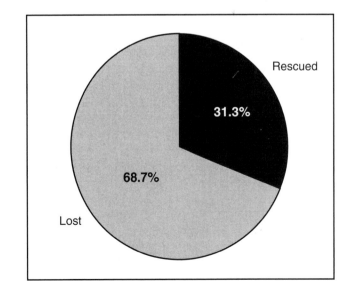

Titanic, passengers and crew.

ship, as did Captain Smith. After the wreck, Ismay retired to his estate and withdrew from public life.

Captain Smith, though perceived as a hero for going down with the liner, also was faulted for apparently allowing *Titanic* to proceed at an unsafe speed through a known ice field, possibly in response to pressure to make a record crossing.

Two official inquiries were held following the wreck, one in Britain and one in the United States. The inquiries proceeded along different lines. The American inquiry was largely informal and allowed witnesses to describe events in their own words, whereas the more structured British proceedings yielded less information. The mere existence of an independent American inquiry drew widespread criticism in Britain, where it was thought that Americans had no business investigating the loss of a British vessel, despite the presence of many Americans aboard.

Various notable pieces of public statuary in Britain and the United States were commissioned and dedicated following the catastrophe. These monuments included a statue of Captain Smith in Lichfield, England; a monument to bandleader Wallace Hartley in Colne, Lancashire; and a memorial to Isidor and Ida Straus at Broadway and West 106th Street in New York City.

Titanic was sister ship to *Olympic,* which was involved in several notable shipwrecks, although never sunk itself. *Titanic*'s other sister ship, *Britannic,* was sunk during World War I while serving as a hospital ship.

The wreck of *Titanic* was discovered at the bottom of the Atlantic in 1985 by a joint American-French expedition using remote-controlled photographic equipment. The wreck was discovered to be in two major pieces. The bow section reached the bottom largely intact and was found upright. The stern section was damaged severely in its descent and was located several hundred yards away from the bow. Debris from the wreck lay scattered around and between the two segments of the wreck. Subsequent expeditions using manned submersibles have explored the wreck and recovered numerous items from the debris field.

See also ALVIN; BRITANNIC; COLLISIONS; CONSTRUCTION; ICEBERGS; OLYMPIC; SMITH, SENATOR WILLIAM ALDEN; SHIPWRECKS, SOCIAL IMPACT OF; SUBMERSIBLES.

Tobago   Located in the Lesser Antilles island chain, Tobago is noted for a major battle that occurred in 1677 between a Dutch and a French fleet in Palmit Bay. The French fleet was destroyed, but no record of the number and names of the sunken ships appears to have survived. Many other shipwrecks have oc-

curred in the waters around Tobago, including the loss of five unnamed Spanish merchant ships that were reportedly wrecked in 1572 while on a voyage to Veracruz, Mexico, from Spain. Much of their cargo is thought to have been salvaged.

tonnage   This measure of a ship's cargo capacity is thought to have originated in the 13th century. At that time, one of the most widely carried cargoes was wine in large casks known as "tuns." An English tun contained approximately 250 gallons of wine and weighed some 2,240 pounds. When European nations started colonizing the Americas, "tun" had become "ton." The weight remained unchanged, but the volume assigned per ton had increased from 57 cubic feet under the old measure to 100 cubic feet by the 17th century. Tonnage of ships using English ports was estimated using a simple formula:

$$\frac{\text{Length of keel} \times \text{width of hull} \times \text{depth of hold}}{\text{constant}} = \text{Tons burden}$$

The constant was changed from time to time, historian J. Richard Steffy points out in an essay in George Bass's 1988 anthology *Ships and Shipwrecks of the Americas.* The constant was 100 for much of the 1600s but was changed to 94 in 1694, when a ton was refigured at 94 cubic feet. Ships of 200 to 400 tons were commonplace in the 17th century, although some comparatively huge ships of 1,000 tons or more existed.

***Tonquin,* American warship**   The tragic story of the *Tonquin* demonstrates how poor leadership, stormy weather and dangerous waters combined to produce catastrophe during an early attempt at colonizing the Pacific Northwest of the United States.

The wealthy New York tradesman John Jacob Astor (one of whose descendants would die in the most famous shipwreck in history, that of the British liner *Titanic,* more than a century later) sent out an expedition in 1810 on the 10-gun *Tonquin* to set up a trading post at the mouth of the Columbia River (Oregon-Washington).

Under command of Captain Jonathan Thorn, the ship had a 33-man crew made up in part of French Canadians and Highland Scots, two peoples not known for their docility. The crew reportedly chafed under the rigid discipline of Captain Thorn until the men were in a mutinous frame of mind.

After about seven and a half months at sea, *Tonquin* reached the mouth of the Columbia River on March 22, 1811. Despite a strong wind that generated a rough sea along the Columbia River bar, Thorn ordered First

Officer William Fox to take a whaleboat to make soundings, or depth measurements.

In view of the rough waters, Fox objected. Thorn responded, in effect, by calling him a coward. Fox then obeyed the captain's orders but evidently paid for his obedience with his life. When Fox and several other men set out in the whaleboat, they were lost in the angry sea.

The wind diminished the next day. *Tonquin* managed to drop anchor in some 84 feet of water north of the river's mouth. At the same time, *Tonquin* came to the attention of natives, who gathered along the shore and made ready to visit the ship in their canoes to trade.

Tonquin, however, still had to cross the dangerous Columbia River bar. Thorn tried again to send out a boat to take soundings. This time, the boat capsized but the men in it were rescued. Another attempt with the same boat also was unsuccessful.

The sea was driving *Tonquin* toward the shore. The men of *Tonquin* quickly assembled a small schooner that they carried on board, and sent the little craft out to seek a safe passage past the bar and into the river. The schooner's crew succeeded in finding a safe channel, but capsized on the way back to *Tonquin* and dumped the men into the water.

Before it could come to the aid of the schooner, *Tonquin* struck a shoal and appeared to be near sinking. Then the tide raised *Tonquin* off the shoal, and the ship passed over the bar intact.

Although the natives wanted to trade, the men of *Tonquin* were preoccupied at first with finding and rescuing the schooner's crew. Two or three of the men turned up alive, but the rest were lost. The schooner was recovered and repaired.

Soon the expedition got down to the business of founding a settlement. They chose a site near Smith Point, on the south bank of the river. After its cargo was unloaded, *Tonquin* set sail again on June 5 for Vancouver Island. On board was one Lamazee, a native who asked, and was given permission, to accompany the ship as interpreter.

More than two years afterward, Lamazee returned to the mouth of the Columbia River with a fantastic story. He was (he said) the only survivor of *Tonquin*. According to Lamazee's story, the ship had encountered natives whose chief had antagonized Captain Thorn. Exasperated, Thorn tossed the chief over the side.

The next day, the enraged natives attacked *Tonquin* and murdered Thorn. Of the men on *Tonquin*, all but Lamazee and four other members of the crew were also killed. Those four survivors used rifle shot to keep the natives at bay. Three of the survivors appar-

ently lost their nerve during the night, however, and tried to escape in a boat. Bad weather drove them to shore, where they were discovered, captured and killed by torture.

One crewman—the ship's clerk, a man named Lewis—remained on *Tonquin*. According to Lamazee, Lewis touched off the ship's magazine as natives swarmed over the ship and looted the vessel. *Tonquin* blew up. The explosion reportedly killed more than 60 natives and injured many others.

See also COLUMBIA RIVER BAR; EXPLOSIONS; NATIVE AMERICANS; SCHOONER; SOUNDINGS; TITANIC.

torpedoes Torpedoes fired by naval vessels have sunk non-combatant ships on numerous occasions. A famous case in point is the sinking of the British liner *Lusitania* in 1917 by a German submarine off Ireland's Old Head of Kinsale. Because a torpedo's high-explosive warhead contains tremendous destructive power, it can blast a hole perhaps 20 feet wide in a typical ship's hull, which is made of steel an inch or less in thickness. The shipwreck widely thought to be the worst of all time in terms of lives lost (6,000–10,000 dead estimated), the sinking of the German liner *Wilhelm Gustloff* in 1945, occurred when a Russian submarine carried out a torpedo attack on the ship.

Despite the torpedo's power, many ships have survived torpedo attack and managed to reach port for repairs. In one highly unusual incident, the American nuclear submarine *Scorpion* is believed to have been sunk by one of its own torpedoes in 1968.

See also MINES; SCORPION; SUBMARINES.

***Toyo Maru*, Japanese ferry** Although this wreck appears to be little known outside Japan, it reportedly killed more people than died on the *Titanic*. Operating between the main Japanese island of Honshu and the northern island of Hokkaido, the ferry was caught in a hurricane in Tsugaru Straits on September 26, 1954. The storm damaged the engines. The ferry reached the harbor at Hakodate, when the ship hit a reef and sank. The wreck allegedly killed 1,600 people.

See also ROCKS AND SHOALS; STORMS.

treasure Rumors of sunken treasure have done much to encourage interest in shipwrecks and salvage, but many tales of such treasure are merely legends. The British liner *Titanic*, for example, was rumored to have sunk in 1912 with great wealth still locked in the purser's safe, but it appears that anything of major value was removed from the purser's keeping before the liner sank.

Numerous stories have circulated of abundant sunken treasure in the Caribbean Sea, where Spanish vessels sank while carrying gold and silver from Spain's American colonies to Europe. Much of the treasure that can be recovered from such wrecks is thought to have been recovered already, however, so that what remains may be of value only to marine archaeologists. In short, reports of sunken treasure seem likely to yield riches only for authors of romantic fiction.

See also ARCHAEOLOGY.

Trenton, **United States Navy corvette**   The 3,900-ton *Trenton* was one of several naval vessels of various nationalities that was caught in a hurricane and sunk off the islands of American Samoa on March 16, 1889. Only one person on *Trenton* was killed, but a total of 147 sailors reportedly died as a result of the storm. Other ships sunk included the American gunboat *Vandalia* and the German ships *Adler*, *Olga* and *Eber*.

Trevessa, **British steamship**   The story of the steamer *Trevessa* is a famous account of survival following shipwreck. *Trevessa* sank in a storm in the Indian Ocean on June 4, 1923. The 48 officers and crewmen escaped in boats. Each boat carried nine gallons of water, 130 tins of condensed milk and six tins of biscuits. Despite the provisions, several men died at sea. Because one boat traveled faster than the other, the two boats separated. They eventually reached land 25 days apart after traveling some 2,300 miles over the Indian Ocean, in one of the most lengthy open-boat journeys ever made.

Trinidad   Located in the Lesser Antilles, Trinidad has been the site of many shipwrecks. Among the most notable of these are five Spanish warships that were burned in February of 1797 to keep them from falling into the hands of an English fleet under command of Sir Henry Harvey. The destroyed Spanish ships included the 80-gun *Capitana* and *San Vicente*, the 74-gun *almiranta Arrogante*, the 74-gun *Gallardo*, the 74-gun *San Damasco* and the 34-gun *Concha*. Some artifacts from the wrecks have been salvaged.

Trinidad, **American schooner**   In one of the most famous rescues in American maritime history, a Coast Guard motor lifeboat saved 21 men from the wreck of *Trinidad* on Willapa bar on the coast of Washington state on May 7, 1937. Caught in a gale, the ship was driven onto a shoal near Willapa Light. Brilliant maneuvering by the Coast Guard boat allowed the rescuers to save all but one person from *Trinidad*. (One crewman was killed in the rescue attempt.) The boat's crew received a Congressional Medal for the greatest act of lifesaving that year.

Trinidad, **Spanish caravel**   Mystery surrounds the alleged loss of this little 35-ton vessel, one of three under command of Captain Francisco de Ulloa on a voyage in 1539–1540 along the western coasts of what are now Mexico and California. Before the three ships entered waters off California, one of the vessels was scuttled and another had to return to Mexico. The third caravel, *Trinidad*, made its way to what is now the San Diego area by mid-1540. All the men on *Trinidad* were sent ashore because of illness. Then the ship was lost when its anchor cable broke during a storm. *Trinidad* reportedly drifted away and was never seen again by its crew. The ship became news in the 20th century in connection with a claim that the wreck had been found and treasure had been recovered from it. Marine archaeologist Robert Marx, in his book *Shipwrecks in the Americas*, discounts those modern claims. Marx writes that no proof was offered of the ship's discovery and the retrieval of the alleged treasure. He adds that it is unlikely the ship carried treasure of any kind, although crewmen may have had belongings of some value aboard.

Triple Hurricanes   A series of severe storms known as the Triple Hurricanes caused tremendous destruction to shipping in the northeastern United States in 1839. The first storm arrived in New England on the night of December 14–15, 1839. The storm began with snow and strong wind, and cast numerous ships at Gloucester, Massachusetts, onto the beach. The beaches of Cape Cod, Massachusetts, were littered with the wreckage of ships, and dozens of vessels were damaged or sunk in Boston harbor. A second storm arrived on December 22, with effects comparable to those of the first storm. The third storm was the most severe and arrived on December 27, but reportedly was not as destructive of life and property, partly because the people of New England were prepared for it and partly because the earlier storms already had destroyed much of what could be wrecked. This third storm involved such a high tide that the mooring lines of a ship in Boston harbor slipped off the pilings to which the ship was tied, and the vessel drifted into a drawbridge, wrecking the bridgetender's house. This series of storms gave rise to Henry Wadsworth Longfellow's famous poem "The Wreck of the *Hesperus*."

See also HESPERUS; NEW ENGLAND; STORMS.

Troy, **British warship**   The sloop-of-war *Troy* was sailing from Campeche, Mexico, to Jamaica when lost on Mexico's Alacran Reef on November 11, 1816. No one on board was killed. The wreck later became a significant archaelogical site under the auspices of CEDAM, Mexico's marine archaeology society.

See also CAMPECHE; CEDAM.

Truculent, British submarine   A Swedish tanker struck *Truculent* on January 12, 1950, during the submarine's trials in the Thames River. The submarine sank. Some men on *Truculent* used escape hatches to make their way to the surface, but some of them died in the cold water. Only 15 of 70 men on board survived the sinking. An investigation concluded that the responsibility for the wreck belonged largely to *Truculent*, because the Swedish ship had displayed warning lights properly.

See also SQUALUS; SUBMARINES; THETIS.

Trumbull, American sloop   Maritime historian Edward Rowe Snow, in his book *Marine Mysteries and Dramatic Disasters*, tells the sad story of the sloop *Trumbull* and the lifesavers that perished while trying to rescue the vessel's crew.

The sloop went aground on a sandbar near the Peaked Hill Bars lifesaving station on Cape Cod, Massachusetts, on November 30, 1880, while on a voyage from Rockport, Maine, to New York with a cargo of granite.

The lifesavers launched a boat and rowed out to *Trumbull*. The lifesavers' captain, one David Atkins, was unable to bring his boat close enough to *Trumbull*, and so he told the sloop's crew to leap into the water, where the boat could pick them up. Three out of five men on board jumped into the sea, but two—the sloop's mate and captain—remained on board, where they felt safer.

After the boat returned to shore, Atkins decided to try again. On this trip, the boat overturned, and Atkins and two surfmen drowned. The three surviving surfmen swam back to shore.

As it happened, there was no need for the second trip to *Trumbull*; the sloop floated free of the sandbar and sailed away.

Truxton, American destroyer   *Truxton* and a companion vessel, the supply ship *Pollux*, sank in a gale off the Newfoundland coast on February 18, 1942. More than 100 men were rescued, but 189 perished, including *Truxton*'s commander.

tsunamis   Better (but inaccurately) known as "tidal waves," tsunamis are seismic sea waves generated by earthquakes or associated disturbances. A tsunami can cause tremendous destruction on shore, and tsunamis have been the cause of numerous shipwrecks. A detailed report of several such incidents is included in the report of Lieutenant J. G. Billings of U.S.S. *Wateree*, a naval vessel that was caught in a tsunami at the port of Arica, Peru, in 1868. Billings described how the wave wrecked several large vessels in the harbor and virtually annihilated the town. Another famous tsunami is the one that followed the Good Friday earthquake in Alaska on March 27, 1964. The wave carried fishing vessels inland at Kodiak, Alaska, and destroyed almost half the local fishing fleet. The wave caused extensive damage as far away as Crescent City, California.

Perhaps the most famous tsunami in history followed the explosion of the volcanic island Krakatoa between Java and Sumatra in Indonesia in 1883. That tsunami caused massive destruction and loss of life along shores in the vicinity of Krakatoa, and was detectable in the English Channel. Estimates of the loss of life from this tsunami range between 30,000 and 80,000, but such estimates are little more than guesses. The crew of the steamer *Loudon*, which was in the Bay of Lampong about 50 miles northwest of Krakatoa at the time of the explosion, saw the wave approaching and hastily turned their vessel bow-on to the wave, hoping to ride up and over it. *Loudon* survived, but the community of Telok Betong, on shore, did not. The wave inundated Telok Betong and destroyed the town completely.

As such cases indicate, a tsunami may travel thousands of miles from its point of origin with much of its initial energy intact, because water is very efficient at transmitting such energy over long distances. The tsunami may not be perceptible as a wave to ships in mid-ocean, because the wave is extremely long in relation to its height. Consequently, a ship at sea may

A tsunami, shown in a diagram, can lift ships out of water and deposit them on land. (D. Ritchie)

ride up and over a tsunami without recognizing what has happened. Only when the wave nears land and starts to "touch bottom" in shallow water does the tsunami resemble the classic picture of a huge breaker. How the tsunami manifests itself on coming ashore, and how much damage the wave may do, depends on many factors, including the configuration of the shoreline. A constriction along the shore may concentrate the wave's energy into a small area and generate a gigantic wave, as happened when a tsunami struck Hilo, Hawaii, in 1946 as a 40-foot wave that wiped out much of the downtown area. Because the Pacific Ocean is surrounded by a belt of intense earthquake and volcanic activity, commonly known as the "Ring of Fire," the nations around the Pacific basin participate in an early warning network that provides warnings of approaching tsunamis in time to allow evacuation of coastal areas that might be in danger.

Much about tsunamis remains mysterious even after many years of study. There is even disagreement about what exactly causes tsunamis. Although they are associated with earthquakes, as in the Good Friday earthquake of 1964, tsunamis sometimes appear to be too large and powerful for the earthquakes that are thought to have generated them. This apparent discrepancy has led some geologists to speculate that certain tsunamis might be produced not directly by displacement of crustal rocks in an earthquake, but rather by release of giant bubbles of methane gas from the earth's interior during a quake. According to this model, the bubbles would rise to the surface, burst, and produce great disturbances in the water. The resulting waves then would radiate out as tsunamis from their point of origin. This explanation, however, is not universally accepted.

See also WATEREE; WAVES.

Tubantia, **Dutch liner**   A mysterious tale of sunken treasure figured in the sinking and salvage of *Tubantia*, a 14,400-ton liner that was sunk by an apparent torpedo attack on a voyage from Amsterdam to Buenos Aires in March of 1916. The ship sank about 30 miles from the Dutch shore, in approximately 120 feet of water. No one was killed in the sinking.

Germany declared that its U-boats had not sunk the liner. The Germans pointed fingers instead at the British, who denied the accusation. Pieces of the torpedo found embedded in the ship's lifeboats, however, indicated the torpedo was indeed German. The Germans tried to explain away that evidence by arguing that *Tubantia* must have struck a torpedo that was drifting on the surface. A court of inquiry cast doubt on that explanation by pointing out that crewmen on the liner had seen the torpedo's wake as it approached them. A drifting torpedo would not have

left a wake behind. Moreover, divers who examined the wreck reported that the hole was amidships and six feet under the waterline: a most unlikely location if the liner had run down a floating torpedo as the Germans had suggested. The International Committee of Inquiry at The Hague sided with the vessel's owners when they entered a claim for compensation; Germany was told to pay £800,000 for the loss of the ship. The Germans paid.

Yet that was not the end of the *Tubantia* incident. In 1922, weeks after the compensation had been paid and the ship's owners thus had given up ownership of the sunken vessel, a salvage operation led by three Frenchmen and an Englishman made its way to the wreck site and remained there from May through November, when stormy weather drove the expedition and its ship away. The following April, the salvage team returned and started using explosives to open a hold that supposedly had contained nothing but Dutch cheeses. A cargo of cheese would hardly have been worth salvaging after years of immersion in the ocean. Yet the salvage operation again remained over the wreck for months, from April through early July of 1923.

On July 9, another salvage operation, this one directed by Italians, arrived on the scene and tried to take over the wreck. The Franco-British operation obtained an order from admiralty court directing the Italians to leave, and the Italians departed. By this time the French and British team had run out of money, however, and had to leave too.

Tubantia apparently went untouched for the next eight years. Then, in 1931, a British salvage ship made a third attempt to reach whatever was in the sunken liner. This effort was unsuccessful. It also cast some light on the curious allure of *Tubantia*. The salvage team sent a wire message to anonymous backers. The message read, FAILED TO FIND BULLION IN THE WRECK OF THE DUTCH LINER TUBANTIA. How this message became public is unclear, but the message dispelled some of the mystery surrounding the repeated salvage attempts. It has been suggested that German gold bullion was packed inside the Dutch cheeses in the ship's hold. The gold supposedly was on its way to Argentina to help finance efforts to prevent the United States from entering World War I on the side of Britain. In that case, however, why would a German submarine have sunk *Tubantia*? Was the torpedo attack merely a mistake, however costly? Some mysteries still appear to surround the *Tubantia* incident.

See also SALVAGE; SUBMARINES; TORPEDOES; TREASURE.

Tulip, **American Union gunboat**   *Tulip* exploded in the Potomac River on November 11, 1864, with the loss of some 50 lives. A tiny vessel, less than 100 feet long and equipped with only three guns, *Tulip* served in the Chesapeake Bay, where the ship's small draft made it ideal for shallow-water duty.

A few months after entering the Union's service, however, it became apparent that the ship needed repairs. Two engineers were so distressed at the condition of *Tulip*'s boilers in mid-1864 that the men declined to operate the vessel. Soon afterward, the ship was designated as unsafe, and preparations were made to send *Tulip* to Washington, D.C., to be repaired.

Although the starboard boiler was in especially bad condition, and orders were given to avoid using it, the ship's commander decided its steam would be needed to maintain a decent speed on the voyage to Washington. He was concerned that Confederate snipers and gunners on shore might find *Tulip* a splendid target if the ship poked along on only one boiler. So, he had both boilers fired up and steamed away.

Off Ragged Point on the Potomac River, clouds of steam billowed from the engine room and fire room. The ship's engineer shouted for someone to activate the safety valve. Then *Tulip* exploded and sank. Eight bodies were recovered later. Ten survivors were found among the wreckage; two of them died hours later. The captain's hat was the only trace of him that could be found.

U

U-44, German submarine *U-44* disabled the freighter *Belgian Prince* in St. George's Channel on July 31, 1917. The freighter was scuttled. The submarine's captain, Paul Wagenfur, had the freighter's crew taken to the submarine. There, the British crew had their life belts, outer clothing and papers taken away. Wagenfur then submerged and left them to die in the sea. Only three men from the freighter survived.

Wagenfur proceeded to carry out mine-laying operations near Waterford, England. His submarine was capable of sowing mines while submerged. *U-44* encountered a British minefield. When a mine from the submarine struck a British mine, both mines exploded. The stern of the submarine was blasted away, and *U-44* sank with the loss of all but one man on board, who was picked up by fishermen and identified the submarine as *U-44*.

The British Admiralty decided to try recovering the wreck for examination, partly in hope of getting a look at Wagenfur's secret orders and code books, if possible. A salvage team located the wreck and moved it, step by step, close to shore with the help of a barge connected with cables that were looped underneath the wreck. Strong local tides of almost 20 feet also helped. The salvage team would flood watertight compartments on the barge, then pump them out again as the tide started rising. The rising tide thus lifted the wreck higher and higher, and allowed the submarine to be moved into progressively shallower water.

At last the British had the wreck in water less than 200 feet deep and sent down a diver to look for the papers. According to one story, finding them was easy. The diver discovered the hatch of the conning tower was propped open by the captain's arm, and in his hand were the papers the Admiralty sought. Apparently Wagenfur had tried to throw them away through the hatch when the submarine started sinking. The incoming torrent of water forced the hatch down upon his arm, trapping him there. The papers remained gripped in his dead fingers until the diver found them.

See also SUBMARINES.

U-307, German submarine An eerie tale from World War II of exploring a ship full of dead men, the case of *U-307* began when the submarine was sunk by British warships in the eastern Mediterranean. Survivors of the sinking said *U-307* had carried a secret infrared tracking device. Apparently the device could "see" heat emanations from ships and thus attack Allied shipping in darkness. The survivors even told where the device was located: attached to a bulkhead in the submarine's control room and protected by a demolition charge that would have to be neutralized.

Thanks to an extremely accurate position report from a destroyer when the submarine was sunk, the British were able to locate the wreck and send down a diver. He entered the submarine through the conning tower and almost immediately had to clear away the body of a German.

Proceeding to the control room, the diver located the tracking device and pried it loose from the bulkhead. At one point, a hand touched him on the helmet. He turned and saw that the hand belonged to another dead German sailor, his body drifting inside the flooded hull. The diver sent the device up to the surface in a bag, and had to undergo decompression later because so much nitrogen had built up in his blood during the dive.

After emerging from a decompression chamber, the diver visited an expert who was taking the device apart for study. The expert wondered aloud how the diver had managed to remove the infrared device without setting off the demolition charge. The diver had to admit he had forgotten about it.

See also SUBMARINES.

Uncle Joseph, German immigrant ship Two hundred and fifty people, including the immigrant vessel's captain, reportedly were killed on November 24, 1880, when the Genoese vessel *Ortiga* rammed *Uncle Joseph* off La Spezia, Italy. The German ship sank in eight minutes. *Ortiga* rescued a small number of survivors.

unidentified Dutch merchant ship   Picking up survivors from a shipwreck could bring the rescuer to destruction too, as one Spanish admiral discovered in 1631. The admiral and ships under his command were chasing a Dutch merchantman off the island of St. Martin's in the Lesser Antilles when the Dutchman was wrecked off the island's southern shore. The admiral was picking up survivors with his own ship when a storm developed suddenly and sank the admiral's vessel. Only eight survivors were reported in all from the two wrecks.

unidentified Japanese vessel   Sometimes a wreck makes a long journey at sea before it finally comes ashore. Described as a "junk," its name unknown, this wreck washed ashore in pieces sometime around the year 1905 near Ocean Park, Washington. Evidently the wreck was carried in the Japanese Current and made its way around the northern rim of the North Pacific Ocean before its travels ended.

unidentified merchant vessel   Part of the New Spain Flota, this craft was wrecked at St. Kitts in the Lesser Antilles in 1630, killing the governor of Santiago, Cuba, and many others.

unidentified ship, 1773   Although the name of this vessel is not recorded, its wreck involved a mutiny and a huge manhunt. The ship sailed from Dublin, Ireland, to Virginia with a load of more than 150 convicts and indentured servants.

The convicts were intended to work as laborers, and the indentured servants were not far above them in social standing. An indentured servant agreed to work for a master in America, practically as slave labor, for seven years in return for passage to the new country.

Apparently the passengers on this voyage did away with the captain and crew en route to Virginia, for the vessel arrived with the convicts and indentured servants in control. A pilot boat that went out to guide the ship on its arrival in Virginia waters was seized and run ashore, and some of the convicts and indentured servants escaped.

About 120 people remained aboard the ship, which wound up stranded near the mouth of the York River. They, or at least the majority of them, also made their way successfully to shore. A massive manhunt followed, but only five people are known to have been recaptured.

***Union*, American steamship**   A misapplied bit of horse dung brought about the destruction of the side-wheel steamer *Union* on July 13, 1837. The steamer operated as a ferry between Alexandria, Virginia, and Prince George's County, Maryland. Around 3 P.M., the ship's boiler exploded and sent a large fragment of metal, along with numerous bolts, flying into the passengers on board. Three people, including the wife of the engineer, were killed immediately. Fifteen other people were injured. Later it was learned that someone had tried to plug a leak in the boiler by applying horse dung to the inside. The dung and other material had clogged the apparatus and led to the explosion.

See also EXPLOSIONS.

unknown sailing vessel, Cape Cod, Massachusetts   This ship, whose name is unrecorded, is one of the oldest shipwrecks in American history. The wreck reportedly occurred in 1616 on Cape Cod, in the vicinity of what is now Chatham, Massachusetts. The vessel went ashore in a storm and was destroyed by waves. Survivors of the wreck encountered a group of hostile natives who attacked them and eventually killed all but five of them. These survivors reportedly were taken prisoner and forced to hand over what provisions they had salvaged from the wreck. The men allegedly lived afterward as slaves of the natives.

See also PORT FORTUNE INCIDENT.

unnamed Chinese troopship   Little information is available about this wreck, which reportedly occurred in November of 1947 when the vessel foundered during the evacuation of Nationalist soldiers from Manchuria. Some 6,000 people are thought to have been killed.

See also KIANGYA.

unnamed Dutch ship, Cuba   That area of numerous shipwrecks, Cuba's Matanzas Bay, was the site of a grisly discovery one day in 1825: a big Dutch vessel with decks covered with blood. No one was found on board. Presumably, pirates attacked the ship, looted it and then cast it adrift.

See also MATANZAS BAY WRECKS.

unnamed English hydrographic vessel, Cuba   The literature on shipwrecks contains numerous accounts of people who were shipwrecked twice on a single voyage. An example is Lieutenant John Payne, whose hydrographic ship was wrecked in 1770 on Cuba's Colorado Reef near Cape Buena Vista. Rescued by the

Spanish, Payne and his men were put aboard a ship bound for Jamaica, but that ship was also wrecked, near Cape San Antonio.

unnamed ferry, Egypt   A ferry at Maghagha, Egypt, sank on May 4, 1963, while carrying more than 200 Moslem pilgrims on a vessel designed to hold fewer than half that many passengers. The overloaded ferry sank several hundred yards from shore. Fifteen people survived.

unnamed Spanish convoy ship, Cuba   This incident in 1748 must have been one of the most spectacular shipwrecks in Cuban history. English warships tried to capture the New Spain Fleet near Havana. The *almiranta* of the Spanish fleet was badly damaged and was run aground on the shore. The Spaniards set fire to the ship, which exploded a few minutes later.

See also ALMIRANTA; CUBA; FLOTA SYSTEM.

unnamed Spanish galleons   Collisions between the slow-moving wooden-hulled ships on Spanish convoys in the days of the flota system could be just as devastating as those between high-powered, steel-hulled craft in our own time. In 1575, for example, when two galleons of the Tierra Firme Armada collided while at anchor in the harbor at Cartagena, Colombia, one galleon sank and took with it a huge sum in silver. The ship sank in water so deep that divers reportedly managed to recover nothing but some cannon and part of the vessel's rigging.

See also COLLISIONS; FLOTA SYSTEM.

unnamed Spanish mail boat   This vessel was wrecked off Cabo de la Vela, Colombia, in 1652. The crew managed to reach shore but were captured, killed and eaten by the native Carib people. The Caribs then salvaged the mail from the boat and sold it to the Spaniards.

unnamed Spanish merchantmen, Cuba   In the war between Spanish ships and the pirates that preyed upon them, the number of ships did not necessarily confer an advantage on one side or another. In 1648, for example, a pirate vessel was seen cruising off Havana, Cuba. The governor sent out two armed merchantmen to destroy or capture the pirate. Both vessels ran aground near Havana, however, and were wrecked. The pirates then murdered numerous survivors of the wrecks.

See also CORSAIRS AND PRIVATEERS; CUBA.

unnamed Spanish merchant ship, Jamaica   This large vessel was reportedly carrying a great cargo of merchandise (as well as missionaries) to Mexico from Spain when the ship was wrecked in a storm on a reef at Pedro Shoals in 1602. Survivors built rafts from the wreckage and used them to reach Jamaica. The ship's owner was Tome Cano, a noted ship designer in Spain.

See also JAMAICA.

unnamed Spanish sailing vessel   If evidence discovered on a beach near the mouth of Oregon's Nehalem River is any indication, some unnamed Spanish sailing vessel was wrecked in that vicinity some time after 1679. Debris from the wreck, including a large piece of beeswax marked with the date 1679, was recovered, along with other fragments of the wreck that indicated the ship might have been Spanish. Marine archaeologist Robert Marx has suggested that the unidentified ship may have been a Manila Galleon that came to grief during a long Pacific journey.

See also MANILA GALLEONS.

unnamed Spanish vessel   A merchant nao whose name is unrecorded was lost on reefs near Veracruz, Mexico, in 1545 with all of its cargo. The people on board were saved.

***Utopia*, British steamship**   *Utopia* was carrying more than 800 immigrants from Italy on a voyage to New York when the ship was driven into the bow of a British battleship and sank in a storm off Gibraltar on March 17, 1891. There were 576 fatalities.

V

Vandalia, American bark A maritime mystery of the Pacific Northwest involves the *Vandalia*, which washed ashore near McKenzie Head, near the mouth of the Columbia River (Oregon-Washington), in mid-January of 1853. A few days earlier, on January 9, the bark was sighted by the brig *Grecian* and did not appear to be in any serious trouble at that time.

What happened to *Vandalia* thereafter is not certain. *Vandalia* came ashore bottom-up. Four bodies also were washed ashore nearby, including that of the ship's captain, E. N. Beard. The other bodies included that of a 14-year-old boy. Twelve people in all are presumed to have died in the wreck.

One possible explanation for the wreck, writes historian James Gibbs in his book *Pacific Graveyard*, is that the ship drifted into breakers at the Columbia River bar, filled with water and capsized.

Vanguard, British battleship An accidental explosion in the ship's magazines is thought to have sunk *Vanguard*, which blew up and sank at Scapa Flow, Scotland, on July 9, 1917. Only two men from a crew of 806 survived.

See also EXPLOSIVES.

Vasa, Swedish warship One of the greatest of all salvage and marine archaeology projects was the raising of the 64-gun Swedish warship *Vasa* (also spelled *Wasa*), which capsized and sank in Stockholm harbor in 1628. The wreck rested on the bottom for more than three centuries, preserved by the absence of teredos, or shipworms, which otherwise would have destroyed the wreck's wooden hull.

An engineer named Anders Franzen used a coring device to obtain a sample of the ship's hull in 1956. Naval divers investigated the wreck and discovered that it was intact. The Swedish government pooled its resources with private groups to fund a salvage operation.

Salvage was difficult in this case, even though the wreck itself was well-preserved. *Vasa* was a very large ship, of some 1,400 tons, and was buried deeply in mud on the harbor floor. Also, because the hull was supposed to be lifted by cables passed beneath it, divers had to dig tunnels beneath the wreck to accommodate the cables. Digging these tunnels was extremely dangerous, because of the risk that the wreck might settle during the digging.

Anything that could be removed from the hull was removed. Gun ports were sealed. Cannon were secured so that they would not shift position and cause damage while the ship was bring lifted. Altogether, this work took five years. The wreck was raised on April 24, 1961, and was taken to a specially built drydock.

Veracruz, Mexico A port city for centuries, and the site of numerous shipwrecks, Veracruz has actually changed location since its founding. Before 1600, Veracruz was located 15 miles west of its present location. Wrecks dating from before 1600 therefore should be assigned to the earlier site.

See also MEXICO; VERACRUZ WRECK.

Veracruz wreck, Mexico Special credit for quick action should go to the men of the New Spain Fleet on a voyage in 1615. One of their ships ran aground on shoals at Veracruz and began to sink in deep water after being pulled off the shoals. As the ship sank, more than 1,000 men were put aboard the 100-ton ship and hastened to toss most of the vessel's cargo into boats.

Vermont, American steamboat The first steamboat to travel on Lake Champlain, *Vermont* was built in 1809 and served until 1815, when the ship threw a connecting rod that made a hole in the hull and caused the ship to sink. The wreck was recovered in 1953 from its site in the Richelieu River, Quebec, and was found to be a long, narrow vessel with a flat bottom. Although what remained of *Vermont* was taken ashore in preparation for becoming a museum exhibit, plans to build a museum for the wreck were never realized, and the remains of the ship eventually were carried away and destroyed.

See also PHOENIX.

verso   A commonly used cannon of the 16th century, the verso was lightweight, portable and able to be aimed and fired quickly. The gun ranged in length from about 6.5 feet to 10 feet and had several parts, including the barrel, a swivel mounting, a breech, and a tiller (an extended iron rod) for aiming. The bore was perhaps two inches. Apparently the versos fired various kinds of shot, including iron cubes. Numerous versos have been recovered from sunken vessels.

See also BOMBARDETA; CANNON; FALCONETE GRANDE.

***Vestris*, British passenger liner**   The 10,000-ton *Vestris* sank in the North Atlantic off Chesapeake Bay on November 12, 1928, on a voyage from New York to Buenos Aires. The ship allegedly was overloaded when it left New York, and water was discovered entering the ship at two points, through an ash ejector discharge and a coal chute door. The ship encountered heavy weather. Apparently, cargo shifted in the hold, and the ship heeled. Pumps were unable to remove enough water to correct the list. For some reason, the captain reportedly delayed sending an S.O.S. distress signal until less than an hour before *Vestris* sank. There were also seemingly inexplicable delays in lowering lifeboats. When lifeboats were lowered, the ship's list resulted in the destruction of many of the boats. Only eight lifeboats were launched successfully and recovered with survivors in them later. More than 100 people were killed in the sinking of *Vestris*. Only eight women on board, and no children, survived the ship's loss. Unofficially, much of the responsibility for the catastrophe was placed on Captain W. J. Carey, who died in the sea. According to one account, the captain's last recorded statement was that he was not to blame for the loss of *Vestris*. Twenty-five survivors of *Vestris* were shipwrecked again only a month later, when the liner *Celtic* was driven onto rocks at Queenstown, Ireland.

See also CELTIC.

***Victoria*, British battleship**   On June 22, 1893, the British battleships *Victoria* and *Camperdown* collided while on maneuvers off Tripoli, Libya, in the Mediterranean. *Victoria* sank in 13 minutes. Three hundred and fifty-eight men were killed, including the fleet commander, Vice Admiral Sir George Tryon. Although the imminent collision was pointed out to Tryon by Captain Archibald Bourke of *Victoria*, the admiral did not give appropriate orders until too late. Tryon later was held responsible for the catastrophe.

video   Remote video cameras have been used for decades to locate and investigate wreckage on the ocean floor. Such technology, in various stages of development, was utilized to locate and photograph wrecks such as those of the British submarine *Affray*, the American nuclear submarines *Thresher* and *Scorpion*, and the British passenger liner *Titanic*. Although video equipment is delicate and must be handled carefully, it can return vast amounts of information to the surface while sparing searchers and explorers the risk and expense of descending to a wreck site in submersibles. Complex, sophisticated communications and guidance equipment may be needed to transmit information to and from an underwater video platform during its operations. The platform itself may take the form of a "sled," or metal framework, with various items of equipment mounted on it, such as cameras and strobe lights for illumination. The sled is towed using a lengthy cable attached to a ship at the surface.

See AFFRAY; SCORPION; SUBMERSIBLES; THRESHER; TITANIC.

***Vindictive*, British cruiser**   A classic of the literature on salvage, the story of *Vindictive* began when Commander A. E. Godsal sailed the ship into occupied Belgium's Ostend Harbor on May 10, 1918. His goal was to block the harbor to German submarines by sinking the cruiser. Godsal was killed when shore batteries began shelling the ship, but his crew carried out the mission successfully and sank *Vindictive* by setting off explosive charges in the bottom. The crew left in a motor launch. To make raising the cruiser more difficult, the British had filled *Vindictive* with sacks of cement before sinking the vessel. After the war, the British had the job of removing the ship they had sunk. The cement was blasted away, a bit at a time, by small explosive charges. Pumps removed sediment from the wreck. Despite the fact that *Vindictive* had broken its back while on the bottom, the British managed to raise the sunken cruiser. The wreck eventually was given to the government of Belgium to be made into a monument.

See also SALVAGE.

***Vineyard*, American lightship**   The *Vineyard* lightship, anchored off the New England coast, was lost in a storm. On September 14, 1944, an intense storm with wind velocities up to 100 miles per hour moved up from the south and struck the vicinity of the lightship. Rather than put into port at New Bedford, Massachusetts, for protection, the lightship was ordered to remain on station to guide any ships that might be at sea during the storm. Seas that night are thought to have reached a height of 20 feet—equivalent to that of a two-story building—where the lightship was anchored. In the morning, the lightship was nowhere to be seen. Wreckage and bodies that drifted to shore later showed that the *Vineyard* lightship had sunk. All 12 crew members died in the storm. The wreck of the lightship was located in 1963 in Buzzards Bay, Massachusetts, in more than 60 feet of water. An examination by a diver indicated that the storm apparently caused a spare anchor to slam into the side of the vessel, knocking a large hole in the hull and causing the lightship to sink.

See also LIGHTSHIPS; STORMS.

Virginia, United States Virginia has an extensive coastline, extending both along the Atlantic Ocean shore and the Chesapeake Bay, and has been the site of numerous shipwrecks since settlement by Europeans in the early 17th century. Many shipwrecks also have occurred on the tributary rivers to Chesapeake Bay, notably the wrecks of several military vessels during the siege of Yorktown, on the York River in 1781.

Frequent storms that sweep Virginia waters have contributed greatly to shipwrecks. In one instance, cited by Robert and Jennifer Marx in their book *New World Shipwrecks 1492–1825,* a powerful storm that struck Portsmouth, Virginia, in 1785 drove several large vessels deep into nearby woods.

Notable examples of Virginia wrecks include the "Switzer ship," an early immigrant vessel that sank near Cape Henry with great loss of life; the aforementioned Yorktown wrecks; and *Nuestra Señora de los Godos,* a New Spain Fleet vessel that was wrecked north of Cape Charles during a hurricane in 1750.

Other significant wrecks in Virginia waters include the 10-gun English warship *Deptford,* lost on August 26, 1689, near Cedar Island; the American vessel *Needham,* which burned and sank at the mouth of the York River in 1738; the English merchant vessel *Sea Nymph,* wrecked on Hog Island in 1741 with the loss of many crewmen; and an unnamed ship, bearing numerous indentured servants from Ireland, that sank in a hurricane on the Rappahannock River on September 3, 1747, with the loss of more than 50 people.

One tantalizing mystery of Virginia waters is the legend of the Tangier Island wreck, believed to have been a Spanish vessel that was lost on the little island in Chesapeake Bay, perhaps in the 17th century. Some artifacts allegedly were recovered from the wreck by locals, but apparently little or no evidence of the wreck remains.

See also CAPE CHARLES; CAPE HENRY; CHESAPEAKE BAY; MIDDLE GROUND SHOAL; TANGIER ISLAND WRECK; YORKTOWN WRECKS.

Virgin Islands Many shipwrecks have occurred in the waters around the Virgin Islands. A notable example is the Spanish warship *St. Auguasies* (the English spelling of its name), which carried between 30 and 60 guns and was wrecked on the island of Anegada on March 20, 1742, with the loss of some 400 of the 600 people on board. Marine archaeologist Robert Marx suggests that this ship may be the same one known as *San Ignacio,* a Spanish ship also reported wrecked on Anegada in 1742.

visibility Reduced visibility has been the cause of many shipwrecks and may have many causes, including nightfall, fog, rain and snow. Ships have many aids to overcome poor visibility and assist navigation, including radar, satellite navigational fixes, lighthouses, radio beacons, and special windows with circular, revolving panels that remove rain and spray as soon as they are deposited. Foghorns also have been widely used in low-visibility conditions to advertise a ship's presence and thus avoid collisions.

Reduced visibility has been an issue, and sometimes a puzzling one, in some famous shipwrecks, notably that of the British passenger liner R.M.S. *Titanic,* which sank in the North Atlantic after colliding with an iceberg in 1912. There are various accounts of visibility on that night in *Titanic's* vicinity.

According to one story, a haze lay over the water and might have made it difficult to sight the iceberg in time to avoid it. Another description of conditions that night, however, indicated that the air was so clear that one could see stars clearly on the horizon.

Moreover, those on *Titanic* evidently had no trouble seeing what they perceived to be the lights of a ship lying several miles away while *Titanic* sank. *Titanic* tried to contact the vessel but was unsuccessful. It is doubtful that a ship miles distant would have been visible from *Titanic* through substantial haze.

Titanic's sister ship, *Olympic,* collided with the Nantucket, Massachusetts, lightship on May 15, 1934, in fog. The liner reportedly was following a radio direction finder signal. Seven on the lightship were killed.

Some ships' masters, contemporaneous with *Titanic,* took an extremely cautious attitude toward haze and fog, and, for safety's sake, slowed down at the first sign of reduced visibility. (One captain named Barr was so careful in this regard that he received the nickname "Foggy.") In many cases, however, a ship's master was under pressure to maintain speed even in fog or haze, so as to meet a schedule.

The distinction between haze and fog may seem academic but traditionally has been a matter of concern to ships' masters, their owners, and investigating boards following shipwrecks. Maritime historian Dwight Boyer, in his history of shipwrecks on the Great Lakes, points out that "hazy" is a less extreme condition than "foggy." A ship therefore might be justified in proceeding at a given speed through haze, but not through fog.

See also COLLISIONS; TITANIC; WEATHER, PROTESTS AGAINST.

Vorovsky, **Russian freighter** On its way outward across the Columbia River (Oregon-Washington) bar on April 3, 1941, *Vazlav Vorovsky* went aground on the dangerous Peacock Spit and was demolished by waves. Laden with heavy machinery for the Soviet Union, the ship developed trouble with its steering mechanism in a gale and was unable to hold its position by dropping anchors. Although motor lifeboats took off 37 crew members, the captain at first declined to leave his ship. He changed his mind, however, and signaled to be taken ashore the following day. *Vorovsky* broke apart on the bar. The cargo of heavy machinery was not salvaged.

W

Wadena, American schooner barge Just how difficult a rescue can be, and how much harm panic can do during a rescue effort, is exemplified by the case of the barge *Wadena*, which was stranded in a gale on a shoal off Monomoy Island, Cape Cod, Massachusetts, early on the morning of March 11, 1902.

At first, all looked well. Lifesavers removed crewmen from the barge. *Wadena* remained intact, and wreckers began removing its cargo of coal.

Six days after the barge stranded, however, Captain Eldredge, keeper of the Monomoy lifesaving station, had a surprise when a message arrived from nearby Hyannis, asking about the situation of the men on the barge. This was the first time the men at Monomoy heard that anyone might be left on *Wadena*.

Captain Eldredge went out to see for himself what was happening. He saw a distress signal flying from the barge, which apparently still had someone on board. Immediately, he placed a call to the station and ordered the surfboat launched from the beach.

Although there was a heavy sea, the barge did not appear to be in danger. The surfmen brought their boat into the lee of *Wadena*. After a line was thrown onto the barge and made fast, the five men remaining on *Wadena*—eager to reach shore—got into the surfboat and left the barge behind.

The rough sea frightened the barge's crew. A large wave struck the boat hard. Seeing water pour into the surfboat, the men from the barge panicked and tried to hold on to the surfmen, so that the rescuers were unable to row. The surfboat thus became helpless among the waves and overturned, throwing all on board into the sea. The men tried to right the boat twice, but each time, the seas overturned it again.

The lifesavers were exhausted. They watched, unable to help, as the five men from the barge were washed away and drowned. The surfmen held on to the overturned boat. Four of the lifesavers were swept away. Soon, only Captain Eldredge and two surfmen remained alive. Then the captain drifted away, hang-ing on to the boat's spar and sail, and was lost. One of the two remaining surfmen, his strength gone, fell off the overturned boat and sank into the sea.

Only a single man, one Seth Ellis, remained alive out of the boat's company. As he clung to the bottom of the overturned boat, it drifted toward another stranded barge, whose captain set out in a dory to rescue Ellis. The captain was an expert boatman and managed to take his little boat through the surf and deposit Ellis on shore. Later, Ellis observed that no one would have died in the rescue attempt if the men from the barge had merely remained calm.

Waratah, British cargo liner Named after an Australian flower, *Waratah* became one of the most widely discussed ships in history after vanishing at sea, within sight of land, on July 27, 1909. Launched in 1908, *Waratah* belonged to the Blue Anchor line, known for the distinctive emblem of an anchor on its ships' funnels. The well-appointed ship was intended to operate between England and Australia by way of South Africa. Although equipped with an impressive array of safety features, including a double bottom and watertight bulkheads, the ship did not carry a wireless set.

Under the command of Captain J. E. Ilbery, *Waratah* began its maiden voyage to Australia on November 6, 1908. From the start, *Waratah* had serious problems. The ship appeared to be top-heavy and had a pronounced roll, even in calm weather. The ship's rolling reportedly interfered with bathing on board, because so much water spilled out of bathtubs.

The next voyage to Australia began on April 27, 1909. Again, the ship appears to have had problems with stability. *Waratah* rolled heavily and reportedly took a long time to recover. Pitching—up-and-down motion of the bow and stern—also allegedly was a problem. *Waratah*, according to one account of the ship's behavior on this voyage, would dip its bow into the trough between two waves, then "plow" through the next wave instead of rising over it. One passenger was so distressed by the apparent top-heaviness of the ship that he got off at Durban, South Africa, and prepared to make other arrangements for travel.

Waratah left Durban on July 26 with 92 passengers and 119 crew members on board. Around 4 A.M. on July 27, the cargo ship *Clan McIntyre*, which had left Durban the same day as *Waratah*, sighted *Waratah* near Cape Hermes. The ships exchanged weather information and greetings. The captain of *Clan Mcintyre* noted that *Waratah* appeared to be in no difficulty, although another observer on *Clan McIntyre* thought *Waratah* was heeled over markedly and was pitching, raising the ship's propellers above the water at times. The weather was turning worse at this time, with strong winds and heavy seas rising.

At approximately 7:30 P.M., the British freighter *Harlow,* passing near Cape Hermes, saw the lights of a ship perhaps eight or 10 miles distant. Next, the ship's master thought he saw flames like those of bush fires on shore, followed by two red flares that rose several hundred feet into the air. Other observers on the freighter also reported seeing flames or a glow at this time. There is some question, however, whether or not these events represented a sighting of *Waratah*, which is thought to have been a considerable distance away by that time.

Another mysterious encounter occurred at 9:51 P.M. The liner *Guelph,* on its way to Durban, saw a large passenger vessel off Hood Point, about 140 miles from Cape Hermes. *Guelph* tried to contact the other ship by signal lamp. The only intelligible letters in the mystery ship's reply were T . . . A . . . H. *Guelph* proceeded on its way. Possibly *Guelph* had encountered *Waratah*, but this cannot be proven.

The weather deteriorated further. When *Waratah* did not arrive in Cape Town, South Africa, as expected on the 29th, a ship was chartered to search the sea between Durban and Cape Town for the missing ship. A tug also went out in search of *Waratah*. This hunt turned up nothing. The Royal Navy then sent three cruisers to look for *Waratah*, and likewise found no trace of the vessel.

A grisly report of floating bodies—and body parts—off the South African coast near East London came from the freighter *Tottenham* several days later. On August 11, one of *Tottenham*'s crew members told the captain and second mate that he had seen the body of a young girl, perhaps 10 or 12 years old, in the water. The girl was wearing a red gown, he added. The captain used binoculars to scan the sea around the ship and saw what looked like numerous chunks of flesh in the water. One piece appeared to be the

trunk of a human body. Other crew members also saw what they took to be human bodies or pieces of bodies. There was some question, however, whether the objects were human remains or fishes. Another ship, the freighter *Insizwa*, also spotted similar objects in the sea, but that ship's crew also disagreed on whether the floating items were from humans or some marine species.

Hope remained for *Waratah* and its people. It seemed just possible that the ship had experienced engine failure and was drifting somewhere, waiting for rescue. Such hope diminished as months passed without any sign of *Waratah*. By December, *Waratah*, in effect, was considered lost. The ship and 211 people on it were never seen again.

Eventually, some items traceable to *Waratah* were found. A deck chair with *Waratah*'s name on it was recovered, as was a lifebelt from the ship. This evidence did not necessarily mean, however, that *Waratah* had sunk. Items such as these might have been thrown or washed overboard even if the ship remained afloat.

More than a year after *Waratah* disappeared, a court of inquiry in Britain investigated the loss of *Waratah* and concluded that the ship was lost in the gale that struck on July 28, 1909. The court did not try to determine precisely how the ship was lost, although it appeared likely that *Waratah* had capsized.

Waratah's disappearance remains a mystery. Colorful stories have arisen about possible mutiny and a postulated collision with floating dynamite that supposedly blew up the ship, but none of these tales has been substantiated.

Did the ship explode? A powerful explosion would account for the flames observed by *Harlow*, and for a floating field of body parts like those supposedly seen from *Tottenham*. One would expect an explosion, however, to cast large amounts of other debris into the water as well. Why was no such debris reported seen along with the alleged fragments of flesh?

Conceivably, *Waratah* sank near shore, in the heavy weather. Yet in such a case, one also would expect debris from the wreck to wash ashore in large quantities. (Shipwrecks along the Outer Banks of North Carolina, for example, cast such large quantities of wreckage ashore that it served as building material.) Apparently, no such wreckage from *Waratah* was found, unless one counts the aforementioned deck chair and lifebelt.

It is also possible that *Waratah*, its engines disabled for some reason, drifted southward into Antarctic waters and was lost there. Because the ship had no wireless, it would have been unable to send a distress signal. Therefore, the ship might have drifted for an indefinite time in the icy southern sea, until the passengers and crew died of hunger or cold, or both. This is, of course, only one of many speculations about what may have happened to *Waratah.*

See also EXPLOSIONS; STORMS.

***Warrington,* American schooner** "Passengers" on ships wrecked on North Carolina's Outer Banks in the late 19th century were not always human. Maritime historian David Stick, in his book *Graveyard of the Atlantic,* tells the story of two such survivors of the schooner *Emma J. Warrington,* which went ashore near Duck, North Carolina, on October 4, 1893.

The captain told the lifesavers that no one on board was injured. Then he asked the lifesavers to check the cabin and see if the ship's passengers had survived. The lifesavers rushed aboard to see if someone at death's door needed their help. The "passengers" turned out to be a pair of tame bears, who were taken ashore.

***Washington,* American steam schooner** A remarkable rescue took place on November 17, 1911, when the tug *Tatoosh* saved the steam schooner *Washington* in the waters of Peacock Spit, on the dangerous Columbia River (Oregon-Washington) bar. Approaching *Washington* in rough seas, Captain C. T. Bailey of *Tatoosh* saw about a dozen passengers wearing life jackets gathered at the schooner's stern. *Washington's* captain informed Bailey that the schooner had no power, for the fires were out beneath the boilers. Despite the danger to his own ship, Bailey proceeded to put a line aboard *Washington* and tow the ship through the breakers to shore. When Bailey looked toward shore, he recalled later, he saw perhaps a thousand onlookers.

Washington, United States A frequently foggy coast has given Washington state its share of shipwrecks. Perhaps the most dangerous part of the state's coastline is the Columbia River bar, at the mouth of the Columbia River between Washington and Oregon. The bar has claimed numerous ships since navigation began on the river. Many wrecks also have occurred along the Long Beach Peninsula between Cape Disappointment and Leadbetter Point at the mouth of Willapa (Shoalwater) Bay.

See also COLUMBIA RIVER BAR.

***Watch and Wait,* American sailing vessel** Thatcher's Island, off the New England coast, was named as a result of this shipwreck, which occurred in August of 1635 off Cape Ann, Massachusetts. One Anthony Thatcher was traveling with his wife and four children on the vessel, along with a number of other passengers, from Ipswich to Marblehead, Massachusetts, when bad weather forced the ship to drop anchor. The vessel dragged its anchor, however, and was driven ashore near an island off Cape Ann. The Thatcher family fell into the sea as the ship broke up. Thatcher managed to save his wife, but all the children were lost. Mr. and Mrs. Thatcher were the only survivors of the wreck. The island where they came ashore came to be known as Thatcher's Woe and later as Thatcher's Island.

See also NEW ENGLAND; STORMS.

***Wateree,* American naval vessel** *Wateree* was not exactly wrecked, but it was lifted out of the water by a tsunami, or seismic sea wave, at the port of Arica, Peru, one afternoon in 1868 and carried far inland. Lieutenant J. G. Billings of *Wateree* recorded his observations of the tsunami and its aftermath. Billings was with the captain when the two men felt the ship vibrate as if it had dropped anchor. No order to drop anchor had been given, so Billings and the captain went to see what was happening. They looked toward shore and saw the land undulating in an earthquake. The hills near shore, Billings said later, appeared to be "capsizing." A cloud of dust arose from the dry soil. When the dust cleared, the men on *Wateree* were amazed to see that the town lay in ruins.

The captain knew that tsunamis often accompany earthquakes in coastal regions, and so he gave orders to prepare *Wateree* for a tsunami. Meanwhile, the ship's crew prepared to rescue survivors of the earthquake, who were standing on the docks and crying out to the ships for help. Before the rescue could be accomplished, however, the tsunami arrived and "swallowed," in Billings's word, the waterfront and the people gathered there. This particular wave did not affect *Wateree,* but a subsequent wave had calamitous effects on ships in the harbor.

The water withdrew from the shore, thus signaling that a big wave was approaching. Ships settled on the bottom, surrounded by fish left behind by the retreating sea. *Wateree* had a flat bottom and settled upright on the seabed, but nearby ships with rounded hulls rolled onto their sides. This difference in construction saved *Wateree,* because the ship remained upright when the wave arrived, whereas the round-hulled ships capsized.

The men on *Wateree* watched as two other ships in the harbor—another American ship, the *Fredonia,* and the Peruvian ironclad *America*—were caught in the wave. *America* had been stranded when the sea withdrew, and the ship's hull was breached. When the sea returned, it carried *America* at great speed toward shore. The captain of *Fredonia*, thinking the Peruvian ship was coming to the rescue of his vessel, called out that *Fredonia* was beyond saving, for the bottom was ruptured. "Save yourselves!" *Fredonia*'s captain cried. The wave then smashed *Fredonia* against a cliff, killing all on board. *America* was caught somehow in a countercurrent and carried in the opposite direction.

Soon after sunset, yet another wave could be seen approaching. In the darkness, the tsunami was visible as a narrow line of phosphorescence along the crest of the wave. With a tremendous noise, the wave struck the shore and engulfed *Wateree*. Once again, the ship survived, and no men were reported killed or missing.

The wave carried *Wateree* two miles inland and deposited the ship upright on its flat underside. The ship came to rest only about 200 feet from a cliff. Had the wave carried *Wateree* just a few moments longer, the ship would have been dashed against the cliff and destroyed.

All around, *Wateree*'s men saw evidence of the terrific destructive power of the tsunami and earthquake. Near *Wateree* lay a British three-master with its anchor chain wrapped several times around its hull. Evidently the British ship had been spun around its long axis in the manner of a rolling pin. Billings reported that nothing at all remained of the town. The tsunami apparently buried the ruins under vast amounts of sand. Billings said that a flat plain of sand covered the former location of the town and left nothing, except a few ruins in outlying areas near the mountains, to indicate where Arica had stood. The wave also deposited great numbers of human bodies near the edge of town. Billings also reported the bizarre sight of a dead woman seated on a dead horse in a crevasse, or large fissure, that had opened in the ground during the earthquake. He presumed that the crevasse had "swallowed" them as they were fleeing.

See also TSUNAMIS.

Water Street ship, sailing vessel, New York City
Finding a ship's hull under the streets of New York may seem unlikely, but it happened in the early 1980s when the "Water Street ship," a merchantman of the mid-18th century, was discovered on a construction site in lower Manhattan near the Brooklyn Bridge. The ship was about 100 feet long and is thought to have been rated at perhaps 200 to 300 tons. The wreck was excavated, and building construction at the site resumed.

The Water Street ship demonstrates a common practice of colonial days, namely filling old ship hulls with debris and using them to reinforce construction along the shore. The wreck's location also showed how far the shoreline had been extended in lower Manhattan

since colonial times; the excavation site was hundreds of feet from the modern Manhattan shoreline.

waves Storm-driven waves can do tremendous damage to, and even sink, ships. A wave may tear open hatch covers, for example, and allow water to flood a ship's hold. Wave action also may cause a ship to capsize, especially if the ship is "beam on" to waves, with its long axis perpendicular to the direction of wave motion. The ship then can roll over in the troughs between waves. In extremely heavy weather, waves may cause such severe damage to a vessel that the ship loses its structural integrity and breaks apart. In a heavy sea, individual waves may become superimposed on one another and "add up" into a single, exceptionally large and powerful wave capable of sinking a ship.

In centuries when wooden ships predominated, the relative fragility of vessels (compared with the strength of modern iron and steel construction) meant that ships were highly vulnerable to wave damage. Even modern vessels, however, have limited resistance to wave damage.

One particular kind of wave, the seismic sea wave, or tsunami, is capable of doing tremendous damage to ships in harbors or near shore by lifting the ships bodily out of the water and casting them onto dry land. A tsunami also may drive ships in harbor against one another with terrific force and correspondingly great damage.

See also STORMS; TSUNAMIS; WATEREE.

Wawaset, American side-wheel steamer In one of the most horrible incidents in the history of the Chesapeake Bay region, *Wawaset* burned on the Potomac River on August 8, 1873, with the loss of 76 lives.

The luxurious vessel set out from Washington, D.C., for Coan River, Virginia, with 117 adult passengers and 20 children on board. This apparently was an unusually large complement of passengers for *Wawaset*. Still more boarded the ship at subsequent stops on the way to Coan River.

On the Potomac River near Chatterton's Landing, Virginia, a fireman discovered the ship was burning. Advised to run the ship ashore at Chatterton's Landing, the captain prepared to beach the vessel. The ship was unable to reach shore, however, because the heat of the fire stopped the engines and left the vessel powerless.

Panic broke out among the passengers, many of whom tried to run forward, only to be stopped by flames. Wind whipped the flames from midships toward the stern, where the clothing of women trapped there caught fire, and the women burned alive.

An attempt to lower a boat ended in failure when a man took out a knife and cut one of the ropes. Passengers spilled from the boat into the water. Donald Shomette, in his history *Shipwrecks on the Chesapeake,* writes that one woman's voluminous skirt acted as a life preserver of sorts by trapping air and keeping her afloat until she could reach shore.

The ship ran aground more than 400 feet from shore. Men on board tried to help people in the water by throwing wooden boxes and planks overboard. A still-turning paddle-wheel drew swimmers beneath the surface. According to one account of the wreck, numerous life jackets floated on the water, unclaimed.

The pilot on *Wawaset* was conspicuous for his heroism. He pulled two women to shore, then went back in a boat to save whom he could.

Many bodies were recovered along the shore following the wreck. Of the dead, 35 were unidentified. Many were buried near Chatterton's Landing, and others at a cemetery in Washington.

An investigation determined that the fire began when a partition near the boiler became overheated. There were no criminal proceedings in the case, although investigators thought the company that owned *Wawaset* should be prosecuted for employing officers who lacked licenses; the captain and mate had not renewed their licenses, and were fined for failure to do so.

See also FIRE.

weather, protests against According to a curious custom, mariners whose ships had wrecked on American shores during storms in the late 18th and early 19th centuries would go before a notary and enter a formal protest against the weather. For example, historian Jeannette Edwards Rattray, in her account of shipwrecks off Long Island, New York, cites a record from the book of John Hulbert, magistrate and notary public at Sag Harbor, New York, from 1770 to 1805. Hulbert's records include a formal protest against a violent storm and heavy seas that destroyed the brig *Ocean,* on a voyage from Bremen, Germany, to Philadelphia. The ship was driven ashore on Long Island on the night of January 17, 1800. The captain was drowned.

***Welsh Prince*, British steamer** Sunk in a collision with the American freighter *Iowan* in fog at the entrance to the Columbia River (Oregon-Washington) on the night of May 28, 1922, *Welsh Prince* was almost cut in two by *Iowan*'s bow. Fire broke out almost immediately on the British ship but was extinguished. Seven men on *Welsh Prince* were killed in the collision.

Welsh Prince settled quickly. *Iowan* was taken to Portland, Oregon, for repairs. Several efforts to raise *Welsh Prince* proved unsuccessful. The wreck was a hazard to navigation and had to be destroyed. After the deck of the sunken ship was removed to take off the ship's cargo of steel, what remained of *Welsh Prince* was blasted to pieces in a spectacular explosion.

whalers In the years before petroleum became a significant energy source, whale oil was a principal source of oil for lamps, and a vast fleet of whaling vessels sailed the world's oceans. Whale oil also had other uses such as lubrication, and "spermaceti," a wax from the heads of sperm whales, had applications including machine oil and detergent. Ambergris, a material found in the stomachs of sick whales, was in great demand as a perfume base.

The whaling industry reached its apex in the 1840s. Although the rise of the oil industry helped ensure the destruction of the 19th-century whaling business in America, the War Between the States did more than perhaps anything else to destroy America's whaling industry. The Union bought aging whaling ships, filled them with rocks and sank them at the mouths of Confederate ports to impede shipping. (This short-term strategy actually hurt the North in the long run by destroying a fleet of ships that would have been of great value after the war.)

Confederate attacks also destroyed numerous whaling vessels from the North during the war. The Confederate raider *Alabama* destroyed a group of 12 whalers off the Azores in 1862. A single Confederate captain, James Waddell, is said to have intercepted 38 ships, including eight New Bedford whalers in the Arctic, during a single cruise in 1864–1865. Waddell burned the whaling ships on June 28, 1865, in what reportedly was the last act of hostility in the war. Waddell knew at that time that General Robert E. Lee, commander of the Confederate armies, had surrendered to General Ulysses S. Grant at Appomattox Courthouse, Virginia, three months before; but Waddell destroyed the whalers anyway, after hearing a report that some Confederate forces remained active.

Whaling ships were, of course, subject to the same hazards as other sailing ships, including storms, grounding and collision. Many whalers operated in the Arctic, which presented the special danger of being trapped in ice. One remarkable shipwreck involved the whaler *Essex,* which was rammed and sunk by a whale.

See also ESSEX.

White Star Line One of Britain's pre-eminent shipping firms in the 19th and early 20th centuries, the White Star Line is perhaps best known as the owner of the liner *Titanic,* whose loss in 1912 made the liner's name a synonym for catastrophe at sea. The chairman of the line at the time of *Titanic's* sinking, J. Bruce Ismay, was aboard *Titanic* on its maiden and final voyage, and was vilified in the press for his perceived cowardice in saving his own life while hundreds of others perished. *Titanic's* sister ship, the White Star Line's *Britannic,* was sunk in 1916 by a German mine. Another famous shipwreck involving a White Star ship was the loss of the liner *Atlantic* in 1873. White Star's great competitor was Cunard.

See also ATLANTIC; BRITANNIC; CUNARD LINE; REPUBLIC; TITANIC.

Wilhelm Gustloff, German passenger ship The liner *Wilhelm Gustloff* sailed from Danzig (now Gdansk, Poland) with an estimated 6,000 to 10,000 passengers on board on January 30, 1945. A Russian submarine sank the ship by torpedo later that day. All but about 1,000 on the liner perished. In terms of lives lost, this is thought to be the single worst shipwreck in history.

William and Ann, British bark The wreck of *William and Ann* illustrates how shipwrecks sometimes led to hostilities between Anglos and Native Americans.

The wreck occurred in March of 1829, when the bark became trapped during a storm in the sands off Clatsop Spit, Oregon, at the mouth of the Columbia River. Despite a rescue attempt by a nearby American schooner, waves swept away all 46 persons on *William and Ann.*

Soon afterward, reports began circulating that the Clatsop Indians had recovered large amounts of cargo from *William and Ann.* According to historian James Gibbs in his book *Pacific Graveyard,* a delegation from Fort Vancouver, sent to the Clatsop village to retrieve the cargo, found large quantities of goods from the wrecked vessel in the possession of the Clatsop people, but the Clatsop chief refused to hand over any of the salvaged cargo. Rebuffed, the whites made plans to take the goods by force.

About this same time, rumors began circulating that a lifeboat from *William and Ann* had wound up in the Clatsop village, and that the Clatsop people had murdered survivors of the wreck. Apparently there was no proof of these reports, but they served to inflame the Anglos even further.

That autumn, the Anglos had assembled a formidable force, including a schooner equipped with cannon. Two parties advanced on the Clatsops, one by sea and the other by land. The schooner bombarded the village and sent the natives fleeing into the woods. One native was reported killed in the assault, and two others injured. The whites recovered the cargo and took prisoners from the Clatsop people. On interrogation, the captured natives reportedly told their captors that the lifeboat was discovered empty.

See also COLUMBIA RIVER BAR; NATIVE AMERICANS.

Williams, American barkentine An exceptional story of bravery in lifesaving involves the sailing vessel *Ephraim Williams,* wrecked off the Outer Banks of North Carolina on December 22, 1884. *Williams* was en route from Savannah, Georgia, to Providence, Rhode Island, with a cargo of lumber when the ship encountered a storm on December 18 and began to take on water. On December 21, *Williams* was sighted off Cape Hatteras. The vessel's decks were barely above water. Someone clearly was still alive aboard the ship, however, because a flag—a distress signal—could be seen as it was hauled up the mast. Although *Williams* needed help urgently, an extraordinarily rough sea made it difficult to launch boats from the beach. Nonetheless, the lifesavers put out successfully in a boat, reached *Williams* and began rescuing survivors, who already had started to abandon ship on makeshift rafts. Had the lifesavers not arrived, the survivors probably would have died in the surf on their way to shore. For this rescue, seven lifesavers—Benjamin Dailey, Patrick Etheridge, Charles Fulcher, Thomas Gray, Isaac Jennett, Jabez Jennett and John Midgett—each received the Gold Lifesaving Medal, the highest such decoration awarded by the United States government. Only 12 of these awards were presented in the entire first 30 years of the lifesaving service on the Outer Banks. More than half of all those awards went to this single team.

Willoughby expedition With a fleet of three ships, the English explorer Sir Hugh Willoughby set out toward Scandinavia and the Arctic coast of Russia in 1553, seeking a northeast passage to the Pacific Ocean. Two of Willoughby's vessels, *Bona Confidentia* and *Buena Esperanza,* halted at the Kola Peninsula to spend the winter there. While at Kola, everyone on the two ships perished, apparently from carbon monoxide released from a stove. The third vessel in Willoughby's fleet, *Edward Bonaventure,* proceeded alone and succeeded in reaching what is now the Arctic port of Archangelsk in Russia. A representative of the expedition traveled from there to Moscow to meet with Czar Ivan the Terrible, and returned with a British-Russian trade agreement that resulted in the founding of the famous Muscovy Company. The expedition did not succeed, however, in completing a passage to the Pacific.

***Wingate*, English steamer** The arrival of *Wingate* off East Hampton, Long Island, New York, on March 14, 1889, illustrated how little its crew apparently knew about the United States. The crewmen, whose ship had been drifting without a rudder for days, had run out of fresh water and food, but had reservations about coming ashore. Apparently they feared that "cannibal Indians" would devour them, writes Jeanette Edwards Rattray in *Ship Ashore!,* her history of shipwrecks on Long Island. The men of the lifesaving station put those fears to rest, and soon the disabled steamer was towed to New York.

wireless Wireless communications allowed ships at sea and stations on shore to communicate by dot-dash code. Messages had to be transmitted one character at a time. To save time and effort, wireless operators often utilized abbreviations. Individual ships identified themselves by call letters, such as MGY for the British liner R.M.S. *Titanic.* One of the most famous wireless messages in history occurred when *Titanic,* on the night of its sinking, apparently became the first ship in history to use the then-new distress code S.O.S. to summon help.

See also REPUBLIC; TITANIC.

***Wisconsin*, Great Lakes steamship** Shifting cargo appears to have destroyed the passenger/freighter *Wisconsin* on October 29, 1929, on Lake Michigan. The ship set out from Chicago in a storm with a cargo that included barrels full of steel castings.

The ship left Chicago on October 28 and began to roll heavily upon passing the seawall. Soon after midnight, the chief engineer was informed that large amounts of water had entered the firehold. *Wisconsin* also began listing to port. The engineer had the pumps started and informed the captain of what was happening.

When the captain inspected the cargo deck, he found that much of the cargo had broken loose and was shifting back and forth with each roll of the ship. The steel castings were resting against the port side of the vessel. Possibly their mass, slamming against the ship's side, dislodged some plates and allowed water to enter.

Wisconsin took on water faster than the pumps could remove it. About half an hour after the water was discovered in the firehold, the ship started sending out distress signals, giving its position as four miles off Kenosha, Wisconsin. By 2:15 A.M., *Wisconsin* signaled that the ship was about to sink. At 2:35, *Wisconsin* reported its fires were out, and there was no steam left. The message at 3:05 was merely a triple S.O.S. The message at 4:32 said the crew was abandoning ship. At 4:32, the Chicago Radiomarine Station tried to reach *Wisconsin* but was unable to do so; the ship's wireless operator had left his post and gone on deck, on orders from the captain.

Conditions on deck must have been nightmarish. The ship rolled in huge waves, in complete darkness, in a powerful, cold wind. Seas swept over the ship, which was practically lying on its port side. The captain ordered the anchors dropped. Men began leaving the ship as best they could, by boat or by life raft. Coast Guard boats stood nearby to rescue survivors. The Coast Guard later was criticized for rescuing men from lifeboats when other men remained in the water; by the time the men were taken off the boats, there was no room left on the Coast Guard craft for the people in the water, who needed help more urgently. A tug also rescued some of the men from *Wisconsin.*

Sixteen lives, including the captain, were lost with *Wisconsin.* Since the captain was not on hand to answer questions at the investigation into *Wisconsin*'s loss, some aspects of the ship's loss remained unclear. In his account of the wreck in his history of Great Lakes shipwrecks, *Ghost Ships of the Great Lakes,* maritime historian Dwight Boyer points out that it seemed unclear why the captain did not beach the ship. He was, after all, only a couple of miles offshore, and *Wisconsin* could have been beached at Kenosha without causing any fatalities. Boyer adds, however, that beaching *Wisconsin* on that stormy night would have exposed a grounded ship to the full force of heavy seas, and destroyed the vessel quickly. Another question is why the captain did not turn around and return to port immediately when he discovered the ship was in trouble. Here again, Boyer points out, the situation was more complicated than it might appear. The leaking ship would have had a much greater draft than usual (that is, would have ridden lower in the water) and might have hit bottom before even reaching the pier. A similar incident had occurred at Duluth, Minnesota, when a ship racing for shelter struck bottom and was stranded offshore, with the loss of part of the crew.

The wreck of *Wisconsin* demonstrated the value of wireless in crisis situations. Without wireless, the ship might have lost all aboard that night, instead of only 16 lives.

See also GREAT LAKES; WIRELESS.

Women's National Relief Association To help relieve the sufferings of shipwreck survivors staying at lifesaving stations, WNRA was organized in the winter of 1882–83. The organization was staffed largely by prominent women in New York City and Washington,

D.C. WNRA's president was Mrs. James Garfield, wife of the then-President of the United States. WNRA provided support in the form of clothing, blankets and other material.

***Wood*, American schooner** Sunken wrecks posed a considerable threat to shipping off the eastern coast of the United States in the late 1800s. The spars of a submerged wreck could puncture a ship's hull and send the vessel to the bottom quickly.

That was what happened to one of the biggest three-masted schooners ever constructed in the United States, the *William B. Wood*. The 599-ton schooner was on a voyage from Cuba to Philadelphia with a cargo of sugar on March 3, 1889, when the ship hit a submerged wreck off Assateague Light on the Eastern Shore of Virginia and started leaking. Wind and seas were high, and the ship headed for the beach.

A surfman on patrol from the lifesaving station at Wallops Beach saw *Wood* proceeding toward the shore. He lighted a flare and went back to the station for help. A surfboat went out to the damaged ship.

Wood sank about 1,700 feet from shore, in 18 feet of water. The nine-man crew gathered on the bowsprit and jib boom to be rescued, but nightfall and the heavy weather complicated the rescue.

Because of rough seas, only five men from *Wood* could be taken to shore in the surfboat. By the time those men were ashore safely, it was dark. Moreover, the wind was rising, and rain was falling. Nonetheless, the surfmen set out in the darkness and storm toward the schooner, which they could see only as a faint light in the distance.

The rescuers were guided to the ship by a line that *Wood*'s captain had trailed in the water. The last four men were taken safely from the schooner and brought ashore.

Although the great schooner was lost along with the crew's personal effects, some good did come out of this wreck. The keeper of the lifesaving station was able to report the position of the dangerous wreck that had destroyed *Wood*.

wracking This English expression for salvage refers to the activities of salvors who set up operations in Bermuda in the early 1600s and performed salvage in the Caribbean Sea. Later in the 1600s, the wrackers moved their base to Port Royal, Jamaica.

See also SALVAGE.

wreckers This name was applied to landsmen who would try to cause shipwrecks by setting up phony lights on shore, in the hope that ships would mistake them for lighthouses and run ashore, where they could be plundered. Such activities helped influence the United States Congress to provide funds for lifesaving stations.

Y

Yarmouth Castle, Panamanian steamship The burning of the cruise ship *Yarmouth Castle* off Nassau in the Bahamas on the night of November 12–13, 1965, was one of the great maritime catastrophes of the 1960s. Built in 1927, the ship originally was named *Evangeline*. It served as a troop carrier in World War II and later was registered in Liberia and finally in Panama. The ship was filled with highly flammable materials.

Around 2 A.M. on November 13, fire started in an unoccupied room. Crew members were unable to put out or contain the fire and it spread through the ship. The captain of the *Bahama Star*, a few miles away, saw the light from *Yarmouth Castle*'s burning and thought at first that the light was the illuminated orange funnel of a Cunard liner. Nonetheless, he went to investigate. Another ship in the vicinity was *Finnpulp*, a Finnish motorship, whose captain saw the fire and went to *Yarmouth Castle*'s aid.

Despite difficulty in lowering lifeboats, the captain of *Yarmouth Castle* managed to board a boat with several members of his crew and left the burning ship. The second mate, who was helping passengers into lifeboats, saw the captain leaving and shouted at him to come back. The captain received the same message when he reached *Finnpulp*, whose master told him and his men to return and help *Yarmouth Castle*'s passengers. Eventually, the fugitive captain went back to *Yarmouth Castle*.

Most of *Yarmouth Castle*'s passengers were transferred to *Bahama Star*, which had its paint blistered by the intense heat of the fire. The burning ship sank at 6:05 A.M. on November 13. Two crewmen and 87 passengers died on *Yarmouth Castle*. The destruction of *Yarmouth Castle* was reminiscent of the burning of the liner *Morro Castle* off the New Jersey coast in 1934.

See also FIRE; MORRO CASTLE.

Yassi Adi Island wreck, Turkey The wreck, which dates from about A.D. 600 to 650, according to coins found on board, provided a particularly close look at the last moments of an ancient vessel. The ship's loss evidently was sudden and unexpected, because the anchors remained grouped together on deck, and dinnerware was discovered where it had been set out in the captain's cabin. In the remains of his cabin, archaeologists found on a beam an inscription in Greek characters referring to "presbyteros," or Captain, George. This inscription has been described as the first known documentation of a ship's master.

See also ARCHAEOLOGY; CAPE GELIDONYA WRECK.

yaw A side-to-side motion of a ship's bow and stern as the ship pivots around a point amidships. Excessive yawing can make a ship difficult to maneuver.

See also PITCH; ROLL.

Yorktown wrecks, Virginia Numerous ships were sunk at Yorktown during the climactic battle of the American Revolution. The destroyed vessels included the 44-gun British warship *Charon*, which burned and sank on October 10, 1781. The British warship *Fowry* also sank at Yorktown, along with several merchant vessels. The British deliberately scuttled some ships to help provide defenses along the shore.

A survey in 1978 indicated six wrecks lay along the shore at Yorktown. These six wrecks brought the total of known wrecks there to nine. One of the wrecks, known as YO 88 and located some 500 feet offshore, was chosen for excavation. Preparations for excavation were extensive. Because conditions for underwater activity were difficult and even dangerous, a cofferdam was built around the wreck to provide clean water in which to work. Completed in 1982, the cofferdam also kept out the dangerous stinging nettles in which the river abounds. A pier was constructed to link the cofferdam with the shore.

Study of YO 88, a vessel about 75 feet long and of some 170 tons capacity, showed that the ship was built sturdily and had unusually elaborate framing at bow and stern. The ship's broad beam shows that it was designed to carry a heavy load of cargo. Examination of barrels from the wreck revealed much about techniques of coopering, or barrel fabrication.

See also ARCHAEOLOGY; CHARON.

Yucatán wrecks, Mexico   Sand has a way of burying wrecks quickly and preventing salvage operations. That was the case with seven ships of the New Spain Fleet that were wrecked on the Yucatán coast of Mexico between Isla Mujeres and Cabo Catoche during a voyage in 1614. By the time a salvage team reached the wreck sites, the cargoes were buried by thick layers of sand.

See also FLOTA SYSTEM; SAND.

Z

Zanzibar wrecks On April 15, 1872, a hurricane struck Zanzibar and destroyed more than 100 ships in the harbor there, including the sultan's private vessel *Sea King*. Some 200 people were reported killed in the storm.

zigzag In World War I and World War II, surface ships often steered a zigzag course to interfere with torpedo attacks by submarines. The zigzag itself could be as dangerous to ships as torpedoes, however, because there was always a danger of collision if a ship should execute a turn poorly and stray into the path of another vessel. A dramatized account of the zigzag and its dangers is contained in British adventure writer Alistair MacLean's wartime novel H.M.S. *Ulysses*. Moreover, a submarine could carry out a torpedo attack successfully despite the zigzag, as in the case of the British liner *Arabic*, sunk in 1915 by the German submarine *U-24*.

See also CURAÇAO.

APPENDIX 1: Fatalities

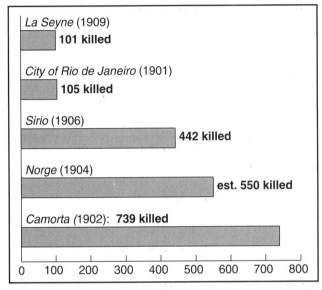

Fatalities, major passenger liner wrecks, 1900–1909. (Bonsall, *Great Shipwrecks of the 20th Century*, 1988)

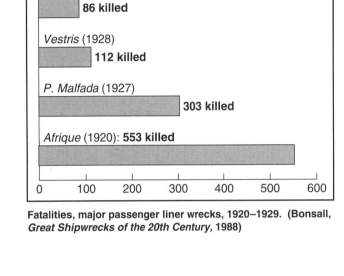

Fatalities, major passenger liner wrecks, 1920–1929. (Bonsall, *Great Shipwrecks of the 20th Century*, 1988)

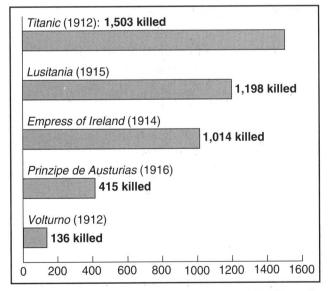

Fatalities, major passenger liner wrecks, 1910–1919. (Bonsall, *Great Shipwrecks of the 20th Century*, 1988)

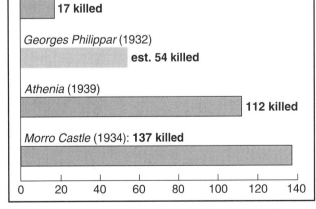

Fatalities, major passenger liner wrecks, 1930–1939. (Bonsall, *Great Shipwrecks of the 20th Century*, 1988)

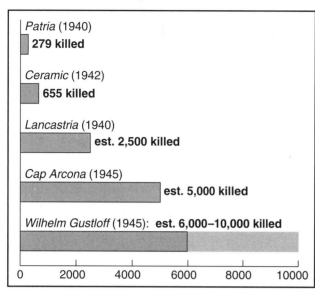

Fatalities, major passenger liner wrecks, 1940–1949. (Bonsall, *Great Shipwrecks of the 20th Century,* 1988)

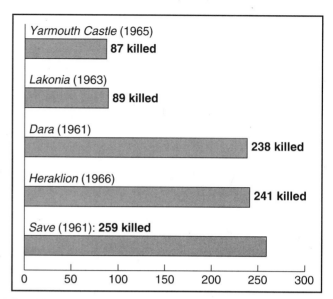

Fatalities, major passenger liner wrecks, 1960–1969. (Bonsall, *Great Shipwrecks of the 20th Century,* 1988)

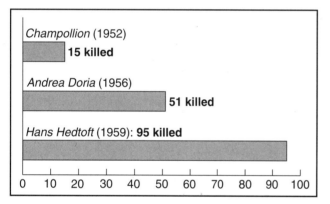

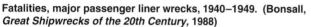

Fatalities, major passenger liner wrecks, 1950–1959. (Bonsall, *Great Shipwrecks of the 20th Century,* 1988)

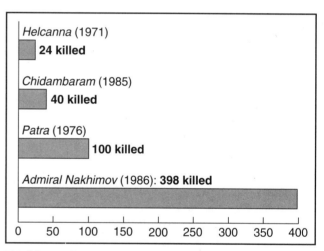

Fatalities, major passenger liner wrecks, 1970–1986. (Bonsall, *Great Shipwrecks of the 20th Century,* 1988)

Chronology of Shipwrecks

The following list represents a selection, though by no means a complete list, of significant shipwrecks. Entries have been selected according to criteria including size of vessel, number of lives lost and historical importance of the shipwreck. In many cases, casualty figures are estimates. Readers should bear in mind that there may be disagreement among various sources where casualty figures are concerned. When a listing reads "no casualty figures available," that does not necessarily mean there was no loss of life; rather, it means that no figures on loss of life accompanied that particular listing.

1492, date uncertain. The caravel *Santa Maria,* flagship of Columbus, was wrecked on a reef near Cape Haitien, Hispaniola.

1494, date uncertain. Two ships from Columbus's second expedition, *Gallega* and *Mariagalante,* are thought to have been lost on the coast of Hispaniola in a storm.

1502, July. A Spanish fleet carrying gold, under command of Admiral Antonio de Torres, encountered a hurricane off Hispaniola. Some 500 men were killed.

1500–1510, date uncertain. According to one account, the island of Bermuda is named for a Spanish vessel, *La Bermuda,* that wrecked there about this time.

1503, date uncertain. Two of Columbus's ships on his fourth voyage were so riddled by teredos that he had them scuttled off Panama, one near Portobello and another in the vicinity of Santa Maria de Belem.

1504, date uncertain. A four-ship flotilla under command of Captain Juan de la Cosa was wrecked in a storm at Bahia de Uraba, Colombia, with the loss of 175 lives.

1508, August 3. A hurricane wrecked numerous ships in the port of Santo Domingo, Hispaniola, and vicinity.

1509, August 8. A hurricane sank as many as 20 ships at Santo Domingo, Hispaniola.

1511, date uncertain. A shipwreck in 1511 on the Alacran Reef in the Gulf of Mexico ultimately left only one survivor, who was rescued at Mexico's Cozumel Island in 1519.

1521, date uncertain. The Spanish merchant vessel *San Anton* was lost in the Florida Keys on a voyage from Cuba to Spain.

1525. A caravel was lost near Cape St. Helen, Florida, with the loss of 200 lives.

1526, date uncertain. The Spanish vessel *La Nicolasa,* carrying supplies of conquistadors, sank at Isla Cancun, Mexico. Cannon from the wreck were recovered in the 20th century.

1526, June. This unidentified vessel, a Spanish brigantine, was on an exploratory voyage when wrecked at what is now Cape Fear, North Carolina.

1527, date uncertain. Two ships of conquistador Francisco de Montejo were burned at Punta Soliman on the Mexican coast.

1540, summer. The 35-ton Spanish caravel *Trinidad* was lost near San Diego, apparently when the ship drifted away during a storm while its crew was ashore.

1545, July 20. The English warship *Mary Rose* foundered in a storm during a voyage from Portsmouth, England, to Spithead, England, killing 73.

1545, August 20. A hurricane struck Santo Domingo, Hispaniola, and destroyed numerous ships in the port there. A second hurricane on September 18 demolished any ships that had survived the previous storm.

1549, date uncertain. Survivors of the wrecks of three Spanish ships near Key Largo had to wait several years for rescue.

1551, date uncertain. The Tierra Firme Armada encountered a prolonged storm near the Bahama Channel, and apparently lost two ships at Bermuda, including the Capitana.

1552, September 2. Twelve ships of a Spanish fleet were sunk at Veracruz, Mexico, by a hurricane before they could sail for Havana.

1553, date uncertain. The New Spain Fleet encountered a hurricane during a voyage from Veracruz, Mexico, to Havana and lost all but two of 20 ships. Survivors from those two ships were reportedly murdered by Native Americans. Several hundred lives were lost altogether.

1553, date uncertain. A hurricane at Santo Domingo, Hispaniola, destroyed 16 merchantmen in the port and four vessels along the coast.

1556 or earlier. One or more ships of the New Spain Fleet reportedly wrecked near Cape Canaveral, Florida.

1556, May 24. The Tierra Firme Armada lost four ships on the Cuban coast between Havana and Cape San Anton in a storm. The vessels included two 220-ton naos and two 80-ton caravels.

1559, date uncertain. The 300-ton Spanish galleon *Santa Maria de los Remedios* was separated from its convoy in a storm, was damaged seriously, and was driven onto a reef in the vicinity of Grand Bahama Bank. Some survivors made their way to Cuba in a boat.

1559, August 20. A Spanish expedition to Florida was wrecked by a hurricane at what is now Tampa Bay, killing some 500 men.

1559, September 19. A Spanish fleet anchored in the Bay of Santa Maria, Florida, lost several ships in a hurricane. The storm carried a caravel far inland and deposited the ship in a grove of trees.

1560, date uncertain. The Capitana of the Tierra Firme Flota vanished in a storm near Bermuda. Evidently no wreckage was ever found.

1563, July 18. Six ships from the New Spain Fleet were wrecked on the Jardines Reefs on the coast of Cuba. The wrecks included the 150-ton Capitana *San Juan Bautista*, and the 250-ton nao *San Juan*.

1564, date uncertain. The 300-ton Spanish galleon *Santa Clara* was wrecked on Little Bahama Bank.

1565, date uncertain. Two ships under command of the French explorer Jean Ribault were lost in a storm near Mosquito Inlet, Florida.

1567, date uncertain. The New Spain Fleet encountered a storm near Puerto Rico, and six ships in the fleet were wrecked near Dominica in the Lesser Antilles. Lost ships included the *capitana*, the 150-ton *San Juan*, and the *almiranta*, the 150-ton *Santa Barbola*.

1568, date uncertain. The *almiranta* of the New Spain Fleet was blown up during hostilities between Spaniards and English forces at San Juan de Ulza, Mexico. Several English ships also were sunk.

1571, date uncertain. The 300-ton Spanish galleon *San Ignacio* and another vessel were wrecked near Cape Canaveral, Florida, with heavy loss of life.

1572, date uncertain. Five merchant ships on a voyage from Spain to Veracruz, Mexico, were reportedly wrecked at Tobago, Lesser Antilles. Divers recovered most of the ships' cargoes in salvage operations.

1572, date uncertain. The galleon *San Felipe* caught fire, was run aground near Colombia's Isla Tesoro, and exploded.

1574, date uncertain. The Spanish nao *Sanct' Ana* and two other, unidentified vessels, all traveling with the New Spain Fleet on a voyage from Spain, encountered a storm in the Gulf of Mexico and were lost.

1582 or earlier. The English warship *Delight* was wrecked on a shoal near Sable Island, off Nova Scotia, Canada. The ship was part of Sir Humphrey Gilbert's fleet.

1582, date uncertain. Three Spanish merchant ships sank in the Plata River near Buenos Aires.

1582, September (?). The New Spain Fleet reached Veracruz, Mexico, on September 18 or 19 after a voyage from Sanlucar. The *almiranta* and a nao were sunk at Veracruz.

1584, September 10. Four ships of the New Spain Fleet were sunk at Las Cabezas, near Veracruz, Mexico.

1585, date uncertain. Nine ships in a Spanish fleet were lost in a storm after the fleet unloaded its cargo at Veracruz, Mexico.

1585, June 29. An English vessel, *Tiger*, was wrecked at Ocracoke Inlet, North Carolina. There were no fatalities.

1586, date uncertain. An earthquake in Peru sank several large merchant ships in the port of Callao.

1586, July 18. Two ships of the New Spain Fleet, *Santa Maria de Begonia* and *Santiago El Mayor*, were wrecked near Cabo Catoche, Mexico.

1588, date uncertain. After surviving a storm in the Gulf of Mexico, the New Spain Fleet lost its *almiranta*, the 500-ton *Ascension*, on a reef at the entrance to the port of Veracruz, Mexico.

1589, date uncertain. A 75-ship Spanish fleet that sailed from Havana on July 27 lost at least 29 ships, many of them off the Florida coast, in storms.

1589, date uncertain. A Spanish convoy that left Havana on September 9 lost several ships, including the *almiranta* of the New Spain Fleet, in the Bahama Channel during a hurricane.

1590, November. The New Spain Fleet was ruined by a storm in the Gulf of Mexico, and about 1,000 people are thought to have been killed.

1597, August 30 or thereabouts. Two ships of the New Spain Fleet were wrecked at the entrance to the port of San Juan de Ulúa, Mexico. The circumstances of the wreck were unusual. An anchor fluke on one ship became entangled in the rigging of the other vessel, so that the two ships collided and sank.

1597, September 22. A hurricane sank the ships *San Buenaventura* and *La Maria* at the port of San Juan de Ulúa, Mexico.

1599, date uncertain. The Manila galleon *San Augustin* foundered near San Francisco while sailing from Acapulco, Mexico, to the Philippine Islands. Hundreds of men were killed.

1599, June. Dutch privateers sank seven Spanish vessels on the Colombian shore.

1600, September 12. The New Spain Fleet ran into a hurricane near Villa Rica, Mexico, then another hurricane on the way to Veracruz, Mexico. Some 1,000 men are thought to have perished.

1603, date uncertain. Three ships of the New Spain Fleet were were wrecked on the southwestern coast of Guadeloupe in the Lesser Antilles. One of the ships was the 700-ton *capitana San Juan Bautista.*

1605, date uncertain. Two Spanish galleons were sunk at or near the port of Trujillo, Honduras. One sank after being struck by lightning, with only 10 of 101 people on board surviving. The other galleon was wrecked in a storm the day after it left Trujillo.

1611, date uncertain. Just before a Spanish fleet was scheduled to leave on a voyage to Havana, four large ships, including the 550-ton *Nuestra Señora del Rosario y Santo Tomas,* were wrecked at Veracruz, Spain.

1614, date uncertain. Several ships of a Spanish fleet sent out against pirates and smugglers were lost on the coast of Campeche, Mexico.

1614, date uncertain. Seven ships in a fleet that left Spain on July 7 were wrecked one night on Mexico's Yucatán coast between Isla Mujeres and Cabo Catoche.

1615, August 30. Off Islas Tranquillas and Arena, Mexico, a 41-ship fleet encountered a storm. Everyone on board, passengers and crew, was lost. Exact casualty figures are unavailable, but hundreds are thought to have been killed.

1616, date uncertain. The New Spain Fleet, on a voyage from Spain, encountered a storm near Veracruz, Mexico, and lost one of its ships, the 200-ton *Nuestra Señora de la Candelaria.*

1616, September. More than 30 ships were reported sunk in a hurricane at Cuba's Oriente province.

1621, date uncertain. *Nuestra Señora del Rosario,* part of the New Spain Fleet, caught fire and sank as the fleet was departing Veracruz, Mexico.

1622, September 6 or 7. A hurricane demolished the Tierra Firme Armada and the New Spain Fleet in the Florida Keys, wrecking at least 12 ships and killing thousands of people.

1623, date uncertain. Dutch forces attacked Callao, Peru, and burned 11 large Spanish vessels in the port.

1623, date uncertain. After the Tierra Firme Flota sailed from Havana on April 26, the fleet encountered a storm and lost two galleons. Where exactly they sank is not certain; some sources say the ships were lost on the high seas, and other say they were wrecked on the Florida coast.

1624, date uncertain. The English ship *Sparrow Hawk* was wrecked near what is now Orleans on Cape Cod, Massachusetts.

1628, August. The Swedish warship *Vasa* capsized and sank on its maiden voyage, in Stockholm harbor. Fifty people were killed.

1628, September 8. A hurricane sank numerous ships along the Yucatán coast in Mexico. (This was not a happy day for the Spaniards in general. Maritime historian Robert Marx notes that on this same day a Dutch privateer and his fleet captured the whole New Spain Fleet at Matanzas, Cuba.)

1629, April. According to the then governor of Yucatán, Mexico, writing to the King of Spain, bad weather took a heavy toll of shipping there in April.

1629, June. The Dutch merchant vessel *Batavia* was wrecked on a reef near Australia. Mutineers reportedly killed some 100 out of 316 people on board.

1630, date uncertain. A merchant ship was lost on the eastern shore of St. Kitts in the Lesser Antilles. Many lives were lost, including the governor of Santiago, Cuba.

1631, date uncertain. Two virtually simultaneous wrecks occurred off the southern shore of St. Martin's in the Lesser Antilles. A Dutch merchantman was wrecked while being chased by Spanish ships from the Windward Armada. When the Spanish admiral in command stopped to pick up survivors from the Dutch vessel, the admiral's ship in turn was sunk by a storm. Only eight people altogether survived the two wrecks.

1631, date uncertain. The Spanish galleon *San Jose* was wrecked on a reef about 120 miles from Panama City, Panama, near the island of La Galera.

1631, October 21. A hurricane that struck the New Spain Fleet between Veracruz, Mexico, and Havana killed some 300 people.

1634, date uncertain. The Spanish galleon *San Juan Agustin* was lost in a storm near Havana, with the loss of 40 lives.

1634, date uncertain. Four ships of the Tierra Firme Armada were lost on arriving at Cartagena, Colombia, including the 600-ton galleon *San Juan Bautista,* which struck a reef. Another ship was lost at the entrance to Boca Chica, and the remaining two vessels leaked so badly that they sank soon after reaching the harbor.

1635, date uncertain. A ship of the New Spain Fleet, *San Juan el Feo,* was burned and destroyed completely at Veracruz, Mexico.

1636, date uncertain. The Spanish warship *San Salvador* was set afire and exploded on the south side of Martinique in the Lesser Antilles.

1640, July 27. The 200-ton British merchant vessel *Mary Rose* exploded and sank off Boston, Massachusetts. Only one person survived.

1642, date uncertain. A hurricane wrecked 23 English ships at Basseterre, St. Kitts, in the Lesser Antilles. Few lives were lost, however, because most of the crewmen were on shore.

1642, date uncertain. The Spanish nao *Nuestra Señora de Atocha y San Josef* encountered a storm near Havana, Cuba, and sank only a few yards from the fort of La Puntal.

1643, date uncertain. Ship Island, Mississippi, was named for the wrecks of two Spanish caravels here in 1643.

1643, November 1. *Nuestra Señora de la Concepcion,* of the Spanish treasure fleet, was lost in a hurricane near Hispaniola. The wreck killed 324 people.

1647, May 13. An earthquake destroyed many ships in ports and along shores of Chile and Peru.

1648, date uncertain. During an engagement between Dutch privateers and Portuguese warships off Salvador, Brazil, the Dutch ship *Utrecht* and the Portuguese ship *Rosarion* both exploded and sank, with more than 550 killed.

1650, date uncertain. Hundreds of lives were lost in a hurricane that destroyed numerous ships of various nationalities off Basseterre, Lesser Antilles.

1650, July 15. Because of a navigational error, an unidentified vessel was wrecked on Mexico's Alacran Reef nine days after leaving Havana. Eight people drowned. The survivors lived on islands in the area for almost two months, then sailed for the mainland on rafts they built from the wreckage of their ship. Along the way, they discovered on an island survivors from another wreck that occurred three years earlier.

1654, August 15. The Dutch ship *Sparrowhawk* broke apart in a hurricane off the coast of Korea, with the loss of 28 lives.

1656, date uncertain. The Spanish galleon *Nuestra Señora de la Marvillas* struck another ship and sank near Memory Rock at Little Bahama Bank. More than 600 people were killed.

1657, date uncertain. The Dutch immigrant ship *Prins Maurits* wrecked on Fire Island, New York. Native Americans saved all on board.

1659, date uncertain. Four ships of the Armada de Tierra Firme were lost on the Yucatán coast in Mexico. Two months later, 300 survivors were rescued.

1666, date uncertain. The day after five English ships captured six French vessels at Bay of All Saints, Barbados, Lesser Antilles, a storm sank all five of the English ships.

1666, date uncertain. A hurricane wrecked two English warships at Antigua in the Lesser Antilles, with numerous lives lost.

1666, September. A hurricane reportedly wrecked numerous French warships at Montserrat, Lesser Antilles.

1668, date uncertain. The ship *John & Lucy* sank at Montauk, New York; casualty figures unavailable.

1668, December 23 or thereabouts. The 1,500-ton galleon *Santa Maria de los Valles* burned and sank rapidly off Acapulco, Mexico. Three hundred and thirty people were killed.

1669, date uncertain. The 650-ton Spanish galleon *Nuestra Señora de Buena Esperanza* was lost on Little Bahama Bank, with the loss of 415 of 478 people on board. A salvage attempt the following year succeeded in recovering only two anchors, because the wreck was mostly buried in sand by that time. A second salvage effort in 1671 failed to find any sign of the wreck at all.

1669, November 1. A hurricane sank numerous ships at Barbados.

1673, date uncertain. The warship *Ogeron*—manned by pirates and built on the order of the French governor of the Island of Tortuga, with the aim of capturing Curaçao—was lost in a storm off the western coast of Puerto Rico. Most of the crew managed to reach land, but the survivors were murdered the following day by Spaniards.

1675, September 1. Twelve English merchantmen were sunk at Bridgetown, Barbados, in a hurricane.

1678, May 3. A French fleet was wrecked at Aves Island, Venezuela, with the loss of some 1,200 lives.

1678, May 3. All but two ships in a 20-ship French fleet sent to take Curaçao from the Dutch wrecked on a reef at Aves Island, Colombia, with the loss of more than 1,200 lives.

1679, date uncertain. The 350-ton Spanish galleon *Je-*

sus, *Maria y Joseph* sank in a storm at the mouth of Argentina's Plata River, with the loss of almost all its crew of 74.

1679, September. The French frigate *Griffon* sank at Birch Island Reef on Lake Huron.

1680, August 3. A hurricane destroyed 20 French vessels and two British ships at Martinique, killing hundreds of people.

1681, date uncertain. Spain's Tierra Firme Armada lost numerous ships on a voyage between Cartagena, Colombia, and Porto Bello, Panama. Hundreds of lives were lost.

1681, date uncertain. Almost 300 people drowned when a galleon of the Tierra Firme Armada broke apart after hitting a reef off Punta de Brujas, Panama.

1682, date uncertain. An unidentified brig was wrecked in a snowstorm while trying to enter the harbor at Boston, Massachusetts. Only a few of the crew survived.

1683, date uncertain. While being careened at Veracruz, Mexico, the 70-ton ship *El Santo Cristobal, San Agustin y La Magdelena* caught fire and was destroyed.

1687, date uncertain. More than 700 were killed when a fleet of 19 Dutch merchantmen was lost in a storm off the coast of French Guiana.

1690, April 6. An earthquake destroyed much of the main settlement on St. Eustatius in the Lesser Antilles. A large part of the town was submerged. Several hundred people died. The sunken city later became the site of marine archaeology studies.

1690, April 6. An earthquake cast much of Charlestown, Nevis, Lesser Antilles, into the sea. Records of this catastrophe are scanty, however, and it is not known how many lives were lost. Some of the sunken town is submerged in less than 10 feet of water.

1692, June 7. Port Royal, Jamaica, was destroyed and partly submerged in an earthquake. More than 2,000 persons were killed in that event, and another 3,000 died in epidemics that followed it.

1695, September. The 60-gun British warship H.M.S. *Winchester* was lost off Key Largo, Florida; some 400 were killed.

1695, October. Numerous French vessels foundered in a hurricane off Martinique, with the loss of some 600 lives.

1698, date uncertain. An unidentified Portuguese vessel was lost on the coast of British Guiana; some 400 were killed.

1698, date uncertain. More than 400 people were killed, and only three survived, when a Portuguese vessel was lost near what is now Georgetown, British Guiana.

1699, March. The 22-gun ship *Adventure,* from London, sank between Block Island, Rhode Island, and Long Island, New York; no casualty figures available.

1700, September 3. *Rising Sun,* a Scottish frigate, was lost off Charleston, South Carolina. Almost 100 were killed.

1702, January 14. The New Spain Fleet lost its *almiranta, Santa Maria de Teasanos,* when the vessel sank at at San Juan de Ulúa, Mexico.

1704, date uncertain. *Castle del Rey,* a 300-ton privateer, was wrecked on shoals off Sandy Hook with more than 100 lives lost.

1705, date uncertain. Four Spanish warships and most of the men on them were lost at Havana in a storm.

1706, date uncertain. A storm destroyed a fleet of more than a dozen merchantmen along the coast near Cape Charles, Virginia.

1709, December 25. The 32-gun British warship H.M.S. *Solebay* was lost with its entire crew at Boston Neck, Massachusetts.

1710, July 7. The German immigrant ship *Herbert* was wrecked on Long Island, New York, but no lives were lost.

1710, November 29. H.M.S. *Garland,* an English warship, wrecked near Currituck Inlet, North Carolina, with 15 lives lost.

1711, August 22. A fleet of eight English transports wrecked in a storm at Egg Island, Labrador, with a loss of some 2,000 lives.

1711, December 16. The New Spain Fleet lost five ships, including the *almiranta,* in a storm near Havana.

1715, March 28. A storm at Veracruz, Mexico, caused great damage to the town and to ships in the harbor. Twelve ships were destroyed, including four belonging to the New Spain Fleet.

1715, July 31. About 1,000 people were killed when a fleet of 11 or 12 Spanish ships was wrecked in a hurricane off the coast of Florida.

1719, date uncertain. A 12-gun Spanish privateer reportedly exploded in a fight with another privateer off Long Island, New York, killing 91 of 133 men on board.

1719, date uncertain. Three large galleons in a Spanish squadron were lost completely on the coast of Campeche, Mexico.

1720, date uncertain. More than 500 men were drowned in the wreck of the warship *Carlos V* in a hurricane at Puerto Rico.

1721, July 2. The French frigate *Le Jean Florin* sank on Lake Erie near Erie, Pennsylvania.

1723, July 29. A unidentified sloop was wrecked at East Hampton, New York; there were several casualties.

1724, September. More than 120 lives were lost when an undetermined number of ships in the New Spain Fleet succumbed to a hurricane in the vicinity of Samana Bay, Hispaniola.

1725, date uncertain. The *capitana* of the New Spain Fleet was lost at Campeche Sound in the Gulf of Mexico; some 400 died.

1725, date uncertain. The French frigate of war *Chameau* was wrecked in a storm off Cape Lornebec, Nova Scotia, on a voyage from Louisbourg, Canada, to Quebec. Most of the passengers and crew were lost.

1726, date uncertain. The 66-gun Portuguese ship *Santa Rosa* sank off the Brazilian coast near Cape San Augustine, with the loss of all but six of more than 700 people on board.

1726, October 22. A hurricane wrecked or sank more than 50 ships at various ports in Jamaica.

1728, September 14. A hurricane destroyed much of Charleston, South Carolina, and sank eight ships in the harbor.

1730, date uncertain. The 54-gun Spanish galleon *Genovesa* hit a reef at Pedro Shoals, Jamaica, and was wrecked.

1732, January. Approximately 500 died when the Spanish galleon *Nuestra Señora de la Concepcion* foundered at Veracruz, Mexico.

1733, June. A storm sank 12 ships at Basseterre, St. Kitts, in the Lesser Antilles. One ship that had arrived at St. Kitts from Philadelphia just before the storm was lost with all lives and cargo.

1738, date uncertain. The German immigrant ship *Princess Augusta* wrecked on Block Island, Rhode Island. Before the wreck, more than 200 passengers and crew reportedly had died from drinking tainted water.

1739, date uncertain. The British merchant vessel *Adriatick* was lost off Cape Hatteras on a voyage from London to Virginia; hundreds are thought to have been killed.

1740, date uncertain. The galleon *Invencible* was struck by lightning in Havana harbor and exploded, causing tremendous damage to the city.

1741, date uncertain. During an attack by English forces, the Spanish sank numerous ships of their own in the harbor at Cartagena, Colombia, including the 70-gun *Galicia* and the 70-gun *San Carlos*.

1742, date uncertain. The British man-of-war *Tyger* was wrecked in the Florida Keys. The crewmen used timber from the wreck to build a fort. When a Spanish admiral sent several small vessels to capture the survivors, the Britons drove the attackers away. The admiral tried again, sending a 60-gun galleon after the British crew. This attempt also was unsuccessful. The galleon was wrecked.

1742, March 20. Four hundred people were drowned when the Spanish warship *St. Auguasies* was wrecked on Anegada Island in the Virgin Islands.

1743, date uncertain. The British warship H.M.S. *Astrea* burned at the Piscataqua River in Maine, with the loss of several lives.

1743, January. The 70-gun British warship H.M.S. *Oxford* was lost in the Gulf of Mexico.

1744, date uncertain. The British warship H.M.S. *Astrea* burned in Boston harbor with no loss of life.

1744, February 5. Looe Reef in the Florida Keys was named for the wreck of H.M.S. *Looe* (also spelled *Loo*) on this date.

1744, October. A hurricane wrecked or sank more than 100 ships at Port Royal and Kingston Harbor in Jamaica. Among the lost ships were the 50-gun British warship H.M.S. *Albans* and the 50-gun H.M.S. *Greenwich*.

1746, date uncertain. Thirteen ships in a Portuguese fleet are presumed to have been lost in a storm, with hundreds of people on board, near Barbados while sailing from Brazil to Portugal.

1746, October 28. A devastating earthquake in Peru destroyed the port of Callao and wrecked or sank 23 ships there, including the 30-gun galleon *San Fermin*.

1747, September 3. A vessel with hundreds of indentured servants from Ireland on board sank in a storm on the Rappahannock River near Urbana, Virginia, with the loss of more than 50 lives.

1747, September 21. A hurricane wrecked eight ships at Nevis, Lesser Antilles.

1747, September 21, October 24. Hurricanes on these dates destroyed 24 ships in all at Basseterre, St. Kitts, in the Lesser Antilles.

1748, February 26. Winds sank almost every French warship and merchant vessel in Louisbourg harbor on Canada's Cape Breton Island in Nova Scotia.

1749, October 7–8. A hurricane destroyed dozens of ships along the coasts of Virginia and North Carolina.

1749, October 8. Seven ships were wrecked, with great loss of life, on Martha's Vineyard, Massachusetts, in a hurricane.

1750, August 18. A hurricane destroyed several ships of the New Spain Fleet along the North Carolina coast.

1751, September 25. The British warship H.M.S. *Fox* was lost in a hurricane at Jamaica, along with two dozen merchant vessels at Port Royal and Kingston Harbor.

1752, September 15. A hurricane destroyed more than 20 English ships in the harbor at Charleston, South Carolina.

1752, September 26. Sixteen ships were lost in the vicinity of Havana in a hurricane.

1752, October 1. A hurricane sank or drove ashore more than 50 merchant vessels and warships at Louisbourg on Cape Breton Island, Nova Scotia, Canada.

1752, October 22. A hurricane in the Gulf of Florida destroyed numerous ships, including the British merchantmen *Alexander, Dolphin* and *Lancaster.*

1753, October 7. More than 40 large vessels were lost during a storm at Cape Breton Island, Nova Scotia, Canada.

1754, date uncertain. The English vessel *Pearl* caught fire and exploded near Cape Charles, Virginia.

1754, September 13. More than 10 vessels were wrecked in a hurricane off St. John's, Antigua, Lesser Antilles.

1755, June. The 64-gun English warship H.M.S. *Mars* was lost at Halifax, Nova Scotia.

1757, date uncertain. The British merchantman *Duke of Cumberland* was wrecked near Cape Henry, Virginia, with 25 lives lost.

1757, July. Eight ships were lost in a hurricane at Barbados.

1757, September 24. Two English warships, the 60-gun H.M.S. *Tilbury* and 10-gun H.M.S. *Ferret,* were wrecked at Louisbourg harbor in Canada during a storm.

1758, June 28. Before an anticipated attack by English forces, the French at Louisbourg, Canada, scuttled several ships including the 50-gun *Apollon* and the 26-gun *Fidele.* At about the same time, three other large French warships caught fire and burned by accident. These were the 64-gun *Capricieux,* the 64-gun *Cilibre* and the 74-gun *Entreprenant.*

1758, August 23. Numerous ships were sunk at Carlisle Bay and Bridgetown, Barbados, in a hurricane.

1758, November 29. The 50-gun British warship *Lichfield* foundered off the Barbary coast with 130 lives lost.

1759, date uncertain. The 74-gun English warship H.M.S. *Terrible* was wrecked in Canada's St. Lawrence River.

1760, July 8. Twenty-five French vessels were sunk at Chaleur Bay, on the Gulf of St. Lawrence in Canada, in an English attack. Three of the destroyed ships were warships, including the 32-gun *Marchault* and the 22-gun *Bienfaisant.*

1760, October 4. The 50-gun English warship H.M.S. *Harwich* was wrecked near Cuba's Isle of Pines.

1761, May 4. A hurricane sank five ships at Charleston, South Carolina.

1761, October 25. The 20-gun British man-of-war *Griffin* sank off Bermuda, with 50 lives lost.

1763, date uncertain. The British ship *Pitt Packet* foundered in Delaware Bay on a voyage from Ireland to Philadelphia; hundreds of lives reportedly were lost.

1764, June 17. The French vessel *Le Blanc Henri* was wrecked on Wolf Island Spit near Kingston, Ontario.

1765, April 1. The schooner *Newport* was wrecked at Setauket, New York, but the crew was rescued.

1766, October. Numerous English merchantmen were wrecked in a hurricane at Montserrat, Lesser Antilles.

1766, October. A hurricane wrecked five English merchantmen at Roseau, Dominica, Lesser Antilles.

1768, date uncertain. A merchantman preparing to sail for Scotland was destroyed by an explosion at Annapolis, Maryland. Some crewmen survived.

1768, October 15. Dozens of ships reportedly were sunk in a hurricane at Havana, Cuba. The storm also destroyed several thousand buildings in Havana and vicinity.

1769, July 26. A hurricane destroyed 13 ships at Roseau, Dominica, Lesser Antilles.

1770, date uncertain. The galleon *Orriflamme* foundered in a storm off Valparaiso, Chile, with 700 people on board. Only a few people survived.

1772, date uncertain. Two big Spanish warships, the 70-gun *El Buen Consejo* and the 40-gun *Jesus, Maria y Joseph,* were sunk off Anguilla in the Lesser Antilles.

1772, January 2. The British merchantman *Intelligence* sank at Cape Francois, Hispaniola, with 21 lives lost.

1772, July 20. A hurricane destroyed more than 150 ships in Cuban waters.

1772, August 30. A hurricane destroyed 18 English merchantmen at Roseau, Dominica, Lesser Antilles.

1773, date uncertain. The ship *Hill,* registry unknown, was struck by lightning and exploded near

Bridgetown, Barbados. Most of the crew was killed.

1775, September 2. The English merchantman *Hibernia* was lost in a storm several miles south of Cape Henry, Virginia. Another English merchantman, *Hector*, was lost on Frying Pan Shoals on the North Carolina coast. Numerous other ships were also wrecked in this storm.

1776, date uncertain. The 30-gun Spanish warship *Clara* was lost near Montevideo, Uruguay; 120 on board were killed.

1776, March 6. The ship *Sally* was wrecked at Montauk, New York, after being captured by the British; the captain and 15 others on board were escorted under guard to New York City.

1776, September 6. Some 6,000 people are thought to have died in a hurricane that sank 100 merchant vessels at Point Bay in Martinique.

1777, date uncertain. The 28-gun American warship *Congress* was burned on New York's Hudson River to avoid capture by British forces.

1777, date uncertain. The British captured and blew up the 24-gun American warship *Montgomery* on the Hudson River in New York.

1777, date uncertain. The 32-gun British warship H.M.S. *Repulse* foundered near Bermuda.

1777, November 11. The British troop transport *Aurora* was wrecked off Cape Hatteras, North Carolina, with hundreds of lives lost.

1778, date uncertain. The 70-gun British frigate of war H.M.S. *Somerset* was wrecked on Cape Cod, Massachusetts, near Provincetown.

1779, date uncertain. A privateer of undetermined nationality was lost near New Smyrna, Florida; 50 crewmen were captured.

1779, date uncertain. A merchantman exploded and was lost completely near Cambridge, Maryland.

1779, May. In a devastating action, British forces destroyed almost 150 American vessels at Norfolk, Virginia, and in the vicinity.

1779, August 14. Several American warships, including the 32-gun *Warren* and the 16-gun *Hazard*, were burned at Portland, Maine, to deprive the British of their use.

1779, August 28. In a repeat of the tragedy of 1776, a hurricane destroyed more than 70 ships at Martinique, with a loss of thousands of lives.

1779, September. The 20-gun British warship H.M.S. *Rose* was sunk intentionally to block the entrance to the harbor at Savannah, Georgia.

1779, September 4. A hurricane wrecked a number of large French warships at Charlestown, Nevis, Lesser Antilles.

1780, February 23. Six large vessels sank in a hurricane at Montego Bay, Jamaica.

1780, October. Numerous ships were lost in a hurricane at Jamaica, including H.M.S. *Badger*, sunk at Lucea Harbor.

1780, October 3. Thirteen British warships, including the 74-gun *Thunderer*, were wrecked in a hurricane on Cuba's Jardines Reefs. Most of the men on the ships were killed.

1780, October 6. Wrecked on Silver Shoals in the Bahamas, the British warship H.M.S. *Sterling Castle* disintegrated within minutes. There were only a few survivors.

1780, October 9. A hurricane at St. Eustatius in the Lesser Antilles wrecked seven Dutch ships completely, with no survivors. Orange Town was demolished totally. Between 4,000 and 5,000 people are thought to have been killed.

1780, October 10. The 74-gun British warship H.M.S. *Cornwall* sank in a hurricane at St. Lucia, Lesser Antilles, along with several other vessels.

1780, October 10. A hurricane sank the 50-gun British warship H.M.S. *Experiment* and a 40-gun French warship at St. Vincent, Lesser Antilles. Almost everyone on board was killed.

1780, October 10. A hurricane wrecked more than 20 ships at Barbados. Many other vessels simply vanished in the storm; presumably they were blown out to sea. Maritime historian Robert Marx writes that two English ships, *Edward* and *Happy Return*, were blown away by the storm, made their way back to the island, and sank on their return. He adds that great waves washed a building at Bridgetown's Naval Hospital into the sea.

1780, October 12. The great hurricane on this date destroyed 19 Dutch merchantmen and numerous other vessels at Grenada, Lesser Antilles.

1780, October 12. A convoy consisting of 40 French troop transports was wrecked completely in a hurricane at Martinique, Lesser Antilles, along with seven English warships. According to some records, more than 150 ships altogether were lost at Martinique in this storm.

1780, October 18. A hurricane demolished or drove aground more than 50 ships at Bermuda.

1780, November 3. The 28-gun British frigate *Hussar* ran aground at Pot Rock in New York's East River, with the loss of 62 lives.

1781, date uncertain. The Santa Ana shoal in Acapulco's harbor was named for a large vessel, *Santa Ana*, that was wrecked there in 1781 on a voyage from Peru.

1781, date uncertain. The 20-gun British warship H.M.S. *Mentor* burned at Pensacola, Florida.

1781, date uncertain. The 32-gun British warship H.M.S. *Thetis* was wrecked at St. Lucia, Lesser Antilles.

1781, January. The British warship *Bedford* was dismasted in a storm between Gardiner's Bay, New York, and Rhode Island, but was repaired several weeks later.

1781, January 23. The 74-gun British warship H.M.S. *Culloden* was wrecked on Long Island, New York.

1781, April 19. The Spanish frigate *Francesca* was wrecked in Pensacola Bay, Florida.

1781, August 1–2. A hurricane destroyed numerous ships at Jamaica, including 90 ships sunk or wrecked at Kingston Harbor alone.

1781, August 9. Two British warships were sunk at their docks in Charleston, South Carolina, by a hurricane.

1782, date uncertain. A British warship, the 74-gun H.M.S. *Hector,* was wrecked on the Grand Banks, Newfoundland, Canada.

1782, date uncertain. The British warship H.M.S. *Rattlesnake* was wrecked at Trinidad, Lesser Antilles, with one life lost.

1782, date uncertain. The 32-gun British warship H.M.S. *Blonde* was wrecked on Nantucket Shoals, Massachusetts, with the loss of several crewmen.

1782, August 15. The 74-gun French warship *Magnifique* was wrecked at Lowell's Island near Boston, Massachusetts, with the loss of seven lives out of a crew of 750.

1782, September. A British fleet was destroyed in an Atlantic storm with the loss of some 3,500 lives. Eight hundred lives were lost on one vessel alone.

1783, date uncertain. The Spanish warship *Dragon* was wrecked in the Gulf of Campeche, Mexico, with 60 lives lost.

1783, date uncertain. The Dutch ship *Erfprinz* sank off Cape Cod, Massachusetts, with the loss of 303 lives.

1783, November 23. The British sloop *Ontario* was lost on Lake Ontario, off Oswego, New York, with 190 killed.

1784, date uncertain. Several large vessels were lost in the harbor at Curaçao, Venezuela, in a hurricane. Other ships were driven out to sea by the storm and were never seen again.

1785, date uncertain. The Scottish immigrant ship *Faithful Stewart* foundered off Cape Henlopen, Delaware, on its way to Philadelphia; some 200 were killed.

1785, date uncertain. A hurricane on some date before October caused the loss of more than 50 ships in Port Royal and Kingston Harbor, Jamaica.

1785, September–October. Storms wrecked several large vessels along the Virginia coast.

1785, December 5. The British ferry *Abermenai* sank in the Menai Strait, with 55 lives lost.

1786, date uncertain. The brig *Peggy*, from Bermuda, was wrecked at Montauk Point, New York, with seven lives lost.

1786, August. A hurricane destroyed numerous ships of various nationalities at St. Eustatius in the Lesser Antilles.

1786, September 2. A hurricane reportedly destroyed every ship at Carlisle Bay, Barbados.

1786, October 20. Approximately 20 ships were lost when a hurricane struck Kingston Harbor, Jamaica.

1787, September 2. Fifteen British merchantmen were wrecked in the port of Belize in a hurricane.

1788, date uncertain. The Spanish galleon *Nuestra Señora de la Balvanera* was lost on the Guapacho Reefs near San Carlos, Chile. There were no survivors.

1788, July 23. A storm demolished numerous ships at Norfolk, Virginia.

1788, July 26. A hurricane wrecked numerous ships at Bermuda.

1788, September. A hurricane destroyed more than 50 large French vessels at Martinique, Lesser Antilles. The hurricane also washed much of the community of Caravel, and most of its people, into the sea.

1790, date uncertain. The British warship H.M.S. *Endymion* was lost on a shoal near Turks Islands in the Bahamas. The crew was rescued.

1790, December. The American brig *Sally* was wrecked on Eaton's Neck Reef, New York, with 10 lives lost.

1792, August 1. A hurricane destroyed 10 ships at St. Barthelemy in the Lesser Antilles, with numerous lives lost.

1792, August 1. Fourteen English ships were lost in a hurricane at Dominica in the Lesser Antilles.

1792, August 29. The British warship *Royal George* capsized at Spithead, England, while undergoing repairs. Some 900 lives were lost.

1793, date uncertain. *General Clark*, a British merchantman, was wrecked on a reef in the Florida Keys, but the crew survived.

1794, date uncertain. The British warship H.M.S. *Placentia* was wrecked near Newfoundland, Canada.

1794, August 27–28. A hurricane destroyed or damaged 76 ships at Havana, including 12 Spanish warships.

1795, August 2. A storm wrecked several ships on the bar at Ocracoke Inlet, North Carolina. This storm also reportedly destroyed a number of Spanish vessels in a fleet off nearby Cape Hatteras.

1796, May 13. The British sloop-of-war *Cormorant* exploded at Port-au-Prince, Haiti, with 95 lives lost.

1796, July 5. The 32-gun British warship H.M.S. *Active* was wrecked in Canada's St. Lawrence River.

1797, December 27. The 18-gun British warship H.M.S. *Hunter* was lost on Hog Island, Virginia, with the loss of all but five of the 80-man crew.

1798, date uncertain. The American brig *Hazard* was sounding the Columbia River (Oregon-Washington) bar when five men in a boat were lost.

1798, June 23. The 16-gun British warship H.M.S. *Rover* was lost in the Gulf of St. Lawrence, Canada.

1798, September 25. Numerous ships were wrecked in a gale that struck Halifax, Nova Scotia, Canada, including the British warship H.M.S. *Lynx*.

1799, March 15. Almost 150 people were killed in the wreck of the Spanish frigate *Guadalupe* at Cape San Antonio, Cuba.

1799, November 5. The British ship *Sceptre* was lost at Table Bay near the Cape of Good Hope, South Africa, with 291 killed.

1800, date uncertain. *St. Nicholas,* a Russian trader, was wrecked at the mouth of the Quillayute River in Washington state.

1800, January 17. The brig *Ocean* was lost off Long Island, New York, on a voyage from Bremen, Germany, to Philadelphia; the captain perished, but the rest of the crew and passengers were rescued.

1800, March 17. The British frigate *Queen Charlotte* burned off Leghorn, Italy. Seven hundred were killed.

1800, August. The British warship H.M.S. *Lowestoffe* and several merchantmen were wrecked on Great Inagua Island in the Bahamas.

1800, November 7. The 34-gun Spanish warship *Leocadia* wrecked near Punta Santa Ilene, Ecuador; 140 on board were lost.

1800, December. The American schooner *Polly* was wrecked on the south shore of Long Island, New York, while on a voyage from Wilmington, North Carolina, to Newport, Rhode Island; one life was lost.

1801, March 16. The 74-gun British warship *Invincible* was wrecked at Harborough Sands, Yarmouth, with 400 killed.

1801, August 10. Six English merchantmen were wrecked simultaneously on reefs at Great Inagua Island in the Bahamas.

1802, date uncertain. The 18-gun British warship H.M.S. *Scout* foundered off the coast of Newfoundland, Canada; all crew members were lost.

1802, date uncertain. The 14-gun British warship H.M.S. *Fly* foundered off Newfoundland, Canada, reportedly with the loss of all on board.

1802, February 23. Numerous ships were lost in a gale at Jamaica.

1802, October 27. The Spanish frigate *Juno* sank off Cape May, New Jersey, killing 425.

1803, November 11. The American sloop *Lady Washington* disappeared on Lake Ontario.

1804, date uncertain. A Portuguese merchantman was wrecked at Barbados during a voyage from Brazil to Portugal, with dozens of lives lost.

1804, February 24. The schooner *Gladiator* was lost on Gardiner's Island, New York; two perished.

1804, September 4. The 32-gun English warship H.M.S. *De Ruyter* sank at Deep Bay, Antigua, Lesser Antilles, in a hurricane. No one was killed.

1804, September 11. Numerous ships were sunk in a hurricane at Savannah, Georgia.

1805, October 23. The British transport ship *Anaeas* was lost off Newfoundland with 340 killed.

1806, date uncertain. The 74-gun French warship *Impetueux* was driven ashore by British vessels and destroyed near Cape Henry, Virginia.

1806, November 4. The 12-gun British schooner of war H.M.S. *Redbridge* was wrecked near Providence, Rhode Island.

1807, date uncertain. The American schooner *Charles* was wrecked on a reef near Portland, Maine, with the loss of 16 lives.

1807, February 1. The 74-gun British warship *Blenheim* sank in a hurricane near the island of Rodriguez in the Indian Ocean, with almost 600 lives lost. Another ship, *Java,* was lost in the same storm with *Blenheim;* 280 perished.

1808, date uncertain. At Veracruz, Spain, the Spanish schooner *Felicidad* was struck by lightning and exploded.

1808, August 22. The 120-ton British vessel *Sea Otter* wrecked near the mouth of Oregon's Umpqua River, with the loss of all but six on board.

1808, December 4. The 22-gun British warship H.M.S. *Banterer* was lost on Canada's St. Lawrence River.

1809, date uncertain. Sixty-two of 65 men on the British war brig *Dominica* were killed when the ship foundered near Tortola in the Virgin Islands.

1809, October 28. The Swedish brig *Fahlum* hit a rock and sank near Sag Harbor, New York.

1810, September 15. The schooner *Sally* was discovered on its beam ends, with no crew on board, near Southampton, New York; three were lost.

1810, October 23–26. A hurricane sank or wrecked 32 ships at Havana and caused extensive damage to the city.

1810, November. The 12-gun British warship H.M.S. *Plumper* sank in Canada's St. Lawrence River.

1810, December 22. The British frigate *Minotaur* was lost of a reef off the coast of Holland; 570 were killed.

1811, March 22. Eight men in boats were drowned when the captain of the American vessel *Tonquin* sent them out in a heavy sea to sound the Columbia River (Oregon-Washington) bar.

1811, June. Most of the crew of the French vessel *Guernsey* died in a wreck at St. Barthelemy in the Lesser Antilles.

1811, August 7. The pirate ship *La Franchise* was burned by its crew near Pensacola, Florida, after a fight with a United States gunboat.

1811, October 7. A hurricane at St. Barthelemy in the Lesser Antilles destroyed 40 ships.

1811, October 8. Several American merchant ships were reported wrecked in a hurricane on the northern side of Anguilla in the Lesser Antilles.

1811, December 23–24. More than 50 large vessels reportedly were wrecked on Long Island, New York, during a storm.

1811, December 24–25. The sloop *Rosette* was wrecked on Long Island, New York, in a snowstorm; all on board were lost.

1812, August 3. The 18-gun English warship H.M.S. *Emulous* was wrecked on Canada's Sable Island.

1812, October 12–14. Numerous ships were lost in a hurricane at Kingston Harbor, Jamaica.

1813, date uncertain. The 10-gun British warship H.M.S. *Subtle* foundered near St. Barthelemy in the Lesser Antilles with the loss of 50 lives.

1813, date uncertain. Before July, five ships were lost in the vicinity of Port Royal, Jamaica, including the 18-gun British warship H.M.S. *Colibri.*

1813, July 26. More than 40 ships were wrecked, or driven ashore, or sunk at Nassau, Bahamas, in a gale.

1813, August. Sixteen ships were wrecked in and around Roseau, Dominica, Lesser Antilles, in a hurricane.

1813, August. Forty-two ships were lost, and more than 3,000 people were killed, in a hurricane that struck Martinique, Lesser Antilles.

1813, August 1. Many ships were sunk or driven ashore at Bermuda in a hurricane.

1813, August 27–28. A hurricane at Charleston, South Carolina, sank many ships in the harbor, in the river and and along the coast.

1813, September. Eleven lives were lost when an unidentified fishing boat was wrecked near Fire Island, New York.

1813, September 27. The 12-gun British warship H.M.S. *Bold* was lost at Prince Edward Island, Canada.

1813, November 5. The 18-gun British warship H.M.S. *Tweed* was wrecked at Newfoundland's Shoal Bay.

1813, November 6. The 40-gun H.M.S. *Woolwich* was wrecked at Barbados in the Lesser Antilles.

1813, November 10. The 18-gun British warship H.M.S. *Atalante* was lost off Halifax, Nova Scotia.

1814, January 14. The British transport *Queen* was lost at Falmouth, with 350 killed.

1814, June 28. The 50-gun British troopship H.M.S. *Leopard* was wrecked at Anticosti Island in the Gulf of St. Lawrence, Canada.

1814, August. The 18-gun British warship H.M.S. *Peacock* foundered off Charleston, South Carolina, with the loss of all on board.

1814, September 15. The 20-gun British warship H.M.S. *Hermes* was sunk at Mobile Bay, Alabama.

1814, November 24. The 18-gun British warship H.M.S. *Fantome* was wrecked near Halifax, Nova Scotia.

1815, March 25. The Spanish ship *Volador* ran aground and broke apart at Pensacola, Florida, with the loss of two crewmen and the entire cargo.

1815, April 24. The 64-gun Spanish warship *San Pedro,* part of a fleet sent from Spain to put down a rebellion in Venezuela, caught fire and exploded off Venezuela's Coche Island. More than 50 men perished.

1815, May 1. The 36-gun British troopship H.M.S. *Penelopee* was lost off Newfoundland.

1815, August 7. The 14-gun British warship H.M.S. *Dominica* was wrecked at Bermuda in a hurricane. Numerous other vessels also were sunk or driven ashore there in this storm.

1815, September. More than 20 vessels were sunk in a storm, either on Ocracoke Island or Ocracoke Inlet, North Carolina.

1815, September 18. A hurricane wrecked or sank 60 vessels, most of them American, at the harbor at St. Barthelemy in the Lesser Antilles.

1815, September 23. Numerous ships were wrecked at Providence, Rhode Island, in a hurricane.

1816, January 30. The British transport *Seahorse* foundered near Tramore Bay, Ireland, with 380 lives lost.

1816, June 5–8. Storms in the Gulf of Florida wrecked numerous ships.

1816, July 1. The French frigate *Medusa* sank off the African coast with the loss of 155 lives.

1816, November 10. The British transport *Harpooner* was wrecked off Newfoundland.

1817, date uncertain. The American brig *Merrimack* was wrecked in the Florida Keys; although the entire cargo was lost, the crew was saved.

1817, October 21. Seven English merchantmen were lost in a hurricane at St. Lucia, Lesser Antilles, with more than 200 men killed.

1819, July. A hurricane wrecked the 12-gun American warship *Firebrand* near Cat Island, Mississippi.

1819, September. A hurricane reportedly wrecked all the ships in the harbor at St. Barthelemy in the Lesser Antilles, and destroyed much of the town as well.

1819, September 20–22. A hurricane destroyed 104 vessels at St. Thomas, Virgin Islands.

1819, December 30. More than 120 men were killed when the Spanish brigantine *Consulado* and the schooner *Guma* sank in a storm at Veracruz, Mexico.

1820, December 28. The English merchant vessel *Caledonia* was wrecked several miles south of Sandy Hook, New Jersey, with three lives lost.

1821, March 6. A storm destroyed three ships at New Orleans, with great loss of life. The French merchantman *Chaureaux* was also lost in this storm, at Chandelier Island, Mississippi.

1821, September 3. A hurricane destroyed two American frigates, *Guerriere* and *Congress,* at Norfolk, Virginia, along with many other vessels.

1821, September 3–5. The schooner *Gloriana* and several other vessels nearby were lost in a storm at Bellport, New York, with 21 killed.

1821, September 4. A hurricane on this date caused heavy damage to shipping in New York City. A total of 22 large ships sank at the Quarantine and at Public Store Dock Number 12, with numerous other wrecks also occurring in the harbor and on the shore of Long Island.

1821, September 10. Numerous ships were destroyed at St. Barthelemy in the Lesser Antilles in a hurricane.

1821, November 5. The ship *Savannah* was wrecked on Fire Island, New York, with 11 lives lost, on a voyage from Savannah, Georgia, to New York.

1822, June 20. The 10-gun British warship H.M.S. *Drake* was wrecked off the coast of Newfoundland, reportedly with great loss of life.

1822, October. The American merchantman *Savannah* was wrecked on Long Island, New York, with the loss of everyone on board.

1822, November 19. Alligator Reef in the Florida Keys was named for the wreck of the 12-gun naval schooner U.S.S. *Alligator.*

1822, December 22. More than 20 large ships were lost in the port of La Guaira, Venezuela, in a storm.

1823, date uncertain. The French merchant vessel *Nereide* foundered off the coast of California, with almost 300 killed.

1823, date uncertain. The Spanish schooner *Ligera* was wrecked at Montauk, New York, on a voyage from Cuba to New York, with seven lives lost.

1825, June 4. A hurricane destroyed more than 25 vessels on the Outer Banks of North Carolina.

1826, March 20. The schooner *Susan* was struck by lightning 100 miles off Montauk Point, New York; was run ashore at Montauk Point and burned; no casualties.

1826, October 7. The sloop *Marietta* capsized off Mattituck, New York, with seven lives lost.

1827, November. The American sloop *Eliza Ann* was wrecked at Southold, New York, with all on board killed.

1829, January 2. Four lives were lost when the sloop *Enterprise* was wrecked at Plum Island, New York.

1829, January 2. An unidentified schooner was wrecked at Plum Island, New York, with two lives lost.

1829, March 10. Forty-six people are thought to have lost their lives when the British bark *William and Ann* was wrecked on Clatsop Spit at the Columbia River (Oregon-Washington) bar.

1829, June 4. The American steam frigate *Fulton the First* blew up at the Brooklyn (New York) Navy Yard; 33 were killed.

1832, April 9. *Brandywine,* a Mississippi River steamboat, burned at Randolph, Tennessee, with 155 lives lost.

1837, January 2. The Mississippi River steamboat *Ben Sherrod* burned at Black Hawk, Louisiana, with 200 killed.

1837, October 31. The sidewheel steamer *Monmouth* struck another vessel, *Tremont,* on the Mississippi River; 300 were killed.

1839, May. The American whaling ship *Edward Quesnel* was wrecked at Napeague, New York, with eight or 10 lives lost.

1839, December 23. The brig *Pocahontas* was wrecked

at Plum Island, New York, while on a voyage from Cadiz, Spain, to Massachusetts; 11 lives were lost.

1840, date uncertain. The American packet ship *Recide* was wrecked at Eaton's Neck, New York, with all lives lost.

1840, January 13. The steamer *Lexington* was wrecked at Eaton's Neck, New York, with more than 100 lives lost.

1841, August 9. The steamer *Erie* burned near Silver Creek, New York, with 242 lives lost.

1841, November. The schooner *Charles & Henry* was wrecked at Old Field Point, New York, in a snowstorm, with four lives lost.

1842, August 27. The convict ship *Waterloo* was lost in a gale off the South African coast; 190 were killed.

1844, March 1. The Mississippi River steamboat *Buckeye* was run down by another steamboat at Atchafalaya, Louisiana, with 80 lives lost.

1844, October 23. The side-wheel steamer *Lucy Walker* blew up at New Albany, Indiana, with 60 killed.

1845, October 27. The side-wheel steamer *Plymouth* collided with another vessel near Shawneetown, Illinois; 25 were killed.

1846, March 17. The ship *Susan* was wrecked at Southampton, Long Island, New York; 100 Irish immigrants on board were rescued and taken by stagecoach to New York City.

1846, August 4. The immigrant ship *Cataraqui* ran aground in a storm in the Bass Strait between Australia and Tasmania, with 414 lives lost.

1846, November 1. The steamer *Rhode Island* was lost off Huntington, New York; 150 on board were rescued.

1846, November 21. Thirty people were killed when the side-wheel steamer *Maria* collided with another vessel at Natchez, Mississippi.

1847, date uncertain. The English vessel *Ashland* was wrecked at Southampton, New York; hundreds were rescued.

1847, March 3. An unidentified ship was wrecked at Montauk, New York, with six lives lost.

1847, June 4. The side-wheel steamer *Edna* blew up at Colombia, Louisiana; 20 were killed.

1847, November 21. The steamer *Phoenix* caught fire and burned at Sheboygan, Wisconsin; 240 were killed.

1847, December 29. The side-wheel steamer *A.N. Johns* blew up at Trinity, Kentucky, killing 60.

1848, January 18. Thirty-five people were killed when the side-wheel steamer *Yalobusha* caught fire at Donaldsonville, Louisiana.

1848, May 27. The side-wheel steamer *Clarksville* burned at Napoleon, Arkansas, with the loss of 21 lives.

1848, August 28. The American sailing ship *Ocean Monarch* sank off Great Orme's Head, North Wales, after catching fire; 178 perished.

1849, March. At least six perished in the wreck of an unknown vessel near Montauk, New York, where the bodies washed ashore on March 3.

1849, March 1. The American bark *Floridian* was wrecked in a gale off Harwich on the British coast, with 193 killed.

1849, October 6. The immigrant ship *St. John* was wrecked near Boston with 27 lives lost.

1849, November 15. The side-wheel steamer *Louisiana* exploded at New Orleans, killing 86.

1850, April 23. The steamboat *Belle of the West* blew up on the Ohio River at Warsaw, Kentucky, killing 34.

1850, June 17. The side-wheel steamer *G.P. Griffith* burned at Mentor, Ohio; almost 300 were killed.

1850, July 19. The bark *Elizabeth* was wrecked at Fire Island, New York, with 10 lives lost.

1850, October 23. More than 500 were killed when the Turkish warship *Neiri Shevket* exploded at Constantinople.

1850, October 29. The side-wheel steamer *Sagamore* exploded at San Francisco, killing 20.

1851, June 10. The Indian sailing vessel *Atiet Rohoman* foundered near Bombay with the loss of 175 lives.

1851, June 25. The bark *Henry* was wrecked at Mecox, New York; the ship was a complete loss, but 104 lives were saved.

1851, August 25. The British ship *Catherine* was wrecked at Amagansett, New York, on a voyage to New York from Dublin; the ship was a complete loss, but 300 Irish immigrants were saved.

1852, January 4. The British passenger liner *Amazon* exploded off the Scilly Isles, killing 140 people.

1852, January 28. The American steamship *General Warren* was wrecked on Clatsop Spit at the Columbia River (Oregon-Washington) bar, with 42 lives lost.

1852, February 26. In one of the most famous shipwrecks in British history, the frigate *Birkenhead* struck a rock and sank off Cape Town, South Africa, with 455 people killed.

1852, August 20. The side-wheel steamer *Atlantic* sank after colliding with another steamer on Lake Erie near Long Point, Ontario, Canada. Between 250 and 350 people drowned.

1852, November 29. The American brig *Marie* was lost

near Cape Disappointment, Washington, with nine killed.

1853, January 9. Nine were lost in the wreck of the American bark *Vandalia* near Cape Disappointment, Washington.

1853, May 4. The immigrant ship *William and Mary* was lost on rocks off the Bahamas; 170 perished.

1853, September 29. *Annie Jane,* an immigrant ship, was lost off the Hebrides; 348 were killed.

1853, November. The captain was drowned in the wreck of the American brig *Palos* at the entrance to Shoalwater Bay, Washington.

1853, December 24. The immigrant ship *St. George* burned in the Atlantic Ocean, with 51 lives lost.

1854, date uncertain. The river steamer *Castle* blew up and sank near Tongue Point, Oregon; no fatalities were reported.

1854, January 14. On its maiden voyage, the steamship *San Francisco* sank in the Atlantic Ocean with 300 lives lost.

1854, January 20. A British passenger ship, *Tayleur* foundered in the Irish Sea; 349 lives were lost.

1854, February 24. Four lives were lost in the wreck of the American steam tug *Firefly* at the Columbia River (Oregon-Washington) mouth.

1854, March 5. The side-wheel steamer *Caroline* burned at White River, Arkansas, with the loss of 45 lives.

1854, March 20. The side-wheel steamer *Monroe* capsized near Natchez, Mississippi, with 30 lives lost.

1854, April 16. The American immigrant ship *Powhatan* was wrecked off Barnegat, New Jersey, with some 250 lives lost.

1854, July 17. The side-wheel steamer *Franklin* was wrecked at Center Moriches, New York; the ship was a complete loss, but 190 were saved.

1854, September 27. In one of the most famous shipwrecks of the 19th century, the liner *Arctic* sank after colliding with the French steamer *Vesta* in the Atlantic Ocean off Cape Race, Newfoundland; 322 were killed.

1855, January 9. The clipper ship *Guiding Star* vanished in an ice field in the South Atlantic; 480 people were lost.

1855, January 27. The side-wheel steamer *Pearl* blew up at Yolo, California, killing 80.

1855, May 3. The British immigrant ship *John* was lost on rocks near Falmouth, England; 200 perished.

1855, June 30. The side-wheel steamer *Lexington* blew up at Rome, Indiana, killing 30.

1856, January 5. The side-wheel steamer *Belle* exploded at Sacramento, California, killing 30.

1856, January 23. The side-wheel steamer *Pacific* disappeared after sailing from Liverpool, England; 186 lives were lost.

1856, January 29. One hundred and thirty-five lives were lost when the American sailing ship *John Rutledge* collided with an iceberg off Newfoundland.

1856, March 30. The Chilean steamship *Cazador* was wrecked on rocks near Constitution, Chile, with 315 lives lost.

1856, July 16. The steamship *Northern Indiana* burned on Lake Erie, with 50 lives lost.

1856, November 2. One hundred and thirty lives were lost when the steamer *Lyonnais* collided with a bark near Nantucket Island.

1857, January 1. The Desdemona Sands on the Columbia River (Oregon-Washington) bar were named for the wreck of the American bark *Desdemona;* one life was lost.

1857, September 12. The American mail steamship *Central America* sank off the Florida coast in heavy seas with a cargo on $1.5 million in gold; 427 perished.

1857, September 23. The Russian warship *Leffort* sank in a storm in the Gulf of Finland; 826 died.

1858, September 13. The Hamburg-Amerika liner *Austria* caught fire and sank in the North Atlantic, killing 471 people.

1859, February 28. The side-wheel steamer *Princess* blew up at Baton Rouge, Louisiana, killing 70.

1859, April 24. The side-wheel steamer *St. Nicholas* blew up at Helena, Arkansas; 60 were killed.

1859, April 28. The American immigrant ship *Pomona* sank off the Irish coast with 386 lives lost.

1860, June 24. The side-wheel steamer *B.W. Lewis* blew up at Cairo, Illinois, killing 40.

1860, September 8. The excursion ship *Lady Elgin* sank in Lake Michigan, with 287 killed, after colliding with the schooner *Augusta.*

1860, September 9. The British sloop *Camilla* was lost in a storm off the Japanese coast; 121 were killed.

1860, October 31. The side-wheel steamer *H.R.W. Hill* blew up at Baton Rouge, Louisiana, killing 39.

1862, July 27. The steamship *Golden Gate* burned near Manzanillo, Mexico, with 198 lives lost.

1862, August 13. Seventy-six people were killed when the side-wheel steamer *West Point* collided with another vessel in the Potomac River.

1862, August 28. The British steamship *Great Eastern* was damaged on a rock at Montauk Point, New York; the rock was subsequently named after the ship.

1862, December 20. The steamship *Lifeguard* was lost at sea off Flamborough Head, England; 46 were killed.

1863, February 7. The British steam corvette *Orpheus* sank off the coast of New Zealand with the loss of 190 lives.

1863, April 27. The passenger ship *Anglo-Saxon* ran onto rocks in fog near Cape Race, Newfoundland; 237 were killed.

1863, August 3. The side-wheel steamer *Ruth* burned at Columbus, Kentucky, with the loss of 30 lives.

1863, September. The ammunition carrier *City of Madison* blew up at Vicksburg, Mississippi, killing 156.

1864, February 22. The liner *Bohemian* sank after striking a rock near Portland, Maine; 20 perished.

1864, June 8. Thirty-five people were killed when the side-wheel steamer *Berkshire* burned at Poughkeepsie, New York.

1864, November 4. The British gunboat *Racehorse* was lost on rocks off Chafee Cape on the Chinese coast; 99 perished.

1864, December 22. The British warship *Bombay* burned off Montevideo, Chile; 92 were killed.

1865, March 15. The American bark *Industry* was wrecked at the Columbia River mouth (Oregon-Washington), with 17 lives lost.

1865, March 25. The steamship *General Lyon* caught fire off Cape Hatteras, North Carolina; 400 were killed.

1865, April 26–27. The side-wheel steamer *Sultana* exploded and burned near Memphis, Tennessee, with more than 1,500 thought to have perished.

1865, July 30. The side-wheel steamer *Brother Jonathan* was lost on rocks off Crescent City, California; 171 were killed.

1865, August 9. The steamship *Pewabic* collided with another vessel near Thunder Bay, Michigan, with 40 lives lost.

1865, August 24. The immigrant ship *Eagle Speed* sank near Calcutta; 265 lives were lost.

1865, October 20. The side-wheel steamer *Niagara* collided with another vessel near Helena, Arkansas; 75 lives were lost.

1865, October 25. The side-wheel steamer *Tennessee* was lost at sea off Savannah, Georgia; 34 perished.

1866, January 11. The British steamship *London* sank shortly after encountering stormy weather in the Bay of Biscay; 220 were lost.

1866, January 30. The side-wheel steamer *Missouri* exploded at Newburg, Indiana; 65 were killed.

1866, April. The steamer *City of Norwich* burned and sank after colliding with a schooner off Huntington, New York; 11 lives were lost.

1866, April 3. The immigrant ship *Monarch of the Seas* was lost in a storm after leaving Liverpool, England; 738 are thought to have been killed.

1866, April 16. The sailing vessel *Jeddo* burned in the Sunda Straits, in what is now Indonesia; 150 were killed.

1866, July 12. The Australian steamship *Cowarra* was lost off New South Wales, with 60 killed.

1866, October 3. The side-wheel steamer *Evening Star* sank near Tybee Island, Georgia, with 261 lives lost.

1866, December 25. The steamer *Commodore Brady* was wrecked at Peconic, New York; some 100 lives were saved.

1867, February 17. The side-wheel steamer *David White* blew up at Columbia, Mississippi, killing 35.

1867, May 21. The steamship *Wisconsin* burned at Grenadine Island on Lake Ontario; 23 were killed.

1867, October 9. The steamship *Home* foundered near Oglethorpe Light off New York harbor; 80 perished.

1867, October 29. The British liner *Rhone* was lost on rocks in the Virgin Islands in a hurricane; 124 perished.

1868, March 18. The side-wheel steamer *Magnolia* blew up at California, Ohio; 80 were killed.

1868, April 9. The steamer *Sea Bird* burned near Evanston, Illinois, with as many as 103 killed.

1868, June 20. Fifty lives were lost when the side-wheel steamer *Morning Star* collided with another vessel near Lorain, Ohio.

1869, January. The American schooner *Anna C. Anderson* disappeared at sea on a voyage from Oysterville, Washington, to San Francisco. One possible explanation for the ship's loss is that the schooner put on a large amount of sail to make a fast passage, but was struck by a strong wind and capsized before the extra canvas could be taken in.

1869, February 20. The Austrian steam frigate *Radetzky* exploded in the Adriatic Sea with 345 lives lost.

1869, September 13. The schooner *Mary Millness* was wrecked at Montauk, New York, with two lives lost.

1869, October 27. The steamer *Stonewall* burned near Cairo, Illinois, with 209 people killed.

1870, January 23. The American frigate *Oneida* collided with the British steamer *Bombay* near Yokohama, Japan; 120 were killed.

1870, January 31. The liner *City of Boston* vanished on a voyage from New York to Liverpool, England; 191 were lost.

1870, September 6. Four hundred and eighty-three people are thought to have perished when the ironclad *Captain* sank in a storm in the Bay of Biscay.

1870, October 19. The steamship *Cambria* was lost on rocks off Donegal, Ireland; 169 were killed.

1870, October 20. The American steamship *Varuna* was lost off the coast of Florida, with 72 lives, on a voyage from New York to Galveston, Texas.

1870, December 18. One hundred and twenty-two lives were lost when the French steam corvette *Gorgone* sank in a storm near Brest, France.

1871, July 30. The ferryboat *Westfield* exploded in New York harbor with 104 lives lost.

1872, August 24. The steamship *America* burned at Yokohama, Japan, with 65 lives lost.

1873, January 22. Three hundred people died when the Spanish steamship *Murillo* collided with the British passenger frigate *Northfleet* off Dungeness, England. The captain of *Northfleet* was among those killed.

1873, April 1. The liner *Atlantic* was wrecked on rocks near Halifax, Nova Scotia; 560 lives were lost.

1873, November 22. The French liner *Ville du Havre* sank after colliding with the clipper *Loch Earn* in the Atlantic Ocean; 226 perished.

1874, May 23. The British liner *British Admiral* was lost on rocks at Bass Strait between Australia and New Zealand; 80 were killed.

1874, October 22. The side-wheel steamer *Brooklyn* exploded on Michigan's Detroit River, killing 20.

1874, November 17. The immigrant ship *Cospatrick* burned off Auckland, New Zealand, with 468 lives lost.

1875, January 8. The steamship *San Marcos* was wrecked at False Cape, Virginia; 66 lives were saved, and none were lost.

1875, January 22. The schooner *C.E. Scammell* was wrecked at False Cape, Virginia; eight lives were saved, and there were no casualties.

1875, February 17. The steamship *Aurora Mills* was wrecked at Cape Henry, Virginia; six people were rescued, and no lives lost.

1875, February 24. The Australian passenger ship *Gothenburg* was wrecked on the Great Barrier Reef with 102 killed.

1875, May 7. The German liner *Schiller* was wrecked near the Scilly Isles; 314 perished.

1875, May 8. The British steamer *Cadiz* was lost on rocks near Brest, France; 62 were killed.

1875, May 31. The liner *Vicksburg* sank off Cape Race, Newfoundland, with 47 lives lost.

1875, November 9. Fifty-three were killed when the ship *City of Waco* was destroyed by fire at Galveston, Texas.

1875, November 22. The American schooner *Sunshine* came ashore bottom-up at North Beach Peninsula, Washington, without its crew of 25; no evidence of what happened to them has been found.

1875, December 6. The German liner *Deutschland* wrecked on Kentish Knock shoals, near Harwich, England, with 157 killed.

1875, December 7. The schooner *N.C. Price* was wrecked at Assateague Beach, Virginia; four lives were saved, none lost.

1875, December 18. The schooner *Anthony Kelley* was lost at Hog Island, Virginia; the ship was a complete loss, but all four people on board were rescued.

1876, January 12. The schooner *Aeolus* was wrecked at Hog Island, Virginia; three lives were saved, none lost.

1876, February. The sloop *Dreadnaught* (or at least a ship to which that name was attributed) was wrecked on Clatsop Spit at the Columbia River (Oregon-Washington) bar, with the loss of all seven on board.

1876, February 18. The schooner *William H. VanName* was wrecked at Smith Island Point, Virginia; six lives were saved, none lost.

1876, February 20. The schooner *Ralph Howes* was lost on Isaac Shoal at Smith Island, Virginia; six lives were saved, none lost.

1876, March 4. The British bark *Nabob* vanished at sea, with the loss of its entire crew, after leaving the Columbia River (Oregon-Washington).

1876, March 28. The schooner *S.E. Barnes* was lost at Cedar Island, Virginia; five were rescued, none lost.

1876, March 28. The schooner *Angie Predmore* was wrecked at Hog Island, Virginia; six were rescued, none lost.

1876, June 30. The schooner *George F. Wright* was lost at Assawoman Inlet, Virginia; five lives were saved, none lost.

1876, August 12. The Australian sailing ship *Great Queensland* exploded near Cape Finisterre, Spain; 569 lost their lives.

1876, December. The ship *Circassian* was wrecked at Mecox, New York; 28 in wrecking crew were lost after the wreck itself occurred.

1876, December 9. The schooner *Fannie K. Shaw* was wrecked at Cape Henry, Virginia; nine were saved, none lost.

1877, January 17. The bark *Carpione* was wrecked at Dam Neck Mills, Virginia; 14 were saved, none lost.

1877, January 20. The schooner *Delphin* was lost at Cobb Island, Virginia; seven were saved, none lost.

1877, January 20. The bark *Lilla* was wrecked at Cape

Henry, Virginia; the ship was a complete loss, but all seven on board were rescued.

1877, January 27. The schooner *George L. Treadwell* was wrecked at Chincoteague Shoal, Virginia; the ship was a complete loss, but all five lives were saved.

1877, February 18. The schooner *Alice Ida* was wrecked on the outer bar at Metomkin Inlet at Cedar Island, Virginia; all six on board were rescued.

1877, March 26. The bark *Pantser* was wrecked off Cape Henry; all 27 on board were saved.

1877, March 26. The bark *Galathea* was wrecked at Smith Island, Virginia; the ship was a complete loss, but all 12 on board were saved.

1877, May 20. The schooner *Armenia Bartlett* was wrecked at Hog Island, Virginia; the schooner was a complete loss, but all six on board were rescued.

1877, November 24. The steamer *Huron* was wrecked off Oregon Inlet, North Carolina, with the loss of 100 lives.

1877, November 25. The brig *Ossipee* was lost near Assateague Beach, Virginia; there were two fatalities.

1877, November 25. The schooner *Frank Jameson* was wrecked at Smith Island, Virginia, with five lives lost.

1878, January 4. The schooner *Montevue* was wrecked at Cobb Island, Virginia; the ship was a complete loss, but all seven on board were rescued.

1878, January 6. The schooner *J.J. Spencer* was wrecked at Hog Island, Virginia; 19 lives were saved (and none lost), but the ship was a complete loss.

1878, March 24. The British frigate *Eurydice* sank off the Isle of Wight, with 398 killed.

1878, May 31. The German ironclad *Grosser Kurfurst* collided with another ship near Folkestone, England; 284 were killed.

1878, September 3. The British excursion ship *Princess Alice* collided with the collier *Bywell Castle* in the Thames River; 645 were killed.

1878, October 22. The sailing ship *A.S. Davis* was wrecked at Virginia Beach, Virginia, with 19 lives lost.

1878, December 1. The schooner *Peerless* was wrecked at Smith Island, Virginia; all eight on board were saved, but the ship was a complete loss.

1878, December 18. The French steamship *Byzantin* collided with the British steamer *Rinaldo* near Gallipoli, Turkey; 210 were killed.

1879, March 1. The steamship *Vingoria* sank near Bombay, with 68 lives lost.

1879, March 2. The bark *Admiral* was wrecked at False

Cape, Virginia; all 14 on board were saved, but the ship was a complete loss.

1879, March 19. The French warship *Arrogante* sank near Toulon, France, with 47 lives lost.

1879, April 19. Eleven crewmen were drowned in the wreck of the side-wheel passenger steamer *Great Republic* on Sand Island at the Columbia River bar (Oregon-Washington).

1879, November 22. Twenty-four lives were lost when the American steamship *Waubuno* vanished on Georgian Bay in the Great Lakes.

1879, November 26. The bark *Jason* was wrecked at Hog Island, Virginia; all 12 on board were rescued, but the ship was a complete loss.

1879, December 2. The liner *Borussia* sank in the Atlantic Ocean with 174 lives lost.

1880, January 31. The British frigate *Atlanta* vanished at sea with 290 on board after leaving Bermuda.

1880, May 4. Two hundred fishermen lost their lives when a storm destroyed a fleet of fishing boats off the Columbia River mouth (Oregon-Washington).

1880, October 15. The steamer *Alpena* sank in Lake Michigan with 101 lives lost.

1880, October 22. The bark *Giambattista Primo* was wrecked near Hog Island and Cobb Island, Virginia; the ship was a total loss, but all 13 on board were rescued.

1880, November 24. The French steamship *Uncle Joseph* collided with the Italian steamer *Ortiga* off La Spezia, Italy; 250 were killed.

1881, January 3. All 16 men on board were killed when the British bark *Lupatia* wrecked off Tillamook Head, Oregon; only a dog survived.

1881, February 7. The British steamer *Bohemian* was lost on a reef near Cork, Ireland; 35 were killed.

1881, February 21. The sloop *Dauntless* was lost near Assateague Beach, Virginia; two lives were lost.

1881, April 26. A British sloop, *Doterel* exploded at Punta Arenas, Chile, with 143 lives lost.

1881, April 29. A New Zealand steamer, *Tararua* was lost on a reef near New Zealand's South Island; 102 were killed.

1882, February 4. The British steamship *Bahama* sank with the loss of 20 lives on a voyage to New York from Puerto Rico.

1882, April 1. Twenty-three perished when the liner *Douro* collided with a Spanish steamship near Cape Finisterre, Spain.

1882, May 18. The American steamship *Manitoulin* burned at Georgian Bay on the Great Lakes, with 30 lives lost.

1882, July 7. The Dutch monitor-ram *Adder* was lost in a storm in the North Sea; 65 were killed.

1882, August 23. The British steamship *Armenian* sank in the Baltic Sea with 23 lives lost.

1882, September 14. The steamer *Asia* was lost in Georgian Bay, Lake Huron, Canada; 123 were killed.

1883, January 7. The schooner *Albert Dailey* was lost at Smith Island, Virginia; there were two fatalities.

1883, January 19. The Hamburg-America liner *Cimbria* collided with the steamer *Sultan* in the North Sea and sank with the loss of 340 lives.

1883, February 1. The steamship *Kenmure Castle* sank during a storm in the Bay of Biscay, with 32 lives lost.

1883, March 17. Twenty-three lives were lost when the sailing ship *Dunstaffnage* sank near Aberdeen, Scotland.

1883, July 3. The British steamship *Daphne* heeled over and sank at launch, killing 195.

1883, July 3. The Belgian liner *Ludwig* vanished at sea during a voyage between Antwerp, Belgium, and Montreal, Canada; 75 lives were lost.

1883, October 7. The pilot schooner *J.C. Cousins* was stranded on Clatsop Spit at the Columbia River mouth (Oregon-Washington), with no sign of the four-man crew on board. No evidence of what happened to them was ever discovered.

1883, November 14. The steamer *Manistree* sank on Lake Superior with the loss of 30 lives.

1884, January 18. The steamer *City of Columbus* sank off Gay Head, Massachusetts, with 97 lives lost.

1884, April 3. The steamship *Daniel Steinmann* was wrecked on a shoal near Halifax, Nova Scotia, with 124 lives lost.

1884, May 6. Sixty-two were killed when the French brig *Senorine* sank off Newfoundland.

1884, July 21. One hundred and sixty-eight were killed when the Spanish steamer *Gijon* collided with a British steamship near Cape Villano.

1884, September 22. The British gunboat *Wasp* was lost off the Irish coast, with 52 killed.

1884, December 27. The bark *Lena* was wrecked at Hog Island, Virginia; there were eight fatalities.

1885, November 7. The Canadian steamer *Algoma* sank in Lake Superior with 54 lives lost.

1886, January 11. The British ship *London* sank in a storm off Land's End, England, with 220 lives lost.

1886, February 9. The side-wheel steamer *W.R. Carter* exploded near Vicksburg, Mississippi; 125 were killed.

1886, August 26. The steamship *Ferntower* sank near Saigon, Vietnam, with 50 lives lost.

1886, December 23. The French liner *Ville de Victoria* sank after colliding with the British warship *Sultan;* 32 were killed.

1887, date uncertain. The pilot boat *Phantom* was lost at sea off Fire Island, New York; all on board perished.

1887, January 8. The schooner *Elizabeth* was wrecked at Little Island, Virginia; 22 were killed.

1887, September 10. The British gunboat *Wasp* vanished at sea on a voyage to Shanghai; 73 were lost.

1887, October 21. The schooner *Manantico* was wrecked at Virginia Beach, Virginia; two perished.

1887, November 15. The steamer *Wah Yeung* burned near Hong Kong with 400 lives lost.

1888, January 28. Three were killed in the wreck of the American river steamer *Gleaner* off Tongue Point, Oregon.

1888, August 14. The liner *Geiser* sank after colliding with another liner near Sable Island, Canada; 119 perished.

1888, October 24. The American barkentine *Makah* was discovered floating bottom-up off Oregon's Tillamook Head. What happened to the 11-man crew is unknown.

1889, March 16. The American corvette *Trenton* and several other ships were destroyed in a hurricane in Samoa; 147 were killed.

1889, April 7. The schooner *Northampton* was wrecked at Virginia Beach, Virginia; three lives were lost.

1889, October 23. The schooner *Henry P. Simmons* was wrecked at False Cape, Virginia; seven were killed.

1890, January 4. The schooner *Douglas Dearborn* was found floating bottom-up off the Columbia River mouth (Oregon-Washington); no sign of what happened to the crew was ever discovered.

1890, March 1. The British steamer *Quetta* was lost on rocks in the Torres Straits (between New Guinea and Australia); 146 perished.

1890, September 19. The Turkish frigate *Ertogrul* was lost in a gale off the coast of Japan; 587 perished.

1890, December 25. The British paddle steamer *Shanghai* burned on the Yangtze River, China; 200 were killed.

1891, March 17. The liner *Utopia* sank after colliding with a battleship at the Bay of Gibraltar; 576 were killed.

1891, March 27. The bark *Dictator* was wrecked at Virginia Beach, Virginia, with seven lives lost.

1891, November 2. The steamer *Enterprise* sank off the Andaman Islands in a storm with 70 lives lost.

1891, November 3. Seven were killed when the British

ship *Strathblane* wrecked near Ocean Park, Washington.

1892, January 10. The Chinese steamship *Namchow* sank off Cupchi Point on the Chinese coast with 414 lives lost.

1892, May 21. The Brazilian ironclad *Solimoes* ran aground and was lost off Cape Polonino, Uruguay; 125 were killed.

1893, June 22. The British battleship *Victoria* sank with the loss of 358 lives after colliding with the warship *Camperdown* on maneuvers off the Cornish coast.

1893, September 19. The Russian warship *Roosalka* foundered in the Gulf of Finland with 178 lives lost.

1894, March. Thirty-one lives were lost when the Scottish ship *Colintrave* vanished at sea during a voyage from Australia to San Francisco.

1895, January 30. The German liner *Elbe* was rammed and sunk off Lowestoft, England, with 335 lives lost.

1895, March 11. The Spanish cruiser *Regina Regente* foundered near Cape Trafalgar, Spain; 402 were killed.

1895, May 22. The Spanish passenger steamer *Gravina* was lost in a storm off the Philippines; 168 perished.

1896, March 18. Two lives were lost in the stranding of the British ship *Glenmorag* near Ocean Park, Washington.

1896, April 15. The liner *Elbe* sank in the North Sea after colliding with the steamer *Crathie*; 334 were killed.

1897, March 8. The French liner *Ville de St. Nazaire* sank in a hurricane off Cape Hatteras, North Carolina, with 34 lives lost.

1897, October. The British ship *Glenfinlas* vanished at sea on a voyage from Manila to Australia; 30 lives were lost.

1898, February 15. The American battleship *Maine* exploded in Havana harbor with 264 lives lost.

1898, July 4. Five hundred and seventy-one people were killed when the French liner *Bourgogne* sank after colliding with the British vessel *Cromartyshire* near Sable Island, south of Nova Scotia.

1898, November 26. The American passenger steamer *City of Portland* was wrecked in a storm off Cape Cod, Massachusetts, with 157 lives lost.

1899, March 5. Storms sank numerous pearling vessels near Cape Meviolle, Queensland, Australia, with some 300 lives lost.

1899, March 30. The steamship *Stella* struck rocks and sank off the French coast with some 100 lives lost.

1899, August 14. Fifty-four perished when the steamship *Resolute* collided with another vessel at Calcutta.

1899, December 17. The French steamship *Pierre le Grand* vanished in the Adriatic Sea; 45 lives were lost.

1900, January 1. All on board were lost when the American steam schooner *Protection* sank off the Columbia River mouth (Oregon-Washington).

1900, February 15. The steamship *Pavillac* vanished during a voyage between New York and Le Havre, France, with 37 lives lost.

1900, June 3. The liner *Devenum* was wrecked at Oporto, Portugal; no casualty figures are available.

1900, June 30. A fire at a Hoboken, New Jersey, pier destroyed the German liners *Main*, *Bremen* and *Saale*, and killed 300 people.

1900, December 11. The British bark *Andrada* disappeared at sea with all on board some miles west of the Columbia River bar (Oregon-Washington). No trace of the ship was ever discovered, although *Andrada* is thought to have foundered in a storm off the coast of Washington state.

1900, December 21. The schooner *Jennie Hall* was wrecked on the Virginia coast; three lives were lost.

1901, January 16. The British bark *Cape Wrath* disappeared at sea off the Columbia River mouth (Oregon-Washington) with 15 crewmen on board. The ship is thought to have been lost in an intense storm.

1901, February 22. The steamship *Rio de Janeiro* sank near San Francisco with more than 100 lives lost.

1901, May 7. The Union-Castle liner *Tantallon Castle* was wrecked near Cape Town, South Africa, but no lives were lost.

1901, June 26. The Elder Dempster liner *Lusitania* (not to be confused with the Cunard liner of the same name, sunk years later by a U-boat off the Irish coast) was wrecked near Cape Race, Newfoundland; there was no loss of life.

1901, July 7. The Spanish Trans-Atlantic Company liner *Mexico* was wrecked off the Portuguese coast, with no loss of life.

1901, August 14. The Canadian steamship *Islander* hit an iceberg and sank at Steven's Passage, Alaska, with 70 lives lost.

1901, August 19. The steamship *City of Golconda* capsized on the Ohio River, killing 40.

1901, August 25. Thirty-nine were killed when the Belgian steamship *Noranmore* capsized in the Black Sea.

1901, December 2. One hundred and four lives were

lost when the British steamship *Condor* vanished off the coast of British Columbia.

1902, date uncertain. The British Indian Steam Navigation Company's liner *Camorta* sank in a storm near Rangoon, Burma (now Myanmar), with 739 lives lost.

1902, January 2. Forty-two lives were lost when the American steamship *Walla Walla* collided with a French vessel near Mendocino, California.

1902, February 9. The Allan liner *Grecian* was wrecked at Halifax, Nova Scotia; no casualty figures are available.

1902, July 21. One hundred and twelve people were killed when the steamer *Primus* collided with another vessel on the Elbe River.

1902, December 8. The Greek steamship *Parthenon* vanished in the Black Sea off the coast of Turkey; 28 were killed.

1903, February 3. Twenty-seven were killed when the French bark *Van Stabel* sank off the Hebrides.

1903, February 9. The German bark *Alsternixe* became one of the few large ships to escape the feared sands of Peacock Spit at the mouth of the Columbia River between Oregon and Washington state. The ship was refloated after being declared a complete loss.

1903, June 2. Sixty-three lives were lost at Valparaiso, Chile, in the sinking of the British steamship *Arequipa*.

1903, June 7. A hundred and fifty lives were lost when the French steamship *Liban* sank near Marseilles, France, after colliding with the steamer *Insulaire*.

1904, May 6. The Hamburg-East Africa liner *Kurfurst* was wrecked off the Portuguese coast with no loss of life.

1904, May 15. Three hundred and twenty-nine lives were lost when the Japanese cruiser *Yoshino* collided with the cruiser *Kasuga* in fog off China's Liao-Tung Peninsula.

1904, June 15. In one of the greatest catastrophes in American maritime history, the steamship *General Slocum* burned in the Hudson River near New York City; more than 1,000 were killed.

1904, June 28. Six hundred and fifty-one people were killed in the wreck of the Danish steamship *Norge*, which was lost on the rocks at Rockall, Scotland.

1904, June 29. The Peninsular and Oriental liner *Australia* was wrecked near Melbourne, Australia, with no loss of life.

1905, July 21. The American gunboat *Bennington* blew up at San Diego, California, killing 65.

1905, September 5. The Booth liner *Cyril* was wrecked in a collision with another ship in the Amazon, no casualty figures are available.

1905, September 10. The Japanese battleship *Mikasa* exploded at the Sasebo naval base, killing 599.

1905, November 5. The Allan Line's *Bavarian* was wrecked near Montreal, but no lives were lost.

1906, January 21. The Brazilian ironclad *Aquidaban* exploded near Rio de Janeiro, killing 212.

1906, January 22. One hundred and twenty-nine lives were lost in the wreck of the American steamship *Valencia* off Vancouver Island, Canada.

1906, August 4. The wreck of the Italian liner *Sirio* on the Hormigas Islands off the coast of Spain killed 442 people.

1906, September 18. A storm destroyed several ships at Hong Kong, with a loss of some 1,000 lives.

1906, October 14. Hundreds were killed when the steamship *Hankow* burned at Hong Kong.

1906, November 21. The North German Lloyd liner *Kaiser Wilhelm der Grosse* was involved in a collision that killed five people, off Cherbourg, France.

1907, February 12. The steamer *Larchmont* collided with a schooner near Block Island, Rhode Island, and sank with 332 lives lost.

1907, February 24. The Lloyd Austriaco liner *Imperatrix* was wrecked off Crete with 40 lives lost.

1907, March 7. The Great Northern Steam Ship Company's liner *Dakota* was wrecked near Yokohama, Japan, with no loss of life.

1907, May 7. The French liner *Poitou* was wrecked off the Uruguayan coast with 20 lives lost.

1907, July 20. Some 100 lives were lost when the steamer *Columbia* collided with another steamship at Point Arena, California.

1907, October 17. The Canadian Pacific liner *Tartar* was involved in a collision off the coast of British Columbia; no lives were lost.

1907, October 22. The Hamburg-America liner *Borussia* sank at Lisbon, Portugal, with three fatalities.

1907, November 26. The steamship *Kaptan* sank in the North Sea with 110 lives lost.

1908, March 12. The Union Castle liner *Newark Castle* was wrecked near Durban, South Africa, with three fatalities.

1908, March 23. The Japanese steamer *Matsu Maru* sank with the loss of 300 lives following a collision at Hakodate, Japan.

1908, April 27. The steamship *Yarmouth* sank en route from Rotterdam, Netherlands, to Harwich, with 20 lives lost.

1908, May 10. The North German Lloyd liner *Hohenzollern* was stranded off Sardinia; no lives were lost.

1908, August 3. The Hamburg-South America Line's

Cap Frio was wrecked off Brazil; no casualty figures are available.

1908, September 30. The Turkish ferry *Stabul* sank following a collision near Smyrna harbor; 140 were killed.

1908, October 16. The Lamport & Holt liner *Velasquez* was stranded near Santos, Brazil; no lives were lost.

1908, October–November. The liner *Neustria* vanished at sea on a voyage between New York and Marseille, France; no casualty figures are available.

1908, December. The British ship *Brodick Castle* vanished at sea after leaving the Columbia River (Oregon-Washington), and is thought to have been lost with all hands in a storm.

1909, January 23. The White Star liner *Republic* sank off New York after a collision; thanks to wireless distress signals, there were only four fatalities.

1909, July 28. In one of the most famous mysteries of the seas, the steamship *Waratah* vanished in a storm near Cape Town, South Africa.

1909, August 4. The Shaw, Savill & Albion Co. Ltd. liner *Maori* was wrecked off Cape Town, South Africa, with 34 lives lost.

1909, August 14. The Cunard liner *Lucania* burned at Liverpool, England, with no fatalities.

1909, August 24. Eight were killed when the Argentine steamer *Colombian* collided with a German steamship near Montevideo, Uruguay.

1909, November 14. The French steamship *La Seyne* collided with a British India liner while en route to Singapore; 101 were killed.

1910, January 12. The steamer *Czarina* was wrecked at Coos Bay, Oregon, with 30 lives lost.

1910, February 10. The French liner *General Chanzy* was wrecked off Minorca, with 93 fatalities.

1910, March 16. The British steamship *Loodiana* vanished with 175 on board during a voyage to Colombo, Ceylon (now Sri Lanka).

1910, October 11. The steamer *Arkadia* vanished at sea after leaving New Orleans.

1910, October 23. The Empresa Nacional liner *Lisboa* was wrecked near Cape Town, South Africa, with seven fatalities.

1910, November 7. Ninety-one were killed when the British India liner *Abhona* sank in a storm on a voyage to Rangoon, Burma (now Myanmar).

1911, February 6. The Norwegian sailing ship *Glenbank* was lost in a storm off New South Wales, Australia; 23 were killed.

1911, February 13. Six lives were lost when the American motor vessel *Oshkosh* wrecked on the Columbia River bar (Oregon-Washington).

1911, March 23. The steamship *Yongala* was lost in a hurricane after sailing from Queensland, Australia; 142 perished.

1911, May 23. Sixty were killed when the steamship *Taboga* was wrecked near Puna Mala, Panama.

1911, September 25. The French battleship *Liberté* exploded in Toulon (France) harbor, killing 235. Unstable ammunition is thought to have been responsible.

1912, March 16. The Peninsular and Oriental Line's passenger liner *Oceana* was involved in a collision in the English Channel, with nine lives lost.

1912, March 21. The Australian vessel *Koombana* was lost in a storm while en route to Western Australia; 125 lives were lost.

1912, April 14–15. The loss of the British liner R.M.S. *Titanic* after striking an iceberg off the Grand Banks of Newfoundland is perhaps the most famous shipwreck of all; 1,517 perished.

1912, June 8. The French submarine *Vendemiaire* was struck and sunk by a battleship during maneuvers near Cape de la Hague; 24 died.

1912, September 28. A thousand lives were lost when the Japanese steamer *Kiche Maru* foundered off Japan's coast.

1912, October 27. Three hundred and forty-six people were killed when the Canadian steamship *Princess Sophia* was lost in a storm on a trip from Skagway, Alaska, to Vancouver.

1912, November 6. The Pacific Steam Navigation Company's liner *Oravia* was wrecked off the Falkland Islands; no casualty figures are available.

1913, January 1. The steamer *El Dorado* vanished at sea after sailing from Baltimore; 39 were lost.

1913, January 7. The American tanker *Rosecrans* was wrecked on Peacock Spit at the Columbia River bar (Oregon-Washington); 33 lives were lost.

1913, January 16. The Lamport & Holt liner *Veronese* was wrecked off the Portuguese coast with 43 lives lost.

1913, October 9. One hundred and thirty-six lives were lost when the liner *Volturno* burned and sank in mid-Atlantic.

1914, March 5. The Spanish liner *Principe de Asturias* was wrecked on rocks at Ponta Boi, Brazil, in fog; 445 died.

1914, May 29. More than 1,000 lives were lost when the Canadian liner *Empress of Ireland* sank in the St. Lawrence River, Canada, after colliding with the collier *Storstad*.

1914, September 18. The American steamship *Francis H. Leggett* sank in a storm off the Columbia River (Oregon-Washington), with 65 lives lost.

1914, November 26. The British battleship *Bulwark*

exploded in Sheerness (England) harbor with 788 lives lost.

1915, July 24. The excursion steamer *Eastland* capsized in the Chicago River in Chicago, Illinois, killing 852.

1915, August. The United Fruit Company liner *Marowijne* vanished in the Caribbean Sea; no casualty figures are available.

1915, September 19. The passenger liner *Athenai,* belonging to the National Steam Navigation Company of Greece, burned in the North Atlantic, but with no loss of life.

1915, October 3. The passenger liner *Highland Warrior,* belonging to the Nelson Line, was wrecked off the Spanish coast; no casualty figures are available.

1915, November 8. The Italia Line's passenger ship *Ancona* was sunk by torpedo in the North Atlantic; almost 200 perished.

1915, December 30. The British cruiser *Natal* caught fire and blew up in Cromarty Harbor, Scotland; 405 perished.

1916, January 5. The National Steam Navigation Company of Greece lost its passenger liner *Thessaloniki* in a storm on the North Atlantic; there was no loss of life.

1916, March 3. The liner *Principe de Austurias,* belonging to Pinillos, Izquierdo y Compania, was wrecked off the Brazilian coast with more than 400 lives lost.

1916, March 31. The Japanese passenger liner *Chiyo Maru* was wrecked off Hong Kong, with no loss of life.

1916, August 30. The New Zealand Shipping passenger liner *Tongariro* was wrecked off New Zealand, with no loss of life.

1916, October 20. The Russian battleship *Imperatriza Maria* exploded after catching fire at a Baltic dockyard; 200 were killed.

1916, December 25. The New Zealand liner *Maitai* was wrecked off Tonga, with no lives lost.

1917, January 14. The Japanese battleship *Tsukuba* exploded in Yokosuka (Japan) harbor; 200 were killed.

1917, July 9. An explosion on the British battleship *Vanguard* at Scapa Flow, Scotland, killed 804 people.

1917, July 15. The Norwegian America Line's passenger liner *Kristianiafjord* was wrecked off Cape Race, Newfoundland, with no loss of life.

1917, December 30. In one of the greatest non-nuclear explosions in history, the steamship *Mont Blanc,* laden with 5,000 tons of high explosive, collided with another vessel in the harbor at Halifax, Nova Scotia, and blew up, killing more than 1,100 people and destroying much of the city.

1918, February 28. The 900-ton American schooner *Americana* disappeared with 11 people on board after crossing the Columbia River (Oregon-Washington) bar. Although no wreckage was ever found, the ship is believed to have foundered in a storm.

1918, May 6. The Nelson Line's passenger liner *Highland Scot* was wrecked off Brazil; no casualty figures are available.

1918, July 12. The Japanese battleship *Kawachi* exploded at Tokoyama Bay, Japan, killing 500.

1919, January 1. The British steam yacht *Iolaire* was wrecked on rocks off the Scottish coast at Stornoway; 300 were killed.

1919, January 17. The French steamer *Chaouia* was wrecked in or near the Strait of Messina, in the Mediterranean, with 460 lives lost.

1919, September 12. *Valbanera,* a passenger liner belonging to Pinillos, Izquierdo y Compania, was lost in a storm near Florida; 488 perished.

1920, January 11. The French liner *Afrique* was wrecked on reefs near La Rochelle, France, killing 553.

1920, March 1. The Leyland Line's passenger liner *Bohemian* was wrecked off Nova Scotia; no lives were lost.

1920, June 23. Six crew members were killed when an explosion destroyed the American river steamer *State of Washington* off Tongue Point, Oregon.

1921, January 20. The British submarine *K-5* vanished in the Bay of Biscay; 57 were lost.

1921, March 14. The Allan Line's passenger liner *Grampion* burned at Antwerp, Belgium; no lives were lost.

1921, March 18. The Chinese steamship *Hong Koh* sank near Swatow (Shan-t'ou); approximately 1,000 were killed.

1921, October 20. The steamer *Santa Rita* vanished at sea after leaving New Orleans; 35 were lost.

1922, March 23. Twenty-six were killed when the British submarine *H-42* collided with a destroyer and sank near Gibraltar.

1922, May 22. The Peninsular and Oriental liner *Egypt* was involved in a collision off the Egyptian coast; 86 were killed.

1922, August 26. The Japanese cruiser *Niitaka* was lost in a storm off the coast of Russia's Kamchatka Peninsula; 300 died.

1922, October 12. The passenger liner *City of Honolulu,* belonging to the Los Angeles Steam Navigation

Company, burned off the California coast, with no loss of life.

1923, March 28. Twenty were killed when the Australian steamer *Douglas Mawson* sank in a storm off Queensland, Australia.

1923, April 24. The liner *Mossamedes* was wrecked on the Angolan coast, with 237 lives lost.

1923, May 21. The Canadian Pacific passenger liner *Marvale* was wrecked off Cape Race, Newfoundland, with no loss of life.

1924, January 10. The British submarine *L-24* sank off Portland Bill, England, with 48 lives lost.

1924, March 19. The Japanese submarine No. 43 sank off Saesebo, Japan, with 46 lives lost.

1924, September 21. The steamer *Clifton* sank on Lake Huron with 27 lives lost.

1925, August 26. Fifty-four lives were lost when the Italian submarine *Sebastiano Veniero* collided with another vessel in the Mediterranean near Sicily.

1925, September 25. The American submarine *S-51* was rammed by the liner *City of Rome* off Montauk, New York, and sank with 132 lives lost; three survivors were rescued by the liner.

1925, November 12. The British submarine *M-1* sank after colliding with a Swedish steamship in the English Channel; 69 were killed.

1926, March 17. The New Zealand Shipping passenger liner *Paporoa* burned in the South Atlantic, with no loss of life.

1926, July 12. The passenger liner *Fontainebleau*, belonging to Messageries Maritimes, burned at Djibouti, with no loss of life.

1926, August 24. The Lloyd Triestino passenger liner *Persia* burned off the coast of India with no loss of life.

1926, August 27. The steamship *Buryvestrick* reportedly struck a pier at Kronstadt, near St. Petersburg, Russia, with 160 killed.

1926, October 16. Twelve hundred are thought to have died when a Chinese troopship on the Yangtze River blew up.

1926, November 26. The passenger liner *Braga*, belonging to the Fabre Line, was wrecked off Greece; no casualty figures are available.

1927, March 18. Some 100 are thought to have been killed when the steamship *Chongfu* was wrecked on China's Yangtze River near Luchow.

1927, August 24. The Japanese destroyer *Warabi* sank with 102 lives lost after colliding with another vessel in the Bungo Channel.

1927, September 20. The Japanese steamship *Gentoku Maru* capsized in Tsingtao (Ch'ing-tao) Bay, China, killing 278.

1927, October 25. The Italian liner *Principessa Malfada* sank off the coast of Brazil with more than 300 lives lost.

1927, December 17. The American submarine *S-4* sank after a collision with a destroyer off Provincetown, Massachusetts; 40 lives were lost.

1928, February 20. The Chinese steamship *Hsin Ta-Ming* sank in the Yangtze River with 300 lives lost after colliding with the steamship *Atsuta Maru*.

1928, July 6. The Chilean naval transport *Angamos* hit rocks in a storm off Punta Morguillas; only eight were saved out of 291 on board.

1928, August 6. Twenty-seven were killed in a collision between the Italian submarine *F-14* and an Italian destroyer in the Adriatic Sea.

1928, August 15. Five hundred reportedly died when the Chinese steamship *Hsin Hsu-Tung* sank on the Yangtze River.

1928, November 12. One hundred and ten people died in the wreck of the steamer *Vestris*, which sank in a storm a day after departing from New York.

1928, December. Sixty people were lost with the Danish motorship *Kobenhavn*, which vanished en route from Buenos Aires to Melbourne, Australia.

1928, December 30. The passenger liner *Paul Lecat*, belonging to Messageries Maritimes, burned at Marseilles, France, with no loss of life.

1929, September 9. The Nelson Line passenger liner *Highland Pride* was wrecked off the Spanish coast with no lives lost.

1929, September 9. The Great Lakes steamship *Andaste* was lost on Lake Michigan with 25 fatalities.

1929, December 16. The Union Steamship Company of New Zealand's passenger liner *Manuka* was wrecked off the New Zealand coast with no lives lost.

1929, December 18. The Furness, Withy & Company passenger liner *Fort Victoria* was involved in a collision off New York, with no lives lost.

1929, December 21. *Lee Cheong*, a Chinese steamship, sank in a gale near Hong Kong with the loss of 200 lives.

1930, January 22. The Hamburg-South America Line's passenger liner *Monte Cervantes* was wrecked in the Straits of Magellan with one life lost.

1930, April 27. Some 100 are thought to have been killed when the British river steamship *Condor* capsized on the Jamuna River in Bengal, India.

1930, May 21. The Fabre Line's passenger liner *Asia* burned at Djibouti with no lives lost.

1930, June 9. The steamer *Lithung* was lost on rocks

in China's Yangtze River; some 100 are believed to have perished.

1930, June 10. Fifty lives were lost when the American tanker *Pinthis* collided with the steamship *Fairfax* near Fall River, Massachusetts.

1931, February 10. The Japanese steamship *Kikusui Maru* sank after colliding with another vessel off Kobe, Japan; 50 were killed.

1931, April 2. The Burns, Philip & Company passenger liner *Malabar* was wrecked off Sydney, Australia, with no loss of life.

1931, June 14. The French passenger ship *St. Philibert* sank in a storm off Noirmoutier Island, France; 368 were killed.

1931, August 8. The steamship *Kwong Sang* ran aground in a storm near Foochow, China; 38 perished.

1931, October 21. The Russian submarine *L-55* sank in the Gulf of Finland with 50 lives lost.

1932, January 26. The British submarine *M-2* sank off Portland Bill, England, with 60 lives lost.

1932, February 15. The Japanese steamship *Taikai Maru* vanished at sea en route from Vladivostok, Russia, to Aomori, Japan; 38 lives were lost.

1932, May 19. The liner *Georges Philippar* caught fire in the Gulf of Aden; 54 lives were lost.

1932, December 6. The Japanese destroyer *Sawarabi* sank in a storm off Formosa (now Taiwan), with 106 lives lost.

1933, January 4. The French passenger liner *L'Atlantique* burned near the English Channel, with 17 lives lost.

1933, January 16. The steamship *Hsin Ningtan* sank in a storm at Hangchow Bay, China; 300 were killed.

1933, June 1. The Union Castle Line's passenger liner *Guildford Castle* was involved in a collision in the Elbe River; two lives were lost.

1933, July 6. The Compagnie de Navigation Paquet's passenger liner *Nicholas Paquet* was wrecked off North Africa; no casualty figures are available.

1933, July 10. The Chinese steamer *Toonan* sank off Shantung, China, after colliding with the Japanese ship *Choshun Maru*; 168 were killed.

1933, November 17. The Japanese ship *Seiten Maru* sank near China's Loochoo Island, with 30 lives lost.

1934, May 3. The Norwegian motorship *Childar* grounded on Peacock Spit at the Columbia River (Oregon-Washington) bar; four were killed.

1934, June 20. The North German Lloyd liner *Dresden* was wrecked off the Norwegian coast with an estimated loss of four lives.

1934, September 8. The liner *Morro Castle* burned off the New Jersey shore; 133 or more were killed.

1935, July 2. The Japanese steamer *Midori Maru* sank after colliding with *Senzan Maru* in the Inland Sea, Japan; 104 were killed.

1935, September 5. The White Star liner *Doric* was involved in a collision off Cape Finisterre, Spain; no casualties were reported.

1935, October 18. The Italian liner *Ausonia* was lost at Alexandria, Egypt, with three killed.

1936, January 12. All 34 on board were lost when the American steamship *Iowa* was wrecked off Peacock Spit at the Columbia River (Oregon-Washington) bar.

1936, May 13. The Chinese motorship *Ming Chiang* was lost near Wanhsien, China; 40 were killed.

1936, September 17. The steamer *Pourquoi Pas* was lost on rocks near Iceland; 33 were killed.

1936, October 24. The Spanish passenger liner *Cristobol Colon* was wrecked off Bermuda, but no lives were lost.

1937, February 10. The Japanese ship *Otaru Maru* sank in a snowstorm off Yatsunobe, with 36 lives lost.

1937, December 10. The Dollar Line's passenger liner *President Hoover* was wrecked near Formosa (now Taiwan), with no lives lost.

1938, February 12. The Belgian training ship *Admiral Karpfanger* was wrecked near Cape Horn, with 60 lives lost.

1938, May 4. The French passenger liner *Lafayette* burned at Le Havre, France, with no loss of life.

1939, May 23. Twenty-six were killed when the American submarine *Squalus* sank off the coast of New Hampshire.

1939, June 1. Ninety-nine perished in the wreck of the British submarine *Thetis* in the Irish Sea.

1939, September 3. The Anchor-Donaldson Line's passenger liner *Athenia* was sunk by torpedo off Ireland, with 112 fatalities.

1939, October 16. Some 300 were killed when the Japanese vessel *Hsin Ta Kou Maru* sank in China's Yangtze River delta.

1939, November 26. *Pegu*, a passenger liner belonging to the Burmah Steamship Company, was wrecked near Liverpool, England, with no loss of life.

1939, December 12. Seven hundred and fifty were killed when the Russian steamship *Indigirka* was wrecked in the Sea of Okhotsk on the northern coast of Japan's Hokkaido Island.

1939, December 29. The passenger liner *Cabo San Antonio*, belonging to Ybarra y Cia, burned in the South Atlantic with five fatalities.

1940, April 20. Some 240 are thought to have died when an unidentified Chinese steamship sank on the Chailing River.

1940, June 28. The Italian troopship *Paganini* burned

and sank near Durazzo, Albania, with 220 lives lost.

1940, October 22. One hundred and forty were killed when the Canadian destroyer *Margaree* collided with a merchant vessel in a convoy in the North Atlantic.

1940, November 25. The French liner *Patria* exploded at Haifa, Palestine (now Israel), killing 280.

1941, April 20. The Norwegian steamship *Blenheim* exploded at the Porsanger Fjord, Norway, with 138 lives lost.

1941, June 16. Thirty-three perished when the American submarine *O-9* sank off the New Hampshire coast.

1941, October 2. Seventy lives were lost when the Japanese submarine *L-61* collided with a gunboat near Japan's Iki Island.

1942, January 8. Two hundred and seventy-seven lives were lost when the French liner *Lamoriciere* sank in a storm off Minorca.

1942, February 7. The American submarine *S-26* sank off the coast of Panama after a collision; 32 were killed.

1942, February 8. Some 200 were killed when an unidentified Chinese steamship sank near Ichang on the Yangtze River.

1942, October 2. The British cruiser *Curaçao* sank with the loss of 338 men after being rammed by the British liner *Queen Mary* in a convoy some 20 miles off the coast of Donegal, Ireland.

1943, April 14. Thirty-three were killed when the Swedish submarine *Ulven* struck a mine off Marstrand, Sweden.

1944, January 3. The American destroyer *Turner* exploded near Ambrose Lightship, New York.

1944, April 14. Three hundred and thirty-six people were killed when the British cargo vessel *Fort Stikine* exploded at Bombay.

1944, December 17. Three American destroyers sank in a typhoon near the Philippine Islands. The destroyer *Spence* sank with 341 lives lost; *Monahan*, 250; and *Hull*, 139.

1945, April 9. The American Liberty ship *John Harvey* blew up in the harbor at Bari, Italy, killing 360.

1945, November 8. When a Chinese river steamer full of soldiers capsized off Hong Kong, 1,550 lives are thought to have been lost.

1946, March 24. *Kinkazan Maru*, a Japanese ferry, sank off the island of Honshu with 170 lives lost.

1946, October 29. The Japanese motorship *Ebisu Maru* hit a wreck and broke apart near Chinampo, Korea; 497 were killed.

1947, January 18. Four hundred people are thought to

have lost their lives when the Chinese steamer *Chekiang* sank following a collision in the Yangtze River near Woosung.

1948, December 3. Some 2,750 people are believed to have died in the wreck of the Chinese ship *Kiangya*, which struck a mine and sank on a journey to Ningpo, China, from Shanghai.

1949, January 27. The wreck of the Chinese steamship *Tai Ping* in Bonham Strait near Chusan Island is thought to have cost 1,500 lives.

1949, April 25. The Royal Mail Line's passenger liner *Magdalena* was wrecked off Rio de Janeiro with no fatalities.

1949, August 23. The Chinese steamship *China Victor* caught fire and exploded at Kaohsiung, Formosa (now Taiwan), killing 500.

1949, November. According to one report, some 6,000 people were killed when a Chinese army evacuation ship exploded and sank.

1950, July 9. Seventy-three were killed when the British ship *Indian Enterprise* blew up in the Red Sea.

1950, November 15. An unidentified Yugoslavian ferry capsized on the Sava River; 94 lives were lost.

1951, April 16. The British submarine *Affray* sank near the Isle of Wight, with 75 lives lost.

1951, September 1. The fishing boat *Pelican* was lost near Montauk Point, New York; 45 perished.

1951, December 20. Eleven people were killed in the burning of the Danish motorship *Erria* near Tongue Point, Oregon.

1952, April 26. One hundred and seventy-five lives were lost when the American destroyer *Hobson* collided with the American aircraft carrier *Wasp* and sank in mid-Atlantic.

1952, September 9. An unidentified Yugoslavian ferry sank in a storm near Belgrade, Yugoslavia, with 86 lives lost.

1952, December 22. The French passenger liner *Champollion*, belonging to Messageries Maritimes, was wrecked off Beirut, Lebanon, with 15 lives lost.

1953, January 9. The South Korean passenger vessel *Chang Tyong-Ho* capsized off Pusan, South Korea; 249 lives were lost.

1953, January 25. The Canadian Pacific passenger liner *Empress of Canada* burned in drydock at Liverpool, England, with no loss of life.

1953, August 1. The French liner *Monique* vanished in the South Pacific Ocean with 120 on board.

1954, September 26. The Japanese ferry *Toyo Maru* capsized in a storm near Hakodate, Japan; 794 lives were lost.

1955, May 11. The Japanese ferry *Shiun Maru* sank after colliding with the freighter *Udaka Maru* on a voyage between the islands of Honshu and Shikoku; 173 perished.

1956, January 12. Seventy were killed when the ship *Taishin-Ho* burned at its dock at Samchopo, South Korea.

1956, April 15. The Rotterdam South America Line's passenger liner *Altair* was wrecked off the Brazilian coast; no casualty figures are available.

1956, July 25. In one of the most famous of 20th-century shipwrecks, the Italian liner *Andrea Doria* sank after colliding with the Swedish liner *Stockholm* near Nantucket Island, Massachusetts; 52 were killed.

1956, November 17. An unidentified Taiwanese ferryboat was wrecked on a reef en route from Taiwan to the Pescadores Islands off the Chinese coast; 102 were killed.

1957, May 17. One hundred were killed when an unidentified Chinese riverboat burned and sank on the Yangtze River near Wuhan, China.

1957, July 14. The Russian fishing vessel *Eshghabad* hit a reef in the Caspian Sea; 270 were killed.

1957, September 25. The Booth Line's passenger liner *Hildebrand* was wrecked near Lisbon, Portugal; no lives were lost.

1958, January 26. The Japanese ferry *Nankai Maru* was lost in a storm between Shikoku and Wakayama; 166 perished.

1958, March 1. The Turkish ferry *Uskudar* sank in a storm in Izmit Bay, Turkey; 350 were killed.

1959, January 30. The Danish ship *Hans Hedtoft* sank after colliding with an iceberg during a voyage from Greenland to Denmark; all 95 on board were killed.

1959, May 8. One hundred and fifty lives were lost when the excursion boat *Dandarah* sank near Cairo, Egypt.

1960, March 4. Seventy-five were killed when the freighter *La Coubre* exploded at Havana.

1960, December 14. The Turkish passenger liner *Tarsus* burned in the Bosporus, with no lives lost.

1960, December 19. Fifty were killed when the American aircraft carrier *Constellation* burned at the Brooklyn (New York) Navy Yard.

1961, April 8. The British India liner *Dara* exploded at Dubai on the Persian Gulf; 236 to 238 were killed.

1961, July 8. The passenger liner *Save*, belonging to the Siucia Oceanica Societa per Azioni, was wrecked off Cannes, Frances, with 259 fatalities.

1962, January 1. Seventy lives were lost when an unidentified Indian riverboat sank near Mhapal on the Savitri River.

1963, February 4. The tanker *Marine Sulphur Queen* vanished with 39 on board while sailing from Texas to Norfolk, Virginia.

1963, April 10. The American nuclear submarine *Thresher* sank in the North Atlantic with the loss of 129 lives.

1963, December 22. The Greek liner *Lakonia* burned at sea north of Madeira, Spain, with 128 lives lost.

1964, February 10. Seventy-nine lives were lost when the Australian destroyer *Voyager* collided with the aircraft carrier Melbourne near Sydney.

1964, July 23. One hundred were killed when a United Arab Republic freighter carrying ammunition exploded at Bone, Algeria.

1965, November 13. In a widely publicized catastrophe, the cruise ship *Yarmouth Castle* burned in the Caribbean Sea near Miami, Florida; 89 lives were lost.

1966, October 25. Some 100 lives were lost when an unidentified Indian riverboat sank near Patna on the Kosi River.

1966, October 26. Forty-three lives were lost in a fire and explosions on the American aircraft carrier *Oriskany* in the Gulf of Tonkin off Vietnam.

1966, December 12. The Greek ferry *Heraklion* sank in a storm in the Sea of Crete, with 230 lives lost.

1967, July 29. In a fire off the coast of Vietnam, 134 were killed on the American aircraft carrier *Forrestal.*

1968, April 11. The New Zealand passenger liner *Wahine* was wrecked off Wellington, New Zealand, with 51 fatalities.

1968, May 21. Ninety-nine perished when the American nuclear submarine *Scorpion* sank off the Azores.

1969, June 2. Seventy-four lives were lost when the Australian aircraft carrier *Melbourne* collided with the American destroyer *Frank E. Evans* in the South China Sea.

1970, December 15. *Namyong-Ho*, a South Korean ferry, sank 50 miles offshore with 308 lives lost.

1971, January 8. The French passenger ship *Antilles* burned off Mustique in the Grenadines with no fatalities.

1971, August 28. Twenty-four were killed when the Greek passenger ship *Helcanna* burned near Brindisi, Italy.

1972, January 9. The liner *Seawise University*, formerly *Queen Elizabeth*, burned at Hong Kong with no fatalities.

1972, August 21. Forty-seven were killed when the tankers *Texanita* and *Oswego Guardian* collided off the South African coast.

1972, September 23. The passenger ship *Caribia* burned off Daytona Beach, Florida, with no fatalities.

1973, May 3. The greek passenger ship *Knossos* burned off the Greek coast with no loss of life.

1973, June 30. The Spanish passenger ship *Satrustegui* burned at Barcelona, Spain, with no lives lost.

1973, July 1. The Homes Lines' passenger ship *Homeric* burned off New York with no fatalities.

1973, December 24. The Ecuadoran ferry *Jambeli* sank between Guayaquil, Ecuador, and Puerto Bolivar, Ecuador, with 163 lives lost.

1974, May 12. The passenger ship *Malaysia Kita* burned at Singapore with no fatalities.

1974, September 12. The Cunard Line passenger ship *Cunard Ambassador* burned off Key West, Florida, with no fatalities.

1974, October 25. Some 200 were killed when a ferry sank near Dacca, Bangladesh.

1975, August 3. Two Chinese excursion boats collided and sank near Canton, with 400 lives lost.

1975, November 10. The ore boat *Edmund Fitzgerald* was lost in a storm on Lake Superior with the loss of 29 lives.

1976, July 30. The passenger ship *Belle Abeto*, belonging to Campania de Navigation Abeto, burned at Sasebo, Japan, with no lives lost.

1976, August 23. The passenger ship *Malaysia Raya* burned at Port Kelang, Malaysia, with no fatalities.

1976, October 20. Seventy-seven were killed in a collision between a ferry and a Norwegian tanker on the Mississippi River near Luling, Louisiana.

1976, December 18. The Orri Navigation Lines passenger ship *Mecca* burned at Jedda, Saudi Arabia, with no fatalities.

1976, December 25. An estimated 100 lives were lost when the Arab Navigators passenger ship *Patra* burned off the coast of Saudi Arabia.

1977, January 11. Thirty-eight were killed when the Panamanian-registered tanker *Grand Zenith* sank off Cape Cod, Massachusetts.

1979, August 14. Eighteen were killed when a storm hit a gathering of yachts during a race in the Irish Sea.

The cruise ship *Prinsendam* burned in the Gulf of Alaska in 1980. (U.S. Coast Guard)

1980, March 3. The Italian passenger liner *Leonardo da Vinci* burned at La Spezia, Italy, with no fatalities.

1980, April 24. The passenger ship *Ernesto Anastasio*, of the Compania Transmediterranea, was wrecked off the Spanish coast with no lives lost.

1980, October 4. The Holland America cruise ship *Prinsendam* burned in the Gulf of Alaska with no fatalities.

1981, January 27. There were 580 fatalities when an Indonesian passenger ship burned and sank in the Java Sea.

1981, August 20. The Egyptian Navigation Company's passenger ship *Syria* was wrecked off Crete with no lives lost.

1982, August 8. The passenger ship *Mediterranean Star* burned in the Aegean Sea with no fatalities.

1982, October 19. The passenger ship *Ciudad de Sevilla*, belonging to the Compania Transmediterranea, was wrecked at Majorca, Spain, with no loss of life.

1983, February 12. Thirty-three perished when the coal freighter *Marine Electric* sank in a storm off Chincoteague, Virginia.

1983, March 7. The passenger ship *Atlantis*, belonging to K-Hellenic Lines, burned at Piraeus, Greece, with no fatalities.

1984, July 29. The passenger ship *Columbus C,* belonging to Costa Armatori, was wrecked at Cadiz, Spain, with no loss of life.

1985, The Shipping Corporation of India's passenger ship *Chidambaram* burned off Madras, India, with 40 reported killed.

1986, February 16. The Soviet passenger ship *Mikhail Lermontov* was wrecked off New Zealand with one fatality.

1986, August 31. The Soviet passenger ship *Admiral Nakhimov* was wrecked in a collision in the Black Sea, with 398 fatalities.

1987, March 6. The ferry *Herald of Free Enterprise* capsized off Zeebrugge, Belgium, with 188 lives lost.

1987, December 20. More than 3,000 lives were lost when the Philippine ferry *Dona Paz* collided with an oil tanker in the Tablas Strait, Philippines.

1988, August 6. More than 400 were killed when an Indian ferry capsized on the Ganges River.

1989, April 7. Forty-two lives were lost when a Soviet submarine sank off the Norwegian coast.

1989, August 20. Fifty-six were killed when a barge collided with the pleasure cruiser *Marchioness* on the Thames River in London.

1991, April 10. One hundred and forty were killed when an oil tanker and auto ferry collided near Livorno Harbor in Italy.

1991, December 14. There were 462 fatalities when a ferry struck a reef near Safaga, Egypt.

1993, February 17. More than 500 lives were lost when a ferry capsized off Port-au-Prince, Haiti.

Selected Bibliography

The literature on shipwrecks is voluminous. The following list represents only a tiny fraction of works for further reading.

Ballard, R. *The Discovery of the Titanic.* New York: Warner Madison Press, 1987.

Barnett, J. *The Lifesaving Guns of David Lyle.* Washington, D.C.: Company of Military Historians, 1974.

Bass, G. *Archaeology Beneath the Sea: A Personal Account.* New York: Harper and Row, 1976.

———. *A History of Seafaring.* New York: Walker and Company, 1972.

———. *Ships and Shipwrecks of the Americas.* New York: Thames and Hudson, 1988.

Beesley, L. *The Loss of the S.S. Titanic.* Boston: Houghton Mifflin, 1912.

Bonsall, T. *Great Shipwrecks of the 20th Century.* New York: Gallery Books, 1988.

Boyer, D. *Ghost Ships of the Great Lakes.* New York: Dodd, Mead and Co., 1968.

Burgess, R. *Sinkings, Salvages and Shipwrecks.* New York: American Heritage, 1970.

Burton, H. *The Morro Castle.* New York: Viking, 1973.

Dalton, J. *The Lifesavers of Cape Cod.* Boston: Barta Press, 1902.

Fish, J. *Unfinished Voyages.* Orleans, Mass.: Lower Cape Publishing, 1989.

Gibbs, J. *Pacific Graveyard.* Portland, Ore.: Binfords & Mort, 1964.

———. *Shipwrecks of the Pacific Coast.* Portland, Ore.: Binfords & Mort, 1957.

Gordon, B., editor. *Man and the Sea: Classic Accounts of Marine Explorations.* Garden City, N.Y.: The Natural History Press, 1970.

Hocking, C. *Dictionary of Disasters at Sea During the Age of Steam, Including Sailing Ships and Ships of War Lost in Action.* London: Lloyd's Register of Shipping, 1969.

Hoehling, A. *Great Ship Disasters.* New York: Cowles, 1971.

———. *They Sailed into Oblivion.* New York: Thomas Yoseloff, 1959.

Howland, S. *Steamboat Disasters and Railroad Accidents in the United States.* Worcester, Mass.: Dorr, Howland and Co., 1840.

Johnson, R. *Guardians of the Seas: History of the U.S. Coast Guard.* Annapolis, Md.: Naval Institute Press, 1987.

Keatts, H. *New England's Legacy of Shipwrecks.* Kings Point, N.Y.: American Merchant Marine, 1988.

Lonsdale, A., and H. Kaplan. *A Guide to Sunken Ships in American Waters.* Arlington, Va.: Compass Publications, 1964.

Lord, Walter. *A Night To Remember.* New York: Holt, 1955.

Marx, R. *Shipwrecks of the Western Hemisphere, 1492–1815.* New York: World, 1971.

Morris, Charles. *The Volcano's Deadly Work.* New York: Scull, 1902.

Moscow, A. *Collision Course: The Andrea Doria and the Stockholm.* New York: Putnam, 1959.

Nash, J. *Darkest Hours.* Chicago: Nelson-Hall, 1976.

Neider, C., editor. *Great Shipwrecks and Castaways: Authentic Accounts of Adventures at Sea.* New York: Harper, 1952.

Padfield, P. *The Titanic and the Californian.* New York: John Day, 1965.

Perkes, D. *Twentieth Century Shipwrecks.* Chicago: Contemporary Books, 1983.

Pouliot, R., and J. Pouliot. *Shipwrecks on the Virginia Coast.* Centreville, Md.: Tidewater Publishers, 1986.

Protasio, J. *The World's Worst Disasters at Sea.* New York: S.P.I. Books, 1993.

Rankin, H. *The Pirates of Colonial North Carolina.* Raleigh, N.C.: Department of Cultural Resources, Division of Archives and History, 1979.

Rattray, J. *Ship Ashore! A Record of Maritime Disasters.* New York: Coward-McCann, 1955.

Shomette, D. *Shipwrecks on the Chesapeake: Maritime Disasters on Chesapeake Bay and its Tributaries, 1608–1978.* Centreville, Md.: Tidewater Publishers, 1982.

Snow, E. *Disaster at Sea.* New York: Avenel Books, 1990.

Stick, David. *Graveyard of the Atlantic: Shipwrecks of the North Carolina Coast.* Chapel Hill, N.C.: University of North Carolina Press, 1952.

Index

This index is designed to be used in conjunction with the cross-references within the A-to-Z entries. The main A-to-Z entries are indicated by **boldface** page references. The general subjects are subdivided by the A-to-Z entries. *Italicized* page references indicate illustrations; "c" following the locator indicates the chronology.